STUDY TEXT

PAPER P5

ADVANCED PERFORMANCE MANAGEMENT

BPP Learning Media is an **ACCA Approved Content Provider**. This means we work closely with ACCA to ensure this Study Text contains the information you need to pass your exam.

In this Study Text, which has been reviewed by **ACCA's examination team**, we:

- **Highlight** the **most important elements** in the syllabus and the **key skills** you need
- **Signpost** how each chapter links to the syllabus and the study guide
- **Provide** lots of **exam focus points** demonstrating what is expected of you in the exam
- **Emphasise key points** in regular **fast forward summaries**
- **Test your knowledge** in **quick quizzes**
- **Examine your understanding** in our **practice question bank**
- **Reference all the important topics** in our **full index**

BPP's **Practice & Revision Kit** also supports this paper.

FOR EXAMS IN SEPTEMBER 2016, DECEMBER 2016, MARCH 2017 AND JUNE 2017

First edition 2007
Ninth edition February 2016

ISBN 9781 4727 4431 9
(Previous ISBN 9781 4727 2683 4)

e-ISBN 9781 4727 4673 3

British Library Cataloguing-in-Publication Data

A catalogue record for this book
is available from the British Library

Published by

BPP Learning Media Ltd
BPP House, Aldine Place
London W12 8AA

www.bpp.com/learningmedia

Printed in the United Kingdom by
Polestar Wheatons

Hennock Road
Marsh Barton
Exeter
EX2 8RP

Your learning materials, published by BPP Learning Media Ltd, are printed on paper obtained from traceable sustainable sources.

We are grateful to the Association of Chartered Certified Accountants for permission to reproduce past examination questions. The suggested solutions in the practice answer bank have been prepared by BPP Learning Media Ltd, unless otherwise stated.

A note about copyright

Dear Customer

What does the little © mean and why does it matter?

Your market-leading BPP books, course materials and e-learning materials do not write and update themselves. People write them on their own behalf or as employees of an organisation that invests in this activity. Copyright law protects their livelihoods. It does so by creating rights over the use of the content.

Breach of copyright is a form of theft – as well as being a criminal offence in some jurisdictions, it is potentially a serious breach of professional ethics.

With current technology, things might seem a bit hazy but, basically, without the express permission of BPP Learning Media:

- Photocopying our materials is a breach of copyright
- Scanning, ripcasting or conversion of our digital materials into different file formats, uploading them to facebook or e-mailing them to your friends is a breach of copyright

You can, of course, sell your books, in the form in which you have bought them – once you have finished with them. (Is this fair to your fellow students? We update for a reason.) Please note the e-products are sold on a single user licence basis: we do not supply 'unlock' codes to people who have bought them second hand.

And what about outside the UK? BPP Learning Media strives to make our materials available at prices students can afford by local printing arrangements, pricing policies and partnerships which are clearly listed on our website. A tiny minority ignore this and indulge in criminal activity by illegally photocopying our material or supporting organisations that do. If they act illegally and unethically in one area, can you really trust them?

Contents

Helping you to pass

BPP Learning Media – ACCA Approved Content Provider

As an ACCA **Approved Content Provider**, BPP Learning Media gives you the **opportunity** to use study materials reviewed by the ACCA examination team. By incorporating the examination team's comments and suggestions regarding the depth and breadth of syllabus coverage, the BPP Learning Media Study Text provides excellent, **ACCA-approved** support for your studies.

The PER alert

Before you can qualify as an ACCA member, you have to not only pass all your exams but also fulfil a three year **practical experience requirement** (PER). To help you to recognise areas of the syllabus that you might be able to apply in the workplace to achieve different performance objectives, we have introduced the **'PER alert'** feature. You will find this feature throughout the Study Text to remind you that what you are **learning to pass** your ACCA exams is **equally useful to the fulfilment of the PER requirement**.

Tackling studying

Studying can be a daunting prospect, particularly when you have lots of other commitments. The **different features** of the Study Text, the **purposes** of which are explained fully on the **Chapter features** page, will help you while studying and improve your chances of **exam success**.

Developing exam awareness

Our Study Texts are completely **focused** on helping you pass your exam.

Our advice on **Studying P5** outlines the **content** of the paper, the **necessary skills** you are expected to be able to demonstrate and any **brought forward knowledge** you are expected to have.

Exam focus points are included within the chapters to highlight when and how specific topics were examined, how they might be examined in the future, and how different topics within the syllabus fit together.

Using the syllabus and study guide

You can find the syllabus and study guide on pages xiii-xxiii of this Study Text.

Testing what you can do

Testing yourself helps you develop the skills you need to pass the exam and also confirms that you can recall what you have learnt.

We include **Questions** – lots of them – both within chapters and in the **Practice Question Bank**, as well as **Quick Quizzes** at the end of each chapter to test your knowledge of the chapter content.

Chapter features

Each chapter contains a number of helpful features to guide you through each topic.

Topic list

Topic list	Syllabus reference

What you will be studying in this chapter and the relevant section numbers, together with ACCA syllabus references.

Introduction

Puts the chapter content in the context of the syllabus as a whole.

Study Guide

Links the chapter content with ACCA guidance.

Exam Guide

Highlights how examinable the chapter content is likely to be and the ways in which it could be examined.

Knowledge brought forward from earlier studies

What you are assumed to know from previous studies/exams.

Summarises the content of main chapter headings, allowing you to preview and review each section easily.

Examples

Demonstrate how to apply key knowledge and techniques.

Key terms

Definitions of important concepts that can often earn you easy marks in exams.

Exam focus points

When and how specific topics were examined, or how they may be examined in the future.

Formula to learn

Formulae that are not given in the exam but which have to be learnt.

Gives you a useful indication of syllabus areas that closely relate to performance objectives in your Practical Experience Requirement (PER).

Question

Gives you essential practice of techniques covered in the chapter.

Case Study

Real world examples of theories and techniques.

Chapter Roundup

A full list of the Fast Forwards included in the chapter, providing an easy source of review.

Quick Quiz

A quick test of your knowledge of the main topics in the chapter.

Practice Question Bank

Found at the back of the Study Text with more comprehensive chapter questions. Cross referenced for easy navigation.

Studying P5

As the name suggests, this paper examines advanced performance management topics and is particularly suited to those who are thinking about a career in management accountancy or are likely to be involved in strategic management decisions.

ACCA expects you to demonstrate a professional approach to all questions – not just presenting information in a professional manner, but also integrating knowledge and understanding of topics from across the syllabus.

The examination team has stressed that candidates should not expect topics in P5 exams to be examined in isolation. One of the major skills you will be expected to demonstrate in the P5 exam is being able to draw on knowledge gained across your studies to date, in order to present complete solutions to relatively broad business issues or problems.

1 What P5 is about

The syllabus for Paper P5 further develops key aspects and skills introduced in **Paper F5**, and it draws on aspects of the material about strategic and operational planning and performance covered in **Paper P3**, Business Analysis.

However, whereas Paper P3 assesses principles of management accounting as part of the wider analysis of a business situation, Paper P5 could examine aspects of management accounting – such as budgeting or costing techniques – in their own right.

The stated aim of the P5 syllabus is:

> '*To apply relevant knowledge, skills and exercise professional judgement in selecting and applying strategic management accounting techniques in different business contexts and to contribute to the evaluation of the performance of an organisation and its strategic development.*'

Read this aim carefully. You are no longer just a 'number cruncher' drawing up budgets and producing calculations to include management reports. You are expected to **understand the wider issues** that affect organisations. These issues are often written about in newspapers and journals such as the *Financial Times* and *The Economist*, so it is important you read the financial press to help you identify how the issues you are studying in P5 relate to the real world context.

At this level in your studies, you also need to recognise how the subjects you previously studied begin to fit together. You need to begin to take a holistic view of an organisation, and to see how the various parts of it and various processes affect overall performance – rather than looking at individual issues in isolation.

Importantly, the P5 exam is likely to also test your ability to assess different approaches to performance **management**, from a variety of perspectives. As well as knowing what the approaches are, you will also need to be able to compare them with one another in the context of a scenario; for example, comparing the long-term and short-term issues affecting an organisation's performance.

Snapshot of the syllabus

The syllabus expects you to understand how organisations set their strategy and the external influences that affect strategic plans and operational outcomes. You will be expected to evaluate different systems of performance management and apply strategic performance measurement techniques in evaluating and improving performance. You may also be expected to advise on strategic performance evaluation and the possibility of corporate failure. Finally, you need to be aware of the current developments in management accounting and performance management, as these affect organisations.

There are **five parts to the syllabus**, as summarised below.

(a) **Use strategic planning and control models to plan** and **monitor organisational performance**

(b) **Assess and identify** relevant **macroeconomic, fiscal** and **market factors** and key **external influences** on **organisational performance**

(c) **Identify and evaluate** the **design features of effective performance management information and monitoring systems**

(d) **Apply** appropriate **strategic performance measurement techniques in evaluating and improving** organisational performance

(e) **Advise** clients and senior management on **strategic business performance evaluation** and on recognising **vulnerability to corporate failure**

We expect most of these capabilities (if not all) to be tested to some extent in every P5 exam.

2 What skills are required?

Look back at the action verbs in the six parts of the syllabus outlined above. You are expected to be able to **assess, advise** and **evaluate**, as well as to **identify** and **monitor**.

The need for these skills of assessing, advising and evaluating highlights that, at P5 level, you are expected to have moved beyond merely demonstrating your knowledge of a model or technique, and instead you have to apply that knowledge to practical situations. For example, the examination team will expect that, by the time you reach P5, you can already calculate basic financial ratios. In P5, though, the examination team will expect you to be able to interpret the information provided by those ratios to understand how an organisation is performing, and to make sensible suggestions (where appropriate) about how its performance could be improved.

The questions set in P5 exams will be based around **case study scenarios** which describe an organisation, its objectives and its business environment. You will need to relate your answers specifically to the scenario given in the question. There will be very few marks available for simply describing models or theories. Evidence from past exam sittings suggests that candidates who simply learn models and theories, but then do not apply their knowledge to the question scenarios, typically score between 20-30% in their P5 exams.

The P5 paper has a large **written element**, with well over half the marks being earned for written answers (discussion, analysis, evaluation) rather than calculations. Again, this is designed to reflect the position of a qualified accountant working in a business. The accountant can expect a number of the routine calculations and figures to be produced by their more junior colleagues, but the accountant should then expect to identify the issues or implications being identified by those figures.

We have summarised here the skills you are expected to demonstrate in P5.

(a) **Core knowledge**. The contents of Paper F5 *Performance Management* – assumed knowledge brought forward for Paper P5.

(b) **Numerical skills.** Those skills demonstrated in Paper F5. You only learn a small number of new mathematical techniques in this paper but, alongside these, you are also expected to remember those you learnt previously.

(c) **Written skills**. These are key skills on this paper. You will be expected to write reports and notes explaining issues you encounter.

(d) **Analysis and interpretation** of question data or calculations. The examination team has stressed that candidates will be expected to analyse (not merely calculate) numerical data given in a scenario.

(e) **Wider business awareness** or application of skills in a practical context.

3 Passing the P5 exam

The examination team provides a lot of useful feedback in the 'Examiner's reports' to past exams. This feedback highlights areas where students have struggled in exams, and also indicates the skills the examination team expects candidates to be able to demonstrate.

Looking at the post exam guidance can also be useful for reminding yourself about essential areas of exam technique. Therefore you are strongly recommended to read these guides which are available in the 'Qualification resources' section of ACCA's website: www.accaglobal.com

The points highlighted in the post exam guidance include the following.

(a) **Read questions very carefully** and answer the question asked, not the question you hoped had been asked. In particular, if a question asks you to 'evaluate' or 'assess' the usefulness of a performance measure for assessing performance in an organisation, this is not asking you to evaluate or assess the **organisation's** performance. Instead, the focus of your answer must be on the performance **measure** itself.

(b) Answers which consist of rote-learned definitions or explanations with no application to the scenario will score very few marks. It is vital that you **apply your knowledge** to the context described by the **question scenario**.

(c) Look at the **mark allocation** to help you manage your time allocation and plan your answer.

(d) Read all the parts of the question before you prepare your answer, so that you **avoid repeating the same points** in answering different parts of the question.

We recommend you read the 'Examiner's approach to P5' article published in October 2012 and available on ACCA's website. This illustrates how some of the skills required to pass P5 have been tested in recent exam sittings, and provides some useful hints about how to approach the paper.

Approach to the exam – In the article, the Examining team suggested that the best approach to the exam can be summarised as:

(a) **Cover the whole syllabus** – Candidates often appear to over-concentrate on Section D of the syllabus (strategic performance measurement). However, it is important to understand how, for example, the choice of performance measures fits with planning and control structures (Section A of the syllabus) or how well the measures chosen relate to external drivers of performance (Section B of the syllabus).

(b) **Be prepared to apply your knowledge of syllabus topics to a business scenario** – answers which provide lists of rote-learned points (or rote-learned advantages and disadvantages for different techniques and approaches) will not earn sufficient marks to pass a question. Candidates will be expected to tailor their knowledge specifically to the situation given in the question scenario.

(c) **Read and answer the question set** – Candidates earn marks where their answers are technically correct **and** relevant to the question asked. However, candidates have a tendency to write answers to the question they wish had been asked, rather than the question the examining team actually set. This approach scores little or no credit though.

(d) **Add value to the organisation that is being advised** – Candidates need to demonstrate their ability to add value by taking data already produced and identifying and analysing the key issues in that data and the commercial implications of it. Candidates need to be prepared to **analyse** numerical data given in a scenario, not merely to perform calculations on it.

Importantly, the article also stresses that P5 is a paper about performance **management**, not simply about performance **measurement**. While it is important for an organisation to measure how well it is performing, this performance measurement takes place within the wider context of strategic planning and control, and is subject to both internal and external factors which can affect performance. In Paper P5 you need to be aware of this context and its impact on performance, not simply how an organisation can measure performance. Performance management also considers how the management of an organisation can be informed by the results of performance measurement; for example, through the way in which staff are rewarded for their performance.

Question practice

The importance of tailoring your answer to the question actually set, rather than simply rote-learning models and theories, also highlights the importance of question practice in preparing for your P5 exam.

You can **develop application skills** by attempting questions in the BPP Learning Media **Practice & Revision Kit**.

4 Brought forward knowledge

You will be expected to build on the skills and knowledge you acquired when you studied Paper F5 *Performance Management*. That paper introduces topics such as **budgeting** and **pricing** that continue into the higher level syllabus. Paper F5 also covers **cost and management accounting techniques** including **activity-based costing** that you will encounter in this paper. You will also be expected to draw on your knowledge of **performance measurement and control techniques** that were introduced in this earlier paper, because candidates sitting P5 will be expected to have a thorough understanding of the F5 syllabus.

In addition, you might be expected to draw on topics covered in Paper P3, *Business Analysis*, particularly in relation to aspects of strategic planning and control, and performance measurement.

ACCA technical article: 'Bringing forward Paper F5 knowledge and skills in Paper P5'

There is an article in the P5 technical articles section of ACCA's website called 'Bringing forward Paper F5 knowledge and skills in Paper P5'. The article highlights the core skills from Paper F5 you will need to bring forward into Paper P5, but also the differences in the depth and application of knowledge required in P5 compared with F5. For example, instead of simply understanding the rationale of the Balanced Scorecard, in P5 you might be asked to evaluate its usefulness to an organisation in a specific scenario.

You are strongly advised to read the article as part of your studies for your P5 exam.

Analysis of past papers

The table below provides details of when each element of the syllabus has been examined and whether it was examined as part of a compulsory (C) or optional (O) question. Further details about questions can be found in the Exam Focus Points in the relevant chapters.

Text chapter		Sept/ Dec 2015	June 2015	Dec 2014	June 2014	Dec 2013	June 2013	Dec 2012	June 2012	Dec 2011	June 2011
	STRATEGIC PLANNING AND CONTROL										
1	Introduction to strategic management accounting		C	C				O	O		
2	Performance hierarchy	C	C			C				C	
3	Performance management and control of the organisation	O			O		O	C			
4	Changes in business structure and management accounting		C	C	O		C				C
5	Environmental and ethical issues			O							O
	EXTERNAL INFLUENCES ON ORGANISATIONAL PERFORMANCE										
6	External influences on organisational performance		C		O	C	O	O		C	
	PERFORMANCE MEASUREMENT SYSTEMS AND DESIGN										
7	Performance management information systems	C,O	O			O				O, O	C
8	Management information, recording and processing and management reports	O	C		C	O			C	O	
	STRATEGIC PERFORMANCE MEASUREMENT										
9	Strategic performance measures in the private sector		O		C			C, O	C		C
10	Divisional performance and transfer pricing issues		O				O				C
11	Strategic performance measures in not-for-profit organisations			O		O					
12	Non-financial performance indicators			O				O	C		
13	The role of quality in management information and performance measurement systems	C,O		C			O		O	O	
14	Performance measurement: and strategic HRM issues		O,O		O	O	C	C		O	O
	PERFORMANCE EVALUATION AND CORPORATE FAILURE										
15	Alternative views of performance measurement and management	O	O	C	C	O	C, O		O	C	C, O
16	Strategic performance issues in complex business structures				O		O		O		O
17	Predicting and preventing corporate failure			O				O			

The exam paper

Format of the paper

The P5 exam paper consists of two sections, and lasts 3 hours and 15 minutes.

Important note: The format of the exam paper changed in June 2013. If you are looking at past exams (on ACCA's website) from 2012 or earlier, it is vital that you remember this point.

Section A

Section A will contain **one compulsory question** comprising **50 marks in total**. This question will comprise several sub-sections, and will usually assess and link a range of subject areas from across the syllabus. The Section A question will require students to demonstrate high-level capabilities to evaluate, relate and apply the information in the case study to the question requirements.

Section B

You need to answer **two questions in Section B from a choice of three**, comprising **25 marks each**. Section B questions are more likely to assess a range of discrete subject areas from the main syllabus section headings. However, they will still require evaluation and synthesis of information contained within the case study scenarios, and will require the application of this information to the question requirements.

A small number of **professional marks** will be available. The examination team has emphasised that in order to gain the marks available, candidates must write in the specified format (such as a report or memo). Reports must have terms of reference, conclusion, appendices and appropriate headings. Make sure you are familiar with how different types of documents are constructed to improve your chances of gaining maximum professional marks.

Syllabus and Study Guide

The P5 syllabus and Study Guide can be found on the following pages.

Syllabus

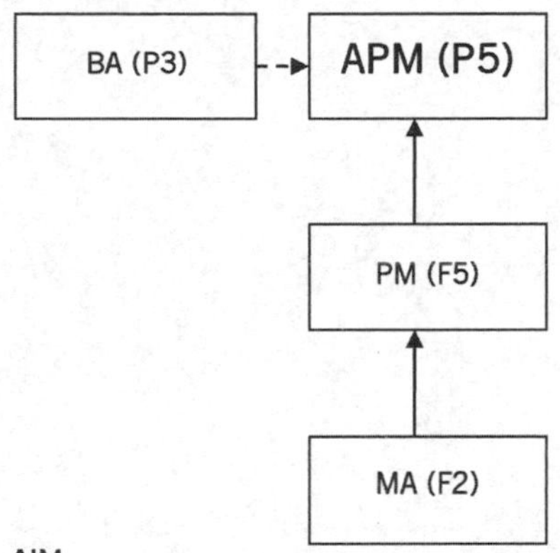

MAIN CAPABILITIES

On successful completion of this paper, candidates should be able to:

A Use strategic planning and control models to plan and monitor organisational performance

B Assess and identify key external influences on organisational performance

C Identify and evaluate the design features of effective performance management information and monitoring systems

D Apply appropriate strategic performance measurement techniques in evaluating and improving organisational performance

E Advise clients and senior management on strategic business performance evaluation and on recognising vulnerability to corporate failure

AIM

To apply relevant knowledge, skills and exercise professional judgement in selecting and applying strategic management accounting techniques in different business contexts and to contribute to the evaluation of the performance of an organisation and its strategic development.

RELATIONAL DIAGRAM OF MAIN CAPABILITIES

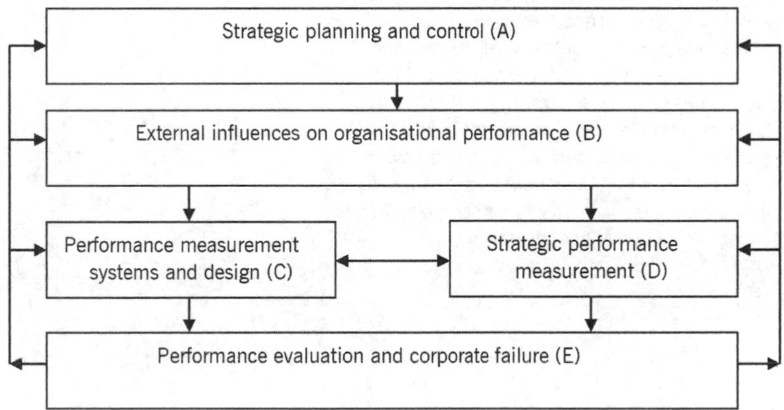

RATIONALE

The Advanced Performance Management syllabus further develops key aspects introduced in Paper F5, *Performance Management*, at the skills level and draws on aspects of the material covered from a more strategic and operational planning perspective in Paper P3, *Business Analysis*.

The syllabus introduces candidates to the strategic role of management accounting as a discipline for planning and controlling performance so that strategic objectives can be set, monitored and controlled. It also covers the impact of external factors on strategic management issues, such as macro-economic, fiscal, market and environmental impacts on performance. From appreciating the strategic context of performance management and the impact of wider factors, the syllabus examines, at an operational level, the issues relating to performance measurement systems and their design.

The syllabus then moves from performance management systems and their design to the scope and application of high-level performance measurement techniques in a variety of contexts, including not-for-profit organisations and multi-national businesses. Having covered the strategic aspects of performance management and operational systems for the measurement and control of performance in a variety of contexts, candidates are then expected to synthesise this knowledge in the role of an advisor to senior management or independent clients on how to assess and control the performance of an entity, including the recognition of whether a business is facing difficulties or possibly failure.

DETAILED SYLLABUS

A. Strategic planning and control

1. Strategic management accounting
2. Performance hierarchy
3. Performance management and control of the organisation
4. Changes in business structure and management accounting
5. Other environmental and ethical issues

B. External influences on organisational performance

1. Impact of risk and uncertainty on performance management
2. Impact of other external factors on performance management

C. Performance measurement systems and design

1. Performance management information systems
2. Sources of management information
3. Recording and processing methods
4. Management reports

D. Strategic performance measurement

1. Strategic performance measures in the private sector
2. Divisional performance and transfer pricing issues
3. Strategic performance measures in not-for-profit organisations
4. Non-financial performance indicators
5. The role of quality in management information and performance measurement systems
6. Performance measurement and strategic human resource management issues
7. Other behavioural aspects of performance measurement

E. Performance evaluation and corporate failure

1. Alternative views of performance measurement and management
2. Strategic performance issues in complex business structures
3. Predicting and preventing corporate failure

APPROACH TO EXAMINING THE SYLLABUS

Paper P5 builds on paper F5, *Performance Management,* and candidates are expected to have a thorough understanding of the paper F5 syllabus. In addition, candidates will also be required to apply the principles and techniques covered in paper F2, *Management Accounting.*

Paper P5 has a link with Paper P3, *Business Analysis,* in the areas of strategic planning and control and performance measurement

EXAMINATION STRUCTURE

The examination will be in two sections, and will last 3 hours and 15 minutes.

Section A

Section A will contain one compulsory question comprising of 50 marks

Section B

In section B candidates will be asked to answer two from three questions comprising of 25 marks each

Total 100 marks

Study Guide

A STRATEGIC PLANNING AND CONTROL

1. Strategic management accounting

a) Explain the role of strategic performance management in strategic planning and control. [2]

b) Discuss the role of performance measurement in checking progress towards the corporate objectives. [2]

c) Compare planning and control between the strategic and operational levels within a business entity. [2]

d) Discuss the scope for potential conflict between strategic business plans and short-term localised decisions. [2]

e) Evaluate how models such as SWOT analysis, Boston Consulting Group and Porter may assist in the performance management process. [3]

f) Apply and evaluate the methods of benchmarking performance. [3]

g) Assess the changing role of the management accountant in today's business environment as outlined by Burns and Scapens. [3]

2. Performance hierarchy

a) Discuss how the purpose, structure and content of a mission statement impacts on performance measurement and management. [2]

b) Discuss how strategic objectives are cascaded down the organisation via the formulation of subsidiary performance objectives. [2]

c) Apply critical success factor analysis in developing performance metrics from business objectives. [3]

d) Identify and discuss the characteristics of operational performance. [2]

e) Discuss the relative significance of planning as against controlling activities at different levels in the performance hierarchy. [3]

3. Performance management and control of the organisation

a) Evaluate the strengths and weaknesses of alternative budgeting models and compare such techniques as fixed and flexible, rolling, activity based, zero based and incremental. [3]

b) Evaluate different types of budget variances and how these relate to issues in planning and controlling organisations. [3]

4. Changes in business structure and management accounting

a) Identify and discuss the particular information needs of organisations adopting a functional, divisional or network form and the implications for performance management. [2]

b) Assess the changing accounting needs of modern service orientated businesses compared with the needs of a traditional manufacturing industry. [3]

c) Assess the influence of Business Process Re-engineering on systems development and improvements in organisational performance. [3]

d) Analyse the role that performance management systems play in business integration using models such as the value chain and McKinsey's 7S's [3]

e) Discuss how changing an organisation's structure, culture and strategy will influence the adoption of new performance measurement methods and techniques. [3]

f) Assess the need for businesses to continually refine and develop their management accounting and information systems if they are to maintain or improve their performance in an increasingly competitive and global market. [3]

g) Highlight the ways in which contingent (internal and external) factors influence management accounting and its design and use. [3]

5. **Other environmental and ethical issues**

a) Discuss the ways in which stakeholder groups operate and how they influence an organisation, its strategy formulation and implementation and business performance (e.g. using Mendelow's matrix). [2]

b) Discuss the social and ethical issues that may impact on strategy formulation, and consequently, business performance. [3]

c) Discuss, evaluate and apply environmental management accounting using for example lifecycle costing and activity-based costing. [3]

B EXTERNAL INFLUENCES ON ORGANISATIONAL PERFORMANCE

1. **Impact of risk and uncertainty on performance management**

a) Assess the impact of the different risk appetites of stakeholders on performance management [3]

b) Evaluate how risk and uncertainty play an important role in long term strategic planning and decision-making that relies upon forecasts of exogenous variables.[3]

c) Apply different risk analysis techniques in assessing business performance such as maximin, maximax, minimax regret and expected values.[3]

2. **Impact of other external factors on performance management**

a) Discuss the need to consider the environment in which an organisation is operating when assessing its performance using models such as PEST and Porter's 5 forces, including such areas as: [2]
   i) Political climate
   ii) Market conditions

C PERFORMANCE MEASUREMENT SYSTEMS AND DESIGN

1. **Performance management information systems**

a) Discuss, with reference to performance management, ways in which the information requirements of a management structure are affected by the features of the structure. [2]

b) Evaluate the compatibility of management accounting objectives and the management accounting information systems. [3]

c) Discuss the integration of management accounting information within an overall information system, for example the use of enterprise resource planning systems. [2]

d) Evaluate whether the management information systems are lean and the value of the information that they provide. [3]

e) Evaluate how anticipated human behaviour will influence the design of a management accounting system. [3]

2. **Sources of management information**

a) Discuss the principal internal and external sources of management accounting information, their costs and limitations. [2]

b) Demonstrate how the information might be used in planning and controlling activities e.g. benchmarking against similar activities. [2]

c) Discuss the development of Big Data and its impact on performance measurement and management, including the risks and challenges it presents. [3]

3. **Recording and processing methods**

a) Demonstrate how the type of business entity will influence the recording and processing methods. [2]

b) Discuss how IT developments e.g. unified corporate databases, RFIDs and network technology may influence management accounting systems. [2]

c) Explain how information systems provide instant access to previously unavailable data that can be used for benchmarking and control purposes and help improve business performance (for example, through the use of enterprise resource planning systems and data warehouses). [2]

d) Discuss the difficulties associated with recording and processing data of a qualitative nature. [2]

4. **Management reports**

a) Evaluate the output reports of an information system in the light of [3]
   i) best practice in presentation;
   ii) the objectives of the report/organisation;
   iii the needs of the readers of the report; and
   iv) avoiding the problem of information overload

b) Advise on common mistakes and misconceptions in the use of numerical data used for performance measurement. [3]

c) Explore the role of the management accountant in providing key performance information for integrated reporting to stakeholders. [2]

D STRATEGIC PERFORMANCE MEASUREMENT

1. **Strategic performance measures in private sector**

a) Demonstrate why the primary objective of financial performance should be primarily concerned with the benefits to shareholders. [2]

b) Discuss the appropriateness of, and apply different measures of performance, including: [3]
   i) Gross profit and operating profit
   ii) Return on Capital Employed (ROCE)
   iii) Return on Investment (ROI)
   iv) Earnings Per Share (EPS)
   v) Earnings Before Interest, Tax, Depreciation and Amortisation (EBITDA)
   vi) Residual Income (RI)
   vii) Net Present value (NPV)
   viii) Internal rate of return and modified internal Rate of Return (IRR, MIRR)
   ix) Economic Value Added (EVA™)

c) Discuss why indicators of liquidity and gearing need to considered in conjunction with profitability. [3]

d) Compare and contrast short and long run financial performance and the resulting management issues. [3]

e) Assess the appropriate benchmarks to use in assessing performance.[3]

2. **Divisional performance and transfer pricing issues**

a) Describe, compute and evaluate performance measures relevant in a divisionalised organisation structure including ROI, RI and Economic value added (EVA). [3]

b) Discuss the need for separate measures in respect of managerial and divisional performance. [2]

c) Discuss the circumstances in which a transfer pricing policy may be needed and discuss the necessary criteria for its design. [2]

d) Demonstrate and evaluate the use of alternative bases for transfer pricing. [3]

e) Explain and demonstrate issues that require consideration when setting transfer prices in multinational companies. [2]

3. **Strategic performance measures in not-for-profit organisations**

a) Highlight and discuss the potential for diversity in objectives depending on organisation type. [3]

b) Discuss the difficulties in measuring outputs when performance is not judged in terms of money or an easily quantifiable objective. [2]

c) Discuss the use of benchmarking in public sector performance (league tables) and its effects on operational and strategic management and client behaviour. [3]

d) Discuss how the combination of politics and the desire to measure public sector performance may result in undesirable service outcomes e.g. the use of targets. [3]

e) Assess 'value for money' service provision as a measure of performance in not-for-profit organisations and the public sector. [3]

4. Non-financial performance indicators

a) Discuss the interaction of non-financial performance indicators with financial performance indicators. [3]

b) Identify and discuss the significance of non-financial performance indicators in relation to employees and product/service quality e.g. customer satisfaction reports, repeat business ratings, customer loyalty, access and availability. [3]

c) Discuss the difficulties in interpreting data on qualitative issues. [2]

d) Discuss the significance of brand awareness and company profile and their potential impact on business performance. [3]

5. The role of quality in management information and performance measurement systems

a) Discuss and evaluate the application of Japanese business practices and management accounting techniques, including: [3]
i) Kaizen costing,
ii) Target costing,
iii) Just-in-time, and
iv) Total Quality Management.

b) Assess the relationship of quality management to the performance management strategy of an organisation including the costs of quality. [3]

c) Justify the need and assess the characteristics of quality in management information systems[3]

d) Discuss and apply Six Sigma as a quality improvement method using tools such as DMAIC for implementation. [2]

6. Performance measurement and strategic Human Resource Management issues

a) Advise on the relationship of HR management to performance measurement (performance rating) and suitable remuneration methods. [3]

b) Advise on the link between achievement of the corporate strategy and the management of human resources (e.g. through the Building Block model) [2]

c) Discuss and evaluate different methods of reward practices. [3]

d) Assess the potential beneficial and adverse consequences of linking reward schemes to performance measurement for example, how it can affect the risk appetite of employees. [3]

7. Other behavioural aspects of performance measurement

a) Discuss the accountability issues that might arise from performance measurement systems. [3]

b) Assess the statement; 'What gets measured, gets done.'[3]

c) Demonstrate how management style needs to be considered when designing an effective performance measurement system. [3]

E PERFORMANCE EVALUATION AND CORPORATE FAILURE

1. Alternative views of performance measurement and management

a) Apply and evaluate the 'balanced scorecard' approach as a way in which to improve the range and linkage between performance measures. [3]

b) Apply and evaluate the 'performance pyramid' as a way in which to link strategy, operations and performance. [3]

c) Apply and evaluate the work of Fitzgerald and Moon that considers performance measurement in business services using building blocks for dimensions, standards and rewards. [3]

d) Discuss and evaluate the application of activity-based management. [3]

e) Evaluate and apply the value-based management approaches to performance management. [3]

2. **Strategic performance issues in complex business structures**

a) Discuss the problems encountered in planning, controlling and measuring performance levels, e.g. productivity, profitability, quality and service levels, in complex business structures. [3]

b) Discuss the impact on performance management of the use of business models involving strategic alliances, joint ventures and complex supply chain structures. [3]

3. **Predicting and preventing corporate failure**

a) Discuss how long-term survival necessitates consideration of life-cycle issues. [3]

b) Assess the potential likelihood of corporate failure, utilising quantitative and qualitative performance measures and models (such as Z-scores and Argenti). [3]

c) Assess and critique quantitative and qualitative corporate failure prediction models. [3]

d) Identify and discuss performance improvement strategies that may be adopted in order to prevent corporate failure. [3]

e) Identify and discuss operational changes to performance management systems required to implement the performance improvement strategies. [3]

SUMMARY OF CHANGES TO P5

ACCA periodically reviews its qualification syllabuses so that they fully meet the needs of stakeholders such as employers, students, regulatory and advisory bodies and learning providers.

There are changes to the syllabus to reflect the latest business and educational developments affecting this paper. These are summarised in the table below.

Section and subject area	Syllabus content
A Strategic planning and control	There are still 5 subject areas, however these have been reordered. A1b has been changed to 'Discuss the role of performance measurement,,,' A1d has been deleted and the subsequent learning outcomes reordered A1e now includes the models from E2a A1g was formerly F2a A2 was formerly D1 D1b, c, e and f have been deleted and the remainder reordered under A2. A3 was formerly A2 A3b is now focused on the use of variance analysis in performance measurement The former A2c has been deleted A4 was formerly A3 There have been some deletions, additions and reordering A4b was A4a from the previous syllabus A4f was A4e from the previous syllabus A4e was F2c A4g was C1e The former A3c and A3e have been deleted The former A4b and A4c have been deleted A5a has been rephrased A5b has been rephrased A5c has been replaced with the former F1b and input/output analysis has been deleted
B External influences on organisational performance	Subject area B1 has been renamed B1a has been deleted and subsequent learning outcomes have been reordered Subject area B2 has been renamed B2aiii has been deleted B2b has been deleted

C Performance measurement systems and design	C1e has moved to A4g C1g has been deleted C2c has been replaced with a new learning outcome C3c was formerly A4d and the previous C3c is now C3d C4b is a new learning outcome focused on how data can be used to misrepresent performance C4c was formerly F2d
D Strategic performance measurement	D1 has moved to A2 and the subject areas have been consequently reordered The former D2b and D2f have been deleted D1bi has been added and the subsequent list of performance measures renumbered D1e was formerly D2g and has been rephrased D3 was formerly D4 The former D4b and D4c have been deleted D3c was formerly F1c D3d has been amended slightly to include 'e.g. the use of targets' The former D5b and D5c have been deleted D5 was formerly D6 The former D6b and D6d have been deleted D5b has been amended to include reference to the costs of quality D6 is now the previous D7 and D8 combined D6a and D6b are new learning outcomes which link together a number of the former learning outcomes D7 was formerly D9 The former D9b has been deleted D7b has been added
E Performance evaluation and corporate failure	E1d has been deleted E2a has been moved to A1e E3 has been reordered
	Former syllabus area (F)

	F1a, F1d, F2b have been deleted F1b has been moved to A5c F1c has been moved to D3c F2a has been moved to A1g F2c has been moved to A4e F2d has been moved to C4c

PART A

Strategic planning and control

1

Strategic management accounting

Topic list	Syllabus reference
1 Planning, control and decision making	-
2 The role of performance management in strategic planning and control	A1(a), A1(b)
3 Planning and control at strategic and operational levels	A1(c)
4 Strategic planning vs short-term localised decisions	A1(d)
5 SWOT analysis and performance management	A1(e)
6 Strategic models and performance management	A1(e)
7 Benchmarking	A1(f)
8 The changing role of the management accountant	A1(g)

Introduction

The syllabus for this paper develops key aspects introduced in **Paper F5 Performance Management** and draws on aspects of the material covered from a more strategic and operational planning perspective in **Paper P3 Business Analysis**.

The opening chapters of this Study Text look at **strategic planning and control**, which is the subject of Part A of the syllabus for P5.

However good an organisation's strategies may be, in principle, the ultimate test of them lies in their impact on an organisation's performance. As such, it is very important that organisations measure how well they are performing in key areas, so that they can take steps to improve performance if necessary.

In relation to this, it is also important that the performance measures organisations focus on are appropriate for their strategies and their competitive position. In this chapter we highlight some of the key models (SWOT analysis; BCG matrix; Porter's five forces) which organisations can use to help them identify which areas of performance it is important for them to measure.

Study guide

		Intellectual level
A1	**Strategic management accounting**	
(a)	Explain the role of strategic performance management in strategic planning and control.	2
(b)	Discuss the role of performance measurement in checking progress towards the corporate objectives.	2
(c)	Compare planning and control between the strategic and operational levels within a business entity.	2
(d)	Discuss the scope for potential conflict between strategic business plans and short-term localised decisions.	2
(e)	Evaluate how models such as SWOT analysis, Boston Consulting Group and Porter may assist in the performance management process.	3
(f)	Apply and evaluate the methods of benchmarking performance.	3
(g)	Assess the changing role of the management accountant in today's business environment as outlined by Burns and Scapens.	3

Exam guide

This paper is a Professional level paper and so there is an emphasis on application and evaluation, and not simply knowledge. You will be expected to know the models and techniques introduced in this chapter and to comment on their use in specific circumstances.

There are some key ideas to keep in mind when studying this syllabus. Firstly, we look at the organisation as a hierarchy from the top where plans are made (strategic level), to the bottom where these are acted out (operational level). Robert Anthony describes this in his hierarchy of information for planning, control and decision making. We look at this later on in the chapter.

Second, although we refer to the rational planning model as a framework for analysing the strategic planning process, it is important to remember that the focus of Paper P5 is on performance management, rather than strategic planning or business analysis in its own right. Whereas in P3 you might use models such as the BCG matrix or Porter's five forces in the context of helping an organisation evaluate different strategic options, the focus in P5 is on how managers could use those models to help understand an organisation's current performance, to identify key areas of performance to measure, or to evaluate the suitability of different performance measures.

Also, remember that although the models can be useful they do have limitations, and you will need to consider these limitations if you are asked to evaluate the models' usefulness in performance management.

As the Study Guide mentions, by name, three models which could assist the performance management process (SWOT analysis, the BCG matrix, and Porter's five forces), you should be prepared for these models to be specifically examined.

Similarly, the Study Guide also mentions Burns and Scapens' work on the changing role of the management accountant, so you should equally be prepared for a question which specifically refers to their work in the requirement.

Performance objective 3 (PO 3) – Strategy and innovation – requires that you 'contribute to the wider business strategy of your organisation through your personal and team objectives, identifying innovative business solutions to improve organisational performance by making or recommending business process changes and improvements.'

Although, as we noted in the Exam Guide above, P5 is not about business analysis and strategy in the sense that P3 was, nonetheless trying to 'improve organisational performance' is a key part of performance management.

Similarly, the skills you need to demonstrate in order to achieve PO 3 include developing 'financial acumen and sound business judgement to anticipate potential business problems and recognise weaknesses that need to be addressed, recommending appropriate solutions.

Again, the notion of identifying potential problems or weaknesses and recommending solutions to them is a key theme throughout P5 so keep this Performance objective in mind as you are studying for your P5 exam.

1 Planning, control and decision making

FAST FORWARD

Strategic planning is the process of deciding on objectives of the organisation, on changes in these objectives, on the resources to attain these objectives, and on the policies that are to govern the acquisition, use and disposal of these resources.

Management control is the process by which managers ensure that resources are obtained and used effectively and efficiently in the accomplishment of the organisation's objectives. It is sometimes called **tactics** or **tactical planning**.

Operational control (or **operational planning**) is the process of assuring that specific tasks are carried out effectively and efficiently.

Within, and at, all levels of the organisation, **information** is continually flowing back and forth, being used by people to formulate **plans** and take **decisions**, and to draw attention to the need for **control** action, when the plans and decisions don't work as intended.

Key terms

Planning means formulating ways of proceeding. **Decision making** means choosing between various alternatives. These two terms are virtually inseparable: you decide to plan in the first place and the plan you make is a collection of decisions.

Strategic decisions are long-term decisions and are characterised by their wide scope, wide impact, relative uncertainty and complexity.

Control is used in the sense of monitoring something so as to keep it on course, like the 'controls' of a car, not (or not merely) in the sense of imposing restraints or exercising power over something.

Question — **Planning, control and decision making**

This simple scenario may help you to understand how these terms are interrelated.

Mr and Mrs Average need to go to a supermarket to buy food and other household items. They make a list beforehand that sets out all the things they need. As they go round the supermarket they tick off the items on the list. If a particular item is not available they choose an alternative from the range on the shelves. They also buy a bottle of wine and two bars of chocolate. These were not on their original list.

(a) What part or parts of this activity would you describe as planning?
(b) There are several examples of decision making in this story. Identify three of them.
(c) What part or parts of this activity would you describe as control?

Answer

We would describe making the list as planning, but it could also be an example of decision making because Mr and Mrs Average have to decide what items will go on the list. Ticking off the items is control and choosing alternatives is 'control action' involving further decision making.

You should be able to answer the various parts of this question without further help.

1.1 Information for planning, control and decision making

Robert Anthony, a leading writer on organisational control, suggested what has become a widely used hierarchy, classifying the information used at different management levels for planning, control and decision making into three tiers: **strategic planning**, **management control** and **operational control**.

Key terms

Strategic planning. The process of deciding on objectives of the organisation, on changes in these objectives, on the resources used to attain these objectives, and on the strategies that are to govern the acquisition, use and disposition of these resources.

Management control. The process by which managers assure that resources are obtained and used effectively and efficiently in the accomplishment of the organisation's objectives. It is sometimes called tactics or tactical planning.

Operational control (or **operational planning**). The process of assuring that specific tasks are carried out effectively and efficiently.

This idea of a hierarchy between strategic and operational levels is an important theme in this Study Text – because an organisation needs to perform well at operational level in order to achieve its strategic objectives. Equally, however, in order for an organisation to achieve its strategic objectives, it is important that the objective and goals at operational level are aligned to those strategic objectives. For example, if an organisation's underlying strategy is based on achieving competitive advantage through the quality of service that it provides its customers, then it needs to ensure that its customer-facing staff deliver the necessary high quality of service to the customers on a day to day basis (ie at operational level).

2 The role of performance management in strategic planning and control

FAST FORWARD

Performance management systems help an organisation measure how well it is **performing against its goals and objectives**, and to identify where **performance can be improved** in order to help the organisation achieve those goals and objectives.

As business environments become increasingly dynamic and competitive, it is increasingly important for managers to develop coherent business strategies and to have tools and processes in place which provide relevant and reliable information to support strategic decision making, planning and control.

This need for information is linked to the importance of performance management in strategic planning and control. **Performance management** is a way of trying to direct and support the performance of employees and departments within an organisation, so that they work as efficiently and effectively as possible. Performance management is also a way of trying to ensure that individual goals are aligned with the organisation's overall goals and business strategy.

Performance management is essentially a set of management processes, often supported by technology, that enable organisations to **define** and **execute their strategies** and to **measure** and **analyse performance** in order to **inform strategic decision making**. The central premise of performance management is to **improve an organisation's performance**.

Performance management systems are plans, with set guidelines and targets, to help organisations measure how efficiently goals are being met, and identify areas where performance can be improved. Performance management systems can also be linked to reward programmes, such that employees are rewarded for helping an organisation to reach its goals (for example through profit-related pay schemes).

Historically, performance management has tended to focus on either people management (eg performance appraisals) or performance monitoring (eg reporting on key performance indicators). However, the concept of performance management is now much wider and includes: strategic planning; performance measurement and monitoring; key performance indicators (KPIs) (covered in Chapter 2); financial planning and budgeting (Chapter 3); business process re-engineering (Chapter 4); risk management (Chapter 6); business intelligence; data warehousing, data mining and analytics (Chapter 8); people management (Chapter 14); and dashboards and scorecards (Chapters 8 and 15).

The reference to KPIs indicates how performance management plays a crucial role in checking an organisation's progress towards its objectives. KPIs should monitor how well a business is performing against its critical success factors (CSFs). In turn, the CSFs are the aspects of an organisation's activity which are central to its future success.

A performance management system should be derived from the company's strategic objectives so that it supports those objectives. It should also change over time as the strategies of the organisation change and should be flexible enough to remain coherent with the objectives of the organisation.

A performance management system should have clear links between **performance measures** at the **different hierarchical levels of the organisation** so that all departments and areas strive towards the same goals. Examples of models of measurement that seek to capture this alignment include the **performance pyramid** and the **balanced scorecard**. These two models are considered later in the Study Text in Chapter 15 but we will look briefly here at how they link the organisation's strategies to its operations and reporting using a performance management system.

The **performance pyramid** is a model of performance management that sets out to relate strategies to operations by translating objectives from the top down and measures from the bottom up, the aim being that these are co-ordinated and support each other. At the top is corporate vision which moves down through market and financial objectives at business unit level, eventually becoming specific operational criteria including quality and delivery at the department and work centre level. The operational measures are reported upward.

The **balanced scorecard** allows top management to review the organisation using four perspectives which provide information on four strategic issues. The financial perspective seeks to resolve how the organisation creates value for its shareholders. The innovation and learning perspective answers the question of how the organisation can continue to improve and create value. The customer perspective looks at what customers value from the organisation and finally the internal perspective considers what internal processes the organisation must do well at to achieve the financial and customer objectives. Under each perspective goals are set, such as manufacturing excellence and specific measures used to monitor outcomes.

2.1 The link between performance management and strategic planning and control

Performance management can be defined as any activity designed to improve an organisation's performance and ensure that its goals are being met.

However, this highlights the fact that an organisation must first have established its goals and objectives, in order to then assess whether they are being met.

In this respect, strategic planning (establishing an organisation's mission, objectives and goals) is necessary before any performance management can take place. Once an organisation's goals have been set, and then its operational performance targets have been set, an organisation can begin to measure whether these goals and targets are being achieved.

In this way, performance **measurement** is an important control in the organisation. However, performance also needs to be **managed** via judicious target setting that reinforces strategic goals and objectives.

Tesco

The Chairman's Statement in Tesco's 2015 Annual Report acknowledges that the 2014/2015 financial year had been 'a difficult year for the company' but he highlights 'As Chairman, my primary duty is to shareholders, and I believe that the best way to deliver shareholder value is to regain our absolute focus on customers and on improving the shopping trip.'

The Annual Report goes on to highlight Tesco's aim is 'to make sure everything in the business is set up in the most efficient way to create value for customers.' Tesco also identifies that it has refocused its business under three operational headlines to try to help it achieve this aim:

- Listening to, understanding and reaching out to customers to create the best possible offer
- Working with growers and suppliers to make great products, and helping to deliver the best value to customers
- Working across different channels to get those products to customers in the most convenient way possible

Tesco acknowledges that the way that it measures performance and rewards success can also play an important part in its aim of creating value for customers. In the light of this it has identified six KPIs:

- Customers recommend us and come back time and again
- Colleagues recommend us as a great place to work and shop – this recognises that Tesco's staff play a key role in customers' shopping experience
- We build trusted partnerships – Tesco needs to build trusted partnerships with its suppliers in order to provide the best offer for its customers
- Grow sales
- Deliver profit
- Improve operating cash flow

The logic for the final three (financial) KPIs is that if Tesco does a better job for its customers, this will help it grow sales and achieve a stronger financial position.

www.tescoplc.com

2.2 The role of management accounting information in performance management

An important point to note from the first section is the fact that managers need information to help them plan and control their businesses effectively. As such, management accounting information can be used for a variety of purposes.

(a) **To measure performance**. Management accounting information can be used to analyse the performance of an organisation as a whole, and/or of the individual divisions, departments or products within the business. Performance reports provide **feedback**, most frequently in the form of comparison between actual performance and budget (as we will discuss in more detail in Chapter 3 of this Study Text).

(b) **To control the business**. Performance reports are a crucial element in controlling a business. In order to be able to control their business, managers need to know the following:

(i) What they want the business to achieve (**targets** or standards; **budgets**)
(ii) What the business is actually achieving (**actual performance**)

By comparing the actual achievements with targeted performance, and identifying **variances**, management can decide whether corrective action is needed, and then take the necessary action when required.

Much control information is of an accounting nature because costs, revenues, profits and asset values are major factors in how well or how badly a business performs.

(c) **To plan for the future**. Managers have to plan, and they need information to do this. Much of the information they use is management accounting information.

(d) **To make decisions**. Managers are faced with several types of decision.

(i) **Strategic decisions** (which relate to the longer-term objectives of a business) require information which tends to relate to the organisation as a whole, is in summary form and is derived from both internal and external sources.

In addition, strategic decision making:

- Is medium to **long term**
- Involves high levels of **uncertainty** and risk (the future is unpredictable)
- Involves situations that **may not recur**
- Deals with **complex** issues

(ii) **Tactical and operational decisions** (which relate to the short or medium term and to a department, product or division rather than the organisation as a whole) require information which is more detailed and more restricted in its sources.

3 Planning and control at strategic and operational levels

FAST FORWARD

An organisation needs to ensure that the controls and performance measures in place at an operational level are **properly aligned** to its strategic goals and objectives in order that it can achieve those strategic goals and objectives.

Although we have already introduced these ideas in Section 1, this section starts by reiterating the main differences between 'strategic' and 'operational' levels of management in an organisation. It then looks at the problems that arise when strategic planning and operational planning are not properly linked or aligned.

Strategic planning is the overall process of deciding the goals of an organisation, and the strategies for attaining those goals.

Strategic control then focuses on questions of whether the strategy is being implemented as planned, and whether the results produced by the strategy are those intended. In both cases, though, strategic control focuses on high level performance, rather than the detail of an organisation's performance. In effect, strategic control is concerned with evaluating the accuracy of a strategic decision – has the decision been justified or not by subsequent performance?

By contrast, **operational control** models tend to be much more precise. Operational control and operational performance measurement tends to focus on much more detailed information, and on a much shorter time period.

Operational control systems should be designed to ensure that day to day actions are consistent with an organisation's overall goals and objectives.

Similarly, **operational planning** needs to be much more systematic and detailed than strategic planning. Operational plans should contain clear objectives, details of activities to be delivered, quality standards, desired outcomes, resource requirements and timetables.

Exam focus point

> Anthony's hierarchy highlights the different levels of decision making and control in an organisation. However, as well as thinking about the characteristics of each level in its own right, it is important to think how the different levels are interlinked – most importantly, through the way in which an organisation's **operational** performance helps it achieve its **strategic** goals.
>
> This idea is also very important in relation to performance measurement, and is emphasised by the **performance pyramid** which we will look at in Chapter 15 later in this Study Text.
>
> If the performance criteria which are being measured and controlled at operational level are not properly aligned to an organisation's overall strategic objectives, this is likely to have an adverse effect on the organisation's ability to achieve those objectives.

3.1 Differences between 'strategic' and 'operational'

We can contrast briefly the differences between planning and control at **strategic** (corporate) and **operational** levels as in the table below.

Strategic	Operational
'Broad brush' targets	Detailed
Whole organisation	Departmental activities
External inputs, with a wide variety of data types from a wide range of sources	Mainly internal information, with less variety of data and from fewer sources
External focus	Internal focus, on actual procedures
Future-orientated, feed-forward control	More concerned with monitoring current performance against plan
Potential for double loop feedback, ie the opportunity to change the plan	Mainly single loop feedback; performance must change, not the plan
Long term	Short term

One of the key challenges that organisations face is linking their (long-term) strategy to their day to day operations. For example, a strategic plan might set revenue growth targets for an organisation over the next five years, but the operational plan will need to consider what practical steps will be taken to generate these revenue increases; in effect, creating a road map that defines the detail of how the overall strategies are going to be put into action.

Exam focus point

> The need to link strategy and operations is also an important idea behind the balanced scorecard (which we will look at in Chapter 15 later in this Study Text).
>
> Kaplan and Norton who developed the scorecard argue that one of the key challenges organisations face is how to align operational improvement activities to strategic priorities.
>
> In other words, there is little point improving an operational process – through total quality management (TQM), Six Sigma, Business Process Re-engineering or any other method – if that process improvement does not translate into tangible results. Instead, organisations should prioritise their operational improvements in the areas which have the largest impact on the organisation's ability to implement its strategy effectively.

3.2 Linking strategy and operations

A member of the examining team for a past syllabus paper similar to Paper P5 wrote an article on this topic. The article included a case study of a fictional company that adopted new management ideas like TQM, just-in-time (JIT) and activity-based costing (ABC) as its strategy for dealing with a high level of customer complaints. The company was trying to improve **quality** and **speed of delivery** while **controlling costs**, but it faced a number of problems.

'The achievement of long-term goals will require strategic planning which is linked to short-term operational planning ... . If there is no link between strategic planning and operational planning the result is likely to be **unrealistic plans, inconsistent goals, poor communication and inadequate performance measurement**.'

(George Brown, 'Management Accounting and Strategic Management', ACCA *Student Newsletter*, March 1994)

3.2.1 Unrealistic plans

Unrealistic operational plans will force staff to **try too hard** with **too few resources**. Mistakes and failure are almost inevitable. This means poor-quality products: costs include lost sales, arranging for returns and time wasted dealing with complaints.

Overambitious plans may also mean that more inventories are produced than an organisation could realistically expect to sell (so costs of write-offs, opportunity costs of wasted resources, and unnecessary inventory holding costs are incurred).

3.2.2 Inconsistent goals

Inconsistent strategic planning and operational planning goals may mean **additional costs** are incurred. An operational plan may require additional inspection points in a production process to ensure that quality products are delivered to customers. The resulting extra costs will be at odds with the strategic planning goal of **minimum cost**.

3.2.3 Poor communication

Poor communication between senior management who set strategic goals and lower-level operational management could mean that operational managers are **unaware** of the strategic planning goal, say to sustain competitive advantage at minimum cost through speedy delivery of quality products to customers.

Some operational managers may therefore choose to focus on quality of product while others attempt to produce as many products as possible as quickly as they can; still others will simply keep their heads down and do as little as possible. This will lead to **lack of co-ordination**: there will be bottlenecks in some operational areas, needing expensive extra resources in the short term, and wasteful idle time in other areas.

3.2.4 Inadequate performance measurement

Inadequate performance measurement will mean that an organisation has little idea of which areas are performing well and which **need to improve**. If quality of product and speed of delivery are the main sources of competitive advantage, a business needs to know how good it is at these things.

For example, if an organisation measures only **conventional accounting results** it will know how much inventory it has and how much it has spent, say, on 'carriage out', but it will not know the **opportunity cost** of cancelled sales through not having inventory available when needed, or not being able to deliver it on time. Equally the **quality** of products needs to be measured not only in terms of sales achieved but also in terms of **customer complaints** and feedback: again the cost is the opportunity cost of lost sales.

3.3 Strategic control

Control at a strategic level means asking the question: **'is the organisation on target to meet its overall objectives and is control action needed to improve performance?'**

Strategic control measures might require **complicated trade-offs** between current financial performance and longer-term competitive position, and **between different desirable ways of building competitive strength**.

3.4 Gaps and false alarms

FAST FORWARD

Strategic control depends on avoiding '**gaps**' and '**false alarms**' and on identifying milestones of performance.

Many firms **measure the wrong things** and **often fail to measure the right things**.

(a) **False alarms** motivate managers to **improve areas** where there are **few benefits** to the organisation.

  (i) Overemphasis on direct costs is foolish when most costs are overheads.
  (ii) Labour efficiency measures are easily manipulated and ignore labour effectiveness.
  (iii) Machine standard hours are irrelevant, as long as the firm has enough capacity.

(b) **Gaps** are important **areas** that are **neglected**.

  (i) New product introduction
  (ii) Customer satisfaction
  (iii) Employee involvement

(c) **Different measures apply to different industries.** In continuous processes, such as chemicals, throughput time is not important, as there will always be buffer inventory. However, it is important in consumer electronics.

3.5 Strategic control systems

To **encourage** the **measurement of the right things**, firms can institute formal or informal systems of **strategic control**. There are four **influences on a strategic control system**:

(a) The **time lag** between **strategic control** measures and **financial results**
(b) The **linkages** with the other businesses in a group
(c) The **risks** the business faces
(d) The **sources** of competitive advantage

3.5.1 Formal systems of strategic control 12/10

Exam focus point

One of the questions in the December 2010 exam looked at a company which produced films for cinema release and DVDs. The company's stated mission is to 'produce fantastic films that have mass appeal' but its aims are primarily concerned with commercial success rather than artistic considerations.

The question highlighted that the company has identified a number of CSFs, but it then goes on to raise concern that the CSFs chosen do not capture all the factors affecting the business performance.

The question also highlighted that there can be two different types of CSFs: **monitoring** CSFs (which can be used for monitoring the performance of ongoing operations) and **building** CSFs (which look at the future of the organisation and its development, for example the launch of new products or the development of new markets).

The examining team commented that students did not appear to be familiar with the distinction between these two different types of CSF (monitoring vs building).

CSFs are those **aspects of a product or service particularly valued by customers** and therefore the business must do well in these areas to outperform competitors. When the business draws up performance measures from its objectives it must make sure that these include measures of the CSFs it has identified as crucial to success. We will look at CSFs again in Chapter 2.

Step 1 Strategy review. Review the progress of strategy.

Step 2 Identify **milestones of performance** (strategic objectives), both quantitative and qualitative (eg market share, quality, innovation, customer satisfaction).

- Milestones are identified after **CSFs** have been outlined.
- Milestones are short-term steps towards long-term goals.
- Milestones enable managers to monitor actions (eg whether a new product has been launched) and results (eg the success of the launch).

Step 3 Set target achievement levels. These need not be exclusively quantitative.

- Targets must be reasonably precise.
- Targets should suggest strategies and tactics.
- Competitive benchmarks are targets set relative to the competition.

Step 4 Formal monitoring of the strategic process. Reporting is less frequent than for financial reporting.

Step 5 Reward. For most systems, there is little relationship between the achievement of strategic objectives and the reward system, although some companies are beginning to use measures of strategic performance as part of the annual bonus calculations.

3.5.2 Informal control

Many companies **do not** '**define explicit strategic objectives** or milestones that are regularly and formally monitored as part of the ongoing management control process'.

(a) Choosing one objective (eg market share) might encourage managers to ignore or downgrade others (eg profitability), or lead managers to ignore wider issues.

(b) Informality promotes flexibility.

(c) Openness of communication is necessary.

(d) Some objectives can be hard to measure quantitatively. An objective like 'employee commitment' is necessary for success, but hard to obtain numerical data on.

Informal control does not always work because it enables managers to skate over important strategic issues and choices.

3.5.3 Guidelines for a strategic control system

The characteristics of strategic control systems can be measured on two axes:

(a) How **formal** is the process?

(b) How many **milestones** are identified for **review**?

As there is no optimum number of milestones or degree of formality, Goold and Quinn suggest these guidelines.

Guideline	Comment
Linkages	If there are linkages between businesses in a group, the formality of the process should be low, to avoid co-operation being undermined.
Diversity	If there is a great deal of diversity, it is doubtful whether any overall strategic control system is appropriate, especially if the CSFs for each business are different.
Criticality	Firms whose strategic stance depends on decisions which can, if they go wrong, destroy the company as a whole (eg launching a new technology) need strategic control systems which, whether formal or informal, have a large number of milestones so that emerging problems in any area will be easily and quickly detected.

Guideline	Comment
Change	Fashion-goods manufacturers must respond to relatively high levels of environmental turbulence, and have to react quickly. If changes are rapid, a system of low formality and few measures may be appropriate, merely because the control processes must allow decisions to be taken in changed contexts.
Competitive advantage	(a) Businesses with few sources of competitive advantage. Control can focus on perhaps market share or quality. (b) Businesses with many sources of competitive advantage. Success over a wider number of areas is necessary and the firm should not just concentrate on one of them.

(Based on*:* Goold, M. & Quinn, J., *Strategic Control: Strategic Milestones for Long-term Performance*)

3.6 Strategic performance measures

3.6.1 Desirable features of strategic performance measures

Role of measures	Comment
Focus attention on what matters in the long term	Shareholder wealth?
Identify and communicate drivers of success	How the organisation generates shareholder value over the long term
Support organisational learning	Enable the organisation to improve its performance
Provide a basis for reward	Rewards should be based on strategic issues, not just performance in any one year

3.6.2 Characteristics of strategic performance measures

(a) Measurable
(b) Meaningful
(c) Defined by the strategy and relevant to it
(d) Consistently measured
(e) Re-evaluated regularly
(f) Acceptable to stakeholders

3.7 Budgeting

Another vital **control mechanism** within organisations, and a key way of **linking strategy to operations**, is budgeting. Budgets provide a quantitative expression of how strategic plans will be implemented over a period of time.

We can summarise the purposes of budgets through the mnemonic 'PRIME'.

Purpose	Comment
Planning	Budget holders are forced to plan how to achieve targets that should ensure the organisation's overall strategic plan is achieved (eg for sales, margins, quality levels).
Responsibility	Budgets help allocate responsibility, and specify which managers control which costs. (We will return to the ideas of accountability and control in Chapter 3, where we highlight that managers' performance should only be assessed in relation to the costs and resources which they control.)

Purpose	Comment
Integration	The process of preparing budgets should help ensure that the planned activities of one area of an organisation do not conflict with another (for example, if the production department forecasts an increase in production, but the sales department forecasts a decrease in sales).
Motivation	If managers and employees are involved in setting the budget targets, this will increase their motivation in trying to achieve the targets. However, it is important that budget targets are felt to be achievable, otherwise they will serve to be demotivating.
Evaluation	Budgets allow trends in performance to be identified and investigated. For example, if actual performance is falling below budget, the reasons for the variance can be investigated, and action taken to correct the shortfall as necessary. In this respect, budgets act as a key strategic control, and they can be used for both financial control (eg sales, profits) and non-financial control (eg error rates, customer satisfaction levels).

Budgets can be used for both planning and control by management, and are widely recognised as management tools which can facilitate the management task of leading a business towards its goals.

In effect, planning and control are two sides of the same coin. The budget reflects an organisation's objectives and targets (plans) – for example, its expected sales for the coming year, and the resources it anticipates it will need to achieve those sales. However, during the year, the organisation's management will compare actual performance to budget, and should take any corrective actions it deems necessary if actual performance is worse than budget.

However, budgets can sometimes also have negative effects. These include the following:

- There is no incentive to try to achieve budgeted figures if the budget is unrealistic.
- A manager may add slack to their expenditure budget to ensure the figure can be met.
- A manager may simply aim to 'achieve' the target but do no more than that.
- A manager may go on a 'spending spree' if budgeted funds remain unspent.
- The budget may focus on short-term results rather than longer-term consequences.

Some of these negative effects also illustrate the distinction between strategic and operational levels of a business. For example, the managers who set the budgets are often not responsible for attaining them, and therefore targets which managers think are realistic at a strategic level may be considered unrealistic once they are translated into an operation level.

Similarly, an operational manager may seek to reduce spending in the short term (for example, on marketing to ensure costs remain below budget) whereas that spending may have generated greater than proportional benefits in the future, and so would have benefited the whole organisation in the longer term.

This again highlights the importance of **goal congruence** within organisations, but the 'integration' aspect of budgeting should also help to encourage **communication** and **co-ordination** between the different parts of an organisation, which will be necessary to achieve goal congruence.

4 Strategic planning vs short-term localised decisions

FAST FORWARD

There is a danger that decisions taken by local managers may not always be aligned with the longer-term strategic plans of an organisation. This highlights the importance of **goal congruence** throughout the organisation.

In the same way Robert Anthony identified a hierarchy of management levels within an organisation (strategic planning, management control, operational control), so we can also identify a hierarchy of objectives within an organisation.

At the top is the overall **mission**, which is then supported by a **small number of wide-ranging goals**. (These may correspond to overall departmental or functional responsibilities within the organisation.)

Each of these goals is supported in turn by **more detailed, subordinate goals** that correspond, perhaps, to the responsibilities of the senior managers in the function concerned. This pattern is continued downwards until we reach the work targets of individual members of the organisation.

As we work our way down this hierarchy we will find that the goals and targets will typically become **more detailed** and will relate to **shorter time frames**. An organisation's mission might be very general and specify no timescale at all, but an individual worker is likely to have very specific things to achieve every day, or even every few minutes.

Note, however, that this description is very simplistic, and the structure of objectives in a modern organisation may be much more complex than this, with the pursuit of some goals involving input from several functions. Also, some goals may be defined in very general terms, so as not to stifle innovation, co-operation and informal ways of doing things.

4.1 The importance of goal congruence

A vital feature in any structure of goals is that there should be **goal congruence**; that is to say, goals that are related to one another should be **mutually supportive**. Goals can be related in several ways:

(a) **Hierarchically**, as in the hierarchical structure outlined above

(b) **Functionally**, as when colleagues collaborate on a project

(c) **Logistically**, as when resources must be shared or used in sequence

(d) In **wider organisational senses**, as when senior executives make decisions about their operational priorities

A good example of the last category is the tension between long- and short-term priorities in such matters as the need to contain costs while at the same time increasing productivity by investing in improved plant and machinery.

4.2 Trade-offs between long-term and short-term objectives

Just as there may have to be a trade-off between different objectives, so too might there be a need to make trade-offs between short-term objectives and long-term objectives. This is referred to as **S/L trade-off**.

Decisions which involve the **sacrifice of longer-term objectives** include the following:

(a) Postponing or abandoning capital expenditure projects, which would eventually contribute to growth and profits, in order to protect short-term cash flow and profits

(b) Cutting research and development (R&D) expenditure to save operating costs, and so reducing the prospects for future product development; in this respect, cost leadership could be seen as a short-term strategy, because it is looking to minimise operating costs rather than develop new products or capabilities as a basis for competitive advantage in the future

(c) Reducing quality control to save operating costs (but also adversely affecting reputation and goodwill)

(d) Reducing the level of customer service to save operating costs (but sacrificing goodwill)

(e) Cutting training costs or recruitment (so the company might be faced with skills shortages)

This relationship between short-term and longer-term objectives also has significant implications for the way organisations **measure performance** and the performance measures they use to do so (something which we will look at in more detail in Chapter 9).

The phrase '**What gets measured, gets done**' is an important one in relation to performance measurement, and its implications are important here as well. For example, if return on investment (ROI) is one of a company's key financial performance measures, then its managers will have a keen interest in maximising the company's ROI.

As a result, however, this choice of performance measure may also encourage the managers to focus on short-term performance rather than longer-term performance. For example, they may decide to dispose of some machinery which is not currently in use, thereby reducing depreciation charges and asset values, and in doing so immediately increasing ROI. However, the potential flaw in such a short-term plan could be exposed if the managers later realise they need to use the machinery again and so have to buy some new equipment (at a higher cost than the equipment they had previously disposed of).

4.3 Centralised strategic planning and short-term, localised decision making

In this context, it is important to remember that corporate strategists will typically be working at the upper end of the hierarchy, and are likely to be taking a relatively **long-term view** of business activity. Similarly, they will typically look at a wider range of measures than the operational decision maker, and adopt a broader and less detailed approach. Many strategic measures are qualitative and less responsive to individual changes in the environment.

For example, a local manager can see how customers are choosing certain products over others from daily feedback. The manager could make a local decision about how best to react to this pattern; for example, by ordering more of the popular product, or offering some kind of incentive on the less popular products to try to increase sales of them.

However, these localised findings will also be reported to the corporate centre and the strategist, whereupon the organisation may make an overall response. Nonetheless, the corporate centre does not have the benefit of the local manager's insight into the local conditions.

Johnson, Scholes and Whittington refer to the idea of 'gut feel'. This is the instinctive response the local decision maker has to the environment, often based on limited data but using their experience and recognising that they must do something. The strategist would prefer to see action based on data, and fitting in with overall goals. Nonetheless, there is room for negotiation if communication channels allow and this could lead to a sensible revision of the long-term plan.

Operational managers will not see any broader trends, so they cannot plan for what is likely to happen in their environment over the longer term. They tend to be more reactive than the strategist, reacting rather than planning ahead, and a conflict arises when the short-term reaction goes against the long-term plan. This can cause conflict, for example where the strategist wants to move into markets but the operational manager does not have the resources to do so at present.

Equally, operational managers may be reluctant to invest in marketing activity, for example, if they are looking only from a very short-term perspective. There will be costs associated with the marketing activity, but the anticipated benefits (for example, from increased sales) will be realised over future periods. In this respect, there could be a lack of **goal congruence** between the strategic plan – for example, to increase market share – and a localised division's focus on maximising profits in the short term.

Also, it is unlikely that the strategic plan and localised decision making will always be in tandem as organisations operate in dynamic environments. Therefore, organisations need to manage any conflicts between the longer-term goals of the strategic plan, and the more immediate goals of the localised decision maker.

However, in many organisations there is an **inherent conflict** between the pressure on management to deliver **short-term results**, and achieving **strategic goals**, which are concerned with the long term.

5 SWOT analysis and performance management 6/15

FAST FORWARD

> Corporate appraisal (**SWOT analysis**) helps an organisation identify the opportunities and threats it faces, and therefore also helps it evaluate the potential strategic options it could pursue. In this respect, corporate appraisal can make an important contribution to improving an organisation's performance. It can also help an organisation identify the key aspects of its performance which need measuring.

When developing its strategic plans, it is important for an organisation to understand its strengths and weaknesses, and to be aware of the opportunities and threats it faces.

SWOT analysis (corporate appraisal) is covered in Paper P3, so you should already be familiar with it as a model. It combines the results of the internal analysis and external environmental analysis into a single framework for assessing an organisation's strengths and weaknesses, and the opportunities and threats offered by the environment. In this way, corporate appraisal allows an organisation to understand its current strategic position as part of preparing its strategic plan.

Key term

> **SWOT analysis** summarises the key issues from the business environment and the strategic capability of an organisation that are most likely to impact on strategy development.
>
> (Johnson, Scholes and Whittington)

5.1 SWOT analysis

Effective SWOT analysis does not simply require a categorisation of information; it also requires some **evaluation of the relative importance** of the various factors under consideration.

(a) These features are only of relevance if they are **perceived to exist by the consumers**. Listing corporate features that internal personnel regard as strengths/weaknesses is of little relevance if they are not perceived as such by the organisation's consumers.

(b) In the same vein, threats and opportunities are conditions presented by the external environment and they should be independent of the firm.

SWOT analysis can then be used to guide strategy formulation. The internal and external appraisals should be brought together so that an organisation can develop its strategies from identifying its own **strengths and weaknesses**, and from identifying **the opportunities and threats** presented by the wider macro-environment. Strengths should be built on and consolidated, while strategies to address any weaknesses can be drawn up. Similarly, strategies should be developed to exploit opportunities, and to provide contingencies against the threats which have been identified.

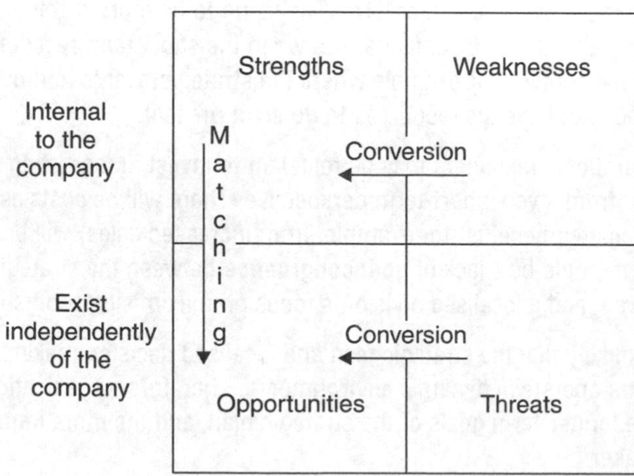

SWOT analysis in strategy formulation

5.2 SWOT analysis and strategic planning

SWOT analysis is usually seen as a key part of strategic analysis. An organisation needs to understand its current strategic position, before evaluating the strategic options available to it. SWOT analysis helps an organisation achieve this understanding in two ways:

(a) It helps the organisation analyse the things it does particularly well (strengths) or badly (weaknesses) at present.

(b) It helps to identify the factors that may give the organisation potential to grow and increase its profits (opportunities) or may make its position weaker (threats).

In this context, it is important to bear in mind what SWOT analysis is for. It is intended to summarise a strategic situation, with a view to deciding what the organisation should do next. Understanding the key opportunities and threats facing an organisation helps its managers identify realistic options from which to choose an appropriate strategy for the firm. A strategy could be drawn up to consolidate the organisation's strengths, improve on its weaknesses, exploit the opportunities available to it, and deal with the threats it faces.

However, it is also important to remember some of the dangers relating to SWOT exercises. As Johnson *et al* highlight in *Fundamentals of Strategy*: 'A SWOT exercise can generate very long lists of apparent strengths, weaknesses, opportunities and threats, whereas what matters is to be clear about what is really important and what is less important. So prioritisation of issues matters.'

Johnson *et al* also highlight two key points, which could be important for SWOT exercises in relation to performance management:

(a) Focus on strengths and weaknesses that differ in relative terms compared to competitors and leave out areas where the organisation is at par with competitors.

(b) Focus on opportunities and threats that are directly relevant for the specific organisation and industry.

5.3 SWOT analysis and the performance management process

The previous sub-section highlights that SWOT analysis is intended to help an organisation decide what to do next.

In this respect, it also plays an important role in the performance management process. Earlier in the chapter we noted that performance management can be defined as any activity designed to improve an organisation's performance and ensure that its goals are being met.

By identifying opportunities and threats, and helping to identify the strategic choices to pursue, SWOT analysis plays an important part in the planning activity designed to improve an organisation's performance.

More specifically, SWOT analysis also assists the performance management process by:

(a) **Identifying shortcomings (weaknesses)** or limiting factors that need to be addressed (this links back to Johnson *et al*'s point about the importance of focusing on areas of weakness relative to competitors)

(b) **Identifying CSFs** which will allow **KPIs** to be created and monitored

(c) **Determining the information needs** of the business to measure and report on the KPIs

(d) **Setting targets**; an organisation should consider what targets would allow it to build on its strengths and/or take advantage of opportunities, as well as minimising its weaknesses and the threats it faces

Equally, however, a consideration of an organisation's strengths and weaknesses, and the opportunities and threats it faces, will also allow the organisation to assess whether targets which have already been suggested are **realistic and achievable**.

5.4 SWOT analysis and performance measurement

As well as helping an organisation decide what to do next, SWOT analysis helps identify the key aspects of performance which an organisation needs to measure.

For example, an organisation may have identified its strengths to be: its reliable products, its well-respected brand name, and the fact it sells its products at competitive prices.

However, this also suggests that in order for the organisation to **continue** to perform well it must maintain its product reliability, reputation and brand name, and it must continue to sell its products at competitive prices.

In turn, in order for the organisation to know whether or not it is achieving its aims it has to measure how well it is performing in these key areas. For example, its key performance measures should include a measure of product reliability, and a comparison of its prices with competitors' prices.

Similarly, if an organisation has identified that one of its weaknesses is its low standard of customer service, then it will be keen to convert this weakness into a strength by improving its levels of customer service. Equally, however, it will be crucial for the organisation to **measure** customer service levels and customer satisfaction, to assess whether or not service levels are improving in the way that the organisation wants.

Case Study **Nike**

A SWOT analysis for Nike could include the following.

Strengths

Market leader – In many countries, Nike is the market leader among sports clothing and footwear businesses.

Strong cash flow – It generates a lot of free cash flow, which enables it to maintain a large R&D budget.

Product innovation – Nike recognises the importance of innovation in maintaining its market position, and is a leading innovator in sports footwear, clothing and accessories (for example, with the NIKEiD service which allows customers to customise their own clothing and footwear, and through the use of NIKE FLYKNIT technology in designing ultra-lightweight footwear).

Branding – Nike is a global brand, and is the most valuable brand among sports businesses, with a brand value (according to Interbrand) estimated at $19.9 billion in 2014. The Nike 'Swoosh' is instantly recognisable, and the organisation pays top athletes in many sports to use its products and promote its technology and designs.

Lean organisation – Nike has no factories of its own, but uses outsourced manufacturing contractors to produce high-quality products at low cost. This gives Nike the flexibility to move production if prices in specific countries rise such that products can be made (to the same quality standards) more cheaply elsewhere.

Weaknesses

Dependence on footwear – Although Nike has diversified into selling a range of sports products and accessories, its revenues are still heavily dependent on its share of the footwear market. This could leave it vulnerable if, for any reason, its share of the footwear market declines.

Dependence on third-party manufacturing – Although Nike's 'lean' structure can be seen as a strength, some people might argue that its dependence on contract manufacturing could be a weakness; for example, Nike may not have the same level of control over the manufacturing process as it would if manufacturing was carried out in-house.

High advertising costs – Although Nike's marketing strategy of signing up major sports stars has been successful in terms of promoting global awareness of its brand, it is expensive. The company's total advertising and promotion expenses were more than 10% of total sales for the year to May 2013.

Opportunities

Industry trends – Nike has traditionally argued that its brand is a sports brand, not a fashion brand. However, its products are worn worldwide as casual clothing and this perception of Nike as a fashion brand creates opportunities for it. For example, customers will buy new sports shoes because they are fashionable, rather than because their existing shoes need replacing.

More recently, Nike has tried to reposition its brand in a way which moves beyond conventional boundaries (eg sports brand vs fashion brand), and instead is trying to move towards creating a single 'lifestyle' brand.

Direct sales – E-commerce offers a major opportunity for Nike to increase sales globally.

International development – Nike's strong global brand recognition could be useful to help it grow internationally, particularly in **emerging markets** such as China, India, and Brazil which have a new, richer generation of consumers with disposable incomes to spend on high value sports goods. In Brazil's case, passion for sports is also high, and global events (such as The Olympics and football World Cups) can be used to promote the brand with a view to increasingly global sales.

Threats

Competitive market – The market for sports shoes and garments is becoming increasingly competitive. In addition to its established rivals (such as Reebok and adidas) Nike now has to deal with competition from newer rivals such as VF Corporation (which owns The North Face and Timberland labels), Skechers and Under Armour. Under Armour, in particular, has been growing rapidly in recent years.

Competitive retail sector – Customers in many countries are also becoming more price sensitive. This means they will shop around for the best deal they can get, and may choose their purchases on the basis of price rather than brand, for example.

In addition, although Nike does have some outlets of its own, the majority of its sales come through third-party retail outlets (which could influence the prices charged for different products). Equally, Nike's sales could be affected by the performance of the retailers which stock its products.

Product cost inflation – Rising raw material costs could be a long-term threat, especially if emerging markets continue to use up more commodities. Labour inflation could also be an issue.

Foreign exchange fluctuations – As an international business, Nike is exposed to the impact of movements in foreign currencies. If it buys and sells in different currencies, then movements in currency exchanges mean that its costs and margins may not be stable over time.

SWOT analysis and performance measurement

You may also be able to think of other factors which could represent strengths, weaknesses, opportunities or threats for Nike. But importantly, in this context, think how these factors could link to performance measurement in Nike.

Here are some possible linkages (although, again, you may have thought of additional ones).

Identifying weaknesses: SWOT analysis has identified that Nike's dependence on revenues from footwear is a weakness. This suggests that Nike needs to try to increase revenues from other products (eg sports clothing) to reduce its dependence on footwear. Equally, it will be important for Nike to measure revenues (and revenue growth) for different product ranges to assess how well it is achieving this goal.

Identifying CSFs: SWOT analysis has identified the importance of innovation and design in enabling Nike to retain its market-leading position. This then suggests that it will be important to have performance measures which look at how effective and efficient Nike's design teams are (and how the development of new products affects consumer demand).

Setting targets: One of the opportunities identified in the SWOT is the growth of revenues in emerging markets. This, in turn, could link to financial objectives, such as revenue growth targets for different markets, and once these targets have been set Nike's managers will then monitor how well actual performance compares to them.

Supply chain management: We have identified Nike's lean organisation and supply chain management as a strength. A key element of performance measurement in relation to this will be looking at how well Nike is able to reduce its product costs, for example through lean manufacturing and eliminating waste in its production processes. Measuring and monitoring the quality of the shoes and garments produced by Nike's manufacturing plants will also be very important – to ensure that quality standards are maintained.

Information needs: As the market leader, Nike is likely to want information about market sales and market growth (to assess its market share and to compare its performance against competitors).

In our brief analysis we have also identified that it will need information about sales from different product types and markets (to assess how well it is taking advantage of potential opportunities there), as well as information about production costs and quality (to ensure it maintains its strength in this aspect of its performance).

Exam focus point

In the June 2015 exam, candidates were asked to use the findings from a SWOT analysis to suggest improvements to the performance metrics an organisation monitors.

The post-exam review highlighted that many candidates focused on the issues arising from the SWOT analysis and how these shape the strategy which the organisation in the scenario should pursue. However, by doing so, candidates were treating this as a P3 question (about strategy) rather than a P5 one (about performance management).

Instead, from a P5 perspective, candidates should have been assessing how well (or not) the organisation's performance metrics enable it to measure how well it is achieving its strategy, or how well they would enable the organisation to identify the impact that the issues identified in the SWOT analysis were having on performance.

6 Strategic models and performance management

In this section, we review two specific models that can be used when appraising an entity's performance. The industry and the markets in which an organisation operates can both influence an organisation's performance, for example due to the intensity of competition in the industry, or the potential for growth within a market.

(a) **Porter's five forces** considers the level **of competition** in an industry or sector, which in turn affect the levels of profit that can be sustained in that industry.

(b) The **Boston Consulting Group matrix** helps the management of an organisation **assess** its products, services and strategic business units in terms of their **market potential**. This is measured in terms of market growth and relative market share and can therefore suggest the attractiveness of entering or remaining in an industry or sector.

You should already be familiar with these models from your P3 studies. However, as we noted in the Exam Guide at the start of the chapter, it is important to remember that the focus in the P5 exam is likely to be on how managers could use the models to understand an organisation's performance, rather than to evaluate different strategic options.

Exam focus point

In their post-exam reviews, the examining team frequently comment that a relatively high number of candidates do not actually answer the question set. A common failing is that candidates write all they know on a particular topic, without **applying** their knowledge to the question set.

The June 2011 exam required candidates to perform a BCG analysis of a company described in the scenario and then use this to evaluate the company's performance. There was no requirement to describe the BCG matrix; instead candidates were asked to apply it to the question scenario.

The June 2013 exam asked candidates to use Porter's five forces model to assess the impact of the external business environment on the performance management at an organisation. This question highlights the difference in the way strategic models (such as Porter's five forces) are likely to be examined in Paper P5 compared with Paper P3.

In P3, you might have expected a question to ask you to use Porter's five forces to assess the opportunities or threats an organisation was facing in its industry environment, or to analyse whether or not to pursue a strategic opportunity.

However, in P5, you should expect the focus of a question to be on how the five forces will affect performance or performance management within an organisation. Continuing the example from the Exam Guide above, if an organisation identifies that the bargaining power of customers is very strong, it will be important not only to monitor the impact this has on performance (eg by measuring gross margins) but also to identify if there are ways of reducing customer bargaining power in order to allow the organisation to improve the gross margins it can earn.

6.1 Porter's five forces model 6/13

FAST FORWARD

Porter's five forces model analyses the factors which determine the intensity of competition within an industry and consequently the level of profits which can be sustained in that industry.

(a) **Threat of new entrants** (which will be affected by barriers to entry and expected reaction from existing firms)

(b) **Threat of substitutes** (which will be determined by the level of innovation of existing producers, the ability of existing competitors to finance responses to the threat and the propensity of buyers to substitute)

(c) **Bargaining power of buyers** (which will be linked to the number of buyers)

(d) **Bargaining power of suppliers** (supplier power and the impact on costs being greater when there are fewer of them)

(e) **Rivalry between existing competitors** (the strength of rivalry being determined by number of competitors, market power, brand identity, producer differences, cost structure and so on)

6.1.1 The threat of new entrants (and barriers to entry to keep them out)

A new entrant into an industry will bring extra capacity and more competition. The strength of this threat is likely to vary from industry to industry and depends on two things:

(a) The strength of the **barriers to entry**. Barriers to entry discourage new entrants.

(b) The likely **response of existing competitors** to the new entrant.

Barriers to entry

(a) **Scale economies**. High fixed costs often imply a high breakeven point, and a high breakeven point depends on a large volume of sales. If the market as a whole is not growing, the new entrant has to capture a large slice of the market from existing competitors. This is expensive (although Japanese companies have done this in some cases).

(b) **Product differentiation**. Existing firms in an industry may have built up a good brand image and strong customer loyalty over a long period of time. A few firms may promote a large number of brands to crowd out the competition.

(c) **Capital requirements**. When capital investment requirements are high, the barrier against new entrants will be strong, particularly when the investment would possibly be high risk.

(d) **Switching costs**. Switching costs refer to the costs (time, money, convenience) that a customer would have to incur by switching from one supplier's products to another's. Although it might cost a **consumer** nothing to switch from one brand of frozen peas to another, the potential costs for the **retailer or distributor** might be high.

(e) **Access to distribution channels**. Distribution channels carry a manufacturer's products to the end-buyer. New distribution channels are difficult to establish and existing distribution channels hard to gain access to.

(f) **Cost advantages of existing producers, independent of economies of scale** include:

   (i) Patent rights
   (ii) Experience and know-how (the learning curve)
   (iii) Government subsidies and regulations
   (iv) Favoured access to raw materials

Entry barriers might be **lowered** by the impact of change:

(a) Changes in the environment
(b) Technological changes
(c) Novel distribution channels for products or services

6.1.2 The threat from substitute products

A **substitute product** is a good or service produced by **another industry** which satisfies the same customer needs.

For example, air travel could be a substitute product for rail travel within the UK. However, video conferencing could be a substitute for business travel as a whole (by allowing colleagues to have a meeting without needing to all be in the same place).

Exam focus point

It is easy to misunderstand the nature of substitute products in Porter's model. While they provide competition, they are **not** goods and services produced by competitors in the same industry. Competition in this way is described by the 'competitive rivalry' force.

However, the example above highlights one of the potential problems in applying the five forces model. At one level of analysis, the 'airline' industry is not the same industry as the 'rail' travel industry. However, at another level of analysis they could both be seen to be part of the 'travel' industry. Defining the scope of the 'industry' under review could therefore be problematic.

6.1.3 The bargaining power of buyers

Customers want better-quality products and services at a lower price. Satisfying this want might force down the profitability of suppliers in the industry. Just how strong the position of customers will be depends on a number of factors:

(a) How much the customer buys

(b) How critical the product is to the customer's own business

(c) Switching costs (ie the cost of switching supplier)

(d) Whether the products are standard items (hence easily copied) or specialised

(e) The customer's own profitability: a customer who makes low profits will be forced to insist on low prices from suppliers

(f) Customer's ability to bypass the supplier (or take over the supplier)

(g) The skills of the customer purchasing staff, or the price awareness of consumers

(h) When product quality is important to the customer, the customer is less likely to be price sensitive, and so the industry might be more profitable as a consequence

6.1.4 The bargaining power of suppliers

Suppliers can exert pressure for higher prices. The ability of suppliers to get higher prices depends on several factors:

(a) Whether there are just **one or two dominant suppliers** to the industry, able to charge monopoly or oligopoly prices

(b) The threat of **new entrants** or substitute products to the **supplier's industry**

(c) Whether the suppliers have **other customers** outside the industry, and do not rely on the industry for the majority of their sales

(d) The **importance of the supplier's product** to the customer's business

(e) Whether the supplier has a **differentiated product** which buyers need to obtain

(f) Whether **switching costs** for customers would be high

6.1.5 The rivalry among current competitors in the industry

The **intensity of competitive rivalry** within an industry will affect the profitability of the industry as a whole. Competitive actions might take the form of price competition, advertising battles, sales promotion campaigns, introducing new products for the market, improving after-sales service or providing guarantees or warranties. Competition can stimulate demand, expanding the market, or it can leave demand unchanged, in which case individual competitors will make less money, unless they are able to cut costs.

Factors determining the intensity of competition

(a) **Market growth**. Rivalry is intensified when firms are competing for a greater market share in a total market where growth is slow or stagnant.

(b) **Cost structure**. High fixed costs are a temptation to compete on price, as in the short run any contribution from sales is better than none at all. A perishable product produces the same effect.

(c) **Switching**. Suppliers will compete if buyers switch easily (eg Coke vs Pepsi).

(d) **Capacity**. A supplier might need to achieve a substantial increase in output capacity, in order to obtain reductions in unit costs.

(e) **Uncertainty**. When one firm is not sure what another is up to, there is a tendency to respond to the uncertainty by formulating a more competitive strategy.

(f) **Strategic importance**. If success is a prime strategic objective, firms will be likely to act very competitively to meet their targets.

(g) **Exit barriers**. Exit barriers make it difficult for an existing supplier to leave the industry. These can take many forms.

   (i) Non-current assets with a low **break-up value** (eg there may be no other use for them, or they may be old)

   (ii) The cost of **redundancy payments** to employees

   (iii) If the firm is a division or subsidiary of a larger enterprise, the **effect of withdrawal on the other operations** within the group

   (iv) The **reluctance of managers** to admit defeat, their loyalty to employees and their fear for their own jobs

   (v) **Government pressures** on major employers not to shut down operations, especially when competition comes from foreign producers rather than other domestic producers

The UK automotive market

The following case study applies the five forces to the UK automotive market.

Competitive rivalry

The UK automotive market is highly consolidated. The major rivalry involves Ford, General Motors (Vauxhall), Volkswagen (VW), Renault, Peugeot, Toyota, BMW, Citroen and Honda. The presence of powerful competitors with established brands creates a threat of intense price wars and poses a strong requirement for product differentiation.

The tough competitive pressure requires increasing promotional costs, but overcapacity also introduces a significant price pressure. Tough market conditions have caused some manufacturers to close certain plants, or reduce working hours, to cut costs and survive on the market.

Firms' competitive strategies have included supply chain improvement, new product development and serving the needs of emerging market segments (eg environmentally friendly or hybrid cars).

Buyers' bargaining power

Due to high intensity of competition on the global scale and increasing overcapacity issues, UK buyers experience very strong bargaining power. This has led to increasing levels of bargain-seeking behaviour among customers.

Suppliers' bargaining power

Though vehicle manufacturers have consolidated (forming large entities) this did not cause a significant shift of bargaining power in supplier relations. The consolidation among vehicle manufacturers has been mirrored by a corresponding consolidation of different supplier groups. However, demand chain partners (car dealerships), especially the large ones, do experience significant bargaining power in the light of the overcapacity issue.

The threat of substitutes

Apart from direct competitors (public transport), cars also compete with other transport services: air, rail and sea. However, the increasing importance of door to door transportation decreases the threat of other means of transportation as substitutes. Ironically, one of the major sources of substitute threats to new cars comes from the sales of secondhand cars. A steady increase in the accumulation of secondhand cars has been one of the reasons behind the fall in new car sales.

Threat of new entrants

The high level of entry barriers (an extremely consolidated industry, well-developed value-added chain, R&D capability, investment capability in promotions and new product development) minimises the threat of new entrants. Nevertheless, due to the globalised nature of the industry the notion of new entrants is not that clear-cut, since existing players might enter new geographical markets. For example, there is the potential for Chinese manufacturers to enter the UK market in future.

6.1.6 Using the five forces model

The five forces model helps determine the **attractiveness of an industry** by assessing the level of profits which can be sustained in an industry. In this respect, it can help support an organisation's decision about whether to enter or leave an industry or market segment.

Moreover, it can reveal some useful insights into the potential attractiveness of an industry in the future, especially if it is used in conjunction with PEST analysis. For example, the analysis might indicate that technological changes are likely to lead to a number of new entrants joining an industry which could reduce the profitability of the industry.

This knowledge about the intensity and power of competitive forces should help organisations develop strategies which help them improve their own competitive position – for example, increasing brand loyalty (to reduce bargaining power of customers or to reduce threat of new entrants), taking over a supplier (to reduce bargaining power of suppliers) or looking at strategic partnerships or alliances with other firms (to reduce competitive rivalry and possibly the threat of substitute products).

It is important to remember, however, that Porter's model is an analytical model. It does not try to simply identify and describe the forces which affect the profitability of an industry, but it looks to analyse the **strength of those forces**.

Understanding the strength of these forces can provide useful background information for performance measurement. For example, if an industry is experiencing fierce competition as rivals attempt to increase market share – with price wars or extensive advertising and promotional campaigns – this might be expected to lead to declining margins.

6.1.7 The five forces model and performance measures 6/13

As we have noted in the previous section, Porter's model looks at **the sources and strength of competition in an industry or sector**. Any organisation needs to understand the nature of its competitive environment if it is to establish appropriate strategies and achieve its objectives.

If an organisation fully understands the nature of the competitive forces it is facing (the five forces), and particularly appreciates which one is the most important, it will be in a stronger position to influence the forces within its strategy and defend itself against any threats to that strategy.

Equally, though, the five forces model can help an organisation understand and measure its performance. We have already identified that the strength of the competitive forces in an industry affects the level of sustainable profits which can be earned in that industry. But this is also relevant when assessing an organisation's performance. If an organisation is operating in an industry which faces strong competitive forces, the profitability of that organisation is likely to be lower than one operating in an industry with weaker competitive forces.

Therefore, as part of their strategic performance evaluation, an organisation could assess the strength of the competitive forces it is facing. (However, as we have already noted, the environment is dynamic, so the nature and relative power of the competitive forces can change.) Nonetheless, some general performance metrics which an organisation might consider looking at are:

Threat of new entrants: percentage of revenue from products protected by patents (as an indicator of how much revenue is protected from new entrants); brand value; customer loyalty; fixed costs as a proportion of total costs (as an indicator of capital requirements); assessment of how unique certain cost advantages are; market share

Threat of substitutes: buyer's propensity to substitute (or conversely, buyer's loyalty to existing products); relative price/performance of substitutes

Bargaining power of customers: number of buyers; size of buyers; price sensitivity; level of discounts offered to customers; switching costs

Bargaining power of suppliers: cost of suppliers' product (or service) relative to ultimate cost or selling price (eg oil companies have high bargaining power in relation to airlines because cost of oil is a major part of the cost of a flight); degree of differentiation between suppliers; level of discounts offered to customers; switching costs

Rivalry between existing competitors: market growth; market capacity; market share; economies of scale; ongoing marketing expenditure

Exam focus point

> A question in the June 2013 exam asked candidates to use the five forces model to assess the impact that the external business environment had on performance management in a company. The 'performance management' element is critical here, and helps to differentiate Paper P5 from Paper P3.
>
> Exam questions in P3 are likely to require candidates to apply Porter's five forces to assess the profitability of an industry, or the desirability of entering an industry.

However, the P5 question requires candidates to consider the aspects of its own performance the organisation needs to manage in order to deal with the five forces. For example, firstly, how can the organisation assess the strength of its customers' bargaining power, and then, if customers have strong bargaining power, how can it try to reduce their bargaining power.

(In the question in the June 2013 exam, candidates were also specifically asked to recommend one new performance measure for each of the five forces areas.)

6.1.8 Potential issues with the five forces model 6/13

However, the five forces model must be used with caution. Its very comprehensiveness can encourage a feeling of false security in those who use it: a sense that all factors have been duly considered and dealt with. Unfortunately, however, no business can be aware of all the threats and opportunities facing it, and it can never have perfect information about their environment.

Moreover, the model **assumes relatively static market structures**. However, this is often not the case in today's markets, which are **increasingly dynamic**, and are also highly influenced by technological progress. For example, the level of rivalry in the fashion retailing industry increased following the entry of online companies (such as Asos and Zalando) that do not operate from physical stores.

Equally, it is important to note that, while the five forces model can provide useful information for strategic planning, the options that an organisation can actually pursue are determined not only by opportunities and threats in the external environment but also by its own **internal resources, competences** and objectives.

Remember also that Porter's five forces model focuses on the profitability of an **industry**. However, by doing so, it underplays the extent to which the **competences and capabilities of individual firms** can determine their profitability within an industry. As such, even though an industry as a whole may be profitable, an individual firm may be less so, if it doesn't have the necessary competences or capabilities to be successful in that industry. Similarly, an individual firm could earn higher margins than its competitors in an industry if it can deal more effectively with key forces, or if it can develop some distinctive competences which provide it with a sustainable competitive advantage in relation to its competitors.

Problem of market definition

Although we noted in the previous paragraph that the five forces model focuses on the profitability of an industry, one of the major problems in using the model could also relate to actually identifying the industry (or market) in question.

It is necessary to define with great care just what market or market segment is being analysed by the five forces. For a large organisation, or one operating in a complex environment, this may be extremely difficult.

BPP's provision of classroom training in accountancy is a good example. The market for training for potential chartered accountants (ICAEW students in the UK) is subject to considerable **customer** bargaining power, since there are a few large accountancy firms that predominate. ACCA and CIMA courses, on the other hand, are more subject to the rivalry from existing **competitors** since, as well as other commercial training providers, universities and local higher education colleges are also sources of competition. In addition, this competition has increased in recent years as **new entrants** have entered the market.

But does BPP have a single market (accountancy training) or does it have different markets according to the different qualifications?

This issue around market definition identifies a potential problem with Porter's model. The model is best used for analysing **simple market structures**, but analysis of the different forces can get very difficult in more complex industries with lots of interrelated segments or product groups.

Competition or co-operation?

Finally it is important to recognise that the model is based on the idea of **competition between firms**. One of the underlying ideas behind Porter's model is that firms are constantly competing against each other, and the intensity of this competition helps to determine the profitability of an industry. The model assumes that companies try to achieve competitive advantages over their rivals in the markets, as well as over suppliers or customers.

However, such an approach does not accurately reflect the context of strategic alliances, electronic linking of information systems of all companies along a value chain (or supply chain), or in a virtual organisation, in which the focus is primarily on **collaboration** rather than competition.

Exam focus point

Part of the question in the June 2013 exam looked at the problems of defining a market in relation to measuring an organisation's market share. The organisation in question made components for eco-friendly vehicles. But this raises the question: is 'the market' being referred to only the market for eco-friendly vehicles, or does it include all vehicles (of which eco-friendly vehicles are only a relatively small part)?

6.2 Boston Consulting Group (BCG) portfolio matrix 6/11

FAST FORWARD

The **BCG portfolio matrix** provides a method of positioning products or strategic business units (SBUs) throughout their life cycles, on the basis of market growth and their relative market share.

Exam focus point

A question in the June 2011 exam asked candidates to perform a BCG analysis of a company's business, and then use this to evaluate the company's performance.

In the second part of the question, candidates were then asked to evaluate the BCG analysis as a performance management system at the company. In their evaluation, candidates should have identified the limitations of the BCG matrix as a performance management tool, as well as its uses.

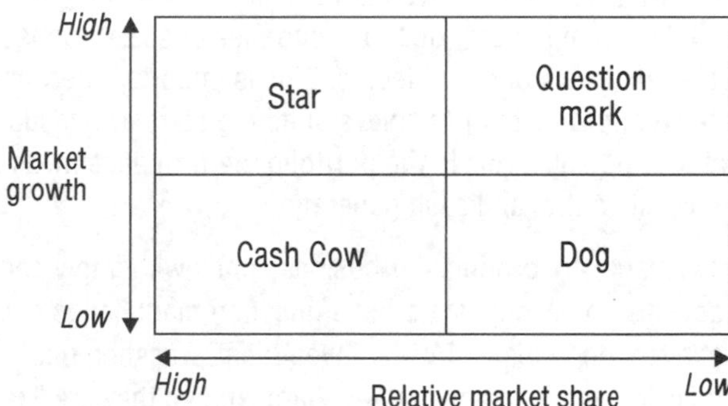

Boston Consulting Group (BCG) matrix

The BCG matrix allows a company to analyse its products or business units in relation to its market share and in relation to market growth (as an indicator of the stage of the market in its life cycle). In this way, the matrix allows a company to assess the balance and development of its portfolio of products or business units.

6.2.1 The axis of the matrix

Horizontal axis: Relative market share

Although the horizontal axis of the matrix is often assumed just to be 'market share', the correct definition of it is actually '**relative** market share'. In other words, an organisation should compare its sales of a product or service in a specified market to the sales earned by the **entity with the largest market share**, not the total sales in the market as a whole.

If an organisation is the market leader, it compares its market share to the entity with the next largest market share. Therefore, a relative market share of **>1** indicates that a product or strategic business unit is the **market leader**, and this is used as the dividing line between high and low relative market share. Therefore, only market leaders (firms with a relative market share of greater than 1) should be said to have a high relative market share.

However, in many cases, although it is not technically correct, a simple measure of market share is used. In other words, an organisation will compare its sales to the total sales from the market as a whole to provide an indication of its relative market share.

Vertical axis: Market growth

Importantly, the vertical axis measures **market growth**, not an individual firm's growth. For example, if we are analysing the performance of a car manufacturer, market growth will be the growth of new car sales as a whole, not the revenue growth of the individual car manufacturer.

The rate of **market growth** can often depend on the stage an industry is at in its life cycle, with new markets often growing rapidly while mature ones hardly grow at all.

As a guide, 10% is often used as a dividing line between high and low growth.

6.2.2 The quadrants of the matrix

(a) **Stars.** Stars are products or business units which have a **high relative market share in** a **high growth market**. In the short term, stars **may require significant investment** in excess of the cash they generate (eg marketing expenditure) in order to maintain their market position. However, stars promise high returns in the future.

(b) **Cash cows.** Over time, as markets become more mature and market growth slows, stars will become **cash cows**. (In effect, cash cows are 'fallen stars'.)

Cash cows are products or business units with a **high market share** in a **low growth** (mature) **market.** Because market conditions are more stable, cash cows should require less investment than stars, and because they have a high relative market share they should be able to maintain unit cost levels below those of their competitors (due to economies of scale). Consequently cash cows should be able to generate high levels of cash income. This is important because they can then **generate cash to finance other products** or business units (eg stars or question marks) in an organisation. Because of their potential role in the portfolio, performance measures for cash cows should therefore focus on cost control and cash generation.

(c) **Question marks.** Question marks are products or business units with a **low share** of a **high growth market**. They have the potential to become stars but a question mark hangs over their ability to achieve sufficient market retention to justify further investment. Question marks may **require significant investment** to help them increase market share, and so they are likely to be cash negative.

(d) **Dogs.** Dogs are products or business units with a **low share** of a **low growth market**. They too may be a drain on cash, and may use up a disproportionate amount of a company's time and resources. In many cases they should be allowed to die, or be killed off. However, in some cases they may have a useful role, either to complete a product range or to keep competitors out, in which case they should be retained in the portfolio.

6.2.3 The BCG matrix and performance measures

The different characteristics of businesses in each of the quadrants means that different financial performance measures are likely to be appropriate depending on a business unit's position in the matrix.

Metrics for business units in high growth industries (question marks or stars) should be based on revenue growth, profit and ROI. Equally, issues such as market share are likely to be important.

Conversely, metrics for business units in low growth industries (in particular, cash cows) should be focused on margins and cash generation. For cash cows and dogs, cost control is likely to be an important issue in preserving profits, indicating a need for performance measures looking at cost.

Question

BCG Matrix

DEF Co is a large company which has three divisions: a restaurants division, a pubs division, and a casino division.

The company's management accountant has prepared the revenue information about the divisions.

	Revenue ($m)	
	Current actual	*3 yr forecast*
Restaurants		
DEF	95	100
Market sector	10,200	10,350
Market leader	295	305
Pubs		
DEF	425	420
Market sector	9,500	9,550
(DEF = Market leader)		
Casino		
DEF	150	195
Market sector	1,800	2,200
Market leader	250	290

Required

Analyse the divisions according to how they fit into the BCG matrix.

Answer

Restaurants

Relative market share is **low**; about 0.3 (95/295).

Market growth is also **low**. The market sector is only forecast to grow about 1.5% (150/10,200) over 3 years.

The restaurant division should be classified as a **dog**.

Pubs

DEF is the market leader, so its relative share must be >1 (because the market leader's sales, by definition, must be higher than any other entity's). Therefore the pub division's relative market share is **high**.

However, market growth is very **low**. Forecast growth in the market sector is only about 0.5% (50/9,500) over 3 years, while DEF's own revenue is actually expected to decline slightly over the 3 years.

The pubs division should be classified as a **cash cow**.

Casino

Relative market share is 0.6 (150/250), so while it is still **low** it is not as low as the restaurant division's market share.

Market growth is **high**. The market sector is forecast to grow about 22% (400/1,800) over 3 years, and DEF's own casino division is forecast to grow even faster than the market.

The casino division is currently a **question mark**, although if it continues to outperform the market it has the potential to become a 'rising star'.

The matrix must be managed so that an organisation's product range is balanced. Four basic strategies can be adopted:

(a) **Build.** This involves increasing the market share, even at the expense of short-term profits. A 'build' strategy might be to turn a question mark into a star. A penetration pricing policy or investment in stabilising quality and brand loyalty may be required to turn a question mark into a star.

(b) **Hold.** This involves preserving market share and ensuring that cash cows remain cash cows. Additional investment in customer retention, through competitive pricing and marketing, may be required to maintain market share if competition is intensifying.

(c) **Harvest.** This involves using funds to promote products which have the potential to become future stars or to support existing stars.

(d) **Divest.** This involves eliminating dogs and question marks which are underperforming.

The suggested strategies for each type of product or business unit are:

(a) **Star**: **Build**

(b) **Cash cow**: **Hold**, or **Harvest** if weak

(c) **Question marks**: **Build** (if it seems likely they can increase their market share) or **Harvest** (if it seems likely they will be squeezed out of the expanding market by rivals)

(d) **Dog**: **Divest** or **Hold**

6.2.4 Using the BCG matrix

The BCG matrix classifies products or strategic business units (SBUs) in terms of their capacity for growth within the market and the market's capacity for growth as a whole.

In doing so it assesses the products or SBUs in relation to their market development potential, and also in terms of their potential to generate profit.

The perceived wisdom is that a firm should have a balanced **portfolio of products** or business units. It needs enough cash generating products (cash cows) to support the cash requirements of question marks or stars (which are cash negative due to the levels of investment they require), and it should have a minimum of dogs.

Some firms may take a different view, though. For example, if a firm's aim is to achieve high growth and it is prepared to invest to achieve that growth, then such a firm may be prepared to support more stars and questions marks than a firm which is concerned with stable cash generation and therefore concentrates on preserving or building its cash cows.

Nonetheless, overall the BCG matrix offers management a simple and convenient way of looking at a diverse range of businesses and products, within a single overall portfolio. In doing so, it encourages management to look at their **portfolio of products or SBUs as a whole** rather than simply assessing the needs and performance of each one independently. For example, the portfolio would allow a group of companies to consider the cash flow requirements of the group as a whole rather than focusing on individual units in isolation.

The BCG matrix should help organisations with their long-term strategic management: for example, by highlighting the need for new question marks or stars to be developed, to eventually replace the current crop of cash cows. But the matrix can also be useful for assessing performance. For example, if a business's portfolio contains primarily cash cows and dogs, this could help explain why its revenue may only be growing slowly, or may even be falling.

However, critics point out the following weaknesses with the matrix:

(a) The model is probably **too simplistic** in the four classifications used. Some divisions or products could fall into more than one category.

(b) Moreover, the axes themselves are too simplistic. A high market share is assumed to indicate competitive strength, but this is not necessarily true. A strong brand may yield competitive strength despite a relatively low market share.

Equally, the matrix uses market share to estimate costs associated with given products or business units. The implication here is that there is a link between higher market share and lower costs (for example, due to economies of scale). However, this is not necessarily always the case.

(c) Equally, high market growth is deemed to indicate an attractive industry. But **fast-growing industries are likely to require significant investment**, so they may not be attractive to a firm with limited capital available. Conversely, markets which are declining or not growing significantly can still provide profit potential for firms, particularly if there are high barriers to entry into the markets. However, if a firm focuses its attention on high growth markets this may lead to the profit potential of declining markets being ignored.

(d) Moreover, the BCG matrix appears to assume that **cash is the critical resource** for organisations (meaning that cash cows are needed to generate cash to fund the growth of question marks or stars). However, this may not be the case. Question marks and stars are also very demanding on the innovative capacity of managers, designers, engineers etc to underpin growth.

(e) The requirement that firms have a high relative market share is justified by the ability of large producers to benefit from economies of scale and experience curve effects (unit costs decline as cumulative volume increases), and thereby to assist in surviving price pressure in late life cycle markets. However, firms following a differentiation strategy or a niche strategy can prosper even if they have a small relative market share.

(f) There is an implicit assumption that the **market** itself can be **easily defined**. This may not be the case. For example, in attempting to calculate the relative market shares of rival supermarkets the following issues may arise.

   (i) Does the market include food products only, or does it also include non-food items such as clothes or electrical items which some supermarkets also stock?

   (ii) Is the market restricted to supermarkets in the 'host' country only or does it look at ones in foreign countries as well?

   (iii) Does the market include all the stores owned by supermarket companies or should it be split to distinguish, for example, out of town megastores and smaller in-town convenience stores?

   (iv) Do all supermarkets aim to serve the same customer market? For example, does a high-quality food store serve the same market as a budget retailer?

Exam focus point

We have already noted that difficulties in defining 'the market' can be one of the problems with using Porter's five forces, but there can be even more of an issue in relation to applying the BCG matrix – given the need to define relative market share.

Therefore the issues which were relevant in the June 2013 exam (looking at the problems of defining a market share) could easily also be relevant to a larger question about using the BCG matrix.

(g) The model fails to consider the **relationship between divisions** or any links between products. However, it is important to consider such links: for example, if a firm stops producing one product will it have a knock-on effect on, say, other products?

Similarly, the position of dogs is often misunderstood in a portfolio. Dogs may be required to complete a product range, and to provide a credible presence in the market. Dogs may also need to be retained in order to reduce the threat from competitors. However, there is often a perception that businesses should divest their dogs.

(h) **Behavioural implications**. When thinking about the relationship between divisions, we also need to consider the potential behavioural implications of the matrix. For example, if the managers of a cash cow see the cash surpluses they earn being invested into other business this could demotivate them, or make them resentful of the other divisions. If the creation of a balanced portfolio leads to jealousy and resentment between divisions, how might this affect performance?

Exam focus point

> There is an article in the P5 Technical Articles section on ACCA's website which discusses the models in this section. You are advised to read the article – 'Business strategy and performance models' – as part of your preparation for your exam.

7 Benchmarking 6/12, 12/14

Performance controls often involve comparing actual results with an internal standard or target, but they can also involve an assessment of performance levels against external benchmarks or comparators.

Exam focus point

> There is a useful article on 'Benchmarking' in the Technical Articles section for Paper P3 on ACCA's website. This article discusses different types of benchmarking and provides some useful examples of the way benchmarking can be used in the strategic planning process. You are encouraged to read this article as part of your preparation for the P5 examination.
>
> It is important to realise that in the P5 exam you shouldn't expect just to have to discuss benchmarking in general terms, but to apply it to a specific organisation given in the case study scenario. The P5 syllabus expects you to be able to '**apply** and **evaluate**' methods of benchmarking performance.
>
> For example, in the June 2012 exam, one of the questions asked candidates to assess the progress of a benchmarking exercise an organisation was carrying out, and then to use the information gained in the benchmarking exercise to evaluate the organisation's strategic position. In the December 2014 exam, part of the compulsory question asked candidates to benchmark the performance of one company against another, in relation to a range of performance measures identified in the question scenario.

Exam focus point

> There is also an article in the Technical Articles section for P**5** (also called 'Benchmarking') which looks more specifically at benchmarking and the use of targets in public sector organisations.
>
> We will also revisit aspects of benchmarking in Chapters 9 and 11 when we consider how benchmarking is used in the context of both private and public/not for profit organisations. We will also look at the idea of public sector league tables (which derive from benchmarking and performance targets) in Chapter 11. This idea of benchmarking in the public sector was examined in the December 2013 exam, in the context of league tables for measuring the performance of different police forces in a country.

7.1 Benchmarking

FAST FORWARD

> **Benchmarking** involves gathering data about targets and comparators such that current levels of performance (especially underperformance) can be identified and evaluated against best practice. Such comparisons can help organisations identify aspects of their performance which need to be improved. However, benchmarking is more useful for helping firms 'catch up' rather than innovating.

Key term

> **Benchmarking** is the establishment, through data collection, of targets and comparators, which will allow relative levels of performance (and particularly underperformance) to be identified.
>
> By adopting identified best practices, it is hoped that performance levels will improve.

Benchmarking provides managers with a means of identifying how well areas of an organisation are performing, with a view to improving the performance of those areas which are currently underperforming.

The sources of data used in benchmarking could include: **internal data** (for example, comparing the performance of different shops in a retail group); **external data** about other companies (for example, those in the same industry); and wider external data (for example, government data about employee sick days).

7.2 Types of benchmarking

(a) **Internal benchmarking**

Internal benchmarking involves comparing one operating unit or function with similar ones within the same organisation. This is easier to do than comparing performance with that of external organisations, and it may be the only approach possible if other companies treat their data as confidential, or if there are no suitable external companies to compare with.

However, using internal benchmarking alone is unlikely to lead to innovative or best-practice solutions, because there is no scope to learn from other organisations.

There is also a danger that, because the focus is internal, an organisation might not pay sufficient attention to the performance levels that other organisations (in particular, competitors) are achieving. However, the nature of competitive advantage means that an organisation's success is likely to depend on its performance in relation to other organisations. For example, if the best performing shop in a retail group earns a profit margin of 20%, the group will not gain any competitive advantage over a rival whose shops earn a margin of 25%, even if the first group improves the margin in all of its shops to 20%.

(b) **Industry benchmarking**

In this approach, benchmarks are set by looking at what other organisations in the same industry as your organisation achieve.

Industry benchmarking can be divided into **competitor** benchmarking and **non-competitor** benchmarking.

Competitor benchmarking: Information is gathered about the performance of direct competitors. From a strategic perspective, the value of competitor benchmarking is that if an organisation can match a competitor's performance in an area which was previously a core competence for the competitor, that area is no longer a source of competitive advantages for the competitor.

At a practical level, the biggest problem with competitor benchmarking could be in obtaining information about the competitor. In particular, a competitor is unlikely to disclose information about a process or area of performance which it knows relates to an area of competitive advantage for it. However, an organisation could overcome this problem through techniques such as reverse engineering (which is the process of buying a competitor's product and dismantling it in order to understand its content and configuration).

Non-competitor benchmarking: This is particularly relevant for not for profit organisations where, for example, it could be useful to compare exam success rates between schools, or mortality rates between hospitals.

Because these organisations do not directly compete with each other, the exchange of data should be more open than in competitor benchmarking. The hope is that by comparing data (and by publishing data as in league tables) poorer performers will be motivated to improve their performance levels.

However, although the comparisons are being made between organisations within the same industry, it is important to recognise that there could be inherent reasons for differences in performance between them. For example, the exam results achieved by different schools could be affected by the socioeconomic backgrounds of their pupils as much as by the teaching the pupils receive in the school.

Benchmarking, by itself, does not explain **why** an organisation might be performing poorly. Instead of using benchmarked results as a motivating factor to improve performance, managers might become defensive and demotivated if they feel they are being judged negatively on results over which they have little or no control.

(c) **Functional benchmarking**

In functional (or 'best in class') benchmarking, internal functions or activities are compared with those of the best external practitioners, regardless of their industry. So, for example, a telephone banking service could compare its call answering times to those in an organisation in another industry which has a very good reputation for answering phone calls quickly and efficiently. Equally, a railway company which provides on-board catering could seek opportunities to improve by sharing information and comparing its catering operations with those of an airline company that has been voted as the 'best' in terms of in-flight catering.

Through functional benchmarking, an organisation can try to find new, innovative ways to create competitive advantage, as well as solving threshold problems. And, because the comparator is not a competitor, there is likely to be less resistance to sharing information than would be the case in relation to competitor benchmarking.

Exam focus point

The P5 syllabus requires you to be able to 'Apply and evaluate the methods of benchmarking performance.' There are various ways this syllabus area could be examined.

On the one hand, a question could require you to use different methods of benchmarking to assess an organisation's performance. For example, if the entity in the scenario has several different operating units, you could be expected to apply internal benchmarking to compare the performance of the different operating units. Equally, however, you may also need to apply competitive benchmarking to compare the entity's overall performance with that of its competitors.

On the other hand, a question requirement focusing more on the 'evaluation' element of the syllabus might require you to identify the benefits as well as the potential limitations of the different methods of benchmarking (internal; industry; functional), or the factors which might affect the appropriateness of the different methods in any given scenario.

A question could look at the process of benchmarking itself, and the different stages involved in a benchmarking exercise; for example, selecting the aspects of performance to compare, and identifying appropriate partners to benchmark against.

7.2.1 Stages of benchmarking

Organisations should begin by asking themselves the following questions:

(a) Is it possible and easy to obtain **reliable competitor** information?

(b) Is there any wide **discrepancy** between different **internal divisions**?

(c) Can **similar processes** be identified in **non-competing environments** and are these non-competing companies willing to co-operate?

(d) Is best practice operating in a similar environmental setting?

(e) Is there time to complete the study?

(f) Is it possible to benchmark companies with similar objectives and strategies?

The benchmarking exercise can then be divided into seven steps.

Step 1 **Set objectives** and determine the areas to benchmark.

Step 2 Establish **key performance measures** or performance drivers which will be measured during the benchmarking exercise.

Step 3 **Select organisations** to compare performance against.

Step 4 **Measure** your own and others' performance, using the measures identified in Step 2 above.

Step 5 **Compare** performances, and identify gaps between the performance of your own organisation and those of the comparator organisations.

Step 6 Design and implement an **improvement programme** to close the performance gaps identified. An important element of this step will also be analysing **how** the comparator organisations achieve superior performance, then assessing whether similar processes and techniques could be introduced into your own organisation.

Step 7 **Monitor** improvements. Benchmarking shouldn't be seen just as a one-off process; its value to an organisation comes from the ongoing improvements in performance which result from the initial comparisons (Steps 4 and 5 above).

Step 1 requires consideration of the **levels of benchmarking**.

Level of benchmarking	Through	Examples of measures
Resources	Resource audit	Quantity of resources • Revenue/employee • Capital intensity Quality of resources • Qualifications of employees • Age of machinery • Uniqueness (eg patents)
Competences in separate activities	Analysing activities	Sales calls per salesperson Output per employee Materials wastage
Competences in linked activities	Analysing overall performances	Market share Profitability Productivity

A key question within Steps 1 and 2 is deciding **what should be benchmarked**. Priority should be given to benchmarking performance areas which are most important to an organisation's success – in other words, its **CSFs**. Another way of identifying performance areas to measure might be to analyse the organisation's value chain, to evaluate which are the key activities that generate value for customers. Additionally, an organisation could choose to benchmark those areas which could bring the greatest benefits to the organisation – for example, through the scope for cost savings.

Importantly, however, an effective benchmarking exercise must focus on performance areas which are **critical to an organisation's success**, not simply those which are easy to measure.

Step 4 requires information. **Financial information** about competitors is **easier** to acquire than non-financial information. Information about **products** can be obtained from **reverse engineering**, **product literature**, **media comment** and **trade associations**. Information about **processes** (how an organisation deals with customers or suppliers) is more **difficult** to find.

Such information can be obtained from **group companies** or possibly **non-competing organisations** in the same industry (such as the train and airline companies mentioned above).

7.2.2 Benchmarking and strategic position

Benchmarking can be useful in helping an organisation assess its current strategic position (as in a SWOT analysis). For example, if an organisation believes that one of its strengths is the reliability of its products, how can it be sure of this unless it has tested the reliability of its products against the reliability of other organisations' products?

Equally, however, if a benchmarking exercise identifies that the organisation's products are more reliable than a competitor's products, the organisation could use these findings as the basis for an advertising campaign, emphasising the greater reliability of its products.

7.2.3 Benchmarking and competitive strategy

Benchmarking could also be useful for assessing the suitability of an organisation's generic competitive strategy (cost leadership or differentiation). For example, before an organisation decides to implement a cost leadership strategy, it would be useful for the organisation to know what its competitors' costs are, and therefore whether it can beat them. If the organisation cannot produce a product or service at a lower cost (or at least the same cost) as its competitors, then it would not seem to be sensible for it to implement a cost leadership strategy.

The same logic applies to differentiation. Whatever an organisation wants its differentiating factor to be, it needs to measure its performance in that area against its competitors before deciding to use that as the basis of its competitive strategy.

7.2.4 Other reasons for benchmarking

(a) **Position audit**. Benchmarking can assess a firm's existing position, and provide a basis for establishing standards of performance.

(b) The sharing of information can be a **spur to innovation**.

(c) Benchmarking can be useful for **setting objectives** and **targets**. Budgets need to be challenging yet attainable; looking at the results comparator organisations achieve can help a company set its own budget targets.

(d) **Cross comparisons** (as opposed to comparisons with similar organisations) are more likely to expose radically different ways of doing things.

(e) It can be an effective method of **implementing change**, people being involved in identifying and seeking out different ways of doing things in their own areas.

(f) It identifies the **processes** to improve.

(g) It helps with **cost reduction**, or identifying areas where **improvement is required**.

(h) It improves the **effectiveness** of operations.

(i) It delivers **services** to a defined standard.

(j) It can provide early warning of **competitive disadvantage**.

7.2.5 Disadvantages of benchmarking

(a) It implies there is **one best way** of doing business – arguably this boils down to the difference between efficiency and effectiveness. A process can be efficient but its output may not be useful. Other measures (such as amending the value chain) may be a better way of securing competitive advantage.

(b) The benchmark may be **yesterday's solution to tomorrow's problem**. For example, a cross-channel ferry company might benchmark its activities (eg speed of turnaround at Dover and Calais, cleanliness on ship) against another ferry company, whereas the real competitor is the Channel Tunnel.

(c) It is a **catching-up exercise** rather than the development of anything distinctive. After the benchmarking exercise, the competitor might improve performance in a different way.

(d) It depends on **accurate** information about comparator companies.

(e) **Potential negative side effects**. There is an old adage (often attributed to the management guru Peter Drucker) that 'What gets measured gets done.' If particular performance targets or objectives are set, employees know that their performance is likely to be appraised against those targets and so they will concentrate on achieving them. However, this could have negative side effects elsewhere. For example, in the UK, there have been concerns that airport passengers are having to queue for too long to get through passport control. Benchmarks for waiting times could result. However, one way to reduce the length of waiting times would be to reduce the quality or thoroughness of the passport checks being carried out, which could then lead to passengers trying to enter the country illegally or without the appropriate documentation not being detected.

8 The changing role of the management accountant 12/12

FAST FORWARD

Burns and Scapens have studied changes in management accounting over a number of years. Their findings are contained in a study that they call the *Accounting Change Project.* One aspect of their study is how the role of management accountant has changed in the past 20 years or so. This changing role arises as a result of environmental pressures.

Management accounting has changed from a focus on **financial control** to a focus on **business support**.

The management accountant has needed to keep up with this shift in focus. Thus the management accountants has have become less of a numbers specialist and more of a generalist. Burns and Scapens have called this new type of accountant the **hybrid accountant**.

The way in which the role of the management accountant has changed in organisations is reflected in Performance Objective 5 – Leadership and management. The performance objective highlights that you will be expected to contribute to the 'leadership and management of your organisation to deliver what is required to meet stakeholder needs and priorities'. Moreover, you will be expected to 'work with others to recognise, assess or improve business performance, using appropriate techniques and IT applications.'

These ideas of the accountant having an important role in improving business performance reflect the ideas discussed in this section – that the accountant's role should no longer simply be to report on financial performance, but that it should also have an increasing business and commercial orientation.

8.1 The traditional view of management accountancy and accountants

Burns and Scapens (in the 1990s) observed that, historically, the **traditional management accountant** had been kept separate from the operational side of the business. This was a physical as well as a psychological separation.

The reason for this derived from the traditional view of accounting as a **mechanism for control**. The accountants needed **their independence** from the operational managers to enable them to **exercise independent and objective judgement** and then report their accounting information up the organisational hierarchy to the divisional managers.

8.2 Why the changes came about

It is interesting to note that Burns and Scapens, in a survey forming part of their study, asked respondents what factors had brought about a change in their management accounting practices.

The main reasons cited were:

(a) That change is important. Burns and Scapens suggest this means that change is regarded as **fashionable**.

(b) That **information needs now differ** as a result of competition, organisation structure and business strategy.

However, respondents did not think that external financial reporting requirements were an important reason. Nor did they think that imposition by a parent company was an important factor.

Burns and Scapens state that there are three main forces for change in the role of the management accountant. These are changes in **technology**, **management structure** and **competition**.

8.2.1 Technology

Probably the most dramatic change in organisations over recent decades has been in **quality** and **quantity** of information technology.

Historically, the management accountant was one of the few people in an organisation who had access to the IT system and the data input generated. The outputs from the IT system were used to prepare financial reports to management. The data input was strictly controlled and only a few people, usually in the accounts department, were allowed to input data.

Nowadays, **sophisticated IT systems** (MIS) allow users across the organisation to input data and run reports giving the type of analysis once only provided by the management accountant.

The management accountant now acts as **another user** of the system, interrogating the MIS to produce management reports based on data often input by other departments.

8.2.2 Management structure

Organisations have experienced a **shift in the responsibility for budgeting** from the centre to operational management. This has occurred as organisations have undergone demergers and the **delayering** of their chain of command, while also increasing **employee empowerment**.

These operational managers are not finance specialists but they have a knowledge of budgeting and cost control. They are accountable for their own budgets and are responsible for managing costs under their control. However, they do not only use financial measures when measuring their performance.

They **produce forecasts** based on their local knowledge of operations and markets. So they tend to look to the future. The forecasts are used with a number of **performance indicators** to give a statement of the performance of the area under their control.

There is still a need for the ongoing comparison of actual performance against target. But this may be over a longer time period than the traditional monthly/annual cycles.

The **management accountant** now has a role as another reporter to senior management. The accountant is expected to produce a financial report but not one that is new to management. Their information is taken along with other measures to give senior management a broad view of the business. Therefore the management accountant's report serves to link the financial outcomes with the strategic consequences of the activities which have been undertaken.

As Burns and Scapens note, 'the monthly management accounts do not provide new information, rather they provide a summary, or breakdown, or benchmark, on how the business is progressing month-by-month'.

8.2.3 Competition

Burns and Scapens asked respondents to their survey what factors had an impact on management accounting. The most frequently cited was the **competitive economic situation** of the 1990s.

The move from financial accounting to a more commercial orientation can be seen to be a consequence of the need to **respond to competition** and deploy a more strategic focus.

The focus on the 'bottom line' has become identified with short-termism. A **commercial orientation** recognises that the future earning capacity of the business is important and not just the profit in the current period.

Organisations now look at a **range of performance measures** to review performance. Many of these are **strategic measures** looking at the organisation's future profitability.

However, Burns and Scapens note that a return to short-termism may occur when economic conditions begin to deteriorate.

8.2.4 Corporate trends and organisational structure

Another relatively recent trend which has also affected the role of accountants has been the creation of business **networks, alliances** and **relationships**, meaning that accounting has had to adapt to new organisational forms involving information sharing, co-operation and flexibility.

Some organisations collaborate in R&D; others are linking up with suppliers in supply chain management and integrating elements of their information systems to support these links.

Also, organisations are increasingly establishing more formal links with customers, due to the increased importance of customer relationship management. As a result, organisations may modify product designs

for customer-specific requirements, provide more flexible delivery methods, and even reshape organisational structures or processes to enable better focus on key customers. However, these developments have all changed information needs and, in doing so, have changed the role of management accountants.

In recent decades, many organisations have also chosen to **outsource** necessary, but non value adding, business activities and processes. This again has implications for management accountants; instead of requiring information about internal processes and internal performance, managers will now need information about how well the outsource partners are performing.

8.3 The modern view of management accountancy and accountants

In their study, Burns and Scapens summarised the changes that have occurred over the past 20 years. They noted the change in management accounting was in **the use** rather than **the form** of accounting. Therefore, even though new accounting techniques may not have been introduced and the traditional accounting systems may continue to be used in an organisation, the management accountant's role in that organisation may still have changed.

The **hybrid accountant** is the modern model of an accountant. This is someone who has **both** accounting knowledge and an in-depth understanding of the operating functions or commercial processes of the business. They are part of a finance function that is becoming **increasingly integrated** into the operations of the business. The accountant is a user of the information system along with other users.

Growing numbers of management accountants spend the majority of their time as internal consultants or business analysts. They spend less time preparing standardised reports, but more time analysing and interpreting information. Moreover, many no longer work in an 'accounting department' but are based in the operating departments with which they work, meaning they are increasingly involved with the operations of their business, and more actively involved in decision making.

An example, quoted in Burns and Scapens' study, highlights a manager who displayed a high level of understanding of accounting systems and accounting information but, nonetheless, still claimed to need a management accountant. The manager regarded the accountant to be important, as the accountant had links to the centralised accounting function. Therefore the accountant had knowledge of interactions with other parts of the business and so was able to provide a much broader understanding of the business.

Exam focus point

A question in the December 2012 exam was focused specifically on Burns and Scapens' work, and asked candidates to use it to describe the changes in the role of the management accountant.

The question then went on to ask candidates to justify why the changes Burns and Scapens identify are appropriate for the management accountant at the organisation described in the scenario.

The examining team's post-exam report noted that while most candidates had a broad grasp of the issues Burns and Scapens addressed, few could remember the detail, and consequently candidates' answers often missed out one or more of the three factors mentioned (technology, management structure and competition).

Chapter Roundup

- **Strategic planning** is the process of deciding on objectives of the organisation, on changes in these objectives, on the resources used to attain these objectives, and on the policies that are to govern the acquisition, use and disposition of these resources.
- **Management control** is the process by which managers assure that resources are obtained and used effectively and efficiently in the accomplishment of the organisation's objectives. It is sometimes called **tactics** or **tactical planning**.
- **Operational control** (or **operational planning**) is the process of assuring that specific tasks are carried out effectively and efficiently.
- Performance management systems help an organisation measure how well it is **performing against its goals and objectives**, and to identify where **performance can be improved** in order to help the organisation achieve those goals and objectives.
- An organisation needs to ensure that the controls and performance measures in place at an operational level are **properly aligned** to its strategic goals and objectives in order that it can achieve those strategic goals and objectives.
- **Strategic control** depends on avoiding '**gaps**' and '**false alarms**' and on identifying milestones of performance.
- There is a danger that decisions taken by local managers may not always be aligned with the longer-term strategic plans of an organisation. This highlights the importance of **goal congruence** throughout an organisation.
- Corporate appraisal (**SWOT analysis**) helps an organisation identify the opportunities and threats it faces, and therefore also helps it evaluate the potential strategic options it could pursue. In this respect, corporate appraisal can make an important contribution to improving an organisation's performance. It can also help an organisation identify the key aspects of its performance which need measuring.
- **Porter's five forces model** analyses the factors which determine the intensity of competition within an industry and consequently the level of profits which can be sustained in that industry.
- The **BCG portfolio matrix** provides a method of positioning products or strategic business units (SBUs) throughout their life cycles, on the basis of market growth and their relative market share.
- **Benchmarking** involves gathering data about targets and comparators such that current levels of performance (especially underperformance) can be identified and evaluated against best practice. Such comparisons can help organisations identify aspects of their performance which need to be improved. However, benchmarking is more useful for helping firms 'catch up' rather than innovating.
- Burns and Scapens have studied changes in management accounting over a number of years. Their findings are contained in a study that they call the *Accounting Change Project*. One aspect of their study is how the role of management accountant has changed in the past 20 years or so. This changing role arises as a result of environmental pressures.
- Management accounting has changed from a focus on **financial control** to a focus on **business support**.
- The management accountant has needed to keep up with this shift in focus. Thus the management accountant has become less of a numbers specialist and more of a generalist. Burns and Scapens have called this new type of accountant the **hybrid accountant**.

Quick Quiz

1 Operational-level planning and control have a mainly external focus. True or false?

2 In the context of SWOT analysis, which one of the following specifically represents a weakness for an organisation?

A Two of its competitors merging
B Inflation rates increasing in its country
C High staff turnover
D The National Government deregulating its industry

3 As well as helping it to monitor its own performance, an organisation uses its key performance indicators (KPIs) to assess the impact that its business environment is having on its performance. One particular area the organisation is interested in is the strength of Porter's five forces, and the impact these could have on the level of profit it can sustain in the longer term.

Among its KPIs, the organisation measures:

- The level of discounts given to customers
- Market share
- The cost of components it has to buy in as a proportion of the total cost of its products

Which of the five forces will these KPIs help the organisation monitor?

KPI	Force(s)
Level of discounts given to customers	
Market share	
Cost of components as a proportion of the total cost of products	

4 Y plc produces and sells a range of confectionery products, including 'Chocaulait', a brand of luxury chocolates. Revenue earned by Chocaulait has increased 11% per year, on average, for the last three years, and in 20X4 annual revenue from the sale of Chocaulait was $55 million.

Total sales of luxury chocolates in Y's country have increased, on average, 2% for the last three years, and for 20X4 were $248 million. The market is very competitive, not least because there are three brands all competing for market leadership. In 20X4, the market leader held a 28% market share.

How should Chocaulait be classified in the BCG matrix?

5 How could benchmarking be useful for an organisation that wants to pursue a cost leadership strategy?

6 According to Burns and Scapens, what are the three main forces for change in the role of the management accountant?

Answers to Quick Quiz

1 False.

Strategic planning and control have a mainly external focus. Operational planning and control have a mainly internal focus; looking at the actual procedures which are used within an organisation to enable it to implement its strategies.

2 C High staff turnover.

Weaknesses have to be **internal** factors. Options A, B and D all relate to factors which are external to the organisation, so they cannot be correct.

High staff turnover is a weakness because when staff leave an organisation they take knowledge with them, thereby reducing knowledge levels within the organisation. In addition, the organisation has to spend time and money recruiting replacements for them, and possibly also training them to get them up to speed with their new job.

3

KPI	Force(s)
Level of discounts given to customers	Bargaining power of customers
Market share	Threat of new entrants; and rivalry between existing competitors
Cost of components as a proportion of the total cost of products	Bargaining power of suppliers

4 Dog

Although Chocaulait's revenues are growing 11% per year, the market is only growing 2%; therefore **market growth** is low.

The market leader's annual revenue for 20X4 was \$69.4m (\$248m × 28%). Therefore Chocaulait's relative market share is 0.79 (\$55m / 69.4m).

Because Chocaulait's relative market share is < 1, it is classified as low according to the BCG matrix.

As Chocaulait has low relative market share in a market with low growth, it would be classified as a dog.

5 For the organisation to be successful in a cost leadership strategy, it needs to be able to produce its goods or services for a lower cost than any of its competitors can. However, in order to assess whether it will be able to do this, the organisation needs to know what its competitors' costs are, so that it can compare its own costs against these.

6 Changes in: (i) the quality and quantity of information **technology** available; (ii) **management structure** and budgetary responsibility within organisations; and (iii) the **competitive environment**, meaning that management accounting needed to take on a more strategic focus.

Now try the question below from the Practice Question Bank

Number	Level	Marks	Approximate time
Q1	Examination	20	40 mins

Performance hierarchy

Topic list	Syllabus reference
1 Mission and mission statements	A2(a)
2 Goals and objectives	A2(b)
3 Objectives, critical success factors and performance metrics	A2(c)
4 Operational performance	A2(d)
5 Planning and control at different levels in the performance hierarchy	A2(e)

Introduction

In Chapter 1, we highlighted the contrast between strategic and operational levels in an organisation, but also the relationship between them.

In this chapter we will now look at the hierarchy of performance (strategic and operational) in more detail.

The chapter begins with a look at **mission and vision**, which identify an organisation's underlying purpose. Then we look at **objectives**, again considering the relationship between objectives at different levels in an organisation.

Study guide

		Intellectual level
A2	**Performance hierarchy**	
(a)	Discuss how the purpose, structure and content of a mission statement impacts on business performance and management.	2
(b)	Discuss how strategic objectives are cascaded down the organisation via the formulation of subsidiary performance objectives.	2
(c)	Apply critical success factor analysis in developing performance metrics from business objectives.	3
(d)	Identify and discuss the characteristics of operational performance.	2
(e)	Discuss the relative significance of planning as against controlling activities at different levels in the performance hierarchy.	3

Exam guide

Remember that the focus of Paper P5 is on performance (performance measurement, and performance management). Therefore, although we are looking at important aspects of strategy – mission, objectives etc – the focus for your exam is on the implications of mission and objectives for **performance management**, rather than for developing strategic options. It is important to remember that P5 is **not a paper about strategy** as such.

Performance Objective 13 (PO 13) – Plan and control performance – requires you to demonstrate that you plan business activities and control performance, making recommendations for improvement.

One of the elements which demonstrate you have fulfilled PO 13 is that you 'contribute to setting objectives for the planning and control of business activities.'

Objectives, and the performance metrics developed from them, are important parts of this chapter of the Study Text. Moreover, identifying performance metrics and key performance indicators is a prerequisite to be able to evaluate performance. If an organisation hasn't set any performance targets then, by definition, it cannot subsequently measure whether it has achieved its targets or not.

1 Mission and mission statements

FAST FORWARD

Mission describes an organisation's basic purpose; what it is trying to accomplish. **Vision** is orientated towards the future, to give a sense of direction to the organisation.

Underlying the behaviour and management processes of most organisations are one or two **guiding ideas**, which **influence the organisation's activities**. Management writers typically analyse these into two categories: mission and vision.

- **Mission:** What is the business for?
- **Vision:** Where is the business going?

Vision and Mission statements

The following are a few examples of vision and mission statements taken from some very different organisations.

Cincinnati Children's Hospital Medical Centre: a not-for-profit hospital and research centre

Mission Statement

Cincinnati Children's Hospital will improve child health and transform delivery of care through fully integrated, globally recognised research, education and innovation.

For patients from our community, the nation and the world, the care we provide today and in the future will achieve the best:

- Medical and quality of life outcomes
- Patient and family experiences
- Value

Vision

Cincinnati Children's Hospital Medical Centre will be the leader in improving child health.

www.cincinnatichildrens.org

Pertamina: a State-owned Indonesian energy company

Mission

To carry out integrated core business in oil, gas, renewable and new energy based on strong commercial principles

Vision

To be a world-class national energy company

www.pertamina.com

Mitsui & Co. Ltd: a Japanese conglomerate (keiretsu) – including chemical, construction, engineering, insurance and banking companies

Mission

Strive to contribute to the creation of a future where the aspirations of the people can be fulfilled

Vision

Aim to become a global business enabler that can meet the needs of our customers throughout the world

www.mitsui.com

The sections below discuss the purpose and context of vision and mission statements. Once you have read them, turn back to the examples in the case study above and consider whether they illustrate these characteristics.

1.1 Vision

A **vision** for the future has three aspects.

(a) What the business **is** now
(b) What it **could** be in an ideal world
(c) What the ideal world would be like

A **vision** gives a **general sense of direction** to the company. A vision, it is hoped, enables **flexibility** to exist in the context of a **guiding idea**.

1.2 Mission

Key term

> **Mission** 'describes the organisation's basic function in society, in terms of the products and services it produces for its clients'. (Mintzberg)

Case Study

The Co-operative Group

The Co-operative Group (Co-op) is the UK's largest mutual business, owned by its consumers rather than by shareholders. Its purpose is 'Championing a better way of doing business for you and your communities.'

Co-op is the UK's leading community food retailer, with approximately 2,800 food stores across the UK – one in every UK postal area. It aims to be at the heart of the communities in which it trades, and the vision of Co-op's food business is 'To be the best local food retailer in the UK.'

The ideas of 'community' and 'local' are important elements in Co-op's food retailing strategy. Instead of operating large supermarkets (to try to compete with Tesco or Sainsbury's) Co-op has focused on convenience stores. In 2014, it acquired 82 new convenience stores, but during the same year it also sold 37 of its larger stores.

Like any business, the Co-operative wants to be a commercial success and therefore issues such as improving product range and product availability throughout the day, ensuring that prices are competitive, and improving customer service are important to Co-op just as they are for other food retailers.

However, although the Co-op Group aims to grow profitability, its mission is not simply to maximise profits. Being owned by suppliers/customers rather than external shareholders has allowed the Co-operative to have a wider social concern, and social responsibility is central to its approach.

The group's website explains the components of its 'purpose' in more detail:

- **Championing** – this is part of Co-op's heritage; 'taking a stand, making a noise on a small number of social issues which are relevant to our businesses and our members' lives.'
- **Better way of doing business** – Co-op recognises the need to be commercially successful but also to build 'a sustainable way of doing business that is mutually beneficial' – using the commercial success to help to strengthen communities. The 'better way of doing business' also underlines the Co-op's continuing commitment to ethical values and sourcing.
- **For you** – providing benefits for Co-op members, and for customers who are not yet members – including 'functional benefits' of better prices; great quality; right location; excellent customer service; as well as the 'emotional benefit' of feeling good.
- **Your communities** – enabling and strengthening communities, being locally relevant, and thereby reinforcing the reasons why members and customers should be loyal to Co-op.

www.co-operative.coop/corporate/aboutus/ourvisionandaims

An expanded definition of mission includes four elements.

Elements of mission	Detail
Purpose	**Why does the organisation exist?** • To create wealth for its owners? • To satisfy the needs of all stakeholders (including employees, society at large, for example)?
Strategy	Mission provides the commercial logic for the organisation, and so defines the following. • Nature of its business • Products/services it offers; competitive position • The competences and competitive advantages by which it hopes to prosper, and its way of competing

Elements of mission	Detail
Policies and standards of behaviour	The mission needs to be converted into everyday performance. For example, a business whose mission covers excellent customer service must deal with simple matters, such as politeness to customers and speed at which phone calls are answered.
Values and culture	Values are the basic, perhaps unstated, beliefs of the people who work in the organisation.

1.3 Mission statements 6/14

FAST FORWARD

A **mission statement** should be brief, flexible and distinctive, and is likely to place an emphasis on serving the customer.

Although many organisations do not have a clearly defined mission, they are becoming increasingly common, especially in larger organisations, and are usually set out in the form of a mission statement. This **written declaration of an organisation's central mission** is a useful concept that can:

(a) Provide a ready reference point against which to make decisions

(b) Help guard against there being different (and possibly misleading) interpretations of the organisation's stated purpose

(c) Help to present a clear image of the organisation for the benefit of customers and the general public

Most mission statements will address some of the following aspects:

(a) The organisation's **reason for existence**

(b) The **identity** of the stakeholder groups for whom the organisation exists (such as shareholders, customers and employees)

(c) The **nature of the firm's business** (such as the products it makes or the services it provides, the markets it produces for, or the business areas in which it will operate)

(d) Ways of **competing** (such as reliance on quality, innovation, technology and low prices; commitment to customer care; policy on acquisition vs organic growth; and geographical spread of its operations)

(e) **Principles of business** (such as commitment to suppliers and staff; social policy, eg on non-discrimination or environmental issues)

(f) **Commitment to customers**

A number of questions need to be considered when a mission statement is being formulated:

(a) Who is to be served and satisfied?
(b) What need is to be satisfied?
(c) How will this be achieved?

Mission statements might be reproduced in a number of places (at the front of an organisation's annual report, on publicity material, in the chairman's office, in communal work areas and so on) as they are used to communicate with those inside and outside the organisation.

There is no standard format, but they should possess certain characteristics:

(a) **Brevity** – easy to understand and remember
(b) **Flexibility** – to accommodate change
(c) **Distinctiveness** – to make the firm stand out
(d) **Open-ended** – not stated in quantifiable terms

They tend to **avoid commercial terms** (such as profit) and **do not refer to time frames** (some being carved in stone or etched on a plaque!).

A mission does not have to be internally orientated. Some of the most effective focus outwards – on customers and/or competitors. Most mission statements tend to place an **emphasis on serving the customer**.

Mission statements

Here are some mission statements from different types of organisations.

(a) **ACCA's mission is to:**

   (i) Provide opportunity and access to people of ability around the world and support our members throughout their careers in accounting, business and finance

   (ii) Achieve and promote the highest professional, ethical and governance standards

   (iii) Advance the public interest

   (iv) Be a global leader in the profession

(b) **Private sector, commercial organisations** traditionally seek to make a profit, but increasingly companies try to project other images too, such as being environmentally friendly, being a good employer, or being a provider of friendly service.

   For example, Coca-Cola's mission statement is:

   - To refresh the world in mind, body and spirit
   - To inspire moments of optimism and happiness through our brands and actions
   - To create value and make a difference

   As another example, Google's mission statement is: 'To organise the world's information and make it universally accessible and useful.'

(c) **Voluntary and community sector organisations** cover a wide range of organisations including charities, trade unions, pressure groups and religious organisations. They usually exist either to serve a particular need or for the benefit of their membership. Such organisations do need to raise funds but they will rarely be dedicated to the pursuit of profit. Their mission statements are likely to reflect the particular interests they serve (and perhaps the values of their organisation). Here is an example (from the World Wide Fund for Nature):

   'WWF's mission is to stop the degradation of the planet's natural environment and to build a future in which humans live in harmony with nature, by:

   (i) Conserving the world's biological diversity
   (ii) Ensuring that the use of renewable natural resources is sustainable
   (iii) Promoting the reduction of pollution and wasteful consumption'

1.4 Mission and strategic planning

Although a mission statement might be seen as a set of abstract principles, it can play an important **role in an organisation's planning process**.

(a) **Inspires planning**. Plans should develop activities and programmes consistent with the organisation's mission. In this way, the mission statement should provide a focus for consistent strategic planning decisions.

(b) **Screening**. Mission also acts as a reference point against which plans are judged – for example, whether the plans are consistent with the mission, and will help an organisation to fulfil its mission.

(c) Mission also affects the **implementation** of a strategy, in terms of the ways in which an organisation carries out its business, and through the culture of an organisation. A mission statement can help to develop a corporate culture in an organisation by communicating the organisation's core values.

1.4.1 Mission and performance management

In Chapter 1, we mentioned that the underlying aim of performance management is to ensure that an organisation meets its goals, and to identify areas where performance needs to be improved in order for it to do so. Equally, we mentioned that an organisation must first have established its goals and objectives in order how to assess well it is performing in relation to them.

In a similar way, by identifying an organisation's key purpose a mission statement can also help to identify – at a high level – the aspects of performance which are important for an organisation, and therefore where its performance needs to be measured.

For example, part of ACCA's mission is to 'Achieve and promote the highest professional, ethical and governance standards.' As such, the mission statement identifies for ACCA the need for performance measures and controls to ensure that it maintains the standards it has set for itself.

1.5 Limitations of mission statements

However, although a number of successful companies have mission statements, the following criticisms and limitations have been raised about them:

(a) They are often perceived to be **public relations** exercises, rather than an accurate portrayal of an organisation's actual values.

(b) They can often be full of **generalisations** which are impossible to tie down to specific strategic implications, and practical objectives. As a result, they may be ignored by the people responsible for formulating or implementing an organisation's strategy.

(c) Mission statements have little value in uniting behaviours and values in an organisation if **employees** are either **not aware of them** or do not understand how they affect them.

(d) Mission statements may **become obsolete** if they are not revised over time to reflect changes in an organisation, its markets, or the external environment.

2 Goals and objectives

FAST FORWARD

Goals and **objectives** derive from an organisation's mission, and support it.

2.1 Goals, objectives and targets

The words 'goal', 'objective' and 'target' are used somewhat imprecisely and, to some extent, interchangeably. However, we suggest the following as possible definitions for them:

A **goal** is often a longer-term overall aspiration. Henry Mintzberg defines **goals** as 'the intentions behind decisions or actions, the states of mind that drive individuals or collectives of individuals called organisations to do what they do.' Goals may be difficult to quantify and it may not be very helpful to attempt to do so. An example of a goal might be to raise productivity in a manufacturing department.

Objectives are often more precise, and should be quantifiable statements of an organisation's goals over a specified period of time. So, an objective for the manufacturing department above might be: to increase productivity by 5% over the next two years.

Targets are generally expressed in concrete numerical terms and are therefore easily used to measure progress and performance. Continuing with the same example, a performance target for the manufacturing department could be: to produce 1,000 units of its finished product per day.

2.2 The need for goals and objectives

Understanding an organisation's mission can be useful when setting and controlling the overall **functioning and progress** of the organisation. However, mission statements themselves are open-ended and are not stated in quantifiable terms, such as profits or revenues. Equally, they are not time bound.

Therefore mission statements can only be seen as a general indicator of an organisation's strategy. In order to start implementing the strategy and managing performance, an organisation needs to develop some more specific and measurable objectives and targets.

Most people's work is defined in terms of specific and immediate **things to be achieved.** If these things are related in some way to the wider purpose of the organisation, this will help the organisation to function more effectively than if these tasks are not aligned to the organisation's overall purpose.

Loosely speaking, these 'things to be achieved' are the goals, objectives and targets of the various departments, functions, and individuals that make up the organisation. In effective organisations, **goal congruence** will be achieved, such that these disparate goals, objectives and targets will be **consistent** with one another and will **operate together** to support progress with the mission.

Equally, while mission statements are high-level, open-ended statements about a firm's purpose or strategy, **strategic objectives** translate the mission into more **specific milestones and targets** for the business strategy to follow and achieve.

2.2.1 A hierarchy of objectives

A simple model of the relationship between the various goals, objectives and targets is a **pyramid** similar to the Anthony hierarchy we looked at in Chapter 1.

When looking at the relationship between mission, goals and the different objectives which can be set in an organisation, we can identify a performance hierarchy as follows.

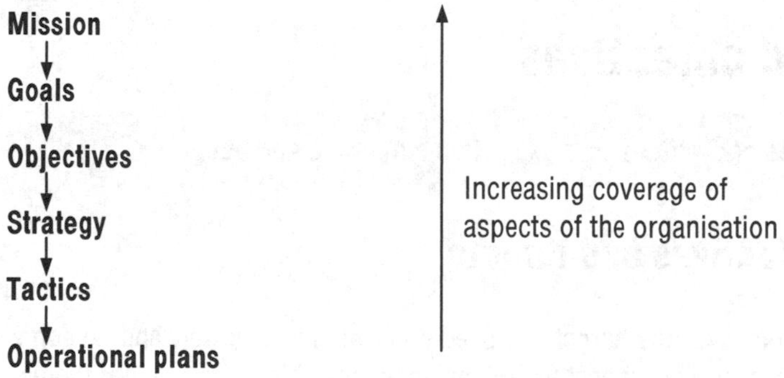

Exam focus point

> This idea of a performance hierarchy underpins the ideas of Lynch and Cross's 'Performance Pyramid' which we will discuss in more detail in Chapter 15 of this Study Text.

At the top of the performance hierarchy is the **overall mission**; this is supported by a **small number of wide-ranging goals**, which may correspond to overall departmental or functional responsibilities. Each of these goals is supported, in turn, by **more detailed, subordinate goals** that correspond, perhaps, to the responsibilities of the senior managers in the function concerned. This pattern is continued downwards until we reach the work targets of individual members of the organisation.

Each level of the hierarchy derives its goals and objectives from the level above, so that all are ultimately founded in the organisation's mission. Objectives cascade down the hierarchy so that, for example, corporate strategies are established to achieve corporate objectives and they, in turn, can be used to set targets for the purposes of tactical planning.

As we work our way down the performance hierarchy, the context in which goals and objectives are set will typically become **more detailed** and will relate to **shorter time frames**. At the top of the hierarchy, an organisation's mission might be very general and specify no timescale at all, but an individual worker is likely to have very specific things to achieve every day, or even every few minutes.

An important feature of any structure of goals is that there should be **goal congruence**; that is to say, goals that are related to one another should be **mutually supportive**. This is because goals and objectives drive actions, so if goals aren't congruent then the actions of one area of a business will end up conflicting with those of another area of the business.

Goals can be related in several ways:

- **Hierarchically**, as in the pyramid structure outlined above
- **Functionally**, as when colleagues collaborate on a project
- **Logistically**, as when resources must be shared or used in sequence
- In **wider organisational senses**, as when senior executives make decisions about their operational priorities

A good example of the last category is the tension between long- and short-term priorities in such matters as the need to contain costs while at the same time increasing productivity by investing in improved plant.

Case Study

Coca Cola

In the previous section, we looked at Coca-Cola's mission statement. In 2010 Coca-Cola launched its '2020Vision', an organisation-wide plan for growth, based around 6 Ps: people, partners, productivity, profit, portfolio and planet.

For Coca-Cola, its '2020Vision' provides a roadmap for converting its long-term aspirations (and its mission) into reality. According to its 2011 Annual Report, the '2020Vision' provides business goals that Coca-Cola needs to accomplish, together with its global bottling partners, customers and consumers, in order to achieve sustainable, measurable growth.

The Annual Report then goes on to list each of the business goals set in the '2020Vision' as identified by the 6 Ps:

- **People**: be a great place to work where people are inspired to be the best they can be
- **Portfolio**: bring to the world a portfolio of quality beverage brands that anticipate and satisfy people's desires and needs
- **Partners**: nurture a winning network of customers and suppliers, together we create mutual, enduring value
- **Planet**: be a responsible citizen that makes a difference by helping build and support sustainable communities
- **Profit**: maximise long-term return to shareowners while being mindful of our overall responsibilities
- **Productivity**: be a highly effective, lean and fast-moving organisation

www.coca-colacompany.com/our-company/

[Accessed 25 January 2016]

Once an organisation has identified its objectives (and **what** it wants to achieve) it can then start to think **how** they are going to be achieved. For example, the organisation then needs to identify the resources (people, machinery, technology, finance) it will need to achieve its objectives, and its marketing plan to make people aware of its products and services.

Conversely, however, if an organisation hasn't identified its strategic goals and objectives, it will be very difficult for that organisation to produce a sensible business plan. A number of the issues which an organisation needs to address in its business plan may also be highlighted in setting its goals and objectives; for example, identifying the characteristics of the business's target markets, identifying the characteristics of the business's product or service that can differentiate it from competitors' offerings, and identifying the level of sales or growth which the business can realistically achieve in its target market.

2.3 Features of goals and objectives in organisations

(a) **Goal congruence.** Goals should be consistent with each other:

  (i) **Across all departments.** There should be **horizontal** consistency. In other words, the goals set for different parts of the organisation should be consistent with each other.

  (ii) **At all levels.** Objectives should be consistent **vertically**; in other words, at all levels in the organisation.

  (iii) **Over time.** Objectives should be consistent with each other over time.

(b) An objective should **identify the beneficiaries** as well as the nature and size of the benefit.

2.4 Setting goals and objectives

Organisations can set goals and objectives in a number of different ways.

Method	Comment
Top down	Goals and objectives are structured from 'top to bottom', a cascading process down the hierarchy, with goals becoming more specific the 'lower' down the hierarchy.
Bottom up	People in individual departments set their own goals, which eventually shape the overall goals of the organisation.
By precedent	Some goals are set simply because they have been set before (eg last year's sales targets plus 5%).
By 'diktat'	A few key individuals dictate what goals should be.
By consensus	Goals and objectives are achieved by a process of discussion among managers – reputedly, Japanese companies employ this approach.

The **setting** of **objectives** is very much a **political process**: objectives are formulated following **bargaining** by the various interested parties.

(a) Shareholders want profits.
(b) Employees want salaries and good working conditions.
(c) Managers want power.
(d) Customers demand quality products and services.

These **conflicting** requirements make it **difficult** to **maximise** the **objectives** of any **one particular group**. The objectives have to **change over time**, too, to reflect the changing membership of the groups.

Exam focus point

Note the link here between these ideas and those of stakeholder management which we will consider in Chapter 5. An organisation needs to consider the interests of its stakeholders (and the relative power of different stakeholder groups) when developing its mission and objectives – to ensure that the mission and objectives are acceptable to the key stakeholders.

2.5 Corporate objectives

When formulating their strategies, organisations have three overall types of strategic choice which they have to make:

(a) **Competitive strategies** – the generic competitive strategies an organisation will pursue in order to achieve competitive advantage; for example, cost leadership or differentiation

(b) **Product-market strategies** – which markets to compete in, and the direction of growth (product-market strategies are illustrated in Ansoff's matrix, which we discuss later in this chapter)

(c) **Method of growth** – whether to grow organically, or through acquisitions or strategic alliances

In turn, the overall strategic choices that an organisation makes will help to shape its objectives and its key performance measures. For example, if an organisation is pursuing a differentiation strategy, based on the quality of its products, then its objectives and performance measures need to encourage the continuing high quality of its products.

2.6 Corporate objectives vs unit objectives

Corporate objectives should relate to the **key factors for business success**:

(a) Profitability
(b) Market share
(c) Growth
(d) Cash flow
(e) Return on capital employed
(f) Risk
(g) Customer satisfaction
(h) Quality
(i) Industrial relations
(j) Added value
(k) Earnings per share

Similar objectives can be developed for each **strategic business unit (SBU)**. (An SBU is a part of the company that for all intents and purposes has its own distinct products, markets and assets.)

Unit objectives, on the other hand, **are specific to individual units of an organisation.**

Types	Examples
Commercial	• Increase the number of customers by x% (an objective of a sales department) • Reduce the number of rejects by y% (an objective of a production department) • Produce monthly reports more quickly, within five working days of the end of each month (an objective of the management accounting department)
Public sector	• Introduce x% more places at nursery schools (an objective of a borough education department) • Respond more quickly to calls (an objective of a local police station, fire department or hospital ambulance service)
General	• Resources (eg cheaper raw materials, lower borrowing costs, 'top-quality college graduates') • Market (eg market share, market standing) • Employee development (eg training, promotion, safety) • Innovation in products or processes • Productivity (the amount of output from resource inputs) • Technology

2.7 Long-term and short-term objectives

One of the key points we have made about goals at different levels of the performance hierarchy is the importance of consistency (goal congruence) between them.

This point also applies to short- and long-term objectives, in the sense that an organisation's short-term objectives should be designed so that they help the organisation achieve its longer-term objectives. However, this is not always possible, and sometimes organisations need to make trade-offs between short-term and long-term objectives; for example, where resources are scarce in the short term. This is referred to as **S/L trade-off**.

The following are examples of decisions which involve the sacrifice of longer-term objectives, as a result of short-term constraints:

(a) Postponing or abandoning capital expenditure projects, which would eventually contribute to growth and profits, in order to protect short-term cash flow and profits

(b) Cutting research and development expenditure to save operating costs, and so reducing the prospects for future product development

(c) Reducing quality control to save operating costs (but also adversely affecting reputation and goodwill)

(d) Reducing the level of customer service to save operating costs (but sacrificing goodwill)

(e) Cutting training costs or recruitment (so the company might be faced with skills shortages)

3 Objectives, critical success factors and performance metrics 12/10, 12/13

FAST FORWARD

Critical success factors are the key activities which will determine whether or not an organisation achieves its objectives. As such, it is very important for an organisation to measure how well it is performing in these key areas.

Exam focus point

One of the questions in the December 2010 exam looked at the relationship between strategy, critical success factors (CSFs) and performance indicators. The question explored the information which an organisation could use to set its CSFs, and then looked at the performance indicators which could be used to measure how well it is achieving its CSFs.

One of the questions in the December 2013 exam also looked specifically at the relationship between CSFs and key performance indicators (KPIs), by asking candidates to evaluate how well the KPIs which had been suggested for an organisation fit to its CSFs.

Critical success factors are those **aspects of a product or service** which are **particularly valued by customers** and therefore those at which a business must excel in order to outperform its competitors.

When a business develops its measures of performance it needs to set them using the particular critical success factors relevant to its performance. For instance, customers may consider technical quality and reliability as particularly important when buying a laptop. Therefore, the performance metrics selected by a laptop manufacturer should include measures relating to quality and reliability. If the manufacturer's performance in these areas is inferior to that of its competitors, then it is likely that consumers will buy the competitors' products in future.

3.1 Objectives, critical success factors and key performance indicators

It is important to understand how objectives, critical success factors (CSFs) and key performance indicators (KPIs) relate to each other.

Once an organisation has established its objectives, it needs to identify the key factors and processes that will **enable it to achieve those objectives**. These key factors are the CSFs. In effect, the CSFs are the building blocks which will enable an organisation to implement its mission and thereby achieve future success.

In an effective organisation, the factors that are crucial to success will influence all aspects of its operations, especially those relating to people. For example, if a company identifies excellent customer service as a CSF, then its recruitment process, training, appraisal and reward systems should all be geared towards promoting customer-service skills in its staff.

However, once an organisation has identified its CSFs, it also needs to know whether it is delivering on them. This is done by using KPIs, which **measure** how well the organisation is performing against its CSFs. The KPIs are the hard data which tells the organisation how well it is performing. KPIs must be measurable.

However, an important point to note about KPIs is that effective KPIs need to tell an organisation something about its **performance**, not simply activity levels. For example, the number of invoices processed by the purchase ledger team is a measure of activity, but it may not be a very useful measure of performance if the team has made errors in the processing of many of the invoices.

Earlier in this chapter we introduced the idea of a hierarchy in which an organisation's goals help support its mission. We could suggest a parallel here, in which the CSFs and KPIs are crucial for enabling an organisation to achieve its mission.

Vision and mission The organisation's vision is a **statement of its aspirations** or what it wants to be in the future. The organisation's mission expresses its **fundamental objectives**; what it wants to achieve.

CSFs The CSFs are the **building blocks** which will enable an organisation to implement its mission and thereby achieve future success.

KPIs KPIs are the **measures** which indicate whether or not the CSFs are being achieved.

For example, if a CSF has been identified as 'We need new products to satisfy market needs', possible KPIs to measure how well this is being achieved could be: 'Number of new products introduced in a period' or 'Proportion of revenue generated from new products.'

Exam focus point

It is vital that you appreciate the difference between CSFs and KPIs, and the relationship between them.

CSFs represent '**what**' must be done to enable an organisation to be successful. KPIs are the '**measures**' of whether or not those CSFs are being achieved.

If an exam question asks you to recommend performance indicators an organisation could use, make sure you recommend KPIs rather than CSFs. For example, 'ensuring high quality' is a CSF because it is what the organisation wants to achieve. By contrast, 'the number of complaints' or 'the number of reported defects' would be KPIs, because these are measurable indicators of the level of quality being achieved.

Example

We can look at the relationship between objectives, CSFs and KPIs by looking at an example of a supermarket.

Let us assume it has defined two of its **objectives** as follows:

- To ensure the loyalty of its customers ('to generate lifetime loyalty')
- To ensure its prices are at least 2% cheaper than the average of rival supermarkets' ('to create value for customers')

The supermarket then needs to identify the **CSFs** which will help it achieve those objectives. These CSFs could be:

- Stocking the goods that customers most want to buy
- Making the shopping experience as pleasant as possible
- Refining internal processes to operate the business on a cost-effective basis
- Using economies of scale to source appropriate goods as cheaply as possible

Then in order to **measure how well it is performing** against these CSFs, the supermarket needs to set **KPIs**. Example KPIs could be:

- The proportion of goods taking more than a week to sell
- Results of customer feedback surveys
- Percentage of customers who are repeat customers
- Market share
- Cost measures and progress against savings targets
- Cost savings in procurement; results of benchmarking prices or costs against rivals

To be 'SMART' (**S**pecific, **M**easurable, **A**ttainable, **R**elevant, and **T**ime-bounded), the KPIs should include numerical targets and deadlines, ideally aiming at continuous improvement.

Exam focus point

There is an article in the P5 Technical Articles section on ACCA's website – 'Defining managers' information requirements' – which explores CSFs further.

The article reiterates the point that CSFs are the few key areas which organisations need to excel at if they are to achieve overall success. In turn, the CSFs dictate the key indicators which need to be measured and monitored to assess whether this success is being achieved.

CSFs and information systems – The article also highlights an important linkage between CSFs and information systems. The CSFs will identify the areas of performance it will be most important to receive management information about, so information systems and control systems will need to highlight performance in these key areas. Managers therefore need to determine in advance what the key indicators are, such that information systems can be designed to provide the managers with the information that is most relevant to them.

However, it is also important to remember the potential impact of CSFs on **behaviour**. Once certain areas of performance are highlighted as key, staff are likely to focus on achieving these. Therefore it is vital that the indicators selected are balanced and consistent across the organisation as a whole.

Sources of CSFs – Another key point the article makes is that CSFs do not relate solely to internal processes or performance. For example, for a road transport company the availability and price of diesel is likely to be vital to operational planning and financial performance. Consequently, external analysis (such as Porter's five forces, or PEST analysis) could play an important role in identifying CSFs, just as much as internal aspects of cost control, product quality, process quality or inventory management.

Perhaps equally importantly, performance measures need to reflect what matters to customers. How well is an organisation performing in those activities which matter most to the customers?

You are strongly advised to read the article in full as part of your preparation for the P5 exam.

3.1.1 Sources of critical success factors (CSFs)

In broad terms, we can identify four **general sources** of CSFs (based on Rockart's work in this area in the 1970s and 1980s):

(a) The **industry** that the business is in; for example, in the supermarket industry, having the right product mix available in each store and having products actually available on the shelves for customers to buy will be prerequisites for an organisation's success, regardless of the detailed strategy it is pursuing

(b) The **company** itself and its situation within the industry (eg market leader or small company; competitive strategy, geographical location)

(c) The **external environment**, for example consumer trends, the economy, and political factors of the country in which the company operates (PEST factors)

(d) Temporal organisational factors, which are **areas of corporate activity** that are currently **unacceptable** and represent a cause of concern, such as high inventory levels; new laws or regulations could also be seen as temporary factors: eg if a regulator has recently fined a financial services company for mis-selling its products, then a possible CSF for the company would be to ensure that similar mis-selling does not occur again in the near future

3.1.2 Types of CSF: Monitoring vs Building

Two distinct types of CSFs can be identified – monitoring CSFs and building CSFs:

(a) **Monitoring.** Monitoring CSFs have a relatively **short-term** focus, and involve the scrutiny of **existing situations**. Managers who are responsible for delivering short-term operating results and maintaining the performance of ongoing activities will invest considerable effort in tracking and guiding their organisation's current performance. They can use monitoring CSFs (such as production costs; actual performance vs budget; or staff turnover rate) to help them scrutinise existing situations.

As such, monitoring CSFs are likely to be used by operational managers in the course of checking and controlling how well their parts of a business are performing.

(b) **Building.** By contrast, building CSFs have a **longer-term** focus, and are **future orientated**. They will be important for helping an organisation adapt to changes in its external environment, and they focus on the future of the organisation and its development.

Building CSFs highlight the factors which underpin the success of new initiatives; for example, the successful launch of new products or services; or the successful implementation of major recruitment and training efforts. As such, building CSFs are more likely to be relevant at senior executive level rather than at operational level.

Exam focus point

There is an article in the P5 Technical Articles section of ACCA's website – 'Performance Indicators' – which explains and illustrates the concepts of:

- Performance
- Objectives
- Critical success factors (CSFs)
- Performance indicators
- Key performance indicators (KPIs)

The article also provides some illustrations of the ways performance indicators relate to topics in the P5 syllabus, and highlights some of the potential problems organisations face when designing performance indicators and measurement systems.

One key point the article stresses is the distinction between KPIs and other (non-key) indicators. As the article highlights, KPIs should measure the most important aspects of performance (ie the CSFs), while other performance indicators should measure how well other, less critical, aspects of performance are achieved.

You are strongly advised to read the article in full as part of your preparation for the P5 exam.

4 Operational performance

FAST FORWARD

Whether strategies are **implemented successfully** or not ultimately depends on operational performance. **Operations** are directly focused on value-adding activities.

The Study Guide requires you to **'identify and discuss the characteristics of operational performance'**.

Operations are the day to day activities that are carried out in order to achieve specific targets and objectives.

Here are some examples.

Sector	Operations carried out by ...
Fast food	Staff employed at a McDonald's checkout
Bank	Dealer on the forex markets
Law	Solicitor finalising the details of a contract for a client
Call centre	People hosting the switchboard
Media	TV cameraperson, or presenter Website construction
Manufacturing	Assembly line worker
Construction	Building site operations

These examples show that operations are directly focused on **activities which immediately add value to the customer**.

Unlike strategy, which involves taking decisions, operations have the following **characteristics**:

(a) **Customer-facing**, in service industries
(b) **Specialised**, as the tasks are closely defined
(c) **More likely to be routine**, but this is not true of all 'operations'
(d) **Limited in scope**
(e) Characterised by **short time horizons**
(f) **Easier to automate** than some management tasks

The significance of operations

(a) Many operational activities require **expert or specialised skills** – such as surgery.

(b) Operations can be areas of **significant risk** for a company and its customers.

(c) Operations are **'moments of truth'** between the firm and its customers. A company's reputation can be made or broken by the quality of its goods and services, which are determined by operational quality and consistency.

These 'moments of truth' are particularly important in service businesses, such as restaurants, hotels and airlines. When travelling on an airline, a passenger has a number of 'moments of truth': booking a ticket, checking in, and being served a meal. These moments are all very important to customers and play an important part in creating the overall image of the airline in their minds. Therefore, if the airline staff focus on improving service, this should improve the airline's performance overall; for example because customers will choose to fly with them again in future rather than looking for an alternative carrier.

(d) The **operational infrastructure** comprises the most **significant element of cost** for most businesses.

(e) The most **well-designed strategy** can be **destroyed by poor implementation** at operational level.

(f) Operations and the deployment of operational activities are a key determinant of **organisation structure**.

4.1 Operational vs strategic and tactical performance

The idea of the three tier hierarchy (the Anthony hierarchy) which we have looked at in relation to information for planning and decision making can also be used when looking at an organisation's performance.

Here again, it can be useful to distinguish between strategic, management (tactical) or operational levels.

Strategic performance is measured over a longer period, often several years, as strategies take time to unfold. It has an external focus looking at the environment of the organisation and incorporating several facets, for instance politics and the economy. It takes account of both quantitative and qualitative outcomes.

Tactical performance is measured over a shorter time than strategic performance and objectives are more detailed. At this level, performance is concerned with how resources are being employed, and the focus is usually on specific departments or activities (for example, tactical performance measures might look at staffing levels or staff turnover in a specific department).

The focus of **operational performance** measures is on day to day activity, to ensure that specific operational tasks are planned and carried out as intended. Therefore operational performance information will be more detailed than information at the other levels (because it is task-specific), and is also likely to be prepared the most frequently (because it is relevant to the immediate term, rather than the medium to long term).

5 Planning and control at different levels in the performance hierarchy

FAST FORWARD

Planning and **control** occur at all levels of the performance hierarchy to different degrees. However, the primary focus of management information at **strategic level** is usually on **planning**, while the primary focus of management information at **operational level** is usually on **control**.

5.1 Planning

The concept of a performance hierarchy which we have discussed earlier describes a cascade of goals, objectives and plans through the different layers of an organisation.

Although this implies a formal, 'top-down' approach to strategic management which is not necessarily the approach to strategy that all organisations pursue, it nonetheless provides a useful framework for evaluating the relative significance of planning compared to control at different levels in an organisation.

The **plans** made at the **higher levels** of the performance hierarchy provide a **framework** within which the plans at the lower levels must be achieved. The **plans** at the **lower levels** are the **means** by which the plans at the higher levels are achieved.

It could therefore be argued that without the plans allied directly to the vision and corporate objective, the operational-level and departmental plans have little meaning. **Planning** could therefore be deemed as **more significant** at the **higher levels** of the performance hierarchy than the lower levels.

This is not to say that planning at an operational level is not important. It is just that the two types of planning are different.

Level	Detail
Corporate plans	• Focused on overall performance • Environmental influence • Set plans and targets for units and departments • Sometimes qualitative (eg a programme to change the culture of the organisation) • Aggregate
Operational plans	• Based on objectives about 'what' to achieve • Specific (eg acceptable number of 'rings' before a phone is answered) • Little immediate environmental influence • Likely to be quantitative • Detailed specifications • Based on 'how' something is achieved • Short time horizons

5.2 Control

Consider how the activities of **planning** and **control** are **interrelated**.

(a) **Plans** set the targets.

(b) **Control** involves two main processes.

  (i) **Measure** actual results against the plan.
  (ii) **Take action** to adjust actual performance to achieve the plan or to change the plan altogether.

Control is therefore **impossible without planning**.

The essence of control is the **measurement of results** and **comparing** them with the original **plan**. Any deviation from plan indicates that **control action** is required to make the results conform more closely with plan.

Exam focus point

> Later in this Study Text, we will discuss the dangers of **information overload**, which occurs when the availability of too much information can hinder managers' decision making.
>
> In relation to performance control, one approach which can be used to reduce the risk of information overload is **management by exception**.
>
> This entails that managers should only be informed of a situation if control data shows a significant deviation from standards or targets (for example, if actual results are significantly different from budget).
>
> In this way, the aim of management by exception is to allow management to focus on the important tactical and strategic tasks, rather than becoming bogged down in operational-level statistics.

5.2.1 Feedback

Key term

> **Feedback** occurs when the results (outputs) of a system are used to control it, by adjusting the input or behaviour of the system.

A business organisation uses feedback for control:

(a) **Negative feedback** indicates that results or activities must be brought back on course, as they are deviating from the plan.

(b) **Positive feedback** results in control action continuing the current course. You would normally assume that positive feedback means that results are going according to plan and that no corrective action is necessary: but it is best to be sure that the control system itself is not picking up the wrong information.

(c) **Feedforward control** is control based on **forecast** results: in other words, if the forecast is bad, control action is taken well in advance of actual results.

There are two types of feedback.

(a) **Single loop feedback** is control, like a thermostat, which regulates the output of a system. For example, if sales targets are not reached, control action will be taken to ensure that targets will be reached soon. The plan or target itself is not changed, even though the resources needed to achieve it might have to be reviewed.

(b) **Double loop feedback** is of a different order. It is information used to **change the plan itself**. For example, if sales targets are not reached, the company may need to change the plan.

5.2.2 Control at different levels

You might think that control can only occur at **the lower levels** of the performance hierarchy, as that is the type of control you have encountered in your studies to date (standard costing, budgetary control). Such **control** has the following **features**.

(a) Exercised internally by management or, in the case of empowered teams, by the staff themselves
(b) Immediate or rapid feedback
(c) Single loop feedback (ie little authority to change plans or targets)

Control does occur at the **higher levels of the hierarchy**, however, and has the following **characteristics**.

(a) Exercised by external stakeholders (eg shareholders)
(b) Exercised by the market
(c) Double loop feedback (ie relatively free to change targets)
(d) Often feedforward elements

A useful way to illustrate the differences between controls at the higher and lower levels of the performance hierarchy is through using **two case study examples**.

Case Study — Controls over performance

(a) **Call centres**

Staff working at call centres in India are subject to precise controls and targets.

(i) The longest time a phone should ring before it is answered
(ii) Speed of dealing with the caller's query
(iii) Rehearsal of a 'script', or use of precise responses or prompts from software

Staff who take too long dealing with queries may be counselled or dismissed. Staff also receive training about UK culture and advice on how to chat with someone from a different culture.

The targets are precise and closely linked to the service provided. They also enable rapid feedback to be gained. Control and planning are exercised over the process of delivery.

(b) **Senior management**

Senior management initiate the planning process, but their time is planned to a far less rigid degree than people at operational level.

For example, the Chief Executive of Network Rail in the UK is responsible to shareholders but, given the nature of the industry and its reliance on government subsidies, must also be accountable to other stakeholders. The market is mainly concerned with results. Controls over corporate governance – over how the company is run – are mainly to do with ensuring the transparency and integrity of the governance process.

Chapter Roundup

- Mission describes an organisation's basis purpose; what it is trying to accomplish. **Vision** is orientated towards the future, to give a sense of direction to the organisation.
- A **mission statement** should be brief, flexible and distinctive, and is likely to place an emphasis on serving the customer.
- **Goals** and **objectives** derive from an organisation's mission, and support it.
- **Critical success factors** are the key activities which will determine whether or not an organisation achieves its objectives. As such, it is very important for an organisation to measure how well it is performing in these key areas.
- Whether strategies are **implemented successfully** or not ultimately depends on operational performance. **Operations** are directly focused on value-adding activities.
- **Planning** and **control** occur at all levels of the performance hierarchy to different degrees. However, the primary focus of management information at **strategic level** is usually on **planning**, while the primary focus of management information at **operational level** is usually on **control**.

Quick Quiz

1 'In ten years' time, all our activities will be web-enabled.' This is a:

A Vision
B Mission
C Goal
D Objective

2 The courier company Federal Express (FedEx) used to have the very brief mission statement 'Absolutely, positively overnight'. FedEx's mission statement was then expanded to highlight that the company remains 'absolutely, positively focused on safety, customers and communities'.

In general terms, which of the following elements should organisations include in their mission statements:

(i) Policies and standards of behaviour
(ii) Profitability
(iii) The organisation's fundamental objectives and the nature of its business

A (i) and (ii)
B (i) and (iii)
C (ii) and (iii)
D (i), (ii) and (iii)

3 Place the terms listed below in the correct boxes of the diagram to show the hierarchy of objectives.

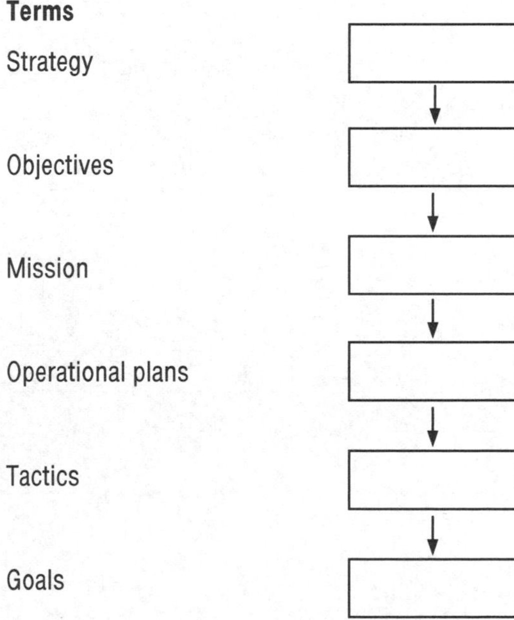

4 Mr Smith is looking to expand his training business, and he has identified that recruiting skilled staff will be vital to the success of the expansion.

Which of the following best describes 'recruiting skilled staff' in this context?

A An objective
B A critical success factor
C A key performance indicator
D A mission statement

5 Which of the following is not a characteristic of operations?

A Specialised
B Long time horizons
C Easy to automate
D Routine

Answers to Quick Quiz

1 A Vision, as the statement is future orientated. We do not know what the organisation actually does so it cannot be a mission.

2 B (i) and (iii)

A mission statement should identify an organisation's fundamental purpose and objectives, and the nature of its business. A mission statement should also identify the organisation's values and culture.

Profitability will be an objective for a business, rather than an element of the mission statement.

3

4 B 'Recruiting skilled staff' is a critical success factor. It is something which Mr Smith has to do in order for his objective of expanding the business to be successful. The KPI related to this CSF would have to include a measurement of how successful Mr Smith is in recruiting new staff; for example, the number of new staff recruited.

5 B Operations and operational controls relate to the routine day to day activities within an organisation. The strategic level (rather than the operational level) of the performance hierarchy focuses on the long term.

Now try the question below from the Practice Question Bank

Number	Level	Marks	Approximate time
Q2	Examination	20	40 mins

Performance management and control of the organisation

Topic list	Syllabus reference
1 Strengths and weaknesses of alternative budget models	A3(a)
2 Evaluating budget variances	A3(b)
3 Responsibility and controllability	A3(b)

Introduction

In Chapter 1 we noted that budgets are an important planning and control mechanism within organisations – setting performance targets for business units and managers to work towards, and then monitoring actual performance against those targets.

In this chapter, we will look at the different models which organisations could use as a basis for preparing their budgets.

Actual revenues and costs can differ from the budget figures for a wide variety of reasons, and budget variance analysis addresses those differences. In many cases, variance analysis can identify issues which are affecting an organisation's actual performance. However, in others, the variances may arise due to problems with the budgets themselves – not the actual performance.

One of the principal aims of Paper P5 is to ensure that you can apply relevant knowledge and skills, and can exercise professional judgement in selecting and applying appropriate strategic management accounting techniques in different business contexts.

In relation to budgets and budgeting, important issues could be identifying whether the budget model being used (or proposed) by an organisation is appropriate to the context of that organisation, and then whether budget variances provide a fair reflection of actual performance.

Study guide

		Intellectual level
A3	**Performance management and control of the organisation**	
(a)	Evaluate the strengths and weaknesses of alternative budgeting models and compare such techniques as fixed and flexible, rolling, activity based, zero based and incremental.	3
(b)	Evaluate different types of budget variances and how these relate to issues in planning and controlling organisations.	3

Exam guide

The examining team for Paper P5 have identified two frequent weaknesses in answers to budgeting questions. These are: (i) lack of lower-level, assumed knowledge and (ii) not observing the specific requirements of questions.

From your earlier studies (in particular from Paper F5) you should be able to explain the different types of budget an organisation could use, and you should be able to indicate the benefits and limitations of using different types of budget.

Make sure you have a good understanding of this assumed knowledge, because in Paper P5 you may be expected to apply it to a scenario in order to evaluate whether or not the type of budget an organisation is using is appropriate to its particular circumstances.

In the same way that you should be familiar with different types of budgets from your earlier studies, you should also be familiar (from Paper F5) with how to calculate variances, and the differences between planning and operational variances. Nonetheless, being able to distinguish the extent to which variances are planning variances and the extent to which they are operational is vital in understanding an organisation's performance, so you should be prepared to apply your knowledge of variance analysis to a scenario in this way in order to help you evaluate how well an organisation is performing.

One of the elements of Performance objective 13 (PO 13) – Plan and control performance – requires you to 'Coordinate, prepare and use budgets selecting suitable budgeting models.'

Another element of PO 13 is that you 'Use appropriate techniques to assess and to evaluate actual performance against plans.'

In this chapter, we discuss the advantages and disadvantages of different budget models, and those advantages and disadvantages which could influence whether a particular budget model is suitable for your organisation or not.

Similarly, variance analysis (which we discuss later in the chapter) is a key technique for assessing actual performance against plan.

1 Strengths and weaknesses of alternative budget models 12/12, 6/13

FAST FORWARD

There are a number of **different techniques** which an organisation could use as the basis for preparing its budgets. It is important to assess the potential **advantages and disadvantages** of each in order to select one which is appropriate for the organisation's circumstances.

In Chapter 1 we identified the role that budgets can play in linking strategy to operations, and we looked at the purposes of budgets as identified by the mnemonic 'PRIME' (for planning, responsibility, integration, motivation and evaluation of performance).

In this chapter, we will review the different models which can be used for preparing budgets, models which you should have encountered earlier in your studies or at work. You will see that there is no 'one size fits all' model and that some models work far better in certain environments. There are also assumptions underpinning these models that may weaken their application, as this section explains.

Budgets are also being improved with new tools and techniques. In particular, forecasting has become essential to managing dynamic environments. Companies are also moving from the traditional **top-down**, centralised budget process to a participative **bottom-up** method.

1.1 Top-down vs bottom-up budgeting

Top-down budgeting – Budgets are prepared centrally by senior management. This should help to ensure that the budgets are consistent with an organisation's longer-term objectives, and should help to ensure co-ordination and avoid inconsistencies between the budgets of different departments.

However, a significant drawback of top-down budgeting is that local budget holders do not have any opportunity to participate in the budgeting process. Instead they have their budget imposed on them, which will not improve their motivation to achieve their budget targets.

Bottom-up budgeting – Local managers prepare their own budgets – or at least participate in the budget-setting process, prior to budgets being reviewed and approved by senior management.

Managers should be motivated to achieve their budgets if they have been involved in setting them. Equally, local managers should have better knowledge than senior management of the conditions their business units face. As a result, the targets and information in the resulting budget should be more realistic and achievable.

However, bottom-up budgeting could lead to dysfunctional behaviour as local managers focus on the individual concerns of their business units rather than overall corporate objectives. Equally, managers may create budgetary slack, and set targets which are too easy to achieve.

1.2 Alternative budget models

Knowledge brought forward from earlier studies

Incremental budgeting

Incremental budgeting is the traditional approach to setting a budget and involves basing next year's budget on the current year's results plus an extra amount (an 'increment') for estimated growth or inflation next year. In the process of preparing budgets, managers might be careful to **overestimate costs**, so that they will **not be blamed** in the future for overspending. 'The personal goals of managers (personal income, size of staff, esteem, and power) will often lead to a "bargained" budget whereby managers intentionally create slack as a protective device.' (Horngren)

Slack is the difference between the minimum necessary costs and the costs built into the budget or actually incurred.

In controlling actual operations, managers must then ensure that their **spending rises to meet their budget**, otherwise they will be 'blamed' for careless budgeting.

A typical situation is for a manager to **waste money on non-essential expenses** so that they **use all their budget allowances**. The reason behind their action is the fear that unless the allowance is fully spent it will be **reduced in future periods** thus making their job more difficult, as the future reduced budgets will not be so easy to attain. Because inefficiency and slack are allowed for in budgets, achieving a budget target means only that costs have remained within the accepted levels of inefficient spending. One approach to the removal of slack is zero based budgeting.

Zero based budgeting

Zero based budgeting (ZBB) involves deconstructing the existing cost base and analysing the fundamental elements that drive each cost category, before preparing the budget for each cost centre from the ground up (ie from a 'zero base'). Every process or expenditure then has to be justified in its entirety in order to be included in the next year's budget.

In ZBB, there should be a positive attempt to **eliminate inefficiency and slack** from current expenditure, not merely to prevent future cost increases. ZBB rejects the idea that next year's budgeted activities should assume that last year's activities will continue at the same level or volume, and that next year's budget can be based on last year's costs plus an extra amount for expansion and inflation.

Case Study

Cisco systems – reducing travel expenses

Instead of managing costs through hundreds of account codes in the general ledger, managers can focus on understanding the root causes of the costs (cost drivers) which they can only see through by taking a process-driven view. While revenues are driven by customer orders, costs are driven by activities and transactions, and the work that people do to fulfil those orders.

One way to tackle expenses in general, and travel in particular, is to change how you describe them, so that people can distinguish between those that 'add value' and those that don't.

In 2008, Cisco Systems cut travel expenses from around $750 million per year to approximately $350 million through challenging whether the travel was necessary to add value for the business. While travel and meetings for sales, new business, and customer opportunities continued unaffected, internal travel and meetings were redirected to Cisco's various virtual meeting technologies.

When staff clicked on internal meetings as a reason for travel in the self-booking tool they were stopped. The system wouldn't let them proceed, and only a senior vice president could approve internal travel.

Cisco found that 49% of travel expenses were being incurred for internal reasons.

Question

ZBB vs incremental budgeting

An organisation used ZBB last year to prepare its budget and is now as efficient, effective and economical as it can possibly be. A manager has put it to the board that, in view of this, a further round of ZBB this year would itself be a wasteful activity and that the time could be more profitably spent on other matters. They propose taking this year's results as the basis for next year's budget and adjusting the figures to allow for planned growth plus inflation at the rate currently indicated by the Retail Price Index, or other more appropriate indices where these are available.

The board has asked you for your opinion.

Answer

Provided that the organisation is indeed already as efficient, effective and economical as possible, and provided that the planned growth or other factors will not have an impact on this, then it would seem perfectly reasonable to use the proposed incremental approach in this case. In practice the conditions described will rarely apply, of course.

Exam focus point

A question in the December 2012 exam asked candidates to evaluate the suitability of incremental budgeting for different divisions in an organisation.

The question then went on to ask candidates to recommend changes to the budgeting method for one of the divisions (where incremental budgeting did not seem to be suitable), as well as asking candidates to assess the use of rolling budgets in a division which had been enjoying significant growth.

Knowledge brought forward from earlier studies (continued)

Rolling budgets

A **rolling budget** is a budget which is continuously updated by adding a further period (a month or quarter) when the earliest period has expired.

Rolling budgets are an attempt to prepare targets and plans which are **more realistic and certain**, particularly with regard to price levels, by shortening the period between preparing budgets.

Instead of preparing a **periodic budget** annually for the full budget period, there would be budgets every 1, 2, 3 or 4 months. Each of these budgets would plan for the next 12 months so that the current budget is extended by an extra period as the current period ends: hence the name **rolling** budgets.

Fixed budgets

A fixed budget is one that is not adjusted to the actual volume of output or level of activity attained in a period. This is **most unrealistic** because the actual level will almost certainly be different from the level of activity originally planned.

This significantly reduces the value of a fixed budget as a cost control technique, as the actual outputs are different from the budgeted level. Consequently, a fixed budget is more useful as a planning tool than as a control tool.

Flexible budgets

A flexible budget, however, recognises the **potential uncertainty in actual output levels**. It is designed to adjust cost levels according to changes in the actual levels of activity and output. In effect, a flexible budget can be seen as a series of fixed budgets – one for each different level of activity.

Flexible budgets may be used in one of two ways:

(a) **Planning** – At the planning stage when budgets are set, to reduce the effect of uncertainty. For example, suppose that a company expects to sell 10,000 units of output during the next year. A master budget (the fixed budget) would be prepared on the basis of this expected volume. However, if the company thinks that output and sales might be as low as 8,000 units or as high as 12,000 units, it may prepare contingency flexible budgets, at volumes of, say, 8,000, 9,000, 11,000 and 12,000 units.

(b) **Control** – Flexible budgets are also used **'retrospectively'** at the end of each month (control period) or year to compare actual results achieved with the results that would have been expected if the actual circumstances had been known in advance. Flexible budgets are an essential factor in **budgetary control** and **variance analysis.**

Activity-based budgeting

Activity-based budgeting involves defining the activities that underlie the financial figures in each function and using the **level of activity** to decide how much resource should be **allocated** and how well it is being **managed** and to **explain variances** from budget.

ABB is based on the following **principles**:

(a) It is activities, which drive costs, and the aim is to control the causes (drivers) of costs rather than the costs themselves, with the result that in the long term costs will be better managed and better understood.

(b) Not all activities are value adding and so they must be examined and split up according to their ability to add value.

(c) Most departmental activities are driven by demands and decisions beyond the immediate control of the manager responsible for the department's budget.

(d) Traditional financial measures of performance are unable to fulfil the objective of continuous improvement. Additional measures which focus on drivers of costs, the quality of activities undertaken, the responsiveness to change and so on are needed.

Example: ABB

A stores department has two main activities, receiving deliveries of raw materials from suppliers into stores and issuing raw materials to production departments. Two major cost drivers, the number of deliveries of raw materials and the number of production runs, have been identified. Although the majority of the costs of the department can be attributed to the activities, there is a small balance, termed 'department running costs', which includes general administration costs, part of the department manager's salary and so on.

Based on activity levels expected in the next control period, the following cost driver volumes have been budgeted.

500 deliveries of raw materials
60 production runs

On the basis of budgeted departmental costs and the cost analysis, the following budget has been drawn up for the next control period.

Cost	*Total* $'000	*Costs attributable to receiving deliveries* $'000	*Costs attributable to issuing materials* $'000	*Dept running costs* $'000
Salaries – management	25	8	12	5
Salaries – store workers	27	13	12	2
Salaries – administration	15	4	5	6
Consumables	11	3	5	3
Information technology costs	14	5	8	1
Other costs	19	10	6	3
	111	43	48	20
Activity volumes		500	60	
Cost per unit of cost driver		$86	$800	$20,000

Points to note

(a) The apportionment of cost will be subjective to a certain extent. The objective of the exercise is that the resource has to be justified as supporting one or more of the activities. Costs cannot be hidden.

(b) The cost driver rates of $86 and $800 can be used to calculate product costs using ABC.

(c) Identifying activities and their costs helps to focus attention on those activities which add value and those that do not.

(d) The budget has highlighted the cost of the two activities.

1.3 Strengths and weaknesses of different budget models 12/12, 12/15

Model	Strengths	Weaknesses
Incremental budgeting	**Easy** to prepare Can be **flexed to actual levels** to provide more meaningful control information	Does not take account of **alternative options** Does not look for ways of **improving performance** Only works if current operations are as **effective, efficient and economical** as they can be Encourages **slack** in the budget setting process
ZBB	Provides a budgeting and planning tool for management that **responds to changes** in the business environment Requires the organisation to look **very closely at its cost behaviour patterns**, and so improves understanding of cost behaviour patterns Should help **identify inefficient or obsolete processes**, and thereby also help reduce costs Helps **eliminate unnecessary costs** Results in a **more efficient allocation of resources** (This can be particularly useful in **not-for-profit organisations** which have a focus on achieving **value for money**.)	Requires a **lot of management time** and effort (The amount of time required for the budgeting process may, in turn, have a demotivating effect on managers.) Requires **training in the use of ZBB techniques** so that these are applied properly Requires a **participative approach** so the organisation must have a suitable culture Questioning current practices and processes **can be seen as threatening** (particularly for managers whose areas are subjected to ZBB)

Model	Strengths	Weaknesses
Rolling budgets	**Reduce the uncertainty** of budgeting for business operating in **an unstable environment**. It is easier to predict what will happen in the short term. The most suitable form of budgeting for organisations in **uncertain environments**, where future activity levels, costs or revenues cannot be accurately foreseen. **Planning and control** is based on a more **recent plan** which is likely to be **more realistic** and more relevant than a fixed annual budget drawn up several months ago. The process of updating the budget means that managers **identify current changes** (and so can respond to these changes more quickly). More realistic targets provide a better basis on which to **appraise managers' performance**. Realistic budgets are likely to have a **better motivational effect** on managers.	They require **time, effort and money** to prepare and keep updating. If managers spend too long preparing/revising budgets, they will have less time to control and manage actual results. **Managers may not see the value** in the continuous updating of budgets. It may be **demotivating** (for managers and staff) if targets are constantly changing. It may **not be necessary** to update budgets so **regularly in a stable operating environment**.
Flexible budgets	It is possible to find out well in advance the **costs of idle time** and so on if the output falls below budget. **It is possible to plan** for the alternative use of spare capacity if output falls short of budget.	As many costs in **modern industry** are **fixed costs**, the **value of flexible budgets** as a **planning tool is limited**. Where there is a **high degree of stability**, the administrative effort in flexible budgeting produces little extra benefit. Fixed budgets can be perfectly adequate in these circumstances.
ABB	It ensures that the organisation's **overall strategy** and **any changes to that strategy will be taken into account**. ABB attempts to manage a business as the sum of its interrelated parts. It identifies **critical success factors** which are activities that a business must perform well if it is to succeed.	As it requires **time and effort to prepare**, it is suited to a more complex organisation with multiple cost drivers. May be difficult to **identify clear individual responsibilities for activities** (and therefore to determine accountability for performance of those activities). ABBs are only suitable for organisations which use an **activity-based costing** (ABC) system. ABBs are not suitable for all organisations, especially ones with significant proportions of fixed overheads.

Model	Strengths	Weaknesses
ABB (cont'd)	As it recognises that activities drive costs, it encourages a focus on **controlling and managing cost drivers** rather than just the costs. **Concentrates on the whole activity** so that there is more likelihood of getting it right first time. As an example, ensuring that goods are produced on time and that the despatch manager has sufficient resources to deliver them.	

1.4 The future of budgeting

As well as looking at the strengths and weaknesses of different budget models, it is important to recognise that many organisations express concern about their planning and budgeting processes in general.

Criticisms of traditional budgeting

(a) Time consuming and costly

(b) Major barrier to responsiveness, flexibility and change

(c) Adds little value given the amount of management time required

(d) Rarely strategically focused

(e) Makes people feel undervalued

(f) Reinforces departmental barriers rather than encouraging knowledge sharing

(g) Based on unsupported assumptions and guesswork as opposed to sound, well-constructed performance data

(h) Developed and updated infrequently

Ways in which companies are adapting planning and budgeting processes

(a) Use of rolling forecasts

(b) Separation of the forecasting process from the budget to increase speed and accuracy and reduce management time

(c) Focus on the future rather than past performance

(d) Use of the balanced scorecard (or other multi-dimensional performance measurement systems)

2 Evaluating budget variances

FAST FORWARD

Analysing the differences between **actual results** and **expected results** – and understanding the reasons for those differences – is a vital part of controlling performance. However, it is inevitable that costs will change as the volume of activity changes. Therefore a **flexible budget** (which takes account of the actual volume of activity) should be used for control purposes, rather than a fixed budget prepared at the beginning of the period under review.

As well as setting performance targets for an organisation, budgets provide a mechanism for **controlling performance** as they provide a yardstick against which to assess performance. This means finding out why actual performance did not go according to plan, and then seeking ways to improve performance for the future.

Budgets enable managers to manage by exception; that is, focus on areas where things are not going to plan (ie the exceptions). This is done by comparing the actual performance to the budgets to identify the **variances**.

However, the reason a budget is not achieved may sometimes be because the budget itself was unrealistic. If this is the case, the budget may need to be revised. Only realistic budgets can form a credible basis for control.

Knowledge brought forward from earlier studies

From Paper F5

The F5 syllabus requires candidates to be able to calculate and explain basic variances such as:

- Sales (including selling price and sales volume variances)
- Materials (including material price and usage variances)
- Labour (including labour rate and labour efficiency variances)
- Variable production overheads (including expenditure and efficiency variances)
- Fixed production overheads (including volume, volume efficiency and volume capacity variances)

The F5 syllabus also requires candidates to be able to:

- Calculate a revised budget, and
- Calculate, identify the cause of, and explain planning and operational variances for sales, materials and labour

As such, the ability to calculate and explain variances is assumed knowledge for Paper P5. We have included a brief recap of the different types of variances here, but if you do not feel comfortable with them you are strongly advised to look again at the F5 study materials.

From Paper P3

From your P3 studies, you should also already be familiar with the role that budgets and variance analysis play in helping management to control an organisation and its performance.

2.1 Variances

When actual performance is compared to standards and budgeted amounts, there will inevitably be **variances**. These may be favourable or adverse, depending on whether they result in an increase to, or a decrease from, the budgeted profit figure.

2.1.1 Sales variances

Sales volume variance is the difference between the original and flexed budget profit figures. This is an important variance because losing sales generally means losing profit as well. If it has the effect of making profit lower than budgeted it is **adverse**, and if it makes profit higher than budgeted it is **favourable**.

Sales price variance is the difference between actual sales revenue and the revenue which should have been earned by selling the actual volume at the standard sales price. Lower sales prices (if all else remains constant) mean a reduction in profit.

2.1.2 Materials variances

Total direct materials variance is the difference between the actual direct materials cost and the expected direct materials cost according to the flexed budget. If the actual material cost is higher than budget, it has an adverse effect on profit.

Direct materials usage variance is the difference between actual usage and budgeted usage for the actual volume of output, multiplied by the standard materials cost. If actual usage is higher than budgeted usage, there will be an adverse effect on profit.

Direct materials price variance is the difference between the actual materials cost and what the materials were expected to cost (ie the actual usage multiplied by the standard materials cost). Again, if actual costs are higher than those budgeted, there will be an adverse effect on profit.

2.1.3 Labour variances

Total direct labour variance is the difference between the actual direct labour cost and the direct labour cost according to the flexed budget. If more is spent on labour than was budgeted, there will be an adverse effect on profit.

Direct labour efficiency variance is the difference between the actual labour time and budgeted time, for the actual volume of output, multiplied by the standard labour rate. The labour efficiency variance looks at the actual versus the budgeted number of hours used to produce the output. If actual time is greater than budgeted time, the effect on the profit will be adverse. The faster people work, the more profit can be made (provided the quality of their work isn't affected by the increased speed, and they continue to produce good-quality output which can be sold).

Direct labour rate variance is the difference between the actual labour cost and the actual labour time multiplied by the standard labour rate. This means it compares the actual cost of the hours worked against the anticipated cost for that number of hours worked. Where the actual hourly rate exceeds the standard, profit will be adversely affected.

2.1.4 Production overhead variances

Variable production overhead variances

The variable production overhead variance is the difference between the actual and budgeted spending on variable overheads, and it can be divided into two sub-variances:

(a) The **variable production overhead expenditure** is the difference between the actual amount of variable production overhead incurred and the amount of production overhead that should have been incurred in the actual hours actively worked.

(b) The **variable production overhead efficiency variance** is the difference between the standard cost of the hours that should have been worked for the number of units actually produced, and the standard cost of the actual number of hours worked.

Fixed production overhead variances

(a) **Fixed production overhead total variance** is the difference between the fixed production overhead incurred and the fixed production overhead absorbed (ie the under- or over-absorbed fixed production overhead).

(b) **Fixed production overhead expenditure variance** is the difference between the budgeted fixed production overhead expenditure, and actual fixed production overhead expenditure.

(c) **Fixed production overhead volume variance** is the difference between actual and budgeted production/volume multiplied by the standard absorption rate per **unit**.

(d) **Fixed production overhead volume efficiency variance** is the difference between the number of hours that actual production should have taken and the number of hours actually taken (that is, worked) multiplied by the standard absorption rate per **hour**.

(e) **Fixed production overhead volume capacity variance** is the difference between budgeted hours of work and the actual hours worked, multiplied by the standard absorption rate per **hour**.

2.2 Flexible budgets and budgetary control

As we have noted earlier in the chapter, flexible budgets are an essential element in variance analysis. An organisation's costs will inevitably be affected if the actual volume of output differs from that in the original budget. As such, unless the actual level of activity and sales in a period are the same as those anticipated in the original budget, a **flexible budget** (which is changed in line with the volume of output and sales) should **be used as the basis for variance analysis**, rather than the original (fixed) budget.

The following example illustrates this point.

Penny manufactures a single product, the Darcy. Budgeted results and actual results for May are as follows.

	Budget	*Actual*	*Variance*
Production and sales of the Darcy (units)	7,500	8,200	
	$	$	$
Sales revenue	75,000	81,000	6,000 (F)
Direct materials	22,500	23,500	1,000 (A)
Direct labour	15,000	15,500	500 (A)
Production overhead	22,500	22,800	300 (A)
Administration overhead	10,000	11,000	1,000 (A)
	70,000	72,800	2,800 (A)
Profit	5,000	8,200	3,200 (F)

Note. (F) denotes a favourable variance and (A) an unfavourable or adverse variance.

In this example, the variances as they are currently presented are meaningless for the purposes of control. All costs were higher than budgeted but the volume of output was also higher. Given this higher volume of output, we should expect that actual variable costs would be greater than those included in the fixed budget. However, it is not possible to tell how much of the increase is due to **poor cost control** and how much is due to the **increase in activity**.

Similarly, it is not possible to tell how much of the increase in sales revenue is due to the increase in activity. Some of the difference may be due to a difference between budgeted and actual selling price but we are unable to tell from the analysis above.

For control purposes we need to know the answers to questions such as the following:

- Were actual costs higher than they should have been to produce and sell 8,200 Darcys?
- Was actual revenue satisfactory from the sale of 8,200 Darcys?

Instead of comparing actual results with a fixed budget which is based on a different level of activity to that actually achieved, the correct approach to budgetary control is to compare actual results with a budget which has been **flexed** to the actual activity level achieved.

Suppose that we have the following estimates of the behaviour of Penny's costs:

(a) Direct materials and direct labour are variable costs.

(b) Production overhead is a semi-variable cost, the budgeted cost for an activity level of 10,000 units being £25,000.

(c) Administration overhead is a fixed cost.

(d) Selling prices are constant at all levels of sales.

Solution

The **budgetary control analysis** should therefore be as follows.

	Fixed budget	*Flexible budget*	*Actual results*	*Variance*
Production and sales (units)	7,500	8,200	8,200	
	$	$	$	$
Sales revenue	75,000	82,000 (W1)	81,000	1,000 (A)
Direct materials	22,500	24,600 (W2)	23,500	1,100 (F)
Direct labour	15,000	16,400 (W3)	15,500	900 (F)
Production overhead	22,500	23,200 (W4)	22,800	400 (F)
Administration overhead	10,000	10,000 (W5)	11,000	1,000 (A)
	70,000	74,200	72,800	1,400 (F)
Profit	5,000	7,800	8,200	400 (F)

Workings

1 Selling price per unit = $75,000 / 7,500 = $10 per unit

Flexible budget sales revenue = $10 × 8,200 = $82,000

2 Direct materials cost per unit = $22,500 / 7,500 = $3

Budget cost allowance = $3 × 8,200 = $24,600

3 Direct labour cost per unit = $15,000 / 7,500 = $2

Budget cost allowance = $2 × 8,200 = $16,400

4 Variable production overhead cost per unit = $(25,000 – 22,500) / (10,000 – 7,500)

= $2,500/2,500 = $1 per unit

∴ Fixed production overhead cost = $22,500 – (7,500 × $1) = $15,000

∴ Budget cost allowance = $15,000 + (8,200 × $1) = $23,200

5 Administration overhead is a fixed cost and hence budget cost allowance = $10,000

Comment

(a) In selling 8,200 units, the expected profit should have been not the fixed budget profit of $5,000, but the flexible budget profit of $7,800. Instead, actual profit was $8,200 ie £400 more than we should have expected.

One of the reasons for this improvement is that, given output and sales of 8,200 units, the cost of resources (material, labour etc) was $1,400 lower than expected.

These total cost variances can be analysed to reveal how much of the variance is due to lower resource prices and how much is due to efficient resource usage.

(b) However, the sales revenue was $1,000 less than expected because the price charged was lower than budgeted.

We know this because flexing the budget has eliminated the effect of changes in the volume sold, which is the only other factor that can affect sales revenue. This means that the adverse variance of $1,000 is a **selling price variance**.

The lower selling price could have been caused by the increase in the volume sold (to sell the additional 700 units the selling price had to fall below $10 per unit). We do not know if this is the case but without flexing the budget we could not know that a different selling price to that budgeted had been charged. Our initial analysis above had appeared to indicate that sales revenue was ahead of budget.

The difference of $400 between the flexible budget profit of $7,800 at a production level of 8,200 units and the actual profit of $8,200 is due to the net effect of cost savings of $1,400 and lower than expected sales revenue (by $1,000).

The difference between the original budgeted profit of $5,000 and the actual profit of $8,200 ($3,200 (F)) is the total of the following:

(a) The savings in resource costs/lower than expected sales revenue (a net total of $400 as indicated by the difference between the flexible budget and the actual results).

(b) The effect of producing and selling 8,200 units instead of 7,500 units (a gain of $2,800 as indicated by the difference in budgeted profit between the fixed budget ($5,000 and the flexible budget ($7,800)). This is the **sales volume** profit variance.

A **full variance analysis statement** would be as follows:

	$	$
Fixed budget profit		5,000
Variances		
Sales volume	2,800 (F)	
Selling price	1,000 (A)	
Direct materials cost	1,100 (F)	
Direct labour cost	900 (F)	
Production overhead cost	400 (F)	
Administration overhead cost	1,000 (A)	
		3,200 (F)
Actual profit		8,200

If management believes that any of the variances are large enough to justify it, they will investigate the reasons for their occurrence to see whether any corrective action is necessary.

2.3 Reasons for variances

Variances may occur for a number of reasons. One possible reason is that the budget itself was not realistic. Unless they are achievable, budgets are not a useful method of control.

Although concerns are often raised when budgets are seen as too challenging (so that they become perceived as unachievable and therefore demotivating), budgets could equally not be a useful method of control if they are not challenging enough. For example, if a division consistently exceeds its budget targets, does this mean it is performing well, or does it mean that there was too much slack in the original budget?

There are many other reasons why variances may arise, however, as shown by the table below. (**Note**. The table looks at the possible reasons for adverse variances; possible reasons for favourable variances would typically be the opposite of these.)

Variance	Possible reason for adverse variances
Sales volume	Poor performance by sales staff Deterioration in market conditions (either due to macro-economic (PEST analysis) factors, or changes in the industry environment (eg entry of new competitors) Deterioration in the company or brand's reputation, making a product less desirable to customers Lack of goods or services to sell as a result of a production problem
Sales price	Poor performance by sales staff Deterioration in market conditions (eg economic downturn) or in the industry environment (eg price wars)

Variance	Possible reason for adverse variances
Direct materials usage	Poor performance by production department staff, leading to high rates of scrap Substandard materials, leading to high rates of scrap Faulty machinery, causing high rates of scrap
Direct materials price	Poor performance by the procurement department's staff (eg failing to negotiate discounts) Using higher-quality material than was planned Price increases by suppliers or other changes in market conditions (eg shortages of a material leading to price increases)
Direct labour efficiency	Poor supervision Having to use less skilled workers than originally intended, meaning they take longer to do the work Low-grade materials, leading to high levels of scrap and wasted labour time Problems with a customer for whom a service is being rendered Problems with machinery, leading to labour time wasted Disruption of materials supply, leading to workers being unable to proceed with production
Direct labour rate	Using more highly skilled labour, or higher grades of workers, than originally planned Change in labour market conditions (eg a shortage of labour, would mean that the rates being paid to recruit and retain labour would have to increase)
Fixed overhead spending	Poor supervision of overheads General increase in costs of overheads not taken into account in the budget

2.4 Standard costing

Knowledge brought forward from earlier studies

From your studies at F5 and P3 you should be familiar with the use of standard costs in preparing budgets, and therefore that variances represent the difference between standard and actual cost.

The process of preparing standard costs is assumed knowledge for Paper P5, so we are not going to cover it again here. If you are not comfortable with standard costing you are strongly advised to look back at your F5 and P3 materials in this area.

Although standard costing can be used in a variety of costing situations (batch and mass production, process manufacture, jobbing manufacture (where there is standardisation of parts) and service industries (if a realistic cost unit can be established)), the **greatest benefit** from its use can be gained if there is a **large amount of repetition** in the production process so that average or expected usage of resources can be determined. It is therefore most suited to **mass production** and **repetitive assembly work**.

By contrast, standard costing is not well suited to production systems where items are manufactured to customer demand and specifications. Therefore, changes in the modern business environment which are leading to shorter product life cycles and an increased emphasis on innovation and flexibility mean that standard costing is becoming less appropriate for modern businesses.

The principles of standard costing are also **inconsistent with the philosophy of continuous improvement**, and the ideas of just-in-time (JIT) production. By definition, the use of a 'standard cost' doesn't provide any incentives to try to reduce costs further – because performance will be seen as acceptable if it meets the standard set.

Two of the underlying principles of standard costing are that:

- A standard set before a period is a satisfactory measure throughout the period
- Performance is acceptable if it meets this standard

As well as being inconsistent with the philosophy of continuous improvement, these principles contradict the idea (held in JIT manufacturing) that normal levels of waste and efficiency are unacceptable, because firms should be trying to obtain zero wastage, and be constantly improving their efficiency.

Exam focus point

We will look at JIT in more detail in Chapter 13, where we also look at the principle of 'Kaizen' (continuous improvement) as one of the key elements of Japanese business practices and management techniques.

More generally, if standards remain unchanged throughout a period, their value as a control mechanism could be reduced in dynamic business environments with rapidly changing conditions. If the changing conditions mean that the standards have become outdated or incorrect, then they lose their control and motivational effects.

2.5 Learning curves

Whenever an individual starts a job, they may be relatively slow at completing the work tasks involved while they are becoming familiar with them. However, as the individual gains experience and becomes more confident and knowledgeable about the task, they become more efficient and can perform the task more quickly. They benefit from 'learning by doing'.

Learning curves are particularly relevant to tasks which are fairly repetitive in nature. However, learning curves are unlikely to be experienced in tasks where the individual's speed of work is dictated by the speed of machinery (as it would be on a production line, for example).

Eventually, however, when they have acquired enough experience, there will be nothing more for the individual to learn, and so **the learning process will stop**.

Key term

Learning curve theory applies to situations where the workforce as a whole improves in efficiency with experience. The **learning effect** or **learning curve effect** describes the speeding up of a job with repeated performance.

Learning curves suggest that labour time should be expected to get shorter, with experience, in the production of items which exhibit any or all of the following features.

- Made largely **by labour effort** (rather than by a **highly mechanised** process)
- Fairly **repetitive** in nature
- Brand **new** or relatively **short-lived** (learning process does not continue indefinitely)

What costs are affected by the learning curve?

(a) **Direct labour** time and costs will be affected because the time taken to complete a task is reduced.

(b) **Variable overhead** costs will also be affected, if they vary with direct labour hours worked.

(c) **Materials costs** are usually **unaffected** by learning among the workforce, although it is conceivable that materials handling might improve, and so wastage costs be reduced.

(d) **Fixed overhead expenditure** should be **unaffected** by the learning curve (although in an organisation that uses absorption costing, if fewer hours are worked in producing a unit of output, and the factory operates at full capacity, the **fixed overheads recovered or absorbed per unit** in the cost of the output **will decline** as more and more units are made).

2.5.1 Application of the learning curve in budgeting and performance management

Learning curve theory can be used to:

(a) **Calculate the marginal (incremental) cost** of making an extra unit of a product.

(b) **Quote selling prices** for orders or new contracts, where prices are calculated at cost plus a percentage mark-up for profit. An awareness of the learning curve can allow an organisation to forecast future cost reductions and any selling price reductions which it may be able to make as a result. This could make the difference between winning contracts and losing them, or between making profits and selling at a loss-making price.

(c) **Prepare realistic production budgets** and more **efficient production schedules**. Understanding the learning curve allows firms to predict their required inputs more accurately. This greater accuracy can benefit both material inputs and the time taken to process products.

Having a better understanding of their production schedules enables an organisation to estimate delivery schedules for customers more accurately. This in turn may lead to improved customer relationships and further sales in future.

(d) **Prepare realistic standard costs** for cost control purposes. For example, if a budget is set without considering the learning curve effect it may be too easy to achieve, and so will not serve to motivate performance.

If an organisation has a culture in which learning is encouraged, then it should also expect improvements in efficiency to occur. These should be reflected in the budgets.

Considerations to bear in mind include:

(a) **Sales projections, advertising expenditure and delivery date commitments**. Identifying a learning curve effect should allow an organisation to plan its advertising and delivery schedules to coincide with expected production schedules. Production capacity obviously affects sales capacity and sales projections.

(b) **Budgeting with standard costs**. Companies that use standard costing for much of their production output cannot apply standard times to output where a learning effect is taking place. This problem can be overcome in practice by:

  (i) Establishing **standard times** for output, once the learning effect has worn off or become insignificant; and

  (ii) Introducing a **'launch cost'** budget for the product for the duration of the learning period.

(c) **Budgetary control**. When learning is still taking place, it would be unreasonable to compare actual times with the standard times that ought eventually to be achieved when the learning effect wears off. **Allowance should be made** accordingly when interpreting labour efficiency variances.

(d) **Cash budgets**. Since the learning effect reduces unit variable costs as more units are produced, this reduction should be allowed for in **cash flow projections**.

(e) **Work scheduling and overtime decisions**. To take full advantage of the learning effect, **idle production time** should be avoided and work scheduling/overtime decisions should take account of the expected learning effect.

(f) **Pay**. Where the workforce is paid a **productivity bonus**, the time needed to learn a new production process should be allowed for in calculating the bonus for a period.

(g) **Recruiting new labour**. When a company plans to take on new labour to help with increasing production, the learning curve assumption will have to be reviewed. (Similarly, if a company has high levels of staff turnover, the learning curve effect will be undermined.)

(h) **Market share**. The significance of the learning curve is that by increasing its share of the market, a company can benefit from shop-floor, managerial and technological 'learning' to achieve greater **economies of scale**.

Learning curve ideas could also be used to help forecast the cost reductions (and consequently reductions in selling price) which **competitors** may be able to achieve. If a competitor is able to reduce its selling price this might enable it to increase its sales and market share.

2.5.2 Limitations of learning curve theory

(a) The learning curve phenomenon is **not always present**.

(b) It assumes **stable conditions** at work which will **enable learning to take place**. This is not always practicable, for example because of **labour turnover**.

(c) It also assumes a certain degree of **motivation** among employees; but if employees have no interest in 'learning' or increasing their efficiency, then there will be no learning effect.

(d) Breaks between repeating production of an item must not be too long, or workers will **'forget'** and the learning process will have to begin all over again.

(e) It might be difficult to **obtain accurate data** to decide what the learning curve is.

(f) **Workers might not agree** to a gradual reduction in production times per unit.

(g) **Production techniques might change**, or product design alterations might be made, so that it takes a long time for a **'standard'** production method to emerge, to which a learning effect will apply.

2.6 Revising a budget or standard cost

FAST FORWARD

There are times when it may be appropriate – or necessary – to **revise a budget or standard cost**. When this happens, variances should be reported in a way that distinguishes between variances caused by the revision to the budget and variances that are the responsibility of operational management.

A planning and operational approach to variance analysis divides the total variance into those variances which have arisen because of inaccurate planning or faulty standards (**planning variances**) and those variances which have been caused by adverse or favourable operational performance, compared with a standard which has been revised in hindsight (**operational variances**).

When variances are reported in a system of budgetary control, it is usually assumed that:

(a) The original budget or standard cost is fairly accurate or reliable

(b) Any differences between actual results and the budget or standard, measured as variances, are attributable to the manager who is responsible for that aspect of performance

The manager responsible will be expected to explain the reasons for any significant variances and, where appropriate, take measures to rectify problems causing an adverse variance.

However, circumstances may occur that make the original budget or standard cost invalid or inappropriate:

(a) The sales budget may have been based on expectations of the total size of the market for the organisation's product. However, due to an unexpected change in economic conditions, an unexpected technological change, a radical change in customer attitudes or unexpected new regulations affecting the marketability of a product, the market size may be much larger or much smaller than assumed when the sales budget was prepared.

(b) The standard cost of materials for a product may have been based on an assumption about what the market price for the materials should be. However, due to a major change in the market, the available market price for the materials may become much higher or much lower than originally expected when the standard cost was prepared.

(c) The standard quantity of materials for a product may be significantly altered due to an unexpected change in the product specification, requiring much more or much less of the material in the product content.

(d) The standard labour rate may become unrealistic due to an unexpected increase in pay rates for employees.

(e) The standard time to produce a unit of product may also change for unexpected reasons (for example, the introduction of new regulations which mean that additional safety features have to be added to the product).

If the budget or standard cost is not revised in these circumstances, variances reported to operational managers will be unrealistic. A large part of the **variances will be due to changes that are outside the control of the operational managers**.

In these circumstances, it may be appropriate – or necessary – to revise the budget or revise the standard cost.

2.6.1 When should budget revisions be allowed?

A budget revision should be allowed if something has happened which is **beyond the control** of the organisation or individual manager and which makes the original budget unsuitable for use in performance management.

Any adjustment should be **approved by senior management** who should look at the issues involved **objectively** and **independently**. **Operational issues** are the issues that a budget is attempting to control so they should **not** be subject to revision. However, it can be very **difficult to establish** what is due to operational problems (controllable) and what is due to planning (uncontrollable).

2.7 The nature of planning and operational variances

When a budget or standard cost is revised, variances are still reported as a **comparison between actual results and the original budget or standard cost**.

However, when variances are reported, a **clear distinction** should be made between:

(a) Variances that have been caused by the revision in the budget or standard cost, for which operational managers should not be held responsible: these are called **planning variances**

(b) Variances that are caused by differences between actual performance and the revised budget or standard, for which operational managers should be held responsible and accountable: these are called **operational variances**

Planning variances are calculated by comparing the original budget/standard cost with the revised budget/standard cost.

Operational variances are calculated in the same way as 'normal' basic variances, except that they are based on a comparison between actual results and the revised budget/standard cost.

2.8 Revising budgets: manipulation issues

When a budget or standard cost is revised, there is a potential problem. The budget or standard cost may be revised in such a way that all the reported operational variances become favourable variances, and the reason why actual results may be worse than budget is attributable entirely to planning variances, for which operational managers cannot be held responsible.

In other words, the revision to the budget or standard cost may be manipulated in such a way as to make operating results seem much better than is really the case.

To prevent manipulation, there should be strict rules about revising a budget or standard cost. In particular, the revision to the budget or standard cost should ideally be based on independent and verifiable evidence that operational managers are not in a position to manipulate.

For example:

(a) If there is an unexpected change in the total size of the market for the company's product, there should ideally be independent evidence from an external source (such as a market research firm) about the revised expectations of the market size.

(b) If there is an unexpected change in the market price for materials, there should ideally be an official price index or price benchmark for the material item.

(c) If there is an unexpected change in the standard material usage for a product, this should ideally be evidenced by a documented change in the product specification.

Independent evidence may be difficult to obtain in many cases. When it is not available, the potential for manipulation of planning and operational variances should be recognised.

3 Responsibility and controllability

FAST FORWARD

The principle of **controllability** is that managers of responsibility centres should only be held **accountable** for areas of performance over which they have some influence.

When measuring the performance of a responsibility centre, one of the key issues is distinguishing which items the manager of that centre can control (and therefore they should be held accountable for) and those items over which they have no control (and therefore they should not be held accountable for).

Responsibility accounting is based on this principle of controllability. This dictates **that managers should only be made accountable for those aspects of performance they can control**. In this respect, the controllability principle suggests that uncontrollable items should either be eliminated from any reports which are used to measure managers' performance, or that the effects of these uncontrollable items are calculated and then the relevant reports should distinguish between controllable and uncontrollable items.

In practice, the controllability principle can be very difficult to apply, because many **areas do not fit neatly into controllable and uncontrollable categories**. For example, if a competitor lowers their prices, this may be seen as an uncontrollable action. However, a manager could respond to the competitor's action by changing the company's own prices, which could then reduce the adverse effect of the competitor's actions. So, in effect, there are both controllable and uncontrollable actions here.

Similarly, if a supplier increased the price of their product, this may be seen as an uncontrollable action. However, a manager could respond by looking to change supplier or using a different product in order to reduce the adverse impact of the supplier's actions. Again, there are potentially both controllable and uncontrollable actions here.

Accordingly, any analysis of performance would need to consider the impact of the competitor or supplier's actions as one element, and then the impact of the manager's response as a second element.

3.1 Controllable costs

Controllability can also be a particular issue when looking at costs within companies.

Consider the following example:

A company has three operating divisions and a head office. The divisional managers think it is unfair that a share of indirect costs – such as central Finance, HR, Legal and Administration costs – are included in their divisional results because the divisional managers cannot control these costs.

Importantly, there is a distinction here between considering the **divisional manager's** performance and the **division's performance** as a whole.

In order to evaluate the **performance of the divisional manager**, then only those items that are directly controllable by the manager should be included in the performance measures. So, in our example, the share of indirect costs reapportioned from the head office should not be included. These costs can only be controlled where they are incurred. Therefore the relevant head office managers should be held accountable for them. As the divisional managers have suggested, it would be unfair to judge them for this aspect of performance.

However, in order for the head office to evaluate the division's overall performance for decision-making purposes (for example, in relation to growth, or divestment) it is appropriate to include a share of the head office costs. If divisional performance is measured only on those amounts the divisional manager can control, this will overstate the economic performance of the division. If the divisions were independent companies, they would have to incur the costs of those services which are currently provided by the head office (for example, finance and HR costs). Therefore, in order to measure the economic performance of the division, these central costs, plus any interest expenses and taxes, should be included within the measure of the division's performance.

3.2 Worked example: controllable costs

TVW is a retail company and has a number of shops across the country.

The managers of the individual TVW shops have little authority. Shop budgets are set centrally by the Finance Director and the senior management team, and shop managers are not consulted in the budget-setting process. Inventory purchasing is controlled by a central purchasing team, and brand marketing is controlled by a central marketing team. The head office also manages the rent agreements and other property costs for the shops. However, each shop has a small marketing budget of its own which it can use to run local promotions.

TVW produces a standard list of selling prices for all the products it sells, although shop managers do have some scope to change prices, and can vary prices by up to 5% from this standard list.

Shop managers also recruit and manage the staff within their shops. However, the wage rates they can offer their staff are fixed by head office, and are not negotiable.

The shop managers are paid a basic salary with bonuses of up to 25%. However, in order for a manager to qualify for a bonus, their shop's profit has to be above budget.

A number of the shop managers have recently complained about this, because they feel that the current remuneration scheme doesn't reflect the effort they are putting in.

The manager of one of TVW's largest stores commented: 'The budget that was set was totally unrealistic in the current economic conditions. Although I have run several promotions, which were well received by my customers, there was no way I could achieve the sales figure in the budget. The budgeted sales figure for my shop was the same as last year, but this year the industry as a whole has seen a 10% fall in revenues.'

The results for the manager's shop for the last year are as follows. These are the figures used as the basis for any bonus calculations.

	Actual	*Budget*	*Variance*
	$	$	$
Sales	261,000	287,000	–26,000
Cost of sales	104,400	124,000	–19,600
Gross profit	156,600	172,200	–15,600
Marketing	12,500	13,000	500
Staff costs (manager)	27,500	27,500	0
Part-time staff	36,500	40,000	3,500
Other running costs (eg rent, heat and light)	26,000	25,000	–1,000
Shop profit	54,100	66,700	–12,600

Question:

What are the problems with using this shop performance information as the basis for assessing the manager's performance?

Problems:

Accountability – The shop manager should only be held responsible for those aspects of performance they can control. However, the branch information used does not appear to distinguish between the factors that the shop managers can control and those which they can't.

Controllable and non-controllable costs – A number of non-controllable costs are currently included in the manager's performance assessment. In particular, the shop manager will have very little scope to control property costs, because the rental contract and other contracted costs (such as heat and light) are managed by the head office. The shop managers may have some control over the amount of heat and light that are used in their shops, but not over the unit prices paid for these utilities.

Similarly, the managers can't control their own wages. However, it is reasonable to classify the **part-time staff costs as controllable**. The managers manage the staffing for their shops, and so they could save on part-time staff costs by working longer hours themselves.

Consequently, a fairer way of assessing the shop managers' performance would be to distinguish costs into two groups: controllable (marketing; part-time staff) and non-controllable (managers' wages; property costs).

Budgets – Another problem with TVW's current performance management process is its budgeting process. If the manager's performance is assessed by comparing actual performance to budget, then it is important that the budgets are realistic and achievable.

However, the original sales budgeted (which showed the same figure as the previous year) seems unrealistic given that there has been a 10% fall in sales across the industry as a whole.

Consequently, it would be useful to break down the overall profit variance ($15,600) into a planning variance (which adjusts for the 10% drop in industry sales) and an operational variance (showing the variance in the shop's own performance after adjusting for the 10%).

Planning variance		$	
Original sales	(1)	287,000	
Revenue variance due to economic conditions (10%)	(2)	28,700	(A)
Planning variance (Gross margin 60%)		**17,220**	(A)
Operational variance			
Actual sales		261,000	
Revised budgeted sales	(1) – (2)	258,300	
		2,700	(F)
Operational variance (Gross margin 60%)		**1,620**	(A)

The operational variance more accurately reflects the shop manager's work in promoting sales, and here we can see that the manager's efforts have actually reduced the fall in gross profit by $1,620. The overall gross profit variance (of $15,600, adverse) reflects an adverse planning variance of $17,220 partially offset by a favourable operational variance of $1,620.

Controllable profit – Following on from this, we could suggest that TVW should show a controllable profit for each shop, as well as the overall shop profit.

The shop manager's performance (and therefore their eligibility for any bonus payments) should then be assessed on the controllable profit performance of their shop only.

If we apply this logic to the manager's shop, then instead of the manager facing an adverse variance of $12,600, they would have achieved a positive variance of $5,620, and would therefore have been entitled to a bonus. This helps explain why the manager is so unhappy about the current way performance is being measured.

Original variance ($)	–12,600
Add back:	
Gross profit planning variance ($)	17,220
Manager's wages ($)	–
Property costs ($)	1,000
	5,620

Discounting – One area where the managers do have a degree of autonomy is in setting prices, because they can vary prices by up to 5% from the standard price list; for example, to reduce prices of a particular product to boost sales of it. Therefore, this is an area of the manager's performance which TVW could justifiably measure; for example, by looking at the sales price and volume for individual product lines, and then looking at the impact of any promotions on gross profit.

However, in this case, it appears that the manager has not made any significant use of this authority because the actual gross margin percentage achieved for the year (60%) has remained constant with the budgeted margin of 60%. If the manager had applied any price discounts this would have led to a reduction in the margin percentage.

Exam focus point

The worked example above is adapted from a scenario in the December 2011 exam in which the managers in a chain of shops are unhappy about their remuneration, which includes a performance-related bonus.

Factors outside a manager's control have led to the manager not being entitled to this bonus. However, if the bonus calculations had been based only on those areas of performance which the manager could control, then they would have been entitled to a bonus.

However, the examining team's report indicated that very few candidates realised that most of the adverse variances (which caused the manager not to receive a bonus) related to aspects of performance the manager could not control.

Chapter Roundup

- There are a number of **different techniques** which an organisation could use as the basis for preparing its budgets. It is important to assess the potential **advantages and disadvantages** of each in order to select one which is appropriate for the organisation's circumstances.
- Analysing the differences between **actual results** and **expected results** – and understanding the reasons for those differences – is a vital part of controlling performance. However, it is inevitable that costs will change as the volume of activity changes. Therefore a **flexible budget** (which takes account of the actual volume of activity) should be used for control purposes, rather than a fixed budget prepared at the beginning of the period under review.
- There are times when it may be appropriate – or necessary – to **revise a budget or standard cost**. When this happens, variances should be reported in a way that distinguishes between variances caused by the revision to the budget and variances that are the responsibility of operational management.
- A planning and operational approach to variance analysis divides the total variance into those variances which have arisen because of inaccurate planning or faulty standards (**planning variances**) and those which have been caused by adverse of unfavourable operational performance, compared with a standard which has been revised in hindsight (**operational variances**).
- The principle of **controllability** is that managers of responsibility centres should only be held **accountable** for areas of performance over which they have some influences.

Quick Quiz

1 Which of the following is/are true:

(i) Incremental budgeting encourages slack in the budgeting process.
(ii) Zero based budgeting helps an organisation reduce costs by identifying inefficient processes.

A Neither of them
B (i) only
C (ii) only
D Both of them

2 Match the description to the type of budget.

Budgets

Incremental
Rolling
Zero based

Descriptions

(a) Next year's budget is based on the current year's results plus an extra amount for estimated growth or inflation.

(b) Each item in the budget is specifically justified, as though each activity were being undertaken for the first time.

(c) The budget is continuously updated by adding a further accounting period when the earliest accounting period has expired.

3 An organisation is operating in an environment which is rapidly changing, with the result that the organisation cannot accurately foresee its future activity levels, costs and revenues.

Which of the following would be the most appropriate type of budget for the organisation to use?

A Activity-based budgets
B Rolling budgets
C Incremental budgets
D Zero based budgets

4 The management accountant's variance analysis identified the following as two main reasons why the actual results for JKL, a confectionery manufacturer, were adverse to the budgeted performance for the year.

(i) The budget had assumed market growth of 4% for the year, but due to tough economic conditions, total market sales have remained static.

(ii) The budget assumed that the price of JKL's main raw material input – cocoa – would rise by 2% over the year. However, shortages in the supply of cocoa mean that prices have risen by nearly 5% over the year.

Are the reasons that have affected performance indicative of operational variances or planning variances?

A Both (i) and (ii) are operational variances.
B (i) is an operational variance; and (ii) is a planning variance.
C (i) is a planning variance; and (ii) is an operational variance.
D Both (i) and (ii) are planning variances.

5 The production department manager at Perspix Co is responsible for recruiting staff for the department. However, the wage rates the manager can offer staff are set by Perspix's head office HR team, and the manager has no authority to amend them.

Maintenance and servicing of the machines is carried out by the maintenance department.

Which of the following aspects of performance should be seen as controllable when assessing the production department manager's performance?

A Increases in raw material costs due to inflation

B Direct labour rate variance

C Increases in overall material costs due to high levels of wastage caused by poor supervision of production workers

D An increase in the level of idle time because of poorly maintained machines

Answers to Quick Quiz

1 D Both of them are true.

Option (i) highlights one of the weaknesses of incremental budgeting, while option (ii) identifies one of the advantages of zero based budgeting.

2 Incremental (a)
Rolling (c)
Zero based (b)

3 B Rolling budgets

The organisation is operating in an unstable environment, and rolling budgets are the most suitable form of budgeting for organisations in this kind of environment. Uncertainty makes it very difficult to try to predict what will happen in the medium to long term, so it is more realistic to focus on the short term instead.

4 D Both (i) and (ii) are planning variances.

Both of the scenarios relate to estimates made when planning the budget which have subsequently proved to be incorrect.

5 C Increases in overall material costs due to high levels of wastage caused by poor supervision of production workers

The performance of the production workers is something which the manager should be able to influence – through the quality (or otherwise) of the supervision the workers are given.

Inflation is an external 'cost' which the manager cannot control. The labour rate variance results from the wage rates set by the head office HR department; and the level of idle time (due to poor maintenance of the machines) reflects the performance of the maintenance department.

Now try the question below from the Practice Question Bank

Number	Level	Marks	Approximate time
Q3	Examination	25	50 mins

Changes in business structure and management accounting

4

Topic list	Syllabus reference
1 Business structure and information needs	A4(a)
2 Information needs of manufacturing and service businesses	A4(b)
3 Business process re-engineering (BPR)	A4(c)
4 Business integration	A4(d)
5 The influence of structure, culture and strategy on performance measurement methods and techniques	A4(e)
6 Developing management accounting systems	A4(f)
7 A contingent approach to management accounts	A4(g)

Introduction

This chapter looks at the relationship between organisational structure and the information needed for performance management in different organisations.

An important theme underlying the chapter is that, in order for it to be useful, the management accounting information an organisation produces must reflect the organisation's structure and its strategy. Equally, therefore, if an organisation makes changes to its structure or strategy, this could have implications for the management accounting information which is required.

Study guide

		Intellectual level
A4	**Changes in business structure and management accounting**	
(a)	Identify and discuss the particular information needs of organisations adopting a functional, divisional or network form and the implications for performance management.	2
(b)	Assess the changing accounting needs of modern service-orientated businesses compared with the needs of traditional manufacturing industry.	3
(c)	Assess the influence of Business Process Re-engineering on systems development and improvements in organisational performance.	3
(d)	Analyse the role that performance management systems play in business integration using models such as the value chain and McKinsey's 7S's.	3
(e)	Discuss how changing an organisation's structure, culture and strategy will influence the adoption of new performance measurement methods and techniques.	3
(f)	Assess the need for businesses to continually refine and develop their management accounting and information systems if they are to maintain or improve their performance in an increasingly competitive and global market.	3
(g)	Highlight the ways in which contingent (internal and external) factors influence management accounting and its design and use.	3

Exam guide

From your studies for Papers F1 and P3 you should be familiar with the range of different structures an organisation could have, and of the relationship between structure and strategy.

One of the key themes in this chapter is how the structure of an organisation affects the information requirements within that organisation, particularly in relation to the way that changing organisational structures could lead to changing information requirements.

Another important issue which this chapter highlights is the way that operational managers (rather than finance specialists) are making increasing use of management information for control purposes, so an organisation's information systems need to be able to provide these users with the information they require. (We have already noted the impact which developments in information systems have had on the role of management accountants in Chapter 1 – in relation to Burns and Scapens' study into the changing role of management accountants in organisations.)

Performance objective 3 – Strategy and innovation – highlights that you should be able to contribute to your organisation by identifying innovative business solutions to improve performance by making or recommending business process changes and improvements. Although these improvements may not be as dramatic as the changes generated by business process re-engineering (which we cover in Section 3 of this chapter), models such as the value chain (covered in Section 4) might identify ways of improving business processes.

A number of the elements in Performance objective 12 (PO 12) – Evaluate management accounting systems – also linked to the topics in this chapter:

PO 12(a): 'Determine the appropriateness and adequacy of management accounting techniques and approaches in an organisation'

PO 12(d): 'Contribute to development and improvements of management accounting systems and internal reporting'

PO 12(e): 'Monitor new developments in management accounting and consider their potential impact on performance and to management accounting systems.'

1 Business structure and information needs

Organisations are not all the same in the way they choose to arrange their activities. Many studies have shown that different organisations arrange their activities according to a variety of influences. We are going to look at three organisational forms, which are described below. We then look at their particular information needs and therefore the implications for performance management. The three types of organisational form are the **functional** form, the **divisional** form and the **network** form.

FAST FORWARD

An organisation's **formal hierarchy** can be arranged by territory, function, product, brand, customer/market, staff numbers and work patterns, and equipment specialisation. In this section we look at three ways of organising the hierarchy. These are: by function, division, and a loose organic form known as a network form.

1.1 Functional form

Functional organisation means that **departments are defined by their functions**; that is, the work that they do. It is a **traditional, common sense approach** and many organisations are structured like this. Primary functions in a manufacturing company might be production, sales, finance and general administration. Sub-departments of marketing might be sales, advertising, distribution and warehousing.

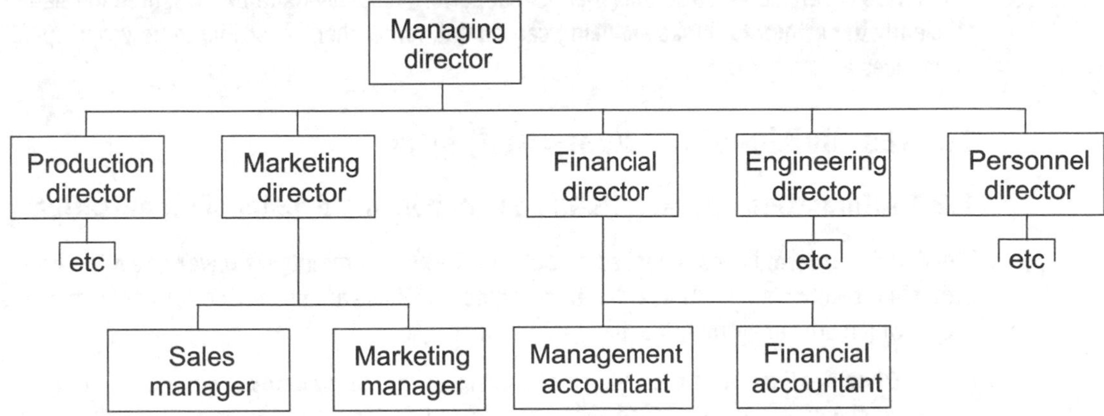

Functional organisation structure

1.1.1 Information characteristics and needs in a functional organisation

Information flows up and down the organisation **vertically**. Senior management communicates strategic plans and decisions downward. Communication upward consists mainly of reports on performance to allow senior management to monitor progress. There is less communication across functions, as control is located higher up the organisation and so functions tend to be **isolated**.

1.1.2 Implications for performance management

(a) The structure is based on **work specialism** and is therefore logical.

(b) The firm can benefit from **economies of scale**.

(c) A functional form does not reflect the actual business processes by which **value is created**.

(d) It is **hard to identify where profits and losses are made** on individual products or in individual markets.

(e) People do not have an understanding of how the **whole business** works.

(f) There are **problems of co-ordinating the work of different specialisms**.

1.1.3 Information needs of functional structures

Functional organisations tend to be **centralised**, meaning that planning and control activities are performed centrally. Senior management at the corporate centre will need information on performance so that they can monitor and control progress. Data about the performance of individual functions is aggregated, before being passed up to senior management. Feedback on performance is given once this information has been aggregated.

However, as we have noted, one of the weaknesses in this structure – looking at performance at an aggregate level – is that it is **hard to know how well individual products are performing**.

Equally, because management and control is centralised it is likely that functional managers only receive limited information about performance. This is likely to add to the feeling that functions are isolated within the organisation. In order to counter this, managers need information which tells them about the performance of other functions and the business overall, so they get a more complete picture of performance and also a greater understanding of how their function affects other parts of the organisation. In this respect, **communication** between functional teams is vital.

However, an important focus in functional structures will be on the **operational efficiency** of each function. Accordingly, organisations need information which indicates how efficiently each department is operating, and highlights **variances** in actual performance against targets or budgets.

The nature of functional structures means that performance needs to be measured in relation to how efficiently **departmental tasks** are being carried out, rather than according to how well specific products or services are performing.

1.2 The divisional (or diversified) form

1.2.1 Information characteristics and needs in a divisional organisation

The **divisional form** is characterised by **autonomy given to managers lower down the line**. The prime co-ordinating mechanism is **standardisation of outputs**. These are usually performance measures, such as profit, which are set at the top of the organisation.

(a) **Divisionalisation** is the division of a business into **autonomous regions** or product businesses, each with its own revenues, expenditures and profits.

(b) **Communication between divisions and head office is restricted, formal and related to performance standards.** Influence is maintained by headquarters' power to hire and fire the managers who are supposed to run each division.

(c) Headquarters management influences prices and therefore profitability in divisions when it sets **transfer prices** between divisions. Here, the **information flow is two-way**, as headquarters relies on the divisions for divisional information to set prices. These transfer prices then give signals to the divisions on their expected performance.

(d) **Divisionalisation** is a **function of organisation size**, in numbers and in product-market activities.

The **multi-divisional structure** might be implemented in one of two forms.

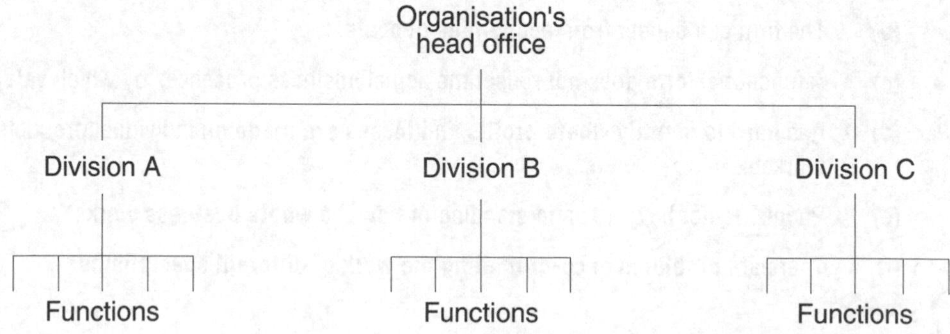

Multi-divisional structure organised by product-market areas

This enables **concentration on particular product-market areas**, overcoming problems of functional specialisation on a large scale. Problems arise with the power of the head office, and control of the resources. Responsibility is devolved, and some central functions might be duplicated.

The **holding company** (group) structure is a radical form of divisionalisation. **Subsidiaries are separate legal entities**. The holding company can be a firm with a permanent investment or one which buys and sells businesses.

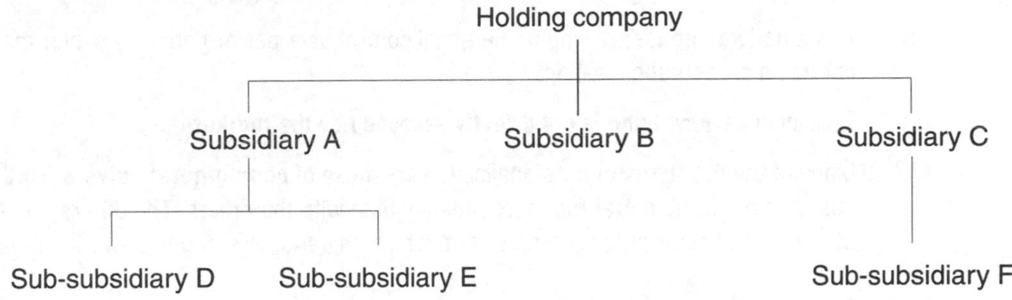

Holding company organisational structure

1.2.2 Implications for performance management

(a) **Divisional management** should be **free to use their authority** to do what they think is right for their part of the organisation, but they must be held accountable to head office (eg for profits earned).

(b) **A division must be large enough to support the quantity and quality of management it needs**. It must not rely on head office for excessive management support.

(c) Each division must have a **potential for growth in its own area of operations**.

(d) There should be **scope and challenge in the job** for the management of the division.

Divisions should exist **side by side with each other**. If they deal with each other, it should be as an arm's length transaction. Where they touch, it should be in competition with each other. There should be no insistence on preferential treatment to be given to a 'fellow unit' by another unit of the overall organisation.

Divisionalisation has some **advantages** in terms of performance management:

(a) It focuses the attention of subordinate management on business performance and results.

(b) Management by objectives can be applied more easily. The manager of the unit knows better than anyone else how they are doing, and needs no feedback from others.

(c) It gives more authority to junior managers and therefore provides them with work, which grooms them for more senior positions in the future.

(d) It tests junior managers in independent command early in their careers and at a reasonably low level in the management hierarchy.

(e) It provides an organisation structure which reduces the number of levels of management. The top executives in each division should be able to report directly to the chief executive of the holding company.

There are also some **inherent problems** for performance management of adopting the divisional form:

(a) A division is partly **insulated** by the holding company from shareholders and capital markets, which ultimately reward performance.

(b) The economic advantages it offers over independent organisations **'reflect fundamental inefficiencies in capital markets'**. (In other words, different product-market divisions might function better as independent companies.)

(c) The divisions are **more bureaucratic** than they would be as independent corporations, owing to the performance measures imposed by the strategic apex.

(d) Headquarters management has a tendency to **usurp divisional profits** by management charges, cross-subsidies, head office bureaucracies and unfair transfer pricing systems.

(e) In some businesses, it **is impossible to identify completely independent products or markets** for which divisions would be appropriate.

(f) Divisionalisation is **only possible at a fairly senior management level**, because there is a limit to how much independence in the division of work can be arranged.

(g) **It is a halfway house**, relying on personal control over performance by senior managers and enforcing cross-subsidisation.

(h) Divisional **performance is not directly assessed by the market**.

(i) Many of the problems of divisionalisation are those of **conglomerate diversification**. Each business might be better run independently than with the others. The different businesses might offer different returns for different risks, which shareholders might prefer to judge independently.

1.2.3 Information needs of divisional structures

In a divisional structure each division is self-contained and based on geography or product/service area.

There is good communication between functions within the division but, crucially, divisional managers have more authority to **act autonomously** than in a functional structure where planning and control are exercised centrally. Divisional organisations tend to be more **decentralised** than functional ones. In this respect, it is important that divisional managers are clear about an organisation's strategy and objectives, so that they can ensure that their divisions perform according to that strategy. Once again, the idea of **goal congruence** is very important here.

Equally, because managers throughout the organisation have a key role in budgeting and monitoring performance, **performance information needs to be available to all these managers** (for example, so that they can monitor costs and revenues for their division).

Conversely, because divisional managers have a relatively high degree of autonomy, the corporate centre (head office) needs to have information about divisional performance, to assess whether the divisions are performing in line with head office's objectives. In this respect, performance will be measured on the basis of divisions or strategic business units, rather than according to business processes.

Managers will be accountable for, and rewarded on the basis of, divisional performance. Accordingly, **divisional performance measures** (such as return on investment (ROI) or residual income (RI)) can be appropriate here.

Whereas in a functional structure performance information tends to be aggregated for the corporate centre to review and then give feedback to functions, in a divisional structure it is important that performance information is available at a lower level so that the divisions can provide feedback on performance upwards to senior management.

1.3 Network organisations

1.3.1 Information characteristics and needs in a network organisation

The idea of a **network structure** is applied both within and between organisations. Within the organisation, the term is used to mean something that resembles both an **organic** organisation (broadly characterised by decentralisation and loose organisational structure) and the structure of informal relationships that exists in most organisations alongside the formal structure. Such a loose, fluid approach is often used to achieve innovative response to changing circumstances.

Communication tends to be lateral and takes this form rather than command. **Information and advice** are given rather than **instructions and decisions**.

The network approach is also visible in the growing field of **outsourcing** as a strategic method. Complex relationships can be developed between firms, which may both buy from and sell to each other, as well as the simpler, more traditional practice of buying in services, such as cleaning.

Organisations have to manage the trade-off between the desire to remain independent and autonomous, and the need to be interdependent and co-operative. Writers such as Ghoshal and Bartlett point to the likelihood of such networks becoming the corporations of the future, replacing formal organisation structures with innovations such as virtual teams. Virtual teams are interconnected groups of people who may not be in the same office (or even the same organisation) but who:

(a) Share information and tasks
(b) Make joint decisions
(c) Fulfil the collaborative function of a team

1.3.2 Implications for performance management

Organisations are now able to **structure their activities very differently**. This will obviously affect the management of performance.

(a) **Staffing**. Freelance or contract workers can undertake certain areas of organisational activity. Charles Handy's shamrock organisation (with a three leafed structure of core, contractor and flexible part-time labour) is gaining ground as a workable model for a leaner and more flexible workforce, within a controlled framework.

(b) **Leasing of facilities** such as machinery, IT and accommodation (not just capital assets) is becoming more common.

(c) **Production itself might be outsourced**, even to offshore countries where labour is cheaper.

(d) **Interdependence of organisations** is emphasised by the sharing of functions and services.

Databases and communication create genuine interactive sharing of, and access to, common data. Network structures are also discerned between competitors, where co-operation on non-core competence matters can lead to several benefits:

(a) Cost reduction
(b) Increased market penetration
(c) Experience curve effects

Typical areas for co-operation between competitors include R&D and distribution chains. The spread of the Toyota system of manufacturing, with its emphasis on JIT, quality and the elimination of waste, has led to a high degree of integration between the operations of industrial customers and their suppliers.

1.3.3 Information needs of network structures

Network structures have developed a sense of collective responsibility between members of the networks; in effect, doing business becomes a process of continuous interaction and collaboration. In network structures, many physical products never touch the 'core' organisation at the centre of the network. For example, most Nike shoes are never touched by a Nike employee and never see the inside of a Nike facility, because they are manufactured and packaged by outsourced network partners.

Similarly, a number of organisations have now outsourced their customer service functions, yet the level of customer service received still plays a vital part in the customer's overall satisfaction with the 'core' company.

The **flow of information between the network partners** plays a key role in connecting all the elements of the network.

While in a traditional organisation managers look to monitor and control the performance of the function or division under their jurisdiction, in a network managers have to rely on contracts, co-ordination and negotiations with their network partners to hold things together. This also means **managing relationships with network partners** and resolving any conflicts.

Information is also required to maintain control across the network, to ensure that all the organisations in the network have common goals. These goals and expectations may be specified in **contractual agreements** or **service level agreements** detailing what the 'core' company in a network requires from its network partners (for example, for establishing quality standards). Equally, management information will also then need to be available to show whether the outsource partners have met the standards required of them. This will be particularly important if the contracts include payment terms which are dependent on results.

Network structures mean that rather than monitoring the performance of divisions or functions, organisations now need to monitor the performance of their outsource partners. At a more strategic level, the 'core' company needs to assess the cost and benefit of outsourcing functions, and therefore to inform resource allocation decision. For example, how do the fees payable to external outsourced partners compare to the costs and overheads saved internally (for example, by reducing headcount) and therefore does an organisation benefit by outsourcing a function?

Importantly, though, performance management initiatives cannot concentrate solely on performance within the 'core' company. Instead, performance management initiatives need to focus **on improving performance across the whole value network**.

Consequently, performance management also needs to recognise the nature of the relationships between the core organisation and its **many stakeholders**. Issues such as transparency between the network partners become important, and performance management needs to focus on **building trust** instead of simply focusing on control. Trust, rather than control, helps to improve performance within a network relationship. Consequently, management processes should aim to build trust in the relationship.

The dynamic of this relationship between the organisations in a network also has important implications for performance measurement. For each key network partner, the 'core' company should monitor not only what it is getting **from** the partner, but also what it is providing **to** the partner (for example, clear instructions for order requirements, or the prompt payment of invoices). Failure to do so could lead to the loss of key network partners, and could leave the 'core' company unable to fulfil its commitments to its customers.

In this respect we can identify different levels of information needs in network structures.

Operational information – typically comprising data on the status of transaction; for example, tracking the progress of a batch of shoes being manufactured by an outsourced partner

Financial information – for example, invoice and payment information

Management information – which supplements operational information and could involve sharing, for example, skills and designs

In order for the output of autonomous network agents to cohere, their various activities must also be integrated. IT systems are likely to play a crucial role here, in relation to data sharing and integration between the 'core' organisation and its network partners. Equally, electronic mail (email) is likely to be important in sharing information and co-ordinating work, regardless of the geographical location of the parties involved.

2 Information needs of manufacturing and service businesses

2.1 Information needs of manufacturing businesses

At the simplest level, all manufacturing businesses follow the same model.

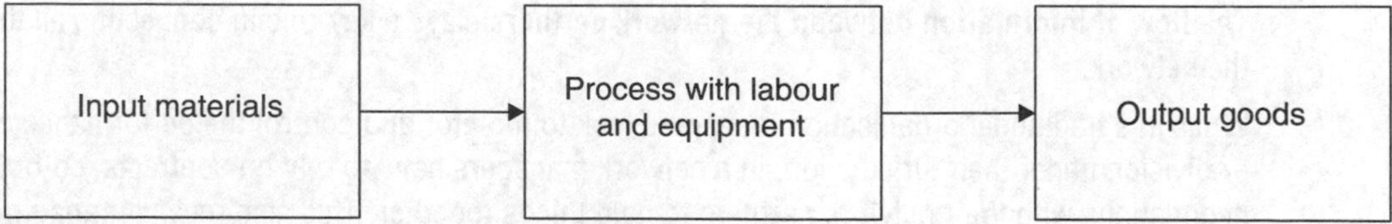

The information required by even modern manufacturing organisations is still based on the demands of this model.

A variety of performance indicators are used by manufacturing businesses, but there are some overriding considerations.

Consideration	Detail
Cost behaviour	Labour is generally a variable cost. Machinery is a fixed cost. Modern technology requires more overheads. (With advanced manufacturing technology, there is a higher proportion of fixed equipment costs compared with variable labour costs.)
Quality	Important in terms of output adherence to production specification. We discuss the importance of quality and quality management in more detail in Chapter 13 of this Study Text.
Time	Production bottlenecks, delivery times, deadlines and machine speed must be considered.
Innovation	This is required in products and processes.
Valuation	Despite the tendency towards low inventory and just-in-time delivery, many businesses still have to give a value to inventory of raw materials or finished goods as a major element in their profit calculations. Whether complicated tracking systems are needed is a different question.

We look at the first four of these considerations in more detail in the following paragraphs.

2.1.1 Cost behaviour, quality, time and innovation

(a) **Cost behaviour**

Uses	Comment
Planning	Standard costs can be outlined, and actual costs compared with them.
Decision making	Estimates of future costs may be needed to assess the likely profitability of a product.
Control	Total cost information can be monitored to ensure the best rates for supplies.

(b) **Quality** information is used to ensure that 'customer satisfaction' is built into the manufacturing system and its outputs.

Uses	Comment
Planning	Ensure that products are well designed and manufactured according to specification.
Decision making	Businesses have a choice as to what level of quality they 'build' into a product. Quality is not perfection, it is 'fitness for use'.
Control	Falling levels of quality are an alarm bell – if products are not manufactured according to their design specification, there will be more rejects, more waste and more dissatisfied customers. This means higher costs and lower profits.

(c) **Time**

Uses	Comment
Planning	Manufacturing time has to be scheduled to ensure the most efficient use of the system; if production can be smoothed over a period, this ensures effective capacity utilisation. Throughput time is thus important.
Decision making	Time is relevant to decision making, as it indicates a firm's ability to keep its promises to its customers for delivery and so on.
Control	• New product development (from conception to implementation) • Speed of delivery • Bottlenecks • In just-in-time systems, where firms hold little material inventories, time is a measure of a factory's ability to function at all. Inventory levels will be measured not in units but in day's supplies • As a measure of efficiency (eg inventory revenue, asset turnover)

(d) **Innovation**

Uses	Comment
Planning	• New product development • Speed to market • New process
Control	This generally refers to the launch and design of new products.

The **experience curve** can be used in strategic control of costs and is relevant to 'time' and 'innovation'. It suggests that as output increases, the cost per unit of output falls, for the following reasons:

(a) **Economies of scale** – in other words, an increased volume of production leads to lower unit costs, as the firm approaches full capacity.

(b) A genuine **'learning effect'** as the workforce becomes familiar with the job and learns to carry out the task more efficiently. As a process is repeated, it is likely that costs will reduce due to **efficiency, discounts** and **reduced waste**.

(c) **Technological improvements**.

This brings us on to **target costing**, covered in your study of Paper F5 *Performance Management.*

(a) In the short run, because of development costs and the learning time needed, costs are likely to exceed price.

(b) In the longer term, costs should come down (for example, because of the experience curve) to their target level.

2.1.2 Strategic, tactical and operational information

The information requirements of manufacturing businesses can also be considered in terms of the three levels we covered in Chapter 1.

Information type	Examples
Strategic	Future demand estimates New product development plans Competitor analysis
Tactical	Variance analysis Departmental accounts Inventory turnover
Operational	Production reject rates Materials and labour used Inventory levels

The information requirements of commercial organisations are influenced by the need to make and monitor profit. Information that contributes to the following measures is important:

(a) Changeover times
(b) Number of common parts
(c) Level of product diversity
(d) Product and process quality

2.2 Service businesses 6/13

FAST FORWARD

Unlike manufacturing businesses, service businesses are characterised by **intangibility, inseparability, variability, perishability** and the **absence of a transfer of ownership**.

Key term

'**Services** are any activity or benefit that one party can offer to another that is essentially intangible and does not result in the **ownership** of anything. Its production may or may not be tied to a physical product.'

(P Kotler, *Social Marketing)*

There are **five major characteristics of services that distinguish services from manufacturing**:

(a) **Intangibility**. This refers to the lack of substance which is involved with service delivery. Unlike goods (physical products such as confectionery), there are no substantial material or physical aspects to a service: no taste, feel, visible presence, and so on. For example, if you go to the theatre, you cannot 'take' the play with you.

(b) **Inseparability/simultaneity**. Many services are created at the same time as they are consumed. (For example, haircuts, medical operations, holidays and concerts are all produced at the same time as they are consumed.) No service exists until it is actually being experienced/consumed by the person who has bought it.

This inseparability also illustrates the importance of the **people** providing the service. The way they provide the service will have a crucial influence on the satisfaction gained by the consumer, and on the consumer's perception of the service experience. In turn, this is likely to have a major impact on the level of repeat business the service provider will generate from its consumers.

(c) **Variability/heterogeneity**. Many services face the problem of maintaining **consistency in the standard of output**. It may be hard to attain precise standardisation of the service offered, but customers expect it (such as with fast food).

(d) **Perishability**. Services are innately perishable, in the sense that consumption cannot be stored for the future. A hotel room that is not occupied on a given day, or an airline seat that is not occupied on any given flight, represents lost income that cannot be made up at a later date. Therefore, it is very important to **match supply and demand** for services. For example, if a hotel has high occupancy levels during the week, but is much less full at weekends, it should try to find ways of increasing the number of guests staying at weekends.

(e) **No transfer of ownership**. Services do not result in the transfer of property. The purchase of a service only confers on the customer access to or a right to use a facility. For example, if a customer rents a car for the duration of their holiday, at the end of their holiday they must return the car to the car hire company – they do not own the car.

Most 'offers' to the public contain a **product** and **service** element.

Exam focus point

Part of a question requirement in the June 2013 exam asked candidates to explain the characteristics which differentiate service businesses from manufacturing ones, using the business described in the scenario (a hotel chain) to illustrate their points.

So, in effect, candidates had to illustrate how the five characteristics listed above are demonstrated in a hotel business.

2.2.1 Types of service business

FAST FORWARD

Mass services are standard services provided for large numbers of people and are often automated. **Personalised services** vary on the circumstances of the service delivery and are often provided on a one to one basis.

With this in mind, we can identify different types of service.

Type	Comment
Mass service	The delivery of the same, very standardised service to many people, as a transaction, for example the checkout process in a supermarket, or public transport. Key information needs here will relate to the process involved in the service: for example, the quality or the cost of the process.

Type	Comment
Personalised service	This service is unique to the recipient, such as financial advice or dentistry (every mouth is different, even though standard procedures are adopted to ensure best practice in dental care). Due to the high degree of interaction and customisation, these services are very labour intensive. Key information needs here will relate to the quality or cost of the inputs to the process, and the quality of the outputs.
Mixed	Some services offer a high degree of interaction and customisation, with a relatively low degree of labour intensity – for example, hospitals and restaurants.

Service activities therefore cut across all sectors of the economy. In the UK, **healthcare** is provided by the **public sector** but also by the **private sector** (for-profit). The objectives may differ even though the activities remain the same.

2.2.2 Quantitative/qualitative information and services

A **dental practice needs** a mix of **quantitative** and **non-quantitative** information to price its services properly, to optimise capacity utilisation and to monitor performance. Many small service businesses have similar concerns, for example garages and beauty parlours.

(a) They need to control the **total cost** of providing the **service operation**.
(b) They need positive **cash flow** to **finance activities**.
(c) They need **operating information** to identify how costs are incurred and on what services.

Arguably, small service businesses, whose expenses are mainly overheads, provide a model, in miniature, of the requirements of **activity-based costing**. As service businesses don't actually 'make' anything, many of the expenses are overheads, meaning that activity-based cost information is very valuable to the business. (We look at activity-based costing in more detail later in this Study Text.)

Are **'mass services'** any different?

(a) Because mass services, such as cheque clearing, are largely automated, there may be a large **fixed cost base**.

(b) Even if a service is heavily automated, each time the service is performed is a '**moment of truth**'* for the customer. Ensuring consistency and quality is important but this is true for small service businesses too.

(* A 'moment of truth' is the instance at which the customer comes into contact with an organisation, and which could therefore shape the customer's impression of the organisation.)

Key terms

Quantitative information is information that can be expressed in numbers. A sub-category of quantitative information is **financial information** (also known as **monetary information**), which is information that can be expressed in terms of money.

Qualitative information is information that cannot be expressed in numbers.

Non-financial information (or **non-monetary information**) is information that is not expressed in terms of money, although this does not mean that it cannot be expressed in terms of numbers.

Question — **Monetary and non-monetary information**

Identify some possible items of **monetary** and **non-monetary information** for a monthly report for a dentist practice. (**Hint**. Ask yourself: What is the key resource of the practice?)

Answer

(a) **Monthly receipts and payments**

(i) Receipts include payments from the Government for publicly funded work, fees for private work, and so on. Dentists are measured on Units of Dental Activity (UDA) and are given annual targets for UDAs that they must undertake.

(ii) Payments include operating costs, such as wages for nursing staff, reception staff, rent, insurance, electricity, telephone expenses, medical equipment and medicine.

(b) **Capacity utilisation**. In other words, how busy has the practice been? Have all available appointments been booked or were there times when the dentist and their staff were kicking their heels? Just by looking at the **appointments diary** you can make comparatives.

(c) **Treatment costs**. Simple treatments such as teeth cleaning can be performed by the dental hygienist. Other treatments, such as root canal surgery, require the dentist and perhaps a dental nurse in attendance.

The cost of providing these different treatments will vary depending on the level of staff and complexity of the treatment.

The **cost driver** is **time**.

The **mix** of treatments offered is thus significant in the total profitability of the practice.

The practice will probably profit more from relatively expensive treatments, such as 'crowns', but these come at a cost. Patients can also have several treatments within a price band and be charged a single fixed price. This may also have an effect on just how much work the dentist is willing to do for a single fixed charge.

However, while this information is useful to monitor the financial health of the practice, it does not give us a sufficiently detailed picture of the operating performance. The key resource is **time**, the dentist's time and staff time.

For the **long-term** business sustainability of the practice, matters such as **customer satisfaction** and **repeat business** must be considered. (Does your dentist remind you to have a check up every six months?)

Question

Quantitative vs qualitative, financial vs non-financial

Categorise the following statements as either financial, qualitative, quantitative or non-financial, whichever **one** of these you think is most appropriate.

(a) I bought four bananas.
(b) I bought $1's worth of bananas.
(c) I like bananas.
(d) I can afford 1lb of bananas.

Answer

We stressed that you should put each statement into one category only to make sure that you take in the essential points. For example, statement (a) is actually both quantitative and non-financial, but we would call it 'quantitative' only because there is no suggestion of money being involved.

If you are uneasy about the idea that the statement 'I like bananas' **cannot** be expressed in monetary terms you are ready to read on.

Colin Drury (in *Management and Cost Accounting*) describes **qualitative factors** as those 'that cannot be expressed in monetary terms.' He cites the decline in employee morale that results from redundancies within an organisation as an example of a qualitative factor.

2.2.3 Example: qualitative information

Consider a firm that is thinking of sacking many of its customer service staff and replacing them with automated telephone answering systems. Now consider how difficult it would be to obtain the following information in order to appraise a decision whether or not to replace staff with an untested system.

(a) The cost of **being sure** that the new system would do the job as well as people can

(b) The potential impact on **customer satisfaction** and **customer retention** if customers do not like the new system

(c) The cost of **loss of morale** among other workers if large numbers are made redundant

(d) The **difficulty of recruiting people** to other parts of the organisation if its reputation is damaged by the redundancies

(e) The **cost to the community** – in social as well as financial terms – of unemployment

These are not just political points. The company's treatment of its staff may have a profound impact on its ability to **recruit** skilled employees in the future and on the way the company is **perceived** by potential **customers**. Whether the costs can be established or not, the questions need to be considered.

Service industries, perhaps more than manufacturing firms, **rely on their staff.** Front-line staff are those who convey the 'service' – and the experience of the brand – to the consumer. They convey the 'moment of truth' with the customer.

Consequently, **employee morale** will be important in a service business. If staff are unhappy, this is likely to adversely affect the service they provide their customers and, as a result, this is likely to adversely affect the overall customer experience.

Management **information** therefore has to include **intangible factors**, such as how customers feel about the service (customer satisfaction) and whether they would use it again. (This reinforces the need for qualitative management information.)

There are some demonstrable relationships between **staff revenue** and **positive customer experiences**. High staff revenue not only means higher recruitment and training costs but it may also have an adverse impact on the firm's ability to **retain** customers (which is cheaper than finding new ones).

For service businesses, **management accounting information** should **incorporate** the **key drivers of service costs**:

(a) Repeat business
(b) Churn rate (for subscriptions)*
(c) Customer satisfaction surveys, complaints
(d) Opportunity costs of not providing a service
(e) Avoidable/unavoidable costs

* The churn rate for any given period of time is the number of participants who discontinue their use of a service divided by the average number of total participants. Churn rate provides insight into the growth or decline of the subscriber base, as well as the average length of time consumers remain loyal to the service provider.

Exam focus point

> One of the key aspects of management information about service businesses is the focus on **customer satisfaction**.
>
> The 'customer perspective' is one of the four perspectives in the **balanced scorecard** which we look at in Chapter 15 later in this Study Text. However, the balanced scorecard highlights the importance of businesses measuring both financial and non-financial performance; and this is a point particularly worth noting when considering the performance of service businesses.
>
> Although it may be easier for service organisations to measure financial performance measures (which are easily quantifiable) than non-financial performance measures (which are often less easily quantifiable), their long-term performance is likely to depend on how well they perform in non-financial areas. Therefore, it is important that service organisations have a range of non-financial performance indicators as well as financial ones.
>
> Fitzgerald and Moon's **building block** model (which we look at in Chapter 15 later in this Study Text) also highlights the importance of these non-financial areas (such as quality of service) as key determinants of an organisation's competitive success. The building block model was developed specifically for use in service businesses, and was designed as a way of trying to overcome the problems associated with performance measurement in service industries.

2.2.4 Strategic, tactical and operational information

In the same way that we did for manufacturing businesses, we can also consider the strategic, tactical and operational information requirements of service businesses.

Information type	Examples
Strategic	Forecast sales growth and market share Profitability, capital structure
Tactical	Resource utilisation such as average staff time charged out, number of customers per hairdresser, number of staff per account Customer satisfaction rating
Operational	Staff timesheets Customer waiting time Individual customer feedback

Organisations have become **more customer and results orientated** in the 21st century. As a consequence, **the differences between service organisations' and other organisations' information requirements have decreased**. Businesses have realised that most of their activities can be measured, and many can be measured in similar ways regardless of the business sector.

3 Business process re-engineering (BPR) 6/14

Process efficiency has become increasingly important in modern business, as increased competition has forced organisations to ask questions such as: 'How should work be designed?', 'Who should do it?' and 'Where should they do it?'

Such questions indicate that process improvement and business process re-engineering (BPR) can play an important part in an organisation's strategy for sustained competitive advantage. However, the link with achieving competitive advantage means that any BPR projects should not be carried out as standalone exercises but in the context of the organisation's overall strategic position and business strategy.

In particular, it is important to identify the organisation's objectives, goals and critical success factors, in order to establish which processes link directly to these. It follows that improvements in these key processes are likely to lead to improvements in the organisation's strategic performance, and therefore suggests that these processes should be the ones which the organisation looks to improve in a BPR exercise.

FAST FORWARD

Business process re-engineering involves focusing attention inwards to consider how business processes can be redesigned or re-engineered to improve efficiency.

BPR involves focusing attention **inwards** to consider how business **processes** can be **redesigned** or re-engineered to **improve efficiency**. It **can** lead to fundamental changes in the way an organisation functions. In particular, it has been realised that processes, which were developed in a paper-intensive processing environment, may not be suitable for an environment that is underpinned by IT.

The main writing on the subject is Hammer and Champy's *Reengineering the Corporation* (1993), from which the following definition is taken.

Key term

Business process re-engineering (BPR) is the fundamental rethinking and radical redesign of business processes to achieve dramatic improvements in critical contemporary measures of performance, such as cost, quality, service and speed.

The key words here are **fundamental, radical, dramatic** and **process**:

(a) **Fundamental** and **radical** indicate that BPR is somewhat akin to zero based budgeting: it starts by asking basic questions such as 'why do we do what we do', without making any assumptions or looking back to what has always been done in the past.

(b) **Dramatic** means that BPR should achieve 'quantum leaps in performance', not just marginal, incremental improvements.

(c) **Process**. BPR recognises that there is a need to change functional hierarchies: 'existing hierarchies have evolved into functional departments that encourage functional excellence but which do not work well together in meeting customers' requirements' (Rupert Booth, *Management Accounting,* 1994).

Key term

A **process** is a collection of activities that takes one or more kinds of input and creates an output.

For example, order fulfilment is a process that takes an order as its input and results in the delivery of the ordered goods. Part of this process is the manufacture of the goods, but under **BPR** the **aim** of **manufacturing** is **not merely to make** the goods. Manufacturing should aim to **deliver the goods that were ordered**, and any aspect of the manufacturing process that hinders this aim should be re-engineered. The first question to ask might be 'Do they need to be manufactured at all?'

A **re-engineered process** has certain **characteristics**:

(a) Often several jobs are **combined** into one.
(b) Workers often **make decisions**.
(c) The **steps** in the process are performed in **a logical order**.
(d) **Work** is performed where it **makes most sense**.
(e) Checks and controls may be reduced, and **quality 'built-in'**.
(f) One manager provides a **single point of contact**.
(g) The advantages of **centralised and decentralised** operations are combined.

3.1 Hammer's principles of BPR

(a) Processes should be designed to achieve a desired **outcome rather than** focusing on existing **tasks**.

(b) **Personnel who use** the **output** from a process should **perform the process**. For example, a company could set up a database of approved suppliers; this would allow personnel who actually require supplies to order them themselves, perhaps using online technology, thereby eliminating the need for a separate purchasing function.

(c) **Information processing** should be **included in the work, which produces the information**. This eliminates the differentiation between information gathering and information processing.

(d) **Geographically dispersed resources** should be **treated** as if they are **centralised**. This allows the benefits of centralisation to be obtained; for example, economies of scale through central negotiation of supply contracts, without losing the benefits of decentralisation, such as flexibility and responsiveness.

(e) **Parallel activities** should be **linked rather than integrated**. This would involve, for example, co-ordination between teams working on different aspects of a single process.

(f) **'Doers'** should be allowed to be **self-managing**. The traditional **distinction** between **workers** and **managers** can be **abolished**: decision aids such as expert systems can be provided where they are required.

(g) **Information** should be **captured once** at **source**. Electronic distribution of information makes this possible.

3.2 Implementing BPR

Davenport and Short recommend a five-step approach for implementing BPR:

(a) **Develop the business vision and process objectives**. BPR is driven by a business vision which implies specific business objectives, such as cost reduction, time reduction, output quality improvement, total quality management and empowerment.

(b) **Identify the processes** to be redesigned. Most firms use the 'high impact' approach, which focuses on the most important processes or those that conflict most with the business vision. Far fewer use the exhaustive approach that attempts to identify all the processes within an organisation and then prioritise them in order of redesign urgency.

(c) **Understand and measure the existing processes**. This is so as to ensure that previous mistakes are not repeated and to provide a baseline for future improvements.

(d) **Identify change levers**. Awareness of IT capabilities could prove useful when designing processes.

(e) **Design and build a prototype of the new process**. The actual design should not be viewed as the end of the BPR process – it should be viewed as a prototype, with successive alterations. The use of a prototype enables the involvement of customers.

Exam focus point

Hammer and Champy envisaged BPR as a way of streamlining work processes and thereby achieving significant improvements in relation to quality, time management and cost.

We look at quality in more detail in Chapter 13 later in this Study Text, where we also discuss Six Sigma as a method for improving existing processes. However, it is important to recognise that the focus of BPR is on fundamentally rethinking and radically redesigning process, whereas Six Sigma (and the DMAIC methodology) is used for improving an existing process when it is not meeting customer needs.

3.3 Business processes and the technological interdependence between departments

The value chain describes a series of activities from input of raw materials to output of finished goods/services for the customers. These activities may be organised into departments even though the actual process of adding value may cross departmental boundaries.

The **links between different departments of a business can vary**, however, and hence the **need to manage the relationships between them. Interdependence** is the extent to which **different departments depend on each** other to accomplish their tasks. It is possible to identify three types of interdependence:

(a) In **pooled interdependence**, each department/section works **independently** of the others, subject to achieving the overall goals of the organisation.

(b) **Sequential interdependence** is when there is a sequence (or a **linked** chain of activities) with a **start** and **end** point. An example is an assembly line: raw materials are taken, moulded to the right sizes and shapes and are assembled into a product. The **outputs** of each stage sequence must be precisely tailored to the **inputs** of the next – standardisation of outputs might be one form of co-ordination used. The first activity must be performed correctly before the second can be tackled. **Management effort** is required to ensure that the **transfer of resources between departments is smooth**. They therefore need information about the process as a whole.

(c) **Reciprocal interdependence** exists when a **number of departments acquire inputs from and offer outputs to each other**. In other words, while resources have to be transferred, there is **no preset sequence**. The output of one department might be sent to another for processing, and then returned to the original department.

You should now have some idea as to the complexities of business processes overlapping different departments. **Some organisations have redesigned their structures on the lines of business processes**, adopting BPR to **avoid** all the co-ordination problems caused by reciprocal interdependence.

3.4 Key characteristics of organisations which have adopted BPR

(a) **Work units change from functional departments (functional structure) to process teams.**

  (i) For example, within a functional framework, a sales order may be handled by many different people, in different departments or business functions. (One person takes the order in the department, and one person delivers.)

  (ii) In process teams, the people are grouped together. A case team might combine to do all the work on a process and this applies not only to one-off projects but also to recurring work.

  Multi-skilling also means that one individual does many of the tasks in a process.

(b) **Jobs change**. People do more, as team members are responsible for results. This ties in with **job enlargement** and **job enrichment**.

(c) **People's roles change**. They are empowered to make decisions relevant to the process.

(d) **Performance measures concentrate on results** rather than activities. Process teams create 'value' which is measurable.

(e) Organisation structures change from **hierarchical** to **flat** (ie delayered).

  (i) When a process becomes the work of a **whole team**, managing the process is the **team's responsibility**. Interdepartmental issues become matters the team resolves itself, rather than matters requiring managerial intervention.

  (ii) Companies require less managerial input. **Managers have less to do**; there are fewer of them and so fewer layers.

  (iii) Organisation structure determines lines of communication, and in many organisations is a weighty issue. This is not the case in process organisations, as **lines of communication 'naturally' develop around business processes**.

3.4.1 Problems with BPR

Although the intended focus of BPR is on improving process efficiency within organisations, there is a danger that, in practice, managers and organisations associate it with narrowly defined targets such as **reductions in staff numbers** and other **cost-cutting** measures.

In addition to the misperception of BPR as being simply a cost-cutting exercise, several other criticisms have been made:

(a) Successful BPR programmes result in significant **changes that affect staff** widely.

  However, writings on BPR appear to overlook the impact of a BPR exercise on the staff involved. A BPR exercise may lead to new patterns of work, changing the composition of work groups and teams, as well as possible redundancies. These changes may come at a cost. This might be the direct costs associated with redundancies or, less immediately obvious, the loss of goodwill among staff, or increased stress among the workforce as a result of the reduction in staff numbers.

(b) BPR **improves efficiency** but may ignore **effectiveness**. For example, fewer managers may lead to reduced innovation and creativity. Hamel and Prahalad call this process **hollowing out**.

(c) While BPR practice generally seeks to empower workers, it assumes they will work within structures and systems imposed by others. This places strict limits on the scope for releasing their potential.

3.5 Implications of BPR for accounting systems

Issue	Implication
Performance measurement	Performance measures must be built around processes, not departments: this may affect the design of responsibility centres.
Reporting	There is a need to identify where value is being added.
Activity	ABC might be used to model the business processes.
Structure	The complexity of the reporting system will depend on the organisational structure. Arguably the reports should be designed around the process teams, if there are independent process teams.
Variances	New variances may have to be developed.

Exam focus point

Benchmarking, which we discussed in Chapter 1 of this Study Text, could also be useful in the context of a BPR exercise.

Once an organisation has identified which its key processes are, it will also then have to decide which of them need to be re-engineered. This will depend on the performance of the organisation's processes compared with those of its competitors or other organisations in different industries which use similar processes.

In order to make this decision, the organisation will need to compare the performance of its processes with the other organisations', which it can do by benchmarking its processes.

Case Study — **Taco Bell**

The case of Taco Bell is one of the examples quoted in Hammer and Champy's seminal text on business re-engineering – *Reengineering the Corporation.*

In the 1980s, Taco Bell was entrenched in a command and control hierarchy that claimed to understand what customers wanted, but did not ask directly. But major re-engineering efforts – automating, changing the organisational structure and management system, reducing kitchen space, and increasing customer space – that focused on what customers really wanted greatly simplified their processes.

These changes had a huge impact on the company. It went from a failing regional Mexican-American fast food chain with $500 million in sales in 1982, to a $3 billion national company 10 years later.

One BPR initiative was the K-Minus programme, or 'kitchenless' restaurant. Based on the belief that they were a service company, not a manufacturer, the K-Minus programme changed the way Taco Bell's food was prepared.

The kitchens in Taco Bell's restaurants became heating and assembly units, while central food production units prepared and cooked the ingredients used to make the meals. The K-Minus programme eliminated 15 hours of work a day from the individual restaurants, improving quality control and employee morale, reducing employee accidents and injuries, and resulting in substantial savings on utilities.

Overall, the K-Minus programme saved Taco Bell about $7 million a year.

3.6 Examples of BPR

(a) A move from a traditional functional plant layout to a JIT cellular product layout is a simple example.

(b) **Elimination of non value added activities**. Consider a materials handling process, which incorporates scheduling production, storing materials, processing purchase orders, inspecting materials and paying suppliers.

This process could be re-engineered by sending the production schedule direct to nominated suppliers with whom contracts are set up to ensure that materials are delivered in accordance with the production schedule and that their quality is guaranteed (by supplier inspection before delivery).

Such re-engineering should result in the elimination or permanent reduction of the non value added activities of storing, purchasing and inspection.

Case Study — **Example of BPR**

A company employs 25 staff to perform the standard accounting task of matching goods received notes with orders and then with invoices. A process review established that 50% of employees' time was spent trying to match the 20% of document sets that do not agree.

One way of improving the situation would be to computerise the existing process to facilitate matching. This would help, but BPR would go further.

A BPR approach may question why any incorrect orders are accepted. To enable incorrect orders to be identified before being accepted, all orders could first be entered into a computerised database. When goods arrive, they either agree to goods that have been ordered (as recorded in the database) or they don't.

Goods that agree to an order are accepted and paid for. Goods that are not agreed are sent back to the supplier. Time is not wasted trying to sort out unmatched documents.

Gains would include staff time saved, quicker payment for suppliers, lower inventory costs and lower investment in working capital.

Exam focus point

Part of a question in the June 2014 exam required candidates to assess the impact of BPR on the culture and management information systems at an organisation.

One of the key issues in the scenario was that the organisation was currently structured on a functional basis, but BPR focuses on processes rather than functions. As a result, performance measures will need to be redesigned around processes rather than departments. Similarly, the change in organisational structure may also have an impact on the organisation's culture.

4 Business integration

Business integration highlights the importance of the linkages between people, operations, strategy and technology in organisations. The goal of business integration is for an organisation to ensure there is a fit between its people, operations and technology and its strategies, such that it can implement its strategies effectively.

Whatever business structure is adopted, there needs to be integration between the parts of the business to ensure that **activities and processes are co-ordinated**, and that the business **creates value**.

In this section we look at two models which highlight the importance of business integration, and which are specifically referred to in the Study Guide: McKinsey's 7S's, and Porter's value chain.

Exam focus point

In Chapter 8 of this Study Text, we discuss the concept of **integrated reporting**. One of the aims of integrated reporting is to demonstrate how an organisation's strategy creates and sustains value for its stakeholders.

In this respect, the ideas we are discussing here (about the way people, operations, strategy and technology come together to create value in an organisation) could also be relevant in the context of the 'business model', and 'strategy and resource allocation' aspects of integrated reporting.

FAST FORWARD

Although it is easy to look at a business as a grouping of specialised departments, in practice value is added by **activities and processes**, which may span a number of departments. These need to be **linked** effectively to **create value**.

Key term

Integration means that all aspects of the business must be aligned to secure the most efficient use of the organisation's resources so that it can achieve its objectives effectively.

4.1 McKinsey's 7S's model

McKinsey's 7S's model provides a way of looking at an organisation as a set of interconnected and interdependent subsystems. This interdependence highlights that strategies adopted in any one area of an organisation (or changes to any of the strategies) will have an impact on other parts of the organisation.

The model was designed to show how the various aspects of a business relate to one another, and it characterises the aspects of the business as seven 'S's.

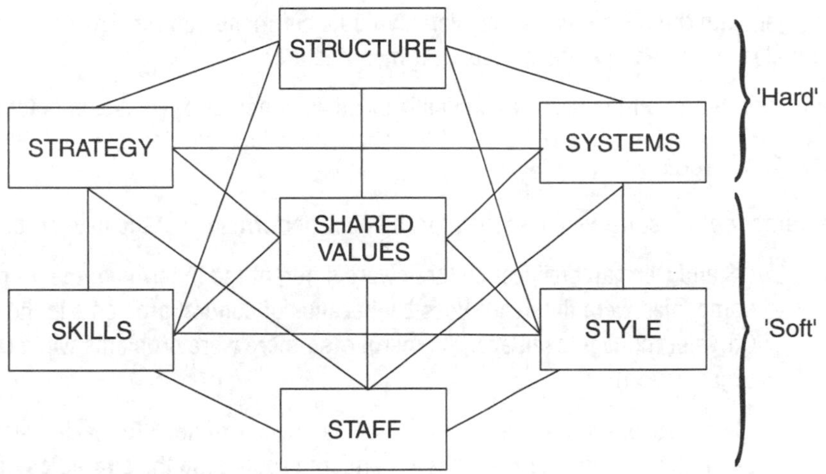

McKinsey 7S model

McKinsey's 7S's model describes the **links** between the **organisation's behaviour** as a whole and the **behaviour of individuals** within it.

There are three **'hard'** elements of business behaviour:

(a) **Structure**. The organisation structure refers to the formal division of tasks in the organisation and the hierarchy of authority from the most senior to junior.

(b) **Strategy**. How the organisation plans to outperform its competitors, or how it intends to achieve its objectives. This is linked to shared values.

(c) **Systems**. These include the technical systems of accounting, personnel, management information and so forth. These are linked to the skills of the staff.

These 'hard' elements are easily quantified and defined, and deal with facts and rules.

'Soft' elements are equally important.

(a) **Style** refers to the **corporate culture** that is the shared assumptions, ways of working, attitudes and beliefs. It is the way the organisation presents itself to the outside world.

(b) **Shared values** are the guiding beliefs of people in the organisation as to why it exists. (For example, people in a hospital seek to save lives.)

(c) **Staff** are the people in the organisation.

(d) **Skills** refer to those things that the organisation does well. For example, the UK telecommunications company BT is good at providing a telephone service but, even if its phone network is eventually used as a transmission medium for TV or films, BT is unlikely to make those programmes itself.

All elements, both hard and soft, **must pull in the same direction for the organisation to be effective**.

For example, an organisation will not benefit if it installs the most sophisticated, up to date management information systems, yet its managers continue to want to receive the same reports as they always have, because they don't understand, or trust, the new technology. In this simple example, there is a **mismatch** between systems and staff/skills.

Case Study

A consideration of the 7S's could also be useful when looking at potential acquisitions or mergers. The following case study illustrates the problems which can arise when there are differences in the business behaviours of the companies joining together in a merger.

Daimler Chrysler

In 1998, Daimler Benz, the German car manufacturer best known for its Mercedes premium brand, merged with the US company Chrysler, a volume car manufacturer. The merged company, Daimler Chrysler, became the world's largest car manufacturer.

However, although the deal was originally billed as a merger of equals, in practice it was a takeover by Daimler. Interestingly, by March 2001 the share price had fallen to just over 60% of what it had been in November 1998.

A number of reasons were identified for the poor performance of the new group.

- US and German business cultures were different (so in terms of the 'S' model, the **styles** of the two companies were different). Possibly because of cultural problems in the new group, many key Chrysler managers left after the merger (so there were problems with **staff** in the merged organisation).
- Mercedes was a premium brand which had been extended to making smaller cars. Chrysler depended on high volumes, not a premium product (so the **strategies** of the two companies were different). Therefore the distinction between 'premium' and 'volume' businesses got blurred.
- The new group did not properly exploit economies of scale, such as sharing components. There was a degree of technology sharing among the engineers, and this did result in some success stories, such as the Chrysler 300 model. However, many critics argued that the merger could not deliver the synergies which had been expected because the businesses were never successfully integrated. In effect, they seemed to be running two independent product lines: Daimler and Chrysler. (So, in terms of the 'S' model, the merger didn't integrate the **systems** of the two companies.)
- Productivity and efficiency at Chrysler was far lower than industry norms. (In 2000, each vehicle took Chrysler around 40 hours to make, compared with approximately 20 for the US factories of competitors such as Honda and Toyota.) In addition, its purchasing was inefficient, and fixed costs were too high for the size of the company. Overall, Chrysler's performance was much weaker than Daimler had realised going into the deal.

Ultimately, the Daimler Chrysler merger failed to produce the transatlantic automotive powerhouse that had been hoped for, and in 2007 Chrysler was sold to a private equity firm that specialises in restructuring troubled companies. In December 2008, Chrysler received a $4bn loan from the US Government to stave off bankruptcy. Nonetheless, Chrysler eventually filed for bankruptcy in April 2009.

While it was by no means the only reason why it failed, the failure to integrate the companies after the merger was a major contributing factor in its failure.

Fiat Chrysler

Despite filing for bankruptcy, Chrysler remained in business, and over the period 2009–2014 Fiat acquired an increasingly large stake in the company. By January 2014, it had acquired all the shares, and Chrysler Group became a subsidiary of Fiat.

In May 2014, a new group – Fiat Chrysler Automobiles (FCA) – was established, with two main operating subsidiaries: FCA Italy (previously Fiat Group Automobiles) and FCA US (previously Chrysler Group).

However, the question now is whether Fiat Chrysler will be any more successful than Daimler Chrysler was.

4.1.1 McKinsey's 7S's model and performance management

As we noted above, the 7S's all need to be aligned for an organisation to be effective; and this point means the 7S's model could have important implications for performance management.

Organisations can use the 7S's model to help identify whether its 'S' elements are **properly aligned** and support each other. For example: are the organisation's shared values consistent with its structure, strategy and systems?

If the organisation identifies that some of the elements are not properly aligned, it can then assess what needs to change, before undertaking the necessary **realignment**. In turn, this realignment should help to improve performance – and improving an organisation's performance is the key purpose of performance management.

4.2 The value chain

A more **sophisticated** model of business integration is the value chain. It offers a bird's eye view of the firm, of what it does and the **way in which its business activities are organised. Business activities** are **not the same as business functions**, however.

(a) **Functions** are the **familiar departments** of a business (production, finance and so on) and **reflect** the **formal organisation structure** and the distribution of labour.

(b) **Activities** are **what actually goes on**, and the **work that is done**. A single activity can be performed by a number of functions in sequence. Activities are the means by which a firm **creates value** in its products. Activities **incur** costs and, in combination with other activities, provide a product or service, which **earns revenue**.

For example, most organisations need to secure resources from the environment. This activity can be called procurement. Procurement will involve more departments than purchasing; however, accounts will certainly be involved and possibly production and quality assurance.

The ultimate **value** a firm **creates** is measured by the **amount customers are willing to pay** for its products or services **above the cost of carrying out value activities**. A firm is profitable if the realised value to customers exceeds the collective cost of performing the activities.

According to Porter, the **value activities** of any firm can be divided into **nine types** and then analysed into a **value chain**. This is a **model of activities** (which **procure inputs, process them** and **add value** to them in some way, to **generate outputs** for customers) and the **relationships between them**.

Key term

> The **value chain** 'disaggregates a firm into its strategically relevant activities in order to understand the behaviour of costs and the existing and potential sources of differentiation. A firm gains competitive advantage by performing these strategically important activities more cheaply or better than its competitors'.
>
> (Michael Porter, *Competitive Advantage*)

4.2.1 Activities

Primary activities are directly related to production, sales, marketing, delivery and service.

Activity	Comment
Inbound logistics	Receiving, handling and storing inputs to the production system: warehousing, transport, inventory control and so on
Operations	Convert resource inputs into a final product; resource inputs are not only materials; people are a resource, especially in service industries; note that this is not just applicable to manufacturing firms, hence the careful choice of name; service companies also have operations
Outbound logistics	Delivering the product to customers; this may include storage, testing, bulk transport, packaging, delivery and so on
Marketing and sales	Informing customers about the product, persuading them to buy it, and enabling them to do so: advertising, promotion and so on
After-sales service	Installing products, repairing them, upgrading them, providing spare parts and so forth

Support activities provide purchased inputs, human resources, technology and infrastructural functions to support the primary activities. The first three tend to provide specific elements of support to the primary activities.

Activity	Comment
Procurement	Acquire the resource inputs to the primary activities (eg purchase of materials, subcomponents equipment)
Technology development	Product design, improving processes and/or resource utilisation
Human resource management	Recruiting, training, developing and rewarding people
Firm infrastructure	General management, planning, finance, quality control, public and legal affairs: these activities normally support the chain as a whole rather than individual activities and are crucially important to an organisation's strategic capability in all primary activities

4.2.2 Linkages

Linkages connect the activities of the value chain, wherever they take place.

(a) **Activities in the value chain affect one another**. For example, more costly product design or better quality production might reduce the need for after-sales service.

(b) **Linkages require co-ordination**. For example, just-in-time requires smooth functioning of operations, outbound logistics and service activities, such as installation.

Because activities can be spread across departments, rather than corresponding to neat, organisation chart boundaries, managing them for best effect can be extremely difficult. Cost control can be a particular problem. The dispersion of activities also complicates the management of linkages.

4.2.3 Value system

Activities and **linkages that add value do not stop** at the organisation's **boundaries**. For example, when a restaurant serves a meal, the quality of the ingredients – although the cook chooses them – is determined by the grower. The grower has added value, and the grower's success in growing produce of good quality is as important to the customer's ultimate satisfaction as the skills of the chef. A **firm's value chain** is **connected** to what Porter calls a **value system**.

4.2.4 How an organisation can use the value chain to secure competitive advantage

The value chain provides a framework for understanding the nature and location of the skills and competences in an organisation that provide the basis for its competitive advantage.

Equally, the value chain provides a framework for cost analysis. Assigning operating costs and assets to value activities is the starting point of cost analysis, so that improvements can then be made or cost advantages defended. For example, if an organisation discovers that it has a cost advantage over its competitors based on the efficiency of its production facilities (operations), it needs to ensure its production facilities remain superior to those of its competitors so that it can maintain its advantage over them.

The value chain can help an organisation to secure competitive advantage in a number of ways:

(a) Invent new or better ways to do activities
(b) Combine activities in new or better ways
(c) Manage the linkages in its own value chain
(d) Manage the linkages in the value system

4.2.5 Example: using the value chain in competitive strategy

The following examples (a) and (b) are based on two supermarket chains, **one concentrating on low prices**, the **other differentiated on quality and service**. See if you can tell which is which.

(a)

	INBOUND LOGISTICS	OPERATIONS	OUTBOUND LOGISTICS	MARKETING & SALES	SERVICE
Firm infrastructure	Minimum corporate HQ				
Human resource management		De-skilled store operatives	Dismissal for checkout error		
Technology development	Computerised warehousing		Checkouts simple		
Procurement	Branded only purchases Big discounts	Low cost sites			Use of concessions
	Bulk warehousing	1,000 lines only Price points Basic store design		Low price promotion Local focus	Nil

(b)

	INBOUND LOGISTICS	OPERATIONS	OUTBOUND LOGISTICS	MARKETING & SALES	SERVICE
Firm infrastructure	Central control of operations and credit control				
Human resource management	Recruitment of mature staff	Client care training	Flexible staff to help with packing		
Technology development		Recipe research	Electronic point of sale	Consumer research and tests	Itemised bills
Procurement	Own label products	Prime retail positions		Adverts in quality magazines	
	Dedicated refrigerated transport	In-store food halls Modern store design Open front refrigerators Tight control of sell-by dates	Collect by car service	No price discounts on food past sell-by dates	No quibble refunds

The two supermarkets represented are based on the following:

(a) The value chain in (a) is similar to that of Lidl, a 'discount' supermarket chain which sells on price. This can be seen in the limited product range and its low-cost sites.

(b) The value chain in (b) is based on Marks & Spencer, which seeks to differentiate on quality and service. Hence the 'no quibble' refunds, the use of prime retail sites and customer care training.

Importantly, the differences between the two different value chains in the example highlight the importance of business integration. The focus of all the activities in chain (a) is on reducing and minimising costs, whereas the focus in chain (b) is on differentiation.

To be successful, an organisation needs to ensure that the 'characteristics' (eg cost leadership or differentiation) of all its activities are consistent with each other. For example, think how the value chain of a fast food restaurant (eg McDonald's) will differ from a Michelin-starred restaurant. The fast food restaurant's focus will be on keeping costs low, while the Michelin-starred restaurant creates value through the high quality of its food and its customer service.

4.2.6 The value chain and performance management

Value chain analysis helps an organisation identify the activities and processes which create value for its customers, and therefore those activities which an activity needs to perform more effectively than its competitors.

This has two important implications for performance measurement and performance management.

(a) The organisation needs to ensure that it is measuring its performance in those **key areas which create value for its customers** (in effect, its critical success factors). If it is not currently doing so, this suggests the organisation needs to revise its performance measures and performance measurement systems, because it needs to know how well it is performing in these key areas.

(b) In order to assess how effectively it is performing activities and processes, an organisation **needs to compare its performance** against others. This suggests that **benchmarking** could be useful here.

5 The influence of structure, culture and strategy on performance measurement methods and techniques

FAST FORWARD

Structure, **culture** and **strategy** all have an impact on the manner in which new performance measurement methods and techniques are adopted by organisations.

The manner in which new methods and techniques are adopted will inevitably vary from organisation to organisation, and from industry sector to industry sector. For example, **service organisations** have historically had relatively unsophisticated budgeting and control systems compared to manufacturing organisations, so the introduction of **activity-based approaches** is likely to be less disruptive to existing systems and therefore may be more easily accepted by managers in service organisations, to whom the whole concept of costing is new.

5.1 The influence of structure

In recent years there has been an emphasis on **flexibility** and **adaptability** in organisational structure, particularly since the pace of change in the technological and competitive environment has put pressure on businesses to innovate, to adopt a market orientation.

Part of this shift in emphasis has been a trend away from function-based structures towards **task-centred structures**, such as **multi-disciplinary project teams**, which draw experience, knowledge and expertise together from different functions to facilitate **flexibility and innovation**. In particular, the concept of the **matrix organisation** has emerged. These involve dual reporting lines, so that an individual reports to a functional manager and an area manager. They therefore divide authority between functional managers and product or project team managers or co-ordinators – thus challenging classical assumptions about 'one man one boss'.

With interdisciplinary co-operation, mixing of skills and expertise, and increased responsibility of managers, such a structure facilitates the adoption of new methods and techniques.

More **formal and constrained structures**, such as heavily **centralised** structures, **restrict the flow of ideas** around the organisation. Managers have **insufficient authority** to try out new methods or techniques.

5.2 The influence of culture

Culture can have a significant impact on an organisation's willingness to embrace new methods and techniques.

For example, **bureaucratic cultures**, in which job descriptions establish definite tasks for each person's job and procedures are established for many work routines, are likely to **constrict the impetus for change**.

Organisations with cultures in which **predictability and reliability** are valued, and in which **formal** ways of behaviour are encouraged, will continue to **use tried and tested methods** and techniques to maintain stability.

On the other hand, cultures in which **innovation** and **creativity** are highly prized, in which individuals are encouraged to **participate** and to get involved and in which **risk taking** is not frowned upon, will tend to be associated with **organisations using activity-based costing** and other new methods and techniques.

Undoubtedly the most profound influences on Western corporate culture since the 1990s were the ideas borrowed from **Japanese management**. 'Philosophies' such as just-in-time (JIT) and Total Quality Management (TQM) have a direct impact on business areas that have long been the preserve of accountants – purchasing and inventory control, quality costs, waste and scrap and so on.

5.3 The influence of strategy

Organisations that hope to compete effectively in today's competitive market need to adopt **strategies** that aim at **satisfying customers**. This requires a focus on **quality**, on **time** and on **innovation**. These key success factors can be most successfully achieved by adopting **TQM and JIT** (and hence throughput accounting).

The focus on customer satisfaction, quality and innovation also highlights the importance of **non-financial aspects of performance** in competitive success, and therefore also the importance of measuring these non-financial aspects of performance.

As we will discuss in more detail later in this Study Text, non-financial performance measures are becoming increasingly significant in contemporary performance management, and therefore an organisation's performance measures should comprise an appropriate mix of financial and non-financial measures (for example, as illustrated in balance scorecard performance measurement systems, or in Lynch and Cross's performance pyramid – which we will look at in Chapter 15).

Organisations pursuing strategies based on **cost efficiency** could find that use of **activity-based approaches**, **life cycle costing** and **customer profitability analysis** provide useful insights.

Exam focus point

> In an exam, if asked how successful the adoption of new methods and techniques are likely to be in a particular organisation, think in terms of structure, culture and strategy. A heavily centralised organisation, where responsibility is vested in a board of ageing directors who have not read a journal or attended a conference in 20 years and who have followed the same strategy during that time, is unlikely to adopt JIT or TQM approaches and philosophies.

6 Developing management accounting systems

FAST FORWARD

> Developments in IT have revolutionised the **potential for management accounting data**, increasing the volume and variety of **possible reports**.
>
> The availability of **timely and reliable information** is becoming an increasingly important asset for managers – to help them make **fact-based decisions** (rather than ones based on intuition) and to control their organisations effectively.

Managers need information for three main reasons:

- To make effective **decisions**
- To **control** the activities of the organisation
- To **co-ordinate** the activities of the organisation

6.1 Information and decision making

Decision making is a key element of management. For example, a marketing manager must decide what price to charge for a product, what distribution channels to use and how to promote the product. Equally, a production manager must decide how much of a product to make, while a purchasing manager must decide how much inventory to hold and whom to buy inputs from.

At a more strategic level, senior managers must decide how to allocate scarce financial resources among competing projects, how the organisation should be structured, or what business-level strategy an organisation should be pursuing.

In order to make effective decisions, managers need information from both inside and outside the organisation. For example, when deciding how to price a product, marketing managers need information about the way consumer demand will vary in relation to different prices, the cost of producing the product and the organisation's overall competitive strategy (since its pricing strategy will need to be consistent with this overall strategy).

6.2 Information and control

The management control process can be summarised in four key steps:

- Establish measurable standards of performance or goals
- Measure actual performance
- Compare actual performance against established goals
- Evaluate the results and take corrective action where necessary

In their text *Contemporary Management*, Jones and George refer to the example of the package delivery company DHL. They note that DHL has a goal to deliver 95% of the packages it picks up by noon the next day. DHL has thousands of branch offices across the US which are responsible for the physical pick-up and delivery of packages, and DHL managers monitor the delivery performance of these offices on a regular basis. If the 95% target is not being achieved, the managers analyse why this is and then take corrective action if necessary.

In order to control operational activity in this way, the managers have to have information about deliveries and performance. In particular, the managers need to know what percentage of packages each branch office delivers by noon, and this information is provided through DHL's IT systems.

All packages to be shipped are scanned with handheld scanners by the DHL drivers, and details of the packages are sent wirelessly to a central computer at DHL's headquarters. The packages are scanned again when they are delivered, with the related delivery time being sent wirelessly back to the central computer. Therefore, managers can identify the percentage of packages which are delivered by noon the day after they were picked up, and can also break down this information to analyse delivery performance on a branch by branch basis.

6.3 Information and co-ordination

Another key element of management is co-ordinating the activities of individuals, departments or divisions in order to achieve organisational goals.

One area where this is particularly important is in relation to managing global supply chains. Organisations are using increasingly sophisticated IT systems to co-ordinate the flow of materials, work in progress and finished products throughout the world.

Jones and George consider the example of Bose, the manufacturers of high-quality music systems and speakers. Almost all the components which Bose uses in its speakers are purchased from external suppliers, and about 50% of its purchases are from foreign suppliers, many in the Middle East.

The challenge for Bose is to co-ordinate its globally dispersed supply chain in a way that minimises inventory and transportation costs. Bose employs a JIT production system, so it needs to ensure that component parts arrive at the relevant assembly plants just in time to enter the production process and not before.

Equally, however, Bose has to be responsive to customer demands. This means that Bose and its supplier need to be able to respond quickly to changes in demand for different kinds of speakers, increasing or decreasing production as necessary.

In order to co-ordinate its supply chain, Bose uses a logistics IT system which provides it with real-time information about parts as they move through the global supply chain. When a shipment of parts leaves a supplier it is logged on the system, and from that point Bose can track the supplies as they move around the globe to the assembly plant.

On one occasion, a significant customer unexpectedly doubled its order for Bose speakers, which meant that Bose had to increase its manufacturing output rapidly. Many of its components were stretched out across the supply chain. However, by using its logistics system Bose was able to locate the parts it needed, and accelerate them out of the normal delivery chain by moving them on air freight. In this way, Bose was able to get the parts it needed at the assembly plant in time to fulfil the customer's order.

6.4 Management information systems (MIS)

Most information is provided by an information system, or management information system (MIS).

Key term

> A **management information system** is 'a system to convert data from internal and external sources into information and to communicate that information, in an appropriate form, to managers at all levels in all functions to enable them to make timely and effective decisions for planning, directing and controlling the activities for which they are responsible'. (Lucey)

A **MIS** is therefore a **system of disseminating information** that will enable managers to do their job. It should provide managers with **data** that they can use **for benchmarking** and **control purposes**.

Management information is by no means confined to accounting information, but until relatively recently accounting information systems have been the most formally constructed and well-developed part of the overall information system of a business enterprise. This is still the case in all but the most advanced organisations.

Most MISs are not designed, but **grow up informally**, with each manager making sure that they get all the information considered necessary to do the job. Much accounting information, for example, is easily obtained, and managers can often get along with frequent face to face contact and co-operation with each other. Such an informal system works best in small organisations.

However, **some** information systems are **specially designed**, often because the introduction of computers has forced management to consider its information needs in detail. This is especially the case in large companies.

Management should try to **develop/implement** an MIS for their enterprise **with care**. If they allow the MIS to develop without any formal planning, it will almost certainly be inefficient because data will be obtained and processed in a random and disorganised way and the communication of information will also be random and hit and miss.

(a) Some managers will keep data in their heads and will not commit information to paper. Stand-ins/successors will not know as much as they could and should because no information has been recorded to help them.

(b) The organisation will not collect and process all the information that it should.

(c) Information may be available but not disseminated to the appropriate managers.

(d) Information is communicated late because the need to communicate it earlier is not understood and appreciated by the data processors.

The **consequences of a poor MIS** might be dissatisfaction among employees who believe they should be told more, a lack of understanding about what the targets for achievement are and a lack of information about how well the work is being done.

Whether an MIS is formally or informally constructed, it should therefore have **certain essential characteristics**:

(a) The **functions of individuals and their areas of responsibility** in achieving company objectives should be **defined**.

(b) **Areas of control** within the company (eg cost centres, investment centres) should also be clearly **defined**.

(c) Information required for an area of control should flow to the manager who is responsible for it. (**Management structure of the organisation should therefore be considered**.)

6.4.1 Types of MIS

Three particular types of MIS deserve special mention.

Type of MIS	Detail
Decision support systems (DSS)	Used by management to help make decisions on poorly defined problems (with high levels of uncertainty). They provide access to information with a wide range of information-gathering and analytical tools. Decision support systems allow the manager to scan the environment, consider a number of alternatives and evaluate them under a variety of potential conditions. There is a major emphasis upon flexibility and user-friendliness.
Executive information systems (EIS)	Give executives a straightforward means of access to key internal and external data. They provide summary-level data captured from the organisation's main systems (which might involve integrating the executive's desktop PC with the organisation's mainframe), data manipulation facilities (such as comparison with budget or prior year data and trend analysis) and user-friendly presentation of data.
Expert systems	These draw on a computerised knowledge base (such as details of the workings of tax legislation) and can give factual answers to specific queries, as well as indicating to the user what a decision ought to be in a particular situation.

Question — Types of management information system

Read the following scenarios.

(a) An insurance company's speed of response and cost advantage derive from its policy of only accepting low risk business and the use of sophisticated computer systems which allow telesales staff to enter essential details, and respond to applications for insurance, instantly rather than having to spend time waiting for a decision from an underwriter.

(b) Instant access to summary information, the potential for highlighting exceptions or variances with budget and the ease with which executives can find the reasons for a variance, in terms of an individual salesperson's performance, have thrown up major implications for entire organisations.

Required

Decide which of these scenarios describes an executive information system and which an expert system.

Answer

The point of exercises like this one is to bring some context to the 'theory' of the different types of information system we are discussing in this chapter.

The answers are: (a) is an expert system, and (b) is an executive information system.

6.5 Setting up a management accounting system

Taking a broad view, the following factors should be considered when setting up a management accounting system (which is just one part of an overall MIS):

(a) The **output required**. This is just another way of saying that the management accountant must **identify the information needs of managers**. If a particular manager finds pie charts most useful the system should be able to produce them. If another manager needs to know what time of day machinery failures occur, this information should be available. Levels of detail and accuracy of output and methods of processing must be determined in each case.

(b) **When the output is required**. If information is needed within the hour the system should be capable of producing it at this speed. If it is only ever needed once a year, at the year end, the system should be designed to produce it **on time**, no matter how long it takes to produce.

(c) The **sources of input information**. It is too easy to state that the outputs required should dictate the inputs made. The production manager may require a report detailing the precise operations of their machines, second by second. However, the management accounting system could only acquire this information if suitable production technology had been installed.

6.6 The need to develop management accounting systems

FAST FORWARD

Globalisation and **competition** require an external, forward-looking focus, with greater facilities for modelling.

In the Study Guide for this paper, ACCA highlights that management accounting systems need to be continually refined and developed in order to help organisations maintain or improve their performance 'in an increasingly competitive and global market'.

Environmental analysis, and models, such as PEST analysis and Porter's five forces, are covered in detail in Paper P3 *Business Analysis* so we are not going to discuss them again here.

What is relevant here, however, is the implications that increasing competition and globalisation might have on the management accounting information which organisations require.

Remember that managers need information (management accounting information) to plan for the future and to make strategic decisions. In turn, management accounting systems play a crucial role in providing that information – which, in the context of strategic decisions, will likely need to come from both internal and external sources.

(a) **Competition**

Impact	Management accounting impact
• More competitors	Better competitor intelligence Model competitor cost structures
• More competing products	Identify which features add most value; model impact on cost
• Faster response	Management accounting information has to be produced speedily and be up to date for decision making

(b) **Globalisation**

Impact	Management accounting impact
• Increases competition	• Similar impact to (a) • Attention to **behavioural** impact on management accounting systems in different markets
• Access to overseas capital	• The cost of operating in different local markets • Aggregating information
• Foreign activities	• Difficulty of comparing performance in different markets • Profit or loss from exchange differences

We consider management accounting systems in more detail later in this Study Text.

7 A contingent approach to management accounts

FAST FORWARD

The **contingency approach to management accounting** is based on the premise that there is no universally appropriate accounting system applicable to all organisations in all circumstances. Efficient systems depend on the system designer's awareness of the specific environmental factors which influence them.

Key term

The **contingency approach to management accounting** is based on the premise that there is no universally appropriate accounting system applicable to all organisations in all circumstances. Efficient systems depend on awareness of the system designer of the specific environmental factors which influence their creation.

The major factors that have been identified by Emmanuel, Otley and Merchant in *Accounting for Management Control* are classified as follows:

(a) **The environment**

(i) Its degree of predictability
(ii) The degree of competition faced
(iii) The number of different product markets faced
(iv) The degree of hostility exhibited by competing organisations

A key issue to consider here is that, if an organisation is operating in an **uncertain/dynamic environment**, then budgets are likely to be a less reliable measure of performance than if the organisation is operating in a more **predictable and static environment**. Therefore, if an organisation is operating in an uncertain/dynamic environment it will need a range of financial and non-financial indicators in order to measure its performance, because simply comparing actual results against budgeted results could be meaningless (if changes in the environment mean that the original budget is no longer realistic).

(b) **Organisational structure**

(i) Size
(ii) Interdependence of parts
(iii) Degree of decentralisation
(iv) Availability of resources

(c) **Technology** (the way in which an organisation organises its production processes, such as mass production or batch production)

(i) The nature of the production process
(ii) The routineness/complexity of the production process
(iii) How well the relationship between ends (finished output) and means (production process) is understood
(iv) The amount of variety or complexity in each task that has to be performed

For example, the level of detail and accuracy that is possible when costing individual jobs cannot be replicated in mass production environments. Production technology is therefore argued to have a significant effect on the type of management accounting information that can be provided.

Competitive strategy

In addition to the factors identified by Emmanuel *et al*, another important factor which could affect the design of an organisation's management accounting system is its competitive strategy; in particular whether it is pursuing a strategy of **cost leadership** or **differentiation**. If an organisation is pursuing a cost leadership strategy, then information about cost control and cost reduction will be vital. Alternatively, if an organisation is following a differentiation strategy, then it will need information about its performance in those areas which it uses to differentiate it from its competitors.

7.1 A simple example

The following example is a highly **simplistic application of the contingency approach** but it may help you to grasp ideas that are generally presented in a highly abstract way by accounting academics.

Stable makes three different products, X, Y and Z. It has **never had any competitors**. **Every month** the managing director receives a **report** from the management accountant in the following form (the numbers are for illustration only).

	$
Sales	10,000
Production costs	5,000
Gross profit	5,000
Administrative costs	1,000
Net profit	4,000

A few months ago **another company**, Turbulence & Co, **entered the market** for products X and Y, **undercutting** the prices charged by Stable. Turbulence has now started to **win some of Stable's customers**.

The managing director asks the management accountant for information about the profitability of its own versions of products X and Y. Sales information is easy to reanalyse, but to analyse production information in this way requires a new system of coding to be introduced. Eventually the management accountant comes up with the following report.

	X	*Y*	*Z*	*Total*
	$	$	$	$
Sales	3,000	3,000	4,000	10,000
Production costs	500	500	4,000	5,000
Gross profit	2,500	2,500	–	5,000
Administrative costs				1,000
Net profit				4,000

As a result of receiving this information the managing director **drops the price** of Stable's products X and Y. They **divide the production function into two divisions**, one of which will concentrate exclusively on reducing the costs of product Z while maintaining quality.

The management accountant is asked to work closely with the division Z production manager in designing a **system that will help to monitor and control costs**. They are also to work closely with the **marketing** managers of products X and Y so that the organisation can **respond rapidly to any further competitive pressures. Reports are** to be made **weekly** and are to include as much information as can be determined about Turbulence's financial performance, pricing, market penetration, and so on.

This **example may be explained in terms of contingency theory**, as follows.

(a) **Originally** the **design of the accounting system** was determined by the facts that Stable faced a **highly predictable** environment, and that it was a **highly centralised** organisation.

(b) The design of the **new system** is the **result of a new set of contingent variables**: the entry of Turbulence into two of Stable's markets requires the system to adopt a product-based reporting structure with more externally derived information in the case of products X and Y and more detailed analysis of internal information in the case of product Z. This is matched by a change in the structure of the organisation as a whole.

To recap, **contingency theorists' aim is to identify specific features of an organisation's context that affect the design of particular features of that organisation's accounting system.**

7.2 Contingent variables

In Emmanuel *et al*'s book there is a review of the major studies in the contingency theory tradition. These are classified under the headings 'environment' and 'technology' (as before), with 'organisation' being subdivided into 'size', 'strategy' and 'culture'. Here we give a summary of the main points made in this discussion.

Many of the points made in the following paragraphs will seem quite stunningly obvious and unsurprising. Some are capable of quite different interpretations. Some contradict others. None of them should be regarded as universal truths: they are simply **observations made by different researchers in the light of investigations into particular cases**.

7.2.1 Environment

In Chapter 6 later in this Study Text, we will look at how the external environment in which an organisation operates can affect its strategic choices and its performance (eg through the impact of the opportunities and threats identified by models such as PEST analysis and Porter's five forces). However, the environment can also affect accounting control systems.

Emmanuel *et al* identify **uncertainty as the major factor in the environment affecting the design of accounting control systems**.

(a) The **sophistication** of an accounting system is influenced by the intensity of **competition** faced. Accounting systems that can produce information that allows for the preparation of an extended trial balance will be insufficient for an organisation that needs to make pricing decisions, analyse market size and market share, and so on.

(b) Organisations use accounting information in different ways depending on the **type of competition faced** (eg competition on price as opposed to product rivalry).

(c) **Budget information is evaluated** by senior managers **rigidly in 'tough' environments**, but more flexibly in 'liberal' environments.

(d) The **more dynamic** the environment (ie the more rapidly it changes), the **more frequently accounting control reports** will be required.

(e) The **larger the number of product markets** an organisation is in, the **more decentralised its control system** will be, with quasi-independent responsibility centres.

(f) The more **severe** the **competition**, the **more sophisticated the accounting information system** will be, for example incorporating non-financial information.

(g) The design of an organisation's accounting system will be affected by its environment. An organisation's **environment** will be somewhere **between** the **two extremes simple/complex** and somewhere between the **two extremes static/dynamic**.

(h) The **more complex the structure** of an organisation, the **more accounting control 'tools'** (such as flexible budgeting and variance analysis) it will have.

(i) **'Turbulence'** or discontinuity in an organisation's environment (say, overseas expansion or the acquisition of a major subsidiary) often requires the **replacement of control tools** (say flexible budgeting) which have been rendered obsolete by new ones.

(j) Control systems are not determined by organisation structure: **both structure and control systems are dependent on the environment**. In an **uncertain environment** more use will be made of **external, non-financial and projected information**.

(k) In conditions of **uncertainty, subjective methods of performance evaluation** (such as a manager's opinion) are more effective because they rely more on qualitative, as opposed to quantitative, information.

(l) Accounting systems are **affected by** the extent to which the organisation is **manipulated by other organisations**, such as competitors, suppliers, customers or government bodies. For example, large supermarkets often insist their (smaller) suppliers adopt particular policies, procedures and techniques.

7.2.2 Technology

(a) The nature of the **production process** (eg jobbing on the one hand or mass production on the other) determines the **type of costing system** that is required and the **amount of cost allocation** rather than **cost apportionment** that can be done. For example, a significant proportion of the total cost of service organisations is overheads. This, together with the fact that services are often consumed at the time of purchase, influences the type of costing system that is most suitable and the extent to which costs can be traced to individual services.

(b) The **complexity of the 'task'** that an organisation performs **affects the financial control structure**. However, it does so via organisation structure. (Eg a railway operator's 'task' of getting people from A to B involves keeping them fed via a catering division that is accounted for differently to the transport division.)

(c) The **amount of data** produced, **what** that data is **about** and **how it is used** closely **correlates** with the **number of things that go wrong in a production process and the procedures used to investigate the problems**. (This correlation exists but the research does not consider whether there is an optimum correlation between data availability and use and problem solving.)

(d) The **more automated** a production process is, the **more 'formality'** there will be in the use of budget systems.

(e) The **less predictable** the production process is, the more likely production managers are to create **budgetary slack**. (The evidence for this is weak, however, as the proponent of the view (Merchant) admits.)

(f) The structure and processes of (and so, presumably, the method of accounting for) **operational units** tend to be related to **technological variables** while the structure and processes of **managerial/planning units** tend to be related to **environmental variables**.

7.2.3 Size

(a) As an organisation grows it will initially organise on a **functional basis**. If it diversifies into different products or markets it will reorganise into **semi-autonomous divisions**. The **same accounting**

system that is used to measure overall performance can then be **applied en bloc to each individual division**.

(b) In larger organisations the greater degree of **decentralisation** seems to lead to greater **participation** in budgeting.

(c) In **large organisations a bureaucratic** approach to budgeting produces the best performance; in **small organisations** a more **'personal' approach** gives better results. (Note that this finding was originally reported in 1981 when bureaucracies were less unfashionable: few modern commentators associate bureaucracy with efficiency.)

(d) Organisations may grow by acquisition: when this occurs, differences in the accounting system used by the **acquired company** disappear, and it **conforms to the practices used by the acquiring company**.

7.2.4 Culture

(a) Control systems which are inconsistent with an organisation's value system or with the language or symbols that help to make up its culture are likely to create **resistance**: typically people would develop informal ways to get round controls that were regarded as intrusive.

(b) New control systems that **threaten to alter existing power relationships** may be **thwarted** by those affected.

(c) Control processes will be most **effective** if they operate by generating a corporate culture that is **supportive** of organisational aims, objectives and methods of working, and which is **consistent** with the demands of the environment in which the organisation operates.

A word of caution

Remember that the points above are observations made by different researchers in the light of investigations into particular cases. They are not universal truths.

7.2.5 The limitations of contingency theory

Logically, one would expect those researching the field of contingency theory and management accounting to have put forward suggestions as to how accounting systems could be improved by demonstrating what systems work well in what circumstances. So far, however, **contingency theory** seems to have **provided no more than a framework for describing existing accounting systems**.

Despite its age now, there has been no better summary of the benefits and limitations of contingency theory than the conclusion to Otley's 1980 article 'The Contingency Theory of Management Accounting: Achievement and Prognosis' *(Accounting, Organizations and Society)* on which much of the relevant chapter in the later book by Emmanuel, Otley and Merchant is based. Otley's conclusion is quoted below:

> 'A contingency theory of management accounting has a great deal of appeal. It is in accord with practical wisdom and appears to afford a potential explanation for the bewildering variety of management accounting systems actually observed in practice. In addition, the relevance of organization theory to management accounting is being increasingly recognized and contingency formulations have been prominent in organization theory. There thus appears to be a prima facie case for the development of a contingency framework for management accounting.'

However, despite the strong arguments for pursuing this line of research, a number of reservations need to be expressed:

(a) Firstly, the nature of appropriate contingent variables has not yet been elucidated and requires greater theoretical, as well as empirical, attention.

(b) Secondly, explicit consideration of organisational effectiveness is a vital part of a true contingency theory of control system design. This has been a much neglected topic from a theoretical stance and its development is urgently needed.

(c) Thirdly, the contingency theory of organisational design is weaker than some of its own literature suggests, its links with organisational effectiveness being, at best, tentative. As the same contingent variables are likely to affect both organisational structure and accounting system design, it appears unwise to use structure as the sole intervening variable between contingent variables and the choice of accounting information system.

(d) Finally, the highly interconnected nature of the components that make up an organisational control package suggests that the management accounting information system cannot be studied in isolation from its wider context.

Some further objections may be added, as follows:

(a) Most, if not all, of the writing on contingency theory and management accounting is written in a **highly abstruse style** and aimed at **fellow academics rather than practising accountants**. A good contrast is provided by the way in which activity-based costing has been popularised by the writings of management consultants.

(b) As Otley implies, it is by **no means clear how the various contingent variables** proposed **affect the management accounting system**. In several of the observations listed above, for example, it seems that it is the organisation structure that adapts to its environment and the management accounting system simply reflects the organisation structure.

(c) As Fincham and Rhodes point out (in *The Individual, Work and Organisation*), contingency theory **plays down the importance** of power, both the **power of the strategically placed managers and the power of the organisation itself**. An example of the former would be the influence of the managing director in our simple example. An example of the latter would be the acquiring company in a takeover imposing its own accounting system on its new subsidiary.

(d) For **financial accounting** purposes accountants are expected to accept the idea of 'best practice' and to follow the rules and regulations of accounting standards and company law. Although financial accounting does not go quite so far as to insist on one best way, it does not allow many alternatives for external reporting purposes. This is quite at **odds with the contingency approach**.

(e) The theory tends to **ignore the influence of aspects of an organisation's context which are more difficult to quantify**. It fails to recognise the impact of the people within an organisation, of management structure, managerial style and, particularly, organisational culture – those factors that make an organisation unique.

Nonetheless, in spite of these many reservations, it should still be clear that there will never be 'one best way' of designing an organisation or its accounting system: otherwise all successful organisations (and their accounting systems) would be identical. Even if this is the only real insight that contingency theory has to offer, it is still a very valuable one.

Chapter Roundup

- An organisation's **formal hierarchy** can be arranged by territory, function, product, brand, customer/market, staff numbers and work patterns, and equipment specialisation. In this section we look at three ways of organising the hierarchy. These are: by function, division, and a loose organic form known as a network form.
- Unlike manufacturing businesses, service businesses are characterised by **intangibility**, **inseparability**, **variability**, **perishability** and the **absence of a transfer of ownership**.
- **Mass services** are standard services provided for large numbers of people and are often automated. **Personalised services** vary on the circumstances of the service delivery and are often provided on a one to one basis.
- **Business process re-engineering** involves focusing attention inwards to consider how business processes can be redesigned or re-engineered to improve efficiency.
- Although it is easy to look at a business as a grouping of specialised departments, in practice value is added by **activities and processes**, which may span a number of departments. These need to be **linked** effectively to **create value**.
- **Structure, culture and strategy** all have an impact on the manner in which new performance measurement methods and techniques are adopted by organisations.
- Developments in IT have revolutionised the **potential for management accounting data**, increasing the volume and variety of **possible reports**.
- The availability of **timely and reliable information** is becoming an increasingly important asset for managers – to help them make **fact-based decisions** (rather than ones based on intuition) and to control their organisations effectively.
- **Globalisation** and **competition** require an external, forward-looking focus, with greater facilities for modelling.
- The **contingency approach to management accounting** is based on the premise that there is no universally appropriate accounting system applicable to all organisations in all circumstances. Efficient systems depend on the system designer's awareness of the specific environmental factors which influence them.

Quick Quiz

1 What are the primary and secondary activities in Porter's value chain model?

2 The new CEO at DJK Co has recently introduced a number of changes which he felt would improve performance at the company, by giving local managers greater authority to make decisions. The changes were based on similar initiatives at the CEO's previous company, which had proved very successful.

Unfortunately, the changes have not been successful at DJK Co. A significant reason for this is that the authority to make decisions at DJK Co has historically been concentrated at head office and among a very small number of regional managers, and so local managers were not used to having any authority to make decisions.

Which one of the following elements of McKinsey's 7S's model best explains why the change initiatives have been unsuccessful at DJK Co?

A Shared values
B Strategy
C Structure
D Systems

3 The introduction of business process re-engineering (BPR) causes organisation structures to change from flat to hierarchical. True or false?

4 Identify **three** changes that have contributed to changes in the business environment that companies operate in.

5 Which of the following are characteristics of services, which distinguish them from manufactured products?

[Select all that apply]

A Inseparability
B Perishability
C Homogeneity
D They involve a transfer of ownership
E Intangibility

Answers to Quick Quiz

1

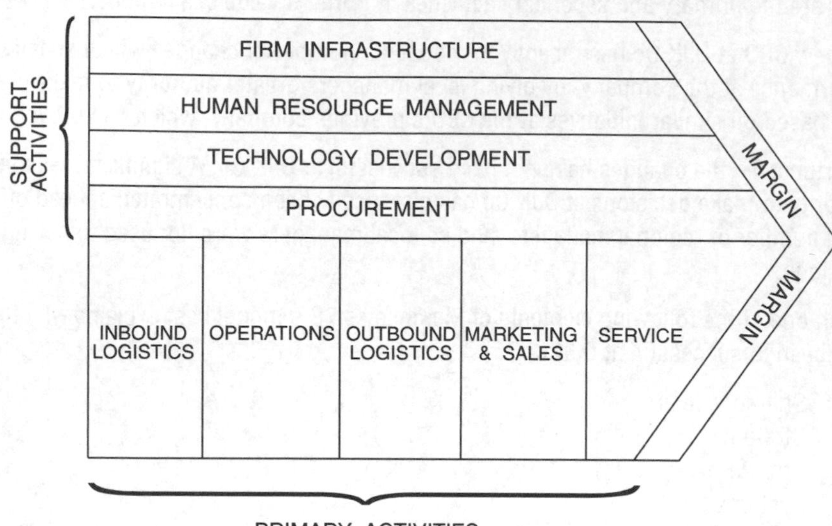

2 C Structure

The previous company appears to have had a relatively decentralised structure, whereas DJK has a very centralised structure.

The scenario does not tell us anything about the company's strategy, shared values or its technical systems.

3 False. It changes from hierarchical to flat.

4 (i) There have been changes in the **competitive environment** such that companies now compete globally and have shorter product life cycles.

(ii) **Customers have become more demanding** and quality and timeliness have become increasingly important to them.

(iii) **Manufacturing has become more diverse and flexible** with shorter product life cycles and greater diversity in the products made.

5 A, B and E Inseparability; Perishability; and Intangibility.

The five characteristics of services that distinguish them from manufacturing are:

- Intangibility
- Inseparability (or simultaneity)
- Variability (or heterogeneity) – not homogeneity, as suggested in Option C
- Perishability
- No transfer of ownership

Now try the question below from the Practice Question Bank

Number	Level	Marks	Approximate time
Q4	Examination	25	50 mins

Environmental and ethical issues

Topic list	Syllabus reference
1 Stakeholders' goals and objectives	A5(a)
2 Stakeholders and business performance	A5(a)
3 Social and ethical issues	A5(b)
4 Environmental management accounting	A5(c)

Introduction

In the previous chapter, we noted that the environment in which an organisation operates is one of the contingent factors which could influence the organisation's management accounting systems.

That environment also contains a number of different **stakeholders** who could influence the organisation's strategy and performance – such as competitors, suppliers, customers, and governments.

In this chapter we are now going to look in more detail at the range of stakeholders who can influence an organisation, and we are also going to look at the impact **social and ethical issues** can have on strategy and performance.

The chapter finishes by looking at **environmental management accounting** and the way organisations can measure their impact on the environment.

Study guide

		Intellectual level
A5	**Other environmental and ethical issues**	
(a)	Discuss the ways in which stakeholder groups operate and how they influence an organisation, its strategy formulation and implementation, and business performance, (eg using Mendelow's matrix).	2
(b)	Discuss the social and ethical issues that may impact on strategy formulation and business performance.	3
(c)	Discuss, evaluate and apply environmental management accounting using, for example, lifecycle costing and activity-based costing.	3

Exam guide

You should already be familiar with stakeholder management (including the application of Mendelow's matrix) if you have studied P3. However, it is important to remember that at P5 we are not looking just at the way stakeholders can influence strategy, but also at how they can influence performance and performance management. For example, if the customers of an organisation are a key stakeholder group, then not only does an organisation's strategy need to be acceptable to its customers, but also the organisation needs to monitor how satisfied its customers are with the way it is performing.

The references to social and ethical issues and environmental management accounting highlight the increasing importance of **sustainability** issues in strategy and performance management. As well as considering the short-term, financial implications of a strategy, organisations need to consider the longer-term, non-financial impacts.

Exam focus point

The June 2011 exam asked candidates to explain environmental accounting techniques and evaluate how they could assist in managing an organisation's environmental and strategic performance. Candidates were then also asked to evaluate a life cycle costing approach compared with an activity-based costing approach.

A question in the December 2014 exam also asked candidates to assess two proposed investment plans in the context of an organisation's environmental goals, and to discuss the life cycle costing issues associated with the plans.

Performance objective 2 – Stakeholder relationship management – requires that you develop and maintain productive relationships with stakeholders, and so some of the issues which we discuss in this chapter (for example, around identifying an organisation's key stakeholders, what their interests are, and how this influences the organisation's strategy) could equally be questions you need to address in the workplace.

1 Stakeholders' goals and objectives

In this section, we look at who the stakeholders are in a business and consider some theories on how stakeholders affect business strategy.

However, it is important to remember that the focus in P5 is on performance management rather than business strategy *per se.* So when looking at different stakeholder groups it is important to consider how the interests and influence of different stakeholder groups can affect an **organisation's performance**, or how the interests of key stakeholder groups might affect which aspects of performance an organisation chooses to measure.

When thinking about the relationship between stakeholders and organisations it is also important to remember that there can be two different aspects of that relationship:

- **Stakeholder satisfaction** – An organisation needs to identify who its key stakeholders are, and what they want from the organisation.
- **Stakeholder contribution** – What the organisation wants and needs from its stakeholders (eg employees; suppliers).

1.1 Stakeholders 6/11, 12/14

FAST FORWARD

Stakeholders have an **interest** in what an organisation does and a degree of **power** to influence it.

Key term

Stakeholders: groups or individuals who have an interest in the strategy and activities of an organisation.

Given that, by definition, stakeholders have an interest in an organisation (and its mission and strategy) then the organisation should bear the interests of its stakeholders in mind when it is developing its mission and objectives.

Here are some stakeholder groups.

Stakeholder group	Example members
• Internal stakeholders	Employees, management
• Connected	Shareholders, customers, suppliers, lenders
• External	The Government, local communities, pressure groups

Stakeholder groups can exert influence on strategy. The **greater the power of a stakeholder group, the greater its influence will be**. Each stakeholder group has different expectations about what it wants, and the expectations of the various groups can often conflict. For example, the shareholders of a company will be interested in the returns it generates, which could be increased (at least in the short term) by restricting the salaries or bonuses paid to staff. On the other hand, the staff will have a vested interest in maximising their incomes or bonuses.

1.2 Stakeholders' objectives

Here is a checklist of some of the more common stakeholders' objectives:

(a) **Employees and managers**

- (i) Job security (over and above legal protection)
- (ii) Good conditions of work (above minimum safety standards)
- (iii) Job satisfaction
- (iv) Career development and relevant training

(b) **Customers**

- (i) Products of a certain quality at a reasonable price
- (ii) Products that should last a certain number of years
- (iii) A product or service that meets customer needs

(c) **Suppliers**: regular orders in return for reliable delivery and good service

(d) **Shareholders**: long-term wealth

(e) **Providers of loan capital (stock holders):** reliable payment of interest due and maintenance of the value of any security

(f) **Society as a whole**

  (i) Control pollution/promote sustainability
  (ii) Financial assistance to charities, sports and local community activities
  (iii) Co-operate with government in identifying and preventing health hazards

Exam focus point

> Part of a question in the June 2011 exam asked candidates to identify and analyse the influence of four different external stakeholders on an organisation.
>
> As the examiner's post-exam report explained, the question sought a description of the power and level of interest that each of the stakeholders would have in the organisation. Although candidates weren't required to refer to Mendelow's matrix, the examination team indicated that many of the better answers used it as a framework.

1.3 The stakeholder view

The **stakeholder view** is that many groups have a stake in what the organisation does. This is particularly important in the business context, where shareholders own the business but employees, customers and government also have particularly strong claims to having their interests considered.

It is suggested that **modern corporations are so powerful, socially, economically and politically, that unrestrained use of their power will inevitably damage other people's rights**. For example, they may blight an entire community by closing a major facility, thus enforcing long-term unemployment on a large proportion of the local workforce. Under this approach, the exercise of **corporate social responsibility** constrains the corporation to act at all times as a good citizen.

Another argument points out that corporations exist within society and are dependent on it for the resources they use. Some of these resources are obtained by direct contracts with suppliers but others are not, being provided by government expenditure. Examples are such things as transport infrastructure, technical research and education for the workforce. Clearly, corporations contribute to the taxes that pay for these things, but the relationship is rather tenuous and the tax burden can be minimised by careful management. The implication is that corporations should recognise and pay for the facilities that society provides by means of socially responsible policies and actions.

Henry Mintzberg (in *Power In and Around Organisations*) suggests **that simply viewing organisations as vehicles for shareholder investment is inadequate.**

(a) In practice, he says, **organisations are rarely controlled effectively by shareholders.** Most shareholders are passive investors.

(b) **Large corporations can manipulate markets**. Social responsibility, forced or voluntary, is a way of recognising this.

(c) **Moreover, as mentioned above, businesses do receive a lot of government support**. The public pays for roads, infrastructure, education and health, all of which benefit businesses. Although businesses pay tax, the public ultimately pays, perhaps through higher prices.

(d) **Strategic decisions by businesses always have wider social consequences**. In other words, says Mintzberg, the firm produces two kinds of outputs: **goods and services** and the **social consequences of its activities** (eg pollution).

1.4 Stakeholder theory 12/14

FAST FORWARD

> Different **stakeholder groups** have different assessments of the risk a strategy poses to their interests. Some are able to **exercise power** over management.
>
> **Stakeholder mapping** may be used to analyse the influence of various stakeholder groups.

Strategies are created and assessed by management. However, the various **stakeholder** groups have more or less influence over what is acceptable.

We may discern two extreme approaches to stakeholder theory for profit-orientated business organisations.

Strong view	Weak view
Each stakeholder in the business has a legitimate claim on management attention. Management's job is to balance stakeholder demands.	Satisfying stakeholders such as customers **is** a good thing but only because it enables the business to satisfy its primary purpose, the long-term growth in owner wealth.

1.4.1 Problems with the strong stakeholder view

(a) Managers who are accountable to everyone are, in fact, accountable to none.

(b) If managers are required to balance different stakeholders' interests there is a danger that they will favour their own interests.

(c) It confuses a stakeholder's interest in a firm with a person's citizenship of a State.

(d) People have interests, but this does not give them rights.

Strategic options pose varying degrees of risk to the **interests** of the different stakeholders. It is possible that they may respond in such a way as to reduce the attractiveness of the proposed strategy.

1.4.2 Stakeholder interests

Stakeholder	Interests to defend	Response to risk
Internal: Managers and employees (eg restructuring, relocation)	• Jobs/careers • Money • Promotion • Benefits • Satisfaction	• Pursuit of systems goals rather than shareholder interests • Industrial action • Negative power to impede implementation • Refusal to relocate • Resignation
Connected: Shareholders (corporate strategy)	• Increase in shareholder wealth, measured by profitability, P/E ratios, market capitalisation, dividends and yield • Risk	• Sell shares (eg to predator) or replace management
Bankers (cash flows)	• Security of loan • Adherence to loan agreements	• Denial of credit • Higher interest charges • Receivership
Suppliers (purchase strategy)	• Profitable sales • Payment for goods • Long-term relationship	• Refusal of credit • Court action • Wind down relationships
Customers (product market strategy)	• Goods as promised • Future benefits	• Buy elsewhere • Damage reputation (eg through negative feedback) • Legal action (eg claims)
External: Government	• Jobs, training, tax • Investment and infrastructure • Aggregate demand • National competitiveness; emerging industries	• Tax increases • Regulation • Legal action • Tariffs

Stakeholder	Interests to defend	Response to risk
Interest/pressure groups	• Pollution • Rights • Other	• Publicity • Direct action • Sabotage • Pressure on government
Industry associations and trade unions	• Members' rights	• Legal action • Direct action (eg strikes)

How stakeholders relate to the management of the company depends very much on what **type of stakeholder** they are – internal, connected or external – and on the **level in the management hierarchy** at which they are able to apply pressure. Clearly a company's management will respond differently to the demands of, say, its shareholders and the community at large.

The way in which the relationship between company and stakeholders is conducted is a function of the parties' **relative bargaining strength** and the philosophy underlying **each party's objectives**. This can be shown by means of a spectrum.

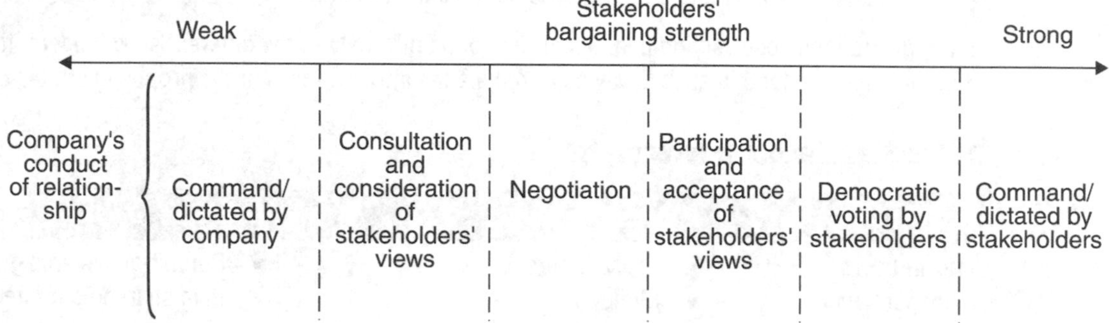

Exam focus point

The case study scenario in one of the questions in the December 2014 exam described the level of interest and power which different stakeholders had in an organisation. Candidates were then asked to justify management approaches which would be appropriate for each of the stakeholder groups, and then to evaluate the appropriateness of the organisation's performance measures. In other words, did the organisation's performance measures address the aspects of performance which its key stakeholders were interested in?

1.5 Stakeholder mapping

Stakeholder mapping – using **Mendelow's matrix** – helps an organisation establish its priorities in relation to managing stakeholder expectations. The matrix classifies stakeholders in terms of the **power** they can exert on the organisation, and the likelihood that they will show an **interest** in the organisation's activities (and therefore exert that power).

These factors (power and interest) will help define the type of relationship the organisation should seek with its stakeholders.

	Level of interest: Low	Level of interest: High
Power: High	Keep satisfied	Key players
Power: Low	Minimal effort	Keep informed

Mendelow's matrix – Stakeholder mapping

(a) Stakeholders with high level of power and interest are **key players**. An organisation's strategy must be **acceptable**, and they need to be managed closely. An example of a key player could be a major customer.

(b) Stakeholders with a **high power**, but **low interest**, must be treated with care. Although they are currently passive (ie have low interest), they are capable of becoming key players if their level of interest increases. Therefore they need to be **kept satisfied**. Large institutional shareholders could be an example of this type of stakeholder – with increasing levels of shareholder activism in recent years also demonstrating their potential to move from 'keep satisfied' to 'key players'.

(c) Stakeholders with **low power** and **high interest** have little ability to influence strategy in their own right, but their views could be important in influencing more powerful stakeholders – perhaps by lobbying, for example. They should therefore be **kept informed**. Community representatives and charities might fall into segment B.

(d) **Minimal effort** is expended on stakeholders who have both **low power** and **low interest**.

Stakeholder mapping is used to assess the significance of stakeholder groups. This in turn has implications for the organisation.

(a) The framework of **corporate governance** should recognise stakeholders' levels of interest and power.

(b) It may be appropriate to seek to **reposition** certain stakeholders and discourage others from repositioning themselves, depending on their attitudes.

(c) Key **blockers** and **facilitators** of change must be identified.

Stakeholder mapping can also be used to establish **political priorities**. A map of the current position can be compared with a map of a desired future state. This will indicate critical shifts that must be pursued.

We can look in detail at the stakeholder groups that not only have an **interest** in an organisation but also **power** over it.

The external coalition	The internal coalition
• Owners (who hold legal title) • Associates (suppliers, customers, trading partners) • Employee associations (unions, professional bodies) • Public (government, media)	• The chief executive and board at the strategic apex • Line managers • Operators • The technostructure • Support staff • Ideology (ie culture)

Each of these groups has three basic choices:

(a) **Loyalty.** They can do as they are told.

(b) **Exit.** For example by selling their shares or getting a new job.

(c) **Voice.** They can stay and try to change the system. Those who choose **voice** are those who can, to varying degrees, influence the organisation. Influence implies a degree of power and willingness to exercise it.

Existing **structures and systems** can **channel stakeholder influence**.

(a) They are the **location of power**, giving groups of people varying degrees of influence over strategic choices.

(b) They are **conduits of information**, which shape strategic decisions.

(c) They **limit choices** or give some options priority over others. These may be physical or ethical constraints over what is possible.

(d) They **embody culture**.

(e) They **determine the successful implementation** of strategy.

(f) The **firm has different degrees of dependency** on various stakeholder groups. A company with a cash flow crisis will be more beholden to its bankers than one with regular cash surpluses.

Different stakeholders will have their own views as to strategy. As some stakeholders have **negative power**, in other words power to impede or disrupt the decision, their likely response might be considered.

2 Stakeholders and business performance

Earlier in the chapter, we noted that stakeholders could influence the **strategy** of an organisation, and we highlighted the importance of understanding the relative power and interest of different stakeholders (Mendelow's matrix).

However, stakeholders can also affect the **performance** of an organisation, and we are now going to consider how different stakeholder groups can affect the performance of organisations.

As we noted, though, it is important to appreciate that the relationship between stakeholders and organisations is a two-way relationship. Stakeholders can have an important impact on the performance of an organisation, but equally the organisation's performance can have an impact on its stakeholders.

2.1 Employees and management

FAST FORWARD

Employees and management are internal stakeholders. They may have considerable power over the performance of the organisation.

We briefly considered the interests of employees and management when we looked at stakeholder theory. Organisations should aim to **align the interests of their staff with those of the organisation**. In other words, they should look at ways of motivating their employees and managers to perform better by agreeing to organisational objectives.

Motivation for employees to perform well comes in a variety of guises. Some will work harder and better for more money whereas others prefer benefits or promotion. Many employees rank the environment in which they work as important for their wellbeing and productivity.

Performance measurement for managers is usually designed so that by attaining targets set by the organisation, they earn rewards. These targets can be negotiated or imposed depending on the culture of the organisation. The rewards are linked to the attainment of the targets using various means.

Simple bonuses can be paid on the achievement of a target return or profit. **Share options** can be granted whereby the reward is linked to the growth in the share price of the organisation. Thus on the exercise of

the option, and receipt of the shares, any growth in the share price from the date of grant is realised by the employee if they sell the shares or earn income from dividends on shares received.

However, there is a danger of **dysfunctional behaviour** – where individuals concentrate on attaining just the measure that leads to the reward, at the expense of other potentially important activities. There is also a risk of the measure being manipulated so that it is achieved whatever the consequences. A good example of this manipulation is return on capital employed (ROCE) where the return can be improved by retaining older written-down assets thereby keeping the capital employed figure low. This may not be the optimum replacement policy for assets but will improve the measure of ROCE.

Exam focus point

The danger that individuals will place undue focus on one performance measure to the detriment of other areas can also be characterised as **tunnel vision**.

In Chapter 14 we will look in more detail at the potential problems of performance measurement in relation to remuneration and reward. Tunnel vision is one of them. If a manager knows that their bonus, for example, depends on achieving performance targets in certain areas, the manager is likely to give more attention to those areas of performance than to other areas.

2.2 Shareholders

FAST FORWARD

Shareholders represent a class of **connected** stakeholder, which provides funds for investment. They often take a short-term view of their involvement in an organisation.

Shareholders can be influential stakeholders, encouraging management to improve performance, by their decision to hold or sell shares.

Institutional shareholders often have significant holdings in companies. They usually hold shares for capital growth or their revenue stream so they tend to monitor performance closely and dispose of underperforming shares. They can be a strong influence on the decisions made by the organisation in which they hold their shares.

By contrast, **private shareholders** typically have little influence over the organisation in which they hold their shares, because they will only hold a very small percentage of the total shares.

Look at the case study below, which gives you an idea of the types of shareholder and the size of shareholdings involved in two **large listed companies**. The first is a large UK retail plc; the second is a Russian oil exploration company.

Look at the mix of shareholdings in the two companies. The mix between the holdings of private individuals and corporate institutions is quite similar despite the two companies being in different industries and on different exchanges.

You may like to analyse a large company of your own choosing and see if this pattern of large institutional shareholdings repeats itself.

Company shareholdings

Tesco plc shareholders at 22 February 2010

Type of shareholder	*Number of shareholders*	*Percentage of shareholders*	*Number of shares*	*Percentage of shares*
Employees	49,050	31.52	49,455,996	2.27
Other individuals	88,739	57.03	185,647,431	8.54
Corporate institutions	17,811	11.45	1,939,823,569	89.19
	155,600	100.00	2,174,926,996	100.00

OAO LUKOIL shareholders and nominees at 30 June 2010

Type of shareholder	*Number of shareholders*	*Percentage of shareholders*	*Number of shares*	*Percentage of shares*
Private individuals	50,231	99.70	26,579,588	3.12
Institutions and entities	151	0.30	823,983,667	96.88
	50,382	100.00	850,563,255	100.00

Sources: www.tesco.com, www.lukoil.com

Exam focus point

We will look at remuneration schemes and reward management in more detail in Chapter 14, but in recent years there have been an increasing number of instances where a company's shareholders have rejected the directors' proposed remuneration packages – with the shareholders arguing that the amounts being proposed are excessive or unduly generous.

2.3 Consumer groups

FAST FORWARD

Consumer groups are a **connected** group representing consumers' interests. They exist to ensure that products give good value. They promote safeguards for consumers against unethical business practice.

Key term

Consumerism reflects the increased importance and power of consumers, and the creation of organised consumer groups. Consumerism also reflects the recognition by producers that consumer satisfaction is the key to long-term profitability.

Consumerism is an attempt to even up the relationship between individual consumers and large powerful corporations. The basis of consumerism is often taken to be President John F Kennedy's **Consumer Bill of Rights**, which highlighted four basic rights.

2.3.1 The right to safety

The right that a product be **safe to use** is covered by legislation in many countries. The main problem is that research may reveal that there are, in fact, specific risks to consumers in using certain products that were at one time thought to be safe: for example, cigarettes. The future may also reveal damage to the wider environment, such as the effect of leaded petrol on the earth's atmosphere.

2.3.2 The right to be informed

This means that **instructions on products** should be **sufficient**, and there should be **clear labelling** of the ingredients that should be used in foodstuffs. This right also covers information about **purchase terms** (excessive small print could be called unfair). It places an obligation on advertisers to make sure that adverts for products are factually correct and are not misleading.

2.3.3 The right to choose

This should encourage **competition**, as marketers will try to influence consumer choice. However, the right to choose might also be interpreted as the right to choose without being unduly pressurised, thus discouraging unsolicited marketing and pressurised selling.

2.3.4 The right to be heard

This includes, in particular, the right to make complaints and know that those complaints will be quickly and fairly answered.

2.4 Consumer safety and fair trading

Many countries have legislation punishing businesses that supply consumer goods which do not comply with safety requirements.

A large number of countries have authorities whose role is to promote fair trading and competition and to act against restrictive practices. Their roles might include:

(a) Various functions in relation to monopolies, mergers, restrictive practices and uncompetitive practices

(b) Review of the carrying on of the commercial supply to consumers of goods and services

(c) Issuing licences

(d) Collation of evidence of harmful practices that may adversely affect the interests of consumers

(e) Taking action against persons who persist in conduct detrimental to the consumer

(f) Encouraging relevant associations to prepare codes of practice

2.5 Consequences of consumer protection legislation

Although managers might complain about the extra costs of consumer protection legislation, there are a number of wider issues to be considered.

(a) Does consumer protection legislation **impede business performance**?

(b) Does consumer protection legislation **put business** at a **competitive disadvantage** from overseas competitors?

Such costs are very hard to quantify but there are features that limit the competitive impact of such legislation.

(a) **Overseas competitors in the domestic market**
Products sold in the local market are subject to local law. The fact that they are imported does not exempt them from domestic consumer protection legislation. Overseas producers may be at a disadvantage, being less familiar with the market. At the very least, there is no obvious gain.

(b) **Domestic businesses in overseas markets**
Domestic businesses are subject to the laws regarding consumer protection prevalent in overseas markets.

There might indeed be burdens, but they are shared equally.

If the effect of consumer protection legislation enhances business's best practice, then **overall**, there may even be a benefit. After all, the US, where the consumer movement first started, was the birthplace of consumerism. Germany, whose export performance is generally impressive, has had some of the most exacting product quality regulations in Europe.

2.6 Self-regulation

The use of law to regulate the relationship between buyers and sellers can often seem unnecessarily forceful. Instead, many organisations regulate their dealings by **voluntary codes of conduct**.

A voluntary code of conduct is a statement by an organisation of the standards by which it seeks to do business. Codes are usually developed by a trade association and individual members incorporate the code into the dealings they have with their customers.

Voluntary codes usually include a mechanism for **resolving disputes** through arbitration.

Many countries have bodies promoting advertising standards. For example, in Singapore, the Advertising Standards Authority of Singapore (ASAS) uses the Singapore Code of Advertising Practice (SCAP) to try to promote a high standard of ethics in advertising.

In addition, at a supranational level, the European Advertising Standards Alliance, for example, brings together national advertising self-regulatory organisations (SROs) and organisations representing the advertising industry in Europe.

Possible sanctions that these self-regulatory bodies might employ include:

(a) **Published disapproval**

The organisations publish reports that detail public complaints and decisions in respect of the complaint.

(b) **Media recommendations**

The organisations will have power to recommend to media owners that certain advertisements or advertisers should not be accepted on their books.

2.7 Consumer protection organisations

As well as government bodies, there are voluntary associations.

An example of such a body is the Citizens Advice Bureau (CAB) in the UK. The CAB is an independent, not-for-profit, volunteer-based, charitable organisation. Its mandate is to help people resolve their legal, money and other problems by providing free, independent and confidential advice, and by influencing policymakers.

CAB focuses its work in the areas of financial and legal aid and other problems as they emerge. It can help with problems in a range of different areas including:

(a) Benefits
(b) Housing
(c) Employment
(d) Legal
(e) Relationships
(f) Tax
(g) Consumer
(h) Debt

2.8 Consumer groups' impact on business

Organisations need to understand how consumer groups can influence the industry environment. Working with consumer groups can have significant advantages, even the **positive endorsement** of products by the groups. A failure to respond to concerns can lead to **boycotts** not just of the products concerned, but also of all other products sold by the organisation. Animal welfare groups have targeted organisations' whole product ranges rather than just those products that have been tested on animals.

2.9 Suppliers

FAST FORWARD

Suppliers are a **connected** group of stakeholders. They can influence the cost and quality of goods and services.

Suppliers can directly influence the performance of an organisation through the **quality** of the goods and services that they supply to an organisation. Poor-quality goods will affect the saleability of the product to the customer, depressing sales and revenues.

The **prices** that suppliers charge will also affect the profitability of the end product if margins are eroded.

Organisations have developed a number of strategies for controlling price and quality from their suppliers. The best known of these is just-in-time, which commits suppliers to supply on-demand zero-defect parts. If an organisation has confidence in its supplier, a long-term relationship will be established.

The impact and importance of suppliers on a business is highlighted by the concept of the supply chain.

A supply chain is a network of facilities and distribution options that performs the functions of procurement of materials, transformation of these materials into intermediate and finished products and the distribution of these finished products and services to customers in order to produce value for the ultimate customer.

(Adapted from: Ganeshan and Harrison, *Supply Chain Management*)

Supply chains connect buyers and sellers in a chain from source materials to the customer. This aspect of supply chains means that buyers and sellers come to rely on each other, and performance can be affected by other partners in the chain.

In this context, three aspects of the supply chain are very important.

(a) **Responsiveness**: The combination of shortening product life cycles and increasing customer expectations means that firms must be able to supply their customers increasingly quickly. Increased integration – for example, Electronic Data Interchanges (EDI) – can be very useful here, allowing orders to be transmitted to suppliers across the chain quickly and accurately.

(b) **Reliability**: Deliveries through the supply chain must be reliable in terms of timeliness, quality and quantity. Reliability will be greatly assisted by transparency in the supply chain: vendors can see orders coming from customers and deliveries coming from suppliers further up the supply chain.

(c) **Relationships**: The need for responsiveness and reliability means that the members of the supply chain need to develop a mutual understanding and trust of each other. In this respect, the supply chain needs to be seen as a **network** based on collaboration and common interest, instead of the traditional dichotomy of the buyer/seller relationship.

The importance of the supply chain to organisations' performance is highlighted if one of these three aspects gets disrupted, as the case study below illustrates.

Case Study **Hornby's supply chain problems**

In 2014, the model train manufacturer, Hornby – which also owns the Airfix and Scalextric brands – announced that its sales for the year ended 31 March 2014 would be lower than expected due to problems with its main Chinese supplier of model railway products – Sanda Kan.

Sanda Kan was a long-standing supplier of Hornby's, but difficulties in obtaining supplies meant that sales of model railway products for the year were approximately 61% of budget in the UK and 68% in Europe.

A major factor in Hornby's poor overall performance was the fact that Sanda Kan failed to deliver products of sufficient quality, while Hornby also found itself opening boxes of models from the supplier which did not contain the full volume of products which had been ordered.

In the light of these problems, Hornby broadened its supplier base to 10 companies in China and India, and ended its relationship with Sanda Kan – which had previously made about 60% of Hornby's train set and Scalextric ranges.

In the 2014 Annual Report, Hornby's Chairman noted that 'The process of recognising the true scale of the issue [with Sanda Kan] and then formulating and executing a risk managed plan to conclude that relationship has been lengthy and complex. But I am confident that we are now on the other side. The corollary of this is the imperative to develop balanced partnerships with a portfolio of manufacturers who have the capacity to support our strategic ambitions over the long term. This piece of work is well under way but will take many months to reach a level of maturity such that the supply chain no longer constrains but positively supports the Group's ambitions to return to sales growth.'

www.hornby.plc.uk/annual-reports/
[Accessed 26 January 2016]

2.10 Government

FAST FORWARD

> **Government** is an **external** stakeholder group. **Central government** sets the regulatory framework in which organisations operate. **Local government** has devolved powers and can raise local revenues from business.

Here we look at how government affects all organisations.

One way in which government can affect organisational performance is in the area of **competition policy**. Competition policy is governed by domestic bodies and also by the wider reach of the transnational bodies such as the European Union.

2.11 Stakeholders' needs and the organisation's needs

In this section we have highlighted the ways that stakeholders may influence business performance. But it is also important to recognise that an organisation's performance also affects its stakeholders, so there is a two-way relationship between organisations and stakeholders, as illustrated in the table below.

Stakeholder	Needs of the organisation	Needs of the stakeholder
Employees	**Hands** – productivity **Hearts** – loyalty and commitment **Minds** – qualifications, teams **Voices** – suggestions and diversity	**Purpose** – support and direction **Care** – respect and fair treatment **Skills** – training and knowledge **Pay** – remuneration package
Investors	**Capital** – to operate and invest **Credit** – facilities from banks **Risk** (taken by the investors) **Support** – loyalty and advice	**Return** – capital appreciation **Reward** – dividends **Figures** – justification of results **Faith** and confidence in management team
Customers	**Profit** – to sustain the business **Growth** – increase of sales **Opinion** – feedback on performance **Trust** – for repeat business	**Fast** delivery **Right** – high-quality products and services **Cheap** – reasonably priced **Easy** – no barriers to buying
Suppliers	**Fast** delivery **Right** – high-quality products and services **Cheap** – reasonably priced **Easy** – no barriers to buying	**Profit** – to sustain the business **Growth** – increase of sales **Opinion** – feedback on performance **Trust** – for repeat business
Government/ Regulators	**Rules** – for fair competition **Reason** – sound purpose and reasonable to implement **Clarity** – no ambiguity **Advice** – on implementing rules	**Legal** – compliance with rules **Fairness** – no monopolistic or anti-competitive behaviour **Safety** – no danger to society **Truth** – openness and honesty

Stakeholder	Needs of the organisation	Needs of the stakeholder
Community	**Image** – being viewed in a positive way **Skills** – availability of workers **Suppliers** – local vendors for particular needs **Support** for organisation's aims	**Jobs** – regional employment **Fidelity** – to sustain and grow employment **Integrity** – openness, honesty and responsibility **Wealth** – bringing health and prosperity to community

Based on: Buytendijk, F. (2009) 'Organisation as network: A modern approach to performance management'

Available from: http://businessfinancemag.com/business-performance-management/organization-network-modern-approach-performance-management [Accessed 26 January 2016]

3 Social and ethical issues

FAST FORWARD

Since the 1990s, businesses have increasingly recognised the importance of acting ethically and in a socially responsible way. Related to this, there has also been an increase in the range of performance metrics that companies report in respect of their social responsibility.

Public opinion and attitudes, and legal and political pressures, mean that organisations can no longer concentrate solely on short-term financial corporate objectives. Environmental and social obligations now play a part in shaping an organisation's objectives (although the case study below provides an example of the way social obligations – to workers – are sometimes sacrificed in the drive for revenue and profit).

Case Study

Apple and Foxconn employees in China

While Apple's iPhones and iPads are becoming 'must-have' consumer items in Western countries, an investigation by two non-governmental organisations (NGOs) into the conditions of Chinese workers has revealed the shocking human cost of producing these items.

The investigation revealed disturbing allegations of excessive working hours and draconian workplace rules at two major plants in southern China. It has also uncovered an 'anti-suicide' pledge that workers at the two plants have been urged to sign, after a series of employee deaths in 2010.

The investigation gives a detailed picture of life for the 500,000 workers at the Shenzhen and Chengdu factories owned by Foxconn, which produces millions of Apple products each year. The report accuses Foxconn of treating workers 'inhumanely, like machines'.

Among the allegations made by workers interviewed by the NGOs – the Centre for Research on Multinational Corporations and Students & Scholars Against Corporate Misbehaviour (Sacom) – are claims that:

- Excessive overtime is routine, despite a legal limit of 36 hours' overtime per month. One payslip indicated that the worker had performed 98 hours of overtime in a month.
- Workers attempting to meet the huge demand for iPads were sometimes pressured to take only 1 day off in 13.
- In some factories, workers who were deemed to be 'performing badly' were required to be publicly humiliated in front of colleagues.
- In the wake of a spate of suicides at Foxconn factories in the summer of 2010, workers were asked to sign a statement promising not to kill themselves and pledging to 'treasure their lives'.

When the allegations uncovered by the NGOs were put to Foxconn, Foxconn manager Louis Woo confirmed that workers sometimes worked more than the statutory overtime limit to meet demand from Western consumers, but claimed that all the extra hours were voluntary. Workers claimed that, if they turn down excessive demands for overtime, they will be forced to rely on their basic wages. Workers in Chengdu are only paid 1,350 yuan (£125) a month for a basic 48-hour week, equivalent to about 65p an hour.

Asked about the suicides that have led to anti-suicide netting being fitted beneath the windows of workers' dormitories, Woo said: 'Suicides were not connected to bad working conditions. There was a copy effect. If one worker commits suicide, then others will follow.'

In a statement, Apple said: 'Apple is committed to ensuring the highest standards of social responsibility throughout our supply base. Apple requires suppliers to commit to our comprehensive supplier code of conduct as a condition of their contracts with us. We drive compliance with the code through a rigorous monitoring programme, including factory audits, corrective action plans and verification measures.'

In April 2012, Apple was finally granted access to the Chinese factories, after it ordered that the Foxconn City plant be opened to independent inspectors. The Washington-based Fair Labour Association has been appointed to interview Foxconn employees and observe their working conditions before continuing inspections at Apple's other Chinese manufacturers.

Based on: Chamberlain, G. (2011) Apple's Chinese workers treated 'inhumanely, like machines', *The Guardian*, 30 April, www.guardian.co.uk

[Accessed 25 January 2016]

3.1 Social responsibility

Why should organisations play an active social role in the society within which they function?

(a) **'The public' is a stakeholder in the business**. A business only succeeds because it is part of a wider society. Giving to charity is one way of **enhancing the reputation** of the business.

(b) **Charitable donations** and artistic **sponsorship** are a useful medium of **public relations** and can reflect well on the business.

(c) Involving managers and staff in **community activities** is good **work experience**.

(d) It helps create a **value culture** in the organisation and a sense of mission, which is good for motivation.

(e) In the long term, upholding the community's values, responding constructively to criticism and contributing towards community wellbeing might be good for business, as it **promotes the wider environment** in which businesses flourish.

(f) There is increasing **political pressure** on businesses to be socially responsible. Such activities help 'buy off' environmentalists.

There are **three contrasting views** about a corporation's responsibilities:

(a) If the company **creates** a social problem, it must **fix** it.

(b) The multinational corporation has the resources to fight poverty, illiteracy, malnutrition, illness and so on. This approach **disregards who** actually **creates** the problem.

Such an approach dates back to Henry Ford, who said 'I do not believe that we should make such an awful profit on our cars. A reasonable profit is right, but not too much. So it has been my policy to force the price of the car down as fast as production would permit, and give the benefits to the users and the labourers, with surprisingly enormous benefits to ourselves.'

(c) Companies **already discharge their social responsibility**, simply by increasing their profits and thereby contributing more in taxes. If a company was expected to divert more resources to solve society's problems, this would represent a double tax.

BP and Deepwater Horizon

In 2010, BP suffered its first annual loss for nearly 20 years, following the catastrophic explosion at the Deepwater Horizon oil rig in the Gulf of Mexico which will cost it at least £25 billion. Although BP agreed, in September 2014, to meet damages claims of $18.7 billion, some analysts think the total cost to shareholders could exceed £40 billion in the 10 years after the explosion (2010 to 2020). The financial cost was not the only reason that made 2010 one of the most damaging years in BP's history, as the devastating explosion, which killed 11 workers and triggered the biggest offshore oil spill in history, also shattered the company's reputation.

In February 2011, BP chief executive Bob Dudley said he was determined to see BP 'emerge from this episode as a company that is safer, stronger, more sustainable, more trusted and also more valuable ... 2011 will be a year of recovery and consolidation as we implement the changes we have identified to reduce operational risk and meet our commitments arising from the spill. But it will also be a year in which we have the opportunity to reset the company, adjusting the shape of our business, and focus on growing value for shareholders.'

Meanwhile, however, the White House oil commission into the fatal blow-out on the drilling rig in April 2010 concluded that it was 'an avoidable disaster caused in part by a series of cost-cutting decisions made by BP and its partners'.

The commission's report argued that 'systemic management failure' at BP, Halliburton and Transocean (the other companies involved with the rig) was ultimately to blame for the blow-out, and many of the poor decisions taken on the drilling rig were made in order to save time and money.

'Whether purposeful or not, many of the decisions that BP, Halliburton, and Transocean made that increased the risk of the blow-out clearly saved those companies significant time (and money),' the report said.

Moreover, investors claimed that BP executives and directors breached their fiduciary duties to the company by ignoring safety and maintenance for years before the well exploded on 20 April 2010. The investors' lawyers argued that, despite warnings about the safety of the well, BP continued to systematically cut budgets.

The investors (who had filed a claim against BP claiming diminished share value) claimed that, in addition to the tragic loss of life which resulted from the blow-out, the disaster is anticipated to cost the company billions of dollars in damages, permanent reputational harm and intense government scrutiny.

The claimants argued that, despite existing concerns raised by federal safety regulators, BP had cut operational costs by 15% in 2009 alone (the year before disaster). In their opinion, 'This reduction in budgets and manpower further undermined the company's ability to operate safely, as personnel were stretched even thinner, and resources that should have been devoted to maintenance, monitoring and addressing crucial safety failures in every aspect of the company's operations were diverted.'

Based on: (i) BP press release, www.bp.com, 1 February 2011;

(ii) 'BP's Pursuit of Cost-Cutting Led to Gulf Spill, Lawyers Say', www.bloomberg.com, 5 February 2011

Exam focus point

In the context of the P5 exam, it is also important to think how failures in performance measurement and performance management led to the failures illustrated in this case study.

For example, the commission report was critical of 'poor decisions taken in order to save time and money'. So, were BP too focused on short-term cost savings to consider the longer-term consequences of their decisions?

Also, were performance measures focused too much on financial factors rather than non-financial ones? For example, there are claims that the cut in operational costs undermined the company's ability to operate safely. But were there any performance measures which looked at safety and maintenance, or the level of resources devoted to safety and maintenance?

3.1.1 The importance of sustainability

In contrast to the BP example above, some companies do realise the importance of responding positively to social and environmental issues in order to protect and sustain their brand, and they can use sustainability issues to help maintain public trust in the brand.

For example, Toyota responded to environmental trends by successfully launching the Prius hybrid car, which supplements normal fuel usage with an electric-powered engine. The battery-powered electric engine starts the car, and operates it at low speeds. At higher speeds, the car switches automatically to a conventional engine and fuel. This combination saves on fuel compared with conventional cars and causes less pollution.

Similarly, environmental and social responsibility can provide marketing opportunities for companies, and companies can even achieve competitive advantage by addressing and accommodating their customers' ethical concerns. For example, in the UK, Innocent Drinks has built its business on corporate social responsibility ideals, with the underlying logic behind its business model being to 'leave things a little bit better than we found them'.

John Elkington, chairman of the think-tank SustainAbility Ltd, has argued that **sustainability** embraces not only environmental and economic questions, but also social and ethical dimensions. He talks of 'the **triple bottom line**', to highlight the fact that business people must increasingly recognise that the challenge now is to help deliver simultaneously:

- Economic prosperity
- Environmental quality
- Social equity

Elkington considers there to be three main forms of capital that businesses need to value:

- **Economic capital** (physical, financial and human skills and knowledge)
- **Natural capital** (replaceable and irreplaceable)
- **Social capital** (the ability of people to work together)

Environmental and social accounting is still embryonic, but Elkington believes that it will eventually develop our ability to see whether or not a particular company or industry is 'moving in the right direction'.

Elkington's concept of the triple bottom line emphasises that, although firms can be capable of socially and environmentally responsible action, many will only take such action if accounting conventions are changed to record and monitor the entire impact of business activities and not just the financial (profit) benefits. If such a change is made, firms may be able to improve their sustainability record without the need for excessive government regulation.

There are potentially a number of ways poor environmental behaviour can affect a firm: it could result in fines (for pollution or damages), increased liability to environmental taxes, loss in value of land, destruction of brand values, loss of sales, consumer boycotts, inability to secure finance, loss of insurance cover, contingent liabilities, lawsuits, and damage to corporate image.

The triple bottom line (TBL) is sometimes summarised as People, Planet, and Profit. It consists of:

(a) **Social justice**: fair and beneficial business practices towards labour and the community and the region in which a corporation conducts its business. A TBL company conceives a reciprocal social structure in which the wellbeing of corporate, labour and other stakeholder interests are interdependent.

(b) **Environmental quality**: a TBL company endeavours to benefit the natural order as much as possible, or at the least do no harm and curtail environmental impact. In this way, the company tries to reduce its ecological footprint by, among other things, carefully managing its consumption of energy and non-renewable resources, and by reducing manufacturing waste, as well as rendering waste less toxic before disposing of it in a safe and legal manner.

(c) **Economic prosperity**: the economic benefit enjoyed by the host society. It is the lasting economic impact the organisation has on its economic environment. Importantly, however, this is not as narrow as the internal profit made by a company or organisation.

For many years, sustainability has been seen from an environmental perspective, but now the social side of sustainability is gaining increasing importance; for example, in relation to such issues as the health and safety of workers, or paying workers a fair wage.

Although health and safety measures do not necessarily add value to a company in their own right, they can help to protect a company against the cost of accidents which might otherwise occur.

Moreover, if a company has poor health and safety controls this might result in, among other things, increased sick leave among staff and possible compensation claims for any work-related injuries, as well as higher insurance costs to reflect the higher perceived risks within the company.

Equally, the issue of social responsibility in relation to consumers has also been highlighted in recent years. The tobacco industry and the food and drink industry have received criticism in relation to the potential harm their products may cause to consumers.

Ultimately, if consumers cease to buy a product because they are concerned about the consequences of consuming a product, that product will not be sustainable because it will not generate any sales. For example, concerns about the high level of sugar in the 'Sunny D' orange drink forced Procter & Gamble to withdraw the drink's original formulation from the market.

Triple bottom line (TBL) and performance management

In this respect, the idea of the TBL has very important implications for performance measurement and performance management. Instead of concentrating on financial performance, and particularly on short-term financial performance, companies should also pay greater attention to the longer-term social, environmental and economic impact that they have on society. And this means that they need to look at performance measures which address these factors, as well as measures focusing on short-term financial performance.

Exam focus point

The reference to environmental performance highlights a potential link to environmental management accounting which we will look at in more detail later in this chapter.

The increased importance of 'sustainability' and reporting on social and environmental aspects of performance could also be seen to support the need for integrated reporting which we look at in more detail in Chapter 8 of this Study Text. Integrated reporting highlights the need to promote financial stability and sustainability, with corporate behaviour and investment decisions being aligned to the aim of long-term value creation.

3.1.2 Business sustainability and performance

Our discussions of TBL and corporate responsibility should have highlighted a key point about sustainability in a business context: that sustainability relates to the social, economic and environmental concerns of a business that aims to thrive in the long term. From a strategic perspective, there is little point in a business being profitable in the short term if it alienates customers, suppliers and/or staff in the process. By doing so, the business will weaken its chance of remaining profitable in the longer term.

In this respect, the idea of business sustainability is central to business strategy. One of the key issues in strategic management is that of how organisations can use their resources and capabilities to develop a **sustainable competitive advantage**. A company's ability to create and sustain a competitive advantage over its rivals is likely to be crucial to its long-term success.

Equally, a sustainable business needs an understanding of the changing business landscape and external environment so that it can respond and adapt to the opportunities and threats presented by it.

In this respect, the idea of sustainability should be seen as a strategic issue for almost every business – for example, in relation to risk mitigation, strategic innovation and the development of new skills and capabilities.

Crucially, however, the concept of sustainability should encourage an organisation to consider long-term orientation in business decisions, rather than purely focusing on short-term (financial) information and performance metrics.

Short-term metrics may push managers towards making decisions that deliver short-term performance at the expense of long-term value creation. Equally, a focus on creating value for shareholders in the short term may result in a failure to make the necessary strategic investments to ensure future profitability.

By contrast, an increased focus on business sustainability will support decisions aimed at attracting human capital, establishing more reliable supply chains, and engaging in product and process innovation, even if those decisions do not necessarily maximise short-term financial performance and profitability.

Equally, however, organisations need good-quality **management information** about social, environmental and ethical performance if they are going to monitor the environmental and social impacts of their operations. For example, company reporting on sustainability needs to provide hard evidence of the actions that companies are taking to address the negative effects of their operations.

Although CSR initiatives and measures can be extremely broad, and will vary from industry to industry, some prevailing themes are likely to emerge – around a company's dealings with its employees and its supply chain, and its impact on society and the environment more generally.

Case Study

CISCO's CSR Report

CISCO's 2014 corporate social responsibility (CSR) review identifies five key elements of the company's CSR strategy – governance and ethics, supply chain, its people, society, and the environment.

The following table identifies some of the CSR performance objectives identified in CISCO's CSR review:

CSR elements	Examples of objectives
Governance and Ethics – Our commitment to ethical conduct and good governance makes us a stronger, more resilient company	Maintain a quarterly review and update of our Human Rights Roadmap, which aligns to the UN Guiding Principles on Business and Human Rights Engage with diverse stakeholder groups to inform our CSR strategy, performance and reporting Augment and deepen engagement with key socially responsible investors for more meaningful dialogue on issues of importance to our investors
Supply Chain – We work closely with the suppliers who make our products to maintain high standards for ethics, labour rights, health, safety and the environment	100% of key suppliers report their greenhouse gas emissions to the Carbon Disclosure Project (CDP) Enhance our supplier engagement by further integrating the Supplier Code of Conduct into day-to-day business operations Gather real-time feedback from supplier workers and management to enhance transparency on labour conditions in the supply chain
Our people – We offer engaging development opportunities, recognise achievement, and foster an inclusive and healthy workplace to help employees achieve their full potential	Improve our employee survey scores in the areas of development, organisational alignment, and recognition Launch a new performance management programme Increase diversity awareness, with an emphasis on gender awareness Launch new rewards and recognition programme that highlights employee contributions

CSR elements	Examples of objectives
Society – Using our expertise and technology, we work with partners to extend access to education and healthcare, create economic development opportunities, respond to disasters and critical human needs, and help communities thrive	Provide at least 7 million meals for people in need through employee donations to our annual Global Hunger Relief Campaign Reach 145,000 employee volunteer hours Support 5,500 remote patient visits worldwide through Cisco collaboration technologies Reach 250,000 factory and farm workers through the Labour Link mobile platform developed by Good World Solutions and supported by Cisco
Environment – We improve our own environmental performance, as well as our customers', by developing products that improve living standards, reduce resource waste, and save energy	Reduce total Cisco greenhouse gas emissions worldwide by 40% absolute by financial year 2017 (compared to FY 2007) Reduce total Cisco operational energy use per unit of revenue worldwide by 15% by financial year 2017 (compared to FY 2007) Use electricity generated from renewable sources for at least 25% of our electricity every year by financial year 2017

3.2 Ethics and ethical conduct

Whereas **social responsibility** deals with the organisation's **general stance towards society**, and affects the **activities** the organisation **chooses** to do, **ethics** relates far more to **how** an organisation **conducts** individual transactions.

Organisations are coming under increasing pressure from a number of **sources** to behave more ethically:

(a) Government
(b) UK and European legislation
(c) Treaty obligations (such as the Kyoto Protocol)
(d) Consumers
(e) Employers
(f) Pressure groups

However, in the same way that social responsibility issues can have a significant impact on a business, so can ethical issues, as the following example illustrates.

Case Study — Volkswagen – emissions scandal

In September 2015 Volkswagen (VW) admitted that up to 11 million diesel-powered vehicles worldwide – manufactured between 2009 and 2015, and also including the company's other brands such as Audi, SEAT and Skoda – could have so-called 'defeat devices' which lowered emissions of nitrogen oxides from their exhausts during laboratory testing.

VW's chief executive resigned after the company admitted the deception, and in November 2015 the ratings firm Moody's Investor Service downgraded some of VW's corporate debt citing mounting risks to the company's reputation and future earnings in the wake of the emissions crisis.

At the same time, VW announced it was offering $1,000 to each of almost 500,000 car owners in the US affected by the scandal, in an attempt to retain customer loyalty.

VW made a €6.7 billion provision in the third quarter of 2014, which caused the company to record its first quarterly loss in more than a decade.

The cost provided for so far relates to the refitting of affected vehicles, but VW's CEO admitted that the costs are likely to rise, but the company was not yet in a position to estimate its potential liabilities from lawsuits. Some analysts think the total cost of the problem could rise to more than €30 billion eventually.

Nonetheless, the crisis had already wiped more than a quarter off VW's stock market value by the end of October 2015.

Based on: Reuters, (2015), Hit by scandal, VW posts first quarterly loss in at least 15 years. Online. Available from: http://in.reuters.com/article/2015/10/28/volkswagen-results-idINKCN0SM0UZ20151028 [Accessed 26 January 2016]

3.3 Fundamentals of ethical theory

Business ethics can be defined as the standards of behaviour in the conduct of business.

Ethics is concerned with right and wrong and how conduct should be judged to be good or bad. It is about how we should live our lives and, in particular, how we should behave towards other people. It is therefore relevant to all forms of human activity.

Business life is a fruitful source of ethical dilemmas because its whole purpose is material gain, the making of profit. Success in business requires a constant, avid search for potential advantage over others and businesspeople are under pressure to do whatever yields such advantage.

3.4 Ethics and strategy

As well as presenting possible threats and dilemmas to a professional accountant, ethics and ethical issues can have a role in strategy and business management more generally. For example, strong ethical policies – that go beyond simply upholding the law – can add value to a brand. Conversely, failing to act ethically can cause social, economic and environmental damage, and in doing so can undermine an organisation's long-term reputation and prospects.

In this respect, a socially and environmentally ethical approach can assist an organisation's ability to thrive in the long run. In this respect, ethical behaviour can help contribute to **sustainable competitive advantage**.

The collapse of Enron (as a result of a massive fraud) clearly showed how unethical behaviour led to a failure to create a sustainable business model. It is also possible to argue that some other corporate failures – such as Lehman Brothers, Bear Stearns and Northern Rock – came about as a result of the organisations focusing too much on the pursuit of short-term gains, but in doing so they jeopardised their longer-term survival.

These examples highlight the importance of organisations not only understanding the **risks** they are taking in their business, but also focusing on long-term sustainability as well as short-term profitability.

Such considerations can be directly relevant in the context of the strategic decisions an organisation makes. For example, how might a consideration of ethical behaviour affect an investment decision? In simple terms, if a project generates a positive net present value (NPV) it is likely to be accepted. If, however, the project involves exploiting cheap labour (or even child labour) it should not be accepted by an organisation; either on ethical grounds, or because of the potential risk to its reputation (and therefore future sales) if its labour practices became more widely known.

Consequently, it is important that ethics are embedded in an organisation's business model, organisational strategy and decision-making processes. Moreover, ethical issues are particularly important when considered alongside aspects of sustainability.

Ethics may have an impact on strategy in various ways.

(a) In the formulation of strategic objectives, some firms will not consider certain lines of business for ethical reasons. For example, in the UK, the Co-operative Bank claims it has turned away over

£1 billion of business from potential customers who do not share its ethical values or who are perceived to act unethically.

(b) External appraisal will need to consider the ethical climate in which the firm operates. This will raise expectations of its behaviour.

(c) Internal appraisal: management should consider whether present operations are 'sustainable', ie consistent with present and future ethical expectations.

(d) Strategy selection: management should consider the ethical implications of proposed strategies before selecting and implementing them.

Ethical issues could arise in a wide range of scenarios, including:

Marketing and the marketing mix: for example, there could be ethical issues relating to the products/services being sold, the price at which they are being sold, or the way in which they are being promoted.

Manufacturing: for example, relating to pollution and environmental ethics, producing defective or inherently dangerous products (such as tobacco), the use of child labour, or product testing (eg testing on animals).

Purchasing and procurement: for example, relating to human rights and working practices with supplier firms; or adopting fair contracting terms and conditions with suppliers (eg Fair Trade principles). Ethical issues could also arise in relation to payments by companies to officials who have the power to influence purchasing decisions – although if a company tries to bribe an official, its behaviour is likely to be not only unethical but also illegal.

3.5 The scope of corporate ethics

Corporate ethics may be considered in three contexts:

(a) The organisation's interaction with **national** and **international society**
(b) The effects of the organisation's **routine operations**
(c) The behaviour of **individual members** of staff

Influencing society. The organisation operates within and interacts with the political, economic and social framework of wider society. It is both inevitable and proper that it will both influence and be influenced by that wider framework. Governments, individual politicians and pressure groups will all make demands on such matters as employment prospects and executive pay. Conversely, organisations themselves will find that they need to make their own representations on such matters as monetary policy and the burden of regulation. International variation in such matters and in the framework of **corporate governance** will affect organisations that operate in more than one country. It is appropriate that the organisation develops and promotes its own policy on such matters.

Corporate behaviour. The organisation should establish **corporate policies** for those issues over which it has direct control. Examples of matters that should be covered by policy include health, safety, labelling, equal opportunities, environmental effects, political activity, bribery and support for cultural activities.

Individual behaviour. Policies to guide the behaviour of individuals are likely to flow from the corporate stance on the matters discussed above. The organisation must decide on the extent to which it considers it appropriate to attempt to influence individual behaviour. Some aspects of such behaviour may be of strategic importance, especially when managers can be seen as representing or embodying the organisation's standards. Matters of financial rectitude and equal treatment of minorities are good examples here.

Corporate ethical codes. Organisations often publish corporate codes of ethical standards. Fundamentally, this is a good idea and can be a useful way of disseminating the specific policies we have discussed above. However, care must be taken over such a document.

(a) It should not be over-prescriptive or over-detailed, since this encourages a legalistic approach to interpretation and a desire to seek loopholes in order to justify previously chosen courses of action.

(b) It will only have influence if senior management adhere to it consistently in their own decisions and actions.

GlaxoSmithKline (GSK) in China

GSK's website (www.gsk.com) contains the following summary statement in relation to ethical conduct and the supply chain.

> 'Ethical conduct is a priority for GSK and we are committed to performance with integrity. We have robust policies and compliance processes covering all our operations, including the way we reward our sales representatives, how we market our medicines and vaccines, and how we work with stakeholders.
>
> Our compliance programmes embed the same standards across our business units in different countries. These include our Code of Conduct, which outlines how all employees should apply our Values and Behaviours, and our Global Code of Practice for Promotion and Customer Interactions, which applies to all employees involved in sales and marketing as well as third parties acting on our behalf.'

In turn, the Code of Conduct makes clear to staff that they are required to read, understand and abide by the Code, such that all of their actions are in line with the company's values and are compliant with the regulations within which GSK has to operate.

Nonetheless, in 2013 GlaxoSmithKline (GSK) was investigated by Chinese police for alleged bribes totalling Rmb 3 billion, over six years, to individuals across every level of the healthcare system in China (from doctors to government officials) in order to help the company win market share and agree higher prices.

In July 2013, Chinese government officials arrested four senior managers from GSK's China business in connection with their investigation, and in May 2014 Mark Reilly – the former head of GSK's operations in the country – was accused of ordering employees to commit bribery on a widespread scale. Chinese police allege that Reilly put pressure on his sales teams to bribe hospitals, doctors and health institutions.

The Chinese State news agency, Xinhua, said 'GSK's practices have eroded its corporate integrity and could cause irreparable damage to the company in China and elsewhere.' Lawyers also warned that, due to Mr Reilly's seniority, the allegations could pave the way for corporate charges against the firm. Moreover, the bribery charges brought against GSK could mean the cancellation of its business licences in China – a major growth market for Western pharmaceutical companies.

GSK's revenues in China fell 61% in the third quarter of 2013, and were down by 20% in the first quarter of 2014 compared with a year earlier. As Xinhua pointed out, the GSK case 'is a warning to other multinationals in China that ethics matter.'

In response to the allegations, GSK said 'The Group takes these allegations seriously and is continuing to co-operate fully with the Chinese authorities in this investigation. The Group has informed the US Department of Justice, the US Securities and Exchange Commission and the UK Serious Fraud Office (SFO) regarding the investigation and is co-operating fully with these agencies.' (This co-operation with the UK and US authorities is required because GSK is listed on the London Stock Exchange and has a secondary listing on the New York Stock Exchange.)

In July 2013 GSK also appointed the US legal firm, Ropes & Gray, to carry out an independent review into the alleged corruption in GSK's Chinese business, and 'to investigate what has happened'.

GSK stressed that the allegations 'are deeply concerning to us, and are contrary to the values of GSK ... We want to reach a resolution that will enable the company to continue to make an important contribution to the health and welfare of China and its citizens.'

Nonetheless, GSK admitted that some of its senior Chinese executives had broken the law. Its head of emerging markets stated: 'Certain senior executives of GSK China, who knew our systems well, appear to have acted outside of our processes and controls which breaches Chinese law'. He promised that the company was taking the charges against it 'extremely seriously' and that 'We have zero tolerance for any behaviour of this nature'.

In the wake of the corruption allegations, GSK's own investigations uncovered evidence of wrongdoing by a small number of sales staff, who were subsequently fired. GSK insisted that these staff were working outside the company's control systems. A company spokesman also noted that 'We routinely monitor and check expenses claims to ensure they adhere to our policies. Since the start of the investigation by the authorities, we have increased this monitoring in China.' Nonetheless, as GSK's CEO, Sir Andrew Witty, admitted: 'This looks like a number of individuals that have worked outside our systems. It would have been difficult to find using our controls.'

As such, although GSK has accepted that individual employees have behaved inappropriately, the company has consistently denied that those individuals acted on its instructions. This is very important, because if the company were found to be liable, it could face enormous fines from the UK and US authorities who have stringent anti-bribery regulations.

However, despite GSK's assertions that the wrongdoing was limited to a small number of staff, who were acting contrary to company policy, a whistleblower within GSK had leaked reports in 2012 that GSK was falsifying its records to conceal illegal practices – including bribery – and the practice of giving cash to doctors to sell products was common. The whistleblower also alleged that GSK fabricated an internal 'compliance' scheme which effectively covered up widespread corruption within its Chinese business.

GSK denied this, and said its own investigation had not found any evidence to support these claims. Moreover, the company pointed to the fact that it had hired an external law firm (Ropes & Gray) to conduct an independent review into its Chinese business for the period under review as evidence that it was not involved in a cover up. (An alternative explanation of this could be that the appointment of Ropes & Gray represented an implicit admission that GSK's own internal investigation had not gone far enough.)

More generally, though, this case highlights that even though a company may have (ethical) processes and controls, they are not always adhered to. And the actions of individual staff not adhering to those controls can lead to very damaging claims against a company. Although GSK claimed it had 'zero tolerance' of the behaviour in question, that behaviour had still taken place.

Sourced from:

Brinded, L. (2014), 'China's crackdown on GlaxoSmithKline bribery scandal is a warning to foreign firms', *International Business Times*, 16 May

Brinded, L. (2014), 'GlaxoSmithKline seeks China bribery scandal resolution as Mark Reilly and execs charged with corruption', *International Business Times*, 14 May

Mitchell, T. & Ward, A. (2014) 'GSK faces questions over direction of China corruption probe', *Financial Times*, 3 July

Roland, D. (2014) 'GSK bribery scandal could cause 'irreparable damage', says China', *The Telegraph*, 16 May

3.6 The ethical stance

FAST FORWARD

An organisation's **ethical stance** is the extent to which it will exceed its minimum obligations to stakeholders. There are four typical stances:

- Short-term shareholder interest
- Long-term shareholder interest
- Multiple stakeholder obligations
- Shaper of society

Key term

Johnson, Scholes and Whittington define an organisation's **ethical stance** as the extent to which the organisation will exceed its minimum obligation to stakeholders.

Johnson, Scholes and Whittington illustrate the range of possible ethical stances by giving four illustrations:

(a) **Short-term shareholder interest (laissez-faire stance)**
(b) **Long-term shareholder interest (enlightened self-interest)**
(c) **Multiple stakeholder obligations**
(d) **Shaper of society**

3.6.1 Short-term shareholder interest

An organisation might limit its ethical stance to taking responsibility for **short-term shareholder interest** on the grounds that it is for **government** alone to impose wider constraints on corporate governance. This minimalist approach would accept a duty of obedience to the demands of the law, but would not undertake to comply with any less substantial rules of conduct. This stance can be justified on the grounds that going beyond it can **challenge government authority**; this is an important consideration for organisations operating in developing countries.

3.6.2 Long-term shareholder interest

The rationale behind the 'enlightened self-interest' stance is that there can be a long-term benefit to shareholders from well-managed relationships with other stakeholders. Therefore, the justification for social action is that it makes good business sense.

There are two reasons why an organisation might take a wider view of ethical responsibilities when considering the **longer-term interest of shareholders.**

(a) The organisation's **corporate image** may be enhanced by an assumption of wider responsibilities. The cost of undertaking such responsibilities may be justified as essentially promotional expenditure.

(b) The responsible exercise of corporate power may prevent a build-up of social and political **pressure for legal regulation**. Freedom of action may be preserved and the burden of regulation lightened by acceptance of ethical responsibilities.

3.6.3 Multiple stakeholder obligations

Organisations adopting this stance accept the **legitimacy of the expectations of stakeholders other than shareholders** and build those expectations into the organisation's stated purposes. Such organisations recognise that, without appropriate relationships with groups such as suppliers, employees and customers, they would not be able to function.

However, organisations adopting a 'multiple stakeholder obligations' stance also argue that performance should not be measured simply through the financial bottom line. They argue that the key to long-term survival is dependent on social and environmental performance as well as economic (financial) performance, and therefore it is important to take account of the views of stakeholders with interests relating to social and environmental matters.

3.6.4 Shaper of society

Shapers of society regard financial considerations as being of secondary importance to changing society or social norms. For such organisations, ensuring that society benefits from their actions is more important than financial and other stakeholder interests.

4 Environmental management accounting 6/11, 12/14

FAST FORWARD

Environmental management accounting (EMA) 'is the generation and analysis of both financial and non-financial information in order to support internal environmental management processes'.

Key term

Environmental management accounting (EMA) 'is the generation and analysis of both financial and non-financial information in order to support internal environmental management processes'.

(Shane Johnson)

The United Nations Division for Sustainable Development (UNDSD) produced a similar definition of environmental management accounting as being the identification, collection, analysis and use of two types of information for internal decision making.

(a) Physical information on the use, flows and destinies of energy, water and materials (including wastes)
(b) Monetary information on environment-related costs, earnings and savings

Environment-related costs could be categorised into four groups.

(a) **Environmental protection costs** – the costs of activities undertaken to prevent the production of waste
(b) **Environmental detection costs** – costs incurred to ensure that the organisation complies with regulations and voluntary standards
(c) **Environmental internal failure costs** – costs incurred from performing activities that have produced contaminants and waste that have not been discharged into the environment
(d) **Environmental external failure costs** – costs incurred on activities' performance after discharging waste into the environment

Exam focus point

When we come to look at 'costs of quality' in Chapter 13 of this Study Text you may notice some overlap with the environment-related costs we have identified here. This should not come as too much of a surprise, though. In effect, we could consider environment-related costs as being the costs of ensuring the quality of an organisation's processes in relation to the environment.

Nonetheless, environment-related costs are specifically to do with the impact of an organisation's processes on the environment. Therefore, if you have an exam question on environment-related costs, make sure you **look specifically at the environmental impact of processes or activities**. For example, an environmental internal failure cost might be the cost of installing filters on a smokestack to reduce the level of carbon dioxide or other gasses emitted into the atmosphere. Equally, an environmental external failure cost might be the cost of cleaning up an oil spill.

4.1 Environmental management accounting – technical article

Exam focus point

There is an article called 'Environmental Management Accounting' in the P5 Technical Articles section on ACCA's website which looks at the increasing importance of environmental management accounting. The main points in the article are summarised below, but you are also strongly advised to read the article in full.

The **main points** made in the article are as follows. (The emphasis is BPP's.)

(a) **Major incidents** like the Exxon Valdez oil spill have significantly **raised the profile of environmental issues** over the last 20 years or so. More recently, the BP Deepwater Horizon oil rig explosion in the Gulf of Mexico (April 2010) also reinforced the importance of environmental issues, and the huge potential costs of environmental disasters.

(b) Poor environmental behaviour can result in '**fines, increased liability to environmental taxes, loss in value of land, destruction of brand values, loss of sales, consumer boycotts, inability to secure finance, loss of insurance cover, contingent liabilities, law suits, and damage to**

corporate image'. In other words, poor environmental behaviour can have a direct impact on a company's financial performance.

Consequently, businesses have become increasingly aware of the environmental implications of their operations, products and services, and recognise that managing environmental risks is now an important part of running a successful business.

(c) Environmental issues need to be **managed before they can be reported** externally, and so changes are needed to management accounting systems.

(d) Management accounting techniques tend to **underestimate** the **cost** of poor environmental behaviour, underestimate the benefits of improvements and can **distort** and **misrepresent** environmental issues, leading managers to make **decisions that are bad** for business and bad for the environment.

(e) Most **conventional accounting systems** are unable to apportion **environmental costs** to products, processes and services and so they are simply **classed as general overheads**. 'Consequently, managers are unaware of these costs, have no information with which to manage them and have no incentive to reduce them.' Environmental management accounting (EMA), on the other hand, attempts to make all relevant, significant costs visible so that they can be considered when making business decisions.

(f) Management accounting techniques which are useful for the identification and management of environmental costs include:

(i) **Input/output analysis** (records material flows with the idea that 'what comes in must go out – or be stored')

(ii) **Flow cost accounting** (aims to reduce the quantities of materials, which leads to increased ecological efficiency)

(iii) **Environmental activity-based costing** (distinguishes between environment-related and environment-driven costs)

(iv) **Life cycle costing**

Input/output analysis records material flows and balances them with outflows on the basis that what comes in must go out, or be stored. This approach is similar to process costing where all materials in a process are accounted for, either as good output or scrap/waste. This forces the business to look at how it uses its resources and focuses it on environmental cost.

So, for example, if 100 kg of materials have been bought (input) and only 80 kg of materials have been produced (output) then 20 kg difference must be accounted for in some way. It may be, for example, that 10% of it has been sold as scrap, leaving 90% as waste. By accounting for outputs in this way, both in terms of physical quantities and, at the end of the process, in monetary terms, businesses are forced to focus on environmental costs, and the levels of waste and externalities being generated by their processes.

The difficulty with adopting this technique is putting monetary values on waste, non-accounted materials and scrap if these previously haven't been accounted for. It also requires additional reporting of factors included, such as water use and energy, which may be difficult to attribute to individual units.

Flow cost accounting takes material flows and combines them with the organisational structure. It evaluates material flows in terms of physical quantities, cost and value. Material flows are classified into material, system and delivery and disposal. The values and costs of each of these are then calculated. This system requires additional reporting which may not be available on existing systems and time consuming to accomplish.

Again, though, it may be difficult to attribute costs to all material flows.

Environmental activity-based costing. Traditional activity-based costing allocates all the internal costs of a business to cost centres and cost drivers on the basis of the activities that caused the costs. Environmental activity-based costing distinguishes between environment-related costs and environment-driven costs.

Environment-related costs are costs specifically attributed to joint environmental cost centres, such as a sewage plant, or a waste filtration plant.

By contrast, **environment-driven costs** are hidden in general overhead costs and do not relate specifically to a joint environmental cost centre, although they do relate to environmental drivers. For example, a company may shorten the working life of a piece of equipment in order to avoid excess pollution in the later years of its working life. As a result, the company's annual depreciation charge will increase. This is an environment-driven cost.

In order for environmental activity-based costing to provide 'correct' information, the choice of allocation basis is crucial. The difficulty in allocating costs correctly could be a major complication in using this method.

Four main bases of allocation are:

- Volume of emissions or waste
- Toxicity of emissions or waste
- Environmental impact added volume (volume × input per unit of volume) of the emissions treated
- The relative costs of treating different kinds of emissions

Life cycle costing records the complete costs of a product 'from cradle to grave' taking into account the environmental consequences across the whole life of the product. Organisations need to have the recording systems to capture all costs, especially those incurred **prior to production** (which is when traditional cost recording commences), and **after production ceases** (for example, the costs of cleaning and decontaminating industrial sites when they are decommissioned at the end of a project).

These costs can often be large sums, and so can have a significant impact on the shareholder value generated by a project. Yet there is a danger that costs which occur after production ceases will be overlooked or given a low priority by managers driven by short-term financial measures. However, it is important that a **project appraisal captures all the costs generated over the whole life cycle** of the project. Life cycle costing will help ensure the full extent of this cost information is included.

Moreover, it is important that potential decommissioning costs and other post-production costs are identified at the start of a project, so that they can be included in the investment appraisal (or similar cost/benefit analysis) to determine whether or not to undertake the project.

(g) The major areas for the application of EMA are 'in the assessment **of annual environmental costs/expenditures, product pricing, budgeting, investment appraisal, calculating costs and savings of environmental projects**, or **setting quantified performance targets**'.

(h) Good environmental management can be seen as a **key component of TQM** (objectives such as zero waste).

In the same way that organisations adopt total quality management to try to reduce defects in production, environmental quality management could be introduced to focus on the 'continuous improvement' of environmental management. Suitable **environmental performance measures** or **targets** will need to be selected to enable a review of environmental performance to be undertaken. For example, performance targets could include: zero spills, zero pollution, zero waste and zero accidents.

(i) Although various classifications have been suggested, 'The most significant **problem** of EMA lies in the **absence of a clear definition of environmental costs**. This means that organisations are not monitoring and controlling such costs.'

Exam focus point

> The Study Guide for Section A5(c) of the syllabus notes that you need to be able to 'Discuss, evaluate and apply environmental management accounting using, for example, lifecycle costing and activity-based costing.'
>
> As such, these two techniques – life cycle costing and activity-based costing – should be the only two specifically required in an exam question about measuring and managing environmental costs.

Exam focus point

> A question in the June 2011 exam asked candidates to evaluate how environmental accounting techniques can assist an organisation (an oil refinery) in managing its environmental and strategic performance.
>
> The question then also asked candidates to evaluate how a life cycle costing approach could affect the forecast profitability of a new product. The key point to note here was the way that traditional product profit analysis overstated profits, because it did not take account of environmental costs and decommissioning costs.

4.2 Environmental concern and performance

Martin Bennett and Peter James (authors of *The green bottom line: management accounting for environmental improvement and business benefit*) looked at the **ways in which a company's concern for the environment can impact on its performance**.

(a) **Short-term savings** through waste minimisation and energy efficiency schemes can be substantial.

(b) Companies with poor environmental performance may face **increased cost of capital** because investors and lenders demand a higher risk premium.

(c) There are a number of **energy and environmental taxes**, such as the UK's landfill tax.

(d) **Pressure group campaigns** can cause damage to reputation and/or additional costs.

(e) Environmental legislation may cause the **'sun-setting'** of products and opportunities for **'sunrise' replacements**.

(f) The cost of processing input which becomes **waste** is equivalent to 5–10% of some organisations' revenue.

(g) The phasing out of chlorofluorocarbons (CFCs) has led to markets for alternative products.

4.2.1 Achieving business and environmental benefits

Bennett and James went on to suggest six main **ways in which business and environmental benefits can be achieved**:

(a) **Integrating the environment into capital expenditure decisions** (by considering environmental opposition to projects which could affect cash flows, for example). There is a feeling that most companies do not know about the extent of their environmental costs, and so tend to underestimate them. This can lead to distorted calculations in investment decisions.

(b) **Understanding and managing environmental costs**. Environmental costs are often 'hidden' in overheads and environmental and energy costs are often not allocated to the relevant budgets.

(c) **Introducing waste minimisation schemes.**

(d) **Understanding and managing life cycle costs.** For many products, the greatest environmental impact occurs upstream (such as mining raw materials) or downstream from production (such as energy to operate equipment). This has led to producers being made responsible for dealing with the disposal of products such as cars, and government and third-party measures to influence raw material choices. Organisations therefore need to identify, control and make provision for environmental life cycle costs and work with suppliers and customers to identify environmental cost reduction opportunities.

(e) **Measuring environmental performance.** Business is under increasing pressure to measure all aspects of environmental performance, both for statutory disclosure reasons and due to demands for more environmental data from customers.

(f) **Involving management accountants in a strategic approach to environment-related management accounting and performance evaluation.** A 'green accounting team' incorporating the key functions should analyse the strategic picture and identify opportunities for practical initiatives. It should analyse the short-, medium- and long-term impact of possible changes in the following:

(i) **Government policies**, such as on transport
(ii) **Legislation and regulation**
(iii) **Supply conditions**, such as fewer landfill sites
(iv) **Market conditions**, such as changing customer views
(v) **Social attitudes**, such as to factory farming
(vi) **Competitor strategies**

Chapter Roundup

- Stakeholders have an **interest** in what an organisation does, and a degree of **power** to influence it.
- Different **stakeholder groups** have different assessments of the risk a strategy poses to their interests. Some are able to **exercise power** over management.
- **Stakeholder mapping** may be used to analyse the influence of various stakeholder groups.
- **Employees and management are internal stakeholders.** They may have considerable power over the performance of the organisation.
- **Shareholders** represent a class of **connected** stakeholder, which provides funds for investment. They often take a short-term view of their involvement in an organisation.
- **Consumer groups** are a **connected** group representing consumers' interests. They exist to ensure that products give good value. They promote safeguards for consumers against unethical business practice.
- **Suppliers** are a **connected** group of stakeholders. They can influence the cost and quality of goods and services.
- **Government** is an **external** stakeholder group. **Central government** sets the regulatory framework in which organisations operate. **Local government** has devolved powers and can raise local revenues from business.
- Since the 1990s, businesses have increasingly recognised the importance of acting ethically and in a socially responsible way. Related to this, there has also been an increase in the range of performance metrics that companies report in respect of their social responsibility.
- An organisation's **ethical stance** is the extent to which it will exceed its minimum obligations to stakeholders. There are four typical stances:
  - Short-term shareholder interest
  - Long-term shareholder interest
  - Multiple stakeholder obligations
  - Shaper of society
- **Environmental management accounting (EMA)** 'is the generation and analysis of both financial and non-financial information in order to support internal environmental management processes'.

Quick Quiz

1. According to Mendelow's matrix, how should an organisation deal with stakeholders which have high power over the organisation, but low interest in it?

2. As part of a restructuring exercise, AB Co will have to make some of its staff redundant. How should AB Co's staff be classified in terms of their levels of power and interest in relation to this decision?

   A Low power; low interest
   B Low power; high interest
   C High power; low interest
   D High power; high interest

3. What are the four typical ethical stances which could be held by an organisation?

4. Large companies often include a reference to social responsibility in their mission statements.

   Which of the aspirations below reflect a genuine concern for socially responsible behaviour?

   (i) To support the local community and preserve the environment
   (ii) To keep employees informed of policy, progress and problems
   (iii) To pay all employees the minimum wage or higher

   A (i) and (ii)
   B (i) and (iii)
   C (ii) and (iii)
   D (i), (ii) and (iii)

5. List **two** management accounting techniques which are useful for the identification and management of environmental costs.

Answers to Quick Quiz

1 Stakeholders with high power but low interest should be **kept satisfied**. While they are often passive, they are capable of becoming key players (high power; high interest) and therefore need to be treated with care.

2 B The staff will have a **high level of interest** in the decision (because it directly affects them) but it is likely that they will only have a **low level of power** to be able to influence it, not least because they don't appear to be able to prevent the redundancies from occurring.

3 Short-term shareholder interest; long-term shareholder interest; multiple stakeholder obligations; and shaper of society.

4 A (i) and (ii)

Social responsibility relates to an organisation's obligation to maximise positive stakeholder benefits while minimising the negative effects of its actions. It reflects the whole range of stakeholders who have an interest in an organisation.

However, social responsibility entails more than simply conforming with legislation, which is what option (iii) is describing. By paying a minimum wage to its employees, an organisation would be fulfilling its legal obligations, not its social responsibilities.

5 You could have selected any two from the following four management accounting techniques we have included in the chapter.

(i) **Input/output analysis** (records material flows with the idea that 'what comes in must go out – or be stored')

(ii) **Flow cost accounting** (aims to reduce the quantities of materials, which leads to increased ecological efficiency)

(iii) **ABC** (distinguishes between environment-related and environment-driven costs)

(iv) **Life cycle costing** (to identify cost incurred before production begins, and after production has ceased)

Now try the question below from the Practice Question Bank

Number	Level	Marks	Approximate time
Q5	Examination	20	40 mins

PART B

External influences on organisational performance

External influences on organisational performance

Topic list	Syllabus reference
1 Risk and uncertainty	B1(a), (b), (c)
2 Factors to consider when assessing performance	B2(a)

Introduction

In the previous chapter, we looked at the relationship between stakeholders and organisations and how stakeholder groups can influence an organisation's strategy and its performance.

In this chapter we now look specifically at how stakeholders' attitudes to risk affect strategic planning and decision making. We also look at the techniques which can be used to assess performance in the context of risk and uncertainty.

You should already be familiar with these techniques from your earlier studies (at F5); it is important to revise them here.

The chapter closes by considering how the external environment in which an organisation operates can affect its performance. This serves as a reminder of the importance of considering this external context when assessing an organisation's performance.

Study guide

		Intellectual level
B1	**Impact of risk and uncertainty on performance management**	
(a)	Assess the impact of the different risk appetites of stakeholders on performance management.	3
(b)	Evaluate how risk and uncertainty play an important role in long-term strategic planning and decision-making that relies on forecasts of exogenous variables.	3
(c)	Apply different risk analysis techniques in assessing business performance, such as maximin, maximax, minimax regret, and expected values.	3
B2	**Impact of other external factors on performance management**	
(a)	Discuss the need to consider the environment in which an organisation is operating when assessing its performance, using models such as PEST and Porter's five forces, including areas such as: (i) Political climate (ii) Market conditions	2

Exam guide

Section B2 of the syllabus looks at the wider external environment in which an organisation operates. You should already be familiar with models such as PEST and Porter's five forces from your studies at Paper P3. Remember, however, that the way you need to apply these models in P5 will be different than in P3.

In P3 the focus was primarily on identifying opportunities and threats in the environment in order to evaluate an organisation's competitive position and then to develop or evaluate strategies designed to help the organisation respond to that position. In P5 the focus is on how the environment can affect the organisation's performance, or how an understanding of the environment will influence the aspects of performance which it is most important for an organisation to monitor. For example, if the bargaining power of customers is increasing, an organisation may need to reduce its selling price to retain those customers. In turn, this could help to explain a decrease in the organisation's gross profit margins, but it could also mean that it becomes increasingly important for the organisation to monitor gross profit margins to ensure they are not reduced so far that the organisation will no longer be profitable.

Exam focus point

In the June 2010 exam, one of the requirements asked candidates to work out expected values and comment on them. This shows that P5 builds on topics from F5, and so it would be worth looking again through your F5 material while preparing for P5 – even if this is just a relatively brief recap.

In the December 2011 exam, one of the requirements asked candidates to evaluate a project using 'metrics and methods for decision making under risk and uncertainty.' (By this, the examination team intended candidates to use maximin, maximax, minimax regret and expected values.) The question then asked candidates to assess the suitability of the different methods used. The examining team's report on the exam pointed out that most candidates knew the techniques they were required to apply, but unfortunately 'were not well practised in applying them'.

One of the elements which support Performance objective 14 – Monitor performance – is the need to 'Advise on the external influences affecting performance' of a department or a business.

Models such as PEST analysis and Porter's five forces, which we discuss in this chapter, could be very useful frameworks for identifying or assessing external influences which could be affecting performance.

1 Risk and uncertainty

FAST FORWARD

Risk and uncertainty must always be taken into account in strategic planning. Many areas of risk and uncertainty are **exogenous**; in other words, outside the control of the organisation.

Strategies, by definition, deal with future events and the future cannot be predicted. Strategic planning must therefore take risk and uncertainty into account.

Key terms

Risk is sometimes used to describe situations where outcomes are not known, but their **probabilities can be estimated**. (This is the underlying principle behind insurance.)

Uncertainty is present when the **outcome cannot be predicted or assigned probabilities**. (Many insurance policies exclude 'war damage, riots and civil commotion'.)

Exogenous variables are variables that are determined **externally**, for example the cost of a raw material imposed by the supplier.

It is important to note the distinction between risk and uncertainty. In a risk situation, the probability of an event occurring can be estimated. However, uncertainty implies a lack of knowledge about potential outcomes such that the probability of an event occurring cannot be predicted.

1.1 Types of risk and uncertainty

The emergence of additional competitors and the increasing globalisation of the marketplace coupled with shortening life cycles and increased dynamism in the business environment all contribute to increases in the potential levels of risk and uncertainty which businesses face.

However, more generally we can identify a number of different types of risk and uncertainty that a business may face.

Risk	Comment
Physical	Earthquakes, fire, flooding, and equipment breakdown. In the long term, risks can include climatic changes: global warming and drought (relevant to water firms).
Economic	Assumptions about the economic environment might turn out to be wrong. Not even the government forecasts are perfect.
Business	This could include lowering of entry barriers (eg new technology); changes in customer/supplier industries leading to changed relative power; new competitors and factors internal to the firm (eg its culture or technical systems); management misunderstanding of core competences; volatile cash flows; uncertain returns; and changed investor perceptions increasing the required rate of return.
Product life cycle	Different risks exist at different stages of the life cycle.
Political	Nationalisation, sanctions, civil war and political instability can all have an impact on the business.
Financial	**Financial risk** has a **specific technical meaning**: **the risk to shareholders caused by debt finance**. The risk exists because the debt finance providers have first call on the company's profits. The need to pay interest might prevent capital growth or the payment of dividends, particularly when trading is difficult. The converse is that when business is buoyant, interest payments are easily covered and shareholders receive the benefit of the remaining profits.

Exam focus point

A question in the December 2011 exam asked candidates to analyse the risks facing an organisation, and then discuss how the management team's attitude to risk might affect their response to those risks.

This requirement highlights the important point that different stakeholder groups are likely to have different attitudes towards risk and this, in turn, could create problems for an organisation when deciding whether or not to undertake a project, or deciding which of a range of different projects to undertake.

Stakeholders who have a high risk appetite (and are prepared to take bold, risky decisions) are likely to want the organisation to pursue different strategic options to stakeholders who are more risk averse, and would therefore prefer it to take more cautious decisions.

1.2 Accounting for risk

A firm might require that all investments make a return of, say, 5%. This can be adjusted for risk.

(a) **Return**. The target return could be raised to compensate for the risk.

(b) **Payback**. To protect cash flows, it might be made a condition of all new investment projects that the project should pay back within a certain period of time.

(c) **Finance**. It might be determined that the investment should be financed under strict conditions (eg only from profits).

Planners try to **quantify the risk** so as to compare the estimated riskiness of different strategies.

(a) **Rule of thumb** methods might express a range of values from worst possible result to best possible result with a best estimate lying between these two extremes.

(b) **Basic probability theory** expresses the likelihood of a forecast result occurring. This would evaluate the data given by informing the decision maker that there is, for example, a 50% probability that the best estimate will be achieved, a 25% chance that the worst result will occur and a 25% chance that the best possible result will occur. This evaluation of risk might help the executive to decide between alternative strategies, each with its own risk profile. A worked example is shown below.

(c) One way of measuring the dispersion or **spread of values** with different possible outcomes from a decision is to calculate a **standard deviation** of the expected value (EV) of profit. The higher the standard deviation, the higher the risk, as the EV is more volatile.

Decision rules are useful in strategic planning because they embody managerial attitudes to uncertainty. The **maximax** approach is optimistic, while the **maximin** is pessimistic. Remember that these rules are used under conditions of **uncertainty**, as is the **minimax regret** rule. If risk can be quantified, probabilistic methods such as decision trees may be used.

In terms of strategic planning, **decision trees** can be used to assess which choices are mutually exclusive, and to try to give them some quantitative value. As such, they are useful for three purposes:

(a) Clarifying strategic decisions when they are complex
(b) Using risk (in probability terms) as an input to quantifying the decision options
(c) Ranking the relative costs and benefits of the options

That said, many of the options in a decision may not be mutually exclusive, and the decision tree may inhibit a creative approach to a problem by assuming that they are. Finally, it is often easy to forget that an **EV is only useful for comparative purposes**, taking probability into account. It is **not a prediction** of an actual outcome. (If you toss a coin, there is a 50:50 chance of it turning heads; but in any one throw it will be either heads or tails, not a bit of both.)

1.3 Basic probability theory and expected values (EVs)

Where probabilities are assigned to different outcomes we can evaluate the worth of a decision as the **EV**, or weighted average, of these outcomes. The principle is that when there are a number of alternative decisions, each with a range of possible outcomes, the decision chosen will be the one which gives the highest EV.

However, a possible problem with using EVs is that assigning probabilities to events can be **highly subjective**. Yet the probabilities assigned to each potential outcome will be crucial in determining which decision is taken.

Formula to learn

The expected value (EV) of a decision is calculated as: **EV = $\sum$ p x**

where 'p' = the probability of an outcome occurring, and 'x' = the value (profit or cost) of that

1.3.1 Example: expected values

Suppose a manager has to choose between mutually exclusive options A and B, and the probable outcomes of each option are as follows.

Option A		*Option B*	
Probability	*Profit* $	*Probability*	*Profit* $
0.8	5,000	0.1	(2,000)
0.2	6,000	0.2	5,000
		0.6	7,000
		0.1	8,000

The EV of profit of each option would be measured as follows.

Option A					*Option B*				
Prob		*Profit* $		*EV of profit* $	*Prob*		*Profit* $		*EV of profit* $
0.8	×	5,000	=	4,000	0.1	×	(2,000)	=	(200)
0.2	×	6,000	=	1,200	0.2	×	5,000	=	1,000
		EV	=	5,200	0.6	×	7,000	=	4,200
					0.1	×	8,000	=	800
							EV	=	5,800

In this example, since it offers a higher EV of profit, option B would be selected in preference to A, unless further risk analysis is carried out.

Question — **Expected Values**

A manager has to choose between mutually exclusive options C and D and the probable costs of each option are as follows.

Option C		*Option D*	
Probability	*Cost* $	*Probability*	*Cost* $
0.29	15,000	0.03	14,000
0.54	20,000	0.30	17,000
0.17	30,000	0.35	21,000
		0.32	24,000

Both options will produce an income of $30,000. Which should be chosen?

Answer

Option C. Do the workings yourself in the way illustrated above. Note that the probabilities are for **costs**, not profits.

1.4 Risk preference

You may remember considering risk and uncertainty in Paper F5. We will revisit this here, as the examining team have indicated that they want students to understand this topic well. We also advise you to go back and read the whole chapter in the F5 Study Text when you have time, as it sets the context for our discussion of risk and uncertainty.

People may be **risk seekers**, **risk neutral** or **risk averse**.

Key terms

A **risk seeker** is a decision maker who is interested in trying to secure the best outcomes, no matter how small the chance that they may occur.

A decision maker is **risk neutral** if they are concerned with what will be the most likely outcome.

A **risk-averse** decision maker acts on the assumption that the worst outcome might occur.

In the previous chapter we identified the range of stakeholders that could influence an organisation's performance – including owners (shareholders) and managers – but it is important to recognise that different stakeholders may have different approaches to risk.

This has clear implications for managers and organisations. A **risk-seeking manager** working for an **organisation** that is characteristically **risk averse** is likely to make decisions that are **not congruent with the goals of the organisation**. There may be a role for the management accountant here, who could be instructed to present decision-making information in such a way as to ensure that the manager considers **all** the possibilities, including the worst.

1.4.1 Stakeholders' risk appetites 6/14

An understanding of risk appetite can be a useful tool for managing risk and enhancing overall business performance, by making sure that business decisions are aligned with risk appetite.

Risk appetite is the amount of risk an organisation is willing to take on or is prepared to accept in pursuing its strategic objectives. Risk appetite can vary between organisations, but it can also vary according to the type of risk incurred.

The concept of risk appetite is important in organisations because it helps to form a link between risk management strategy, target setting and business strategy.

However, it is also important to recognise that **different stakeholders have different risk appetites** or different perspectives on risk.

For example, equity investors are likely to want to see a return on their investments and may be prepared to support relatively high risk strategies if these strategies offer the prospect of high returns. By contrast, employees may prefer to see a lower risk strategy because they may feel it offers them greater security.

Consequently, articulating risk appetite is a complex task which requires the views of many different stakeholders to be considered (employees and management, shareholders, customers, suppliers, government and regulators, local community). Organisations need to take time to define the level and type of risk they are prepared to accept.

Equally importantly, there needs to be **clarity** over the **level of risk an organisation is prepared to accept**, so this needs to be communicated consistently to the different stakeholder groups.

This idea of risk appetite also has important consequences for management information and performance management requirements. On the one hand, it will mean that risks need to be measured and reported; but perhaps more importantly, new management information may be required to monitor risks across an organisation.

A critical issue is that management are able to gather sufficient data so that they can take **pre-emptive action before risk appetites are breached**. It is little use to report at the end of a month that risk appetite has been breached. However, it is of much greater value to take preventive action: for example through risk transfer (eg derivatives or swaps) or risk mitigation (eg insurance).

We can also look at the idea of risk appetite in relation to business strategy. For example, an organisation may have a management team that is very good at maintaining the business's current position, and ensuring that operations are run smoothly. However, such a company may find itself underperforming in terms of shareholder returns; and the management team may need to review its risk appetite in order to find new growth opportunities (for example, in terms of Ansoff's matrix, whether to pursue a market penetration strategy which is relatively low risk or whether to pursue a market development strategy which is higher risk but potentially offers greater rewards).

Exam focus point

> As the Exam focus point at the end of Section 1.1 noted, the level of risk which different stakeho' are prepared to accept could have a significant impact on their decisions as to whether or not a should be undertaken, or which projects should be chosen from a range of possible projects.
>
> This could be a particular issue where the directors and management team of an organisation have a differing attitude to risk to that of the shareholders. The concept of agency theory highlights that managers (agents) have a duty to act in the best interests of the owners of a company (shareholders; principals). However, if the two groups have significantly different attitudes to risk, this could mean, for example, that managers' decisions to accept or reject certain projects will differ from the decisions which the shareholders would have taken themselves. As such, are the managers still acting in the best interests of the shareholders?
>
> This issue of attitude to risk also has implications for the reward and remuneration systems in organisations (which we will look at in more detail in Chapter 14 of this Study Text). One of the key characteristics of reward systems is that they should help to align the risk preferences of directors and managers with those of the organisation and its owners, and one way which can help to achieve this is by granting share options to management.

Exam focus point

> One of the question scenarios in the June 2014 exam featured a joint venture in which the two venture partners had different risk appetites. The venture partners were in the process of evaluating different options for a capital investment, but their different risk appetites mean each would choose to use a different basis (eg maximax or maximin) for evaluating the options.
>
> The implication of this is that the differences in their risk appetites (and therefore the bases they used for evaluating the options) lead to the two venture partners each preferring a different option to the other. In turn, this creates problems for the joint venture as a whole in deciding which option to choose.

1.5 Decision rules 12/11

FAST FORWARD

> The 'play it safe' basis for decision making is referred to as the **maximin basis**. This is short for '**maximise the minimum achievable profit**'.
>
> A basis for making decisions by looking for the best outcome is known as the **maximax basis**, short for '**maximise the maximum achievable profit**'.
>
> The 'opportunity loss' basis for decision making is known as **minimax regret**.

When looking at potential business decisions, a decision maker has to consider both the potential downsides (risks and losses which could be incurred) and the potential upsides (gains) of a particular course of action.

However, the decision outcome resulting from the same information may vary from one decision maker to another as a result of their individual attitude to risk and reward.

As we noted in the previous section, we can distinguish (in general terms) between people who are risk averse and those who are risk seeking. However, more specifically, an individual's attitude to risk can also determine the decision-making criteria which they think are most appropriate to make decisions.

We can illustrate this by looking at three different criteria: maximin, maximax and minimax regret.

1.5.1 Maximin decision rule

Key term

> The **maximin decision rule** suggests that a decision maker should select the alternative that offers the least unattractive worst outcome. This would mean choosing the alternative that **maximises** the **minimum** profits.

Suppose a businessman is trying to decide which of three mutually exclusive projects to undertake. Each of the projects could lead to varying net profit under three possible scenarios.

		Profits		
			Project	
		D	*E*	*F*
	I	100	80	60
Scenarios	II	90	120	85
	III	(20)	10	85

The maximin decision rule suggests that he should select the 'smallest worst result' that could happen. This is the decision criterion that managers should 'play safe' and either minimise their losses or costs, or else go for the decision which gives the higher minimum profits. If he selects project D the worst result is a loss of 20. The worst results for E and F are profits of 10 and 60 respectively. The best worst outcome is 60 and project F would therefore be selected (because this is a better 'worst possible' than either D or E).

However, Maximin has its problems:

(a) It is a risk-averse approach, but this may lead to it being **defensive** and **conservative**, a safety-first principle of avoiding the worst outcomes without taking into account opportunities for maximising profits.

(b) It ignores the **probability** of each different outcome taking place.

1.5.2 Maximax

Key term

> The **maximax criterion** looks at the best possible results. Maximax means 'maximise the maximum profit'.

Using the information above, the maximum profit for D is 100, for E is 120 and for F is 85.

Project E would be chosen if the maximax rule is followed.

Maximax also has its problems:

(a) It ignores probabilities.
(b) It is **over-optimistic**.

Question

Maximax and maximin

A company is considering which one of three alternative courses of action, A, B and C, to take. The profit or loss from each choice depends on which one of four economic circumstances, I, II, III or IV, will apply. The possible profits and losses, in thousands of pounds, are given in the following payoff table. Losses are shown as negative figures.

			Action	
		A	*B*	*C*
	I	70	60	70
Circumstance	II	–10	20	–5
	III	80	0	50
	IV	60	100	115

Required

State which action would be selected using each of the maximax and maximin criteria.

Answer

(a) The **best possible outcomes** are as follows.

A (circumstance III): 80

B (circumstance IV): 100

C (circumstance IV): 115

As 115 is the highest of these three figures, action C would be chosen using the maximax criterion.

(b) The **worst possible outcomes** are as follows.

A (circumstance II): –10

B (circumstance III): 0

C (circumstance II): –5

The best of these figures is 0 (neither a profit nor a loss), so action B would be chosen using the maximin criterion.

1.5.3 Minimax regret rule

Key term

The **minimax regret** rule aims to minimise the regret from making the wrong decision. **Regret** is the opportunity lost through making the wrong decision.

We first consider the extreme to which we might come to regret an action we had chosen.

Regret for any combination of action and circumstances	=	Profit for best action in those circumstances	–	Profit for the action actually chosen in those circumstances

The minimax regret decision rule is that the decision option selected should be the one which **minimises the maximum potential regret** for any of the possible outcomes.

Using the example in Section 4.1, a table of regrets can be compiled as follows.

		Project		
		D	*E*	*F*
Scenario	I	0	20*	40**
	II	30***	0	35
	III	105	75	0
Maximum regret		105	75	40

* 100 – 80 ** 100 – 60 *** 120 – 90

The **lowest** of maximum regrets is 40 with project F so project F would be selected if the minimax regret rule is used.

1.5.4 Contribution tables

Questions requiring application of the decision rules often incorporate a **number of variables, each with a range of possible values**. For example, these variables might be:

- Unit price and associated level of demand
- Unit variable cost

Each variable might have, for example, three possible values.

Before being asked to use the decision rules, exam questions could ask you to **work out contribution** for each of the possible outcomes. (Alternatively, profit figures could be required if you are given information about fixed costs.)

The **number of possible outcomes** = number of values of variable 1 × number of values of variable 2 × number of values of variable 3 etc

So, for example, if there are **two** variables, each with **three** possible values, there are **3 × 3 = 9 outcomes**.

Perhaps the easiest way to see how to draw up contribution tables is to look at an example.

Example: contribution tables and the decision rules

Suppose the budgeted demand for product X will be 11,500 units if the price is $10, 8,500 units if the price is $12 and 5,000 units if the price is $14. Variable costs are estimated at either $4, $5 or $6 per unit. A decision needs to be made on the **price** to be charged.

Here is a contribution table showing the budgeted contribution for each of the nine possible outcomes.

Demand	*Price*	*Variable cost*	*Unit contribution*	*Total contribution*
	$	$	$	$'000
11,500	10	4	6	69.0
11,500	10	5	5	57.5
11,500	10	6	4	46.0
8,500	12	4	8	68.0
8,500	12	5	7	59.5
8,500	12	6	6	51.0
5,000	14	4	10	50.0
5,000	14	5	9	45.0
5,000	14	6	8	40.0

Once the table has been drawn up, the decision rules can be applied.

Solution

Maximin

We need to maximise the minimum contribution.

Demand/price	*Minimum contribution*
11,500/$10	$46,000
8,500/$12	$51,000
5,000/$14	$40,000

Set a price of $12.

Maximax

We need to maximise the maximum contribution.

Demand/price	*Maximum contribution*
11,500/$10	$69,000
8,000/$12	$68,000
5,000/$14	$50,000

Set a price of $10.

Minimax regret

We need to minimise the maximum regret (lost contribution) of making the wrong decision.

Variable cost		*Price*	
$	$10	$12	$14
4	–	$1,000	$19,000
5	$2,000	–	$14,500
6	$5,000	–	$11,000
Minimax regret	$5,000	$1,000	$19,000

Minimax regret strategy (**price of $12**) is that which minimises the maximum regret ($1,000).

Sample working

At a variable cost of $4, the best strategy would be a price of $10. Choosing a price of $12 would mean lost contribution of $69,000 – $68,000, while choosing a price of $14 would mean lost contribution of $69,000 – $50,000.

Exam focus point

At this point we also suggest you read the two articles 'The risks of uncertainty' (parts 1 and 2), available in the Technical Articles section for P5 on ACCA's website.

The first article looks at the use of probability in decision making, and revises expected values, dispersion (standard deviation), decision rules and decision trees. The second looks at the value of perfect information compared with the value of imperfect information, as well as the concept of value-at-risk.

At this level the articles should largely be revision, but it should still be useful to read them and work through the examples given in them.

2 Factors to consider when assessing performance

FAST FORWARD

A wide variety of **economic (market), political, cultural and legal factors** need to be taken into consideration when assessing performance. **PEST** (or PESTEL) analysis can be a useful framework for analysing the opportunities and threats present in the **macro-environment**.

Similarly, **Porter's five forces model** is a useful framework for analysing the **industry environment**, and the level of profits which can be sustained in an industry.

When we assess business performance, typically we look at how well an **individual organisation** is performing. Nonetheless, it is also important to consider the **context** in which that organisation operates, because that context has an impact on the organisation's own performance.

Two models which can be used to assess the context in which an organisation is operating are: **PEST** analysis (or PESTEL analysis), and **Porter's five forces** model.

You should be familiar with both of these models from your studies at P3 *Business Analysis*, but we will recap them here to illustrate why external factors need to be considered when assessing an organisation's performance.

2.1 PEST analysis

PEST analysis seeks to identify the main factors in the **macro-environment** which will affect an organisation's performance.

These factors have traditionally been broken down into four segments:

(a) Political
(b) Economic
(c) Socio-cultural
(d) Technological

Increasing public concern for the natural environment, corporate social responsibility and sustainability in recent years has led to the inclusion of a second 'E' in the mnemonic, standing for '**environment**'. Equally, when **legal** matters are now given their own heading (instead of being included with 'political'), the mnemonic becomes expanded to 'PESTEL'.

We will look at some of these factors in more detail in the rest of this section, but remember that in P5 the focus will not primarily be on how environmental factors will shape an organisation's strategic choices but rather on how the factors could help managers assess an organisation's performance. For example, if the Government in a country has just increased sales tax (a political factor, or possibly an economic factor), this could help explain a slowdown in an organisation's sales.

Nonetheless, do not forget that the factors identified through PEST analysis represent **opportunities** and **threats** which an organisation could face. These are likely to affect the strategy and behaviour of the organisation which, in turn, will affect the organisation's performance. Equally, an organisation's ability to respond more quickly to market opportunities or threats than its rivals could help give that organisation a competitive advantage over its rivals – with a corresponding improvement in the organisation's performance.

2.2 Political factors

(a) Does government policy encourage firms to increase/reduce capacity? Are incentives being offered to locate in a particular area?

(b) Is the organisation affected by government plans for divestment/rationalisation?

(c) Is government policy discouraging entry into an industry by restricting investment or competition or by making it harder, by use of quotas and tariffs, for overseas firms to compete in the domestic market?

(d) Is government policy affecting competition?

  (i) A government's purchasing decisions will have a strong influence on the strength of one firm relative to another in the market (such as in the armaments industry).

  (ii) Regulations and controls in the industry will affect the growth and profits in the industry (such as minimum product quality standards).

  (iii) Governments and supra-national institutions such as the EU might impose policies which keep an industry fragmented and prevent the concentration of too much market share in the hands of one or two producers.

(e) Does government regulate new products (such as pharmaceuticals)?

2.3 Economic environment

Gross domestic product

(a) Has it grown or fallen?
(b) How has demand for goods/services been affected by the growth/fall?

Local economic trends

(a) Are local businesses rationalising or expanding?
(b) Are office/factory rents increasing/falling?
(c) In what direction are house prices moving?
(d) Are labour rates on the increase?

Inflation

(a) Is a high rate making it difficult to plan, owing to the uncertainty of future financial returns? Inflation and expectations of it help to explain short-termism.

(b) Is the rate depressing consumer demand?

(c) Is the rate encouraging investment in domestic industries?

(d) Is a high rate leading employees to demand higher money wages to compensate for a fall in the value of their wages?

Interest rates

(a) How do these affect consumer confidence and liquidity, and therefore demand?
(b) Is the cost of borrowing increasing, thereby reducing profitability?

Exchange rates

(a) What impact do these have on the cost of overseas imports?
(b) Are prices that can be charged to overseas customers affected?

Government fiscal policy

(a) Are consumers increasing/decreasing the amount they spend due to tax and government spending decisions?
(b) How is the Government's corporation tax policy affecting the organisation?
(c) Is sales tax (VAT in the UK) affecting demand?

Government spending

Is the organisation a supplier to the Government and therefore affected by the level of spending?

Business cycle

(a) Is the economy booming or in recession?
(b) Does the organisation follow the business cycle or is it in a counter-cyclical industry?
(c) What is the forecast state of the economy?

International factors

How do the characteristics of overseas markets affect demand/supply?

2.4 Socio-cultural factors

Culture in a society can be divided into **subcultures** reflecting social differences.

Subculture	Comment
Class	People from different social classes might have different values reflecting their position of society.
Ethnic background	Some ethnic groups can still be considered a distinct cultural group.
Religion	Religion and ethnicity are related.
Geography or region	Distinct regional differences might be brought about by the past effects of physical geography (socio-economic differences etc). Speech accents most noticeably differ.
Age	Changing age profiles in a country could change the demand for different products and services (for example, pensions and life insurance).
Gender	Some products are targeted directly at women or at men.
Work	Different organisations have different corporate cultures, in that the shared values of one workplace may be different from another.

Cultural change might have to be planned for. There has been a revolution in attitudes to female employment, despite the well-publicised problems of discrimination that still remain.

Knowledge of the culture of a society is clearly of value to businesses in a number of ways. These have an **effect on performance**.

(a) **Culture influences tastes and lifestyles** and therefore influences the sorts of products and services a business should offer.

(b) **Marketers** can adapt their products accordingly, and be fairly sure of a sizeable market. This is particularly important in export markets.

(c) **Human resource managers** may need to tackle cultural differences in recruitment. For example, some ethnic minorities have a different body language from the majority, which may be hard for some interviewers to interpret.

Socio-cultural factors as threats and opportunities

Pension funds

In the UK, medical advances over the last few decades which have prolonged life spans have led to an ageing population.

This ageing population means that the pensions industry now has to support a greater number of pensioners for longer periods than it has historically had to. In turn this has raised concerns over an impending pensions crisis, in which there is not enough money invested in pension funds to guarantee a comfortable retirement for today's working population.

The Government's Actuarial Department calculated that, in 2001, there were 3.32 people of working age to support every State pensioner. However, it has estimated that by 2060 this ratio will have fallen to 2.44 people of working age for every State pensioner.

However, the problems facing the pensions industry don't only come from demographic factors. The problems have been exacerbated in recent years by falling stock market returns. Pension funds depend on steady stock market returns to pay policyholders, but when share prices fall (as they have done during and after the global economic downturn from 2007 to 2010) it becomes harder for pension funds to meet their obligations.

Saga

Although the ageing population is causing problems for pension funds, companies like The Saga Group are benefiting from the change.

Saga has focused its business on providing a wide range of services (from insurance to cruise holidays) exclusively for people aged 50 and over.

Saga is therefore in a prime position to take advantage of the increasing numbers of older people as consumers, especially as they could become a dominant segment of the consumer market in the future.

2.5 Technological factors

Organisations have to adapt themselves in response to technological change in the environment.

Technological change can affect the activities of organisations in a number of ways.

(a) **The type of products or services** that are made and sold. For example, in recent years, consumer markets have seen the emergence of smartphones, tablet computers, e-books and 3D television, while car manufacturers are looking at alternative sources of fuel to petrol. Technological change can have a direct impact on a product's life cycle and, consequently, demand for the product.

(b) **The way in which products are made**:

   (i) Modern production equipment reduces the need for labour. Also, as technology increases manufacturing productivity, more people become involved in service jobs rather than manufacturing ones.

   (ii) Technology can also develop new raw materials.

(c) The **way in which services are provided**; for example, rather than booking a holiday through a travel agency, consumers can now book holidays directly over the internet.

(d) The **way in which firms are managed**. IT has helped in the 'delayering' of organisational hierarchies, and it has also facilitated the emergence of network and virtual organisations.

(e) The means and extent of **communications** with external clients can be affected by technological change.

(f) The **way in which products are sold** – particularly the growth of e-commerce.

2.6 Legal factors

(a) **Employment law.** What is the impact of Social Charter provisions? Minimum wage? Anti-discriminatory legislation?

(b) **Marketing and sales.** How do laws that protect consumers (such as on refunds and replacements) affect the organisation?

(c) **Environment.** Do laws on pollution control and waste disposal affect the organisation?

(d) **Regulators.** Is the organisation in an industry subject to regulators (such as electricity, gas and water) who have influence over market access, competition and pricing policy?

2.7 Porter's five forces model

In the same way that factors in the macro-environment can affect an organisation's performance, so can the level of competition in the industry in which the organisation operates.

Porter argued that the state of competition in an industry, and therefore the ability of that industry **as a whole to sustain profits**, is determined by **five competitive forces**.

(a) The threat of **new entrants** to the industry
(b) The threat of **substitute** products or services
(c) The bargaining power of **customers**
(d) The bargaining power of **suppliers**
(e) The **rivalry** among current competitors in the industry

In turn, the threat of new entrants depends on the extent of the **barriers to entry** to the industry. These might be, for example, the economies of scale of existing producers, the level of capital expenditure required to enter the industry, or regulation such as patents or copyrights held by existing organisations.

Porter argues that the **stronger each of the five competitive forces**, the **lower the profitability of an industry**. For example, if there are a number of competitors of a similar size in an industry, but the industry is in the mature stage of its life cycle and the rate of market growth is low, there is likely to be high rivalry between the competitors. One firm can only grow by obtaining market share at the expense of its competitors, so firms will be keen to ensure that the price of their products and the quality or features of their products matches that of their competitors. However, this intensity of competitors between the firms in this industry is likely to mean that profitability levels are lower than in an industry dominated by a monopoly producer and therefore in which there is no significant competitive rivalry.

The significance of Porter's model for assessing an organisation's own performance is that it reminds us that the organisation's **performance needs to be assessed in the context of its industry**. For example, if a government is about to deregulate an industry, it is likely that there will be a number of new entrants into the industry. This could lead to the pre-existing organisations in the industry reducing their prices to deal with the threat from the new entrants, which could in turn lead to lower margins and profitability.

Simply looking at the firm's results (lower margins and profitability) might suggest that there are problems with the firm's operational processes which have led to a decline in performance. However, considering the external environment will help explain the reasons for the lower margins and profitability, especially if the other pre-existing organisations in the industry have experienced similar reductions in margins and profitability.

Telecommunications in Zambia

The telecommunications market in Zambia is dominated by three operators, MTN Zambia, Airtel, and Zamtel (the government-run Zambia Telecommunication Company). MTN Zambia is the market leader, with just over 50% of the country's mobile phone market. Airtel is the second largest provider, holding around 35% market share, while Zamtel has approximately 15%.

In 2012 the Zambian Government appeared to have cleared the way for a fourth mobile service provider, and by early 2013 bids had been received from five telecom operators, including Vodacom of South Africa.

The Government believed that the entry of a fourth provider would increase competition in the sector, generate sustainable improvements in the quality of services, reduce tariffs, and extend service outreach to more areas. In particular, the Government was concerned with the high cost of making phone calls, and felt that the increased competition from a fourth mobile service provider could help reduce call tariffs.

However, in August 2013, the Zambian Government announced that plans to award the fourth mobile licence had been put on hold until the completion of the country's digital migration project in 2015. (In line with the Southern African Development Community's deadline, Zambia plans to migrate to digital television services by 2015.)

In July 2015, ZICTA (the Zambia Information and Communication Technology Authority) noted that the country's mobile phone market had been growing at a faster than expected rate in recent months. The Authority also said that increased competition in the provision of mobile phone services had resulted in the reduction of the tariffs and the growth of the subscriber base. ZICTA highlighted how the liberalisation of the international gateway for the three operators has promoted competition in Zambia's information and communication technology sector.

Prior to 2010, Zamtel had monopoly rights over the international gateway – the satellite system for making international calls – so the other providers had to pay a gateway fee to Zamtel for using the system. However, in 2010, the Zambian Government awarded the private mobile phone operators licences to operate their own international gateways, in order to force down the high costs of communication and thereby to make international calls and international roaming more attractive.

In mid-2010 a majority stake in Zamtel was sold to LAP Green of Libya (although this sale was subsequently challenged, and Zamtel reverted to a State-owned company). One of Zamtel's key assets is a national fibre optic cable network, because cable networks are required to develop internet usage in the country.

Internet penetration in Zambia is still very low. Market research in 2014 suggested that only 16% of the country's population had internet access, compared to 91% of them using mobile phones. There is still a perception that data services are the preserve of the elite, and ZICTA has said that there is a need for heavy investment in broadband and cable networks to alleviate the country's digital divide, and to help Zambian companies to grow and compete on a global level.

Analysing the five forces

As you read the case study, try to think about what the key forces are that might influence the profitability of the mobile telecommunications industry in Zambia – for example regulatory environment and structural reform; infrastructure development; competitive rivalry between key players; development of new technologies; pricing trends – and think about how these could affect the profitability of the industry.

Threat of new entrants – Two main barriers to entry into the telecoms industry can be distinguished.

Firstly, in order to assume the high fixed costs characteristic of this capital intensive industry, potential new entrants must have a high level of cash in hand. The availability of funds, or the ability to raise funds through capital markets, can therefore exert a direct influence on the industry players.

Secondly, regulatory approval and licensing can be seen as a massive barrier to entry. However, the liberalisation of the markets opens up the opportunity for new entrants to join the market.

Suppliers' power – Key suppliers will be the telecommunication equipment makers (for example, suppliers of fibre optic cables and handset manufacturers). Their bargaining power is likely to be determined by how

many alternative suppliers exist for each type of equipment. If there are a number of competing suppliers, this will reduce their bargaining power over the telecoms companies. However, because the manufacturing and delivering of some of these products requires a high degree of knowledge and expertise, this could sometimes increase the suppliers' bargaining power.

Customers' power – Market liberalisation is likely to increase competition and broaden consumers' choice of supplier. This increased choice is also likely, in turn, to boost technology advances and enhance services, but it will also drive prices down. Therefore liberalisation will increase customers' power in the telecommunications industry. Nevertheless, high switching costs on certain market segments, such as business segments, can reduce buyers' power.

Threat of substitutes – The threat of multiple products and services from non-traditional telecoms industries has raised serious challenges to telecommunications players. For example, the development of the Voice over Internet Protocol (VoIP) has meant that the internet has become a way of making cut-price (and in some cases, free) phone calls, to the detriment of the more traditional phone business (delivered by telecoms companies).

Competitive rivalry – Market liberalisation (industry deregulation), breakthrough innovations and new technologies, together with attractive economic indicators (eg growth rates), can contribute to the creation of intense rivalry between players in the industry.

2.8 Government – a sixth force?

The activities and influence of government would normally be analysed using the PEST model but it could also be useful to reconsider the influence of government in the context of a particular industry and market.

There is also the consideration that competition itself is often the target of specific government policies, either to encourage it or, quite often, to restrict it.

Porter argues that the best approach is to assess the impact of government on one or more of the five forces, rather than viewing it as a separate sixth force. However, some commentators have argued that the five forces should be extended to include the influence of government as a separate 'sixth' force.

Exam focus point

It is important that you understand how the impact of a particular force, or a PEST element, could vary over time.

The environmental context in which organisations operate is dynamic rather than static, and changes in the environment could have a significant impact on an organisation's performance.

Chapter Roundup

- **Risk and uncertainty** must always be taken into account in strategic planning. Many areas of risk and uncertainty are **exogenous**; in other words, outside the control of the organisation.
- The 'play it safe' basis for decision making is referred to as the **maximin basis**. This is short for '**maximise the minimum achievable profit**'.
- A basis for making decisions by looking for the best outcome is known as the **maximax basis**, short for '**maximise the maximum achievable profit**'.
- The 'opportunity loss' basis for decision making is known as **minimax regret**.
- A wide variety of **economic (market), political, cultural and legal factors** need to be taken into consideration when assessing performance. **PEST** (or PESTEL) analysis can be a useful framework for analysing the opportunities and threats present in the **macro-environment**.
- Similarly, **Porter's five forces model** is a useful framework for analysing the **industry environment**, and the level of profits which can be sustained in an industry.

Quick Quiz

1 When choosing between different strategic options to pursue, the CEO of a company always makes their decision based on the best outcomes that could occur from each option, however small the chance that those outcomes will occur.

(a) What is the CEO's attitude to risk?
(b) Which decision rule is the CEO most likely to use for evaluating different options?

2 The senior management team at BNM Co, who have a risk-neutral attitude to decision making, are trying to decide which one of four mutually exclusive projects to invest in.

BNM Co's management accountant has identified three possible outcomes for each project: worst, most likely and best.

He has constructed the following payoff table:

	Net profit in $'000 if outcome turns out to be:		
Project	**Worst**	**Most Likely**	**Best**
A	80	150	290
B	90	180	270
C	100	160	250
D	120	140	230

Which project should the management team choose to invest in?

3 A company needs to invest in a new machine, but is currently trying to decide whether to buy a like for like replacement for its existing medium-sized machine, or to buy a new, larger machine instead which can also make a more advanced version of its products.

The company is unsure what the level of demand for the products will be, but has estimated three possible levels of demand: high, medium and low. The probability of achieving the high demand is 0.3; medium is 0.4 and low is 0.3.

The table below shows the expected profits from production using the two machines at each of the three levels of demand.

$'000	High demand	Medium demand	Low demand
Medium-sized machine	300	270	240
Larger machine	400	250	200

Which machine has the higher expected value for the company?

4 CMN Co's profitability has fallen in recent years, as has the profitability of the other companies in the industry in which CMN Co operates.

Which of the following is the most likely explanation for the reduction in profitability in the industry?

A Two of CMN's competitors in the industry have recently ceased trading.

B The industry is supplied by a large number of suppliers who are relatively small compared to CMN.

C Several key patents held by existing firms in the industry (including CMN) have recently expired.

D Potential new entrants need to commit a high level of capital expenditure in order to establish themselves in the industry.

5 Which one of the following would be most likely to result in a company's customers having a low bargaining power?

A The company's product is a luxury item rather than a necessity.
B The company is the sole supplier of a product with no apparent substitutes.
C The company is suffering financial difficulties.
D Information about alternative products is readily available to customers, and switching costs are low.

Answers to Quick Quiz

1 (a) **Risk seeker**. The CEO is trying to secure the best outcome, even if there is only a very small chance that this outcome may actually occur.

(b) **Maximax**. The CEO focuses on the best possible results, which suggest they are likely to want to maximise the maximum profit available.

2 B

The management team are risk neutral, and are therefore concerned with the most likely outcomes, and Project B offers the most profitable outcome here (of $180,000).

3 The **larger machine** has the higher expected value.

Medium-sized machine: (300 × 0.3) + (270 × 0.4) + (240 × 0.3) = 270

Larger machine: (400 × 0.3) + (250 × 0.4) + (200 × 0.3) = 280

4 C Several key patents held by existing firms in the industry (including CMN) have recently expired.

The expiry of a patent would remove a key barrier to entry into the industry, and would therefore allow new entrants to join the industry. The arrival of new competitors would increase the level of competition in the industry which in turn would be expected to reduce the level of profitability which can be sustained.

If existing competitors leave the industry (as in Option A) the level of competition could be expected to reduce.

Option B describes a situation in which the bargaining power of suppliers would be low (which should enable the level of profits to be maintained).

Option D describes a situation in which the barriers to entry are high, and therefore the threat of new entrants should be low.

5 B The company is the sole supplier of a product with no apparent substitutes.

In these circumstances, a customer cannot buy the product – or a substitute product – from an alternative supplier, meaning that the customer has a low bargaining power.

The other options would create a high bargaining power for customers.

Now try the question below from the Practice Question Bank

Number	Level	Marks	Approximate time
Q6	Examination	20	40 mins

P A R T C

Performance measurement systems and design

7

Performance management information systems

Topic list		Syllabus reference
1	Accounting information needs for planning, control and decision making	-
2	Information requirements and management structure	C1(a)
3	Objectives of management accounting and management accounting information	C1(b)
4	Management accounting information within the management information system	C1(c)
5	Lean management information systems	C1(d)
6	Human behaviour and management accounting systems	C1(e)
7	Information and responsibility accounting	-

Introduction

This chapter is the first of two covering Part C of the syllabus – discussing issues relating to **performance measurement systems and their design**.

This chapter looks primarily at the systems themselves, while the next chapter looks at the sources of information which goes into the systems and the outputs from them.

We begin with a look at the **accounting information needs** at all levels of the organisation. Then we consider how information needs are **shaped by the organisational structure**. Moving on, we look at **the objectives of management accounting information** and the importance of ensuring that an organisation's information systems can produce the management accounting information required.

As you work through this chapter, try to think how the information systems we are discussing could help an organisation with the issues of strategic planning, management control and operational control which we considered in Chapter 1.

Study guide

		Intellectual level
C1	**Performance management information systems**	
(a)	Discuss, with reference to performance management, ways in which the information requirements of a management structure are affected by the features of the structure.	2
(b)	Evaluate the compatibility of management accounting objectives and management accounting information systems.	3
(c)	Discuss the integration of management accounting information within an overall information system, for example the use of enterprise resource planning systems.	2
(d)	Evaluate whether management information systems are lean and the value of the information they provide.	3
(e)	Evaluate how anticipated human behaviour will influence the design of a management accounting system.	3

Exam guide

Management accounting and information systems are an important part of the P5 syllabus, because they play an integral part in producing the information which managers use for performance measurement and performance management.

Performance management information systems provide the information which enables performance measurement to take place. The syllabus for P5 requires that candidates should be able to 'evaluate the compatibility of management accounting objectives and the management accounting information systems' in an organisation. One of the key issues this could raise in an exam question scenario is: To what extent does an organisation's management accounting information system provide managers with the information they need for planning, control and decision making within the organisation?

Performance objective 12 (PO 12) of the PER requires you to evaluate management accounting systems.

Two elements of the objective are particularly relevant to the issues we will discuss in this chapter and the following chapter in the Study Text:

PO 12(c): 'Assess and advise on the impact of the output of an organisation's management accounting and information systems'

PO 12(d): 'Contribute to development and improvements of management accounting systems and internal reporting'

A key point to note in this context is that the quality of an organisation's management information systems are likely to have a significant impact on the accountant's ability to provide managers with the information they require. This could be an issue which you face in the workplace, just as much as it could be an issue with the information systems being described in a case study scenario in an exam question.

Exam focus point

Exam questions on the topics in this chapter are likely to require written rather than computational answers, as the topics mainly require you to **discuss, evaluate** or **assess** certain aspects of management accounting and information systems. For example, as we noted in the Exam Guide above, how well does the system in an organisation provide management with the information they need?

Part of one of the compulsory questions in the December 2010 exam asked candidates to discuss the implications of a business's key performance indicators for the design and use of a company's website, management information system and executive information system. In effect, the question is asking how the systems can help provide performance information which management can then use to monitor how well the business is performing against its key indicators.

1 Accounting information needs for planning, control and decision making

FAST FORWARD

Management accounting information can be used to support strategic planning, control and decision making. Strategic management accounting differs from traditional management accounting because it has an **external** orientation and a **future** orientation.

Management control is at the level below strategic planning in Anthony's decision-making hierarchy and is concerned with decisions about the efficient and effective use of resources to achieve objectives.

Operational control, the lowest tier in Anthony's hierarchy, is concerned with ensuring that specific tasks are carried out effectively and efficiently.

Knowledge brought forward from earlier studies

The syllabus for **F5** identifies that candidates need to be able to identify the accounting information requirements for **strategic** planning, **management** control and **operational** control and decision making.

However, we will recap some of the key points here, because it is important to recognise that the **level** at which information is being used (ie strategic, management or operational) will affect the **nature** of the information required.

The Anthony hierarchy provides a useful framework for distinguishing between the levels at which information could be required in an organisation.

Strategic planning. Strategic planning is concerned with setting a future course of action for an organisation. This often includes defining an organisation's strategy and its objectives (or any changes to those objectives) and allocating the resources required to achieve its objectives.

Management (or **tactical**) **control**. Management control is concerned with the decisions managers take about the way resources are obtained and used effectively and efficiently in order to achieve an organisation's strategic objectives.

Operational control (or **operational planning**). Operational controls are concerned with ensuring that specific tasks are carried out effectively and efficiently.

	Focus of information	Nature of information	Sources of information
Strategic level	Focus on planning; future orientation	Broad brush; relatively unstructured Long term (usually between one and five years) Uncertain	Mostly external
Tactical (management) level	Some planning, but greater focus on control Focus on resources, and the efficiency and effectiveness of their use	Concerned with how to use resources to achieve targets set at strategic level Setting benchmarks and performance yardsticks (eg budgets) Short to medium term	Largely internal (and usually prepared regularly; perhaps weekly or monthly; eg variance reports vs budget)
Operational level	Focus on control (rather than planning)	Narrowly defined, highly structured Short term (day to day) Detailed; high level of accuracy (needs to be consolidated into totals in order to prepare management control information) Often expressed in terms of units, hours, quantities of material etc rather than in monetary terms	Internal Often includes 'transaction data': customer orders, purchase orders, receipts, payments etc

This comparison between the three levels illustrates the importance of ensuring that the information is tailored to the needs of the manager or decision maker who is going to be using it. For example, detailed operational performance information is unlikely to be any help for members of the board who are considering growth strategies for the next five years.

We can illustrate the link between strategic plans and operational/management control decisions in the following simple example.

Senior management may decide that the company should increase sales by 5% per year for at least the next five years. This is a **strategic plan**.

The sales director and senior sales managers will make plans to increase sales by 5% in the next year, with some provisional planning for future years. This involves planning direct sales resources, advertising, sales promotions, and so on. Sales quotas are assigned to each sales territory. These are **tactical management control** decisions.

The manager of a sales territory specifies the weekly sales targets for each sales representative. This is an **operational control** decision. Individuals are given specific targets and tasks which they are expected to achieve.

However, alongside the general distinction between the different levels of information, it is also important to consider how information requirements might vary in different types of organisation.

For example, in decentralised organisations, divisional performance measures become particularly important for control purposes.

2 Information requirements and management structure

FAST FORWARD

Each manager needs to be given information according to what their **responsibilities** are.

Management structure varies considerably between different types of entity, but information requirements also vary considerably between different types of structure.

We looked at different organisation forms in Chapter 4, and suggested some of the information requirements for each type of structure, so this section should recap some of those ideas.

(a) A company might be structured on a **divisional** basis as follows:

   (i) A **holding company** board of directors.

   (ii) **Subsidiary companies**, each with its own board of directors. Each subsidiary might be either a division of the company, or a separate company in its own right.

   For example, the Berkshire Hathaway group has a diverse range of subsidiaries which include:

   (1) Insurance – General Re, Guard Insurance Group
   (2) Clothing – Fruit of the Loom
   (3) Building products – Johns Manville; Acme Brick Company
   (4) Retail – The Pampered Chef
   (5) Private airlines – NetJets

   In such a structure, information will be needed to measure **how well each division is performing**; for example, by looking at the return on investment (ROI) of each division.

(b) By contrast, a company might be organised on a **functional** basis as follows:

   (i) Manufacturing
   (ii) Sales and marketing
   (iii) Administration

   Under this type of structure, information will be needed to measure the **operational efficiency** of each of the functions.

   How does this affect the information requirements of managers in the different structures?

   The **divisional manager** needs to be fully informed about all aspects of the division's activities because they are responsible for selling strategy, manufacturing strategy, investment policy, and so on.

   The **functional manager** is only responsible for a part of their organisation's activities, and so only needs to be supplied with detailed information if it concerns their own function. The functional manager needs to be aware of how other functions are performing only insofar as their own function's activities need to be co-ordinated with those of other functions.

(c) **Network organisations**

   Network organisations combine a central 'core' with a mosaic of productive relationships outside the formal structure of the core organisation.

   This provides a looser, more fluid structure than can be achieved under organic structures (functional or divisional structures), and so can allow organisations to achieve innovative responses to changing circumstances.

   The network approach is also visible in the growing field of **outsourcing** as a strategic method. Complex relationships can be developed between firms, which may both buy from and sell to each other, as well as the simpler, more traditional practice of buying in services such as cleaning.

   Virtual teams are interconnected groups of people who may not be in the same office (or even the same organisation) but who:

   - Share information and tasks
   - Make joint decisions
   - Fulfil the collaborative function of a team

Organisations are now able to structure their activities very differently and this has **consequences for their information requirements**. The **interdependence** of organisations is emphasised by the sharing of functions and services. Databases and communication tools (such as extranets) create genuine interactive sharing of, and access to, common data.

In a network structure it is important that information is available to show how each of the network partners is performing. And details of this actual performance should be measured against goals and targets, for example those set in a service level agreement.

(d) **Virtual organisations**

Virtual organisations can be seen as an extension of the idea of network organisations, although truly virtual organisations do not have any physical presence.

There is some disagreement among academics as to a precise definition of the virtual organisation, but a consensus exists with regard to **geographical dispersion** and the centrality of **information technology** to the production process. Many also agree that the virtual organisation has a temporary character. Other characteristics are a **flexible structure** and a **collaborative culture**.

However, an organisation is not a virtual organisation merely because it uses IT extensively and has multiple locations.

Certainly **information requirements** would require the **integration of IT systems** so that information is communicated across the virtual organisation equally to all members. One aspect of virtual organisations is the remoteness of personnel. This means that collecting data, especially on performance, relies on excellent links, setting measures that can capture outworker performance such as regular reporting and some degree of trust that people are performing. However, because virtual teams can be composed of people working remotely, then selecting the members of virtual teams can sometimes be just as important an issue as managing and assessing their performance.

Case Study — **Amazon.com**

Amazon.com is the most commonly cited example of a virtual organisation.

Customers come to the Amazon website via Internet Service Providers (ISPs), often from links on other (affiliate) websites. Amazon processes the customer orders; it does not hold the inventory itself. If a customer orders a book through Amazon it is likely the book will be despatched from the publisher's warehouse, and the delivery will be handled by a logistics or mail company. Nonetheless, the customer feels they are dealing with one organisation (Amazon), not many different companies.

But for this relationship to work, Amazon needs information from its partners – for example, it needs to know inventory availability and an estimate of delivery times so that it can provide this information for the customer when they make their order. Equally, Amazon needs to be confident that its partners will deliver the service they have agreed to provide (for example, if a partner says inventory will be available in 48 hours, then it needs to be available in 48 hours).

(e) **Flexible firms**

Network structures are also discerned between competitors, where **co-operation on non-core competence matters** can lead to several benefits.

- Cost reduction
- Increased market penetration
- Experience curve effects

A growth in the proportion of the workforce employed on temporary contracts, or on a freelance basis, has produced the phenomenon of the **flexible firm** or, as Handy calls it, the **shamrock organisation**.

Handy defines the **shamrock organisation** as a 'core of essential executives and workers supported by outside contractors and part-time help'. This structure permits the buying-in of services as needed, with consequent reductions in overhead costs.

The first leaf of the shamrock is the **professional core**. It consists of professionals, technicians and managers whose skills define the organisation's core competence. This core group defines what the company does and what business it is in. They are essential to the continuity and growth of the organisation. Their pay is tied to organisational performance and their relations will be more like those among the partners in a professional firm than those among superiors and subordinates in today's large corporation.

The next leaf is made up of **self-employed professionals or technicians** or smaller specialised organisations that are hired on contract, on a project by project basis. They are paid in fees for results rather than in salary for time. They frequently **telecommute**. No benefits are paid by the core organisation, and the worker carries the risk of insecurity.

The third leaf comprises the **contingent workforce**, whose employment derives from the external demand for the organisation's products. There is no career track for these people and they perform routine jobs. They are usually temporary and part-time workers who will experience short periods of employment and long periods of unemployment. They are paid by the hour or day or week for the time they work.

A fourth leaf of the shamrock may exist, consisting of **consumers** who do the work of the organisation. Examples are shoppers who bag their own groceries and purchasers of assemble it yourself furniture.

(f) **Alliances**

The very great cost advantages available from economies of scale are a major driver of expansion. Indeed, the minimum efficient scale for capital intensive industries such as motor vehicle manufacture is so high that operations on at least a continental scale are necessary to achieve it. Such a degree of expansion requires huge amounts of capital; various forms of **complex organisation** result from the pressure to pool resources. These include relatively informal relationships (such as alliances in which the research and development (R&D) departments of the partners work together to improve technologies), as well as **joint ventures** and more formalised link-ups, such as **takeovers** and **mergers**. However, formalised alliances do not always lead to an integration of the structures and organisations involved.

An example of this was the merger between Daimler and Chrysler (which we mentioned in Chapter 4). The merged entity preserved much of the structure of the two companies involved, to the extent of having two chief executives and, in effect, running two independent production lines. (Ultimately, the failure to integrate the two companies meant that the Daimler Chrysler merger failed to produce the transatlantic automotive powerhouse that had been hoped for, and Chrysler was sold to a private equity firm in 2007, before eventually filing for bankruptcy in April 2009.)

Structures such as franchises and joint ventures inevitably depend on the **management of relationships**, though the legal form can vary from loose co-operation on more or less market terms to joint ownership.

The main problem of such structural relationships is the **integration of knowledge** to create a successful product. This becomes more difficult as the number of partners increases. Information requirements for performance management centre on the sharing of profits and losses, recording of data agreed by all parties and the sharing of that data. However, information requirements are not confined solely to financial performance: alliance partners may also need to agree a common approach to marketing for example.

In some cases, the alliances may also involve the integration of core operating systems. For example, the Oneworld alliance brings together ten of the world's biggest airlines, including American Airlines, British Airways, Cathay Pacific and Qantas. The alliance allows them to offer an integrated service, including code-sharing and the common use of passenger terminals. In order to achieve this, each individual airline's booking system needs to be linked to its partners' systems.

3 Objectives of management accounting and management accounting information

FAST FORWARD

Management accounting information is used by managers for a variety of purposes: performance measurement and **control, planning, and decision making**. The effectiveness of the management accounting systems in an organisation can be assessed in relation to how well they provide managers with the information they need.

As an introduction to this section, let us consider a definition of accounting.

'The process of identifying, measuring and communicating economic information to permit informed judgements and decisions by users of the information.' (American Accounting Association)

This definition reinforces the role that accounting plays in providing information **to enable decision makers to make good decisions**.

3.1 The objectives of management accounting

As its name implies, management accounting involves the **provision of information for managers to use** to assist in their decision making and to help ensure the smooth running of their organisations. The main distinction between management accounting, financial accounting and cost accounting is:

Management accounting systems provide information specifically for the use of managers within the organisation.

Financial accounting provides information to shareholders and to other interested parties who are external to the organisation.

Cost accounting systems aim primarily to accumulate costs for inventory valuation to meet the requirements of external reporting to shareholders.

However, the need for management accounting information is clear, because managers need information that financial accounting systems and cost accounting systems on their own do not provide.

(a) Managers need more **detailed** information, to help them to run the business.
(b) They also need **forward-looking** information, for planning.
(c) They will want data to be **analysed differently**, to suit their specific requirements for information.

3.2 The objectives of management accounting information

Management accounting information is used by managers for a variety of purposes.

(a) **To measure performance**. Management accounting information can be used to analyse the performance of the business as a whole, or that of individual divisions, departments or products within the business. Performance reports provide **feedback**, most frequently in the form of comparison between actual performance and budget.

Management accounting information can also be used to assess the performance of individuals within an organisation; for example, whether a manager has achieved certain goals or targets which they need to achieve in order to earn a bonus.

(b) **To control the business**. Performance reports are a crucial element in controlling a business. In order to be able to control their business, managers need to know the following:

(i) What they want the business to achieve (targets or standards; budgets)
(ii) What the business is actually achieving (actual performance)

By comparing the actual achievements with targeted performance, management can decide whether corrective action is needed, and then take the necessary action when required.

Much control information is of an accounting nature because costs, revenues, profits and asset values are major factors in how well or how badly a business performs.

(c) **To plan for the future**. Managers have to plan (for example, about how to allocate resources most efficiently), and they need information to do this. Much of the information they use is management accounting information.

(d) **To make decisions**. As we have seen, managers are faced with several types of decision.

  (i) **Strategic decisions** (which relate to the longer-term objectives of a business) require information which tends to relate to the organisation as a whole, is in summary form and is derived from both internal and external sources.

  (ii) **Tactical and operational decisions** (which relate to the short or medium term and to a department, product or division rather than the organisation as a whole) require information which is more detailed and more restricted in its sources.

3.3 Evaluating management accounting information

The objective of **management accounting** and **management accounting systems** is to provide information for managers to use, for planning, control and performance measurement. In order to evaluate how well management accounting systems are providing this, managers need to assess whether the information available to them gives them what they need to know for planning, control and making decisions. The management accountant's role is to provide managers with feedback information in the form of periodic reports – suitably analysed and at an appropriate level of detail – to determine whether the business is performing according to plan.

It may be the case that there is too much information available and in an unsuitable format for management to use. For instance, a production manager needs to know about outputs and costs in their department but not immediately about marketing data or even necessarily summarised data that would go into a board report. Information overload can sometimes be as much of a problem as having too much information. Accounting information needs to be distilled in a manner that makes it clear and concise and does not overwhelm the user.

In this context it is important to highlight that, while management accounting involves the process of transforming data about an organisation's performance into information that managers can use for many reasons, management accounting only produces good information if it is useful and relevant to its users.

Sub-objective	Detail
The provision of good information	This requires supplying information that is **relevant** to the needs of the users (which involves identifying the user, getting the **purpose** right and getting the **volume** right), that is **accurate** within their needs, **inspires their confidence** (so it should not be out of date, badly presented or taken from an unreliable source), is **timely** (it must be in the right place by the right time) and is **appropriately communicated** (since it will lose its value if it is not clearly communicated to the user in a suitable format and through a suitable medium).
The provision of a value for money service	User departments are likely to be charged in some way for the management accounting service and are therefore likely to require that the **charge incurred is reflected in the level of service and the quality of information provided.** **Cost efficiency** – Valuable information should not cost more to produce than it is worth. Equally, management reports that are produced more regularly than required are likely to be less useful/valuable than information that is produced to satisfy a specific request for information.
The availability of informed personnel	Users will require management accounting staff to be available to **answer queries and resolve problems** as and when required.

Sub-objective	Detail
Flexibility	Management accountants should be flexible **in their response to user requests** for information and reports. (But remember the point about cost efficiency, above.)

4 Management accounting information within the management information system

FAST FORWARD

As we have already identified in Chapter 1, in relation to the works of Burns and Scapens, the **role of the management accountant** and the **type of information** they are expected to provide is **changing**. Management accounting information does not exist in isolation but is part of the wider information system within an organisation, as illustrated by **enterprise resource planning systems** (ERPS).

4.1 Management accounting information within the management information system

The management accountant's traditional role in an organisation is to provide information to help with planning and control decisions by other managers throughout the organisation.

Management accounting can **provide a basis for much control reporting** by doing the following.

Step 1 Recording actual results

Step 2 Analysing actual results and comparing them with the target, plan or budget

Step 3 Reporting actual results and the comparisons with plan to the managers who are responsible for whatever control action might be necessary

Management accountants are **not the only people** in an organisation **who provide control information**:

(a) Salespeople or market researchers will provide control information about customers and sales demand.

(b) Quality controllers will provide control information about product quality.

(c) Maintenance staff will provide information about the amount of maintenance and repair work, and reasons for breakdowns.

(d) R&D staff will provide control information about the progress of product development projects.

Such information tends to be **highly user-specific and localised**, whereas **management accounting systems** provide feedback on **every aspect** of an organisation's operations using the **common denominator, money**.

The diagram below shows the **division of responsibilities in a typical system**.

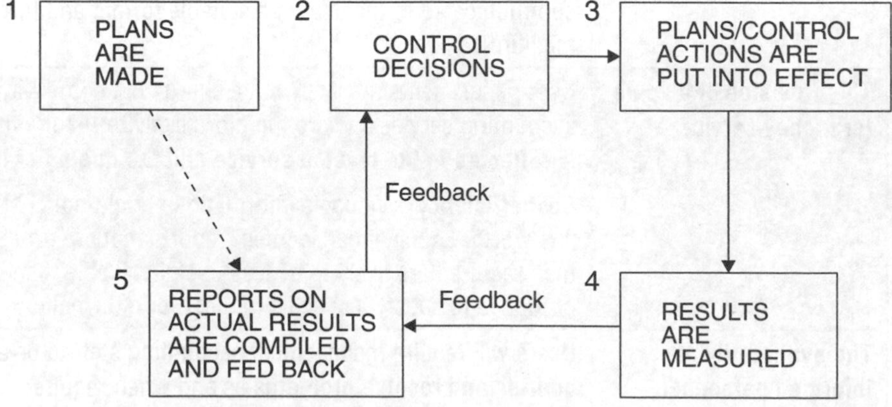

Planning, control and feedback system

Activities 1, 2, 3 and some of 4 will be done by line managers and their subordinates.

Activity 5 and some of 4 will be done by the management accountant, whose main role is to **provide feedback**. In budgeting, the management accountant, in the role of budget controller, may be required to co-ordinate and consolidate the plans of the various departments into a single master budget. The comparison of actual results with plan is a task that is begun by the management accountant (Activity 5) but completed by the line manager (Activity 2).

4.2 Enterprise Resource Planning Systems (ERPS) 6/15, 12/15

It is also important that the management accounting information does not exist in isolation, but is also part of the wider information system in an organisation. A good illustration of the way organisations are increasingly using integrated software systems can be seen by looking at Enterprise Resource Planning Systems and Strategic Enterprise Management Systems.

Enterprise Resource Planning Systems (ERPS) are software systems designed to support and automate the business processes of medium-sized and large enterprises. ERPS are accounting-orientated information systems which aid in identifying and planning the enterprise-wide resources needed to resource, make, account for and deliver customer orders. They aid the flow of information between all business functions within an organisation, as well as managing connections to outside stakeholders (such as suppliers).

ERPS handle many aspects of operations including **manufacturing, distribution, inventory, invoicing** and **accounting**. They also cover support functions, such as **human resource management** and **marketing**. **Supply chain management** software can provide links with **suppliers** and customer relationship management with **customers**.

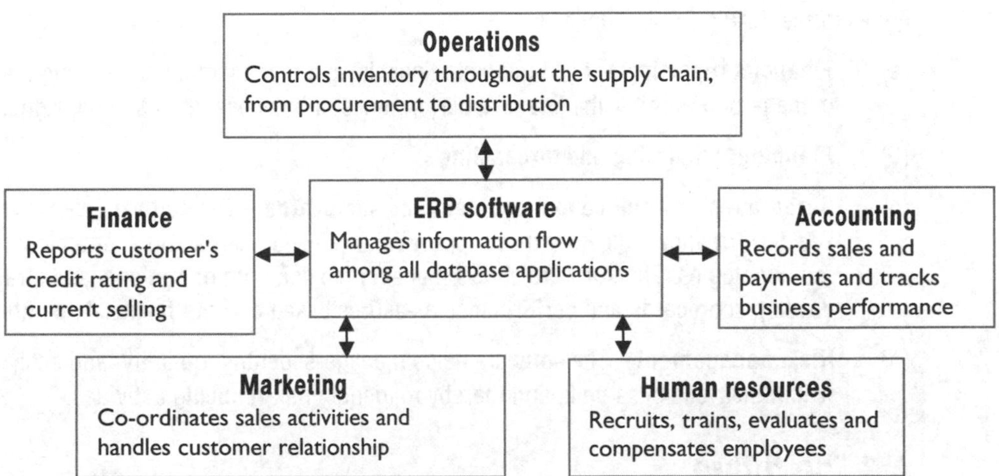

Integration of information systems in an enterprise resource planning system

ERPS thus operate **throughout the whole organisation** and **across functions**. All departments that are involved in operations or production are **integrated** into one system. In this way, adopting ERPS makes firms more agile in the way they use information, meaning they can process that information better and integrate it into business procedures and decision making more effectively.

Some ERPS software is custom built, and often now ERPS software is written for organisations in particular industries. ERPS can be configured for organisations' needs and software adapted for circumstances. The data is made available in data warehouses, which can be used to produce customised reports containing data that is consistent across applications. They can **support performance measures** such as **balanced scorecard** and **strategic planning**.

ERPS should result in **lower costs** (for example, through workforce analytics and workforce redeployment) and lower **investment required** in assets. ERPS should increase **flexibility** and **efficiency of production**, for example by co-ordinating procurement and logistics functions; and they should increase **customer to cash processes**, and thereby improve control of cash flow.

Their disadvantages include cost, implementation time and lack of scope for adaptation to the demands of specific businesses. In addition, a **problem** with one function can affect all the other functions. ERPS linked in with supply chains can similarly be vulnerable to problems with any links in the chain, and switching costs may be high. The blurring of boundaries can also cause accountability problems.

Exam focus point

> One the question scenarios in the June 2015 exam described a company which was suffering a number of operational problems as a result of poor information sharing within the company. The scenario also indicated that the company was considering the purchase of an ERPS, and part of the requirement asked about the impact the ERPS could have on the performance management issues within the company.
>
> In the post-exam report, the examining team noted that this part of the requirement was answered fairly well, with candidates recognising how an ERPS could help to address the specific problems relating to information management which had been described in the scenario.

As well as ERPS (which focus primarily on operational management), firms can use **Strategic Enterprise Management Systems** (SEMS) for making high-level strategic decisions.

SEMS focus primarily on strategic management, with a view to allowing organisations to improve their business processes and procedures, and their business decision making, in order to sustain a competitive advantage in a competitive business environment.

SEMS can be seen as an extension of the balanced scorecard approach, because they encourage senior managers to combine financial and strategic measures when formulating business decisions. And SEMS provide organisations with the capability to support financial consolidation and to manage strategy and performance through a single piece of software (such as SAP Strategic Enterprise Management; **SAP SEM**).

For example, SAP's SEMS supports:

(a) **Financial reporting** – It can generate financial and management accounting information to allow managers to monitor the financial performance of business units and divisions.

(b) **Planning, budgeting and forecasting.**

(c) **Corporate performance management and scorecards** – The software allows managers to develop key performance indicators that support balanced scorecards and economic value-added scorecard methodologies. The software allows managers to link both operational and strategic plans and to develop scorecards and performance measures based on both financial and non-financial data.

(d) **Risk management** – The software helps managers identify, quantify, and analyse business risks within their business units and thereby to identify risk-reducing activities.

4.3 The future

For as long as budgetary control **based on money** remains central to the co-ordination and control of organisations, management accounting information will retain its **central place** within the overall management information system. Financial information will always be extremely important because commercial organisations aim to make profits and even non profit making organisations or public sector bodies must break even financially or keep spending within budgeted limits.

The **role of the management accountant** and the **type of information** they are expected to provide is changing. **Developments in information technology** mean that almost instantaneous feedback can in theory be obtained at the touch of a button. The impact on the traditional management accounting function could be profound.

5 Lean management information systems 12/13, 12/15

FAST FORWARD

Lean production is a manufacturing methodology developed originally at Toyota. It is also known as the Toyota Production System. Its goal is 'to get the right things to the right place at the right time, the first time, while **minimising waste** and being open to change'. This lean philosophy can also be applied to services and systems.

In this section we start off with a quick overview of lean systems in general terms, before we move on to look at how the concepts of 'lean' would be used in a management information context. The syllabus reference in P5 talks specifically about evaluating whether management information systems and the information they provide are lean. We finish with a look at some general benefits and criticisms of lean systems.

Exam focus point

There is an article called 'Lean enterprises and lean information systems' available in the Technical Articles section for P5 on ACCA's website.

As we do in this Study Text, the article looks at the development of 'lean' as a production system, and then looks at the way the ideas of lean can be applied to information systems.

The article discusses six innovations at Toyota which have come to be seen as important aspects of 'lean' production:

- More flexible production lines allowing smaller batch sizes
- Greater involvement of employees in the continuous improvement of operations
- Elimination of non value adding functions
- Identifying the root causes of problems
- Constructive relations with suppliers
- Greater contact with customers

You are strongly encouraged to read the article to supplement your reading from this Study Text.

Lean production is a philosophy of production that aims to minimise the amount of resources (including time) used in all activities of an enterprise. It involves identifying and eliminating all non value adding activities.

The concepts behind lean production may also be applied to services and systems in the organisation. To summarise, the lean philosophy (lean) requires the organisation to focus on:

- Continuous improvement
- Increased productivity
- Improved quality
- Improved management

Lean involves the systematic elimination of waste, and Toyota identified aspects of this as:

- **Over-production** and early production
- **Waiting** – time delays, idle time, any time during which value is not added to the product
- **Transportation** – multiple handling, delay in materials handling, unnecessary handling
- **Inventory** – holding or purchasing unnecessary raw materials, work in process and finished goods
- **Motion** – actions of people or equipment that do not add value to the product
- **Over-processing** – unnecessary steps or work elements/procedures (non value added work)
- **Defective units** – production of a part that is scrapped or requires rework

Lean should eliminate waste, and lead to improved product flow and improved quality. Instead of devoting resources to planning what would be required for future manufacturing, lean production focuses on reducing system response time so that the production system is capable of rapid change to meet market demands.

5.1 Characteristics of lean (based on lean production)

The characteristics of lean are:

(a) Integrated single piece continuous work flow

(b) Integration of the whole value chain through partnerships with suppliers and distributors

(c) Just-in-time processing: a part moves to a production operation, is processed immediately, and moves immediately to the next operation

(d) Short order to ship cycle times and small batch production capability synchronised to shipping schedules

(e) Production is based on orders rather than forecasts and is driven by customer demand or 'pull'

(f) Minimal inventories at each stage of the production process

(g) Quick changeovers of machines and equipment

(h) Production layout based on product flow

(i) Active involvement by workers in problem solving to improve quality and eliminate waste

(j) Defect prevention (rather than inspection and rework) by building quality into the process

(k) Team-based work with multi-skilled staff empowered to make decisions

Supporters of lean production believe that it enables a company to deliver on demand, minimise inventory, maximise the use of multi-skilled employees, flatten the management structure and focus resources where they are most effective.

Other benefits include:

- Waste reduction
- Production cost reduction
- Manufacturing cycle times decreased
- Labour reduction while maintaining or increasing throughput
- Inventory reduction while increasing customer service levels
- Capacity increase in current facilities
- Higher quality
- Higher profits
- Higher system flexibility in reacting to changes in requirements improved
- More strategic focus
- Improved cash flow through increasing shipping and billing frequencies

5.2 Applications of lean to management information systems

During the 1980s, lean production methods were adopted by many manufacturing plants in the US and Europe, with varying degrees of success. More recently, there has been a renewed interest in the principles of lean production, particularly since the 'lean' philosophy encourages the reduction of inventory, and also promotes the idea of 'continuous improvement'.

Lean techniques are applicable not only in manufacturing, but also in a service environment, since every system contains waste (ie something that does not provide value to the customer).

An article by Hicks in the *International Journal of Information Management* ('Lean information management: Understanding and eliminating waste') considers the way 'lean' ideas can be applied to information management and information systems.

Lean thinking in this context aims to add value to the information provided by the system, and there are three levels at which it can do this.

First, lean can enhance the value of the data in the system and how it is **organised, exchanged and retrieved**. Waste arises from effort or difficulties in retrieving and accessing information. It also arises from having to correct inaccurate information.

At a second level, lean thinking can add value to information by virtue of how the information is organised, and **presented**; for example, by not including unnecessary detail, or presenting the same information in different reports (ie duplication).

Thirdly, value can be added by enabling the information to **flow to the users of the information more efficiently**; by addressing the processes of exchange, sharing and collaboration between the management accountants and the managers in a business.

Overall, the lean approach would seek to identify and concentrate improvements on eliminating waste and improving the flow of value from the management information system. The ultimate aim is to improve efficiency, productivity and quality of information. However, measuring waste and defining value are more difficult when looking at information systems compared with manufacturing where there are established methods for identifying waste and measuring performance.

Moreover, there is always **scope for improvement** in the way information is managed and shared with users. As such, the providers and users of information should meet regularly to review the usefulness of the information currently being provided and to identify potential improvements to it.

The article on ACCA's website – 'Lean enterprises and lean information systems' – which we referred to earlier highlights some additional features of lean information systems:

Value adding – Reports should only be produced if they add value, ie if they are useful to decision makers or other recipients.

Reports should only be sent to those who need them. Sending reports to people who do not need them is an example of waste.

Information should be processed quickly so that users do not have to wait for it (because time spent waiting for a report is another example of waste). In this respect, real-time processing should be encouraged in preference to batch processing because batch processing involves delays.

Flexibility – Information systems need to be flexible enough to respond to ad hoc requests or to meeting the changing needs of managers over time. A system which can only produce a standard set of reports characterises the principles of mass production rather than lean production. A system which allows managers to create their own customised reports – focusing specifically on the information which is relevant and valuable to them – is more likely to be lean.

5.3 Lean management

In a paper looking at the lean management enterprise, the management consultants McKinsey & Company also argue that applying lean principles to the management of organisations as a whole, rather than just to individual processes and operations, can help organisations improve the ways in which they work.

As such, McKinsey & Company suggest that there are four key disciplines in lean management.

(a) **Delivering value efficiently to the customer** – There are two important issues here: first, an organisation has to understand what its customers really value; and then second, it must configure the way it works so that it can deliver that value with the fewest resources possible. To do this requires co-ordination across processes, elimination of non value adding processes, and building quality into every process. Equally, however, understanding the customer's exact requirements is vital so that the organisation doesn't waste resources in delivering additional features or quality which the customer doesn't need or want.

(b) **Enabling people to lead and contribute to their fullest potential** – For example, through providing them with the support and resources they need to master their work.

(c) **Discovering better ways of working** – As competitors, customers, and the broader business environment change, organisations need to think continually about how they could improve their ways of working. Problem identification, and more importantly resolution, should become part of everyone's roles, supported by structures in which problems are reported to the people best able to solve them.

(d) **Connecting strategy, goals and meaningful purpose** – Organisations which are successful in the long term have a clear direction – a vision which shapes their strategy and objectives in ways which, in turn, give meaning and context to daily work. This final link is important because it aligns individual goals to the overall strategy and vision, so that individual employees understand their role in the organisation, and why it matters.

By definition, in a lean organisation, each individual's role matters, because roles which do not add value will have been made redundant.

5.4 Implementing lean principles – the 5 'S's

In many situations, an organisation supposedly using lean principles has not experienced the improvements in productivity and profitability expected. It is difficult to know whether this is due to shortcomings in the lean philosophy or whether the techniques involved are being **interpreted and applied correctly**.

For example, the **5 'S's** concept is often associated with lean principles and is underpinned by the idea that there is 'a place for everything and everything goes in its place.' The 5 'S's concept should be used with the aim of creating a workplace with real organisation and order, which creates employee pride in their work, improves safety, and results in better quality.

The 5 'S's are:

Seiri (Structurise, or Sort) – Introduce order where possible. Identify the things which are important in a process and which are not, so that items which are unimportant or not needed can be discarded. The aim of this first stage of the 5 'S's is to remove any items that do not add value to a process, and to leave only those which are required.

In relation to information systems, this stage of the 5 'S's could involve identifying what information is actually required for planning, controlling and decision-making, and whether there are parts of the information which are less valuable than others (or possibly not really needed at all) and so could be removed.

Seiton (Systemise, or Simplify) – Arrange the items which are required for a process in the most efficient manner, so that they can be accessed quickly and easily. The notion that 'everything has a place, and everything is in its place' would be especially relevant here. This aspect of the 5 'S's also highlights the need to approach tasks systematically.

In relation to information systems, this aspect of the 5 'S's could involve identifying the most efficient ways of storing information – for example, by having a clearly defined file structure, so that users can easily find the information they need. 'Simplify' could also mean identifying the most suitable methods of communicating information to different groups of recipients.

Seiso (Sanitise, or Scan) – Ensure the working environment is kept clean. Be tidy, avoid clutter. This cleanliness and tidiness will help to ensure that any non-conformity (or item which is out of place) stands out.

In relation to information systems, an important aspect of sanitisation could be removing obsolete data from a firm's records, or removing sections of a report that no one reads.

Seiketsu (Standardise) – Be consistent in your approach, and maintain consistent standards, procedures and ways of working. For example, this could involve defining a standard structure for an organisation's reports and a timetable for producing them, or setting up user groups to receive different reports.

Shitsuke (Self-discipline, Sustain) – Sustain via motivation, for example by conducting performance audits or by reporting on performance. The purpose of this stage is to ensure that an organisation continuously improves by using the previous stages; and also that 'lean' becomes part of the culture of an organisation and is seen as the responsibility of everyone in the organisation.

Exam focus point

> The December 2013 exam question included a requirement in which candidates were asked to evaluate whether introducing a new asset tagging (RFID) system in a group of hospitals will help to make the management of the hospitals leaner.
>
> Although the post-exam report acknowledged that candidates did not specifically need to refer to the 5 'S's to answer this question, the 'S's could provide a useful framework for evaluating how 'lean' a system is: for example, how well structured tasks and processes are; whether key items or key information can be accessed quickly and easily; and is clutter and waste avoided?

5.5 Difficulties with implementing lean principles

The reference within 'Shitsuke' to the 5 'S's becoming part of the culture of an organisation is important, because it highlights that 'lean' shouldn't simply be seen as some kind of cleaning and housekeeping exercise.

However, in some organisations, this is what they become – meaning that the underlying philosophy behind the 'lean' concept has been lost.

To be successful, lean techniques should be seen and treated as outward signs of a more **fundamental approach** to operations and quality. However, many organisations seem to treat the techniques as the end in themselves. These organisations have a mistaken belief that simply putting structures and mechanisms (eg quality circles) in place will improve efficiency and quality. **Sustainable differences** require a change in thinking and in culture – which is difficult to achieve.

Lean production is often viewed as a simple **cost-cutting exercise** rather than a fundamental commitment to eliminating waste and adding value. Many companies use lean manufacturing and Six Sigma techniques (which we discuss in Chapter 13) to improve quality and reduce costs. But the benefits most businesses realise are only a fraction of what could be achieved if these strategies were applied over a better foundation of business plan deployment, levelling of resources and an engaged workforce.

6 Human behaviour and management accounting systems

FAST FORWARD

> Management accounting systems have to develop ways of overcoming the problems of **human behaviour** – in particular, how to deal with the contrast between people who take a broad-brush approach to interpreting information and those who focus on the fine detail of any information presented.

Managers have an impact on information, whether they intend to or not, simply because they are people.

(a) As people, they have **personal needs and motivations** which are quite **separate from the objectives of the organisation** but which cannot fail to influence the workings of it.

(b) People are the receivers of information, but because they are people they do **not all necessarily respond in the same way to the same information**.

(c) People are also the senders of information, but because they are people they do **not necessarily send** the **information they ought to send**.

Management accounting **systems** have to **develop ways of overcoming the problems of human behaviour** – by allocating responsibility, encouraging participation in decision making, devising ways of measuring and rewarding behaviour that contribute to organisational objectives, and so on. Much has been written on this subject, and we shall return to it in later parts of the Study Text.

Exam focus point

> In Chapter 14, we look in more detail at the possible problems which can accompany the use of performance measures.
>
> Berry, Broadbent and Otley have identified a number of specific problems which can arise in this context. However, it is also important to remember the more general issue of **goal congruence** when designing performance reward systems. In particular, reward systems need to be designed in such a way that individuals' goals (in order to earn their rewards) are aligned to team goals and the organisation's goals overall.
>
> In Chapter 14, we will also look at the different categories of control mechanism which can be used to help control employees' performance in an organisation, and to ensure that they are working towards the objectives of the organisation.
>
> - Behavioural (or action) control
> - Personnel and cultural control
> - Results (or output) controls

6.1 Dual-process framework

When designing management accounting systems, accountants should also be aware of how the outputs from the system will be used. The dual-process framework summarises scientific research into thinking and reasoning, and highlights how people will respond and react to stimuli – with the stimulus, in this case, being the management accounting information presented to them.

The dual-process framework presents the contrast between **heuristic/holistic** processing and **analytic/systematic** processing.

Heuristic processing occurs when the respondent adopts a broad-brush or rule of thumb approach to interpreting information. The heuristic approach takes less effort than analytic processing, and normally occurs when an individual has low levels of motivation or ability.

By contrast, **analytic/systematic processing** occurs when an individual responds to the detail of the information presented. However, this kind of response requires significantly more effort than heuristic processing, and only occurs when individuals are both **willing** and **able** to perform the task at hand.

In this way, the dual-process framework highlights that an individual's response to a stimulus is determined by both **cognitive ability** and **motivational factors**. Importantly, the framework also suggests that, in situations where cognitive ability is not constrained, the determining factors behind how much effort individuals give to a task is how relevant they think that task is to them. As the relevance of a task or a decision increases, so does the amount of time the individual is willing to give it. And as the amount of time and effort the individual gives to the task increases, so does the likelihood of analytical/systematic processing.

6.1.1 Implications for management accountants

The importance of this for management accountants is it suggests that if the recipients of management accounting information feel the information is relevant to them they will look at it carefully and in detail. By contrast, if the users feel they are being given information which has little relevance to them – or if they do not have the cognitive ability to analyse it in detail – they will only look at it briefly, and will adopt a broad-brush approach to making any decisions based on it.

The dual-process framework also highlighted another feature which accountants should recognise. People who adopt a heuristic/holistic approach (and therefore don't analyse information in detail) are also influenced by contextual cues, such as the way a decision is framed. For example, if a decision is presented in terms of controlling expenditure, their response is likely to be different than if a similar decision is presented in terms of maximising sales.

However, the key issue to consider in terms of **designing management accounting systems** is that the accountant should consider how outputs and reports may need to be tailored for particular types of recipients. Some user groups are likely to prefer summarised data that supports their inclination to make

broad-brush decisions, whereas others may prefer longer reports presenting figures in detail and explaining the background to data, trends and analysis.

6.1.2 Ways of presenting information

The previous section highlighted the distinction between presenting high-level summary reports, and more detailed figures. However, another important consideration in deciding how to present management accounting information is whether it should be presented in a written format, or as a **table, graph** or **chart**.

The use of charts, graphs and tables can often make it **easier for people to understand** accounting information and other quantitative information. In particular, charts or graphs can be effective ways of communicating information, and focusing readers' attention on **key aspects of the information**.

However, it is important to remember that the usefulness of different types of chart or graph (for example, pie charts, bar graphs and line charts) depends on the sort of information being communicated. Therefore, it is important to select the most suitable type of chart or graph in any given situation.

Pie charts can be particularly useful in reflecting percentage or other proportional relationships; for example, the proportion of total expenses associated with each function or department in an organisation; and the proportion of revenues generated by different products or services within an organisation.

Bar charts (or column charts) are useful for making comparisons between two or more items when absolute amounts are being presented instead of proportional or percentage figures. In this way, bar charts provide a useful way of making direct comparisons between the different items. For example, bar charts would be useful for highlighting changes in revenue over two or three periods.

Line charts (or similar scatter plots) are most useful for presenting a trend (or a combination of trends) over a period of time. For example, a line chart could be a useful way of illustrating how monthly sales have varied over a year. However, equally, by combining trends in cost information and revenue information a line chart would be an effective way of illustrating that cost increases over a period have been greater than revenue increases over the same period.

However, it is important not to use too many charts or graphs in a report. If too many charts are used, they are likely to lose their effectiveness, because the reader will be likely to end up ignoring some of them.

On the other hand, if a smaller number of graphs and charts is used to communicate significant points only, readers are more likely to pay closer attention to them.

6.1.3 Interactive reports

In the next chapter, we will look in more detail at the impact technology has had on the ways management information is processed and reported. However, one of the key recent developments in the way management information is reported is the use of **dashboards**.

Importantly, dashboards mean that reports are no longer a 'one way' transfer of information between the producer and the reader/user. Instead, dashboards allow reports to become more interactive. For example, the users of a report (which could be presented on screen as a number of high-level indicators) can filter data within it or drill down into the data to look at specific aspects of it in more detail.

Equally, some dashboard reporting systems allow users to create their own display panel, which can incorporate elements – for example specific tables or graphs – which are particularly important to them.

7 Information and responsibility accounting 12/15

FAST FORWARD

The management accountant has to learn from managers of **responsibility centres** what information they need, in what form and at what intervals, and then design a system that enables this information to be provided.

Key terms

Responsibility accounting is a system of accounting that segregates revenues and costs into areas of personal responsibility in order to monitor and assess the performance of each part of an organisation.

A **responsibility centre** is any part of an organisation which is headed by a manager who has direct responsibility for its performance.

If a manager is to bear responsibility for the performance of their area of the business they will need information about its performance. In essence, a manager needs to know three things.

Requirements	Examples of information
What are their resources?	Finance, inventories of raw materials, spare machine capacity, labour availability, the balance of expenditure remaining for a certain budget, target date for completion of a job
At what rate are their resources being consumed?	How fast is their labour force working, how quickly are their raw materials being used up, how quickly are other expenses being incurred, how quickly is available finance being consumed?
How well are the resources being used?	How well are their objectives being met?

This is the content of the information provided, but decisions must also be made as to the **level of detail** that is provided and the frequency with which information is provided. Moreover, the **cost** of providing information must be **weighed against the benefit** derived from it.

In a traditional system managers are given monthly reports, but there is no logical reason for this except that it ties in with financial reporting cycles and may be administratively convenient. With **modern systems**, however, there is a danger of **information overload**, since information technology allows the information required to be made available much more frequently.

The **task of the management accountant**, therefore, is to learn from the managers of responsibility centres **what information** they need, in **what form** and at **what intervals**, and then to design a system that enables this to be provided.

It is to this end that responsibility centres are usually divided into four **different categories**.

Cost centres – where managers are normally accountable for the costs that are under their control. Cost centre managers are not accountable for sales revenues.
(However, it is important to note that cost centres can still affect the amount of sales revenues generated if quality standards are not met, or if goods are not produced on time.)

Revenue centres – where managers are only accountable for sales revenues, and possibly directly related selling expenses (eg salesperson salaries). However, revenue centre managers are not accountable for the cost of the goods or services they sell.

Profit centres – managers are given responsibility for both revenues and costs.

Investment centres – managers are responsible not only for revenues and costs, but also for working capital and capital investment decisions, production and sales.

7.1 Controllability

We have already looked at the ideas of responsibility and controllability in Chapter 3 in relation to variance analysis. The key point we highlighted in Chapter 3 is that when measuring the performance of a

responsibility centre, it is necessary to distinguish which items the manager of that centre can control (and therefore they should be held accountable for) and those items over which they have no control (and therefore they should not be held accountable for).

7.1.1 Impact on information requirements

The potential need to measure different aspects of performance (eg manager's performance; divisional performance) could have important implications for a management accounting system. In such circumstances, the system will need to be able to produce the different types of report required, or distinguish between controllable and non-controllable costs as necessary. If the management accountant cannot produce the reports required, then any performance measurement based on those reports also cannot be undertaken.

7.1.2 Responsibility centres and information requirements

It is also important to think how information requirements will vary for different types of responsibility centre.

The focus of management information in **cost centres** should be on costs; for example, comparing actual costs against budgeted or standard costs.

By contrast, the focus of management information **in revenue centres** should be on the revenues generated.

However, if managers are evaluated solely on the basis of sales revenue (as in a revenue centre) there is a danger that they will concentrate on maximising sales at the expense of profitability. This can occur when sales are not all equally profitable, and managers can achieve higher sales revenues by promoting low-profit products rather than trying to sell higher-profit products.

This problem can be overcome by introducing **profit centres** instead of revenue centres. In a profit centre, managers are responsible for both revenues and costs. Consequently, management information will be required which monitors performance in respect of **both revenues and costs**.

Chapter Roundup

- **Management accounting information** can be used to support strategic planning, control and decision making. Strategic management accounting differs from traditional management accounting because it has an **external** orientation and a **future** orientation.
- **Management control** is at the level below strategic planning in Anthony's decision-making hierarchy and is concerned with decisions about the efficient and effective use of resources to achieve objectives.
- **Operational control**, the lowest tier in Anthony's hierarchy, is concerned with ensuring that specific tasks are carried out effectively and efficiently.
- Each manager needs to be given information according to what their **responsibilities** are.
- Management accounting information is used by managers for a variety of purposes: performance measurement and **control, planning and decision making**. The effectiveness of the management accounting systems in an organisation can be assessed in relation to how well they provide managers with the information they need.
- As we have already identified in Chapter 1, in relation to the work of Burns and Scapens, the **role of the management accountant** and the **type of information** they are expected to provide is **changing**. Management accounting information does not exist in isolation but is part of the wider information system within an organisation, as illustrated by **enterprise resource planning systems** (ERPS).
- **Lean production** is a manufacturing methodology developed originally at Toyota. It is also known as the Toyota Production System. Its goal is 'to get the right things to the right place at the right time, the first time, while **minimising waste** and being open to change'. This lean philosophy can also be applied to services and systems.
- Management accounting systems have to develop ways of overcoming the problems of **human behaviour** – in particular, how to deal with the contrast between people who take a broad-brush approach to interpreting information and those who focus on the fine detail of any information presented.
- The management accountant has to learn from managers of **responsibility centres** what information they need, in what form and at what intervals, and then design a system that enables this information to be provided.

Quick Quiz

1 Which of the following are characteristics of features of operational information rather than strategic information?

[Select all that apply]

A Internally generated
B Focus on planning
C Routine and frequent
D Largely qualitative
E Long time frame

2 Which of the following is the best description of an ERPS?

An ERPS is a system that:

A Plans the materials and inventories required for manufacturing processes to avoid stock outs

B Operates across functions to plan the resources needed to record, produce, distribute and account for customer orders

C Manages the customer ordering process efficiently to improve customer service

D Tracks purchasing and payments so that outstanding debts can be chased up

3 Which of the four general objectives of management accounting information is missing from the list below?

- To measure profits and put a value to inventories
- To control the business
- To make decisions

4 As part of an initiative to improve the usefulness of the monthly management accounts, the management accountant has asked senior managers to identify which parts of the accounts are valuable to them, and which are less valuable, or of no value to them at all.

Which of the lean principles (the 5 'S's) does this initiative demonstrate most clearly?

A Sanitise
B Standardise
C Structurise
D Systemise

5 The new Managing Director (MD) of a company has commented to the management accountant that they feel the regular management accounts show far too much detail. The MD feels that the accounts should give a broad-brush overview of business performance, to allow the senior management team to see how the business is performing overall.

What is the Managing Director's approach to information processing: heuristic or analytic?

Answers to Quick Quiz

1 The correct answers are: A, C

Operational information is typically internally generated, and is routine and frequent.

B, D and E all characterise strategic information.

Operational information tends to focus on control (rather than planning), it is largely quantitative (rather than qualitative) and it has a short (rather than long) time frame.

2 B Operates across functions to plan the resources needed to record, produce, distribute and account for customer orders

As its title (Enterprise Resource Planning System) suggests, an ERPS is used for resource planning, and one of the key features of an ERPS is that it operates across functions. The activities covered in A, C and D could all be elements within an ERPS, but B provides the best description of an ERPS overall.

3 To plan for the future

4 C Structurise

The main purpose of the initiative is to identify the parts of the report which are important and those which are unimportant and which can therefore be discarded.

This reflects the first stage of the 5 'S's – Structurise – whose aim is to ensure that only those parts of a process which add value to it are prioritised.

5 **Heuristic**. The Managing Director seems to be taking a broad-brush approach to interpreting information. If they had been taking an analytic approach we would expect them to focus more on the detail of the information presented.

Now try the question below from the Practice Question Bank

Number	Level	Marks	Approximate time
Q7	Practice	20	40 mins

Management information, recording and processing and management reports

Topic list	Syllabus reference
1 Sources of management accounting information	C2(a)
2 Costs of information	C2(a)
3 Information for planning and control	C2(b)
4 Big Data and performance management	C2(c)
5 Recording and processing methods in business entities	C3(a)
6 Developments in IT and recording and processing systems	C3(b)
7 Instant access to data	C3(c)
8 Recording and processing qualitative data	C3(d)
9 Output reports and information systems	C4(a)
10 Potential issues with numerical performance information	C4(b)
11 Key performance information and integrated reporting	C4(c)

Introduction

Having looked at performance measurement systems in the previous chapter, we will now look at the information which they produce – the **sources** of that information, how it is **recorded** and **processed**, and how it can be used to help with **planning** and **control** in an organisation.

Management information needs to be **accessible** or available to the relevant people, and must be in a suitable format to allow them to make decisions. If it is not, then its usefulness is severely curtailed. Therefore the nature of the **outputs** from a management information system is an important aspect of the system.

However, controls over the information in the system, and **data security**, are also important; for example, to prevent confidential information being distributed to people who should not receive it.

Study guide

		Intellectual level
C2	**Sources of management information**	
(a)	Discuss the principal internal and external sources of management accounting information, their costs and limitations.	2
(b)	Demonstrate how the information might be used in planning and controlling activities, eg benchmarking against similar activities.	2
(c)	Discuss the development of Big Data and its impact on performance measurement and management, including the risks and challenges it presents.	3
C3	**Recording and processing methods**	
(a)	Demonstrate how the type of business entity will influence the recording and processing methods.	2
(b)	Discuss how IT developments eg unified corporate databases, RFIDs and network technology may influence management accounting systems.	2
(c)	Explain how information systems provide instant access to previously unavailable data that can be used for benchmarking and control purposes and help improve business performance (for example, through the use of enterprise resource planning systems and data warehouses).	2
(d)	Discuss the difficulties associated with recording and processing data of a qualitative nature.	2
C4	**Management reports**	
(a)	Evaluate the output reports of an information system in the light of: (i) Best practice in presentation (ii) The objectives of the report/organisation (iii) The needs of the readers of the report; and (iv) Avoiding the problem of information overload	3
(b)	Advise on common mistakes and misconceptions in the use of numerical data used for performance measurement.	3
(c)	Explore the role of the management accountant in providing key performance information for integrated reporting to stakeholders.	2

Exam guide

We have already highlighted that managers need information for planning and decision making in order for them to manage and control their organisations effectively. We have also highlighted (in the previous chapter) that information requirements vary according to the type of decisions being taken (for example, strategic or operational). Therefore managers are likely to need a range of internal and external information in the course of their planning, decision making and control functions.

In very simple terms, we can look at a management information system in terms of: inputs (sources of information), processing information, and outputs (reports). In this chapter we look at these three aspects of management information, as illustrated in the diagram on the next page.

The syllabus for **Paper F5** requires candidates to be able to discuss the sources of management information which could be used for control purposes, and the costs of capturing and producing management accounting information. It also requires candidates to be able to discuss the controls

required in generating and distributing information, and the procedures that may be necessary to ensure the security of confidential information.

Students taking Paper P5 will be assumed to have this knowledge from Paper F5. However, we have included some material on these subjects in this chapter for you to recap, to ensure that you could draw on these areas of assumed knowledge if they were relevant to a P5 exam question.

Questions in the P5 exam regularly ask candidates to evaluate performance reports, and it is important to appreciate the importance of performance reports in performance management. If performance reports do not provide managers with the information they need to control their business, or to assess how well it is performing, this will significantly reduce the managers' ability to manage the business effectively.

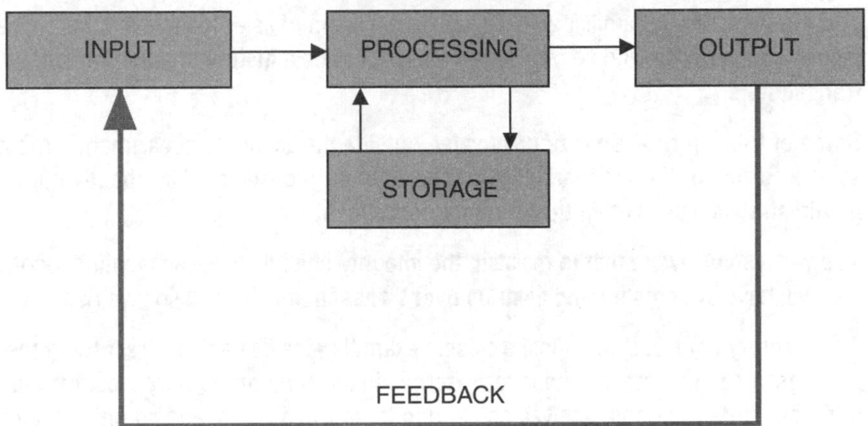

Information flows in performance management

Exam focus point

Evaluating performance *reports* vs evaluating *performance*

Crucially, however, if you are asked to evaluate a performance report, you must focus on the report itself and the information it provides to management – not on the underlying performance of the organisation. We will return to this point towards the end of the chapter, but candidates frequently answer questions about performance reports very poorly because they focus their answers on the underlying performance of the organisation which the reports are about, not on the reports themselves.

As we noted in the previous chapter, your ability to advise on the impact which information systems have on an organisation's ability to measure or manage its performance could help you fulfil elements (c) and (d) of Performance objective 12 – Monitor performance:

PO 12(c): 'Assess and advise on the impact of the output of an organisation's management accounting and information systems'

PO 12(d): 'Contribute to development and improvements of management accounting systems and internal reporting'

1 Sources of management accounting information

Internal sources of **information** include the financial accounting records and other systems closely tied to the accounting system.

Capturing data/information from inside the organisation involves the following:

(a) A **system for collecting or measuring transactions data** – eg sales, purchases, inventory and revenue – which sets out procedures for **what** data is collected, **how frequently**, **by whom** and by **what methods**, and how it is **processed**, and **filed** or **communicated**

(b) **Informal communication** of information between managers and staff (eg by word of mouth or at meetings)

(c) **Communication between managers**

1.1 Sources of monetary and non-monetary information

1.1.1 The financial accounting records

You are by now very familiar with the idea of a system of sales ledgers and purchase ledgers, general ledgers, cash books, and so on. These records provide a **history of an organisation's monetary transactions.**

Some of this information is of great value outside the accounts department – most obviously, for example, sales information for the marketing function. Other information, like cheque numbers, is of purely administrative value within the accounts department.

You will also be aware that to maintain the integrity of its financial accounting records, an organisation of any size will have systems for and **controls over transactions**. These also give rise to valuable information.

An inventory control system is the classic example: besides actually recording the monetary value of purchases and inventory in hand for external financial reporting purposes, the system will include purchase orders, goods received notes, goods returned notes, and so on, and these can be analysed to provide management information about **speed** of delivery, say, or the **quality** of supplies.

1.1.2 Other internal sources

Much information that is not strictly part of the financial accounting records nevertheless is closely tied in to the accounting system.

(a) Information about personnel will be linked to the **payroll** system. Additional information may be obtained from this source if, say, the cost of a project is being budgeted and it is necessary to ascertain the availability and rate of pay of different levels of staff.

(b) Much information will be produced by a **production** department about machine capacity, movement of materials and work in progress, set up times, maintenance requirements, and so on.

(c) Many service businesses – notably accountants and solicitors – need to keep detailed records of the **time** spent on various activities, both to justify fees to clients and to assess the efficiency of operations.

(d) It will also be useful for organisations to assess the volume and value of purchases they are making, to ensure they are getting value for money on their purchases without compromising quality. If an organisation has a **procurement** (or purchasing) department, it should be able to provide this information.

More generally, a **marketing or sales department** can provide valuable information; for example, about sales for recent years, and forecasts of future sales. The marketing department can also provide valuable information from market research (for example, about customers' tastes or potential demand for new products). It will also be useful to assess what **impact marketing campaigns have had on sales** or contributions from different products.

Staff themselves, throughout an organisation, are an important source of internal information. Information may be obtained either **informally** in the course of day to day business or **formally** through **meetings, interviews** or **questionnaires**.

Question — **Sources of information**

Think of at least one piece of non-monetary information that a management accountant might obtain from the following sources in order to make a decision about a new product.

(a) Marketing manager
(b) Vehicle fleet supervisor
(c) Premises manager
(d) Public relations officer
(e) Head of research

1.2 External sources of information

FAST FORWARD

External information tends to be more relevant to strategic and tactical decisions than to operational decisions. (Benchmarking is an exception.)

Capturing information from outside the organisation might be carried out formally and entrusted to particular individuals, or might be 'informal'. We will look at one particular external source of information – **Big Data** – separately in more detail later in this chapter.

1.3 Formal collection of data from outside sources

(a) A company's **tax specialists** will be expected to gather information about changes in tax law and how this will affect the company.

(b) Obtaining information about any new legislation on health and safety at work, or employment regulations, must be the responsibility of a particular person – for example the company's **legal expert** or **company secretary** – who must then pass on the information to other managers affected by it.

(c) Research and development (R&D) work often relies on information about other R&D work being done by another company or by government institutions. An **R&D official** might be made responsible for finding out about R&D work outside the company.

(d) **Marketing managers** need to know about the opinions and buying attitudes of potential customers. To obtain this information, they might carry out market research exercises.

Informal gathering of information from the environment **goes on all the time, consciously or unconsciously**, because the employees of an organisation learn **what is going on in the world around** them – perhaps from the media, meetings with business associates or the trade press.

Organisations hold external information, such as invoices and advertisements, **from customers and suppliers**. But there are many occasions when an active search outside the organisation is necessary.

1.4 Specific external sources

FAST FORWARD

Secondary data, such as government statistics or data provided by online databases, is not collected by or for the user. **Primary data** – more expensive than secondary data – is more tailored to the user's exact needs. Market research is an example.

1.4.1 Directories

Examples (of business directories) include the following (although there are many others).

(a) Kompass Register (Kompass)
(b) Who owns Whom (Dun & Bradstreet)
(c) Key British Enterprises (Dun & Bradstreet)

1.4.2 Associations

There are associations in almost every field of business and leisure activity, and ACCA itself is an organisation. Associations collect and publish data for their members that can be of great interest to other users. For example, although the services of the Road Haulage Association (RHA) are geared towards transport businesses, their analysis of fuel price rises could be useful to all motorists.

1.4.3 Government agencies

Governments are a major source of economic information and information about industry and population trends, as well as more general economic data (such as economic growth, employment figures, consumer spending statistics and imports/exports). Many government publications are available online, and can often be accessed or downloaded for free.

In addition to information published by national governments, official statistics are published by local authorities and supra-national bodies, such as the European Union and the United Nations.

1.4.4 Other published sources

This group includes all other publications, including some **digests** and **pocket books** and **periodicals** (often available in the public libraries).

1.4.5 Syndicated services

The sources of secondary data we have looked at so far have generally been **free** because they are **in the public domain**. Inexpensiveness is an advantage that can be offset by the fact that the information is **unspecific** and needs **considerable analysis** before being useable. A middle step between adapting secondary data and commissioning primary research is the **purchase of data collected by market research companies**. The data tend to be expensive but less costly than primary research.

1.4.6 Consumer panels

A form of continuous research which results in secondary data often bought in by marketers is that generated by **consumer panels**. These constitute a representative sample of individuals and households whose buying activity in a defined area is monitored either continuously (every day, with results aggregated) or at regular intervals, **over a period of time**. There are panels set up to monitor purchases of groceries, consumer durables, cars, baby products and many others.

1.5 Information from customers

Customers can provide useful information.

(a) Firms send out satisfaction questionnaires and market research.
(b) Customer comments and complaints sent voluntarily can suggest improvements.

1.6 Information from suppliers

Supplier information comes in several categories.

Information	Comment
'Bid' information	A supplier pitching for a product will detail products, services and prices. This is before a deal is done.
Operational information	If a firm has placed a particular job or contract with a supplier, the supplier may provide details of the stages in the manufacturing process, eg the delivery time.
Pricing information	Component prices vary from industry to industry; some are volatile.
Technology	Technological developments in the supplier's industry can affect the type of input components, their cost and their availability.

1.7 The internet

FAST FORWARD

The **internet** increases the richness of external data and reduces the cost of searching for it.

The internet offers efficient, fast and cost-effective **email**, and massive information **search and retrieval facilities**. There is a great deal of financial information available and users in the UK can also access publications and news releases issued by the Treasury and other government departments.

Businesses are also using it to **provide information (cheaply) about their own products and services** and to conduct **research** into their competitors' activities.

The internet offers a **speedy** and **impersonal** way of getting to know the basics (or even the details) of the services that a company provides.

The internet is commonly used to **access information about suppliers**.

(a) A firm can visit a supplier's website for details of products and services.

(b) The user can search a number of websites through a browser. Note that the internet may not contain every supplier; arguably it should not be relied on as the sole source.

(c) A number of business to business sites have been opened. Participating members offer their services, and can offer quotes. (This can help to reduce the time taken to find potential suppliers).

1.8 Database information

A **management information system** or **database** should provide managers with a **useful flow** of **relevant information** which is **easy to use** and **easy to access**. Information is an important corporate resource. Managed and used effectively, it can provide considerable competitive advantage and so it is a worthwhile investment.

It is now possible to access large volumes of generally available information through databases held by public bodies and businesses.

(a) Some **newspapers** offer computerised access to old editions, with search facilities looking for information on particular companies or issues.

(b) **Public databases** are also available for inspection.

Dun & Bradstreet provides general business information. Nielsen is a world leader in consumer measurement. It measures what consumers buy and how they behave; and Nielsen's researchers examine key business trends by product or market, using sales information gathered from thousands of retail outlets.

Developments in information technology allow businesses to have access to the databases of **external organisations**. Reuters, for example, provides an online information system about money market interest rates and foreign exchange rates to firms involved in money market and foreign exchange dealings, and to the treasury departments of a large number of companies. The growing adoption of technology at **point of sale** provides a potentially invaluable source of data to both retailer and manufacturer.

1.8.1 Online databases

Most external databases are online databases, which are very large computer files of information, supplied by **database providers** and managed by **'host'** companies whose business revenue is generated through charges made to **users**. Access to such databases is open to anyone prepared to pay, and who is equipped with a PC plus internet access and communication software. These days there are an increasing number of companies offering free internet access. Most databases can be accessed around the clock.

1.9 Data warehouses

We will look at data warehouses in more detail later in the chapter, when we look at the way organisations record and process data.

A **data warehouse** contains **data from a range of internal** (for instance sales order processing system, nominal ledger) **and external sources**. One reason for including individual transaction data in a data warehouse is that the user can drill down to access transaction-level detail if necessary. Data is increasingly obtained from newer channels, such as customer care systems, outside agencies or websites.

The warehouse provides a coherent **set of information** to be **used across the organisation** for management **analysis** and **decision making**. The reporting and query tools available within the warehouse should facilitate management reporting and analysis. This analysis can be enhanced through the use of **data mining** software to identify trends and patterns in the data.

2 Costs of information

FAST FORWARD

The costs of information come not only from the costs of **capturing** and **processing** information, but also from the potential costs of **using information inefficiently**.

The costs to an organisation of the collection, processing and production of internal information can be divided into three types. These are: direct data capture costs, direct processing costs, and the indirect costs of producing internal information.

Cost	Examples
Direct data capture	• Use of bar coding and scanners (eg in retailing and manufacturing) • Employee time spent filling in timesheets • Secretary time spent taking minutes at a meeting
Processing	• Payroll department time spent processing and analysing personnel costs • Time for personnel to input data (eg in relation to production) into the management information system (MIS)
Inefficient use of information	• Information collected but not needed • Information stored long after it is needed • Information disseminated more widely than necessary • Collection of the same information by more than one method • Duplication of information
System change	• Modifying existing systems to facilitate data capture and processing (eg to ensure compatibility between software or systems used by different departments)

2.1 Costs of external information

There are effectively five types of cost associated with external information.

Cost	Examples
Direct search costs	• Cost of a marketing research survey (these can be considerable) • Subscriptions to online databases • Subscriptions to magazines, services • Download fees

Cost	Examples
Indirect access costs	• Management and employee time spent finding useful information • Wasted management and employee time on unsuccessful searches for information • Time theft – using office equipment and facilities for private internet activity during working hours • Spurious accuracy/redundancy • Wasted management and employee time on excessive searching • Wasted time on trying to find spurious accuracy
Management costs	• Recording, processing and dissemination of external information • Wasted time due to information overload • Wasted time on excessive processing
Infrastructure costs	• Installation and maintenance of computer networks, servers, landlines etc to facilitate internet searching and internal electronic communication
Time theft	• Wasted time caused by abuse of internet and email access facilities • Lost time • Cost of monitoring and disciplinary procedures • Information overload

In some cases, the **internet** can significantly reduce search time and search cost – more information can be had for less money. However, there may be concerns over the quality and reliability of information obtained, and there could also be a danger of information overload, if the volume of information available means that organisations gather too much information without thinking critically about what they actually need.

2.2 Benefits and limitations of external data

The **benefits** can be quantified in the following terms:

(a) The quality of **decisions** that the data has influenced

(b) **Risk/uncertainties** avoided by having the data

(c) The organisation's ability to **respond** appropriately to the environment or to **improve** its performance

One of the principal **limitations** of external data is that its **quality** cannot be guaranteed. Its **quality** will depend on the following characteristics:

(a) The **producers** of the data. (How reliable are they? Are they neutral or might they be biased? For example, trade associations may not include data which runs counter to the interests of their members. In this respect, when looking at any external data an important consideration is the data's **completeness**. Is it complete, or have the producers of the data been selective in what they report?)

(b) The **reason for the data** being collected in the first place. This might also affect the **level of detail** available in the data.

(c) The **collection method**. (Random samples with a poor response rate are particularly questionable.)

(d) The **age** of the data. Is it still current/relevant, or is it out of date now? (Government statistics and information based on them are often relatively dated, though information technology has speeded up the process.)

(e) **How parameters were defined**. (For instance, the definition of family used by some researchers could well be very different to that used by others.)

Using poor-quality external data can have disastrous consequences: projects may proceed on the basis of overstated demand levels; opportunities may not be grasped because data is out of date and does not show the true state of the market.

2.2.1 Advantages arising from the use of secondary (as opposed to primary) data

(a) The data may solve the problem without the need for any primary research: **time and money is thereby saved**.

(b) **Cost savings** can be substantial because secondary data sources are a great deal **cheaper** than those for primary research.

(c) **Secondary data**, while not necessarily fulfilling all the needs of the business, can be of great use in:

 (i) **Setting the parameters**, defining a hypothesis, highlighting variables; in other words, helping to focus on the central problem

 (ii) **Providing guidance**, by showing past methods of research and so on, for primary data collection

 (iii) **Helping to assimilate the primary research** with past research, highlighting trends and the like

 (iv) **Defining sampling parameters** (target populations, variables and so on)

2.2.2 Disadvantages to the use of secondary data

(a) **Relevance**. The data may not be relevant to the research objectives in terms of the data content itself, classifications used or units of measurement.

(b) **Cost**. Although secondary data is usually cheaper than primary data, some specialist reports can cost large amounts of money. A cost/benefit analysis will determine whether such secondary data should be used or whether primary research would be more economical.

(c) **Availability**. Secondary data may not exist in the specific product or market area.

(d) **Bias**. The secondary data may be biased, depending on who originally carried it out and for what purpose. Attempts should be made to obtain the most original source of the data, to assess it for such bias.

(e) **Accuracy**. The accuracy of the data should be questioned.

The golden rule when using secondary data is **use only meaningful data**. It is obviously sensible to begin with internal sources and a firm with a good MIS should be able to provide a great deal of data. External information should be consulted in order of ease and speed of access.

3 Information for planning and control

FAST FORWARD

Controls are applied at three levels in an organisation: strategic, tactical (management) and operational. Much control is achieved through the **feedback** of internal information.

We have already noted, in Chapter 4, that managers need management accounting information to make effective decisions and to control the activities of their organisation.

Managers can use this information for a variety of purposes:

(a) **To measure performance**. Management accounting information can be used to analyse the performance of the business as a whole, and of the individual divisions, departments or products within the business. Performance reports provide **feedback**, most frequently in the form of comparison between actual performance and budget.

(b) **To control the business**. Performance reports are a crucial element in controlling a business. In order to be able to control their business, managers need to know the following:

 (i) What they want the business to achieve (targets or standards; **budgets**)
 (ii) What the business is actually achieving (**actual performance**)

By comparing the actual achievements with targeted performance, and identifying **variances**, management can decide whether corrective action is needed, and then take the necessary action when required.

Much control information is of an accounting nature because costs, revenues, profits and asset values are major factors in how well or how badly a business performs.

(c) **To plan for the future**. Managers have to plan, and they need information to do this. Much of the information they use is management accounting information.

(d) **To make decisions**. As we have seen, managers are faced with several types of decision:

   (i) **Strategic decisions** (which relate to the longer-term objectives of a business) require information which tends to relate to the organisation as a whole, is in summary form and is derived from both internal and external sources.

   (ii) **Tactical and operational decisions** (which relate to the short or medium term and to a department, product or division rather than the organisation as a whole) require information which is more detailed and more restricted in its sources.

3.1 Control and feedback

Control is dependent on the **receipt and processing of information**, both to plan in the first place and to compare actual results against the plan, so as to judge what control measures are needed.

Plans will be based on an **awareness of the environment** (from externally sourced information) and on the **current performance of the organisation** (based on internal information such as, for example, sales volumes and costs).

Control is achieved through **feedback** – information about actual results produced from within the organisation (that is, internal information) such as variance control reports for the purpose of helping management with control decisions.

The sources of information outlined earlier in the chapter are used to supply **management with data for control**.

For instance, **payroll records** give information on the total cost of staff and a breakdown into cost by function, role, bonuses, taxes and so on which can show management how different cost areas are performing. As payroll is often a large cost, and to some extent discretionary or variable, it is important to monitor and control.

Equally, information on **wage payments** will also be relevant to an organisation's cash flow planning. As far as possible, organisations like to keep their cash balances within certain limits. So, by knowing the amount and timing of wages and salary payments the organisation can make any adjustments to ensure that cash balances remain within the desired limits.

Information about **inventory** levels can also be instructive. For example, some lines of inventory may be slow moving, but management will need to establish why this is. Has a competitor introduced a rival product, or reduced its prices? Have there been any quality issues with the product which have damaged its reputation in the marketplace? Is the product in a long-term decline and should production of it be discontinued? In this respect, information about quantities of a product sold compared to quantities produced could also be very useful. For example, if a product is selling very well, production may need to be increased so that demand can be satisfied and any stock-outs avoided.

Customer data is vital in any business that strives to focus on customers. Thus data on buying habits, where customers shop, what they buy and who the main customers are all gives feedback for control purposes.

Equally, data from customer sales accounts can provide useful information on how customer debts are aged. A report on the ageing of debt can provide management with information on how successful its receivables control policy is. Management's response will be different if half the customer debt has been outstanding for more than, say, 60 days, compared with only 5% of the debt being outstanding for more than 60 days.

3.2 Control and benchmarking

One of the key aims of performance controls is to promote efficiency, and in order to do this managers need to evaluate how efficiently a department (or employee) is currently working.

Comparing actual performance against targets or budgets could be one way to determine how effectively a task is being performed. However, another way would be to benchmark performance against suitable comparators; by comparing performance between departments (internal benchmarking), or by comparing performance in key areas against other organisations (either competitors, or best in class performers).

3.3 External information for planning and control

In addition to internal information extracted from an organisation's operating systems, external information can also be useful for planning, decision making and control.

Management function	Type of information	Example
Planning	• Demand estimates • Market research	For example, if an organisation is considering expansion into a foreign market, external information which would be useful to it includes: Expected demand for its products in that market Social and economic factors in the target country which could affect future demand for products The number and strength of the competitors already in the market, and their future plans Barriers to entry which might prevent it entering the market, including government policies
Decision making	• Demand estimates • Market research • Competitor research	For example, an organisation is reviewing the prices it charges for its products, and is considering an increase in its prices. External information which would be useful to it includes: Market research into the impact that (changes in) price will have on the demand for the product Market research into the price that customers are willing to pay for the product Competitors' pricing policies Government policies which have an impact on the price paid by the customer (eg duties or sales tax levied on the product) Competitors' plans for launching new products or improving competitor products
Control	• Benchmarking • Customers' expectations	If an organisation is looking to pursue a cost leadership strategy, it will need to ensure its costs are kept as low as possible. One way of checking this is by comparing the cost and efficiency of key processes against external benchmarks.

As we mentioned earlier, however, the **value of external information for planning, control and decision making** will very much **depend** on the **quality of the information**, which is very **difficult to assess and/or guarantee**.

Clearly, **some external information**, such as 'technological' or 'political' developments, **does not feed into the management accounting system**, even though it can be in a broader category of management information.

External information of a **quantitative** nature is **easier to feed into the management accounting system**. For example, forecasts of revenues, costs and profits derived from market research and targets based on competitors' performance (the information having been sourced from the internet) are easier to incorporate than qualitative information.

3.4 Benchmarking

Traditionally, control involves the comparison of actual results with an internal standard or target. The practice of **setting targets using external information** is known as benchmarking. We considered benchmarking in more detail in Chapter 1. Refer back to that chapter to remind yourself of what benchmarking is. Remember that benchmarking is a tool for **external** comparison and that it has **weaknesses** as well as strengths. The examination team will expect you to bring this out in any answer you give.

The case study below looks at one particular way in which benchmarking has been applied in a consumer environment. In this case, it is not processes which are being compared between companies, but prices.

Case Study — **Price comparison websites**

Since the late 1990s, as increased internet usage has encouraged greater price transparency, a number of price comparison websites have been set up which allow consumers to compare products between different retailers.

For example, in the UK, mySupermarket is a grocery shopping and comparison website which allows customers to compare prices between Tesco, Asda, Sainsbury's, Ocado, Waitrose, Morrisons and Aldi. In turn, the supermarkets themselves also compare the prices of their goods against their competitors to ensure that their prices are competitive. For example, Sainsbury's 'Brand Match' compares the price of branded products in its stores against those at Asda; and customers receive a coupon for the difference if they could have bought the equivalent products more cheaply in the other store.

However, as well as using comparison websites for simple comparisons on the prices of grocery shopping, millions of people are using comparison websites for choosing financial products: loans, credit cards, insurance and energy tariffs.

Consumers are clearly attracted by the prospect of being able to save money and find a product or service at the cheapest available price.

However, in the UK the Financial Services Authority (FSA) has raised concerns that customers could end up buying inappropriate insurance products because the comparison websites do not take responsibility for checking customers' eligibility for particular products.

Also, there has been growing concern that the websites usually list policies according to price, with the cheapest first, such that customers may be misled into thinking that cost is the most important criterion when choosing insurance, and therefore they may end up buying policies that do not provide the protection they need.

4 Big Data and performance management

FAST FORWARD

The amount of data available to organisations is increasing ever more rapidly, and Big Data – with its characteristics of **volume, velocity and variety** – highlights both the opportunities and challenges which new sources of data present to organisations.

The ability to analyse large, and unstructured, data sets and to uncover previously hidden patterns of information could be an important element of an organisation's competitive advantage. However, as a prerequisite for this, organisations need to have the capacity to store and – more importantly – to analyse these data sets.

One of the key themes in this chapter and the previous one has been the way organisations collect and use information to support their strategic, tactical and operational decision making. Crucially, though, organisations today have more transactional data than they have ever had before – about their customers, their suppliers and their operations.

The growth of the internet, multimedia, wireless networks, smartphones, social media, sensors and other digital technologies are all helping to fuel a data revolution. In the so-called 'Internet of Things', sensors embedded in physical objects, such as mobile phones, motor vehicles, smart energy meters, RFID tags, tracking devices and traffic flow monitors, all create and communicate data which is shared across wired and wireless networks that function in a similar way to the internet. The timing and location of cash withdrawals from ATM machines could also be a potential source of data.

Key term

Internet of things: A situation in which everyday objects have network connectivity, allowing them to send and receive data over the internet.

Furthermore, consumers using social media, smartphones, laptops and tablets to browse the internet, to search for items, to make purchases and to share information with other users all create trails of data. Similarly, internet search indexes (such as Google Trends) can be a source of data for 'Big Data analytics'.

Consequently, whereas intuition has historically played a large part in business decisions (in the absence of reliable and timely data) organisations now expect business decisions to be based on robust data analytics, supported by intuition and experience.

One of the key challenges facing today's business managers is how they can use data and information about current performance to leverage additional value throughout an organisation's value chain (for example, through identifying greater operational efficiencies, or enhancing customer relationships) or to identify new sources of competitive advantage.

4.1 What is Big Data?

In a June 2011 report, 'Big data: The next frontier for innovation, competition and productivity', McKinsey Global Institute defined Big Data as 'datasets whose size is beyond the ability of typical database software to capture, store, manage and analyse'.

However, the most widely cited definition of Big Data is that given by the technology research firm, Gartner.

Key term

Big Data is 'high-volume, high-velocity and high-variety information assets that demand cost-effective, innovative forms of information processes for enhanced insight and decision making.' (Gartner)

4.2 Characteristics of Big Data

Volume – Perhaps the main benefit of Big Data analytics comes from the ability to process very large amounts of information. The bigger the data, the more potential insights it can give in terms of identifying trends and patterns, and in terms of getting a deeper understanding of customer requirements. For example, as most customers use the internet, smartphones and social media in their everyday lives, these can now also be sources of data for organisations alongside any data they may capture internally – for example, from customer loyalty cards or the transactions recorded in EPOS tills.

However, the 'volume' aspect of Big Data also presents the most obvious challenges to conventional IT structures, due to volume of storage space required for the data. If organisations are capturing increasing volumes of data, this has implications for the capacity of the information systems needed to store and analyse that data.

In this respect, the use of external capacity (ie cloud computing) could be a useful way for organisations to increase the amount of data they can store.

Velocity – Refers to the increasing speed with which data flows into an organisation, and with which it is processed within the organisation.

Online retailers are able to compile records of each click and interaction a customer makes while visiting a website, rather than simply recording the final sale at the end of a customer transaction. Moreover, retailers who are able to utilise information about customer clicks and interactions quickly – for example, by recommending additional purchases – can use this speed to generate competitive advantage.

It is important to recognise that the competitive advantage an organisation can gain from 'velocity' relates to the speed with which data is processed and the velocity of a system's outputs, as well as the speed with which data initially flows into it.

Variety (or variability) – A common theme in relation to Big Data is the diversity of source data, with a lot of the data being unstructured (ie not in a database). For example, keywords from conversations people have on Facebook or Twitter, and content they share through media files (tagged photographs, or online video postings), could be sources of unstructured data.

However, this variety presents a challenge to organisations, as they need to find ways of capturing, storing and processing the data. If data is too big, moves too fast, or doesn't fit with the structures of an organisation's existing information systems, then in order to gain value from it an organisation needs to find an alternative way to process that data.

In this respect, 'Big Data analytics' is likely to be crucial to making use of the potential value of Big Data.

Big Data analytics – Refers to the process of collecting, organising and analysing large sets of data ('Big Data') to discover patterns and other useful information which an organisation can use in its future business decisions.

Big Data analytics should help an organisation to reveal insights in data which had previously been too difficult or costly to analyse – due to the volume and variability of the data involved. These insights can be historical, real-time or predictive.

Being able to extract insights from the data available is crucial for organisations to benefit from the availability of Big Data – for example, to help them understand the complexity of the environment in which they are operating, and to respond swiftly to the opportunities and threats presented by it; or to develop new insights and understanding into what customers need or want.

However, the value of any insights which can be gained from Big Data also depends on the quality and accuracy of the underlying data. This highlights another 'V' characteristic of Big Data: veracity.

Veracity (truthfulness) – Although the volume of data available to organisations is greater than ever before, for that data to be beneficial for decision making it needs to be reliable and truthful. If the data is not truthful (for example, due to bias or inconsistencies within it) this could reduce the value of any decisions which are informed by it. Moreover, hidden biases in the data could present significant risks to an organisation – for example, if the organisation develops a new product believing there is sufficient customer demand to make the product viable, when in fact that demand does not exist.

Poor data quality can often be the main barrier to executives integrating more data and analytics into their decision making.

4.3 Making use of Big Data

Historically, only the largest corporations have had sufficient resources to be able to process Big Data. Now, however, it is becoming possible for all organisations to access and process the volumes of Big Data potentially available to them, due to cost-effective approaches such as cloud-based architectures and open source software.

McKinsey's 'Big Data' report suggests that 'Big data has now reached every sector in the global economy. Like other essential factors of production such as [physical] assets and human capital, much of modern economic activity simply couldn't take place without it.'

This suggests that the ability to capture and analyse Big Data, and the information gained by doing so, have become important strategic resources for organisations. Making effective use of Big Data could confer competitive advantage for an organisation. Alternatively, in time, competitors who fail to develop their capabilities to use Big Data and information as strategic resources could be left behind by those who do.

While these might initially seem to be quite bold claims, Big Data can certainly create value for organisations through its ability to drive innovation and by helping organisations gain greater and faster insights into their customers.

Similarly, analysing data from as many sources as possible when making decisions can also increase the amount of useful information available to managers when they are making decisions.

However, the distinction between simply having 'data' and having 'useful information' is important here. Simply having more data available does not, in itself, benefit organisations or provide them with any competitive advantage. Instead, organisations benefit if that data is converted into valuable information and managers then use that information to make effective decisions – which, for example, improve operational efficiency and the customer experience, or which enable new business models to be created.

Case Study — Big Data and the logistics industry

Logistics providers, such as DHL, manage a massive flow of goods around the globe, and at the same time create vast data sets; for example, from recording the origin and destination, size and weight of millions of shipments every day, and then from tracking their location across global delivery networks.

Big Data can also provide a number of potential benefits to logistics providers, and this case example highlights three of these.

Last-mile optimisation

A major constraint on the levels of operational efficiency in a distribution network is the so-called 'last mile' – the final stage of a supply chain in which goods are handed over to the recipient. This final stage can often be one of the most expensive in the supply chain (for example, if a delivery driver becomes stuck in a traffic jam, or if a recipient is not present when a courier attempts to deliver their package, and so the delivery has to be rearranged).

However, analysis of Big Data can help to increase last-mile efficiency, through route optimisation aimed at saving time in the delivery process. Rapid processing of real-time information assists route optimisation in a number of ways.

When the delivery vehicle is loaded and unloaded, sensors detect the destinations of the packages and the optimal delivery sequence is then calculated for the driver.

Once the delivery vehicle has begun its journey, telematics databases are used to automatically change delivery routes according to current traffic conditions. For example, if heavy traffic is causing delays on the route originally scheduled, a revised route is generated for the driver to avoid those delays.

In addition, routing intelligence makes use of availability and location information posted by recipients in order to avoid unsuccessful delivery attempts.

The 'Big Data' aspects of this scenario are that the driver's control systems make use of a number of different optimisation procedures, fed by correlated streams of real-time events, to dynamically re-route vehicles while they are on the road. As a result, each driver receives instant driving direction updates from their onboard navigation system, guiding them to the next best point of delivery.

Capacity planning

Effective capacity planning can be an important competitive advantage for logistics providers. Excess capacities reduce profitability, while capacity shortages affect service quality and potentially jeopardise customer satisfaction (eg by increasing delivery times).

Resource planning is therefore an important consideration for logistics planners at both strategic and operational levels. At a strategic level, the topology (links, nodes etc) and the capacity of the distribution network need to be adapted according to anticipated future demand. The results from capacity planning often lead to capital expenditure, such as investments in warehouses, distribution centres and vehicles. Therefore, more precise capacity demand forecasting can increase efficiency and lower the risks attached to investing in storage and fleet capacity (either by overinvesting or underinvesting).

Big Data can support such capacity planning by analysing data about the historical capacity and utilisation rates of transit points and transportation routes. In addition, it can take account of seasonal factors and emerging freight flow trends (which are affected by external economic information, such as industry or regional growth forecasts).

As well as identifying potential under-capacity, planners can expose any potential overcapacity, and identifying this should provide a trigger to try to increase sales volumes – for example, by using dynamic pricing mechanisms.

Risk evaluation and resilience planning

Business to business logistics providers know their customers' supply chains in great detail, and customers rely on the providers' predictive risk assessment.

In order to be able to identify potential threats to the supply chain, logistics providers need to maintain a model which not only describes all the elements of the supply chain topology but also monitors the forces which could affect the performance of that supply chain – for example, local developments in politics, economy, or events in the natural environment.

Data on these environmental factors can come from a number of sources (eg weather forecasts, new sites, social media and blogs) but must then be aggregated and analysed. Much of this data stream is unstructured and continuously updating, so the power of Big Data analytics in dealing with velocity and variability could be invaluable in detecting supply chain risks. For example, if there is a tornado warning in the region where a transhipment point is located, the logistics company will need to alert its customer to this risk, as well as suggesting suitable counter-measures to mitigate against potential disruption (for example, either re-planning the transport route, or else increasing substitute supplies from another area).

Based on a research paper produced by DHL (2013): 'Big Data in Logistics', www.dhl.com [Accessed 20 January 2016]

4.4 The value of Big Data

The case study above (about Big Data in the logistics industry) illustrates some of the ways Big Data can help an organisation, but more generally, DHL's report 'Big Data in Logistics' suggested that one of the main ways in which Big Data can create value for organisations is through improving operational efficiency. Data can be used to make better decisions, to optimise resource consumption and to improve process quality and performance. In this respect, Big Data provides similar benefits to automated data processing, although Big Data can increase the level of transparency in the data.

McKinsey's 'Big Data' report also highlights its ability to create transparency as one of five broad ways in which Big Data can create value for organisations:

(a) **Creating transparency** – Making data more easily accessible to relevant stakeholders, in a timely manner, can create value in its own right – for example, by revealing insights from data which had previously been too costly or complex to process. This transparency could relate to data within an organisation as well as external data – through better integration and analysis of data produced by different parts of an organisation. For example, within a manufacturing company, integrating data from research and development, engineering and manufacturing units to enable concurrent engineering could significantly reduce time to market as well as improving quality.

However, in many cases the increased transparency resulting from Big Data is likely to relate to external data. For example, analysing shoppers' transactions, alongside social and geographical data, can reveal peer influence among customers – ie the extent to which shoppers' choices are shaped by their friends and neighbours as well as by the marketing efforts of the company itself.

Another important context in which transparency can be valuable for an organisation is in relation to **fraud**. For example, having real-time information available from a variety of sources could help an organisation expose fraud and irregular business practices among customers, employees, suppliers or other partners more quickly than it would otherwise have been able to do.

(b) **Performance improvement** – The increasing amount of transactional data they store in digital form provides organisations with an increasing amount of accurate and detailed performance data – in real or almost real time. By analysing variability in performance – and the causes of that variability – organisations then manage performance to higher levels. For example, identifying what customers are saying in social media about an organisation's products or its customer service could help the organisation identify how well it is meeting customers' needs. Customers' conversations could help the organisation identify potential changes which are needed to its products, or the way they are delivered, in order to meet customers' needs more effectively – and thereby to increase sales.

In addition to increasing revenues, cutting costs is also likely to be a key component of increasing profits. Having a complete picture of operational activities – and a detailed picture of costs – can help an organisation identify patterns that indicate wasteful or inefficient processes. Similarly, understanding the dynamics of the supply chain in more detail could help an organisation optimise its costs, capacity and inventory levels, as well as the service it provides customers (for example, through improved product availability).

(c) **Market segmentation and customisation** – The volume and variety within Big Data enables organisations to create highly specific segments within its markets and to tailor its products and services precisely to meet those needs.

The idea of market segmentation is already a key concept within strategic marketing, which you should be familiar with from your studies in Paper P3. However, Big Data could facilitate the real-time micro-segmentation of customers for targeted promotions and advertising – for example, by sending tailored recommendation to customers' mobile devices while they are in the right area to take advantage of the offers.

The ability to perform precise customer segmentation and targeting could be used to help organisations improve customer loyalty and retention, as well as in attracting new customers.

McKinsey's report highlights that Big Data could also be valuable in segmenting public sector markets. Traditionally, public sector markets have not segmented citizens (service users) in the same way that private sector companies have segmented customers and potential customers. However, Big Data could enable public sector organisations to also tailor products and services more effectively.

(d) **Decision making** – The sophisticated analytics tools which are used to uncover previously hidden patterns and trends in data could also be used to improve decision-making. For example, trends identified by a retailer in in-store and online sales – in real time – could be used to manage inventories and pricing. In some cases, decisions will be made by managers in store (based on analytics from the data sets) but in other cases the decisions themselves could even become automated. So for example, a retailer could use algorithms to optimise decisions about inventory levels and pricing in response to current and predicted sales data.

(e) **New products and services** – Entities can use data about social trends and consumer behaviours to create new products and services to meet customers' needs, or to enhance existing products and services so that they meet customers' needs more exactly. For example, the emergence of real-time location data, from traffic light sensors and satellite navigation systems, could enable insurance companies to refine the pricing of their insurance policies according to where, and how, people drive their cars.

More generally, Big Data could also provide new business opportunities in their own right. For example, Facebook's advertising business incorporates analysis of a user's actions as well as their friends' actions. Equally, Amazon could be seen as an example of a company which has built its business – and serves its customers – using data and analytics; for example, through the way it makes recommendations for customers linked to the purchases made by other customers with similar interests.

4.5 Potential risks and challenges of Big Data

Some critics have argued that Big Data is simply a buzzword, a vague term which has turned into an obsession in large organisations and the media. However, the critics argue that very few instances exist where analysing vast amounts of data has resulted in significant new discoveries of performance improvements for an organisation.

Correlation not causation – The primary focus within Big Data is on finding correlations between data sets, rather than focusing on the cause of any trends and patterns. It can often be easier to identify correlations between different variables than to determine what – if anything – is causing that correlation. Correlation does not necessarily imply causality.

Similarly, if an organisation does not understand the factors which give rise to a correlation, it will equally not know what factors may cause the correlation to break down.

Case Study

Google Flu Trends

Google Flu Trends was presented as a means of tracking and predicting the spread of influenza across the US.

The program used algorithms which identified correlations between the symptoms people searched for online and flu symptoms.

However, after providing a swift and accurate account of flu outbreaks for several winters, in the 2012–3 season Flu Trends overstated the spread of flu-like illnesses across the US by almost a factor of two.

The cause of this problem was that ultimately Google did not know what linked the search terms with the spread of flu, and Google's algorithms weren't designed to identify what caused what. They were simply finding statistical patterns in the data; and as such they focused on correlation rather than causation.

One explanation of the Flu Trends failure in 2012–3 is that there were a number of news stories in December about the dangers of flu, and these provoked internet searches by people who were healthy.

Sample population – While the data sets available through Big Data are often very large, they are still not necessarily representative of the entire data population as a whole. For example, if an organisation uses 'tweets' from the social networking site Twitter to provide insight into public opinion on a certain issue, there is no guarantee the 'tweets' will accurately represent the view of society as a whole. (For example, according to the Pew Research Internet Project, in 2013, US-based Twitter users were disproportionately young, urban or suburban, and black.)

Data vs relevant information – More generally, in a review article 'Two dogmas of Big Data', the accountancy firm Deloitte also notes that there is a misconception that 'more bytes yields more benefits'. In other words, management decisions are based on relevant information, not raw data. Therefore, by itself, increasing the volume of data available to an organisation does not necessarily provide managers with better information for decision making.

Deloitte's article also suggests that, given the time and expense involved in gathering and using Big Data, entities need to consider whether 'big data yields commensurately big value'. As the article points out, the paramount issue when gathering data is not volume, variety or velocity *per se*, but 'gathering the right data that carries the most useful information for the problem at hand'.

Data silos – Furthermore, an organisation's ability to maximise the value it obtains from Big Data could be restricted by 'data silos' within the organisation (although this issue represents a problem with the ways organisations share data and information between departments rather than a specific limitation of the value of Big Data). For example, insurance companies are aware that Big Data could have a significant effect on their industry – through helping to combat fraud or through enabling them to understand customers better and to price premiums more accurately. Equally, however, insurers are aware that data silos persist within their organisations which reduce the value they can extract from the data, with communication channels between the risk department and the sales and marketing departments, in particular, often being inadequate.

Volume and variety – We highlighted that volume and variety are two of the key characteristics of Big Data. Yet these characteristics also contribute to the challenges of using Big Data. The enormous volumes of data pouring into organisations mean that traditional information systems architectures and infrastructures are not able to record and process the data. As such, IT teams or business analysts may become burdened with increasing requests for data, ad hoc analysis and one-off reports. Equally, this will mean that the information and analysis will not be available to decision makers as quickly as the 'velocity' aspect of Big Data may initially imply.

4.6 Ethics and governance

Potential ethical issues

Although Big Data can help entities gather more information about their customers and understand customer behaviour more precisely, gathering this data could also raise significant ethical and privacy issues. In particular, to what extent should information about individuals remain private (or confidential) rather than being shared across analytical systems?

Organisations' demand for Big Data has led to data itself becoming a business – with entities such as data brokers collecting massive amounts of data about individuals, often without their knowledge or consent, and being shared in ways they don't want or expect. However, critics argue that in order for Big Data to work in ethical terms, the individuals whose data is being collected need to have a transparent view of how their data is being used or sold.

On the one hand, if organisations have access to personal data – such as health records and financial records – this could help them to pinpoint the best medical treatment for a patient or the most appropriate financial products for a customer. On the other hand, however, these categories of personal data are those which consumers regard as being the most sensitive. In this respect, Big Data raises questions around how organisations and individuals will manage the trade-offs between privacy and utility of data.

If companies are using Big Data properly, it will be vital for them to consider data protection and privacy issues. On the one hand, they must ensure they comply with any legislation about these areas. But even if they comply with prevailing laws, the large-scale collection and exploitation of data could still arouse public debate, which could subsequently damage corporate reputation and brand value.

The issue of **data security** is also closely linked to issues of privacy. What steps – and technologies – are organisations taking to prevent breaches of data security which could expose either personal consumer information or confidential corporate information?

The significance of data security as a potential issue could also be increased if organisations want to use third-party cloud service providers to store their data. Although using an external service provider ('cloud computing') could be an effective way of increasing the volume of data an organisation can store, the organisation needs to be sure that the provider can protect their data.

Potential governance issues

The use of Big Data also requires organisations to maintain strong governance on data quality. For example, the validity of any analysis of that data is likely to be compromised unless there are effective cleansing procedures to remove incomplete, obsolete or duplicated data records.

Similarly, it is very important for organisations to ensure that the overall data quality from different data sources is high because the volume, variety and velocity characteristics of Big Data all combine to make it difficult to implement efficient procedures for validating data or adjusting data errors.

5 Recording and processing methods in business entities

FAST FORWARD

The **type of business entity** will influence the recording and processing methods adopted.

(a) A factory which runs a **single continuous production line** may have relatively **simple, structured information requirements** and hence will **not** require **sophisticated recording and processing methods**. The **information cycle** and hence **management accounting reporting** may only be required on a **monthly** or **quarterly** basis.

(b) A **modern 'world class' manufacturer** is likely to operate in an environment in which **product life cycles** are very **short** and a high level of **flexibility** is required to satisfy sophisticated customer requirements. A **large range** of customised products will be produced. **Information requirements** are thus **less structured**, **ad hoc reports** will be required and the **information cycle** will need to be very **short**. Significant **investment** in **IT** will be required to provide the necessary information.

(c) Organisations that need **accurate** and **up to date** information on, say, inventory levels need to use some form of **online real-time** approach. Large retail stores, for example, use **electronic point of sales** (EPoS) devices, which include **bar code readers**, providing immediate sales and inventory level information.

(d) If **accuracy** and **processing volume** is important, as in the banking sector, **magnetic ink character recognition (MICR)** can be used to process thousands of cheques and deposit slips quickly and accurately.

(e) Other organisations might record and process information periodically rather than in real time. **Batch processing**, for example, might be used by a small bookshop to update its inventory records at the end of a day.

(f) Smaller organisations might rely on **manual** recording and processing methods, although advances in information technology mean that computerised methods are at everyone's disposal.

Case Study

EPoS Systems

Virtually all major retail stores now use electronic point of sales (EPoS) systems, which give them a fast and convenient way of transacting sales, and at the same time recording vital business information.

At the most basic level, EPoS systems total up a customer's bill, calculate any change due and issue receipts in the same way that cash tills have historically done.

However, EPoS systems can also keep track of inventory levels and can record customer information. This ability to manage inventory and to promote customer relationship management (CRM) helps EPoS systems improve a retailer's performance.

For example, by keeping track of the products sold, an EPoS system can assist inventory management by ensuring that the retailer has adequate supplies of a product to meet demand, and reorders top performing products as necessary. However, the system could also highlight which product lines are not selling very well, such that the retailer may question whether it wants to continue selling them, or whether it discounts their price to try to encourage demand.

Equally, if management wants to change the price of an item, or run a special offer on it, this can be done very easily with an EPoS system. Importantly, from a performance measurement perspective, the system can also record data on how the price changes have affected sales.

The data from EPoS systems can also be used for marketing purposes, particularly when used in conjunction with store loyalty cards (such as Tesco's Clubcard). The systems can record trends and patterns in individual customers' behaviour, and in doing so they can provide valuable data for personalised marketing campaigns.

5.1 Factors affecting the choice of processing methods

As a general point, it is important to note that the methods used for recording and processing information should suit:

- The **volume** and **complexity** of data being processed
- The level of **accuracy** or the **quality of data** required
- The **speed** with which the information is required

The **size and structure** of an organisation also affects the choice of processing method; for example, whether the organisation is centralised or decentralised. Equally, the information requirements of a large multinational corporation (with managers in different countries) are likely to be very different to those of an owner-managed business, based on a single site.

The **nature of the business** could also affect the information required. For example, the requirements in a manufacturing business will be different to those for a service business.

The following table provides examples of the typical information requirements of organisations operating in different sectors.

Sector	Information type	Example(s)	General comment
Manufacturing	Strategic	Future demand estimates New product development plans Competitor analysis	The information requirements of commercial organisations are influenced by the need to make and monitor profit. Information that contributes to the following measures is important. • Changeover times • Number of common parts • Level of product diversity • Product and process quality
	Tactical	Variance analysis Departmental accounts Inventory turnover	
	Operational	Production reject rate Materials and labour used Inventory levels	
Service	Strategic	Forecast sales growth and market share Profitability, capital structure	Organisations have become more customer and results orientated over the last decade. As a consequence, the difference between the information requirements of service organisations and those of other organisations has decreased. Businesses have realised that most of their activities can be measured, and many can be measured in similar ways regardless of the business sector.
	Tactical	Resource utilisation such as average staff time charged out, number of customers per hairdresser, number of staff per account Customer satisfaction rating	
	Operational	Staff timesheets Customer waiting time Individual customer feedback	

Sector	Information type	Example(s)	General comment
Public	Strategic	Population demographics Expected government policy	Public sector (and non profit making) organisations often don't have one overriding objective. Their information requirements depend on the objectives chosen. The information provided often requires interpretation (eg student exam results are not affected by the quality of teaching alone). Information may compare actual performance with: • Standards • Targets • Similar activities • Indices • Activities over time as trends
	Tactical	Hospital occupancy rates Average class sizes Percentage of reported crimes solved	
	Operational	Staff timesheets Vehicles available Student daily attendance records	
Non-profit/ charities	Strategic	Activities of other charities Government (and in some cases overseas government) policy Public attitudes	Many of the comments regarding public sector organisations can be applied to not-for-profit organisations. Information to judge performance usually aims to assess economy, efficiency and effectiveness. A key measure of efficiency for charities is the percentage of revenue that is spent on the publicised cause (eg rather than on advertising or administration).
	Tactical	Percentage of revenue spent on admin Average donation 'Customer' satisfaction statistics	
	Operational	Households collected from/approached Banking documentation Donations	

6 Developments in IT and recording and processing systems

The management accounting information system might be **connected to and able to receive data from other information systems** within the firm, such as the purchasing system, the production planning and scheduling system and the firm's overall financial system. These various systems may be found on mainframe computers or networked personal computers, and may be geographically close or distant. **Unified corporate databases** allow users to access the same information across the organisation. For instance, employees across the organisation may see data on jobs and projects and make reports. These can be read by top management who can use the system to integrate corporate planning. **Network technology** is used by organisations to integrate workers across sites and working at home. Developments in broadband, particularly improved capacity, and protecting the security of data have improved the ability to communicate across sites and from home. Multiple-use applications, for instance telephone and email, can be handled by enhanced networks.

Nowadays, **broadband** and **commercial telecommunications systems allow** distant computers to **communicate** with each other and to send and receive information. This information can then be **downloaded** onto personal computers (PCs) using compatible software.

6.1 Information overload

In general, developments in IT have had a positive impact on organisations. However, in looking at the impact of technology it is also worth considering the potential dangers of information overload.

Nowadays, where mobile phones, computers and tablets and the internet have become such an intrinsic part of our social and working lives, we have numerous potential sources of information all fighting to be heard at once, including websites, emails, Twitter feeds and social networking updates. However, the volume of potential information available means that people may be unable to assimilate information effectively. Consequently, if information is not presented clearly and coherently within organisations, there is a danger that managers and staff will overlook it, with the related danger that they will subsequently be ill-informed about important issues.

This has important implications for the way management information is presented: the key points need to be presented in such a way that they are clearly communicated to their audience and do not get overlooked.

A related consequence of information overload is that people's attention spans appear to have shortened. This again has important implications for the way management information is presented and distributed. Instead of presenting long, detailed reports, users are now more likely to value shorter reports, indicating key points of interest.

6.2 Personal computers (PCs)

FAST FORWARD

The availability of cheap and powerful **PCs** has transformed the role of management information systems.

High volumes of data can be sourced from outside the organisation (using **Electronic Data Interchange**) or from within it (from the computers running the automated production process). Such data can be stored, retrieved and processed into information and reported in a timely and ultimately cost-effective manner.

Electronic Data Interchange (EDI) involves the computer to computer exchange of documents, in a standardised electronic format, between business partners. By using electronic exchange instead of paper-based exchange of business documents, organisations can benefit from reduced processing costs, increased processing speed, reduced errors and improved relationships with business partners.

6.3 Spreadsheet packages

The availability of spreadsheet packages means that managers are able to **download data** from a **database** and **manipulate** it as they like. The speed, ease of use and capacity of PCs is such that, when combined with the power of the spreadsheet, most of the business **analysis** problems that a manager might wish to tackle can be dealt with. This means that managers can carry out their **own investigations and analyses** as and when they wish. In the recent past, it was necessary to design and develop purpose-built information processing and reporting systems that were inflexible, took months or years to become available and were extremely expensive.

6.4 Database packages

Networked PCs containing spreadsheet software which are connected to databases enable managers to **access and manipulate data** far more effectively and at a **fraction of the cost** of previous generations of MISs. Both standard and ad hoc **reporting is facilitated** and any number of managers can make use of the data, thereby **reducing duplication** of effort and speeding up the control and decision-making process.

6.5 Software packages

Modern **management accounting techniques** (such as activity-based costing) and modern **production methods** (such as just-in-time) require MISs that can access **large amounts of data** and report **accurate detailed information frequently**. In the past, the excessive cost and time to carry out the necessary tasks manually meant this sort of information simply could not be provided.

Advances in the **power of PCs** and the **sophistication of software packages** mean that MIS are a necessary part of the organisational framework in the modern business environment.

Enterprise Resource Planning Systems (ERPS) were discussed in Chapter 7. To remind you, they are an advanced MIS that have the following features:

(a) **Integration and control** of all information flows in the organisation using a common database. ERPS provide an integrated corporate information system, helping organisations to control their operations – including inventory, purchasing, manufacturing, finance and personnel operations. ERPS allow an organisation to automate and integrate most of its business processes, and to share common data and practices across the whole organisation.

(b) **Accessible** by users across the organisation. Managers can obtain information previously only available from the finance function. ERPS may also incorporate transactions with an organisation's suppliers.

(c) **Real-time** information. ERPS allow organisations to produce and access information on all aspects of operations in a real-time environment.

(d) **Once-only data entry** typically where the data originates. So information on a purchase of a computer would be entered on the purchase ledger and fed through to assets, suppliers, cash book and so on.

One of the key benefits of ERPS is that they help large national and, in particular, multinational companies to manage geographically dispersed and complex operations. For example, an organisation's UK sales office may be responsible for marketing, selling and servicing a product assembled in China using parts manufactured in France and Hong Kong. ERP enables the organisation to understand and manage the demand placed on the various plants in the supply chain.

6.6 Email systems

These allow information to be transmitted **quickly** throughout an organisation and **around the world**, considerably improving an organisation's efficiency and effectiveness, its response to problems and its decision-making process.

6.7 Computer Telephony Integration (CTI)

CTI systems **gather information** about callers, such as their telephone number and customer account number or demographic information (age, income, interests and so on). This is stored on a customer **database** and can be **called up and sent to the screen** of the person dealing with the call, perhaps before the call has even been put through.

Order forms with key details entered already can be displayed on screen automatically.

6.8 WiFi

WiFi allows computers with wireless network adapters to connect to the internet when within range of a wireless network connected to the internet. The coverage of one or more (interconnected) access points or hotspots can comprise an area as small as a few rooms or as large as many square miles. It means that users can still connect to the internet while travelling around. This gives them more flexibility over where they do their work and where they view data and reports produced by the information systems in their organisations.

6.9 Radio frequency identification (RFID) 12/13

Radio frequency identification (**RFID**) allows organisations to keep track of assets by tagging them with small radio receivers (typically referred to as an RFID tag) applied to or incorporated into an asset, product, animal or person.

RFID is becoming increasingly widely used in **supply chain management**. RFID tags attached to materials or inventory enable an entity to track the movement of that inventory between locations more accurately, and to get an exact count of items coming into storage and items held in storage.

6.9.1 Example uses of RFID

RFID systems can be used just about anywhere, from clothing tags to vehicles to pet tags – anywhere that a unique identification system is needed. Here are a few examples of how RFID technology is being used in everyday places.

(a) RFID systems are being used in some hospitals to track a patient's location, and to provide real-time tracking of the location of doctors and nurses. In addition, the system can be used to track the whereabouts of expensive and critical equipment, and even to control access to drugs, paediatrics, and other areas of the hospital that are considered 'restricted access' areas.

(b) RFID in retail stores offers real-time inventory tracking that allows companies to monitor and control inventory supply at all times.

(c) A major benefit could be in the consumer goods supply chain, where an RFID tag attached to a consumer product could be tracked from manufacturer to the retail store right to the consumer's home.

Inventory management systems

The co-operative 'Granada La Palma' (GLP), located in the Granada province in the South-East of Spain, is the world's largest grower and dealer of speciality tomatoes, including cherry tomatoes.

The co-operative comprises a group of more than 600 farmers, selling to markets in the UK, France, Germany and the Scandinavian countries, as well as in Spain.

The co-operative's main aim is to deliver a steady supply of fresh tomatoes to its customers, which requires it to have accurate information about product inventory and its supply chain processes.

In September 2013, GLP deployed an RFID inventory-management system to help manage its cherry tomato products.

Prior to implementing the RFID system, GLP used to track the pallets and boxes filled with cherry tomatoes using either manual processes or bar code scanners – both of which methods were subject to problems with human error, lack of accuracy and high operational costs. The co-operative's operations manager said that one of the main problems leading to high costs was that, using the bar code system, each batch of tomatoes needed a different bar code label. In addition, the labels often got damaged due to the working environment, leading to errors when they were read.

The operations manager also pointed out two further problems with the old system.

Identifying the location of inventory in the warehouse was almost impossible.

The system was not integrated with the co-operative's ERPS, which meant the bar code information 'could not be leveraged for the purposes of inventory management and production planning.'

However, the new RFID solution allows the pallets of cherry tomatoes to be tracked from the cold warehouse where they are temporarily stored when they arrive from the farms, to the production line where they are sorted and packaged for customers. In turn, the RFID solution then monitors the movement of the tomatoes to the logistics area, from where they are shipped to customers.

Exam focus point

> One of the questions in the December 2013 exam asked candidates to assess the impact of an RFID system on performance management in a group of hospitals.
>
> The scenario highlighted that the current asset registers in the hospitals were often unreliable because equipment is used but then not replaced in the correct location – therefore one clear benefit of an RFID system should be that it enables staff to find the equipment they need to treat patients more quickly and easily.

Real-time processing

RFID technologies and the 'velocity' aspect of Big Data both highlight another characteristic of modern IT processing systems: real-time processing. In real-time processing, transactions and data are processed as soon as they arise. For example, if a passenger buys an airline ticket, the airline company needs to update its records for this instantly, to prevent another passenger from being able to double-book a seat.

The key benefit of real-time processing is that it provides organisations with the most up to date information possible about their performance.

6.10 Network technology

Network technology has evolved from early LAN-connected computers to systems allowing home workers to connect to the organisation's systems using virtual private network (VPN) links which treat home workers as if they were on site.

In Chapter 4, we noted the development of network organisational structures, and the emergence of virtual organisations. Network technology has played a vital role in the development of these new organisational structures.

6.11 Unified corporate databases

Unified corporate databases integrate data from subsystems (for instance, production and sales) allowing management to see an overall picture of where performance is, and thereby help inform future business decisions.

A unified corporate database provides a single software solution that uses an organisation's existing databases and financial models to improve control over budgeting, forecasting and planning; reporting, consolidations and scorecards; or financial analysis and modelling.

Unified corporate databases could also permit links to be made between different sets of data, such as payroll and HR records. We covered ERPS earlier in this chapter and in Chapter 7. They are a good example of an integrated database.

6.11.1 Task databases

Also, if an organisation (for example, an audit firm) undertakes multiple projects and tasks (ie audits for different clients) it could benefit from using a corporate database which employees can all access to find information about the jobs assigned to them, to view the overall progress of projects in which they are involved, and to make reports about their work performance. At the same time, such a database can be useful for company co-ordinators for general unified planning of a company's activities.

7 Instant access to data

Exam focus point

> In this section we will look at some of the ways IT systems have facilitated access to management accounting data in organisations. However, remember that in the context of Paper P5 your main focus should not be on the details of the technology itself, but rather on how instant access to data can help performance management.
>
> For example, one of the question requirements in the June 2011 exam asked candidates to evaluate the potential impact of a new executive information system on an organisation's performance management.

FAST FORWARD

> **Access to data** has been facilitated by **groupware**, **intranets**, **extranets**, **databases**, **data warehousing** and **data mining**.

7.1 Distribution of data

Developments in IT have facilitated the distribution of data, making it instantly available to those who require it. Such developments are known generally as office automation systems.

(a) Word processing
(b) Electronic schedules
(c) Desktop databases (see below)
(d) Web publishing
(e) Voicemail
(f) Email

7.2 Sharing of data

There have also been significant developments in the ways in which data can be shared.

7.2.1 Groupware

Key term

> **Groupware** is a term used to describe software that provides functions that can be used by collaborative work groups.

Typically, groups using groupware are small project-orientated teams that have important tasks and tight deadlines.

Features might include the following:

(a) A **scheduler** allowing users to keep track of their schedule and plan meetings with others

(b) An **address book**

(c) '**To do**' lists

(d) A **journal**, used to record interactions with important contacts, items (such as email messages) and files that are significant to the user, and activities of all types and track them all without having to remember where each one was saved

(e) A **jotter** for jotting down notes as quick reminders of questions, ideas, and so on

(f) File sharing and distribution utilities

There are clearly advantages in having information such as this available from the desktop at the touch of a button, rather than relying on scraps of paper, address books and corporate telephone directories. It is when groupware is used to **share information** with colleagues that it comes into its own. Here are some of the features that may be found.

(a) **Messaging**, comprising an **email** inbox which is used to send and receive messages from the office/home/on the road and **routing** facilities, enabling users to send a message to a single person, send it sequentially to a number of people (who may add to it or comment on it before passing it on), or sending it to everyone at once.

(b) Access to an **information database**, and customisable **'views'** of the information held on it, which can be used to standardise the way information is viewed in a workgroup.

(c) **Group scheduling** can be used to keep track of colleagues' itineraries.

(d) **Public folders**. These collect, organise, and share files with others on a team or across the organisation.

(e) **Hyperlinks** in mail messages. The recipient can click the hyperlink to go directly to a web page or file server.

7.2.2 Intranets

Key term

> An **intranet** is an internal network used to share information. Intranets utilise internet technology. A firewall surrounding an intranet fends off unauthorised access.

The idea behind an 'intranet' is that companies set up their own **mini version of the internet**. Intranets use a combination of the organisation's own networked computers and internet technology. Each employee has a browser, used to access a server computer that holds corporate information on a wide variety of topics, and in some cases also offers access to the internet.

Potential applications include company newspapers, induction material, online procedure and policy manuals, employee web pages where individuals post details of their activities and progress, and **internal databases** of the corporate information store.

The **benefits** of intranets are diverse.

(a) Savings accrue from the **elimination of storage**, **printing** and **distribution** of documents that can be made available to employees online.

(b) Documents online are often **more widely used** than those that are kept filed away, especially if the document is bulky (eg manuals) and needs to be searched. This means that there are **improvements in productivity** and **efficiency**.

(c) It is much **easier to update** information in electronic form.

(d) Wider access to corporate information should open the way to **more flexible working patterns**, as material available online may be accessed from remote locations.

Remote access to intranets can be available **quickly** and **easily**. This means that people working at different parts of the organisation or away from the office can access data when they need it. Developments in IT allow information from a data warehouse (see below) to be displayed and Excel has facilities to post spreadsheets straight to the intranet and for users to drill down to the detail from a summary level.

7.2.3 Extranets

Key term

> An **extranet** is an intranet that is accessible to authorised outsiders.

Whereas an intranet resides behind a firewall and is accessible only to people who are members of the same company or organisation, an extranet provides various levels of accessibility to outsiders.

Only those outsiders with a valid username and password can access an extranet, with varying levels of access rights enabling control over what people can view. Extranets are becoming a very popular means for **business partners to exchange information**.

7.3 Databases

A **typical accounting application package** processes only one sort of data. A payroll file processes only payroll data and an inventory file only inventory data. An organisation might end up with separate files and processing subsystems for each area of the business. However, in many cases the underlying data used by each application might be the same. A major consequence is that data items are duplicated in a number of files (**data redundancy**). They are input more than once (leading to **errors and inconsistencies**) and held in several files (**wasting space**). For example, data relating to the hours which an hourly paid employee has worked on a particular job is relevant both to the payroll system, as the employee's wages will be based on the hours worked, and to the job costing system, as the cost of the employee's time is part of the cost of the job.

The **problem of data redundancy is overcome**, partly at least, by an **integrated system**. An integrated system is a system where **one set of data is used for more than one application**. In a cost accounting context, it might be possible to integrate parts of the sales ledger, purchase ledger, inventory control systems and nominal ledger systems, so that the data input to the sales ledger updates the nominal inventory ledger automatically.

The integrated systems approach, where different applications update each other, is a halfway house between a system based on separate application-specific files and a database approach.

Key term

> Broadly speaking, a **database** is a file of data organised in such a way that it can be used by many applications.

Using the example of hours worked given above, the following situations are possible:

(a) The employee's hours are **input twice**, once to the payroll application, once to the job costing system, in a non-integrated system of **application-specific files**.

(b) In an **integrated system**, the data would have been **input once**, to the payroll application. The payroll application would have been used to update the job costing application.

(c) In a **database system** it would only be **input once** and would be **immediately available to both systems**.

A database provides a **comprehensive file of data for a number of different users. Each user will have access to the same data**, and so different departments **cannot keep their own data files**, containing duplicate information but where the information on one file disagrees with the corresponding information on another department's file.

7.4 Database management systems

The database management system (DBMS) is a complex **software** system **that organises the storage of data in the database in the most appropriate way** to facilitate its storage, retrieval and use in different applications. It also provides the **link between** the **user and the data**.

7.4.1 Data warehousing

A **data warehouse** contains **data from a range of internal** (eg sales order processing system, nominal ledger) **and external sources**. One reason for including individual transaction data in a data warehouse is that if necessary the user can drill down to access transaction-level detail. Data is increasingly obtained from newer channels, such as customer care systems, outside agencies or websites.

The warehouse provides a coherent **set of information** to be **used across the organisation** for management **analysis** and **decision making**. The reporting and query tools available within the warehouse should facilitate management reporting and analysis.

The reporting and query tools used within the warehouse need to be flexible enough to allow multi-dimensional data analysis, also known as online analytical processing (**OLAP**). Each aspect of information (eg product, region, price, budgeted sales, actual sales and time period) represents a different dimension. OLAP enables data to be viewed from each dimension, allowing each aspect to be viewed in relation to the other aspects. So, for example, information about a particular product sold in a particular region during a particular period would be available online and instantly.

Organisations may build a single central data warehouse to serve the entire organisation or may create a series of smaller **data marts**. A data mart holds a selection of the organisation's data for a specific purpose.

A data mart can be constructed more quickly and cheaply than a data warehouse. However, if too many individual data marts are built, organisations may find it is more efficient to have a single data warehouse serving all areas.

Advantages of setting up a data warehouse system include:

(a) Decision makers can access data without affecting the use of operational systems.

(b) Having a wide range of data available to be queried easily encourages the taking of a wide perspective on organisational activities.

(c) Data warehouses have proved successful in a number of areas:

(i) Quantifying the effect of marketing initiatives
(ii) Improving knowledge of customers
(iii) Identifying and understanding an enterprise's most profitable revenue streams

(d) Information can be made available to business partners. For example, if customer sales order information is in the data warehouse, it could be made available to customers and even suppliers. Internal information on products and services could also be provided.

Case Study **Tesco Clubcard**

'Clubcard' is Tesco's loyalty card, and customers earn loyalty points whenever they make purchases using their Clubcard.

However, by rewarding customers with Clubcard points when they make purchases using their card, Tesco is not solely rewarding customers for their loyalty. At the same time, the Clubcard programme provides Tesco with insight into millions of customer transactions.

From this, Tesco can develop tailored ranges, promotions and marketing by country or region. Perhaps even more valuably, Tesco can tailor its marketing, right down to individual customers, via its Clubcard mailings.

Loyalty card programmes (such as Tesco's Clubcard) are also linked to data warehouses, and the data stored in them can be analysed to provide retailers with valuable information about individual customers' spending patterns. This information enables retailers to send personalised marketing messages to customers with offers relating to products which they have bought previously or may be likely to buy in the future.

7.4.2 Data mining

Key term

Data mining software looks for hidden patterns and relationships in large pools of data.

True data mining software discovers **previously unknown relationships**. Data mining provides insights that cannot be obtained through OLAP. The hidden patterns and relationships the software identifies can be used to guide decision making and to **predict future behaviour**.

Case Study **Data mining**

(1) In the Tesco 'Clubcard' example, we noted that the supermarket can use the loyalty card to create a record of the items each customer has bought. Tesco can then use the details about the purchasing behaviour of its customers to create a profile of what kind of people they are, and to identify trends in the items they buy.

A popular illustration of this principle being applied in practice comes from the US retailer Wal-Mart which discovered an unexpected relationship between the sale of **nappies** and **beer**! Wal-Mart found that both tended to sell at the same time, just after working hours, and concluded that men with small children stopped by to buy nappies on their way home, and bought beer at the same time. Logically, therefore, if the two items were put in the same shopping aisle, sales of both should increase. Wal-Mart tried this and it worked.

(2) Some credit card companies have used data mining to predict which customers are likely to switch to a competitor in the next few months. Based on the data mining results, the bank can take action to retain these customers.

7.5 Enterprise Resource Planning Systems (ERPS)

We discussed **ERPS** in Chapter 7, but their value in relation to processing information in organisations comes from the way they integrate information flows from different parts of an organisation.

ERPS assist in identifying and planning the resources needed to deal with many aspects of operations including manufacturing, distribution, inventory, invoicing and accounting. They also cover support functions, such as human resource management and marketing. Supply chain management software can provide links with suppliers and with customers.

ERPS thus operate **over the whole organisation** and **across functions**. All departments that are involved in operations or production are **integrated** into one system. Some ERPS software is custom-built, and often now ERPS software is written for organisations in particular industries. ERPS can be configured for organisations' needs and software adapted for circumstances. They can **support performance measures** such as **balanced scorecard** and **strategic planning**.

Using ERPS should result in **lower costs** and lower **investment required** in assets; they should also increase the **flexibility** and **efficiency of production**. However, there are also some disadvantages with ERPS: these include cost and lack of scope for adapting to the demands of specific businesses. Another problem is getting end users to accept the new technology.

Case Study — **Enterprise Resource Planning Systems**

In their text, *Management Information Systems*, Laudon and Laudon offer the following illustration to show how organisations can benefit from ERPS.

Imagine a company has ten different major product lines, each produced in separate factories, and each with separate, and incompatible, sets of systems controlling production, warehousing and distribution.

As a result of this, it will be difficult for managers to really understand what is happening in the business as a whole, and it is likely that their decision making could be based on manual hard-copy reports, many of which will be out of date.

At the time they place an order, sales personnel might not know whether the items being ordered are in stock, and manufacturing staff will not easily be able to use sales data to plan for new production.

The company could benefit from an ERPS which collects data from the different product lines and factories, as well as from a number of key business processes – not just in manufacturing and production (including inventory management), but also in sales and marketing, finance and accounting, and human resources. The benefit of such an integrated system is that when new information is entered by one process, that information is immediately made available to other business processes.

For example, imagine if the company makes automobile components. If a sales representative places an order for tyre rims for a customer, the system verifies the customer's credit limit, schedules shipment of the parts to the customer, and reserves the necessary items from inventory. If inventory stock is not sufficient to fulfil the order, the system schedules the manufacture of more rims, and orders any material or components needed from suppliers. Sales and production forecasts are immediately updated to reflect the customer order. General ledger and cash levels are automatically updated with the revenue and cost information from the order.

Users across the company could log in to the system and find out the status of the order at any time. In addition, management could obtain information at any point in time about how the business was operating. The system could also generate company-wide data for management analyses for product cost and profitability.

7.6 Impact of instant access to data on the business

Instant access to data, coupled with **real-time billing** and **transaction processing**, allows organisations to monitor their performance much more rapidly than they have traditionally been able to. For example, the impact of transactions on performance is now **visible as soon as the transactions occur**, whereas previously managers might have had to wait until the month-end accounts to know how the business is performing.

The ability to monitor performance almost on a real-time basis allows managers to take **preventative** or **corrective action** much more quickly.

Having instant access to data may also be used for planning and decision making, and can allow managers to **update targets or strategies more rapidly** as new information becomes available.

Equally, having instant access to data could help in staff management, for example by allowing managers to provide staff with timely and accessible feedback on their performance. Performance management systems are often used in call centres: to consolidate performance data for employees and groups of employees, and to align performance with company goals. In this way, all the staff have an up to date picture of current achievement levels and what they could do to improve.

However, in order to be useful, the data must be reliable – providing good-quality and **accurate** information about the activity taking place. **Thus speed should not be at the expense of quality and accuracy**. Information needs to be reported in a form that is appropriate for the end user, or else the message risks becoming distorted or misunderstood.

Many businesses now use **dashboards** as a means of reporting business data on a real-time basis. Dashboards provide a **visual representation** of key business data, and in doing so allow managers to monitor key elements of performance from all areas of the business. Because the dashboards have real-time updates, as soon as new data is available it updates the dashboard.

Another feature of many dashboard displays is that they allow users to **drill down** and see the detailed data behind the summary graphs. In this way, managers can investigate the reasons why areas of the business are performing as they are.

Another feature of current management information systems is that they have **user-defined displays**. In other words, a sales manager can choose only to receive information about sales performance. One of the dangers of having instant access to data is that managers could become swamped with too much data, but by filtering the data they can focus only on the data which is important to their job.

In some performance management systems, staff can even **self-manage** their performance by having access to their own performance information. For example, employees could measure their current performance levels against target levels, team averages or historical information. In this way, management can create a culture of accountability, by making sure their staff understand expectations, have the opportunity to meet them, and have the data to see whether they are meeting them or not.

7.7 Using data warehouses and ERPS

It is also worth considering how data warehouses and ERPS (which we looked at respectively in Sections 7.4 and 7.5) can help provide access to data, and hence to improve business performance.

As the case study illustration in Section 7.5 above shows, ERPS can offer managers access to previously unavailable data, which they can then use for control purposes and improving business performance.

7.7.1 Using data warehouses

Data warehouses allow organisations to store vast amounts of data which can then be analysed on a timely basis. However, one of the key objectives of data warehouses is to support business intelligence. Business intelligence is the art of analysing large amounts of data, extracting useful information from that data, and then turning that information into actionable knowledge.

For example, business intelligence can be used to help improve business performance by allowing managers to understand how their business is doing; what the underlying issues are which are affecting their business's performance; and how they can improve their performance.

7.7.2 Using ERPS

ERPS potentially plays a more direct role in improving performance. By providing the software that enables all the departments in a business to run from a single database, ERPS allows the different departments to share information and communicate with each other more easily.

We can illustrate this by looking at a simple example of a customer order, in a company in which the different departments all have their own individual information systems.

For example, when the customer places an order the order will be processed by the warehouse. However, the finance department will not be able to see whether the item has been shipped. Similarly, if a customer phones the customer service department to enquire about the status of the order, that department will then have to call the warehouse to find out.

However, the integrated nature of ERPS means that these problems can be overcome. Finance, customer services and the warehouse could still have their own software, but this will now be linked together so that someone in finance can look into the warehouse software to see if an order has been shipped.

In effect, ERPS provides organisations with a way of improving their order fulfilment processes (from taking a customer order, fulfilling that order, and then raising an invoice to turn that order into revenue). ERPS provide a software route map for organising the steps along the path to fulfilling the order; but they also provide a mechanism for staff to process and monitor the order as efficiently as possible. For example, if a customer service representative enters a customer order into an ERP system, they have all the information necessary to complete the order – for example, the customer's credit rating and order history from the finance module, the company's inventory levels from the warehouse module, and the outbound logistics delivery schedule from the logistics module.

7.8 Information, information systems and business performance

Developments in information and communications technologies have reduced the **cost** of storing and transmitting information, but they have also increased organisations' **capacity** for storing, processing and communicating information.

As access to information becomes easier and less expensive, skills and competences relating to the selection and efficient use of information become increasingly important to organisations. For some organisations, information and information management could even become a core competence in its own right, and a source of competitive advantage for the organisation.

The resource-based approach to strategy highlights that a successful organisation acquires and develops resources and competences over time, and exploits them to create competitive advantage.

The ability to capture and harness corporate knowledge has become critical for organisations as they seek to adapt to changes in the business environment, particularly those businesses providing financial and professional services.

Managing information effectively can help to promote competitive advantage through:

- The fast and efficient exchange of information
- Effective channelling of the information to:
  - Improve processes, productivity and performance
  - Identify opportunities to meet customer needs better than competitors
  - Promote creativity and innovation

Equally, the importance of meeting customer needs better than competitors means that organisations need to capture and analyse information about customers and potential customers (for example, through the use of customer databases) rather than simply looking at internal processes.

Customer and supplier engagement

Like other high-end hotels, the Mandarin Oriental in Manhattan uses information systems and technologies to develop detailed knowledge of its customers. The hotel uses computers which keep track of guests' preferences, such as room temperature, check-in time and television programmes, and store these in a large data repository.

Individual rooms in the hotels are networked to a central network server computer so that they can be remotely monitored or controlled. When a customer arrives at one of the hotels, the system automatically changes the room conditions, such as dimming the lights, setting the room temperature or selecting appropriate music based on the customer's digital profile. The hotels also analyse their customer data to identify their best customers, and to develop individualised marketing campaigns based on customers' preferences.

7.9 Remote input of data

It is no longer the case that data input requires someone to sit at a desk and tap away at a keyboard. There is a wide range of data capture techniques, a number of which allow staff to input data into the organisation's system whether or not they are in the office.

(a) Sales staff can communicate sales orders directly to head office using **laptop computers**. A number of restaurants have now started a similar logic, with the waiting staff recording customers' orders on hand-held personal digital assistants (**PDAs**) which then relay the orders to the kitchen and automatically add them onto the customer's bill.

(b) The use of **hand-held computers**, often with touch sensitive screens, means there is no need for subsequent manual entry of data, speeding up processes and reducing the chance of error because there are no transcription errors and computerised data validation techniques can be employed.

(c) **EPOS** systems (**bar code** scanners and tills) are primarily intended to speed up and avoid error in the checkout process in supermarkets, to allow customers to complete transactions and to manage inventories. In addition, however, they collect precise and detailed information about **how many** of **what products** are being bought at **what times**. If linked to a **loyalty scheme, 'and by whom' can be added** since this allows the purchase data to be combined with demographic data.

(d) Items such as **pressure mats** that sound a buzzer in smaller shops or **sliding doors** in larger ones have the practical purpose of either alerting staff to the fact that there is someone in the shop or simply of letting customers in and out, but if linked to a computer they also collect information about the number and movements of customers. The same applies to ticket scanners in car parks, stations, and leisure facilities like sports venues.

8 Recording and processing qualitative data

FAST FORWARD

There are difficulties associated with the recording and processing of qualitative data. This is due to the **subjective** and **judgemental** nature of this type of data.

We looked at service businesses in Chapter 4. This chapter introduced the idea of **qualitative data being used to measure performance**.

Given that qualitative data is **subjective and judgemental**, its recording is likely to be problematic. The number of sales made is easy to record; the reasons why sales are lost are not.

To overcome this problem **quantitative surrogates** are often used for important qualitative information, for instance number scales ranking preferences. For example, customer satisfaction surveys might ask customers to indicate how satisfied they are with a recent purchase or service they have received, using a scale of 1 to 5, with '1' indicating 'Very satisfied' and '5' indicating 'Not at all satisfied'.

However, although this kind of number scale allows qualitative information to be recorded in a structured way, it can still have its problems, as individuals can be highly personal in what they decide is, say, a '1' or a '5' – even if they have all had the same guidance about how to apply their scoring. Some people may naturally be tougher scorers than others. Equally, others may feel uncomfortable scoring the extreme marks (ie '1' or '5') and they may feel more comfortable scoring marks nearer the middle of the spectrum.

9 Output reports and information systems 12/11, 6/12, 6/14

FAST FORWARD

The output reports from a management information system need to be tailored to **suit the needs of the users** of those reports.

Access to greater volumes of data is having an effect on business.

A report in *The Economist* (27 February 2010, 'A special report on managing information') presented the findings of a study by IBM in which half the managers questioned said they did not trust the data they had to make decisions. As *The Economist* report notes, the managers felt that 'instead of finding a needle in a haystack, they are making more hay.'

Clearly there is a need to make sure data is 'fit for purpose': usually this means providing data that is accurate and relevant without being overwhelming.

The Economist report notes the importance of improving the **accuracy** of the data used as the input for information systems. Nestlé used SAP software and overhauled its bank of nine million records for consumers, vendors and materials, ridding these of duplication, inaccuracies and obsolete records.

Another way to improve the data used is to make it more up to date – or even using **real-time** information where possible. Wal-Mart offers its suppliers real-time access to the inventory in its stores. Effectively, the suppliers manage the inventory and ownership passes to Wal-Mart on sale.

Processing more data more quickly allows users access to more **timely data**. The capacity of computers to process data continues to improve dramatically permitting users to have more depth and accuracy of data, provided they have asked the right question of course! Users need not rely on their own computing capacity alone. Cloud computing uses the internet to collect, store and process data and users can lease computing power when they need it from large computer users, such as Amazon.

Google, Yahoo and other internet search engines already **rank data by relevance** when a user searches for data.

Analytics enables correlations between data to be revealed that may be used for focusing effort, say, on marketing to specific customers. The Royal Shakespeare Company sifted through more than two million records to identify data on customers that allowed it to promote its productions to customers more likely to respond. In fact, this marketing campaign saw an increase in regular visitors by 70%.

Case Study — Benefits of data analytics

La Tienda aims to deliver the best of Spanish food and wine (produced by artisanal and small family firms across Spain) to customers throughout the US, Canada and Europe. It guarantees that customers will receive quality products delivered in excellent condition. If this is not the case, La Tienda will either replace or refund the purchase.

The company, which has been delivering products to homes since 1996, has grown successfully, and now ships hundreds of thousands of orders. It claims to have the largest selection of Spanish food online. However, La Tienda's management recently faced an issue in relation to the delivery charges they added to the cost of customer orders.

The company's main warehouse in the US is based in Virginia, and one of its key product categories required more expensive shipping methods for destinations above a certain distance from the Virginia warehouse. The question facing management was whether this increased cost could be passed on to customers, and the management team wanted to understand the potential impact on sales if varying shipping rates were introduced for this product category.

To analyse the impact, La Tienda classified customers into two 'regions': those who lived close enough to the warehouse to use the existing shipping methods on all products (Region A); and those who lived further away (Region B) and so had to use the more expensive shipping method (and possibly to incur a higher charge) for the key product category.

La Tienda introduced the higher delivery charge for customers in Region B for the key product category on a trial basis and employed a marketing and sales analytics company to measure the impact on sales whenever one of the key products was placed in a customer's online shopping cart. The analytics company tracked the behaviour of customers in the two different groups (Region A and Region B) and found that customers from Region B were 48% less likely to make a purchase once they placed an item from the key product category in their shopping cart, and thereby triggering the higher total shipping costs.

Following this initial change, La Tienda then implemented a less expensive, flat rate shipping model for all products delivered to customers in Region B, but continued to monitor the number of customers who proceeded to the online checkout. Following the change to the shipping costs, the number of visitors from Region B who completed their purchase increased by nearly 70% compared to the previous cost model.

Over the same period, the conversion rate for customers in Region A only fluctuated about 3%, which suggested that the overwhelming impact on shopping cart behaviour in Region B had come from the changes to product shipping charges.

9.1 Reports and the dangers of information overload

Developments in IT systems mean that, in many organisations, there is potentially a vast range of different reports and statistics which managers can refer to.

With this increase in information comes the risk of **information overload**: the difficulty managers can have in understanding an issue or making a decision due to the presence of **too much information**.

Moreover, there is a danger that alongside this increase in measurement and reporting, senior managers can also start to micro-manage their organisations, and lose sight of the strategic side of management.

It is important to realise that managers do not need more reports *per se*; they just need to know what is going on in their organisations. In this respect, it is vital that management information systems are focused around gathering management **information**, not simply taking more and more measurements.

Exam focus point

In this context, it is worth noting that some commentators have noted that many organisations have become obsessed with **measurement** rather than **management**. Instead of scrutinising lots of numbers that provide very little information to managers, it could be more beneficial for them to take a step back and ask pertinent questions about how well their organisation is performing, or how its performance could be improved.

If a case study scenario describes the reports and information produced by an organisation and asks you to evaluate them, remember that having too much information to look at can be counterproductive for managers (just as having too little information can also be).

As well as recognising the potential dangers of having too much information in general, be aware of the danger that **strategic** managers end up focusing too much on detailed **operational** data – rather than obtaining the information they need to manage their organisations more effectively at a strategic level.

9.1.1 Evaluating output reports

Exam focus point

The P5 syllabus requires you to be able to evaluate the performance **reports** produced by an organisation, as well as being able to evaluate the organisation's performance itself.

There is an article – 'Reports for Performance Management' – in the Technical Articles section for P5 on ACCA's website which discussed the factors which should influence the design of a performance report, and which can be used to evaluate how good, or useful, a performance report is for an organisation.

The article highlights four basic criteria which can be used to evaluate an organisation's performance reports.

- **Purpose**: What is the fundamental purpose of the report? Does the report provide information which is relevant to the organisation's performance against its mission or objectives?
- **Audience**: Who is the report produced for? Is the report appropriate for its audience and their requirements?
- **Information**: What information is needed – financial and non-financial; quantitative and qualitative? Does the report provide the information which is needed?
- **Layout**: Does the report make it clear for readers to identify the most important information, plus any caveats and conclusions?

You are strongly encouraged to read the article in full as part of your preparations for your P5 exam.

Output reports from an information system might include overall performance reports for managers (for example, weekly or monthly management account reports) or they might be more specific, such as reports showing the inventory which should be ordered, analyses of credit customers whose accounts are overdue, or payroll summary reports. Interestingly, although a payroll report might initially be produced for an accounting manager, it could also be useful for a production manager to help control labour and job costs.

However, considering the output from an information system, a key point is that the output must be **evaluated for its suitability to the recipient**.

Good reporting is that which is **timely, accurate** and **tailored** to the user, measuring where they are accountable. An example would be a monitoring report to production managers produced monthly straight after the month end and showing statistics on good production, waste and scrap, possibly data from individual machines where there may be problems in production. Data would be summarised and managers could '**drill down**' into the detail. Financial data would also be available, as this ties into budget targets where managers are accountable.

Bad reporting may involve flawed input data, or data that is not tailored to the user, too detailed or too summarised, or out of date.

In this respect, key factors to consider when evaluating the suitability of a report include:

(a) The level of management requiring the report
(b) The nature of the information required (eg strategic vs operational; real time vs historical)
(c) The frequency of the report
(d) The model of circulation (for example, hard copy; soft copy; dashboard)

Exam focus point

The case study scenario for one of the questions in the December 2011 exam described the management information pack which is produced for the board of governors of a school, and which is only reviewed once a year.

This pack contains a detailed income and expenditure statement, as well as detailed information (by department) showing the marks obtained by pupils in their exams.

The case study scenario mentioned that the board is concerned that the information they are receiving does not meet their needs, and the question requirement then asked candidates to evaluate the usefulness of the pack that is provided to the board.

Similarly, in June 2012 candidates were presented with an extract from a performance report which showed extensive amounts of revenue and cost information (but didn't include, for example, any cash flow information or non-financial performance indicators). Candidates were then asked to critically assess the report and suggest improvements to its content and presentation.

A number of developments in output reporting from information systems have been driven by the need to provide timely and tailored information, but also to avoid swamping the user with too much information.

9.1.2 Dashboards

Increasingly, companies are looking at ways of reducing the number (and size) of paper reports which are produced, and of providing the necessary information to decision makers in an easy to read manner.

One of the ways of doing this is through the use of 'Executive Dashboards' which show current data, pictures, graphs and tables to illustrate how a business is performing and to help managers make better decisions. For example, if a retail chain is expanding, and preparing to open new stores, it could use dashboards to monitor the progress of the new stores. The dashboards could display geographical areas and the new stores that are being developed. By clicking on an individual store, executives can see details of how the new stores are being constructed and if any are being delayed. Once the new stores have opened, the executives could then also use the dashboards to see how well each store is performing – for example, when sales are in line with expectations.

Historically, there have been criticisms of information systems and reports that people were getting tied in knots trying to produce the reports they wanted from the systems available. Reporting tools tended to be rigid, and had lots of requirements about the way reports were produced. However, current reports offer a lot more flexibility, and thereby allow managers to get the reports they actually need, or want.

9.1.3 Drill-down reports

Dashboards are often also combined with drill-down reports. Drill-down reports provide users with the capability to look at increasingly detailed data about a situation. For example, the sales managers could first look at data for a high level (such as sales for the entire company) and then drill down to a more detailed level (such as sales for individual departments of the company) if they are concerned about sales performance. The manager should then also be able to drill down to a very detailed level, possibly to look at sales for an individual sales representative. In this way, the manager can dictate the level of detail and information presented, and can avoid being overloaded with too much detail initially.

9.1.4 Exception reports

Another way of managing the amount of information being presented, and thereby **preventing information overload**, is through the use of exception reports. Exception reports are reports that are only triggered when a situation is unusual or requires management action. For example, the parameters could be set so that exception reports are generated for all capital projects which exceed budget by greater than $100,000.

However, the key to using exception reports successfully is setting the parameters carefully. The aim of an exception report is only to highlight the situations which require management action. If the parameters are set too low (for example, all capital projects which exceed budget by over $100) then the manager will end up looking at too many items. Conversely, if the parameters are set too high (for example, capital projects which exceed budget by over $10 million) then situations which should receive management attention will not do so.

Because the aim of exception reports is to highlight situations which require management attention or action, they are best used to monitor aspects of performance which are important to an organisation's success. In this respect, exception reports could be used to report against key performance indicators (KPIs), or other aspects of an organisation's performance relating to its critical success factors.

Finally, in relation to the outputs of information systems as a whole, **users need to get involved when scoping what they require from their information systems**. If an MIS has immense capacity but does not give users the data they need individually, then the system is making life harder for the user.

9.1.5 The presentation of reports

Although organisations may be able to use dashboards and exception reports to help improve the suitability of the management information they produce, there are also some more basic factors which can affect the quality of their output reports.

Presentation. Taking care with presentation can make a significant difference to the professionalism and appearance of a report. For example, a well-presented report, which is clearly structured and written in a logical order, is more likely to be well received than one which isn't.

Standard format. Some organisations have 'house rules' which determine the format and style of reports. This might be to promote a corporate image within the organisation. However, it might also be to allow ease of comparison between reports, or to ensure that the managers do not miss key pieces of information because they do not know where to look for them.

Length. The length of a report should be appropriate to its purpose. So, for example, a summary report should be concise, but a detailed review should be comprehensive. However, whatever the length of the report, it is important that the material contained in it should be relevant.

Exam focus point

Evaluating performance *reports* vs evaluating *performance*

The P5 exam regularly includes questions which ask candidates to assess or evaluate the design of performance reports. However, these questions are often answered poorly, because candidates focus their answer on the underlying performance of the organisation, rather than on the report itself.

For example, a question in the June 2012 exam asked candidates to 'Critically assess the existing performance report and suggest improvements to its content and presentation.' Similarly, in June 2014, candidates were asked to evaluate an organisation's current performance report.

As the examiner's report from the June 2014 exam stresses, the requirement was to 'Evaluate the current performance report' – not 'Evaluate the current performance of the organisation' using the information provided in the report as the basis for doing so.

The examining team also identified that candidates seem reluctant to use an entity's mission or strategy to help them evaluate a report. A report – particularly to senior levels of management – should help to identify how well an entity is performing in relation to achieving its mission/strategy. For example, if part of an organisation's mission is 'to supply good value products for its customers', do its performance reports provide any information about how effectively the organisation is providing value to its customers?

Equally, the examiner's report highlighted that, in the scenario from the June 2014 exam, the report in question had three different groups of readers, requiring different levels of detail in the report. As such, an important factor to consider when evaluating the report is how well a single report can meet the requirement of all its readers.

These points echo the ones made in the technical article – 'Reports for Performance Management' – on ACCA's website which we referred to earlier.

More generally, the importance of reading the question requirement carefully, and then answering the question actually asked, is also covered by a P5 technical article on ACCA's website: 'Reading the question requirements of Paper P5'. The article looks at a selection of past exam requirements and then highlights the correct interpretation of them as well as some of the ways they were incorrectly interpreted by candidates. You are strongly advised to read this article as part of your preparation for the P5 exam.

Exam focus point

The question from the June 2014 exam referred to above is also the subject of a two-part technical article on ACCA's website: 'Improving Your P5 Answers' (Parts 1 and 2).

In this article, a member of the P5 examining team highlights some of the errors which students made when answering the requirement to evaluate an organisation's current performance report. The article then goes on to demonstrate the sorts of points which candidates would have been expected to make in order to score well in this part of the question.

You are strongly advised to read this article as part of your preparation for the P5 exam.

10 Potential issues with numerical performance information

FAST FORWARD

Performance information is only useful to the users of that information if it is **credible** and **reliable**.

If a report misrepresents how well an organisation has actually performed, then that report's value as a basis for planning, decision making or control is significantly reduced.

The difficulties we identified in Section 8 in relation to recording and processing qualitative information might suggest that numerical (quantitative) performance information is inherently more robust than qualitative information. However, as the quotation 'Lies, damn lies and statistics' suggests, numerical data could also be presented in ways which make it unreliable or misleading.

There are a number of possible reasons why this could be the case.

(a) **Data is incomplete**. For example, if the trading results from some stores are omitted from the consolidated results for a retail company, this will give a misleading impression of the group's performance.

Such an omission could be a particular problem if the stores omitted were ones which performed particularly well or particularly poorly, because their omission would distort average performance figures across the group.

(b) **Lacks neutrality**. If data is based on a sample population but that sample has not been picked at random, this could be misleading.

(c) **Inconsistencies in basis of preparation**. Managers can often gain more insight into performance by looking at performance trends rather than one-off figures. However, the validity of these trends will be reduced if the basis on which the figures are prepared is not consistent. For example, in the retail group above, if one of the group's KPIs is the average revenue per store but in one year the group includes all its stores when calculating the KPI, but in the following year it excludes stores which opened or closed during the year, this reduces the comparability of the KPI results between the two years.

This point about inconsistency raises three further issues:

(i) The definition of any performance measures needs to remain constant over time in order for them to be comparable.

(ii) The choice of performance indicators needs to remain constant over time in order to be able to identify trends in performance (rather than, for instance, changing KPIs from one year to the next to ensure that the KPIs focus on areas where an organisation has performed well).

(iii) Performance measures need to be calculated on a 'like for like' basis in order to be comparable.

The issue of inconsistency in the way performance measures are calculated could also cause problems when benchmarking performance externally. If a supermarket group is comparing average sales per store against its competitors, but it includes online sales in its total revenue whereas some of its competitors base average revenue only on in-store sales, the validity of the comparison is significantly reduced.

Case Study **Retailers' sales statistics**

In its report *Audit Insights: Retail* ICAEW's Audit and Assurance Faculty notes that, although like for like sales figures are the most prominent KPI for the retail sector, they are not comparable on a consistent basis.

Instead, many retailers use their judgement to calculate movements in like for like sales by identifying and removing any distorting elements from the calculation. There is no standard basis for calculating like for like sales, nor is there any standard agreement as to what factors should be classified as 'distortions' and therefore excluded from like for like sales.

Figures may not be calculated in the same way between different retailers. Perhaps even more importantly, the basis of the calculation may change from year to year within the same business.

The report points out, 'Without an understanding of the adjustments and judgements in each case, the public may place greater significance on comparisons between like for like sales than is warranted'.

Factors that may lead to stores being excluded from like for like sales include:

- Stores undergoing a refurbishment or a refit
- Stores undergoing a resize (eg where adjustment to floor space is greater than 5% of the original floor space)
- Stores due to be closed in the near future
- Stores opened during the period under review
- Stores suffering from a major disruption to trading (eg flood; fire; roadworks in the immediate vicinity leading to a significant decline in footfall; redevelopment; or opening of a direct competitor's store nearby)
- Impact of one-off events (eg impact of the Olympic Games on sales in London in 2012)

The judgement involved in determining which stores classify as 'like for like', and the lack of standardisation, means the performance measure is less valuable to the public than it might otherwise be.

The ICAEW report suggests that the fundamental judgements required to develop an approach to like for like sales in each period depend on a fully developed understanding of sale activity across the business. Unfortunately, however, one reason for the variations in like for like calculations may simply be the range of data available to different retailers.

Finally, the report suggests that the usefulness of like for like sales as a performance measure is further reduced because the core relationship between like for like sales and profitability has changed, due to increasingly widespread deep discounting. As a result, sales numbers can be pushed upwards at the expense of profitability. But retailers rarely link data on profitability (such as movements in profit margins) to like for like sales.

(d) **Not verifiable**. Some data or information may not be verifiable. Management may want corroboration of a fact or allegation, but there may not be an alternative source for checking its accuracy. This could be a particular problem with secondary data from external sources.

However, the issue of verification could equally apply to internally generated figures. For example, the readers of an organisation's corporate social responsibility report might wonder what assurance they have that information about the organisation's greenhouse gas emissions have been correctly recorded. For example, have they been independently validated?

(e) **Level of detail**. The reliability and usefulness of numerical data can be affected by the level of detail presented. This could be the case if too much detail is provided as well as if too little detail is provided. For example, if lots of detailed information is provided about relatively unimportant issues, this could distract the reader's attention away from potentially more significant areas of a report.

(f) **Out of date**. When events in the business environment are changing rapidly, information may get out of date very quickly. There is a risk that any data in a report or statement is no longer accurate because it is no longer up to date.

(g) **Deliberately distorted**. Although in many cases the problems we have highlighted above are not the result of a conscious decision to mislead, in a small number of cases, numerical data could be

misleading because it has been deliberately distorted. For example, in September 2015 it was revealed that the German car manufacturer Volkswagen had rigged emissions tests for about 500,000 diesel cars in the US.

Case Study **Hospital waiting times**

One of the indicators which is often used to measure the performance of hospitals in the UK is 'waiting time' – the length of time patients have to wait before they are treated.

NHS guidelines determine that a patient's waiting time ends if no treatment is necessary, or when their treatment begins. This could include:

- Being admitted to hospital for an operation or treatment
- Starting treatment, such as taking medication, that doesn't require you to stay in hospital
- Beginning your fitting of a medical device, such as leg braces
- Agreeing to your condition being monitored for a time to see whether you need further treatment
- Receiving advice from hospital staff to manage your condition

However, there have been examples where hospitals have tried to manipulate performance against the guidelines to improve their reported waiting times. For example:

- Holding patients in ambulances to delay their point of registration
- Counting triage or preliminary examinations as 'being seen'

Exam focus point

ACCA's examining team has written an article 'Reading the question requirements of Paper P5' (available on ACCA's website) which you are strongly advised to read in full before you sit your exam.

However, one section in particular is relevant here.

The article notes that there appears to be a common misconception among candidates that financial performance indicators are **always** being manipulated and that non-financial performance indicators are **less** open to manipulation than financial ones.

However, this implies both that the people that prepare financial reports are generally unethical and that controls over financial information systems are less stringent than those over non-financial information systems.

Hopefully you will recognise that both of these implications are false. There may be a **danger** of manipulation in financial information systems, and this **may** be exacerbated by inappropriate reward systems (creating a 'bonus culture'). However, this does not mean that financial performance indicators are inherently more vulnerable to manipulation than non-financial performance indicators.

11 Key performance information and integrated reporting

FAST FORWARD

The aim of **integrated reporting** is to communicate how an organisation's strategy, governance, performance and prospects, in the context of its external environment, create value for the organisation's stakeholders – in the short, medium and long term. An integrated report should help to explain how an organisation is developing and implementing its strategies for **sustainable value creation**.

The increased importance of environmental management accounting (as discussed in Chapter 5) reflects the increasing awareness of the impact businesses have on their environment, and the increasing importance of issues around environmental sustainability.

The issue of sustainability is also an important aspect in integrated reporting, although here 'sustainability' relates to the wider concept of business sustainability rather than simply environmental sustainability.

However, this also has implications for the performance information organisations produce – because the aspects of performance covered in integrated reports extend well beyond the traditional measures of short-term financial performance.

11.1 Integrated reporting

The International Integrated Reporting Council (IIRC) has defined an integrated report as a concise communication about how an organisation's strategy, governance, performance and prospects, in the context of its commercial, social and environmental context, lead to the creation and enhancement of value over the short, medium and long term.

According to the IIRC, integrated reporting combines the different strands of reporting (financial, management commentary, governance and remuneration, and sustainability reporting) into a coherent whole that explains an organisation's ability to create and sustain value. As such, integrated reporting (IR) also highlights the need to embed the concept of **long-term business sustainability** within the organisation.

By encouraging organisations to focus on their ability to create and sustain value, IR should help them take decisions which are more sustainable and which ensure a more effective allocation of scarce resources.

IR should also help providers of financial capital (primarily shareholders), and other stakeholders, to better understand how an organisation is performing and creating value over time. In particular, IR should help stakeholders make a meaningful assessment of the long-term viability of an organisation's business model and its strategy.

At the same time, IR should help to simplify annual reports, by highlighting critical information and by removing excessive detail.

It is also important to consider IR as a **process**, not a product. The report periodically delivered to stakeholders (reporting on an organisation's current state and future prospects) requires a comprehensive understanding of the strategies being adopted, the risks the organisation is facing, the opportunities it is pursuing, and details of its operations, as well as the organisation's impact on the environment and the wider society.

The IIRC highlights that **integrated *reporting*** also reflects **integrated *thinking*** within an organisation – management's ability to understand the interconnections between the range of functions, operations, resources and relationships which have a material effect on the organisation's ability to create value over time.

Exam focus point

The focus within IR of understanding how different elements of an organisation create value could also link back to the idea of the value chain which we have discussed earlier in this Study Text.

Equally, the importance of understanding the interconnections between different functions and how they contribute to the performance of an organisation could also link to the ideas of multi-dimensional performance measurement systems (such as the performance pyramid and the balanced scorecard) which we will discuss later (in Chapter 15).

IR allows a company to better understand and manage the multiple dimensions of value. As a result, this can help companies make better decisions, and manage their business in a way that creates value for their key stakeholders.

11.1.1 Six capitals

All organisations depend on different forms of capital for their success, and these different capitals should be seen as part of the organisation's business model and strategy. These capitals are an important part of an organisation's value creation.

The IR framework identifies six categories of capital and refers to six categories of 'capital': financial; manufactured; human; intellectual; natural; and social.

Category of capital	Characteristic elements of the category of capital
Financial	Funds available for use in production or service provision, obtained through financing or generated through operations
Manufactured	Manufactured physical objects used in production or service provision; including buildings, equipment, and infrastructure
Human	Skills, experience and motivation to innovate: Alignment and support for an organisation's governance framework and ethical values Ability to understand and implement organisation's strategies Loyalties and motivations for improvements
Intellectual	Intangible assets, providing competitive advantage: Patents, copyrights, software and organisation systems Brand and reputation
Natural	Inputs to goods and services, and natural environment on which an organisation's activities have an impact: Water, land, minerals and forests Biodiversity and health of ecosystems
Social	The institutions and relationships established within and between each community, stakeholder group, and network to enhance individual and collective wellbeing Includes an organisation's social licence to operate

By implication, identifying these six different categories of capital suggests that an integrated report will describe an organisation's performance in relation to the different capitals – in contrast to 'traditional' annual reporting which focuses primarily on financial performance.

Similarly, an organisation will need information about its performance in relation to each of the different capitals, in order to be able to report on them. As a result, introducing IR could have important implications for the information systems in an organisation. For example, does the organisation currently record non-financial (social; environmental) performance in a way which provides it with suitable information to include in its integrated report?

11.1.2 Guiding principles of integrated reporting (IR)

The IIRC has identified seven **guiding principles** for IR.

Strategic focus and future orientation – An integrated report should provide insight into an organisation's strategy, and how that strategy relates to the organisation's ability to create value in the short, medium and long term, and to the organisation's use of, and effects on, the six capitals.

IR is designed to highlight the capitals (resources and relationships) on which an organisation depends, how the organisation uses those capitals, and its impact on them.

Connectivity – An integrated report should show a holistic picture of the relationships and dependencies between the factors which affect an organisation's ability to create value over time.

Stakeholder relationships – An integrated report should provide an insight into the nature and quality of an organisation's relationships with its key stakeholders, including an insight into how the organisation recognises and responds to the interests of its stakeholders.

Materiality – A report should disclose information about matters which substantively affect an organisation's ability to create value over the short, medium and long term.

Reliability and completeness – An integrated report should include all material matters, both positive and negative, and should present them in a balanced way and without material error.

Conciseness – An integrated report should be concise.

Consistency and comparability – Information in an integrated report should be presented in a way which enables comparison with other organisations, to the extent it is material to the organisation's own ability to create value over time.

11.1.3 Aspects of an integrated report

In addition to the guiding principles, the IIRC has suggested that, in general terms, an integrated report should answer the following questions:

(a) What does an organisation do, and what are the circumstances under which it operates?

(b) **Governance** – How does the organisation's governance structure support its ability to create value in the short, medium and long term?

(c) **Opportunities and risk** – What are the specific opportunities and risks which affect the organisation's ability to create value over the short, medium and long term; and how is the organisation dealing with them?

(d) **Strategy and resource allocation** – Where does the organisation want to go, and how does it intend to get there?

(e) **Business model** – What is the organisation's business model, and to what extent is it resilient?

(f) **Performance** – To what extent has the organisation achieved its strategic objectives and what are the outcomes in terms of effects on the capitals?

(g) **Future outlook** – What challenges and uncertainties is the organisation likely to encounter in pursuing its strategy, and what are the potential implications for its business model and its future performance?

Exam focus point

In an article available on ACCA's website ('ACCA embeds integrated reporting'), ACCA's Qualifications Development Manager points out that the P5 syllabus is already firmly structured around several of the elements in the IIRC's Framework.

The most obvious one is the '**Performance**' element, linking to issues such as measurement systems and design, performance evaluation, and prediction of corporate failure. However, the earlier sections of the P5 syllabus (Sections A and B) also cover strategic aspects of performance relating to '**Opportunities and Risks**' and to '**Strategy and resource allocation**'.

As such, while 'Integrated Reporting' is being talked about as a new initiative, a number of the elements within it should actually be elements that a strategic management accountant has already been considering.

11.1.4 Implications of IR for the management accountant

As yet, there is no standard, accepted format for an integrated report, so the detailed implications of the information required for an integrated report will vary from organisation to organisation. However, the general principles and aims of IR suggest that a management accountant will need to consider the following issues when preparing information for an integrated report.

Forward-looking information

In their 2012 report 'What is Integrated Reporting', UBS noted that 'there is a gap between the information currently being reported by companies and the information investors need to assess business prospects and value.'

The reference to 'prospects' highlights that IR information should be forward looking as well as historical. The focus of IR is how an organisation's strategy, governance and performance can lead to the creation of value in the future. Equally, therefore, the performance information produced by an organisation needs to give an insight into an organisation's prospects and future performance – how it can create value in the future – as well as reporting its past performance.

However, an organisation needs to think carefully about what kind of 'forward looking' information it discloses. Any material providing information about the future prospects and profitability of the entity (particularly a listed company) is likely to be regulated, and it could also be commercially sensitive. For example, an organisation needs to consider the balance between disclosure and the loss of competitive edge.

Equally, the inherent danger of producing forward-looking information is that no one can predict the future: forecasts are inevitably wrong to some degree, and are necessarily dependent on the assumptions an organisation's management team have made about the future.

While management is likely to have (and will want to have) the best information available to make such predictions, they still need to ensure that investors do not place undue reliance on that information.

Long-term performance

The idea of sustainability also highlights the need to evaluate performance and strategic decisions on a long-term basis as well as in the short term. This idea of the potential for conflict between long-term and short-term decisions is one which we will discuss in more detail in the next chapter, in relation to the choice of metrics which an organisation uses to measure its performance.

One of the key aims of IR is to reflect the longer-term consequences of the decisions which organisations make, in order that decisions should be sustainable and create value over time. Therefore, the IR process highlights that when making a (strategic) decision, an organisation needs to consider the long-term consequences of that decision – and its effect on the six capitals, both positive and negative – as well as its short-term consequences.

Similarly, in order to implement IR successfully, an organisation will need to select a range of performance measures which promote a balance between achieving short-term and long-term performance.

Again, in this respect, the use of non-financial performance indicators is likely to be important, since aspects of non-financial performance (for example, environmental performance) have a long-term time frame.

Non-financial information

One of the main potential benefits of IR is that it helps organisations identify more clearly the links between financial and non-financial performance.

In particular, by focusing on value generation in a broader sense (rather than focusing on narrower goals of revenue generation, for example) IR will also encourage organisations to review the set of performance measures they use to monitor and manage performance.

Therefore, one of the main consequences of IR is likely to be the increased use of non-financial data to gain a clearer picture of an organisation and its performance.

Multi-dimensional performance measurement systems (such as the balanced scorecard and the performance pyramid, which we will discuss in Chapter 15) already recognise the importance of looking at an appropriate mix of non-financial measures alongside financial ones. Introducing IR will reinforce this. For example, IR highlights the need to obtain a wider understanding of value creation in an organisation, beyond that which can be measured through traditional financial terms.

Equally, IR should also encourage greater attention being paid to non-financial data in strategic decision making. For example, investment appraisals may need to include non-financial costs and benefits (and sustainability information) as well as traditional financial costs and benefits.

Strategy, not just reporting

The guiding principles of IR note that an integrated report needs to provide insight into an organisation's strategy rather than simply reporting figures. So, rather than simply presenting the figures, an integrated report should highlight the significance of the figures being presented, and how they affect an organisation's ability to create value.

In their report 'Integrated Reporting: Performance Insight through Better Business Reporting' KPMG argued that 'Successful Integrated Reporting is not just about reporting, but about co-ordinating different disciplines within the business, and focusing on the organisation's core strategy'.

Connecting different teams within the business is an important step to achieving the integrated thinking necessary to underpin IR.

The IIRC's own website also notes that: 'Businesses need a reporting environment that is conducive to understanding and articulating their strategy, which helps to drive performance internally and attract financial capital for investment. Investors need to understand how the strategy being pursued creates value over time.'

As such, the management accountant's role should no longer be simply to report on financial performance, but also to provide information which can provide insight into an organisation's strategy.

In this respect, IR could be seen as reinforcing the changes in an accountant's role which Burns and Scapens identified (as we discussed in Chapter 1). By developing their understanding of the operating functions and commercial processes of a business, a management accountant may be better able to identify which aspects of the business can help to drive performance.

Focusing on key aspects of performance

One of the guiding principles of IR is **conciseness**, and therefore one of the potential benefits of IR is that it encourages organisations to produce shorter, more streamlined communications.

Crucially, IR should not be seen as a reason for simply producing more information or longer reports. Instead, it requires organisations to identify which aspects of performance are truly key to their future success – and then focus its performance metrics on them.

Although we have noted that IR encourages the use of non-financial data as well as financial data, the range of data used needs to be considered within the context of brevity. Overall, organisations should be looking to reduce the amount of information which is published, in order to make their 'story' more accessible to stakeholders.

In this respect, there could also be links between IR and the ideas of **'lean'** which we considered earlier in this Study Text.

11.1.5 Potential benefits of IR

The introduction of IR could have the following benefits for an organisation.

- Streamline performance reporting, and find efficiencies within the organisation, so that data sets can be used in a range of different ways
- Reduce duplication of information and ensure consistency of messaging
- Align and simplify internal and external reporting – for consistency and efficiency

IR also leads to a greater **focus on what is material** to an organisation and – perhaps equally importantly – helps an organisation identify what is not material to it. This means that less time and effort is wasted on reporting unimportant issues and, instead, the focus is on those activities and processes through which an organisation creates value (for example, activities linked to the organisation's critical success factors).

Similarly, this focus only on key activities should reduce the risk of information overload.

Selection of performance metrics

One of the main benefits of IR is expected to come from the more rigorous preparation of performance metrics, and the insights those metrics can bring to an organisation's stakeholders.

Focusing on the performance metrics which truly deliver value provides the managers of an organisation with both the ability and the incentive to improve performance. Once again, the idea 'What gets measured, gets done' is pertinent here. If the areas being measured are those which are critical to the organisation's performance then, by implication, this should also focus attention on improving performance in these key areas.

Accordingly, an important part of the management accountant's role in relation to IR will be working with the board or with operational managers to identify material issues (critical business issues) and then to identify appropriate KPIs which can be used to monitor performance in relation to those issues.

IR should lead to an increased focus among the directors of an organisation on exactly what the organisation's KPIs should be. In particular, additional non-financial KPIs can help to highlight areas of poor performance – or areas where there is scope for improvement – which financial metrics alone might not reveal.

Recognition of stakeholder interests

The guiding principles of IR highlight the importance of developing relationships with stakeholders and responding to their interests. In relation to performance measurement and performance management, as part of its preparation for producing an integrated report, an organisation could consult with its key stakeholders, to identify what they want to know about the performance and direction of the organisation. This consultation could then help to identify possible areas of performance which the organisation should monitor, and report on in its integrated report.

11.1.6 Information requirements

If an organisation needs to include forward-looking information and information about its long-term performance in its IR, this could also have important implications for the information which the organisation's management accountant produces.

In particular, the introduction of IR may require management accounting information to become more strategic, rather than simply reporting on historical, internal, financial performance. For example, since an integrated report should highlight the opportunities and risks an organisation faces, there is likely to be a need for external analysis in order to identify the opportunities, threats and risks presented by the external environment.

Implications of increased importance of non-financial information

Although including non-financial performance metrics in performance reports can help provide a clearer picture of an organisation and its performance, there could be a number of practical considerations linked to providing non-financial performance information. In particular:

(a) Can the organisation's information systems supply the full range of non-financial data which stakeholders wish to see in an integrated report?

(b) If this data cannot currently be obtained from an organisation's information systems, how can the management accountant get the information wanted for the report?

(c) Can non-financial issues be embedded into existing financial systems?

(d) How can the organisation's information systems be improved in order to allow the required non-financial information to be collected?

(e) Can non-financial information be gathered and verified within financial reporting timelines?

(f) How can the management accountant ensure that non-financial data is reliable and, more generally, what assurance is there over non-financial data in a report? (Non-financial data is typically not audited in the same way that financial data is; but if stakeholders are going to rely on this data then should an organisation obtain some kind of assurance over the data?)

In its paper 'Understanding Transformation: Building the Business Case for Integrated Reporting' the IIRC notes that one organisation has developed a non-financial dashboard for its Executive Committee, linked directly to remuneration packages.

If organisations are going to use non-financial information in this way, they will need assurance over the accuracy and robustness of the figures, given their potential impact on the executives' remuneration.

Chapter Roundup

- **Internal** sources of **information** include the financial accounting records and other systems closely tied to the accounting system.
- **External information** tends to be more relevant to strategic and tactical decisions than to operational decisions. (Benchmarking is an exception.)
- **Secondary data**, such as government statistics or data provided by online databases, is not collected by or for the user. **Primary data** – more expensive than secondary data – is more tailored to the user's exact needs. Market research is an example.
- The **internet** increases the richness of external data and reduces the cost of searching for it.
- The costs of information come not only from the costs of **capturing** and **processing** information, but also from the potential costs of **using information inefficiently**.
- Controls are applied at three levels in an organisation: strategic, tactical (management) and operational. Much control is achieved through the **feedback** of internal information.
- The amount of data available to organisations is increasing ever more rapidly, and Big Data – with its characteristics of **volume, velocity and variety** – highlights both the opportunities and challenges which new sources of data present to organisations.
- The ability to analyse large, and unstructured, data sets and to uncover previously hidden patterns of information could be an important element of an organisation's competitive advantage. However, as a prerequisite for this, organisations need to have the capacity to store and – more importantly – to analyse these data sets.
- The **type of business entity** will influence the recording and processing methods adopted.
- The availability of cheap and powerful **PCs** has transformed the role of management information systems.
- **Access to data** has been facilitated by **groupware, intranets, extranets, databases, data warehousing** and **data mining**.
- There are difficulties associated with the recording and processing of qualitative data. This is due to the **subjective** and **judgemental** nature of this type of data.
- The output reports from a management information system need to be tailored to **suit the needs of the users** of those reports.
- Performance information is only useful to the users of that information if it is **credible** and **reliable**.
- If a report misrepresents how well an organisation has actually performed, then that report's value as a basis for planning, decision making or control is significantly reduced.
- The aim of **integrated reporting** is to communicate how an organisation's strategy, governance, performance and prospects, in the context of its external environment, create value for the organisation's stakeholders – in the short, medium and long term. An integrated report should help to explain how an organisation is developing and implementing its strategies for **sustainable value creation**.

Quick Quiz

1 Provide an example for each of the following costs of obtaining external information.

Direct search costs ....

Indirect access costs ....

Management costs ....

Infrastructure costs ....

Time theft ....

2 Organisations have many sources they can use for external data. List six of these.

3 Supermarkets rely on up to date and accurate recording of inventory levels, as stock-outs can be very expensive. What devices enable them to do this?

4 The article on ACCA's website – 'Reports for Performance Management' – identifies four basic criteria which can be used to evaluate an organisation's performance reports.

What are they?

5 Which of the following statements about Integrated Reporting are true:

(i) An integrated report should provide an insight into an organisation's ability to create value in the short, medium and long term.

(ii) An integrated report should provide an insight into how an organisation recognises and responds to the interests of its stakeholders.

(iii) The primary focus of an integrated report is an organisation's financial performance.

A (i) and (ii) only
B (i) and (iii) only
C (ii) and (iii) only
D (i), (ii) and (iii)

Answers to Quick Quiz

1 See Section 2.1.

2 Directories, trade associations, government agencies, periodicals/journals, market research data, and consumer panels

3 Large retail stores use **Electronic Point of Sale** or **EPoS** devices including bar code readers. These record units sold and update inventories on a real-time basis.

4 Purpose – what is the purpose of the report?

Audience – who is the report produced for?

Information – what information is needed? Does the report provide the information which is needed?

Layout – does the report help readers to identify the key information?

5 A

One of the main potential benefits of integrated reporting is that it helps organisations identify more clearly the links between financial and non-financial performance. Integrated reporting focuses on value generation in a broad sense, not only in a narrow financial sense (eg in terms of revenue or profit). Therefore option (iii) is not true.

Option (i) reflects the guiding principle that an integrated report should provide an insight into an organisation's strategic focus and future orientation.

Option (ii) reflects the guiding principle that an integrated report should provide an insight into an organisation's relationships with its key stakeholders.

Now try the question below from the Practice Question Bank

Number	Level	Marks	Approximate time
Q8	Examination	20	40 mins

PART D

Strategic performance measurement

Strategic performance measures in the private sector

Introduction

In your P5 exam, you may be required to look at performance measurement in a variety of contexts. In this chapter we look at the principal **financial measures** used by the **private sector** to assess performance.

There are three main groups of such measures:

- Those addressing profitability
- Those addressing liquidity
- Those addressing gearing

You should already be familiar with most of these measures from your previous studies, but at P5 level you will be expected not only to be able to calculate the measures correctly but also to discuss the advantages and disadvantages of different measures.

Make sure you are clear about the distinction between **short-run** and **long-run** performance measures. The decisions an organisation takes could be very different if it has a short-term focus as opposed to a long-term one.

In the final part of the chapter, we revisit **benchmarking** as we look at how an organisation's financial performance might be compared against that of other organisations.

Study guide

		Intellectual level
D1	**Strategic performance measures in the private sector**	
(a)	Demonstrate why the primary objective of financial performance should be primarily concerned with the benefits to shareholders.	2
(b)	Discuss the appropriateness of, and apply different measures of performance including: (i) Gross profit and operating profit (ii) Return on Capital Employed [ROCE] (iii) Return on Investment [ROI] (iv) Earnings per share [EPS] (v) Earnings before Interest, Tax, Depreciation and Amortisation [EBITDA] (vi) Residual income [RI] (vii) Net Present Value [NPV] (viii) Internal Rate of Return [IRR] and Modified Internal Rate of Return [MIRR] (ix) Economic Value Added [EVA™]	3
(c)	Discuss why indicators of liquidity and gearing need to be considered in conjunction with profitability.	3
(d)	Compare and contrast short- and long-run financial performance and the resulting management issues.	3
(e)	Assess the appropriate benchmarks to use in assessing performance.	2

Exam guide

This part of the syllabus lends itself to a range of possible question styles, which could include calculations as well as more discursive elements. Given the intellectual level of the syllabus elements, you should expect to have to discuss the elements and their appropriateness for a given organisation or context – even in a question which contains a degree of calculation.

Note that Part D of the syllabus, overall, also covers performance measurement in public sector and non-profit organisations. So you may be asked to comment on performance measurement systems in a wide variety of organisations.

Exam focus point

The examining team have highlighted that the increased use of technology by accountants (eg spreadsheets) means there should be less need, particularly at a strategic level, for accountants to perform calculations manually. Equally, qualified accountants might reasonably expect to have more junior members of staff supporting them, who can perform some of the more routine calculations.

Consequently, candidates should not expect there to be significant amounts of computational work in the P5 exam. Instead, the focus is more likely to be on analysing the results of performance measurement calculations which have already been carried out, or on evaluating the choice of different performance measures which organisations can use to measure and control their performance.

For example, a compulsory question in the June 2011 exam included a requirement to evaluate how well a division is performing, and then discuss proposed alternative measures of divisional performance (which were identified in the scenario as RI and EVA).

Equally, in the June 2012 exam candidates were asked to use NPV and MIRR to appraise a project, and then also to evaluate the use of NPV, MIRR, EVA and profit-based measures for assessing the performance of a business.

Although you should expect that Paper P5 will require you to undertake some calculations and computations, you should also be prepared to link this to the interpretation and further analysis of data provided in the question. The examining team have highlighted that candidates will need to demonstrate their ability to add value to their advice, by taking information already produced and identifying the important features of it. Because this is a Professional level paper, you should also think about the commercial implications of the information being discussed.

Finally, remember it is important to apply your calculations specifically to the scenario if you are asked to assess or evaluate an organisation's performance, and then make sure you comment on what the calculations indicate about the organisation's performance. ACCA's examining team often refer to candidates' inability to do this, and the fact that candidates lose valuable marks as a result.

The examining team have published an article outlining the intended approach to the paper – 'P5 Examiner's approach article' – which is available on ACCA's website. **You are strongly advised to read this article as part of your preparation for your exam.**

The examining team have repeatedly stressed that candidates will be expected to **analyse numerical data** given in a scenario, **not merely to perform calculations**. While candidates will be expected to use various techniques to perform calculations, they also need to be able to explain what the results of those calculations indicate, and what importance can be given to them. In other words, candidates need to explain how the calculations will help managers manage performance in an organisation. Remember that Paper P5 is ultimately about **performance *management***, not just performance **measurement**.

The topics covered in Section 5 of the P5 syllabus as a whole – Strategic performance measurement – could all help you fulfil Performance objective 14: Monitor performance. The objective requires you to 'measure and assess department and business performance.'

The topics we cover in this chapter are particularly relevant to element (c) of the objective: 'Identify and use appropriate performance measurement techniques to assess aspects of performance within the organisation.'

However, element (e) also reiterates the importance of performance **management**, rather than just measurement: 'Advise on appropriate ways to maintain and improve performance'.

1 The private sector: shareholder benefits

FAST FORWARD

The overriding **purpose** of a company is to **increase long-term owner wealth**.

Carefully read the case study below.

Case Study — Corporate performance

The strategic report extracts below are adapted from the published accounts of a UK company, listed on the stock exchange (ie a plc), with revenue in the year under review of $110m, operating profits of $16m, and post-tax profit of $10m.

As you are reading through the case study, think which aspects of performance it is highlighting, and also what insights the report gives into the company's priorities.

Dragon Press plc

Group Strategy

(1) Our strategy is to build on our position as one of the leading printers of magazines, brochures etc offering a complete service for the customer from pre-press and printing to finishing and despatch. We remain focused on making acquisitions to assist in achieving our goal as well as developing our existing businesses.

Capital investment – investment criteria and budgeted expenditure

(2) As referred to in the Chairman's and the Chief Executive's review, the last year has been a period of considerable investment for your company. We purchased new presses, finishing equipment and pre-press equipment, at a total cost of $14.1m. We plan to invest a further $14m this year on upgrading existing equipment and expanding capacity by installing additional machines.

Funding structure

(3) Our closing level of debt is $26.7m, of which $23.2m is at fixed rates ranging from 5.9% to 8.1%. The balance is at 1% over base rate and this averaged 6.4% during the period. Given the high level of **operating gearing** within a printing business, we believe our **optimal level of debt/equity** is between 50% and 70%.

See section 3

(4) **Interest cover** has reduced from 14 times to 10.3 times, which is still a very healthy level, and **gearing increased to 56%**. Both ratios are well within our **targets** of a minimum of 8 times interest cover and a maximum of 70% gearing. The **covenants under our debt facilities** require a gearing of less than 85% and debt of less than twice **EBITDA** (earnings before interest, tax, depreciation and amortisation).

(5) The Group has a progressive dividend policy. **Dividend growth** will follow **earnings growth** and we will maintain **dividend cover at our target of three times**. We believe this level of cover should generate sufficient **retained capital** to support the **equity component** of our investment programme.

Key performance indicators and benchmarking of performance

See sections 2 & 7

(6) We benchmark our performance against a peer group of comparable businesses (A, B, C, D). We aim for **top quartile performance** compared to this group in the following categories: **operating profit** as a percentage of sales, **return on capital employed, profit per employee, proportion of repeat business**. We believe we currently rank in the top quartile of the printing sector on all these criteria.

(7) The group achieved a **return on capital** employed of 29%. In the **long term, our objective** is a steady rise in return on capital employed as a result of acquisitions, capital expenditure programmes and improvements in efficiency and machine utilisation.

See Section 5

Risks and sensitivities

(8) The commercial risks we face in the coming year are:

(i) If sterling continues to increase in value, overseas companies will become even more competitive on the non-magazine work.

(ii) While we expect a very modest growth in the economy, if economic activity contracts there will be a resultant decline in demand for our services.

Trading prospects

(9) Our prospects for the current year are dependent on prices achieved and volume of work. We believe that volume of work will move ahead this year arising from the increased capacity generated by the installation of new plant.

(10) We remain confident about the prospects for our business.

1.1 Why are shareholders important?

In the case example above, the majority of the extracts from the strategic report are expressed in financial terms. The reference to dividend policy and earnings growth also highlights that the report is reporting not only on the company's performance but also on the prospects for the shareholders who have invested in it.

As we saw in the previous chapters, organisations are likely to have a number of goals, objectives and targets which, despite managerial effort to attain goal congruence, are at times likely to conflict. This is often due to the difficulty in satisfying the differing objectives of the organisation's various stakeholder groups.

Nonetheless, performance reports in profit-making organisations often tend to focus on financial performance in general, and on the interests of shareholders in particular. The logic for this is that shareholders are the legal owners; the company belongs to them, and so their interests are paramount. Consequently, the underlying financial objective of commercial organisations should be to **maximise the wealth of their shareholders**.

Although the dividends they receive provide one source of wealth for shareholders, the main source of shareholder wealth – particularly in the longer term – comes through increases in the value of the shares. As a firm's share price increases, the value of the firm increases, and therefore the wealth of the shareholders who hold shares in the firm also increases.

Question

Long-term owner value

Go back to the case example above. Identify factors which indicate that maximising long-term owner value is the company's objective.

Answer

(a) The group strategy – to serve customers – is undertaken with profit in mind.

(b) Capital investments generate future profits by raising productivity.

(c) Funding structure. There is generally an optimum mix of debt and equity capital. The firm monitors this to raise capital and funds at the cheapest cost – in the shareholders' interests.

(d) Benchmarking of performance. Although these are accounting measures, they do contribute to the long-term performance of the company. Raising return on capital employed means rewarding shareholders more each year for their investment.

1.2 Significance of long-term owner focus

(a) As maximising shareholder wealth is a **long-term** goal for a business, inevitably managers must decide between **what funds** they want to **disburse now** and **what funds** need to be **maintained** in the business to ensure the prospects of long-term profitability.

(b) Shareholders **own the business** and so the directors of the company have a **duty** to safeguard their interests.

(c) What the shareholders require as a **return** is used to judge the **validity of investment projects**.

(d) Shareholders assess the **quality of management** by how well the **business performs financially**.

(e) Shareholders are the principal **source of capital investment** in a business. They provide funds on share issues or permit managers to retain profits for investment.

1.3 What are shareholders interested in?

(a) Current earnings
(b) Future earnings
(c) Dividend policy
(d) The relative risk of the investments compared with other investments and the return available

1.4 Difficulties of incorporating shareholder concerns in performance measurement for managers

(a) **Accounting.** Shareholders are interested in **future returns** whereas accounts generally provide **historic information**. Accounting measures such as return on capital employed (ROCE) do not measure shareholder wealth.

(b) **Shareholders** have a different assessment of risk to managers. Managers typically worry about their careers, which don't concern shareholders at all. Shareholders are concerned about the security of the investment and the likelihood of making a return.

(c) At **operating** level, it is not easy to identify exactly how well a business is doing in relation to other businesses.

(d) Any other yardstick than shareholders' objectives effectively means that managers may run an organisation in their **own** interests.

1.5 Why should managers bother to know who their shareholders are?

A company's senior management should remain aware of who its major shareholders are, and it will often help to retain shareholders' support if the chairman or the managing director meets occasionally with the major shareholders, to exchange views.

(a) The company's management might learn about **shareholders' preferences** for either high **dividends** or high **retained earnings** for profit growth and capital gain.

(b) For public companies, changes in shareholdings might help to explain recent share price movements.

(c) The company's management should be able to learn about **shareholders' attitudes to both risk and gearing**. If a company is planning a new investment, its management might have to consider the relative merits of seeking equity finance or debt finance and shareholders' attitudes would be worth knowing about before the decision is taken.

(d) Management might need to know its shareholders in the event of an unwelcome takeover bid from another company, to identify key shareholders whose views on the takeover bid might be crucial to the final outcome.

1.6 Aligning shareholder and managerial goals

Although companies are owned by their shareholders, the responsibility for running and controlling a company rests with its board and senior management. This separation of ownership and control gives rise to the problem of ensuring that companies are managed in such a way that the economic interests of their principals (shareholders) are promoted rather than the interests of their agents (company executives and managers).

This issue of resolving the differing interests of principals and agents is known as **agency theory**.

The importance of agency theory here is that it highlights the importance of evaluating strategic decisions taken by managers in terms of the potential those decisions have to maximise the wealth of a company's shareholders.

We will see the significance of this point later in the chapter, in relation to the relative merits of using **economic value added** (EVA) as a measure of performance instead of profit-based measures.

The implications of agency theory are also relevant in relation to **reward and remuneration systems** (which we will discuss in Chapter 14).

One way of rewarding managers is **share options**.

(a) This is regarded as a **good thing**, as it means that managers have a direct financial interest in increasing owner wealth, ensuring goal congruence between principals and agents.

(b) However, although share options and employee share schemes **can** improve the alignment of the interests of staff and managers with those of shareholders, this is not necessarily the case.

   (i) Managers are rewarded for **past** performance and the rewards are often **immediate**. They may be incentivised to take **short-term measures** and ignore the long term.

   (ii) There may be a **general** rise in share prices which is not performance related.

Case Study

From *The Times*, 13 November 2007

Bonnie Brown was not in a position to haggle. She was recently divorced and living with her sister so when a small technology start-up offered her a job in 1999 as a part-time masseuse she took it. The post paid $450 a week, plus a pile of what were then worthless stock options.

However, by 2007 as a result of that package, Ms Brown, Google employee No 41, was a multimillionaire.

This story gives a flavour of some of the rewards possible from owning options. However, no one would suggest that Ms Brown, or indeed the other 1,000 or so Google employees who are multimillionaires, put in as much as they have reaped in rewards. The dramatic rise in Google's share price was due to a range of factors from the hard work of its employees to market fever for Google shares.

1.6.1 Internet businesses

Between 1995 and 1999, investors in internet companies offered managers share options, in return for a lower salary and long hours. By offering managers a stake in the company, they were given an incentive to work to boost the share price, and then – in theory – enjoy a significant cash return when they exercised their share options in future.

The share options, potentially, could have made the managers into millionaires. For several years, managers worked long hours for reward that correlated neatly with the rewards offered to shareholders.

However, around the year 2000, the market lost confidence in internet companies. Managers saw their potential rewards wiped out. For the thousands of people who had left safe jobs to try their luck in the 'new economy', and with the hope of making a fortune through stock options, the downturn in the markets came as a very nasty shock. Many people came to rue their decision to rely on the stock market for their pay day, instead of taking home a regular monthly income.

One of the key lessons of the 'dot.com' boom and bust is that it may now be unrealistic to expect managers to take the same risks with their rewards as investors, who are able to spread risks.

Managers and staff now have a more realistic outlook about the level of risk they are prepared to accept. Basic salaries now figure more highly in job negotiations. Stock options may still be an attraction for some people, but the options are now seen as the 'icing on the cake' rather than as a guaranteed source of income. People will want a regular monthly income alongside the options.

Exam focus point

Notice the link from the example about internet businesses to the ideas about stakeholders and their attitudes to risk which we discussed in Chapter 4. Managers and staff (as stakeholders) can either accept a relatively high level of risk (stock options) or they may prefer a lower level of risk (a regular monthly salary).

2 Profitability 6/12

FAST FORWARD

Measures relating to profit include sales margin, EBITDA and EPS. More sophisticated measures (ROCE, ROI) take the size of investment into account. Later on in the chapter we consider how measures of profitability are used for **short-run** or **long-run performance measurement**. Bear this in mind particularly when you study the sections on RI, ROI and NPV and go through the examples covering these.

Knowledge brought forward from earlier studies

You should already be familiar with how to calculate many of the performance measures in this section (profitability, sales margin, EPS, ROCE) from your studies at F5.

The focus at P5, however, is likely to be less on the calculations themselves, but rather on what different measures may indicate about an organisation's performance, along with the benefits and limitations of using different performance measures.

You need to be able to discuss the **appropriateness** of the measures of 'profitability' specifically identified in the P5 Study Guide and covered in this section.

As a general principle, these measures of performance we will be looking at are only meaningful if they are used for comparison.

(a) Over time (equivalent time periods)
(b) With other measures of performance
(c) With other companies
(d) With other industries

2.1 Profitability

A company ought of course to be profitable, and there are obvious checks on **profitability**:

(a) Whether the company has made a profit or a loss on its ordinary activities
(b) By how much this year's profit or loss is bigger or smaller than last year's profit or loss

It is probably better to consider separately the profits or losses on exceptional items if there are any. Such gains or losses should not be expected to occur again, unlike profits or losses on normal trading.

Question **Profitability**

A company has the following summarised statements of profit or loss for two consecutive years.

	Year 1	*Year 2*
	$	$
Revenue	70,000	100,000
Less cost of sales	42,000	55,000
Gross profit	28,000	45,000
Less expenses	21,000	35,000
Net profit	7,000	10,000

Although the net profit margin is the same for both years at 10%, the gross profit margin is not.

Year 1 $\frac{28,000}{70,000} = 40\%$ Year 2 $\frac{45,000}{100,000} = 45\%$

Is this good or bad for the business?

Answer

An increased profit margin must be good because this indicates a wider gap between selling price and cost of sales. Given that the net profit ratio has stayed the same in the second year, however, expenses must be rising. In year 1 expenses were 30% of revenue, whereas in year 2 they were 35% of revenue. This indicates that administration, selling and distribution expenses or interest costs require tight control.

Percentage analysis of profit between year 1 and year 2

	Year 1	*Year 2*
	%	%
Cost of sales as a % of sales	60	55
Gross profit as a % of sales	40	45
	100	100
Expenses as a % of sales	30	35
Net profit as a % of sales	10	10
Gross profit as a % of sales	40	45

Profit on ordinary activities before taxation is generally thought to be a better figure to use than profit after taxation, because there might be unusual variations in the tax charge from year to year which would not affect the underlying profitability of the company's operations.

Another profit figure that should be calculated is **PBIT**: **profit before interest and tax**.

(a) This is the amount of profit which the company earned **before having to pay interest to the providers of loan capital**. By providers of loan capital, we usually mean longer-term loan capital, such as debentures and medium-term bank loans, which will be shown in the statement of financial position (balance sheet) as 'Suppliers: amounts falling due after more than one year.' This figure is of particular importance to bankers and lenders.

(b) How is profit before interest and tax calculated?

PBIT = profit on ordinary activities before taxation + interest charges on long-term loan capital

In effect, PBIT is often the same as **operating profit**. As such, PBIT is: **Gross profit less other operating costs.**

2.2 Profit margins

Key term

Gross profit margin is calculated as gross profit (ie revenue less cost of sales) divided by revenue.

Operating profit margin is calculated as operating profit (PBIT) divided by revenue.

Look at the following examples.

(a) European communications and information technology company: for the year ended 31 December

	20X4	*20X3*
	€m	€m
Revenue	12,732	12,709
Cost of sales	(7,094)	(7,364)
Gross profit	**5,638**	**5,345**
Research and development	(2,493)	(2,619)
Selling, general and administrative expenses	(1,634)	(1,671)
Impairment of goodwill	(1,209)	-
Other income and expenses	(132)	(536)
Operating profit	**170**	**519**

Gross profit in 20X4 had risen to 44.3% (5,638/12,732), compared to 42.1% in 20X3 (5,345/12,709). By contrast, operating profit fell from 4.1% (519/12,709) to 1.3% (170/12,732).

(b) South African energy and chemical company: for the year ended 30 June

	20X5	*20X4*
	Rm	Rm
Revenue	185,266	202,683
Cost of sales (materials, energy and consumables used)	(80,169)	(89,224)
Gross profit	**105,097**	**113,459**
Selling and distribution expenditure	(6,041)	(5,762)
Administrative expenditure	(29,724)	(36,859)
Exploration expenditure and feasibility costs	(554)	(604)
Depreciation and amortisation	(13,567)	(13,516)
Other expenses, net	(9,912)	(7,415)
Operating profit	**45,299**	**49,303**

Gross profit margin increased slightly from 56.0% (20X4) to 56.7% (20X5). Operating profit was virtually the same for both years: 24.4% (20X5) compared to 24.3% (20X4).

(c) **Lessons to be learnt**

(i) Profit margins as a performance measure are **not really much use when comparing different industries**. (The examples above are denominated in different currencies as well, which would also make comparison more difficult).

(ii) Gross profit margin is influenced by the level of **direct costs**, and the **selling price** of products or services.

(iii) **Trends** in margins are potentially more useful than one-off margins. A falling gross profit margin suggests that an organisation has not been able to pass on input price rises to customers.

(iv) **Comparisons** with similar companies are of interest. If an organisation has a lower gross profit margin than a similar business, this could suggest problems in controlling input costs. Alternatively, it could suggest an organisation is selling its product at a lower price than its competitors (and therefore earning a lower margin than them, even if its input costs are the same as theirs).

2.2.1 Profit margins and performance management

Often, companies' strategies will focus on growth. However, it is important that revenue growth is also profitable.

Consider the following simple example:

A company currently sells 1,000 units of a product per week, for $20 each. The costs of manufacturing and selling the product are $15. In order to boost sales the company decides to reduce the selling price to $17 per unit. Following the reduction in price, the company now sells 2,000 units per week.

	After price change	*Before price change*
	$	$
Revenue	34,000	20,000
Cost of sales	(30,000)	(15,000)
Gross profit	**4,000**	**5,000**
Gross profit %	11.8%	25.0%

Crucially, although the company's revenue has increased following the change, its gross profit (and its gross profit margin) have actually decreased. If the company only measured revenue growth as one of its key performance indicators, it would appear to be performing well. Therefore, it would be important for the company to measure profitability as well as revenue growth, to ensure that profitability isn't sacrificed for revenue growth.

Measuring profit margins can also be important in relation to monitoring and controlling costs.

Consider the following results for a manufacturing company that has expanded during the year 20X5, but that has also been affected by rising costs:

	20X5	*20X4*
	$	$
Revenue	1,724,000	1,570,000
Operating costs	(1,382,500)	(1,229,800)
Operating profit	**341,500**	**340,200**

Although the company's operating profit increased slightly from 20X4 to 20X5, operating profit margin has fallen from 21.7% (340,200/1,570,000) to 19.8% (341,500/1,724,000).

The fall in margin (%) highlights the impact of the rising costs, in a way which the absolute operating profit figure doesn't.

Although in the example above the company has expanded, operating profit margin could be a particularly important performance metric for organisations which have limited opportunities for revenue growth – for example, because they are operating in industries which have reached the mature stage of their life cycle. In order to maximise their profits, these companies will have to control their costs as efficiently as possible – and operating profit margin could be a key indicator for measuring how well they are achieving this.

More generally, operating profit margin provides a useful indicator for measuring how efficiently and effectively management are controlling the costs in a business. In this respect, operating profit margin could also be affected by the bargaining power of an organisation's suppliers. If the bargaining power of the suppliers is weak, this might help an organisation sustain a higher margin than one whose suppliers have higher bargaining power (for example, as in the relationship between supermarkets and the farmers who supply their agricultural products).

Equally, however, an organisation's profit margin could also be affected by its ability to pass on rising costs to its own customers. If the cost of raw materials used by a manufacturing company is increasing, but the company has little scope to increase the prices it charges its own customers, then the costs could lead to a significant reduction in its profit margin. As such (and as Porter's five forces suggests) the bargaining power of an organisation's customers (as well as its suppliers) could be a factor which influences its profit margins.

2.3 EBITDA

Key term

EBITDA is earnings before interest, tax, depreciation and amortisation.

EBITDA is essentially net income with interest, taxes, depreciation and amortisation added back to it, and can be used to analyse and compare profitability between companies and industries because it eliminates the effects of financing and accounting decisions.

To see what EBITDA actually does, it is worth identifying **what it omits**.

Item	Comment
Earnings	In practice this equals **profit after tax** for the financial year with some **adjustments**, as you should be aware from your financial accounting studies.
Interest	Essentially this is a **financing cost**. In essence, EBITDA is a measure of operating profit, but interest is a non-operating cost. A business will need to generate sufficient profit (and cash) from its operations to be able to repay the interest on its loans.
Tax	The Government's take is not relevant to the operating performance of the business.
Depreciation and amortisation	This is the income statement charge for **tangible** and **intangible** assets. Depreciation generally represents the writing off of expenditure incurred several years ago, not in itself relevant to performance in any particular financial year.

2.3.1 Advantages of EBITDA

(a) It is a good proxy for **cash flow from operations**, and therefore is a measure of underlying performance. It can be seen as the proportion of operating profits converted to cash.

(b) Tax and interest, while important, are effectively distributions to the Government (tax) and a finance charge (interest). By stripping out these expenses, EBITDA offers a clearer reflection of how the companies' operations are performing.

(c) EBITDA is easy to calculate and understand.

(d) EBITDA can be used to assess the performance of a manager who has no control over acquisition and financing policy, as it excludes costs associated with assets (depreciation) and debt (interest). Depreciation and amortisation also relate to historic decisions – for example, depreciation charges could relate to an asset acquired a relatively long time ago. By stripping out costs relating to historic decisions, EBITDA can help get a better understanding of an organisation's current performance.

(e) In addition, EBITDA removes the subjective judgement that can go into calculating depreciation and amortisation, such as useful lives and residual values. By eliminating these, EBITDA makes it easier to compare the financial performance of different companies. In a similar way, EBITDA is useful for evaluating the performance of firms with different capital structures, tax rates or depreciation policies.

EBITDA has become a popular measure in capital intensive industries or ones where companies have high levels of debt. In some of these industries companies struggle to make profits once interest and depreciation charges have been deducted from earnings. However, EBITDA allows a company to make its financial picture more attractive by removing these costs from the measures of its performance.

Note, however, that although EBITDA can be a good proxy for cash flow from operations, critics of EBITDA argue that for an organisation as a whole EBITDA is only a good metric for evaluating **profitability**, not **cash flow**. They argue that it doesn't take account of the cash required to fund working capital or to replace or acquire assets which can be significant.

2.3.2 EBITDAR

EBITDAR adds back operating lease **rental** costs to the EBITDA figure. Certain user groups view operating leases as a form of finance which is not recognised in the statement of financial position. By adding back operating lease rentals, consistency is achieved between companies, whether they use finance or operating leases.

Worked example: EBIT, EBITDA and EBITDAR

Fin Co and Op Co both operate in the same industry and are of similar size. Both have entered into a number of significant lease arrangements to obtain the use of key operating assets. Under IAS 17 *Leases* Fin Co's leases are finance leases, while Op Co's are operating leases. The following amounts have been extracted from the income statements of Fin Co and Op Co.

	Fin Co	*Op Co*
	£'000	£'000
Gross profit	350	320
Depreciation of owned assets	(50)	(20)
Depreciation of leased assets	(60)	–
Operating lease rentals	–	(80)
Other operating expenses	(100)	(100)
Operating profit	140	120
Finance lease interest expense	(20)	–
Other interest expense	(30)	(30)
Profit before taxation	90	90

The profitability measures can be calculated as follows.

	£'000	£'000
EBIT	140	120
EBITDA (140 + 60 + 50)/(120 + 20)	250	140
EBITDAR (140 + 60 + 50)/(120 + 80 + 20)	250	220

Question — **The relevance of interest**

When might interest be relevant in a significant way to the **operating** performance of the business?

Answer

- It depends. Short-term bank interest can be a significant operating expense.
- Also, a bank itself earns money from an interest margin so interest is at the heart of what it does.

2.4 Earnings per share (EPS)

Earnings per share (EPS) is a convenient measure, as it shows how well the shareholder is doing.

EPS is widely used as a **measure of a company's performance**, especially in **comparing** results over a period of **several years**. A company must be able to sustain its earnings in order to pay dividends and reinvest in the business so as to achieve future growth. Investors also look for **growth in the EPS** from one year to the next.

Key term

Earnings per share (EPS) is defined (in Financial Reporting Standard 3) as the profit in cents attributable to each equity (ordinary) share. EPS is calculated as follows.

$$\frac{\text{Profit of the period after tax, minority interests and extraordinary items, and after deducting preference dividends}}{\text{Number of equity shares in issue and ranking for dividend}}$$

Extraordinary items are unusual, non-repeating items that affect profit but have effectively been outlawed by FRS 3.

Question — **EPS**

Walter Wall Carpets plc made profits before tax in 20X8 of $9,320,000. Tax amounted to $2,800,000.

The company's share capital is as follows.

	$
Ordinary share (10,000,000 shares of $1)	10,000,000
8% preference shares	2,000,000
	12,000,000

Required

Calculate the EPS for 20X8.

Answer

	$
Profits before tax	9,320,000
Less tax	2,800,000
Profits after tax	6,520,000
Less preference dividend (8% of $2,000,000)	160,000
Earnings	6,360,000
Number of ordinary shares	10,000,000
EPS	63.6c

EPS on its own does not really tell us anything. It must be seen **in context**.

(a) EPS is used for comparing the results of a company **over time**. Is its EPS growing? What is the rate of growth? Is the rate of growth increasing or decreasing?

(b) Is there likely to be a significant **dilution of EPS** in the future, perhaps due to the exercise of share options or warrants, or the conversion of convertible loan stock into equity?

(c) EPS should not be used blindly to compare the earnings of one company with another. For example, if A Co has an EPS of 12c for its 10,000,000 10c shares and B Co has an EPS of 24c for its 50,000,000 25c shares, we must take account of the numbers of shares. When **earnings are used to compare one company's shares with another**, this is done **using** the **P/E ratio or perhaps the earnings yield**.

(d) If EPS is to be a reliable basis for comparing results, it **must be calculated consistently**. The EPS of one company must be directly comparable with the EPS of others, and the EPS of a company in one year must be directly comparable with its published EPS figures for previous years. Changes in the share capital of a company during the course of a year cause problems of comparability.

Note that EPS is a figure based on past data, and it is easily manipulated by changes in accounting policies and by mergers or acquisitions. **The use of the measure in calculating management bonuses makes it particularly liable to manipulation.** The attention given to EPS as a performance measure by City analysts is arguably disproportionate to its true worth. Investors should be more concerned with **future earnings**, but of course estimates of these are more difficult to reach than the readily available figure.

A **fully diluted EPS** (FDEPS) can be measured where the company has issued securities that might be converted into ordinary shares at some future date, such as convertible loan stock, share warrants or share options. The FDEPS gives investors an appreciation of by how much EPS might be affected if and when the options, warrants or conversion rights are exercised.

2.5 Profitability and return: the return on capital employed (ROCE)

It is impossible to assess profits or profit growth properly without relating them to the amount of funds (the capital) employed in making the profits. An important profitability ratio is therefore **ROCE**, which states the profit as a **percentage of the amount of capital employed.**

Profit is usually taken as PBIT, and capital employed is shareholders' capital plus 'suppliers: amount falling due after more than one year' plus long-term provisions for liabilities and charges. This is the same as total assets less current liabilities. The underlying principle is that we must compare like with like, and so if capital means share capital and reserves plus long-term liabilities and debt capital, profit must mean the profit earned by all this capital together. This is PBIT, since interest is the return for loan capital.

Key term

Return on capital employed (ROCE) indicates the productivity of capital employed. It is calculated as:

$$\frac{\text{Profit before interest and tax} \times 100}{\text{Average capital employed}}$$

The denominator is normally calculated as the average of the capital employed at the beginning and end of the year. Problems of seasonality, new capital introduced or other factors may necessitate taking the average of a number of periods within the year.

2.5.1 Evaluating the ROCE

What does a company's ROCE tell us? What should we be looking for? There are three **comparisons** that can be made.

(a) The change in ROCE from **one year to the next**

(b) The ROCE being earned by **other companies**, if this information is available

(c) A comparison of the ROCE with **current market borrowing rates**

   (i) What would be the cost of extra borrowing to the company if it needed more loans, and is it earning an ROCE that suggests it could make high enough profits to make such borrowing worthwhile?

   (ii) Is the company making an ROCE which suggests that it is making profitable use of its current borrowing?

Exam focus point

In Section 5 later in this chapter we look at issues surrounding short-termism in decision making.

One of the main criticisms of ROCE as a performance measure is that it can encourage **short-term decision making**.

If a company's (or a division's) performance is being assessed on the basis of ROCE, this may discourage capital investment, because an increase in capital will lead to a fall in ROCE if PBIT remains the same.

However, such a failure to invest is likely to have an adverse effect on a business's performance in the **longer term**.

2.5.2 Analysing profitability and return in more detail: the secondary ratios

We may analyse the ROCE, to find out why it is high or low, or better or worse than last year. There are two factors that contribute towards a return on capital employed, both related to revenue.

(a) **Profit margin**. A company might make a high or a low profit margin on its sales. For example, a company that makes a profit of 25c per $1 of sales is making a bigger return on its revenue than another company making a profit of only 10c per $1 of sales.

(b) **Asset turnover**. Asset turnover is a measure of how well the assets of a business are being used to generate sales. For example, if two companies each have capital employed of $100,000, and company A makes sales of $400,000 a year whereas company B makes sales of only $200,000 a year, company A is making a higher revenue from the same amount of assets and this will help company A to make a higher ROCE than company B. Asset turnover is expressed as 'x times' so that assets generate x times their value in annual revenue. Here, company A's asset turnover is four times and company B's is two times.

Profit margin and asset turnover together explain the ROCE, and if the ROCE is the primary profitability ratio, these other two are the **secondary ratios**. The relationship between the three ratios is as follows:

Profit margin × **Asset turnover** = **ROCE**

$$\frac{\text{PBIT}}{\text{Sales}} \times \frac{\text{Sales}}{\text{Capital employed}} = \frac{\text{PBIT}}{\text{Capital employed}}$$

It is also worth commenting on the **change in revenue** from one year to the next. Strong sales growth will usually indicate volume growth as well as revenue increases due to price rises and volume growth is one sign of a prosperous company.

2.6 Return on investment (ROI)

Key term

> **Return on investment (ROI)** is a form of ROCE and is calculated as:
>
> $$\frac{\text{Profit before interest and tax} \times 100}{\text{Operations management capital employed}}$$

The ROI compares income with the operational assets used to generate that income. Profit is taken before tax and interest because tax is an appropriation of profit made from the use of the investment, and the introduction of interest charges introduces the effect of financing decisions into an appraisal of operating performance.

ROI is normally used to apply to investment centres or profit centres. These normally reflect the existing organisation structure of the business.

2.6.1 Main reasons for the widespread use of ROI

(a) **Financial reporting**. It ties in directly with the accounting process, and is identifiable from the income statement and statement of financial position (balance sheet), the firm's most important communications media with investors.

(b) **Aggregation**. ROI is a very convenient method of measuring the performance for a division or company as an entire unit.

Other advantages include its ability to permit comparisons to be drawn between investment centres that differ in their absolute size.

2.6.2 Measurement problems: non-current assets

(a) It is probably most common to use **return on net assets**.

(i) If an investment centre maintains the **same annual profit**, and keeps the **same assets** without a policy of regular non-current asset replacement, its **ROI** will **increase year by year as the assets get older**. This can give a false impression of improving 'real' performance over time.

Using ROI as a performance measure may also encourage **short-termism**, because managers may choose not to replace assets. ROI increases as the assets get older, because depreciation reduces the net book value of the assets.

(ii) It is **not easy** to **compare fairly** the performance of one investment centre with another. Non-current assets may be of different ages or may be depreciated in different ways.

(iii) **Inflation and technological change** alter the cost of non-current assets. If one investment centre has non-current assets bought ten years ago with a gross cost of $1 million, and another investment centre, in the same area of business operations, has non-current assets bought very recently for $1 million, the quantity and technological character of the non-current assets of the two investment centres are likely to be very different.

(iv) Measuring ROI as return on **gross assets ignores the age factor**. Older non-current assets usually cost more to repair and maintain. An investment centre with old assets may therefore have its profitability reduced by repair costs.

(b) **Measurement problems: what are 'assets' anyway?**

Prudence and other accounting principles require that items such as research and development should only be carried forward as an investment in special circumstances. Many 'costs' do have the effect of enhancing the long-term revenue-earning capacity of the business. A good example is **brands**: many firms have capitalised brands for this reason. For **decision-making** and **control** purposes, the expenditure on brands might be better treated as an investment.

2.6.3 The target return for a group of companies

If a group of companies sets a **target return** for the group as a whole, or if a company sets a target return for each strategic business unit, it might be company policy that no investment project should go ahead in any subsidiary or investment centre unless the project promises to earn at least the target return. Here is an example.

(a) There should be no new investment by any subsidiary in the group unless it is expected to earn at least a 15% return.

(b) Similarly, no non-current asset should be disposed of if the asset is currently earning a return in excess of 15% of its disposal value.

(c) Investments which promise a return of 15% or more ought to be undertaken.

Problems with such a policy include:

(a) **Investments** are **appraised by discounted cash flow (DCF)** whereas **actual performance** will probably be **measured on the basis of ROI**.

(b) The **target return** makes **no allowance** for the different **risk** of each investment centre.

(c) In a **conglomerate**, an **identical target return** may be **unsuitable** to many businesses in a group.

Since **managers** will be judged on the basis of the ROI that their centre earns each year, they are likely to be **motivated** into taking those decisions which **increase** their centre's **short-term ROI**.

(a) An investment might be desirable from the group's point of view, but would not be in the individual investment centre's 'best interest' to undertake. Thus there is a lack of **goal congruence**.

(b) In the short term, a desire to increase ROI might lead to projects being taken on without **due regard to their risk**.

(c) Any decisions which **benefit** the company in the **long term** but which **reduce** the ROI in the immediate **short term** would **reflect badly** on the manager's reported performance.

2.7 Divisional performance: residual income (RI)

An alternative way of measuring the performance of an investment centre, instead of using ROI, is residual income (RI).

Key term

Residual income is a measure of the centre's profits after deducting a notional or imputed interest cost.

Its use highlights the finance charge associated with funding.

The **imputed cost of capital** might be the organisation's **cost of borrowing** or its **weighted average cost of capital**. Alternatively, the cost of capital can be adjusted to allow for the risk characteristics of each investment centre, with a higher imputed interest rate being applied to higher **risk** centres.

2.8 Example: calculation of ROI and RI

Division M is a division of MR Co. The following data relate to Division M.

Capital employed (net assets)	$20m
Annual profit	$5m
Cost of capital	15% per annum

MR Co is considering two proposals.

Proposal 1

Invest a further $2m in fixed assets to earn an annual profit of $0.30m.

Proposal 2

Dispose of fixed assets at their net book value of $5.5m. This would lead to profits falling by $0.8m per annum. Proceeds from the disposal of these fixed assets would not be credited to Division M (but to the Holding Company of MR Co instead).

Required

(a) Calculate the current return on investment and residual income for Division M.

(b) Consider each of the two proposals and show how the return on investment and residual income would change if these proposals were adopted.

2.9 Solution

(a) **Current return on investment**

Return on investment $= \dfrac{\text{Profit before interest and tax}}{\text{Operations management capital employed}} \times 100\%$

$= \dfrac{\$5m}{\$20m} \times 100\%$

$= 25\%$

Residual income = Annual profit – Imputed interest charge on net assets
= $5m – (15% × $20m)
= $5m – $3m
= $2m

The return on investment (25%) exceeds the cost of capital (15%) and the residual income is positive (+$2m) and therefore Division M is performing well.

(b) Let us now look at the situations that would arise if proposals 1 and 2 were to be adopted.

Proposal 1

New profit = $5m + $0.3m
= $5.3m

∴ New capital employed = $20m + $2m
= $22m

∴ **New return on investment** $= \dfrac{\$5.3m}{\$22m} \times 100\%$
= 24.1%

∴ **New residual income** = $5.3m – (15% × $22m)
= $5.3m – $3.3m
= $2m

Proposal 2

New profit = $5m – $0.8m
= $4.2m

New capital employed = $20m – $5.5m
= $14.5m

∴ **New return on investment** $= \dfrac{\$4.2m}{\$14.5m} \times 100\%$
= 29%

∴ **New residual income** = \$4.2m – (15% × \$14.5m)
= \$4.2m – \$2.18m
= \$2.02m

Summary

	Current	*Proposal 1*	*Proposal 2*
Return on investment (%)	25	24.1	29
Residual income (\$m)	2	2	2.02

On first inspection it appears that proposal 2 should be adopted as the ROI increases from 25% to 29% and the RI also increases slightly from \$2m to \$2.02m. However, divisional managers should also consider the asset rate of return relevant to proposal 2.

$$\text{Asset rate of return} = \frac{\text{Change in profit}}{\text{Change in investment}}$$

$$= \frac{\$0.8\text{m}}{\$5.5\text{m}} \times 100\%$$

$$= 14.5\%$$

Since MR Co's current rate of return is 25%, any asset which has a rate of return less than this should be disposed of. It is important to remember, therefore, that whichever proposal is accepted, it should lead to **goal congruence**.

2.10 The advantages and weaknesses of RI compared with ROI

2.10.1 Advantages of RI

(a) **RI increases in the following circumstances:**

(i) Investments earning above the cost of capital are undertaken.
(ii) Investments earning below the cost of capital are eliminated.

(b) RI is more **flexible** since a different cost of capital can be applied to investments with different risk characteristics.

2.10.2 Weaknesses of RI

The first is that it **does not facilitate comparisons** between investment centres nor does it relate the size of a centre's income to the size of the investment, other than indirectly through the interest charge. The second is that it can be **difficult to decide on an appropriate and accurate measure of the capital employed** on which to base the imputed interest charge (see comments on ROI).

2.11 Cash flows: net present value (NPV) and internal rate of return (IRR)

Although net present value (NPV) and internal rate of return (IRR) are often used alongside business cases to evaluate whether or not to undertake new capital investments, the Study Guide also specifically mentions them as measures of performance.

In this context, they can be useful as controls by comparing actual results to those planned.

Moreover, they are useful because they focus on **future cash flows** and make allowance for **risk** (through the use of discount factors).

2.11.1 The advantages and weaknesses of NPV compared with ROI and RI

Advantages include:

(a) Cash flows are less subject to manipulation and subjective decisions than accounting profits.
(b) It considers the opportunity cost of not holding money.
(c) Risk can be allowed for by adjusting the cost of capital.
(d) Shareholders are interested in cash flows (both in the short term and long term).

The **disadvantages** of the NPV approach are centred on the assumptions underlying the values of critical variables within the model. For example:

(a) The duration of the cash flows
(b) The timing of the cash flows
(c) The appropriate cost of capital

2.11.2 Cash flows and NPVs for strategic control: shareholder wealth

Control and performance measures at a strategic level do need to pay some attention to wealth. Shareholders are interested in cash flow as the safest indicator of business success. According to one model of share valuations, the market value of the shares is based on the expected future dividend.

Control at a **strategic level** should be **based** on measurements of **cash flows** (actual cash flows for the period just ended and revised forecasts of future cash flows). Since the objective of a company might be to maximise the wealth of its shareholders, a control technique based on the measurement of cash flows and their NPV could be a very useful technique to apply. A numerical example might help to illustrate this point.

Suppose that ABC Co agrees to a **strategic plan from 1 January 20X1** as follows.

Year	*20X1*	*20X2*	*20X3*	*20X4*	*20X5*	*Total*
Planned net cash inflow ($'000)	200	300	300	400	500	1,700
NPV at cost of capital 15%	174	227	197	229	249	1,076

Now suppose that ABC Co **reviews** its position **one year later**.

(a) It can measure its actual total cash flow in 20X1: roughly speaking, this will be the funds generated from operations minus tax paid and minus expenditure on non-current assets and plus/minus changes in working capital.

(b) It can revise its forecast for the next few years.

We will assume that there has been **no change in the cost of capital**. Control information at the end of 20X1 might be as follows.

Year	*20X1 (actual)*	*20X2 (forecast)*	*20X3*	*20X4*	*20X5*	*Total*
Net cash inflow ($'000)	180	260	280	400	540	1,660
NPV at cost of capital 15%	180	226	212	263	309	1,190

A **control summary** comparing the situation at the start of 20X1 and the situation one year later would now be as follows.

	$'000
Expected NPV as at 1.1.20X1	1,076
Uplift by cost of capital 15% *	161
What NPV should have been at 31.12.20X1 **	1,237
Expected NPV as at 31.12.20X1	1,190
Variance	47 (A)

* You might wonder why we are doing this. Each cash flow in the original calculation was × by discount factor of $1/(1.15)^N$, where N = number of years between 20X1 and the cash flow. If we were to calculate the NPV starting at a point a year later, the discount factor for each of the cash flows would be $1/(1.15)^{N-1}$ (ie a cash flow at year 2 (31 December 20X2) from 1 January 20X1 would have a discount factor of $1/1.15^2$, but when NPV is recalculated at 31 December 20X1 the discount factor for 31 December 20X2 cash flow = 1/1.15). So each discount factor for recalculating is multiplied by 1.15 (changing $1/1.15^N$ to $1/1.15^{N-1}$). We can therefore multiply total NPV at 1 January 20X1 by 1.15 to get what NPV should have been at 31 December 20X1.

** The uplifting shows by how much the expected NPV would change if we were doing the calculation 12 months later.

The control information shows that by the end of 20X1, ABC Co **shows signs of not achieving the strategic targets** it set itself at the start of 20X1. This is partly because actual cash flows in 20X1 fell short of target by (200 – 180) $20,000, but also because the revised forecast for the future is not as good now either. In total, the company has a lower NPV by $47,000.

The **reasons for the failure** to achieve target should be investigated. Here are some possibilities.

(a) A higher than expected pay award to employees, which will have repercussions for the future as well as in 20X1

(b) An increase in the rate of tax on profits

(c) A serious delay in the implementation of some major new projects

(d) The slower than expected growth of an important new market

Strategic progress can therefore be measured by reconciling successive net present values and the intervening cash flows.

2.11.3 IRR

IRR is another way of reviewing investments. The IRR of a project can be compared to the cost of capital. A project's IRR is the required rate of return (or cost of capital) which leads to the project having an NPV of zero when that rate of return is used to discount the project's cash flows.

An organisation should undertake a project if the IRR of that project is greater than the organisation's cost of capital.

2.12 Modified internal rate of return (MIRR) 6/12

One of the weaknesses of IRR is that it assumes that cash flows after the investment phase are **reinvested at the project's IRR** over the life of the project (the reinvestment assumption). However, a better assumption is that funds will be reinvested at the investor's required return (or cost of capital).

The problem of the **reinvestment assumption** can be addressed by using the modified internal rate of return (MIRR). The MIRR distinguishes between the **investment phase** of a project and the **return phase**, and is calculated as follows.

Formula to learn

$$\left(\frac{PV_R}{PV_I}\right)^{\frac{1}{n}} \times (1+r_e) - 1$$

Where PV_R = the present value of the return phase (the phase of the project with cash inflows)
PV_I = the present value of the investment phase (the phase of the project with cash outflows)
r_e = the cost of capital
n = the life of the project (in years)

We can look at an example to compare IRR and MIRR.

Consider a project requiring an initial investment of $24,500, with cash inflows of $15,000 in years 1 and 2 and cash inflows of $3,000 in years 3 and 4. The **cost of capital** is 10%.

If we calculate the IRR:

Year	*Cash flow*	*Discount factor*	*Present value*	*Discount factor*	*Present value*
	$	10%	$	25%	$
0	(24,500)	1.000	(24,500)	1.000	(24,500)
1	15,000	0.909	13,635	0.800	12,000
2	15,000	0.826	12,390	0.640	9,600
3	3,000	0.751	2,253	0.512	1,536
4	3,000	0.683	2,049	0.410	1,230
			5,827		(134)

$$IRR = 10\% + \left[\frac{5{,}827}{5{,}827 + 134} \times (25\% - 10\%)\right] = 24.7\%$$

Now we will calculate MIRR, by calculating the **present value** of the investment phase and the return phase. Note that the MIRR is calculated on the basis of **investing the inflows** at the **cost of capital**.

Year	*Cash flow*	*Discount factor*	*Present value*
	$	10%	$
0	(24,500)	1.000	(24,500)
1	15,000	0.909	13,635
2	15,000	0.826	12,390
3	3,000	0.751	2,253
4	3,000	0.683	2,049

PV_R = Total PV for years 1–4 (the return phase) = $30,327

PV_I = Cost of investment (the investment phase) = $24,500

MIRR = $[30{,}327/24{,}500]^{¼} \times (1 + 0.1) - 1 = 16\%$

In this example, the MIRR of 16% is likely to be a **better measure** than the IRR of 24.7%. The MIRR is **invariably lower than the IRR**.

2.12.1 Return and investment phases

Note that when preparing an MIRR calculation it is vital to distinguish the cash flows from a project into the **return** and the **investment phases**. The initial cash outflows at the start of a project represent the 'investment' phases, and then subsequent cash inflows represent the 'return' phase.

2.12.2 MIRR with different rates for return and investment phases

This distinction between the two phases (return and investment phases) becomes vital if a company applies different discount rates for each phase. This means there is no longer one single cost of capital which can be applied to work out the rate of return.

Consequently, the formula used to calculate the MIRR also has to be changed.

Formula to learn

$$MIRR = \left[\frac{-FV}{PV}\right]^{1/(n-1)} - 1$$

Where:

FV = the future value of cash inflows (the return phase)
PV = the net present value of cash outflows (the investment phase)
n = the number of time periods

We can illustrate this by looking at an example.

Consider a project requiring an initial investment of $100,000, with subsequent cash inflows of $40,000 in year 1, $35,000 in year 2, $40,000 in year 4, $38,000 in year 5 and $40,000 in year 6. However, in year 3 there is expected to be an outflow of $20,000.

The finance rate (discount rate for the investment phase) is 13%, but the reinvestment rate (discount rate for the return phase) is 11%.

To calculate the MIRR, we **discount** each of the **negative net cash flows** (the investment phase) at the finance rate to get an NPV, and we **compound** each of the **positive net cash flows** at the reinvestment (return) rate to get a net future value.

Net cash **outflows** discounted at finance rate **(investment phase)** (at 13%):

Year	Cash flow	Discount factor	Present value
	$	13%	$
0	(100,000)	1.000	(100,000)
3	(20,000)	0.693	(13,860)
			(113,860)

Positive net cash inflows in **return (reinvestment) phase** (at 11%):

Year	Cash flow	Factor	Compound rate	Value
	$			$
1	40,000	$(1 + 11\%)^5$	1.685	67,402
2	35,000	$(1 + 11\%)^4$	1.518	53,132
3	[outflow]			
4	40,000	$(1 + 11\%)^2$	1.232	49,284
5	38,000	$(1 + 11\%)^1$	1.11	42,180
6	40,000	$(1 + 11\%)^0$	1	40,000
				251,998

MIRR = $(-FV/PV)^{1/n-1}-1$

MIRR = $(-251{,}998/-113{,}860)^{1/6}-1$ **[Note**. There are 7 time periods in total, not 6. '0' and then 1 to 6.]

MIRR = 1.1416 – 1

MIRR = 0.1416 = 14.16%

2.12.3 Advantages of MIRR

One obvious advantage of MIRR over IRR is that MIRR does not give the multiple answers which can sometimes arise with the conventional IRR.

MIRR also has the advantage that it assumes the **reinvestment rate** is the **company's cost of capital**. IRR assumes that the reinvestment rate is the IRR itself, which is usually untrue.

In many cases where there is conflict between the NPV and IRR methods, the MIRR will give the same indication as NPV, which is the **correct theoretical method**. This helps when explaining the appraisal of a project to managers, who often find the concept of rate of return easier to understand than that of NPV.

2.12.4 Disadvantages of MIRR

However, MIRR, like all rate of return methods, suffers from the problem that it may lead an investor to reject a project which has a **lower rate of return** but, because of its size, generates a **larger increase in wealth**.

In the same way, a **high-return** project with a **short life** may be preferred over a **lower-return** project with a longer life.

2.13 Summary

When compared with the NPV method, the **IRR method** has a number of **disadvantages**:

(a) It ignores the relative size of investments.

(b) There are problems with its use when a project has non-conventional cash flows or when deciding between mutually exclusive projects.

(c) Discount rates which differ over the life of a project cannot be incorporated into IRR calculations.

The MIRR is calculated on the basis of investing the inflows at the cost of capital.

2.14 Economic value added (EVA) 12/10, 12/12, 6/14, 12/15

Exam focus point

In a question in the December 2010 exam, the case study scenario described a company which had traditionally used earnings per share (EPS) and share price to assess performance. Candidates were then asked to assess the financial performance of a company using EVA, and then evaluate their results compared with those indicated by EPS and share price performance.

A question in the December 2012 exam asked candidates to evaluate the performance of an organisation using EVA. In effect, candidates had to calculate EVA, and then comment on the findings of their calculation. The examination team commented that, overall, candidates appeared well prepared for a calculation of EVA, although the weakest areas of their calculations related to the adjustments to capital employed.

As part of the compulsory question in the June 2014 exam, candidates were again asked to evaluate the EVA of a company, while in the September/December 2015 exam, candidates were asked to evaluate the accuracy of an EVA calculation which had been prepared by a junior management accountant.

FAST FORWARD

EVA™ is an absolute performance measure. It is similar to RI because both are calculated by subtracting an imputed interest charge from the profit earned by a company or division.

EVA is calculated as follows:

EVA = net operating profit after tax (NOPAT) less capital charge

where the capital charge = weighted average cost of capital × net assets

The key differences between EVA and RI are:

(a) The profit figures are calculated differently. EVA is based on '**economic profit**' which is derived by making a series of **adjustments to accounting profit**.

(b) The notional capital charges in EVA use **different bases for net assets** compared to those used in RI. The replacement cost of net assets is usually used in the calculation of EVA.

EVA is a specific performance measure, developed and registered as a trade mark by the Stern Stewart consulting organisation. EVA is an extension of the traditional income method, but it incorporates adjustments to adjust perceived distortions introduced by generally accepted accounting principles.

The logic behind EVA is that if the primary objective of commercial organisations is **to maximise the wealth of their shareholders**, then performance measures should evaluate how well they are doing this. Profit-based measures, which many organisations use as their primary measure of financial performance, do not do this because:

(a) Profit ignores the cost of equity capital. Financial statements take account of the cost of debt finance when calculating profit, but ignore the cost of equity finance.

(b) Profits calculated in accordance with accounting standards do not truly reflect the wealth that has been created.

The way EVA is calculated takes account of these concerns.

EVA = net operating profit after tax (NOPAT) less capital charge

(where the capital charge = weighted average cost of capital (WACC) × net assets)

Although the logic behind EVA is similar to that of RI (in other words, subtracting an imputed interest charge from the profit earned by a company or division), the calculation of EVA is different to RI because the net assets used as the basis of the imputed interest charge are usually valued at their **replacement cost** and are **increased by any costs that have been capitalised** (see below).

There are also **differences in the way that NOPAT is calculated**, compared with the profit figure that is used for RI. There are three main reasons for adjusting accounting profits to derive NOPAT.

(a) Costs which would normally be treated as expenses in the financial statements, but which are considered within an EVA calculation as **investments building for the future**, are added back to derive a figure for 'economic profit'. These costs are included instead as assets in the figure for net assets employed; in other words, they are deemed to be investments for the future. Costs treated in this way include such items as **research and development expenditure**, and **advertising costs**.

(b) **Cash accounting versus accruals**. Investors are primarily interested in cash flows, so accounting adjustments for non-cash items, such as allowances for doubtful debts, are eliminated.

(c) Investors, who are interested in maximising their wealth, will be interested in the continuing performance of the company. Therefore **one-off, unusual items** of profit or expenditure should be ignored.

Another point to note about the calculation of NOPAT, which is the same as the calculation of the profit figure for RI, is that **interest is excluded from NOPAT** because interest costs are taken into account in the capital charge.

However, note that because NOPAT is after tax, any adjustments to add back interest charges must also adjust the tax figure **to include the tax benefit of the interest**.

Exam focus point

There are two articles in the P5 Technical Articles section of ACCA's website, looking at 'Economic value added versus profit-based measures of performance' (Part 1 and 2). You are strongly advised to read these as part of your preparation for the exam.

The first of the articles points out that, in practice, there could be a very large number of adjustments required to accounting profits when calculating NOPAT.

The examination team will, however, only expect you to be aware of the most common adjustments. These are summarised in the table below.

2.14.1 Accounting adjustments

Types of item	Comment
Value-building expenditure	Expenditure on **marketing and promotions, research and development**, and **staff training** which will generate value for the business in future periods should be capitalised. If any such expenditure has been **charged as an expense** in the income statement, it should be **added back to profit**, and also **added to capital employed** in the year in which the expenses were incurred.
Depreciation	The charge for depreciation in the income statement should be **added back to profit**, and a **charge for economic depreciation** made instead. The value of non-current assets (and therefore capital employed) should also be adjusted to reflect the revised charge. Economic depreciation reflects the true change in value of assets during the period. However, if no detail is given about economic depreciation in a question scenario, then you should assume that accounting depreciation is a reasonable approximation for it, and therefore you should not make any change to the depreciation figure.
Provisions	Provisions, allowances for doubtful debts, inventory write-downs, and deferred tax provisions are deemed to represent over-prudence on the part of the financial accountant, and lead to the true value of capital employed being understated. Therefore they should all be **added back to capital employed**. Any movements in provisions recognised as income or expenses in the income statement also need to be **removed from NOPAT**.

Types of item	Comment
Non-cash expenses	All non-cash items (eg goodwill) are treated with suspicion, on the basis that if the costs were 'real', cash would have been paid for them. Any non-cash expenses should be **added back to profits**, and to **capital employed**.
Operating leases	Operating leases should be **capitalised** and **added to capital employed**. Otherwise, the inconsistency in treatment between operating and finance leases means that firms can take advantage of operating leases to reduce the capital employed figure, and in doing so increase EVA. In effect, EVA treats all leases **as finance leases**. Any **operating lease charges** in the income statement should be added back and removed from NOPAT. In principle, **depreciation** should then be charged on the assets acquired under finance leases. However, remember that accounting depreciation is replaced with **economic depreciation** when calculating EVA.

However, note that **no additional adjustments are made to the tax charge** in relation to the tax on other adjustments made when calculating NOPAT (eg adding back value-building expenditure to profit).

2.14.2 Example: calculating EVA

A company has reported operating profits of $21 million. This was after charging $4 million for the development and launch costs of a new product that is expected to generate profits for four years. Taxation is paid at the rate of 25% of the operating profit.

The company has a risk-adjusted WACC of 12% per annum and is paying interest at 9% per annum on a substantial long-term loan.

The company's non-current asset value is $50 million and the net current assets have a value of $22 million. The replacement cost of the non-current assets is estimated to be $64 million.

Required

Calculate the company's EVA™ for the period.

Solution

Calculation of NOPAT

	$m
Operating profit	21
Add back development costs	4
Less one year's amortisation of development costs ($4 million/4)	(1)
	24
Taxation at 25% (of original operating profit)	(5.25)
NOPAT	18.75

Calculation of economic value of net assets

	$m
Replacement cost of net assets ($22 million + $64 million)	86
Add back investment in new product to benefit future	3
Economic value of net assets	89

Calculation of EVA

The capital charge is based on the **WACC**, which takes account of the cost of share capital as well as the cost of loan capital. Therefore the correct interest rate to use is 12%.

	$m
NOPAT	18.75
Capital charge (12% × $89 million)	(10.68)
EVA	8.07

2.14.3 Example: calculating EVA

Read the articles on ACCA's website referred to in the last Exam Focus Point, and then try the following question.

Question

Calculating EVA

B division of Z Co has operating profits and assets as below.

		$'000
Gross profit		156
Less:	Non-cash expenses	(8)
	Amortisation of goodwill	(5)
	Interest @ 10%	(15)
Profit before tax		128
Tax @ 30%		(38)
Net profit		90
Total equity		350
Long-term debt		150
		500

Z Co has a target capital structure of 25% debt/75% equity. The cost of equity is estimated at 15%. The capital employed at the start of the period amounted to $450,000. The division had non-capitalised leases of $20,000 throughout the period. Goodwill previously written off against reserves in acquisitions in previous years amounted to $40,000.

Required

Calculate EVA™ for B division.

Answer

	$'000	$'000
NOPAT		
Net profit		90
Add back:		
Non-cash expenses	8	
Amortisation of goodwill	5	
Interest (net of 30% tax) 15 × 0.7	10.5	23.5
		113.5
Assets		
At start of period		450
Non-capitalised leases		20
Amortised goodwill		40
		510

	$'000	$'000
WACC		
Equity 15% × 75%		0.1125
Debt (10% × 0.7) × 25%		0.0175
WACC		0.13
EVA NOPAT	113.5	
Capital charge 13% × $510	(66.3)	
	47.2	

2.14.4 Replacement costs or balance sheet costs?

In the earlier example 2.14.2, the scenario identified that the replacement cost of the non-current assets was estimated to be $64 million, which meant we were able to use the replacement cost figure in the calculation.

However, **balance sheet costs** (costs on the statement of financial position) **will often be used as an estimate of replacement costs**. The other adjustments (for example, adding back research and development costs) will still be made to calculate the economic value of net assets, as in the example in 2.14.2.

However, if balance sheet costs are used instead of replacement costs, EVA will be distorted because there is no attempt to adjust for inflation. The cash costs and revenues in the calculation will be measured in current prices, but the non-current asset costs and depreciation charges will be based on historical prices from the year in which the assets were acquired. Consequently, the asset costs and depreciation charges are likely to be understated if they are not adjusted to reflect inflationary price movements. As a result, EVA is likely to be overstated.

2.14.5 Using EVA as a performance measure

EVA (like RI) gives an absolute measure, rather than a percentage value of performance, and if EVA is positive it indicates that an organisation is generating a return greater than that required by the providers of finance. In other words, a positive EVA indicates that an organisation is creating wealth for the shareholders.

Consequently, directors should be encouraged to either:

(a) Invest in divisions where the returns from those divisions exceed the cost of capital; or

(b) Close down divisions, or harvest assets, where the return is less than the cost of capital. In turn, the proceeds from any sales can either be reinvested in other divisions, or returned to shareholders as dividends.

2.14.6 Evaluation of EVA

The advantages of EVA include the following:

(a) **Real wealth for shareholders.** Maximisation of EVA will create real wealth for the shareholders. Maximising the present value of future cash flows will help **maximise shareholders' wealth**.

(b) **Less distortion by accounting** policies. The adjustments within the calculation of EVA mean that the measure is based on figures that are **closer to cash flows than accounting profits**.

(c) **Consistent with NPV.** EVA is consistent with the idea of NPV, showing the return on projects in excess of the cost of financing them. Any projects which would generate a positive NPV will also increase EVA.

(d) **An absolute value.** The EVA measure is an absolute value, which is easily understood by non-financial managers.

(e) **Treatment of certain costs as investments thereby encouraging expenditure.** If management are assessed using performance measures based on traditional accounting policies, they may be unwilling to invest in areas such as advertising or research and development because the costs incurred by those activities **will reduce the current year's accounting profit**. EVA recognises such costs as investments for the future and thus they do not immediately reduce the EVA in the year of expenditure. This will **reduce the temptation to short-termism** (which may occur under ROCE or ROI).

EVA does have some drawbacks, though.

(a) **Dependency on historical data**. EVA is based on historical accounts, which may be of **limited use as a guide to the future**. In practice, the influences of accounting policies on the starting profit figure may not be completely negated by the adjustments made to it in the EVA model.

(b) **Number of adjustments needed to measure EVA**. Making the necessary adjustments can be problematic, as sometimes a **large number of adjustments** are required.

(c) **Comparison of like with like**. EVA is an absolute measure, so larger companies in size may have larger EVA figures than smaller companies, simply because they are bigger, not because they are performing better. **Allowance for relative size** must be made when comparing the relative performance of companies. In this respect, ROI (which shows a percentage measure) may be better for comparing performance between companies of different size.

(d) **Difficulty in estimating WACC**. Many organisations use models such as the capital asset pricing model for estimating WACC. However, this is not a universally accepted method of determining the cost of equity.

3 Gearing 12/12

FAST FORWARD

As well as profitability, **liquidity** and **gearing** are key measures of performance.

Exam focus point

There could be a danger that companies concentrate too much on profit-related aspects of their performance and, by doing so, end up neglecting liquidity and gearing. However, liquidity is equally important for a business as profit, and many business failures are the result of liquidity problems rather than profit issues.

One of the questions in the December 2012 exam built on this idea, and asked candidates to discuss why it was important for an organisation to consider indicators of liquidity and gearing in conjunction with profitability. At P5 level, you need to be able to explain why it is important for organisations to measure different aspects of their performance, and not simply to be able to calculate different performance measures or ratios.

The examining team noted, however, that while many candidates successfully dealt with issues around **financial gearing**, only a few addressed the **operational gearing** issues in the business. The examining team also noted that candidates appeared not to identify the mix of variable and fixed costs in the business, although this ought to be an integral part of a management accountant's financial assessment of a business.

3.1 Capital structure

The assets of a business must be financed somehow and, when a business is growing, the additional assets must be financed by additional capital. **Capital structure** refers to the **way in which an organisation** is **financed**, by a combination of long-term capital (ordinary shares and reserves, preference shares, debentures, bank loans, convertible loan stock and so on) and short-term liabilities, such as a bank overdraft and trade suppliers.

3.1.1 Debts and financial risk

There are two main **reasons why companies should keep their debt burden under control**.

(a) When a company is heavily in debt, and seems to be getting even more heavily into debt, banks and other would-be lenders are very soon likely to refuse further borrowing and the company might well find itself in trouble.

(b) When a company is earning only a modest PBIT, and has a heavy debt burden, there will be very little profit left over for shareholders after the interest charges have been paid. And so, if interest rates were to go up or the company were to borrow even more, it might soon be incurring interest charges in excess of PBIT. This might eventually lead to the liquidation of the company.

A high level of debt creates financial risk. **Financial risk** can be seen from different points of view.

(a) **The company** as a whole. If a company builds up debts that it cannot pay when they fall due, it will be forced into liquidation.

(b) **Suppliers**. If a company cannot pay its debts, the company will go into liquidation owing suppliers money that they are unlikely to recover in full.

(c) **Ordinary shareholders**. A company will not make any distributable profits unless it is able to earn enough PBIT to pay all its interest charges, and then tax. The lower the profits or the higher the interest-bearing debts, the less there will be, if there is anything at all, for shareholders.

When a company has preference shares in its capital structure, ordinary shareholders will not get anything until the preference dividend has been paid.

3.1.2 The appraisal of capital structures

One way in which the financial risk of a company's capital structure can be measured is by a **gearing ratio**. A gearing ratio should not be given without stating how it has been defined.

3.2 Gearing ratios

FAST FORWARD

Gearing ratios measure the financial risk of a company's capital structure. Business risk can be measured by calculating a company's **operational gearing.**

Key term

Financial leverage/gearing is the use of debt finance to increase the return on equity by using borrowed funds in such a way that the return generated is greater than the cost of servicing the debt. If the return on borrowed funds is less than the cost of servicing the debt, the effect of gearing is to reduce the return on equity.

Gearing measures the **relationships between shareholders' capital plus reserves, and either prior charge capital or borrowings or both**.

Key term

Prior charge capital is capital which has a right to the receipt of interest or preference dividends before any claim is made by ordinary shareholders on distributable earnings. On winding up, the claims of holders of prior charge capital rank before those of ordinary shareholders.

Prior charge capital is:

(a) Any preference share capital

(b) Interest-bearing long-term capital

(c) Interest-bearing short-term debt capital with less than 12 months to maturity, including any bank overdraft

However, (c) might be excluded.

Below are some commonly used measures of financial gearing, which are **based** on the **statement of financial position (balance sheet) values (book values)** of the **fixed interest and equity capital**.

$$\frac{\text{Prior charge capital}}{\text{Equity capital (including reserves)}} \qquad \frac{\text{Prior charge capital}}{\text{Total capital employed}}$$

With the **first definition** above, a company is **low geared** if the **gearing ratio** is **less than 100%**, highly geared if the ratio is over 100% and neutrally geared if it is exactly 100%.

Question

Financial gearing ratio

From the statement of financial position (balance sheet) below, compute the company's financial gearing ratio.

	$'000	$'000
Assets		
Non-current assets		12,400
Current assets		1,000
		13,400
Equity and liabilities		
Equity		
Called up share capital		
Ordinary shares		1,500
Preference shares		500
Share premium account		760
Revaluation reserve		1,200
Retained earnings		2,810
Non-current liabilities		
Debentures	4,700	
Bank loans	500	
		5,200
Deferred tax		300
Deferred income		250
Current liabilities		
Loans	120	
Bank overdraft	260	
Trade suppliers	430	
Bills of exchange	70	
		880
		13,400

Answer

	$'000
Prior charge capital	
Preference shares	500
Debentures	4,700
Long-term bank loans	500
Prior charge capital, ignoring short-term debt	5,700
Short-term loans	120
Overdraft	260
Prior charge capital, including short-term interest-bearing debt	6,080

Either figure, $6,080,000 or $5,700,000, could be used. If gearing is calculated with capital employed in the denominator, and capital employed is net non-current assets plus **net** current assets, it would seem more reasonable to exclude short-term interest-bearing debt from prior charge capital. This is because short-term debt is set off against current assets in arriving at the figure for net current assets.

Equity = 1,500 + 760 + 1,200 + 2,810 = $6,270,000

The gearing ratio can be calculated in one of the following ways.

(a) $\frac{\text{Prior charge capital}}{\text{Equity}} \times 100\% = \frac{6,080}{6,270} \times 100\% = 97\%$

(b) $\frac{\text{Prior charge capital}}{\text{Total capital employed}} \times 100\% = \frac{5,700}{12,520} \times 100\% = 45.5\%$

There is **no absolute limit** to what a **gearing ratio** ought to be. Many companies are highly geared, but if a highly geared company is increasing its gearing, it is likely to have difficulty in the future when it wants to borrow even more, unless it can also boost its shareholders' capital, either with retained profits or with a new share issue.

3.3 The effect of gearing on earnings

The level of gearing has a considerable effect on the earnings attributable to the ordinary shareholders. A **highly geared** company must **earn enough profits to cover its interest charges before anything is available for equity**. On the other hand, if borrowed funds are invested in projects which provide returns in excess of the cost of debt capital, then shareholders will enjoy increased returns on their equity.

Gearing, however, also **increases the probability of financial failure** occurring through a company's inability to meet interest payments in poor trading circumstances.

3.4 Example: gearing

Suppose that two companies are identical in every respect except for their gearing. Both have assets of $20,000 and both make the same operating profits (profit before interest and tax: PBIT). The only difference between the two companies is that Nonlever Co is all-equity financed and Lever Co is partly financed by debt capital, as follows.

	Nonlever Co	*Lever Co*
	$	$
Assets	20,000	20,000
10% loan stock	0	(10,000)
	20,000	10,000
Ordinary shares of $1	20,000	10,000

Because Lever Co has $10,000 of 10% loan stock it must make a profit before interest of at least $1,000 in order to pay the interest charges. Nonlever Co, on the other hand, does not have any minimum PBIT requirement because it has no debt capital. A company which is lower geared is considered less risky than a higher geared company because of the greater likelihood that its PBIT will be high enough to cover interest charges and make a profit for equity shareholders.

3.5 Operating gearing

Financial risk, as we have seen, can be measured by financial gearing. **Business risk** refers to the **risk of making only low profits**, or even losses, **due to the nature of the business** that the company is involved in. One way of measuring business risk is by calculating a company's **operating gearing** or **'operational gearing'**.

Key term

Operating gearing or leverage = $\frac{\text{Contribution}}{\text{Profit before interest and tax (PBIT)}}$

A key factor in determining the level of operational gearing in a business will be the **mix between fixed and variable costs** in the business.

If contribution is high but PBIT is low, fixed costs will be high, and only just covered by contribution. **Business risk**, as measured by operating gearing, will be **high**.

If contribution is not much bigger than PBIT, fixed costs will be low, and fairly easily covered. Business risk, as measured by operating gearing, will be **low**.

Exam focus point

> Note that there are important links between operating gearing and breakeven analysis or CVP (cost-volume-profit analysis).
>
> A firm with high fixed costs is likely to have high operating gearing, but it is also likely to have a high breakeven point (because it will need to sell a large number of units in order to cover its fixed costs).

Operational gearing can be a very useful indicator of a firm's ability to survive a reduction in sales. In the example below, Company A has a higher operating gearing than Company B because it has higher fixed costs. However, notice how the operating gearings (and the PBIT figures) for the two companies change if sales fall by 10% (from $100,000 to $90,000).

	Company A	*Company B*
	$	$
Sales	100,000	100,000
Variable costs	(20,000)	(70,000)
Contribution	80,000	30,000
Fixed costs	(70,000)	(20,000)
PBIT	10,000	10,000
Operating gearing	8	3

	Company A	*Company B*
	$	$
Sales	90,000	90,000
Variable costs	(18,000)	(63,000)
Contribution	72,000	27,000
Fixed costs	(70,000)	(20,000)
PBIT	2,000	7,000
Operating gearing	36	3.9

Company A's relatively high fixed costs make it more vulnerable to a reduction in sales than Company B.

The link to CVP analysis is instructive here.

Breakeven sales (in $'000) for Company A is 70,000/0.8 = 87,500.
Breakeven sales (in $'000) for Company B is 20,000/0.3 = 66,667.

Company B (which has the lower operating gearing) can afford sales revenues to drop 33% (from $100,000 to $66,667) and it will still break even. However, Company A can only afford sales revenues to drop 12.5% (from $100,000 to $87,500). If sales fall below this point, the contribution it makes will no longer be sufficient to cover its fixed costs.

4 Liquidity

12/12

FAST FORWARD

A company can be profitable but at the same time get into cash flow problems. Liquidity ratios (**current** and **quick**) and **working capital turnover ratios** give some idea of a company's liquidity.

Knowledge brought forward from earlier studies

As with the measures of profitability earlier in this chapter, you should also be familiar with the ratios used to calculate liquidity (current ratio, quick ratio, accounts receivable days etc) from your studies at F5 and P3. Again, however, exam questions in P5 are more likely to focus on what indicators of liquidity can tell us about an organisation's performance, or why it is important for organisations to monitor their liquidity, rather than simply calculating the ratios themselves.

Profitability is of course an important aspect of a company's performance and debt or gearing is another. Neither, however, directly addresses the key issue of liquidity. A company needs liquid assets so that it can meet its debts when they fall due. In the short term, liquidity is likely to be more important to a business than profitability.

Key term

Liquidity is the amount of cash a company can obtain quickly to settle its debts (and possibly to meet other unforeseen demands for cash payments too).

4.1 Liquid assets

Liquid funds include:

(a) Cash

(b) Short-term investments for which there is a ready market, such as investments in shares of other companies (NB **not** subsidiaries or associates)

(c) Fixed-term deposits with a bank or building society, for example six-month deposits with a bank

(d) Trade receivables

(e) Bills of exchange receivable

Some assets are more liquid than others. Inventories of goods are fairly liquid in some businesses. Inventories of finished production goods might be sold quickly, and a supermarket will hold consumer goods for resale that could well be sold for cash very soon. Raw materials and components in a manufacturing company have to be used to make a finished product before they can be sold to realise cash, and so they are less liquid than finished goods. Just how liquid they are depends on the speed of inventory **turnover** and the length of the production cycle.

Non-current assets are not liquid assets. A company can sell off non-current assets, but unless they are no longer needed, or are worn out and about to be replaced, they are necessary to continue the company's operations. Selling non-current assets is certainly not a solution to a company's cash needs, and so although there may be an occasional non-current asset item which is about to be sold off, probably because it is going to be replaced, it is safe to disregard non-current assets when measuring a company's liquidity.

In summary, **liquid assets are current asset items that will or could soon be converted into cash, and cash** itself. Two common definitions of liquid assets are **all current assets** or **all current assets with the exception of inventories**.

The main source of liquid assets for a trading company is sales. A company can obtain cash from sources other than sales, such as the issue of shares for cash, a new loan or the sale of non-current assets. But a company cannot rely on these at all times and, in general, obtaining liquid funds depends on making sales and profits.

4.2 Why does profit not provide an indication of liquidity?

If a company makes profits, it should earn money, and if it earns money, it might seem that it should receive more cash than it pays out. In fact, **profits are not always a good guide to liquidity**. Two examples will show why this is so.

(a) Suppose that company X makes all its sales for cash, and pays all its running costs in cash without taking any credit. Its profit for the year just ended was as follows.

		$	$
Revenue			400,000
Less costs:	running costs	200,000	
	depreciation	50,000	
			250,000
Profit			150,000
Less dividends (all paid)			80,000
Retained profits			70,000

During the year, the company purchased a non-current asset for $180,000 and paid for it in full.

Depreciation is not a cash outlay, and so the company's 'cash profits' less dividends were sales less running costs less dividends = $120,000. However, the non-current asset purchase required $180,000, and so the company's cash position worsened in the year by $60,000, in spite of the profit.

(b) Suppose that company Y buys three items for cash, each costing $5,000, and resells them for $7,000 each. The buyers of the units take credit, and by the end of the company's accounting year, they were all still customers.

(i) The profit on the transactions is $2,000 per unit and $6,000 in total.

(ii) The company has paid $15,000 to buy the goods, but so far it has received no cash back from selling them, and so its cash position is so far $15,000 worse off from the transactions.

(iii) The effect so far of the transactions is:

Reduction in cash	$15,000
Increase in customers	$21,000
Increase in profit	$6,000

The increase in assets is $6,000 in total, to match the $6,000 increase in profit, but the increase in assets is the net change in cash (reduced balance) and customers (increased balance).

Both of these examples show ways in which a **company can be profitable but** at the same time **get into cash flow problems**. If an analysis of a company's published accounts is to give us some idea of the company's liquidity, profitability ratios are not going to be appropriate for doing this. Instead, we look at liquidity ratios and working capital **turnover** ratios.

4.3 Liquidity ratios

4.3.1 Current ratio

The standard test of liquidity is the current ratio. It can be obtained from the statement of financial position (balance sheet), and is **current assets/current liabilities**.

A company should have enough current assets that give a promise of 'cash to come' to meet its commitments to pay its current liabilities. Obviously, a **ratio in excess of 1 should be expected**. Otherwise, there would be the prospect that the company might be unable to pay its debts on time. In practice, a ratio comfortably in excess of 1 should be expected, but what is 'comfortable' varies between different types of businesses.

Companies are not able to convert all their current assets into cash very quickly. In particular, some manufacturing companies might hold large quantities of raw material inventories, which must be used in production to create finished goods. Finished goods might be warehoused for a long time, or sold on lengthy credit. In such businesses, where inventory **turnover** is slow, most inventories are not very liquid assets, because the cash cycle is so long. For these reasons, we calculate an additional liquidity ratio, known as the quick ratio or acid test ratio.

4.3.2 Quick ratio

The quick ratio, or **acid test ratio**, is **(current assets less inventories)/current liabilities**.

This ratio should ideally be **at least 1** for companies with a **slow inventory turnover**. For companies with a **fast inventory turnover**, a quick ratio can be **less than 1** without suggesting that the company is in cash flow difficulties.

Do not forget the other side of the coin. The current ratio and the quick ratio can be bigger than they should be. A company that has large volumes of inventories and customers might be overinvesting in working capital, and so tying up more funds in the business than it needs to. This would suggest poor management of customers or inventories by the company.

4.3.3 Turnover periods

We can calculate **turnover periods** for inventory, customers and suppliers (the question below revises these calculations). The time taken to collect amounts due from customers is known as the **accounts receivable collection period**. Credit from suppliers is known as the **accounts payable payment period**. If we add together the inventory days and the days taken to collect accounts owed from customers, this should give us an indication of how soon inventory is convertible into cash. This gives us a further indication of the company's liquidity.

Question — **Liquidity and working capital ratios**

Calculate liquidity and working capital ratios from the accounts of a manufacturer of products for the construction industry, and comment on the ratios.

	20X8	*20X7*
	$m	$m
Revenue	2,065.0	1,788.7
Cost of sales	1,478.6	1,304.0
Gross profit	586.4	484.7
Assets		
Current assets		
Inventories	119.0	109.0
Customers (note 1)	400.9	347.4
Short-term investments	4.2	18.8
Cash at bank and in hand	48.2	48.0
	572.3	523.2
Equity and liabilities		
Non-current liabilities		
Loans and overdrafts	49.1	35.3
Taxes	62.0	46.7
Dividend	19.2	14.3
Suppliers (note 2)	370.7	324.0
	501.0	420.3
Net current assets	71.3	102.9

Notes		20X8	20X7
1	Trade customers	329.8	285.4
2	Trade suppliers	236.2	210.8

Answer

	20X8	20X7
Current ratio	572.3/501.0 = 1.14	523.2/420.3 = 1.24
Quick ratio	453.3/501.0 = 0.90	414.2/420.3 = 0.99
Accounts receivable collection period	329.8/2,065.0 × 365 = 58 days	285.4/1,788.7 × 365 = 58 days
Inventory turnover period	119.0/1,478.6 × 365 = 29 days	109.0/1,304.0 × 365 = 31 days
Accounts payable payment period	236.2/1,478.6 × 365 = 58 days	210.8/1,304.0 × 365 = 59 days

As a manufacturing group serving the construction industry, the company would be expected to have a comparatively lengthy accounts receivable collection period, because of the relatively poor cash flow in the construction industry. It is clear that the company compensates for this by ensuring that it does not pay for raw materials and other costs before it has sold its inventories of finished goods (hence the similarity of accounts receivable and accounts payable turnover periods).

The company's current ratio is a little lower than average but its quick ratio is better than average and very little less than the current ratio. This suggests that inventory levels are strictly controlled, which is reinforced by the low inventory turnover period. It would seem that working capital is tightly managed, to avoid the poor liquidity which could be caused by a high accounts receivable collection period and comparatively high suppliers.

The accounts payable payment period is ideally calculated by the formula (trade accounts payable/purchases) × 365.

However, it is rare to find purchases disclosed in published accounts and so cost of sales serves as an approximation. The ratio often helps to assess a company's liquidity; an increase is often a sign of lack of long-term finance or poor management of current assets, resulting in the use of extended credit from suppliers, increased bank overdraft and so on.

Exam focus point

Although we have been looking at a range of different ways of measuring financial performance in this chapter, it is important to reiterate that Paper P5 is ultimately about performance **management** and not simply performance **measurement**.

An important issue in performance management could be selecting the 'right' aspects of performance to measure, and it is likely that this selection will include a range of financial measures looking at liquidity, profitability and returns for shareholders.

However, when looking at financial performance measures, it is very important to analyse what the figures indicate, rather than simply performing the calculations. For example, do they highlight any significant changes compared with previous years, or with competitors, which need to be investigated further?

Also, it is important to look at financial performance in the context of the wider environment in which an organisation operates. For example, how might any political, economic, social or technological (PEST) factors have affected its performance?

5 Short-run and long-run financial performance

FAST FORWARD

Short-termism can often occur if managers' performance is measured on short-term results.

We identified in Chapter 2 that organisations often have to make a trade-off between short-term and long-term objectives, and financial performance is likely to be an important factor in this trade-off. For example, advertising expenditure may be cut to increase short-term profit, but this is likely to be at the expense of long-term financial results (ie future growth generated by the advertising).

There is a danger that if organisations focus too much on achieving short-term financial results this could lead to them underinvesting in the assets required to create **long-term value** (such as new product development, or human resource development and training). Consequently, a focus on short-term performance could ultimately hinder a company's ability to create long-term value for its shareholders.

EVA tries to recognise this weakness in short-term performance measures by adding back 'value-building expenditure' (such as marketing and promotions, or training and development) to profit. In this way, EVA tries to align the organisation's performance measures more closely with shareholders' interests.

However, ROCE, ROI, RI and EVA are ultimately all still **measures of short-term performance**. Therefore they may not be appropriate performance measures to use in organisations that have long-term objectives, such as sustained, long-term growth. In order to support such growth, an organisation is likely to need to expand its asset base. However, in the short term, ROCE, ROI, RI and EVA will show relatively poor results as a result of the increase in the asset base.

By contrast, discounted cash flow techniques, such as NPV and IRR, may be more appropriate as long-term profitability measures, since they recognise the future economic benefits of current investments.

Case Study

Short-term decision making

The downturn in world economies in 2008/9 made businesses focus on cutting costs. However, unscrupulous cost cutting can be a misguided decision because the cuts can impair future business. IT departments serving the finance industry expressed concerns about the cuts they were being asked to make following the economic slowdown.

Many banks had made substantial investments in IT infrastructure, but then started asking how costs can be cut. However, they didn't appear to realise that systems couldn't just be switched off. Moreover, while it might be possible to migrate to cheaper IT systems, the cost of doing so is likely to be prohibitively high. And, perhaps most importantly, the infrastructure that the banks initially invested in, such as data centres, is likely to become necessary again once the economy recovers.

A second concern IT departments raised was that many ongoing projects were being stopped, which posed a risk in relation to the loss of future capability.

One IT director commented: 'Our business is very short sighted. In two years' time, we'll probably be spending twice as much as we are now, to get back the kind of service we can provide today, having cut costs now.'

Based on: Robinson, J, (2008) Cost-cutting conundrum. *Information Age*. Available from: http://www.information-age.com/technology/applications-and-development/825127/cost-cutting-conundrum [Accessed 26 January 2016]

5.1 Using ROI

Suppose that an investment in a non-current asset would cost $100,000 and make a profit of $11,000 p.a. after depreciation. The asset would be depreciated by $25,000 p.a. for four years. It is group policy that investments must show a minimum return of 15%. The DCF net present value of this investment would just about be positive, and so the investment ought to be approved if group policy is adhered to.

Year	*Cash flow (profit before dep'n)*	*Discount factor*	*Present value*
	$	15%	$
0	(100,000)	1.000	(100,000)
1	36,000	0.870	31,320
2	36,000	0.756	27,216
3	36,000	0.658	23,688
4	36,000	0.572	20,592
		NPV	2,816

If the investment is measured year by year according to the accounting ROI it has earned, its return is less than 15% in year 1, but more than 15% in years 2, 3 and 4.

Year	*Profit*	*Net book value of equipment (mid-year value)*	*ROI*
	$	$	%
1	11,000	87,500	12.6
2	11,000	62,500	17.6
3	11,000	37,500	29.3
4	11,000	12,500	88.0

In view of the low accounting ROI in year 1, should the investment be undertaken or not?

(a) Strictly speaking, **investment decisions should be based on DCF yield**, and should not be guided by short-term accounting ROI.

(b) Even if accounting ROI is used as a guideline for investment decisions, ROI should be looked at **over the full life** of the investment, not just in the short term. In the short term (in the first year or so of a project's life) the accounting ROI is likely to be low because the net book value of the asset will still be high.

Question

DCF

Why are DCF techniques not commonly used?

Answer

Because they are perceived as being difficult to calculate and understand and because it is difficult in practice to establish an accurate cost of capital.

5.1.1 DCF vs ROI

In spite of the superiority of DCF yield over accounting ROI as a means of evaluating investments, and in spite of the wisdom of taking a longer-term view rather than a short-term view with investments, it is nevertheless an uncomfortable fact that the consideration of short-run accounting **ROI does often influence investment decisions.**

In our example, it is conceivable that the group's management might disapprove of the project because of its low accounting ROI in year 1. This approach is short-sighted, but it nevertheless can make some sense to a company or group of companies which has to show a satisfactory profit and ROI in its **published accounts** each year to keep its **shareholders** satisfied with performance.

A similar misguided decision would occur where a divisional manager is worried about the low ROI of their division, and decides to reduce their investment by **scrapping some machinery** which is not currently in use. The reduction in both depreciation charges and assets would immediately improve the ROI. When the machinery is eventually required the manager would then be obliged to buy new equipment. Such a situation may seem bizarre, but it does occur in real life.

ROI should not be used to guide management decisions but there is a difficult motivational problem. If **management performance** is measured in terms of ROI, any decisions which benefit the company in the long term but which reduce the ROI in the immediate short term would reflect badly on the manager's reported performance. In other words, good investment decisions would make a manager's performance seem worse than if the wrong investment decision were taken instead.

6 Comparisons of accounting figures

FAST FORWARD

Comparisons might be made between a company's results and the results of the most recent year/previous years, other companies in the same industry, or other companies in other industries.

6.1 Results of the same company over successive accounting periods

Although a company might present useful information in its five-year or ten-year summary, it is quite likely that the only detailed comparison you will be able to make is between the current year's and the previous year's results. The comparison should give you some idea of whether the company's situation has improved, worsened or stayed much the same between one year and the next.

Useful comparisons over time include:

(a) Percentage growth in profit (before and after tax) and percentage growth in revenue

(b) Increases or decreases in the debt ratio and the gearing ratio

(c) Changes in the current ratio, the inventory turnover period and the accounts receivable collection period

(d) Increases in the EPS, the dividend per share and the market price

The principal advantage of making comparisons over time is that they give some indication of progress: are things getting better or worse? However, there are some weaknesses in such comparisons.

(a) The effect of **inflation** should not be forgotten.

(b) The progress a company has made needs to be set **in** the **context** of what other companies have done, and whether there have been any special environmental or economic influences on the company's performance.

6.1.1 Putting a company's results into context

The financial and accounting ratios of one company should be looked at in the context of **what other companies have been achieving**, and also any **special influences** on the industry or the economy as a whole. Here are two examples.

(a) If a company achieves a 10% increase in profits, this performance taken in isolation might seem commendable, but if it is then compared with the results of rival companies, which might have been achieving profit growth of 30%, the performance might seem very disappointing in comparison.

(b) An improvement in ROCE and profits might be attributable to a temporary economic boom, and an increase in profits after tax might be attributable to a cut in the rate of corporation tax. When improved results are attributable to factors outside the control of the company's management, such as changes in the economic climate and tax rates, other companies might be expected to benefit in the same way.

6.2 Comparisons between different companies in the same industry

Making comparisons between the results of different companies in the same industry is a way of assessing which companies are outperforming others.

(a) Even if **two companies are in the same broad industry (eg retailing) they might not be direct competitors**. For example, in the UK, the Kingfisher group (DIY stores) does not compete directly with the Arcadia group (clothes shops). Even so, they might still be expected to show broadly **similar performance**, in terms of growth, because a boom or a depression in retail markets will affect all retailers. The results of two such companies can be compared, and the company with the better growth and accounting ratios might be considered more successful than the other.

(b) If two companies **are direct competitors**, a comparison between them would be **particularly interesting**. Which has achieved the better ROCE, sales growth, or profit growth? Does one have a better debt or gearing position, a better liquidity position or better working capital ratios? How do their P/E ratios, dividend cover and dividend yields compare? And so on.

Comparisons between companies in the same industry can help investors to rank them in order of desirability as investments, and to judge relative share prices or future prospects. It is important, however, to make comparisons with caution: a large company and a small company in the same industry might be expected to show different results, not just in terms of size, but in terms of:

(a) Percentage rates of growth in sales and profits

(b) Percentages of profits reinvested (Dividend cover will be higher in a company that needs to retain profits to finance investment and growth.)

(c) Non-current assets (Large companies are more likely to have freehold property in their statement of financial position (balance sheet) than small companies.)

6.3 Comparisons between companies in different industries

Useful information can also be obtained by comparing the financial and accounting ratios of companies in different industries. An investor ought to be aware of how companies in one industrial sector are performing in comparison with companies in other sectors. For example, it is important to know:

(a) Whether sales growth and profit growth is higher in some industries than in others (eg how does growth in the financial services industry compare with growth in heavy engineering, electronics or leisure?)

(b) How the ROCE and return on shareholder capital compare between different industries

(c) How the P/E ratios and dividend yields vary between industries (eg if a publishing company has a P/E ratio of, say, 20, which is average for its industry, whereas an electronics company has a P/E ratio of, say, 14, do the better growth performance and prospects of the publishing company justify its higher P/E ratio?)

7 Using benchmarks to assess performance

In Chapter 1 of this Study Text we looked at benchmarking as a means of making comparisons and setting targets using external data. We then assessed the advantages and disadvantages of benchmarking. Bear these in mind here as we consider **financial benchmarking**.

Financial data for benchmarking can be obtained from a variety of sources, many of which are publicly available. For instance, a company may compare its profitability with other companies which have **published accounts**. **Analysts' reports** are another useful source of data, as these look at companies across sectors. However, it is **important for the benchmarks to be valid** (ie comparable) or else the comparison is misleading.

For example, comparing the ROCE of a manufacturing company (which has a high level of capital employed) with a service company (with a low level of capital employed) is unlikely to be a valid comparison. The difference in the levels of capital employed will mean that the service company would be expected to have a higher ROCE than the manufacturing company.

Equally, if a company is benchmarking its performance with other companies in the same industry, it is important that the companies are pursuing similar generic strategies in order for the benchmarks to be comparable. For example – regardless of how well the two companies are performing in their respective sectors of the market – we might expect a supermarket which is pursuing a low price, high volume strategy to have a lower gross profit margin (%) than a retailer pursuing a differentiation strategy based on the high quality of their products and the service they provide for their customers.

The company also has **to decide which areas to benchmark**, and for what purposes. An **internal benchmarking** exercise between functions is likely to use data which is operational and short-term in focus. **Strategic benchmarking** for the whole organisation will seek data that helps in making long-term decisions on change.

Benchmarking can be difficult to do in practice and companies often have to **select their data carefully**. Of course, published data is backward looking so a company seeking to improve cannot only rely on data that is several months out of date. Where companies seek more up to date financial information, this may rely on **sharing information systems** with companies which could be rivals. There may be mutual benefits from doing this but the participants need to be confident that the risks to their confidential data are outweighed by the benefits from obtaining the financial data.

Chapter Roundup

- The overriding **purpose** of a company is to **increase long-term owner wealth**.
- **Measures relating to profit** include sales margin, EBITDA and EPS. More sophisticated measures (ROCE, ROI) take the size of investment into account. Later on in the chapter we consider how measures of profitability are used for **short-run** or **long-run performance measurement**. Bear this in mind particularly when you study the sections on RI, ROI and NPV and go through the examples covering these.
- EVA™ is an absolute performance measure. It is similar to RI because both are calculated by subtracting an imputed interest charge from the profit earned by a company or division.
- EVA is calculated as follows:

  EVA = net operating profit after tax (NOPAT) less capital charge

  where the capital charge = weighted average cost of capital × net assets
- The key differences between EVA and RI are:

  (a) The profit figures are calculated differently. EVA is based on an '**economic profit**' which is derived by making a series of **adjustments to accounting profit**.

  (b) The notional capital charges in EVA use **different bases for net assets** compared to those used in RI. The replacement cost of net assets is usually used in the calculation of EVA.
- As well as profitability, **liquidity** and **gearing** are key measures of performance.
- **Gearing ratios** measure the financial risk of a company's capital structure. Business risk can be measured by calculating a company's **operational gearing**.
- A company can be profitable but at the same time get into cash flow problems. Liquidity ratios (**current** and **quick**) and **working capital turnover ratios** give some idea of a company's liquidity.
- **Short-termism** can often occur if managers' performance is measured on short-term results.
- **Comparisons** might be made between a company's results and the results of the most recent year/previous years, other companies in the same industry, or other companies in other industries.

Quick Quiz

1 In the last year, an increase in interest rates has meant that the interest charges X Co has incurred have increased, despite its level of borrowing remaining constant.

Assuming other aspects of its business remain constant, what impact will this change in the interest rates have on the ROCE figure for X Co?

2 Choose the correct words from those highlighted.

ROI based on profits as a % of net assets employed will (a) **increase/decrease** as an asset gets older and its book value (b) **increases/reduces**. This could therefore create a(n) (c) **incentive/disincentive** to investment centre managers to reinvest in new or replacement assets.

3 An investment centre with capital employed of $570,000 is budgeted to earn a profit of $119,700 next year. A proposed non-current asset investment of $50,000, not included in the budget at present, will earn a profit next year of $8,500 after depreciation. The company's cost of capital is 15%. What is the budgeted ROI and residual income for next year, both with and without the investment?

	ROI	*Residual income*
Without investment	………………..	………………..
With investment	………………..	………………..

4 'The use of residual income in performance measurement will avoid dysfunctional decision making because it will always lead to the correct decision concerning capital investments.' True or false?

5 The income statement for Beta Co for the year ended 31 December 20X1 showed the following.

	$m
Operating profit	650
Interest expenses	(90)
Profit before tax	560
Tax (at 25%)	(140)
Profit after tax	420

The operating profit included $5m expenditure for research and development costs which have not been capitalised, in accordance with financial reporting standards.

Calculate Beta's NOPAT for the year ended 31 December 20X1.

Answers to Quick Quiz

1 ROCE will remain unchanged.

The profit figure used to calculate ROCE is profit before interest and tax. Therefore, the change in interest charges will not affect the calculation.

2 (a) increase
(b) reduces
(c) disincentive

3

	ROI	*Residual income*
Without investment	21.0%	$34,200
With investment	20.7%	$35,200

4 False

5

	$m
Operating profit	650
Add back research costs	5
Less cash taxes (working)	(162.5)
NOPAT	**492.5**

Taxes:

Tax charge per income statement	140
Add tax relief on interest	22.5
Cash taxes	162.5

Now try the question below from the Practice Question Bank

Number	Level	Marks	Approximate time
Q9	Examination	40	80 mins

Question 9 has been annotated to help you to get to grips with analysing a question scenario, which you will have to do in your exam.

Note, however, that this question is only worth 40 marks, whereas the Section A question in your P5 exam is worth 50 marks.

Divisional performance and transfer pricing issues

10

Topic list	Syllabus reference
1 Divisional structure and performance measures	D2(a)
2 Measuring performance	D2(b)
3 The need for transfer pricing	D2(c)
4 The 'general rule'	D2(c)
5 The use of market price	D2(d)
6 Cost-based approaches to transfer pricing	D2(d)
7 Fixed costs and transfer pricing	D2(d)
8 Standard cost versus actual cost	D2(d)
9 Cost-based approaches with no external market	D2(d)
10 Opportunity costs and transfer prices	D2(d)
11 Transfer pricing when intermediate products are in short supply	D2(d)
12 Transfer pricing and a range of limiting factors	D2(d)
13 Shadow price and transfer prices	D2(d)
14 Negotiated transfer prices	D2(d)
15 Multinational transfer pricing	D2(e)

Introduction

The focus of the previous chapter was measuring financial performance in organisations as a whole. In this chapter, the focus switches to measuring the performance of divisions within an organisation.

The main focus of this chapter is **transfer pricing** – looking at why transfer pricing may be needed in order to evaluate divisional performance accurately, and then looking at different bases for calculating transfer prices.

A lot of the material in this chapter about transfer pricing methods should be revision from your studies at F5. However, in the P5 context, it is important that you understand not only the basis for calculating transfer prices but also the impact which transfer pricing and different transfer pricing methods have on divisional performance.

Study guide

		Intellectual level
D2	**Divisional performance and transfer pricing issues**	
(a)	Describe, compute and evaluate performance measures relevant in a divisionalised organisation structure including ROI, RI and Economic Value Added [EVA^{TM}].	3
(b)	Discuss the need for separate measures in respect of managerial and divisional performance.	2
(c)	Discuss the circumstances in which a transfer pricing policy may be needed and discuss the necessary criteria for its design.	2
(d)	Demonstrate and evaluate the use of alternative bases for transfer pricing.	3
(e)	Explain and demonstrate issues that require consideration when setting transfer prices in multinational companies.	2

Exam guide

The topics in this chapter provide plenty of material for an exam question. Indeed, you may find a full question testing your knowledge of transfer pricing, and you should be prepared for a discussion question about the role of transfer pricing in performance measurement, or the issues that transfer pricing raises for performance measurement.

As you are reading through the sections of the chapter on transfer pricing, try to remember the following, and consider how well it is being addressed.

The aims of transfer pricing are to try to **resolve the conflict between decision-making and performance evaluations**, and to achieve **goal congruence** between individual divisions and an organisation as a whole.

Also, remember that in Paper P5 the primary focus of questions is unlikely to be detailed transfer pricing calculations in their own right. Instead, you are more likely to be asked to comment on the transfer pricing system being used in an organisation – for example, how useful is it in allowing managers to measure and evaluate divisional performance, or how well does it ensure that decisions taken by individual divisions (with a view to maximising their own divisional profits) also help to maximise group profit as a whole.

There is a useful article (called 'Transfer Pricing') in the P5 Technical Articles section of ACCA's website which summarises why transfer prices are needed, and discusses different approaches to transfer pricing. This article is well worth reading (if you haven't already done so) and gives some examples to work through.

Exam focus point

One of the questions in the June 2011 exam asked candidates to evaluate the divisional performance of a company described in the question scenario, and then to discuss the proposed measures of divisional performance (which were residual income (RI) and economic value added (EVA)). The question then asked candidates (for 12 marks) to outline the criteria for designing a transfer pricing system, and then to evaluate two transfer pricing approaches (market price and cost plus) identified in the scenario.

Exam focus point

One of the questions in the June 2013 exam asked candidates to evaluate the system of transfer pricing being used in an organisation, in which the transfer price for one product was determined by market price while the transfer price for another product was determined by total actual production costs. The question then asked candidates to assess the impact of changing the basis of the transfer price for the second product so that it was determined by variable costs only. Crucially, however, the revised basis for the transfer price led to a reduction in profits for the division which provided the organisation's key competitive advantage (while increasing the profit of a division which was not as important strategically). As such, how well does the revised basis fit with the aims of transfer pricing?

1 Divisional structure and performance measures

FAST FORWARD

We considered the **divisional form or structure** for an organisation in Chapter 4, when we looked at the information needs of businesses adopting this form. That chapter also discussed the pros and cons of adopting the divisional form, including ease of performance measurement.

In this section we look at three performance measures relevant in a divisionalised structure. These are return on investment, residual income and economic value added™.

Return on investment (ROI) and **residual income (RI)** were discussed in Chapter 9 when we considered the scope of strategic performance measures in the private sector. In this chapter we will just pick out the salient features that apply to their use in divisionalised structures.

1.1 Divisional performance: return on investment (ROI)

Key term

Return on investment (ROI) is a form of ROCE and is calculated as:

$$\frac{\text{Profit before interest and tax} \times 100}{\text{Operations management capital employed}}$$

ROI is normally used to apply to investment centres or profit centres. These normally reflect the existing organisation structure of the business.

1.1.1 Evaluation of ROI

You may like to consider the following factors when evaluating the use of ROI as a divisional performance measure.

(a) **Comparisons**. It permits comparisons to be drawn between investment centres that differ in their absolute size.

(b) **Aggregation**. ROI is a very convenient method of measuring the performance for a division or company as an entire unit.

(c) **Using an identical target return**. This may not be suitable for many divisions or investment centres, as it makes **no allowance** for the different **risk** of each investment centre.

(d) **Misleading impression of improved performance**. If an investment centre maintains the **same annual profit**, and keeps the **same assets** without a policy of regular non-current asset replacement, its **ROI** will **increase year by year as the assets get older**. This can give a false impression of improving 'real' performance over time.

(e) **Valuation and classification of assets**. Many of the criticisms of ROI arise from the valuation of assets used in the denominator. Refer back to Chapter 9 for a full explanation of the problems in measuring asset values. Chapter 9 also refers to the tricky decision of when to classify expenditure as assets.

(f) **Short-term perspective**. Since **managers will be judged** on the basis of the ROI that their centre earns each year, they are likely to be **motivated** into taking those decisions, which **increase** their centre's **short-term ROI**. So, in the short term, a desire to increase ROI might lead to projects being taken on without **due regard to their risk**.

(g) **Sub-optimal decisions**. Similarly, if ROI is used to evaluate divisional performance it may encourage managers to make sub-optimal decisions. For example, managers may choose, incorrectly, not to undertake a project with a return greater than the cost of capital simply because it has a lower projected ROI than the current ROI for the division as a whole.

(h) **Lack of goal congruence**. An investment might be desirable from the group's point of view, but would not be in the individual investment centre's 'best interest' to undertake. Furthermore, any decisions which **benefit** the company in the **long term** but which **reduce** the ROI in the immediate **short term** would **reflect badly** on the manager's reported performance.

1.2 Divisional performance: residual income (RI)

Key term

> **Residual income** is a measure of the centre's profits after deducting a notional or imputed interest cost.

Its use highlights the finance charge associated with funding.

1.2.1 Evaluation of RI

You may like to consider the following factors when evaluating the use of RI. Think about how it compares to ROI as a possible divisional performance measure.

(a) **Usefulness in decision making.** RI **increases in the following circumstances**:

  (i) Investments earning above the cost of capital are undertaken.
  (ii) Investments earning below the cost of capital are eliminated.

  Thus it leads managers to make the correct investment decision to benefit the company as a whole.

(b) **It has flexibility compared to ROI** since a different cost of capital can be applied to investments with different risk characteristics.

(c) **Does not allow comparisons between investment centres.** RI cannot be used to make comparisons between investment centres, as it is an absolute measure of performance.

(d) **Difficulty in deciding on an appropriate and accurate measure of the capital employed**. As we discussed above, there can be some difficulty in knowing what values to place on assets.

(e) **It does not relate the size of a centre's income to the size of the investment**, other than indirectly through the interest charge.

1.3 Divisional performance: economic value added (EVA)

We looked at EVA in detail in the previous chapter, and noted that its underlying approach is similar to RI. However, we also noted that the objective of EVA was to focus on the ways in which corporate value (shareholder value) can be added or lost.

Therefore, by linking divisional performance to EVA, divisional managers should also be motivated to focus on maximising the wealth of their division and in turn **increasing shareholder value**.

Divisional managers are unlikely to be able to change the weighted average cost of capital for a company as a whole, but using EVA should ensure that divisional managers only invest in projects where their return exceeds **the costs of the company's capital**.

2 Measuring performance

FAST FORWARD

> One of the problems of measuring managerial performance is **segregating managerial performance from the economic performance of their department or division**.

Exam focus point

> We have already discussed the ideas of responsibility and controllability in Chapters 3 and 7 in the context of variance analysis (Chapter 3) and performance reports (Chapter 7). The questions that we raised in those chapters are also relevant here though: in particular, the extent to which it is fair to use performance reports focusing on divisional performance and including factors outside a manager's control as a basis for assessing a manager's performance.

2.1 Managerial performance

The distinction between the **manager's performance** and the **performance of the division** is very important. The following short example provides a good illustration.

One of a company's most skilful divisional manager is often put in charge of a struggling sickest division in an attempt to change its fortunes. Such a turnaround may often take years, not months. Furthermore, the manager's efforts may merely result in bringing the division up to a minimum acceptable ROI. The division may continue to be a relatively poor profit performer in comparison with other divisions. As such, if top management relied solely on the absolute ROI to judge management, the skilful manager would be unwilling to accept such a trouble-shooting assignment. However, the manager's reluctance to take on the assignment would not be in the best interests of the company as a whole.

The distinction between **managerial performance** and **divisional performance** means that a division might be unprofitable because of external market conditions (such as overcapacity or a declining market) yet the manager may still be performing well. Conversely, another division might report significant profits, but management may not be performing well; for example, if a favourable economic environment means it should have been able to generate even greater profits than it did.

It is difficult to devise performance measures that relate specifically to a manager to judge their performance as a manager. It is possible to calculate statistics to assess the manager as an employee like any other employee (days absent, professional qualifications obtained, personability and so on), but this is not the point. As soon as the issue of **ability as a manager** arises it is necessary to **consider them in relation to their area of responsibility**. If we want to know how good a manager is at marketing, the only information there is to go on is the marketing performance of their division (which may or may not be traceable to their own efforts).

In summary, then, **managers** should only be assessed on **results within their control**. (This is based on the idea of the **controllability principle**: managers should only be held accountable for the results that they can significantly influence.)

Divisional performance should be based on **total economic performance** (including central service and administration costs) to provide an assessment of the measure of the worth of the division to the organisation.

This is an important distinction. If divisional performance were measured only on the amounts directly controllable by the divisional manager, this would **overstate the economic performance** of the division. If the divisions were independent companies, they would have to incur the cost of those services currently provided by head office. Therefore, to measure the economic performance of a division, many items that the divisional manager cannot influence (such as interest charges, taxes and the allocation of central administrative staff expenses) should be included in the profitability measure.

2.2 Profit statement

A possible profit statement for a division might look as follows.

	$'000
Sales revenue	X
Variable costs	(X)
Contribution	X
Controllable fixed costs	(X)
Controllable profit	X
Non-controllable fixed costs	(X)
Divisional profit	X

Contribution should be an acceptable measure of managerial performance unless it contains imposed transfers and transfer prices.

Controllable profit may be a more appropriate measure of managerial performance where managers can make decisions about equipment rental or labour costs. It is more acceptable when managers are free to secure services either in-house or from third parties. Depreciation is likely to be included and this will only be controllable to the extent that managers control investment decisions.

Divisional profit is unlikely to be an acceptable managerial measure. It is suitable for assessing the economic performance of the divisions provided the allocation of fixed costs is reasonable.

3 The need for transfer pricing

FAST FORWARD

It is necessary for **control purposes** that some **record** of the market in inter-divisional goods or services should be kept. One way of doing this is through the accounting system. Inter-divisional work can be given a cost or a charge: a transfer price.

3.1 Introduction to transfer pricing

Where there are transfers of goods or services between divisions of a divisionalised organisation, the **transfers could be made 'free' or 'as a favour'** to the division receiving the benefit. For example, if a garage and car showroom has two divisions, one for car repairs and servicing, the other for car sales, the servicing division will be required to service cars before they are sold and delivered to customers. There is no requirement for this service work to be charged for: the servicing division could do its work for the car sales division without making any record of the work done.

Unless the cost or value of such work is recorded, however, management cannot keep a proper check on the amount of resources (like labour time) being used on servicing cars for the sales division. It is necessary for **control purposes** that some **record** of the inter-divisional services should be kept, and one way of doing this is **through the accounting system**. Inter-divisional work can be given a cost or charge: a transfer price.

Key term

A **transfer price** is the price at which goods or services are transferred from one department to another, or from one member of a group to another.

The simple example of the garage and the car showroom also illustrates the need for transfer pricing to help **evaluate the performance of the two divisions** more fairly. For example, if the service division does not receive any credit for the work it does for the sales division, then its revenue and profitability are effectively understated. Conversely, the performance of the sales division is effectively overstated.

Therefore, transfer prices are required to prevent the performance of the two divisions being distorted.

Preventing distortion in this way should also help maintain the **motivation** of the divisional managers. For example, if the selling division (in our example, the service division) doesn't get any credit for the work it does, this could demotivate the manager and staff of that division. Equally, however, if the charge to the purchasing division (in our example, the car sales division) was too high, this could serve to demotivate the manager and staff of that division.

3.1.1 Aims of transfer pricing

There are three main aims of transfer pricing.

Aim	Achieved by
To preserve goal congruence	Aligning divisional behaviour with the best interests of the group as a whole – by setting a transfer price which reflects the true cost to the group of products or services being transferred between divisions
To allow managers to retain autonomy	Allowing divisions to decide who they buy from, or who they supply, and in what quantities
To permit performance evaluation of divisions	Preventing divisional performance being unfairly distorted (for example, by not receiving credit for work they do for other divisions)

Exam focus point

> Part of the question on transfer pricing in the June 2013 exam asked candidates to advise how changing the basis for setting transfer prices between two divisions in a company will affect the results of the two divisions and the company.
>
> This question highlights the potential impact that transfer pricing can have on the profits of different divisions within a company, and therefore the impact it could have when evaluating the performance of those different divisions.
>
> Importantly, however, despite what some candidates claimed in their answers to this question, changing the transfer pricing policy will not, by itself, change a company's overall profit. The increased profitability of one division following the change in transfer pricing policy will be matched by an equivalent decline in profitability in the other division.
>
> In the longer term, changes to the transfer pricing policy may result in divisions making different decisions (for example, whether to buy internally or externally) and the results of these decisions might affect the company's overall profit. However, simply changing the basis on which transfer prices are calculated will not, in itself, affect the company's profit.

3.2 Criteria for designing a transfer pricing policy

FAST FORWARD

> Transfer prices are a way of promoting **divisional autonomy**, ideally without prejudicing **divisional performance measurement** or discouraging overall **corporate profit maximisation (goal congruence)**.

3.2.1 Divisional autonomy

Transfer prices are particularly appropriate for **profit centres** because if one profit centre does work for another the size of the transfer price will affect the costs of one profit centre and the revenues of another.

However, a danger with profit centre accounting is that the business organisation will divide into a number of **self-interested segments**, each acting at times against the wishes and interests of other segments. A profit centre manager might take decisions in the best interests of their own part of the business, but against the best interests of other profit centres and possibly the organisation as a whole.

A task of head office is therefore to try to prevent dysfunctional decision making by individual profit centres. To do this, it must reserve some power and authority for itself and so profit centres **cannot** be allowed to make entirely **autonomous decisions**.

Just how much authority head office decides to keep for itself will vary according to individual circumstances. A **balance** ought to be kept between **divisional autonomy** to provide incentives and motivation, and retaining **centralised authority** to ensure that the organisation's profit centres are all working towards the same target, the benefit of the organisation as a whole (in other words, retaining **goal congruence** among the organisation's separate divisions).

3.2.2 Divisional performance measurement

Profit centre managers tend to put their **own profit performance** above everything else. Since profit centre performance is measured according to the profit they earn, no profit centre will want to do work for another and incur costs without being paid for it. Consequently, profit centre managers are likely to dispute the size of transfer prices with each other, or disagree about whether one profit centre should do work for another or not. Transfer prices **affect behaviour and decisions** by profit centre managers.

3.2.3 Corporate profit maximisation (goal congruence)

When there are disagreements about how much work should be transferred between divisions, and how many sales the division should make to the external market, there is presumably a **profit-maximising** level of output and sales for the organisation as a whole. However, unless each profit centre also maximises its own profit at this same level of output, there will be inter-divisional disagreements about output levels and the profit-maximising output will not be achieved.

In this respect, one of the key aims of transfer pricing is to preserve goal congruence: to align the interests of the individual divisions with the interests of the group as a whole, by setting a price which reflects the **true cost to the group** of the transfer.

3.3 The ideal solution

Ideally a transfer price should be set at a level that overcomes these problems.

(a) The transfer price should provide an 'artificial' selling price that enables the transferring division to **earn a return** for its efforts, and the receiving division to **incur a cost** for benefits received.

(b) The transfer price should be set at a level that enables profit centre performance to be **measured 'commercially'** (that is, it should be a **fair** commercial price).

(c) The transfer price, if possible, should encourage profit centre managers to agree on the amount of goods and services to be transferred, which will also be at a level that is consistent with the organisation's aims as a whole, such as **maximising company profits**.

In practice it is very difficult to achieve all three aims.

Question — **Problems with transfer pricing**

(a) What do you understand by the term 'divisional autonomy'?

(b) What are the likely behavioural consequences of a head office continually imposing its own decisions on divisions?

Answer

(a) The term refers to the right of a division to govern itself; that is, the freedom to make decisions without consulting a higher authority first and without interference from a higher body.

(b) Decentralisation recognises that those closest to a job are the best equipped to say how it should be done and that people tend to perform to a higher standard if they are given responsibility. Centrally imposed decisions are likely to make managers feel that they do not really have any authority and therefore that they cannot be held responsible for performance. They will therefore make less effort to perform well.

4 The 'general rule'

We shall see eventually that the **ideal transfer price** should **reflect the opportunity cost of sale to the supplying division and the opportunity cost to the buying division**. We look at this in detail in Section 10. However, this 'general rule' needs to be measured against the three criteria we looked at in the previous section. When setting a transfer price, management must always seek to reconcile the three criteria of goal congruence, managerial effort and divisional autonomy simultaneously. As we work through the different methods of transfer pricing we will consider how each method meets the three criteria.

Knowledge brought forward from earlier studies

There are various bases which can be used for deciding a transfer price, which can be summarised as:

- Market-based transfer prices
- Cost-based transfer prices
- Negotiated transfer prices

You should already be familiar with the bases for calculating transfer prices from your studies for Paper F5. However, you also need to be able to 'Demonstrate and evaluate the use of alternative bases for transfer pricing' in Paper P5, so we will discuss them again here.

However, as we highlighted earlier, in P5 you are unlikely to be asked simply to calculate a transfer price. You are more likely to be asked to evaluate the suitability of different bases of transfer pricing in a given situation, or to analyse the impact of different methods of transfer pricing on divisional performance and motivation.

5 The use of market price 6/11, 6/13

FAST FORWARD

Transfer prices may be based on **market price** (or an **adjusted market price**) where there is an external market for the item being transferred.

5.1 Market price as the transfer price

If an **external market** price exists for transferred goods, profit centre managers will be aware of the price they could charge or the price they would have to pay for their goods on the external market, and so will **compare** this price with the internal transfer price.

5.1.1 Example: transferring goods at market value

A company has two profit centres, A and B. Centre A sells half of its output on the open market and transfers the other half to B. Costs and external revenues in an accounting period are as follows.

	A	*B*	*Total*
	$	$	$
External sales	8,000	24,000	32,000
Costs of production	12,000	10,000	22,000
Company profit			10,000

Required

What are the consequences of setting a transfer price at market value?

Solution

If the transfer price is at market price, A would be happy to sell the output to B for $8,000, which is what A would get by selling it externally instead of transferring it.

		A		*B*	*Total*
	$	$	$	$	$
Market sales		8,000		24,000	32,000
Transfer sales		8,000		–	
		16,000		24,000	
Transfer costs	–		8,000		
Own costs	12,000		10,000		22,000
		12,000		18,000	
Profit		4,000		6,000	10,000

The consequences, therefore, are as follows:

(a) A earns the same profit on transfers as on external sales. B must pay a commercial price for transferred goods, and both divisions will have their profit measured fairly.

(b) A will be indifferent about selling externally or transferring goods to B because the profit is the same on both types of transaction. B can therefore ask for and obtain as many units as it wants from A.

A **market-based** transfer price therefore seems to be the **ideal** transfer price. However, a market-based transfer price can only be applied if a valid market price is available for the goods being transferred between the divisions.

5.2 Adjusted market price

However, internal transfers are often **cheaper** than external sales, with **savings** in selling and administration costs, bad debt risks and possibly transport/delivery costs. It would therefore seem reasonable for the buying division to expect a **discount** on the external market price.

The transfer price might be slightly less than market price, so that A and B could **share the cost savings** from internal transfers compared with external sales. It should be possible to reach agreement on this price and on output levels with minimum intervention from head office.

5.3 The merits of market value transfer prices

5.3.1 Divisional autonomy

In a decentralised company, divisional managers should have the **autonomy** to make output, selling and buying **decisions, which appear to be in the best interests of the division's performance**. (If every division optimises its performance, the company as a whole must inevitably achieve optimal results.) Thus a **transferor division should be given the freedom to sell output on the open market**, rather than to transfer it within the company.

'Arm's length' transfer prices, which give profit centre managers the freedom to negotiate prices with other profit centres as though they were independent companies, will tend to result in a market-based transfer price.

5.3.2 Corporate profit maximisation

In most cases where the transfer price is at market price, **internal transfers** should be **expected**, because the **buying division** is likely to **benefit** from a better quality of service, greater flexibility and dependability of supply. **Both divisions** may **benefit** from cheaper costs of administration, selling and transport. A market price as the transfer price would therefore **result in decisions, which would be in the best interests of the company or group as a whole**.

5.3.3 Divisional performance measurement

Where a **market price exists**, but the **transfer price is a different amount** (say, at standard cost plus), divisional managers will **argue** about the volume of internal transfers.

For example, if division X is expected to sell output to division Y at a transfer price of $8 per unit when the open market price is $10, its manager will decide to sell all output on the open market. The manager of division Y would resent the loss of their cheap supply from X, and would be reluctant to buy on the open market. A wasteful situation would arise where X sells on the open market at $10, where Y buys at $10, so that administration, selling and distribution costs would have been saved if X had sold directly to Y at $10, the market price.

5.4 The disadvantages of market value transfer prices

Market value as a transfer price does have certain disadvantages.

(a) The market price may be a **temporary** one, induced by adverse **economic conditions**, or dumping, or the market price might depend on the volume of output supplied to the external market by the profit centre.

(b) A transfer price at market value might, under some circumstances, act as a disincentive to use up any **spare capacity** in the divisions. A price based on incremental cost, in contrast, might provide an incentive to use up the spare resources in order to provide a marginal contribution to profit.

(c) Many products **do not have an equivalent** market price so that the price of a similar, but not identical, product might have to be chosen. In such circumstances, the option to sell or buy on the open market does not really exist.

(d) The **external market** for the transferred item might be **imperfect**, so that if the transferring division wanted to sell more externally, it would have to **reduce** its price.

6 Cost-based approaches to transfer pricing 6/11, 6/13

FAST FORWARD

Problems arise with the use of **cost-based** transfer prices because one party or the other is liable to perceive them as unfair.

Cost-based approaches to transfer pricing are often used because, in practice, the following conditions are common.

(a) There is **no external market** for the product that is being transferred.

(b) Alternatively, although there is an external market, it is an **imperfect** one because the market price is affected by such factors as the amount that the company setting the transfer price supplies to it, or because there is only a limited external demand.

In either case there will not be a suitable market price on which to base the transfer price. **When a transfer price is based on cost, standard cost should be used, not actual cost**. We will look at this in more detail in Section 8 but first of all we will run through the possible cost-based transfer prices.

6.1 Transfer prices based on full cost

Under this approach, the **full cost** (including fixed overheads absorbed) incurred by the supplying division in making the 'intermediate' product is charged to the receiving division. If a **full cost plus** approach is used a **profit margin** is also included in this transfer price.

Key term

An **intermediate product** is one that is used as a component of another product, for example car headlights or food additives.

6.2 Example: transfers at full cost (plus)

Consider the example introduced in Section 5.1.1, but with the additional complication of imperfect intermediate and final markets. A company has two profit centres, A and B. Centre A can only sell **half** of its maximum output externally because of limited demand. It transfers the other half of its output to B, which also faces limited demand. Costs and revenues in an accounting period are as follows.

	A	*B*	*Total*
	$	$	$
External sales	8,000	24,000	32,000
Costs of production in the division	12,000	10,000	22,000
Profit			10,000

There are no opening or closing inventories. It does not matter here whether marginal or absorption costing is used and we shall ignore the question of whether the current output levels are profit maximising and congruent with the goals of the company as a whole.

6.2.1 Transfer price at full cost only

If the transfer price is at full cost, A in our example would have 'sales' to B of $6,000 (costs of $12,000 × 50%). This would be a cost to B, as follows.

	A		*B*		*Company as a whole*
	$	$	$	$	$
Open market sales		8,000		24,000	32,000
Transfer sales		6,000		–	
Total sales, inc transfers		14,000		24,000	
Transfer costs			6,000		
Own costs	12,000		10,000		22,000
Total costs, inc transfers		12,000		16,000	
Profit		2,000		8,000	10,000

The transfer sales of A are self-cancelling with the transfer costs of B so that total profits are unaffected by the transfer items. The transfer price simply spreads the total profit of $10,000 between A and B.

The obvious drawback to the transfer price at cost is that **A makes no profit** on its work, and the manager of division A would much prefer to sell output on the open market to earn a profit, rather than transfer to B, regardless of whether or not transfers to B would be in the best interests of the company as a whole. Division A needs a profit on its transfers in order to be motivated to supply B; therefore transfer pricing at cost is inconsistent with the use of a profit centre accounting system.

6.2.2 Transfer price at full cost plus

An obvious way of solving this problem, however, is to include a margin in the price which A charges to B for its work. If the transfers are at cost, plus a margin of 25% for example, A's sales to B would be $7,500 ($12,000 × 50% × 1.25).

	A		*B*		*Total*
	$	$	$	$	$
Open market sales		8,000		24,000	32,000
Transfer sales		7,500		–	
		15,500		24,000	
Transfer costs			7,500		
Own costs	12,000		10,000		22,000
		12,000		17,500	
Profit		3,500		6,500	10,000

Compared to a transfer price at cost, **A gains some profit** at the expense of B. However, A makes a bigger profit on external sales in this case because the profit mark-up of 25% is less than the profit mark-up on open market sales. The choice of 25% as a profit mark-up was arbitrary and unrelated to external market conditions.

6.2.3 Divisional autonomy, divisional performance measurement and corporate profit maximisation

In the above case the transfer price **fails on all three criteria** for judgement.

(a) Arguably, it does not give A fair revenue or charge B a reasonable cost, and so their profit **performance** is distorted. It would certainly be unfair, for example, to compare A's profit with B's profit.

(b) Given this unfairness it is likely that the **autonomy** of each of the divisional managers is under threat. If they cannot agree on what is a fair split of the external profit a decision will have to be imposed from above.

(c) It would seem to give A an incentive to sell more goods externally and transfer less to B. This may or may not be in the best interests of the **company as a whole**.

Question

Transfer pricing

Suppose, in the example, that the cost per unit of A's output is $9 in variable costs and $6 in fixed costs. B's own costs are $25 including a fixed element of $10. What is the minimum price that B should charge for its products to break even?

Answer

A produces $12,000/($9 + $6) = 800 units and transfers half of them to B for $6,000. The cost for each unit that B buys is therefore $6,000/400 = $15. From B's perspective this is a **variable** cost. B's costs are as follows.

	Cost per unit
	$
Variable cost: transfers from A	15
Own variable costs	15
	30

From B's perspective it must charge more than $30 per unit to earn a contribution. However, from the overall perspective, $6 of the 'variable' cost of transfers is **fixed**. The variable cost is really $9 + $15 = $24, and any price above this will earn a contribution for the organisation as a whole.

6.3 Transfer price at marginal cost

A marginal cost approach entails charging the marginal cost that has been incurred by the supplying division to the receiving division. As above, we shall suppose that A's cost per unit is $15, of which $6 is fixed and $9 variable.

	A		*B*		*Company as a whole*	
	$	$	$	$	$	$
Market sales		8,000		24,000		32,000
Transfer sales ($6,000 × 9/15)		3,600		–		
		11,600		24,000		
Transfer costs	–		3,600			
Own variable costs	7,200		6,000		13,200	
Own fixed costs	4,800		4,000		8,800	
Total costs and transfers		12,000		13,600		22,000
(Loss)/Profit		(400)		10,400		10,000

6.3.1 Divisional autonomy, divisional performance measurement and corporate profit maximisation

(a) This result is deeply unsatisfactory for the manager of division A who could make an additional $4,400 ($(8,000 – 3,600)) profit if no goods were transferred to division B.

(b) Given that the manager of division A would prefer to transfer externally, head office are likely to have to insist that internal transfers are made.

(c) For the company overall, external transfers only would cause a large fall in profit, because division B could make no sales at all.

The problem is that with a transfer price at marginal cost the **supplying division does not cover its fixed costs**.

7 Fixed costs and transfer pricing

FAST FORWARD

Fixed costs in the supplying division can be accounted for in a number of ways to ensure that it at least breaks even.

There are a number of ways in which this problem could be overcome.

7.1 Sharing contribution

Each division can be given a **share** of the overall contribution earned by the organisation, but it is probably necessary to decide what the shares should be centrally, undermining **divisional autonomy**. Alternatively, central management could impose a range within which the transfer price should fall, and allow divisional managers to **negotiate** what they felt was a fair price between themselves.

7.2 Two-part charging system

Transfer prices are set at variable cost and once a year there is a transfer of a fixed fee to the supplying division, representing an allowance for its fixed costs. Care is needed with this approach. It risks sending the message to the supplying division that it need not control its fixed costs because the company will **subsidise any inefficiencies**. On the other hand, if fixed costs are incurred because spare capacity is kept available for the needs of other divisions, it is reasonable to expect those other divisions to pay a fee if they 'booked' that capacity in advance but later failed to utilise it. The main problem with this approach once more is that it is likely to conflict with **divisional autonomy**.

7.3 Dual pricing

Be careful not to confuse this term with 'two-part' transfer pricing. Dual pricing means that two separate transfer prices are used.

(a) For the transfer of goods from the supplying division to the receiving division the transfer price is set at variable cost. This ensures that the receiving division makes optimal **decisions** and it leads to corporate profit maximisation.

(b) For the purposes of **reporting results** the transfer price is based on the **total** costs of the transferring division, thus avoiding the possibility of reporting a loss.

This method is not widely used in practice.

7.4 Addressing organisational structure

There is one final possibility that may be worth mentioning. Given that the problems are caused by the divisional structure, might it not be better to address the **structure**, for example by **merging the two divisions**, or ceasing to treat the transferring division as a profit centre? This may not be practical. Some would argue that the benefits of decentralisation in terms of motivation outweigh any costs that might arise due to slight inefficiencies.

8 Standard cost versus actual cost

FAST FORWARD

Standard costs should be used for transfer prices to avoid encouraging inefficiency in the supplying division.

When a transfer price is based on cost, **standard cost** should be used, not actual cost. A transfer of actual cost would give no incentive to **control costs**, because they could all be passed on. Actual cost-**plus** transfer prices might even encourage the manager of A to overspend, because this would increase the divisional profit, even though the company as a whole (and division B) suffers.

Suppose, for example, that A's costs should have been $12,000, but actually were $16,000. Transfers (50% of output) would cost $8,000 actual, and the cost plus transfer price is at a margin of 25% ($8,000 × 125% = $10,000).

	A		B		Total
	$	$	$	$	$
Market sales		8,000		24,000	32,000
Transfer sales		10,000		–	
		18,000		24,000	
Transfer costs	–		10,000		
Own costs	16,000		10,000		26,000
		16,000		20,000	
Profit		2,000		4,000	6,000

A's overspending by $4,000 has reduced the total profits from $10,000 to $6,000.

In this example, B must bear much of the cost of A's overspending, which is clearly unsatisfactory for responsibility accounting. If, however, the transfer price were at standard cost plus instead of actual cost plus, the transfer sales would have been $7,500, regardless of A's overspending.

	A		B		Total
	$	$	$	$	$
Market sales		8,000		24,000	32,000
Transfer sales		7,500		–	
		15,500		24,000	
Transfer costs	–		7,500		
Own costs	16,000		10,000		
		16,000		17,500	26,000
Profit/(loss)		(500)		6,500	6,000

The entire cost of the overspending by A of $4,000 is now borne by division A itself, as a comparison with the first table of figures in this section will show.

Question — Standard cost vs actual cost

Why has A's profit fallen by $2,500, not $4,000?

Answer

A was already bearing 50% of its overspending. The fall in profit is $2,000 × 125% = $2,500, which represents the other 50% of its overspending and the loss of the profit margin on transfers to B.

The advantage of using standard costing is that it avoids any inefficiencies from the selling division (in this case, division A) being transferred to the purchasing division (here, division B). As a result, this will encourage the selling division (division A) to be as efficient as possible, because any inefficiencies in its performance will impact directly on its own results.

Conversely, however, the standard costing method does not reflect the efforts of the selling division, so it will not be favoured by that division. For example, if raw material costs have increased since the standard cost was set, the selling division's cost will have increased, but it will not be able to transfer any of this increase to the purchasing division. Do you think this will seem fair to the manager of the selling division (ie division A)?

9 Cost-based approaches with no external market

With **no external market**, the transfer price should be set in the range where variable cost in the supplying division is less than or equal to net marginal revenue in the receiving division.

9.1 Unlimited capacity and no external market

So far we have considered the use of cost-based approaches where the following factors applied.

(a) There was a **limit on the maximum output** of the supplying division.
(b) There was a **limit** to the amount that could be sold in the **intermediate market**.

We found that a **marginal cost**-based approach led to the **best decisions** for the organisation overall, but that this was **beset with problems** in maintaining divisional autonomy and measuring divisional performance fairly.

We shall now consider whether this finding changes in different conditions. We shall remove the limit on output and demand for the final product, but assume that there is **no** intermediate market at all.

9.2 Example: unlimited capacity and no intermediate market

Motivate Ltd has two profit centres, P and Q. P transfers **all** its output to Q. The variable cost of output from P is $5 per unit, and fixed costs are $1,200 per month. Additional processing costs in Q are $4 per unit for variable costs, plus fixed costs of $800. Budgeted production is 400 units per month, and the output of Q sells for $15 per unit. The transfer price is to be based on standard full cost plus. From what **range** of prices should the transfer price be selected, in order to motivate the managers of both profit centres to both increase output and reduce costs?

Solution

Any transfer price based on **standard** cost plus will motivate managers to cut costs, because favourable variances between standard costs and actual costs will be credited to the division's profits. Managers of each division will also be willing to increase output above the budget of 400 units provided that it is profitable to do so; that is:

(a) In P, provided that the transfer price exceeds the variable cost of $5 per unit.

(b) In Q, provided that the transfer price is less than the difference between the fixed selling price ($15) and the variable costs in Q itself ($4). This amount of $11 ($15 – $4) is sometimes called **net marginal revenue**.

The range of prices is therefore between $5.01 and $10.99.

Let's do a check. Suppose the transfer price is $9. With absorption based on the **budgeted** output of 400 units, what would divisional profits be if output and sales are 400 units or 500 units?

Overheads per unit are $1,200/400 = $3, so the full cost of sales is $(5 + 3) = $8 in division P. In division Q, full cost is $(4 + 2) = $6, plus transfer costs of $9.

At 400 units:

	P	*Q*	*Total*
	$	$	$
Sales	–	6,000	6,000
Transfer sales	3,600	–	
Transfer costs	–	(3,600)	
Own full cost of sales	(3,200)	(2,400)	(5,600)
	400	0	400
Under-/over-absorbed overhead	0	0	0
Profit/(loss)	400	0	400

At 500 units:

	P	*Q*	*Total*
	$	$	$
Sales	–	7,500	7,500
Transfer sales	4,500	–	–
Transfer costs	–	(4,500)	–
Own full cost of sales	(4,000)	(3,000)	(7,000)
	500	0	500
Over-absorbed overhead (100 × $3; 100 × $2)	300	200	500
Profit/(loss)	800	200	1,000

Increasing output improves the profit performance of both divisions and the company as a whole, and so decisions on output by the two divisions are likely to be **goal congruent.**

9.3 Summary

To summarise, the **transfer price should be set in the range** where:

Variable cost in supplying division ≤ **Selling price minus variable costs (net marginal revenue) in the receiving division**

In fact, if there is no external market, and if the transferred item is the major product of the transferring division, there is a strong argument for suggesting that profit centre accounting is a waste of time.

Profit centres cannot be judged on their commercial performance because there is no way of gauging what a fair revenue for their work should be. It would be more appropriate, perhaps, to treat the transferring 'division' as a cost centre, and to judge performance on the basis of cost variances.

10 Opportunity costs and transfer prices

FAST FORWARD

If a profit-maximising output level has been established, the transfer price should be set such that there is not a more profitable opportunity for individual divisions. In other words, transfer prices should include **opportunity costs** of transfer.

10.1 The ideal transfer price

Ideally, a transfer price should be set that enables the individual **divisions** to maximise their profits at a level of output that maximises profit for the **company as a whole**. The transfer price which achieves this is unlikely to be a market-based transfer price (if there is one) and is also unlikely to be a simple cost plus based price.

10.2 An opportunity cost approach

If optimum decisions are to be taken transfer prices should reflect **opportunity costs**.

(a) If profit centre managers are given sufficient autonomy to make their own output and selling decisions, and at the same time their performance is judged by the company according to the profits they earn, they will be keenly aware of all the commercial opportunities.

(b) If transfers are made for the good of the company as a whole, the commercial benefits to the company ought to be **shared** between the participating divisions.

Transfer prices can therefore be reached by:

(a) Recognising the levels of output, external sales and internal transfers that are best for the **company as a whole**; and

(b) Arriving at a transfer price that ensures that all divisions maximise their profits at this same level of output. The transfer price should therefore be such that there is **not a more profitable opportunity** for individual divisions. This in turn means that the opportunity costs of transfer should be covered by the transfer price.

11 Transfer pricing when intermediate products are in short supply

FAST FORWARD

When an **intermediate resource is in short supply** and **acts as a limiting factor** on production in the supplying division, the cost of transferring an item is the variable cost of production plus the contribution obtainable from using the scarce resource in its next most profitable way.

11.1 Example: scarce resources

Suppose, for example, that division A is a profit centre that produces three items, X, Y and Z. Each item has an external market.

	X	*Y*	*Z*
External market price, per unit	$48	$46	$40
Variable cost of production in division A	$33	$24	$28
Labour hours required per unit in division A	3	4	2

Product Y can be transferred to division B, but the maximum quantity that might be required for transfer is 300 units of Y.

The maximum **external** sales are 800 units of X, 500 units of Y and 300 units of Z.

Instead of receiving transfers of product Y from division A, division B could buy similar units of product Y on the open market at a slightly cheaper price of $45 per unit.

What should the transfer price be for each unit if the total labour hours available in division A are 3,800 hours or 5,600 hours?

Solution

Hours required to meet maximum demand:

	Hours
External sales:	
X (3 × 800)	2,400
Y (4 × 500)	2,000
Z (2 × 300)	600
	5,000
Transfers of Y (4 × 300)	1,200
	6,200

Contribution from external sales:

	X	*Y*	*Z*
Contribution per unit	$15	$22	$12
Labour hours per unit	3 hrs	4 hrs	2 hrs
Contribution per labour hour	$5.00	$5.50	$6.00
Priority for selling	3rd	2nd	1st
Total hours needed	2,400	2,000	600

(a) If only **3,800 hours** of labour are available, division A would choose, **ignoring transfers** to B, to sell:

	Hours
300 Z (maximum)	600
500 Y (maximum)	2,000
	2,600
400 X (balance)	1,200
	3,800

To transfer 300 units of Y to division B would involve forgoing the sale of 400 units of X because 1,200 hours would be needed to make the transferred units.

Opportunity cost of transferring units of Y, and the appropriate transfer price:

	$ per unit
Variable cost of making Y	24
Opportunity cost (contribution of $5 per hour available from selling X externally): benefit forgone (4 hours × $5)	20
Transfer price for Y	44

The transfer price for Y should, in this case, be less than the external market price.

(b) If **5,600 hours** are available, there is enough time to meet the full demand for external sales (5,000) and still have 600 hours of spare capacity, before consideration of transfers. However, 1,200 hours are needed to produce the full amount of Y for transfer (300 units), and so 600 hours need to be devoted to producing Y for transfer instead of producing X for external sale.

This means that the **opportunity cost** of transfer is:

(i) The variable cost of 150 units of Y produced in the 600 'spare' hours ($24/unit)

(ii) The variable cost of production of the remaining 150 units of Y ($24 per unit), plus the **contribution forgone** from the external sales of X that could have been produced in the 600 hours now devoted to producing Y for transfer ($5 per labour hour). An average transfer price per unit could be negotiated for the transfer of the full 300 units (see below), which works out at $34 per unit.

	$
150 units × $24	3,600
150 units × $24	3,600
600 hours × $5 per hour	3,000
Total for 300 units	10,200

In both cases, the opportunity cost of receiving transfers for division B is the price it would have to pay to purchase Y externally – $45 per unit. Thus:

Maximum labour hours in A	*Opportunity cost to A of transfer*	*Opportunity cost to B of transfer*
	$	$
3,800	44	45
5,600	34 (average)	45

In each case any price between the two opportunity costs would be sufficient to persuade B to order 300 units of Y from division A and for division A to agree to transfer them.

11.2 Central information

The only way to be sure that a profit-maximising transfer policy will be implemented is to **dictate the policy from the centre**. This means that the following information must be available centrally:

(a) A precise **breakdown of costs in each division** at all levels of output

(b) **Market information** for each market, indicating the level of demand at a range of prices

(c) Perhaps most vitally, knowledge of the **likely reaction of divisional managers** to a centrally imposed policy that undermines their autonomy and divisional profits

12 Transfer pricing and a range of limiting factors

FAST FORWARD

If a supplying division is subject to a **range of limiting factors**, the optimum production plan can be derived using a **linear programming model**.

12.1 Example: transfer pricing with a range of limiting factors

LP Ltd has two divisions, division 1 and division 2. Division 1 produces liquid A, all of which is transferred to division 2, and liquid B which can either be sold externally or transferred to division 2. Division 2 uses these liquids to produce its powdered products, X and Y.

Production of liquid A is restricted due to a shortage of skilled labour so that only 4,000 litres can be produced. Liquid B can also only be produced in limited numbers due to a scarcity of ingredients. Only 6,000 litres of liquid B can be made. Details of costs and revenues are as follows.

	A	*B*	*X*	*Y*
	$	$	$	$
Variable cost (division 1)	4	6	–	–
Variable cost (division 2)	–	–	7	5
Selling price	–	9	30	35

One sachet of powder X requires 1 litre of liquid A and 2 litres of liquid B.

One sachet of powder Y requires 2 litres of liquid A and 2 litres of liquid B.

Required

Formulate a linear programming model to determine the optimum production levels and transfer prices.

Solution

Step 1 **Work out the contribution obtained from each product**

This needs to take account of the usage of A and B by X and Y.

	B	*X*	*Y*
Variable costs	6	7	5
Liquid A (1 litre/2 litres)	–	4	8
Liquid B (2 litres/2 litres)	–	12	12
	6	23	25
Selling price	9	30	35
Contribution	3	7	10

Step 2 **Formulate objective function**

The objective is to maximise the corporate contribution by producing the optimum quantities of products B, X and Y. Algebraically this is expressed as follows.

Maximise 3B + 7X + 10Y

Step 3 **Define constraints**

The constraints are as follows.

1X + 2Y	≤	4,000	(labour shortage)
B + 2X + 2Y	≤	6,000	(ingredients shortage)
B, X, Y	≥	0	

Note. You are only required to be able to formulate the model, not solve it.

In practice, as you probably remember, where there are **more than two variables** in the objective function and more than a few constraints a **computer software package** is needed.

The **output** from the model will show **how many sachets of X and Y should be produced and how many litres, if any, of B should be sold externally**. The output also provides a means of calculating the ideal transfer price, because it indicates the shadow price of scarce resources.

13 Shadow price and transfer prices

FAST FORWARD

Shadow prices replace opportunity costs when determining transfer prices if there are constraints on production.

Key term

The **shadow price** is the maximum amount that a division would be prepared to pay to obtain one extra unit of a scarce resource.

Alternatively, a shadow price could be seen as the opportunity cost of that scarce resource; or the amount of benefit forgone by not having the extra unit of the scarce resource available.

We know already that an **optimal transfer price** can be calculated by **adding together the variable cost of the intermediate product and the opportunity cost of making the transfer**. In our example, let us suppose that the shadow price of liquid A is \$3 and of liquid B, \$2.

	A	*B*
	\$	\$
Variable cost	4	6
Shadow price	3	2
Transfer price	7	8

This solution might be tested by the divisional manager of the supplying division by applying their own linear programming model attempting to maximise the contribution from external sales of B (which we shall call B1) and from transfers of A and B.

$$\text{Maximise } 3A + 2B + 3B1$$

$$\begin{aligned} \text{Subject to} \quad A &\leq 4{,}000 \\ B + B1 &\leq 6{,}000 \\ A, B, B1 &\geq 0 \end{aligned}$$

This would give the same optimum production levels as the original linear programme, because it is derived from the same information.

For division 2, however, these transfer prices would result in each product yielding a contribution of nil. In effect, this means that the **optimal solution must be centrally imposed**, otherwise the manager of division 2 will have no incentive to produce X and Y at all.

14 Negotiated transfer prices

FAST FORWARD

In practice, **negotiated** transfer prices, **market-based** transfer prices and **full cost-based** transfer prices are the methods normally used.

A transfer price based on opportunity cost is often **difficult to identify**, for lack of suitable information about costs and revenues in individual divisions. In this case it is likely that transfer prices will be set by means of **negotiation**. The agreed price may be finalised from a mixture of accounting arithmetic, politics and compromise.

The process of negotiation will be improved if **adequate information** about each division's costs and revenues is made available to the other division involved in the negotiation. By having a free flow of cost and revenue information, it will be easier for divisional managers to identify opportunities for improving profits, to the benefit of both divisions involved in the transfer.

A negotiating system that might enable **goal congruent plans** to be agreed between profit centres is:

(a) Profit centres **submit plans** for output and sales to head office, as a preliminary step in preparing the annual budget.

(b) Head office **reviews these plans**, together with any other information it may obtain. Amendments to divisional plans might be discussed with the divisional managers.

(c) Once divisional plans are acceptable to head office and **consistent** with each other, head office might let the divisional managers arrange budgeted transfers and transfer prices.

(d) Where divisional plans are **inconsistent** with each other, head office might try to establish a plan that would maximise the profits of the company as a whole. Divisional managers would then be asked to negotiate budgeted transfers and transfer prices on this basis.

(e) If divisional managers fail to agree a transfer price between themselves, a head office **'arbitration' manager** or team would be referred to for an opinion or a decision.

(f) Divisions **finalise their budgets** within the framework of agreed transfer prices and resource constraints.

(g) Head office **monitors the profit performance** of each division.

15 Multinational transfer pricing

FAST FORWARD

Multinational transfer pricing needs to take account of a range of factors:

- Exchange rate fluctuations
- Taxation in different countries
- Import tariffs
- Exchange controls
- Anti-dumping legislation
- Competitive pressures
- Repatriation of funds

Globalisation, the rise of the **multinational corporation** and the fact that more than **60% of world trade takes place within multinational organisations** mean that international transfer pricing is very important.

15.1 Factors to consider when setting multinational transfer prices

The level at which a transfer price should be set is even less clear-cut for organisations operating in a number of countries, when even more factors need to be taken into consideration. Moreover, the manipulation of profits through the use of transfer pricing is a common area of confrontation between multinational organisations and host country governments.

Factors to consider	Explanation
Exchange rate fluctuation	The value of a transfer of goods between profit centres in different countries could depend on fluctuations in the currency exchange rate.
Taxation in different countries	If taxation on profits is 20% of profits in Country A and 50% on profits in Country B, a company will presumably try to 'manipulate' profits (by means of raising or lowering transfer prices or by invoicing the subsidiary in the high-tax country for 'services' provided by the subsidiary in the low-tax country) so that profits are maximised for a subsidiary in Country A, by reducing profits for a subsidiary in Country B. Some multinationals set up marketing subsidiaries in countries with low tax rates and transfer products to them at a relatively low transfer price. When the products are sold to the final customer, a low rate of tax will be paid on the difference between the two prices.

Factors to consider	Explanation
Import tariffs	Suppose that Country A imposes an import tariff of 20% on the value of goods imported. A multinational company has a subsidiary in Country A which imports goods from a subsidiary in Country B. In such a situation, the company would minimise costs by keeping the transfer price to a minimum value.
Exchange controls	If a country imposes restrictions on the transfer of profits from domestic subsidiaries to foreign multinationals, the restrictions on the transfer can be overcome if head office provides some goods or services to the subsidiary and charges exorbitantly high prices, disguising the 'profits' as sales revenue, and transferring them from one country to the other. The ethics of such an approach should, of course, be questioned.
Anti-dumping legislation	Governments may take action to protect home industries by preventing companies from transferring goods cheaply into their countries. They may do this, for example, by insisting on the use of a fair market value for the transfer price.
Competitive pressures	Transfer pricing can be used to enable profit centres to match or undercut local competitors. (For example, if a transferee division (receiving goods from another division within a company) is facing intense competition in its local market, its 'costs' could be reduced by adjusting the transfer price, thereby allowing it to be more competitive in its local market.)
Repatriation of funds	By inflating transfer prices for goods sold to subsidiaries in countries where inflation is high, the subsidiaries' profits are reduced and funds repatriated, thereby saving their value.

15.2 Transfer prices and tax

Tax authorities obviously recognise the **incentive to set transfer prices to minimise taxes and import tariffs**. Many **tax authorities** have the **power** to **modify transfer prices in computing tariffs or taxes on profit**, although a **genuine arm's length market price should be accepted**.

(a) UK government legislation restricts how far companies can declare their profits in a low taxation country. However, some scope for profit apportionment between divisions clearly exists. HM Revenue & Customs has the power to adjust the taxable income of the UK party to a cross-border transaction to the figure that would have resulted if the **prices actually used had been between two unrelated parties ('arm's length' price)**.

(b) In the US, multinational organisations must follow an Internal Revenue Code specifying that transfers must be priced at 'arm's length' market values, or at the values that would be used if the divisions were independent companies. Even with this rule, companies have some leeway in deciding an appropriate 'arm's length' price.

To meet the multiple objectives of transfer pricing, companies may choose to maintain **two sets of accounting records, one for tax reporting and one for internal management reporting**. However, the tax authorities may interpret the use of two sets of records as **suggestive of profit manipulation**.

Double taxation agreements between countries mean that companies pay tax on specific transactions in one country only. If a company sets an unrealistically low transfer price, however, the company will pay tax in both countries (double taxation) if it is spotted by the tax authorities.

Most countries now accept the Organisation for Economic Co-operation and Development (OECD) 2010 guidelines *Transfer Pricing for Multinational Enterprises and Tax Administrations.* These aim to standardise national approaches to transfer pricing and provide guidance on the application of the 'arm's length' price.

15.2.1 Example: arm's length transfer price

Suppose division A produces product B in a country where the income tax rate is 30% and transfers it to division C, which operates in a country with a 40% rate of income tax. An import duty equal to 25% of the price of product B is also assessed. The full cost per unit is $290, the variable cost $160.

Required

The tax authorities allow either variable or full cost transfer prices. Determine which should be chosen.

Solution

Effect of transferring at $290 instead of $160

	$
Income of A is $130 higher and so A pays $130 × 30% more income tax	(39.0)
Income of C is $130 lower and so C pays $130 × 40% less income tax	52.0
Import duty is paid by C on an additional $130, and so C pays $130 × 25% more duty	(32.5)
Net effect (cost) of transferring at $290 instead of $160	(19.5)

15.3 The pros and cons of different transfer pricing bases

(a) A transfer price at **market value** is usually encouraged by the tax and customs authorities of both host and home countries, as they will receive a fair share of the profits made, but there are problems with its use.

- (i) Prices for the same product may vary considerably from one country to another.
- (ii) Changes in exchange rates, local taxes and so on can result in large variations in selling price.
- (iii) A division will want to set its prices in relation to the supply and demand conditions present in the country in question to ensure that it can compete in that country.

(b) A transfer price at **full cost** is usually acceptable to tax and customs authorities since it provides some indication that the transfer price approximates to the real cost of supplying the item and because it indicates that they will therefore receive a fair share of tax and tariff revenues.

(c) Transfer prices at **variable cost** are unlikely to be acceptable to the tax authorities of the country in which the supplying division is based, as all the profits are allocated to the receiving division and the supplying division makes a loss equal to the fixed costs incurred.

(d) In a multinational organisation, **negotiated** transfer prices may result in overall sub-optimisation because no account is taken of such factors as differences in tax and tariff rates between countries.

Question

Multinational transfer pricing

RBN is a Polish parent company with an overseas subsidiary. The directors of RBN wish to transfer profits from Poland to the overseas company. They are considering changing the level of the transfer prices charged on goods shipped from the overseas subsidiary to Polish subsidiaries and the size of the royalty payments paid by Polish subsidiaries to the overseas subsidiary.

Required

In order to transfer profit from Poland to the overseas subsidiary, explain very briefly what the directors of RBN should do.

Answer

They should increase both the transfer prices and the royalty payments.

To increase the overseas subsidiary's profit, the transfer price needs to be higher (since it is the overseas subsidiary doing the selling) and the royalty payments by the Polish subsidiaries to the overseas subsidiary company should also be higher. Both would add to the overseas subsidiary's revenue without affecting its costs.

Question — More multinational transfer pricing

LL Multinational plc transferred 4,000 units of product S from its manufacturing division in the US to the selling division in the UK in the year to 31 December.

Each unit of S cost $350 to manufacture, the variable cost proportion being 75%, and was sold in the UK for £600. The UK division incurred marketing and distribution costs of £8 per unit. The UK tax rate was 30% and the exchange rate £1 = $1.50.

The market price for each unit of product S in the US was $600. The US division's profit after tax for its sales to the UK division for the year just ended was $750,000.

Required

(a) If the transfers were at variable cost, calculate the UK division's profit after tax.

(b) Calculate the tax rate in the US if product S was transferred at the US market price.

Answer

(a)

	£
External sales (£600 × 4,000)	2,400,000
Variable cost (transfer price of ($350 × 75%/$1.5) × 4,000)	700,000
Marketing and distribution costs (£8 × 4,000)	32,000
Profit before tax	1,668,000
Tax at 30%	500,400
Profit after tax	1,167,600

(b)

	$
Transfer sales ($600 × 4,000)	2,400,000
Costs ($350 × 4,000)	1,400,000
Profit before tax	1,000,000
Tax	?
Profit after tax	750,000

Therefore tax = $(1,000,000 – 750,000) = $250,000

Therefore tax rate = ($250,000/1,000,000) = 25%

Case Study — Starbucks

In 2011, Starbucks's UK sales were worth £398m. Costa's UK sales in the same year were worth £377m. However, while Costa paid £15m in corporation tax in 2011/12, Starbucks did not pay any. In fact, Starbucks in the UK reported a loss of £28.2m, following recorded costs of £426.2m for the year.

Does this mean that Starbucks's operations in the UK are a commercial failure, though? No, Starbucks regards its UK operations as a highly profitable part of its business.

You might then question how a profitable operation can make losses, but the answer lies in transfer pricing.

The Starbucks corporation (based in the US) charges the UK operation high prices for various services, such as royalties for the use of branding and logos. Similarly, the Swiss-based firm, Starbucks Coffee Trading Co, earns a 'moderate profit' on the price it charges Starbucks UK for its coffee beans.

As such, the Starbucks corporation moves all of its profits out of the UK and thereby avoids paying UK corporation tax. However, the tactics that Starbucks uses are entirely legal, and there is no suggestion that Starbucks has broken any laws.

Chapter Roundup

- We considered the **divisional form or structure** for an organisation in Chapter 4, when we looked at the information needs of businesses adopting this form. That chapter also discussed the pros and cons of adopting the divisional form, including ease of performance measurement.
- One of the problems of measuring managerial performance is **segregating managerial performance from the economic performance of their department or division**.
- It is necessary for **control purposes** that some **record** of the market in inter-divisional goods or services should be kept. One way of doing this is through the accounting system. Inter-divisional work can be given a cost or a charge: a transfer price.
- Transfer prices are a way of promoting **divisional autonomy**, ideally without prejudicing **divisional performance measurement** or discouraging overall **corporate profit maximisation (goal congruence)**.
- Transfer prices may be based on **market price** (or an **adjusted market price**) where there is an external market for the item being transferred.
- Problems arise with the use of **cost-based** transfer prices because one party or the other is liable to perceive them as unfair.
- **Fixed costs** in the supplying division can be accounted for in a number of ways to ensure that it at least breaks even.
- **Standard costs** should be used for transfer prices to avoid encouraging inefficiency in the supplying division.
- With **no external market**, the transfer price should be set in the range where variable cost in the supplying division is less than or equal to net marginal revenue in the receiving division.
- If a profit-maximising output level has been established, the transfer price should be set such that there is not a more profitable opportunity for individual divisions. In other words, transfer prices should include **opportunity costs** of transfer.
- When an **intermediate resource is in short supply** and **acts as a limiting factor** on production in the supplying division, the cost of transferring an item is the variable cost of production plus the contribution obtainable from using the scarce resource in its next most profitable way.
- If a supplying division is subject to a **range of limiting factors**, the optimum production plan can be derived using a **linear programming model**.
- **Shadow prices** replace opportunity costs when determining transfer prices if there are constraints on production.
- In practice, **negotiated** transfer prices, **market-based** transfer prices and **full cost-based** transfer prices are the methods normally used.
- **Multinational transfer pricing** needs to take account of a range of factors:
  - Exchange rate fluctuations
  - Taxation in different countries
  - Import tariffs
  - Exchange controls
  - Anti-dumping legislation
  - Competitive pressures
  - Repatriation of funds

Quick Quiz

1 To prevent dysfunctional transfer price decision making, profit centres must be allowed to make autonomous decisions. True or false?

2 Which of the following is/are true:

(i) Controllable profit is an acceptable measure of divisional performance.
(ii) Divisional profit is an acceptable measure of managerial performance.

A (i) only
B (ii) only
C (i) and (ii)
D Neither of them

3 Which of the following is not a disadvantage of using market value as a transfer price?

A The market price might be a temporary one.
B Use of market price might act as a disincentive to use up spare capacity.
C Many products do not have an equivalent market price.
D The external market might be perfect.

4 Fill in the blanks.

Ideally, a transfer price should be set that enables the individual divisions to maximise their profits at a level of output that maximises ....

The transfer price which achieves this is unlikely to be a .... transfer price or a .... transfer price.

If optimum decisions are to be taken, transfer prices should reflect ....

5 Choose the appropriate word(s) from those highlighted.

When an intermediate resource is in short supply and acts as a limiting factor on production in the **transferring/receiving** division, the cost of transferring an item is the **variable/fixed/opportunity** cost of production **plus/less** the **contribution obtainable/opportunity cost** from using the scarce resource in its next most profitable way.

6 Which of the following is/are true:

(i) Transfer prices based on standard costs provide an incentive for the receiving division to control costs.

(ii) One of the disadvantages of using negotiated transfer prices to evaluate divisional performance is that the price depends on the negotiating skills of the divisional managers.

A Neither of them
B (i) only
C (ii) only
D Both of them

Answers to Quick Quiz

1 False. They cannot be allowed to make entirely autonomous decisions.

2 D Neither of them.

Controllable profit may be an acceptable measure of managerial performance, while divisional profit may be an acceptable measure of divisional performance. Divisional performance should be based on the total economic performance of a division, whereas managers should only be assessed on results within their control.

3 D The external market might be perfect.

4 profit for the company as a whole; market-based; cost-based; opportunity cost

5 transferring
variable
plus
contribution obtainable

6 C Option (i) is false. Transfer prices based on standard costs provide an incentive for the **transferring** division to control costs (not the **receiving** division).

Option (ii) is true. A negotiated transfer price is the result of a bargaining procedure between the selling unit and the purchasing unit, so there is a danger that the price may be decided by the negotiating skills and bargaining power of one of the divisions, rather than being an 'optimal' price.

Now try the question below from the Practice Question Bank

Number	Level	Marks	Approximate time
Q10	Examination	20	40 mins

Strategic performance measures in not-for-profit organisations

11

Topic list	Syllabus reference
1 The objectives of not-for-profit organisations	D3(a)
2 Performance measurement in not-for-profit organisations	D3(b)
3 The use of benchmarking and league tables in public sector organisations	D3(c)
4 Politics, performance measurement and undesirable service outcomes	D3(d)
5 Value for money	D3(e)

Introduction

In Chapter 9 we looked at performance measurement in profit-seeking organisations in the private sector. However, while the primary objective of such organisations is to generate value for their shareholders, that is not the primary objective for all organisations.

In your P5 exam you may need to discuss performance measurement and strategic performance measurement techniques in a range of different organisations. Therefore, in this chapter we now focus on performance measurement in not-for-profit organisations.

We will start by looking at the range of different objectives these organisations may have, and we then go on to discuss the implications this can have for performance measurement in them.

Study guide

		Intellectual level
D3	**Strategic performance measures in not-for-profit organisations**	
(a)	Highlight and discuss the potential for diversity in objectives depending on organisation type.	3
(b)	Discuss the difficulties in measuring outputs when performance is not judged in terms of money or an easily quantifiable objective.	2
(c)	Discuss the use of benchmarking in public sector performance (league tables) and its effect on operational and strategic management and client behaviour.	3
(d)	Discuss how the combination of politics and the desire to measure public sector performance may result in undesirable service outcomes; eg the use of targets.	3
(e)	Assess 'value for money' service provision as a measure of performance in not-for-profit organisations and the public sector.	3

Exam guide

One of the main capabilities which candidates need to demonstrate in the P5 exam is an ability to **apply appropriate strategic performance measurement techniques in evaluating and improving organisational performance**.

This means you must be able to assess performance in a range of different organisations – including not-for-profit organisations as well as 'for-profit' ones – using **suitable performance measures** to do so. Notice also that, as well as evaluating current performance, you should be prepared to suggest ways the organisation could improve performance in future.

Notice that in this case the focus is on ways of **improving performance**. However, in earlier chapters we have identified that you could also be asked to suggest **improvements to the measures** being used to assess performance, as well as **management reports**.

Exam focus point

The Pilot Paper asked candidates to consider performance measures in a not-for-profit organisation in contrast to a profit-seeking organisation, and then asked candidates to state performance measures appropriate to either type of organisation.

A question in the December 2014 exam looked at value for money in the provision of public services, and asked candidates to suggest relevant performance indicators which could assess how an organisation is performing in terms of the value for money it provides. The question also asked candidates to explain why non-financial indicators are particularly important for public sector organisations, and to discuss the difficulties of measuring qualitative factors of performance.

There are also two useful articles about not-for-profit organisations in the P5 Technical Articles section of ACCA's website. The first article – 'Not-for-profit organisations – Part 1' – explains what not-for-profit organisations are, while Part 2 looks in more detail at charities as a specific type of not-for-profit organisation. You should read these articles as background reading, and as an introduction to not-for-profit organisations if you are not familiar with them.

Element (b) of Performance objective 14 – Monitor performance – identifies that you should 'Analyse and provide appropriate information to measure performance.'

The issue of identifying 'appropriate information' to measure can sometimes be a particular challenge in not-for-profit organisations due to the number of different objectives they can have, and therefore the number of different aspects of performance which could potentially be measured.

1 The objectives of not-for-profit organisations

FAST FORWARD

One possible definition of a **not-for-profit organisation** is that the attainment of its **primary goal is not assessed by economic measures**. However, not-for-profit organisations may nonetheless sometimes undertake profit-making activities in the pursuit of that goal.

Note. In this chapter we use the terms 'not-for-profit' and 'non-profit-seeking' interchangeably, and many writers use one or the other to mean the same type of organisation. The P5 syllabus refers to 'not-for-profit' organisations, though.

Bois has suggested that non-profit-seeking organisations are defined by recognising that their first objective is to be involved in **non-loss operations** in order to cover their costs and that profits are only made as a means to an end (such as providing a service, or accomplishing some socially or morally worthy objective).

Key term

A **not-for-profit organisation** is an organisation whose attainment of its prime goal is not assessed by economic measures. However, in pursuit of its primary goal it may undertake profit-making activities, and then use any surplus funds to help pursue its goal.

1.1 Objectives and not-for-profit organisations

A major problem with many not-for-profit organisations, particularly government bodies, is that it is extremely **difficult to define their objectives** at all. In addition, they tend to have **multiple objectives**, so that even if they could all be clearly identified it is impossible to say which the overriding objective is.

Question — Objectives

What objectives might the following not-for-profit organisations have?

(a) An army
(b) A local council
(c) A charity
(d) A political party
(e) A college

Answer

Here are some suggestions.

(a) To defend a country
(b) To provide services for local people (such as the elderly)
(c) To help others/protect the environment
(d) To gain power/enact legislation
(e) To provide education

More general objectives for not-for-profit organisations include:

(a) Surplus maximisation (equivalent to profit maximisation in commercial organisations)
(b) Revenue maximisation (as for a commercial business)
(c) Usage maximisation (as in leisure centre swimming pool usage)

(d) Usage targeting (matching the capacity available, as in hospitals)
(e) Full/partial cost recovery (minimising subsidy)
(f) Budget maximisation (maximising what is offered)
(g) Producer satisfaction maximisation (satisfying the wants of staff and volunteers)
(h) Client satisfaction maximisation (the police generating the support of the public)

It is difficult to judge whether **non-quantitative objectives** have been met. For example, assessing whether a charity has improved the situation of those benefiting from its activities is difficult to research. Statistics related to product mix, financial resources, size of budgets, number of employees, number of volunteers, number of customers serviced and number and location of facilities are all useful for this task.

1.2 Stakeholders in not-for-profit organisations

The reason for the potential **diversity** in the objectives of not-for-profit organisations is linked to the range of **stakeholders** they have. We discussed, in Chapter 5, the way stakeholder groups influence an organisation and its strategy formulation, and this idea is important here.

One of the main reasons why not-for-profit organisations have different objectives to profit-seeking, commercial ones is because of the differences in the key stakeholders between the two types of organisation.

The primary objectives of commercial organisations are likely to be fairly similar, and will be based around maximising the profit they generate for their shareholders. As such indicators such as earnings and profitability will also be measures for assessing performance in commercial organisations.

However, not-for-profit organisations **do not have shareholders**. Consequently (as their name suggests) their primary objective is not to make a profit. Instead, they provide value in other ways – for example through healthcare or education. As such, there is rarely an equivalent financial measure of performance which can be applied to not-for-profit organisations, in the way that earnings or profitability can be used to assess the performance of commercial organisations.

Exam focus point

As we noted in the Exam focus point at the start of the chapter, one of the question requirements in the December 2014 exam asked candidates to explain why non-financial indicators are particularly useful for public sector organisations.

The absence of the underlying objective which commercial organisations have – to make a profit (or to generate value for shareholders) – is an important factor in the relative importance of non-financial indicators in public sector, and other not-for-profit, organisations.

Another characteristic of not-for-profit organisations is the **range of different stakeholders** they have – for example, beneficiaries; local authorities; managers; staff; financial backers – who all have an interest in their activities.

1.2.1 Diversity of stakeholders and their objectives

Managers in not-for-profit organisations need to take account of the range of stakeholders and stakeholder views when setting objectives and making strategic decisions. However, the number of different stakeholder groups involved means there can be considerable scope for conflict between the interests and objectives of those different stakeholders.

We can illustrate this by looking at an example of a hospice in the UK.

The **stakeholders** include the **trustees** who are responsible for overseeing the running of the hospice and reporting to the Charity Commission. **Clinical staff** provide medical care for the terminally ill patients the hospice looks after. **Therapists** provide therapies including massage and aromatherapy. The **National Health Service (NHS)** contracts with the hospice to provide care for terminally ill patients. **Support staff** will also be stakeholders and they include marketing, human resources, and finance staff. The **patients** who attend either full-time or respite care are important stakeholders, as are their relatives. **Fund raisers** who are volunteers are unpaid stakeholders. A **medical director** who is responsible for ensuring the upkeep of medical standards is an essential stakeholder.

Possible conflicts that might occur include those between stakeholders with commercial and charitable interests. The **trustees** may want the hospice to cut back on spending but the **clinical staff** will see quality of care as a priority. **Patients** (and their friends and relatives) as well as the **medical director** will monitor service standards and will veto anything that compromises the quality of clinical care offered; for instance, permitting open days that allow visitors to tour certain private therapy areas. The **NHS**, as a contractor and also a provider of funding, may want some say in how the hospice is run and how much it is willing to pay for funding patient care.

2 Performance measurement in not-for-profit organisations

FAST FORWARD

Not-for-profit organisations often have **multiple objectives** which are **difficult to define**. There are a range of other problems in measuring performance.

Exam focus point

There is an article in the P5 Technical Articles section on ACCA's website looking at 'Benchmarking and the use of targets in public sector organisations'.

One of the issues this article highlights is the difficulty of deciding which aspects of performance to measure; for example, due to the number of stakeholders who are interested in the performance of public sector organisations.

You are advised to read this article as part of your preparation for your P5 exam.

Commercial organisations generally have market competition and the profit motive to guide the process of managing resources economically, efficiently and effectively. However, not-for-profit organisations **cannot by definition be judged by profitability** and do not **generally have to be successful against competition**, so other methods of assessing performance have to be used. If an organisation is not expected to make a profit or to generate revenue, it follows that financial indicators may have less relevance to that organisation than in commercial organisations.

As we have already noted in Section 1, a major problem with many not-for-profit organisations is that they have multiple objectives. This makes it extremely **difficult to define their overriding objective** at all, let alone find one which can serve a yardstick function in the way that profit does for commercial bodies.

Question — Objectives for not-for-profit organisations

One of the objectives of a local government body could be 'to provide adequate street lighting throughout the area'.

(a) How could the 'adequacy' of street lighting be measured?

(b) Assume that other objectives are to improve road safety in the area and to reduce crime. How much does 'adequate' street lighting contribute to each of these aims?

(c) What is an excessive amount of money to pay for adequately lit streets, improved road safety and reduced crime? How much is too little?

Answer

Think over these questions and discuss them in class or with colleagues if possible.

It is possible to suggest answers, perhaps even in quantitative terms, but the point is that there are no **easy** answers, and no right or wrong answers.

Given the potential difficulty in defining the objectives of not-for-profit and public sector organisations precisely, you might feel there is little scope for measuring their performance. However, there is equally little scope to argue that such organisations should just be given whatever amount of money they say they need to pursue their aims, with no check on whether it is spent well or badly.

(a) Without information about what is being achieved (outputs) and what it is costing (inputs) it is impossible to make **efficient resource allocations**. These allocation decisions rely on a range of performance measures which, if unavailable, may lead managers to allocate resources based on subjective judgement, personal whim or in response to political pressure.

(b) Without performance measures managers will not know the **extent to which operations are contributing to effectiveness and efficiency**; when diagnostic interventions are necessary; how the performance of their organisation **compares** with similar units elsewhere; and how their performance has **changed** over time.

(c) **Government** may require performance information to decide how much to spend in the public sector and where, within the sector, it should be allocated. In particular they will be interested to know what results may be achieved as a consequence of a particular level of funding, or to decide whether or not a service could be delivered more effectively and efficiently in the private sector. Likewise, **people who provide funds for** other kinds of non-profit-seeking organisations are entitled to know whether their money is being put to good use.

Some kind of measure of '**value for money**' becomes particularly important in the context of **funding constraints** or limited funding which we referred to in the previous section.

Question — Performance measures in a charity

What performance measures might be used by a famine relief charity?

Answer

Some measures that might be used include:

- Income in donations, and changes in income over time
- Income by source – personal donations, corporate donations, etc
- Responses to campaign initiatives, such as television or newspaper advertisements, or appeals relating to specific crises
- Cost containment measures – such as management costs and other operating expenses (This is particularly important, as donors want to know that as much of their donation as possible is going to the famine relief, and charities are likely to be criticised if administration costs absorb a high proportion of income.)
- Income from commercial activities (for example, charity shops)
- Number of volunteers attracted
- Changes in mortality and sickness rates in areas where relief has been provided

You may have thought of other measures, but this list is an indicator of some of the measures which you could have suggested.

This question and answer are taken from the article 'Not-for-profit organisations – Part 2' which is available from the Technical Articles section on ACCA's website. This article, and the companion article ('Not-for-profit organisations – Part 1'), provide some useful background information about objectives and management in not-for-profit organisations.

2.1 How can performance be measured? 12/14

FAST FORWARD

Performance is judged in terms of inputs and outputs and hence the **value for money criteria** of **economy, efficiency** and **effectiveness.**

As the performance of not-for-profit organisations cannot be properly assessed by using conventional accounting ratios (such as ROCE and ROI), it is usually judged in terms of **inputs and outputs** instead, and this ties in with the 'value for money' criteria that are often used to assess non-profit-seeking organisations. (We look at 'value for money' in more detail in Section 5.)

(a) **Economy** (spending money frugally)
(b) **Efficiency** (getting out as much as possible for what goes in)
(c) **Effectiveness** (getting done, by means of the above, what was supposed to be done)

More formal definitions are as follows.

Key terms

Economy is the ability of the organisation to optimise its use of its productive resources; achieving the appropriate quantity and quality of inputs at the lowest cost possible.

Efficiency is the relationship between inputs and outputs; the 'output' of the organisation per unit of resource consumed.

Effectiveness is the relationship between an organisation's outputs and its objectives; the extent to which the organisation achieves its objectives.

We will look at these concepts in more depth in Section 5.

2.2 Problems with performance measurement of not-for-profit organisations

(a) **Multiple objectives**

As we have said, not-for-profit organisations tend to have multiple objectives. Consequently, even if the different objectives can all be clearly identified it is impossible to say which is the overriding objective, and therefore what are the most important aspects of performance to measure.

(b) **Measuring outputs**

Outputs can seldom be measured in a way that is generally agreed to be meaningful. (For example, are good exam results alone an adequate measure of the quality of teaching?)

Equally, data collection can be problematic. For example, unreported crimes are not included in data used to measure the performance of a police force.

(c) **Lack of profit measure**

If an organisation is not expected to make a profit, or if it has no sales, indicators such as ROI and RI are meaningless.

(d) **Nature of service provided**

Many non-profit-seeking organisations provide services for which it is difficult to define a cost unit. For example, what is the cost unit for a local fire service? This problem does exist for commercial service providers but problems of performance measurement are made simple because profit can be used.

(e) **Financial constraints**

Although every organisation operates under financial constraints, these are more pronounced in non-profit-seeking organisations. For instance, a commercial organisation's borrowing power is effectively limited by managerial prudence and the willingness of lenders to lend, but a local authority's ability to raise finance (whether by borrowing or via local taxes) is subject to strict control by central government.

(f) **Political, social and legal considerations**

(i) Unlike commercial organisations, public sector organisations are subject to strong political influences. Local authorities, for example, have to carry out central government's policies as well as their own (possibly conflicting) policies.

(ii) The public may have higher expectations of public sector organisations than commercial organisations. A decision to close a local hospital in an effort to save costs, for example, is likely to be less acceptable to the public than the closure of a factory for the same reason.

(iii) The performance indicators of public sector organisations are subject to far more onerous legal requirements than those of private sector organisations. We consider this point in more detail in Section 4.

(iv) Whereas profit-seeking organisations are unlikely in the long term to continue services making a negative contribution, non-profit-seeking organisations may be required to offer a range of services, even if some are uneconomical.

2.3 Possible solutions to these problems

2.3.1 Inputs

Performance can be judged in terms of inputs. This is very common in everyday life. If somebody tells you that their suit cost $750, you would generally conclude that it was an extremely well-designed and good-quality suit, even if you did not think so when you first saw it. The drawback is that you might also conclude that the person wearing the suit had been cheated or was a fool, or you may happen to be of the opinion that no piece of clothing is worth $750. So it is with the inputs and outputs of a non-profit-seeking organisation.

2.3.2 Judgement

A second possibility is to accept that performance measurement must to some extent be subjective. Judgements can be made by **experts** in that particular not-for-profit activity or by the **persons who fund the activity**.

2.3.3 Comparisons

We have said that most non profit seeking organisations do not face competition but this does not mean that all are unique. Bodies like local governments and health services can judge their performance **against each other** and **against the historical results of their predecessors**. Furthermore, since they are not competing with each other, there is less of a problem with confidentiality and so **benchmarking** is easier.

2.3.4 Quantitative measures

Unit cost measurements like 'cost per patient day' or 'cost of borrowing one library book' can fairly easily be established to allow organisations to assess whether they are doing better or worse than their counterparts.

Efficiency measurement of inputs and outputs is illustrated in three different situations as follows.

(a) **Where input is fixed**

$$\frac{\text{Actual output}}{\text{Maximum output obtainable for a given input}}$$ 25/30 miles per gallon = 83.3% efficiency

(b) **Where output is fixed**

$$\frac{\text{Minimum input needed for a given output}}{\text{Actual input}}$$ 55/60 hours to erect scaffolding = 91.7% efficiency

(c) **Where input and output are both variable**

Actual output ÷ actual input	\$9,030/7,000 meals = \$1.29 per meal
compared with	
standard output ÷ standard input	\$9,600/7,500 meals = \$1.28 per meal
	Efficiency = 99.2%

As a further illustration, suppose that at a cost of \$40,000 and 4,000 hours (inputs) in an average year two policemen travel 8,000 miles and are instrumental in 200 arrests (outputs). A large number of possibly meaningful measures can be derived from these few figures, as the table below shows.

	\$40,000	*4,000 hours*	*8,000 miles*	*200 arrests*
Cost \$40,000		\$40,000/4,000 = \$10 per hour	\$40,000/8,000 = \$5 per mile	\$40,000/200 = \$200 per arrest
Time 4,000 hours	4,000/\$40,000 = 6 minutes patrolling per \$1 spent		4,000/8,000 = ½ hour to patrol 1 mile	4,000/200 = 20 hours per arrest
Miles 8,000	8,000/\$40,000 = 0.2 of a mile per \$1	8,000/4,000 = 2 miles patrolled per hour		8,000/200 = 40 miles per arrest
Arrests 200	200/\$40,000 = 1 arrest per \$200	200/4,000 = 1 arrest every 20 hours	200/8,000 = 1 arrest every 40 miles	

These measures **do not necessarily identify cause and effect** (do teachers or equipment produce better exam results?) **or personal responsibility and accountability**. Actual performance needs to be compared as follows:

(a) With standards, if there are any
(b) With similar external activities
(c) With similar internal activities
(d) With targets
(e) With indices
(f) Over time, as trends

2.4 Not-for-profit organisations and profit-seeking bodies

If it has struck you when reading the previous sections that the main issue in the performance measurement of not-for-profit organisations is one of **quality**, you may be wondering whether the distinction between profit-seeking and not-for-profit in this context is worth making.

Although the primary objectives between the types of organisations remain different, in many other respects the distinction is becoming less useful. The commercial sector's increasing focus on customer satisfaction and quality of service (and non-financial aspects of performance) has much in common with the aims of non-profit-seeking organisations. Conversely, non-profit-seeking organisations (in particular government bodies) have increasingly been forced to face up to elements of competition and market forces.

The distinctions are thus becoming blurred. The problems of performance measurement in not-for-profit organisations are to a great extent the problems of performance measurement generally.

Question

Profit-seeking vs not for profit

Can you think of some issues which would impact on the different performance indicators used by a public sector hospital (eg an NHS hospital in the UK) and a private sector hospital?

Answer

- The private sector hospital would be focused on maximising **profit**, the NHS hospital on **cost efficiency**.
- Managers within a private sector hospital are likely to have far greater autonomy than those working in the NHS.

- A private sector hospital has far greater **freedom in selecting its patients** and the types of **treatment** offered. It can choose to specialise in the most profitable areas. An NHS hospital, unless it is a specialist centre, must treat all patients and offer a huge range of treatments.
- Private sector hospitals can **market** their services.

Case Study — Performance measurement in police forces

Public sector performance has become an increasingly important issue in the Western world since the 1980s, as advocates of a new approach to public service – referred to as 'New Public Management' (NPM) – have tried to propel organisations which have traditionally been seen as slow-moving, inefficient and overly bureaucratic closer to a private sector model. The logic behind NPM was that bringing public services more in line with a private sector, corporate model would hopefully enable them to deliver better services for less money.

A key part of NPM was a push towards greater accountability, but this in turn required the development of performance measurement frameworks in public sector organisations.

A lot of attention is given to the publication of crime statistics, and statistical systems (such as COMPSTAT) have become increasingly common, focusing on the occurrence of specific crimes, in defined areas, over a particular time frame.

As a result of this statistical focus, the rate of recorded and resolved crime has become the primary performance measure for police forces around the world. In many police organisations, aggregated crime data is presented in league table formats showing the (perceived) comparative performance of different jurisdictions.

However, the use of statistics in this way has led to a debate about the applicability of numerical performance schemes in the policing environment. For example, crime rates will be affected not only by the actions of the police forces but also by much wider economic and socio-demographic factors.

Also, commentators on police performance have begun to emphasise that the way the police act is as important as the statistics they achieve. For example, mass random stop and searches might improve performance in relation to crime rates, but they would harm the image and legitimacy of the police force in the eyes of local communities.

Moreover, some commentators have concerns about the alignment between what police forces perceive to be good performance, and what the public think. Police forces may focus on resolved crime rates, but the public may not perceive this as good performance if they continue to feel unsafe. In addition, the public are often sceptical that improvements in crime statistics are often merely the result of manipulation of recording practices by the police.

In a report looking into the factors which citizens should value and measure in police performance, Braga and Moore highlight that while 'controlling crime is the single most important core function of the police, there are many other dimensions of performance that are valued'.

In this respect, Braga and Moore suggest that any performance scheme needs to incorporate seven dimensions:

- Reducing crime and criminal victimisation
- Effectiveness in calling offenders to account
- Reducing fear and enhancing personal security
- Ensuring civility in public spaces
- Using force and authority fairly, efficiently and effectively
- Using financial resources fairly, efficiently and effectively
- Providing quality services/customer satisfaction

Braga and Moore argue that it is important to measure performance in all of these dimensions, because ignoring one or more of them would result in a failure to appreciate the complexity of police work.

As such, their approach could be seen as a detailed balanced scorecard, and highlights the importance of multi-dimensional approaches to performance measurement in the public sector.

We will look at multi-dimensional performance measurement systems (including the balanced scorecard) in more detail in Chapter 15 later in this Study Text.

2.5 Comparing performance of profit-seeking organisations with not-for-profit organisations

A valid comparison between such organisations (for example, between a private hospital and a public sector one) may **require adjustments** to be made to data provided for analysis purposes. Here are some examples.

(a) If the not-for-profit organisation does not **charge for services**, a hypothetical amount may need to be included in profit calculations, possibly based on the number of customers who would be willing to pay.

(b) The not-for-profit organisation may have no debt (perhaps because it has been paid off by a governing body, a local authority and so on). Any **interest paid on debt** by the profit-seeking organisation may therefore need to be removed from profit calculations.

(c) Any **loss attributable to uneconomical sections/divisions/services** of the not-for-profit organisation (which it may be required to continue for social or legal purposes) may need to be removed for comparison purposes.

3 The use of benchmarking and league tables in public sector organisations 12/13

FAST FORWARD

The desire to improve the overall efficiency and effectiveness of public sector organisations has led to the increasing use of **performance measures and targets** to evaluate their performance, and to enable **comparison of their performance** with that of other similar organisations.

We discussed benchmarking in Chapter 1 where we noted its potential value to organisations in comparing their performance with other organisations, and then using the results as an incentive to improve their own performance. However, benchmarking can be equally relevant to not-for-profit organisations as it is to profit-orientated ones: comparing operating performance and identifying the best practices can be beneficial to an organisation whatever its objectives.

Benchmarking can have a **positive effect on behaviour**. By sharing data on performance against appropriate benchmarks, organisations can improve their own performance. (This is a crucial point to remember about benchmarking. The value of benchmarking comes not simply from comparing performance against other organisations, but also from then taking steps to improve your own performance in the light of the findings from the benchmarking exercise.)

Benchmarking also encourages management to concentrate on what is important (based on the benchmarked measures in league tables) and to devise strategies aimed at improving performance in those key areas. Operational targets should then also be set to achieve the benchmarked measure(s).

However, while benchmarking can have a positive impact on behaviour (for example, in setting operational targets to help achieve levels of performance identified in the benchmarks), it could also have less favourable consequences. For example, benchmarking could actually serve to demotivate staff, rather than to motivate them, if their organisation's performance is being highlighted as inferior to the ones being benchmarked against.

An organisation has to be selective in what aspects of performance to benchmark, but there is a danger it may focus on areas that are easy to measure rather than being critical business processes. In a similar vein, benchmarking may allow a business to carry out a process more **efficiently**, but if the output of that process is not very important then the **effectiveness** of the improvement is limited. In effect, there is a danger that benchmarking can concentrate on 'doing things right' rather than 'doing the right thing'.

Management may also concentrate on achieving specific benchmarks while neglecting others. For example, in the UK, university league tables are produced based on nine selected aspects of the universities' performance.

- Student satisfaction – measure of the view of students of the teaching quality at the university
- Research assessment/quality – measure of the average quality of the research undertaken in the university
- Entry standards – the average exam grades in their final school- or college-level exams (A Levels) that students have to achieve to secure their place
- Student/staff ratio – measure of the average staffing level in the university
- Academic Services spend – the expenditure per student on all academic services
- Facilities spend – the expenditure per student on staff and student facilities
- Good honours – proportion of first and upper-second class degrees
- Graduate prospects – measure of the employability of a university's graduates
- Completion – measure of the completion rate of those studying at the university

As a result, universities are likely to focus mainly on improving their performance in these areas of activity, and less attention will be given to other areas. This highlights the adage (which we will look at again in the next chapter in relation to non-financial performance indicators) that '**What gets measured, gets done.**' If an organisation has chosen to benchmark certain aspects of performance, then the organisation's focus is likely to be on improving performance in those areas.

Exam focus point

There is an article in the P5 Technical Articles section about 'Benchmarking and the use of targets in public sector organisations'.

This article looks in general at some of the difficulties of using targets and of measuring performance in public sector organisations, before looking more specifically at some of the issues relating to benchmarking performance in public sector organisations.

You are strongly advised to read this article if you have not already done so.

3.1 Difficulties in deriving performance measures

We looked at the features of services in Chapter 4 earlier in this Study Text. The four facets of services – **simultaneity, heterogeneity, perishability** and **intangibility** – can make them difficult to measure quantitatively. These four facets are also characteristic of the activities in the majority of not-for-profit organisations, because they are service-providing organisations. This adds another level of complication to measuring the performance of not-for-profit organisations.

A hospital could report the **number** of operations it has carried out in a month, but this would not measure the quality of its procedures or patient care, nor would it take account of the complexity of the operations being carried out. Often qualitative measures are used to capture aspects of service – such as quality and reliability. And it seems likely that some kinds of qualitative measures will also be necessary to supplement quantitative measures of performance.

Patient rating systems

The NHS has announced plans to introduce a 'patient rating system' to improve the quality of nursing care in England.

From April 2013, patients will be asked if they would recommend the hospital they were treated in to their friends and family, and the results will be made public.

However, these proposals highlight the potentially subjective nature of any such rating systems. In particular, what factors would determine whether a patient would 'recommend' a hospital to friends and family? The quality (and success) of any medical treatment received? The quality of the care the patient received from the staff looking after them? How quickly they were treated? Factors relating to the hospital itself (eg cleanliness, how crowded it was)?

3.2 Using league tables 12/13

League tables are a readily available data bank for users of public services ranking not-for-profit organisations on a range of measures, such as exam results for schools. They are compiled using benchmarks against comparative organisations and then ranked on the measures used.

Question

League tables

What do you think might happen if a senior school (for pupils aged 11+) chooses to concentrate on its ranking in a league table for students achieving a set number of good passes (grades A to C in the UK) in their final exams?

Answer

The school may succeed in getting students to pass the exams, but at the expense of other priorities. It is a criticism of league tables in the UK that where schools focus on this measure, they omit to help students who are not likely to meet the grades by making their priority the students who are likely to pass and boost this measure.

The benefit of league tables is that different areas of performance can be summarised into a final score, showing how well an organisation has performed overall. League tables are also intended to inspire competition among organisations, and to provide an incentive to those performing relatively poorly to improve their performance and thereby improve their ranking in the table.

However, a number of criticisms have also been raised against league tables. We can illustrate some of these by continuing our example of school league tables.

If the league tables are produced on the basis of academic results alone, they may reflect the **capability of the students** as much as the **quality of teaching** provided by the school. A school with academically gifted students is likely to show better results than a school with less talented students. Headline academic results in themselves do not provide a measure of the **value added** by the school, or the **effectiveness** of the education provided by the school. However, these ideas of 'value added' and 'effectiveness' are also much harder to quantify and measure.

Another issue is that each year, several organisations produce academic school league tables, as well as giving schools 'value-added' scores. However, each organisation has its own criteria and methodology for calculating which school is the 'best'. Therefore, the rankings are likely to differ from one league table to the next.

A common criticism of league tables is that they apply **weightings** to different factors used in the calculation of the final performance score. These weightings are arbitrary; however, the rankings in the table could often be different if different weightings were used.

Finally, it is worth remembering that the primary focus of the league tables is on academic performance. However, the league table does not necessarily indicate that a school which ranks highly in the league tables will be the 'best' one for a specific child to go to. A pupil who is a gifted sportsperson but not particularly academic will not necessarily benefit from being at a school that is consistently at the top of the league table but which places little emphasis on sports and physical education.

Ultimately, the league tables can help parents who want to find out about the academic standing of a school, but the parents have to use this information in conjunction with other research activities about the school.

Exam focus point

The December 2013 exam featured a scenario in which league tables had been proposed as a means of improving the performance of the police forces in a country.

The first part of the question focused on the way in which the league tables were being produced, and the performance measures included in them. One of the issues the question raised was whether the measures included were appropriate or not.

The second part of the question looked more generally at the merits of league tables in performance management, as well as possible disadvantages of using them.

Exam focus point

In Chapter 14, we will look at the potential problems which can arise in relation to the choice of measures used to assess staff performance. One of the problems is '**tunnel vision**', where staff focus on one particular aspect of performance at the expense of other aspects, knowing that they are being assessed on that particular area.

The issues which we look at in Chapter 14 could equally be relevant to the potential pitfalls of introducing public sector league tables.

For example: might league tables encourage **measure fixation** – an emphasis on measures rather than underlying objectives? Or might they encourage **misrepresentation** – the deliberate manipulation of data to improve an organisation's position in the league table?

4 Politics, performance measurement and undesirable service outcomes

FAST FORWARD

The combination of politics and the desire to measure public sector performance may result in **undesirable service outcomes**.

4.1 Performance measurement in the public sector

Performance measurement in the public sector has traditionally been perceived as presenting four **special difficulties**: how to assess performance; stakeholder expectations; the influence of government; and problems of defining 'performance'.

4.1.1 How to assess performance

With public sector services, there has rarely been any market competition nor any underlying profit motive. In the private sector, these two factors (competition and profit) help to guide the process of fixing proper prices and managing resources economically, efficiently and effectively. Since most public sector organisations cannot be judged by their success against competition or by profitability, other methods of assessing performance have to be used.

4.1.2 Stakeholder expectations

Different stakeholders hold different expectations of public sector organisations. For example, parents, employers, the community at large and central government might require different things from the education sector. And even within groups of stakeholders, such as parents, there might be a mix of requirements. Priorities of all the groups might change over time. Schools have to reconcile the possibly conflicting demands made on them but to make explicit statements of objectives might show that they are favouring one group of stakeholders at the expense of another.

4.1.3 Influence of government

Given the role of government in public sector organisations, long-term organisational objectives are sometimes sacrificed for short-term political gains.

4.1.4 Defining performance measures

In the public sector, **performance measures are difficult to define**. Measures of output quantity and output quality themselves provide insufficient evidence of, for example, a local authority's success in serving the community.

4.1.5 Ways in which these problems could be managed/overcome

(a) Set up systems for regional benchmarking (making allowances for known regional differences)

(b) Change the way in which such organisations are controlled to restrict political interference

(c) Carry out cost/benefit analyses in an attempt to place a financial value on services being provided

(d) Use independent agencies (of experts) to make objective decisions based on their experience and information provided

4.2 Performance indicators

During the 1980s, however, the increased availability of information technology led to a dramatic reduction in the cost of collecting data. This fuelled the practice of publishing information (**performance indicators**) about the performance of public sector bodies. This aimed to **overcome** the traditional **problems** of public sector performance measurement and enable various interested parties to **secure control** of public sector resources.

Whether within central government, local government or other public services (such as the NHS in the UK), public sector bodies are required to produce and publish key indicators on a variety of fronts.

4.3 Examples of indicators

To assess **overall performance** of a public service (ie those areas/issues generally considered to be important), indicators can be usefully divided into three groups.

(a) **Financial indicators to measure efficiency**

  (i) Cost per unit of activity; eg cost per arrest (for a police force); cost per bed per night (in a hospital); or cost per pupil (for a school)

  (ii) Variance analysis

  (iii) Comparisons with benchmark information

  (iv) Cost component as a proportion of total costs (eg administration costs as a proportion of total costs)

  (v) Costs recovered as a proportion of costs incurred (eg payment received from householders requesting collection of bulky/unusual items of refuse)

(b) **Non-financial (quantifiable) indicators to measure effectiveness**
   (i) Quality of service/output measures (eg exam results, crime rates)
   (ii) Utilisation of resources (eg hospital bed occupancy ratios; average class sizes in a school)
   (iii) Flexibility/speed of response (eg hospital waiting lists)

(c) **Qualitative indicators to measure effectiveness**
   (i) Workplace morale
   (ii) Staff attitude to dealing with the public (eg can they provide the correct information in a helpful and professional manner)
   (iii) Public confidence in the service being provided (eg will a pupil be well educated, a patient properly cared for)

We will be looking in more detail at various indicators later in this Study Text.

4.4 Undesirable service outcomes

We have already noted that the publication of league tables, such as those for schools, can encourage **dubious comparisons** and/or can lead to a **competitiveness which does not fit** with the nature of many of the services being provided.

For example, extra effort and expenditure on disruptive pupils may represent the **best way for a society as a whole** to deal with them, but a **school's best managerial strategy** is to exclude such pupils (and there has been a sharp rise recently in such exclusions) so as to improve performance for league table purposes.

Hospitals are under increasing pressure to **compete on price and delivery** in areas such as elective surgery (planned, non-emergency surgery) such as hip and knee replacements. Although this **reduces waiting lists**, it may represent a **shift of resources from other, less measurable areas**, such as emergency services. In attempting to reach a target of ensuring that no patient waits more than a certain number of years for an operation, patients awaiting serious surgery are said to have suffered longer waiting times as hospitals have concentrated on reducing the longer waiting times of those in need of relatively minor surgery. (This is an example of the problem of **measure fixation**, which we will discuss further in Chapter 14.)

4.5 Undesirable outcomes and the use of targets

What gets measured, gets done

The management guru, Tom Peters, asserts that one of the best pieces of advice he has heard is that 'What gets measured, gets done.'

Although this adage is appropriate for both profit and not-for-profit organisations, it is perhaps particularly important in connection to performance measurement and reward systems in not-for-profit organisations.

In the UK, the Government issues performance targets for government departments and public sector organisations and the level of resources allocated to the organisations is linked to how well they perform against the targets. In addition, individual providers of public services may also get specific rewards linked to their performance, either directly (the top performing hospitals gain 'earned autonomy' to authorise their own capital investments without having to gain approval from central government, for example) or indirectly (schools that perform well attract more students and hence more resources).

Not surprisingly, therefore, if the **targets focus on a particular aspect of performance**, that will be the aspect of performance the organisation will most want to try to achieve.

This is particularly important in public sector organisations which often have a number of **different stakeholders** with interests in different aspects of an organisation's performance. However, if management start to concentrate on certain target areas (at the expense of others) it seems likely that the interests and objectives of some stakeholders will have to be sacrificed in order to achieve this.

For example, a hospital's stakeholders would include:

(a) **Patients** (and their relatives) – whose focus will be on waiting times, quality of surgery and successfulness of outcome, quality of care in the hospital

(b) **Hospital management** – focus on performance (medical performance; cleanliness and hygiene; customer service), costs and volume of activity with a view to deciding 'best' use of resources

(c) **Central government** – focus on value for money from central funding, accountability for performance and potential cost savings

(d) **Staff** – training to provide clinical excellence, or customer care; job security; working conditions (eg hours worked); wages and salaries

In this example, if central government is looking to cut costs, this could lead to cuts in the hospital's budgets which in turn could force the local hospital managers to reduce the number of beds available in their hospital. This could either lead to longer waiting times or else potentially a decline in the quality of surgery or the quality of care (if operations and post-operation recovery times become rushed).

As with this hospital example, targets are often set by central government but then implemented by local services. This means local management usually have little discretion about what to implement or the means by which targets are implemented.

This reveals a difference in **relative power** between central and local services which can result in little questioning of the targets and a tendency to concentrate on achieving them. This relationship between central and local bodies embodies the **political stance** of politicians by way of central government which is the means by which politicians communicate their policies. In the UK, the political system has seen a shift towards centralising decision making and making local bodies responsible for attaining targets centrally set and intended to drive them towards achieving selected goals, with the aim of seeing an improvement in service standards.

In addition, as well as illustrating the political influences which can constrain public sector organisations, the hospital example highlights the wider issue of organisational politics and relationships between different layers of management (and staff) in an organisation.

5 Value for money (VFM) 12/14

FAST FORWARD

Public sector organisations are now under considerable pressure to prove that they operate economically, efficiently and effectively, and are encouraged from many sources to draw up action plans to achieve **value for money** as part of the continuing process of good management.

Although much has been written about value for money (VFM), there is no great mystique about the concept. The term is common in everyday speech and so is the idea. If you have studied Paper F5, you should be familiar with the three 'E's of economy, efficiency and effectiveness.

Key term

Value for money means providing a service in a way which is economical, efficient and effective.

Case Study — Value for money

To drive the point home, think of a bottle of Fairy Liquid (washing up liquid). If we believe the advertising, Fairy is good 'value for money' because it washes half as many plates again as any other washing up liquid. Bottle for bottle it may be more expensive than some other brands of washing up liquid, but plate for plate it is cheaper. Not only this, but Fairy gets plates 'squeaky' clean. To summarise, Fairy gives us VFM because it exhibits the following characteristics:

(a) **Economy** (more clean plates per pound)
(b) **Efficiency** (more clean plates per squirt)
(c) **Effectiveness** (gets plates as clean as they can be)

The assessment of economy, efficiency and effectiveness should be a part of the normal management process of any organisation, public or private.

(a) Management should carry out **performance reviews** as a regular feature of their control responsibilities.

(b) Independent assessments of management performance can be carried out by 'outsiders', perhaps an internal audit department, as **value for money audits (VFM audits)**.

VFM is important **whatever level of expenditure** is being considered. Negatively it may be seen as an approach to spreading costs in public expenditure fairly across services but positively it is necessary to ensure that the desired impact is achieved with the minimum use of resources.

5.1 Studying and measuring the three Es

Economy, efficiency and effectiveness can be studied and measured with reference to the following:

(a) **Inputs**

(i) Money
(ii) Resources – the labour, materials, time and so on consumed, and their cost

For example, a VFM audit into State secondary education would look at the efficiency and economy of the use of resources for education (the use of schoolteachers, school buildings, equipment, cash) and whether the resources are being used for their purpose: what is the pupil/teacher ratio and are trained teachers being fully used to teach the subjects they have been trained for?

(b) **Outputs**; in other words, the **results of an activity**, measurable as the services actually produced, and the quality of the services.

In the case of a VFM audit of secondary education, outputs would be measured as the number of pupils taught and the number of subjects taught per pupil; how many examination papers are taken and what is the pass rate; what proportion of students go on to further education (eg at university).

(c) **Impacts**, which are the **effect that the outputs** of an activity or programme have in **terms of achieving policy objectives**.

Policy objectives might be to provide a minimum level of education to all children up to the age of 16, and to make education relevant for the children's future jobs and careers. This might be measured by the ratio of jobs vacant to unemployed school leavers. A VFM audit could assess to what extent this objective is being achieved.

As another example from education, suppose that there is a programme to build a new school in an area. The **inputs** would be the **costs of building** the school, and the resources used up; the **outputs** would be the **school building** itself; and the **impacts** would be the **effect that the new school has on education in the area** it serves.

5.2 Potential problems with VFM

As with many other aspects of performance management, however, there could be conflicts between the different elements of VFM.

Continuing the example of schools and exam results, the quality of education pupils receive and the exam results they achieve (effectiveness) is likely to be improved by reducing the ratio of pupils to teachers and keeping class sizes relatively low. However, in terms of efficiency, the school's efficiency will be improved by having a higher ratio of pupils to teachers.

5.3 VFM audits and objectives

In a VFM audit, the objectives of a particular programme or activity need to be specified and understood in order for the auditor to make a proper assessment of whether VFM has been achieved.

(a) In a **profit-seeking organisation**, objectives can be expressed financially in terms of target profit or return. The organisation, and profit centres within it, can be judged to have operated **effectively** if they have **achieved a target profit** within a given period.

(b) In **non-profit-seeking organisations**, effectiveness cannot be measured this way, because the organisation has non-financial objectives. The **effectiveness** of performance in such organisations could be measured in terms of whether **targeted non-financial objectives have been achieved**, but as we have seen there are several problems involved in trying to do this.

Chapter Roundup

- One possible definition of a **not-for-profit organisation** is that the attainment of its **primary goal is not assessed by economic measures**. However, not-for-profit organisations may nonetheless sometimes undertake profit-making activities in the pursuit of that goal.
- Not-for-profit organisations tend to have **multiple objectives** which are **difficult to define**. There are a range of other problems in measuring performance.
- Performance is judged in terms of inputs and outputs and hence the **value for money criteria** of **economy, efficiency** and **effectiveness**.
- The desire to improve the overall efficiency and effectiveness of public sector organisations has led to the increasing use of **performance measures and targets** to evaluate their performance, and to enable **comparison of their performance** with that of other similar organisations.
- The combination of politics and the desire to measure public sector performance may result in **undesirable service outcomes**.
- Public sector organisations are now under considerable pressure to prove that they operate economically, efficiently and effectively, and are encouraged from many sources to draw up action plans to achieve **value for money** as part of the continuing process of good management.

Quick Quiz

1 Which one of the following groups are **not** stakeholders in not-for-profit organisations?

A Employees
B Volunteers
C Shareholders
D Funding providers

2 Identify two potential problems which reduce the validity of public sector league tables.

3 Match the definition to the term.

Term		*Definition*	
(a)	Economy	(1)	Ensuring outputs succeed in achieving objectives
(b)	Efficiency	(2)	Getting out as much as possible for what goes in
(c)	Effectiveness	(3)	Spending money frugally

4 List three sources of funds for not-for-profit organisations.

5 Six problems of measuring performance in non-profit-seeking organisations were described in this chapter.

Four are: multiple objectives; the absence of a profit measure; the difficulty of measuring output; the nature of the service provided.

What the other two which are missing from this list?

Answers to Quick Quiz

1 C One of the key distinctions between not-for-profit (NFP) organisations and commercial, private sector companies is that NFPs do not have shareholders, and consequently they do not have to earn profits for their shareholders.

2 Two possible answers here would be:

They do not take into account differences between the organisations being measured. (In the example in the chapter of school exam results, the exam results do not take account of the underlying academic ability, or aptitude, of the pupils at a school.)

They apply arbitrary weightings to the factors used in calculating the final scores.

(You may have identified others from your reading of Section 3.2 of the chapter.)

3 (a) (3); (b) (2); (c) (1)

4 Possible answers include:

Government funding (eg grants)
Donations (eg bequests from individuals, or corporate donations)
'Self'-funding (eg charity shops raise money for charities; universities charge fees to students)
Fundraising activities (eg sponsored events)

5 Financial constraints
Political/social/legal considerations

Now try the question below from the Practice Question Bank

Number	Level	Marks	Approximate time
Q11	Practice	20	40 mins

12

Non-financial performance indicators

Topic list	Syllabus reference
1 Financial and non-financial performance indicators	D4(a)
2 The significance of non-financial performance indicators	D4(b)
3 Interpreting data about qualitative issues	D4(c)
4 Branding and brand awareness	D4(d)

Introduction

In Chapters 9 and 10 we looked at measures which could be used to assess the financial performance of organisations and divisions.

However, some of the issues we identified in Chapter 11 in relation to performance measurement in not-for-profit organisations have highlighted the importance of qualitative and non-financial measures in assessing performance, rather than relying solely on financial measures.

In this chapter we are going to look at non-financial performance indicators (NFPIs) in more detail. NFPIs are becoming increasingly important in organisations, in particular where they are looking to measure how well they are performing in relation to critical success factors (such as customer satisfaction and product quality) which are non-financial in nature.

Study guide

		Intellectual level
D4	**Non-financial performance indicators**	
(a)	Discuss the interaction of non-financial performance indicators with financial performance indicators.	3
(b)	Identify and discuss the significance of non-financial performance indicators in relation to employees and product/service quality eg customer satisfaction reports, repeat business ratings, customer loyalty, access and availability.	3
(c)	Discuss the difficulties in interpreting data on qualitative issues.	2
(d)	Discuss the significance of brand awareness and company profile and their potential impact on business performance.	3

Exam guide

As we noted in the previous chapter, one of the main capabilities which candidates need to demonstrate in the P5 exam is an ability to apply appropriate strategic performance measurement techniques in evaluating and improving organisational performance.

Ultimately, an organisation's financial performance is likely to be a reflection of how well it is performing in key non-financial activities: for example, an organisation's revenue will be the result of it developing products or services that customers want to buy, and then attracting – and retaining – customers who buy those products and services. Therefore non-financial aspects (of product development; quality; or customer service) could all be crucial elements of sustaining and improving the organisation's performance. Similarly, when evaluating an organisation's performance it is crucial to look at non-financial performance indicators (NFPIs) as well as financial ones.

Performance measurement systems such as the balanced scorecard and the performance pyramid (which we will look at in Chapter 15) explicitly highlight the role of non-financial factors in shaping an organisation's performance.

We will also look in more detail at the impact of quality on an organisation's performance in Chapter 13, and the importance of employees and human resource management in organisations' performance in Chapter 14 of this Study Text.

More generally, note that most of the requirements in the section of the Study Guide covered by this chapter require you to 'discuss' the significance of NFPIs in different circumstances, or the difficulties in interpreting data on qualitative issues. In other words, you need to be able to do more than just list potential NFPIs which could be useful to an organisation. Instead you will need to apply your knowledge to specific scenarios, and discuss **how** the NFPIs could be useful in those scenarios.

Exam focus point

A question in the June 2012 exam provided candidates with a range of operational data for three airline companies and then asked candidates to use appropriate performance indicators in order to analyse the airlines' performance.

1 Financial and non-financial performance indicators

FAST FORWARD

If organisations concentrate solely on financial performance indicators, important goals and objectives may get overlooked. And, although financial indicators can be used to measure performance, they give little insight into the drivers which have caused an organisation to perform as it has.

While it is important for organisations to measure and monitor their financial performance, there may be disadvantages to focusing solely on financial performance.

1.1 Concentration on too few variables

If performance measurement systems focus entirely on those items which can be expressed in monetary terms, managers will **concentrate solely on those variables** and **ignore** other important variables that cannot be expressed in monetary terms.

For example, pressure from senior management to **cut costs and raise productivity** will produce **short-term benefits** in cost control but, in the **long term**, managerial performance and motivation is likely to be affected, labour turnover will increase and product quality will fall.

Reductions in cost can easily be measured and recorded in performance reports; employee morale cannot. **Performance reports** should therefore **include** not only costs and revenues but also **other important variables**, to give an indication of expected future results from present activity.

1.2 Lack of information on quality

Traditional responsibility accounting systems also fail to provide **information on the quality or importance of operations**. Consider the following brief example.

The purchasing department in an organisation regularly achieved its budget targets for the cost of all the expense items it purchased. Looking at the department's performance purely in financial terms (eg actual expenditure vs budget) might suggest that the department was well managed and effective. However, the department provided a poor service to the other departments in the organisation which produced finished goods. The purchasing department had selected low-cost suppliers who provided poor quality materials and frequently failed to deliver materials on time. This caused much wasted effort in chasing up orders and jeopardised the company's ability to deliver to its customers on time, and to provide them with products which met their quality expectations.

(We will look at the relationship between quality management and performance management in more detail in Chapter 13.)

1.3 Measuring success, not ensuring success

Financial performance indicators have been said to simply **measure success**. What organisations also require, however, are performance **indicators that ensure success**. Some of these indicators, which are **linked** to an organisation's **critical success factors** such as quality and flexibility, will be **non-financial** in nature.

For example, consider a pizza delivery company. When a customer is choosing which pizza company to buy their pizza from, key factors in their decision will be the price of the pizza, the toppings available and the taste of the pizza. However, they could also be influenced by the time they will have to wait for their pizza to be delivered. If one company can deliver their pizza in 20 minutes, but another one says they will only be able to deliver the pizza in an hour, there is a good chance the customer will choose to place their order with the first company.

It is possible that the speed of delivery could even become a factor which one of the pizza delivery companies uses to differentiate itself from its rivals, in which case it will be very important for that company to measure how long it takes to deliver its pizzas to its customers, because 'delivery time' has effectively become one of its critical success factors.

Equally, NFPIs can identify areas where an organisation's **performance is currently relatively weak**, and therefore need to be improved in order to make the organisation more competitive. For example, in the pizza delivery example, the second company might find that it needs to reduce the time it takes to deliver its pizzas to make itself more competitive.

1.3.1 Competitive position

As the previous point suggests, in an increasingly competitive business environment, non-financial aspects of performance are likely to be crucial to maintaining a company's competitive success.

Companies (particularly those pursuing differentiation strategies) are also competing in terms of **product quality, delivery, reliability, after-sales service** and **customer satisfaction**. If these variables are important elements in a company achieving its strategy successfully, then it follows that the company should also measure its performance in respect of them.

In this context it could also be useful to think of a company's relationship with its customers.

Many companies are now looking to use **relationship marketing** techniques to help build longer-term relationships and loyalty among their customers. The quality of service given to customers (including after-sales service) and customer satisfaction are likely to be very important in maintaining these relationships with customers.

This again highlights the importance of measuring how well a company is performing in such areas.

1.3.2 Leading and lagging indicators

The way in which non-financial indicators can allow an organisation to assess how well it is performing against its critical success factors also means they can act as leading indicators, whereas most traditional financial indicators tend to be lagging indicators, reporting on past performance and past events.

As such, lagging indicators do not necessarily help managers or directors to understand the future challenges an organisation will face. By contrast, leading indicators can point to future performance successes or problems. For example, declining customer satisfaction levels could point to future revenue issues and a longer-term erosion of the value of a company's brand.

1.4 Link to long-term organisational strategies

Another issue is that financial performance measurement systems generally focus on **annual or short-term performance** (against financial targets) so they may not be directly linked to longer-term organisation objectives. For example, financial performance measures will not assess how well an organisation is **meeting customer requirements**.

However, non-financial objectives (such as achieving customer loyalty and new product development) may be vital in achieving – and sustaining – profitability, competitiveness and other longer-term strategic goals.

Once again, there is potentially a **trade-off between the short term and the long term** here. For example, new product development may be an important strategic goal, but the costs involved in research and development may hinder short-term accounting performance.

1.5 Interaction of financial and non-financial performance indicators

The reference to new product development in the previous section also highlights the **importance of the interaction between financial and non-financial performance indicators**. For example, measuring the number of new products developed in a period is an NFPI, but developing new products is only valuable to an organisation if they help it to increase revenue and profitability.

Financial and non-financial performance indicators interact with each other even though they measure separate activities or aspects of performance.

NFPIs looking at production performance, for example, **measure activity but not cost**. However, activity and cost are linked. For instance, if there are problems with the **quality** of output from a production process, then the goods produced will have to be reworked and fixed before they can be shipped to customers. This reworking will add to **production costs**. Therefore, if the organisation improves quality standards in its processes, reworking costs will be reduced.

Equally, if the company is having to rework goods, this may delay production schedules. However, if the organisation also has a target for **on-time deliveries** it could face a dilemma. If the goods are delayed in production, then they may have to be delivered by express courier or some other out of hours delivery service to ensure they are delivered on time. However, this would increase delivery cost compared with a standard delivery service. So, if management want to focus on the cost of deliveries, they may have to accept a lower number of on-time deliveries. However, in turn, if customers do not receive their goods on time, they may not place any repeat orders with the company.

This illustrates the different aspects of both financial and non-financial performance that management need to consider, but also indicates that they may, on occasion, need to accept a trade-off between the two.

Another common example of this is the relationship between market share (non-financial) and profit margin (financial). If an organisation is trying to increase its **market share**, it may try to do this by **discounting** its products or offering some kind of **special offers** on them. While the discounts and offers may enable the organisation to gain market share (at least in the short term before competitors react) they may also lead to lower profit margins (for example as discounts reduce the revenue received per product sold).

We can also see the link between financial and non-financial performance in relation to **customer service**. For example, if customers receive good-quality service from an organisation, they are more likely to be loyal to that organisation and use it again than if they have received poor service. In this way, there can be a direct link between good-quality service, customer retention, and future sales revenue.

Exam focus point

An approach which explicitly combines **financial** and **non-financial performance indicators** is the **balanced scorecard**, with its four perspectives of: financial; customer; internal business; and innovation and learning. By integrating the four perspectives, the scorecard highlights the importance of satisfying customer needs, internal business process efficiency, and learning and development in contributing to the overall financial success of a company. As such, the scorecard suggests the importance of setting non-financial performance targets, and measuring performance against those targets, as well as measuring traditional financial performance targets.

We will look at the balanced scorecard in more detail in Chapter 15 later in this Study Text.

The **performance pyramid** (which we also look at in more detail in Chapter 15) also highlights the way that a range of objectives focusing on customer satisfaction, flexibility and productivity will be necessary in order to support an organisation's financial performance and market position.

Exam focus point

In a similar way, Fitzgerald *et al*'s **results and determinants analysis** also explicitly combines financial and non-financial aspects of performance in relation to **service industries**.

This analysis looks at the **competitive** and **financial results** which can be used to measure an organisation's performance, and then the **determinants** which underpin that performance.

Results

(a) **Competitive performance**, focusing on factors such as sales growth and market share
(b) **Financial performance**, concentrating on profitability, liquidity, capital structure and market ratios

Determinants (of those results)

(a) **Quality of service** looks at matters like reliability, responsiveness, courtesy, competence and availability/accessibility. These can be measured by customer satisfaction surveys.

(b) **Flexibility** relates to an organisation's ability to deliver at the right speed to meet customer requirements, to respond to precise customer specifications, and to cope with fluctuations in demand.

(c) **Resource utilisation** considers how efficiently resources are being utilised. This can be problematic because of the complexity of the inputs to a service and the outputs from it and because some of the inputs are supplied by the customer.

(d) **Innovation** is assessed in terms of both the innovation process and the success of individual innovations. Individual innovations can be measured in terms of whether they have improved the organisation's ability to meet the other five performance criteria.

We will look at the importance of results and determinants again in Chapter 15 of this Study Text, alongside our analysis of Fitzgerald and Moon's building block model.

2 The significance of non-financial performance indicators

For many organisations, their employees are vital assets in enabling them to implement their strategies successfully. As such, given the importance of employees to an organisation's competitive success, it is therefore equally important that the organisation gathers, and monitors, information about its employees.

2.1 Performance indicators in relation to employees

FAST FORWARD

Non-financial performance indicators can usefully be applied to **employees**. This could be particularly important in service industries, where the staff providing a service, and the way that service is provided, can have a significant impact on a customer's impression of the service, and their satisfaction with it.

One of the many criticisms of traditional accounting performance measurement systems is that they do not measure the **skills, morale and training of the workforce**, which can be as valuable to an organisation as its tangible assets. For example, if employees have not been trained in the manufacturing practices required to achieve the objectives of the new manufacturing environment, an organisation is unlikely to be successful.

Employee attitudes and morale can be measured by **surveying** employees. Education and skills levels, promotion and training, absenteeism and labour turnover for the employees for whom each manager is responsible can also be monitored. For example, if the level of employee turnover in a department is high, an organisation should investigate why. Is it because of poor management in that department, or because of issues with job design? Either way, having a high labour turnover is likely to be disadvantageous for the organisation – due to the time and costs involved in continually having to recruit and train new employees.

2.1.1 Service industries

As we discussed in Chapter 4, one of the characteristics of service industries is inseparability, and this inseparability means that the employees providing the service to customers are likely to have a significant influence on the satisfaction gained by the customer, and on the customer's perception of the service.

As such, employee-based performance indicators should be seen as particularly important in service industries.

For example, the **morale** of restaurant staff could directly affect the welcome and the service they give to customers, which in turn could affect the customers' impression of the restaurant and whether they choose to eat there again.

Aviva

The insurance company Aviva has recognised that as well as reporting on financial performance it is also important to report on the non-financial aspects of its business.

It considers that its employees and customers are fundamental to the success of its business, so they form the basis of its non-financial performance measures which include employee engagement and customer advocacy.

Employee engagement represents the degree to which people believe Aviva is a great place to work, and are contributing to help meet the company's collective goals and ambitions.

Customer advocacy provides an indication of expected customer retention levels and the opportunities for cross-selling of the company's portfolio of products.

2.2 Performance indicators in relation to product/service quality

FAST FORWARD

Indicators such as **customer satisfaction scores** and **repeat business ratings** can act as useful surrogates for product/service quality. If customer satisfaction scores or customer retention levels are falling, this could be a warning that the underlying quality of an organisation's product/service is also deteriorating.

The quality of a product that a customer buys from an organisation, or of the service they receive from the organisation, will be critical in determining the customers' satisfaction level. In turn, a customer's degree of satisfaction with a product or service will determine whether they will make a repeat purchase.

2.2.1 Measuring customer satisfaction

However rigorous an organisation's quality procedures are, sometimes substandard products will be produced, or the level of service a customer receives will be below the standard they expect. On such occasions, customers may complain about the product/service they have received.

'Complaints' – in the form of letters of complaint, returned goods, penalty discounts, claims under guarantee or requests for visits by service engineers – should be monitored, because the volume of complaints could provide an indicator of the standard of the underlying product/service. (Customer comments on social media should also be monitored, because this could also highlight areas where customers have been dissatisfied with a product or service.)

However, monitoring complaints does not necessarily give an accurate picture of quality. Some customers may not bother to complain about a product or service they were not satisfied with; they will simply choose to buy it from an alternative supplier in future.

Consequently, many organisations adopt a more proactive approach to monitoring customer satisfaction – by surveying their customers on a regular basis. They use the feedback to obtain an index of customer satisfaction which is used to identify quality problems before they affect profits (through lost sales).

2.2.2 Customer satisfaction, repeat business and loyalty

Maintaining customer satisfaction levels is very important to a business, because satisfied customers are most likely to be loyal and make repeat orders with that business. As a result, high levels of customer satisfaction should lead to higher and more stable revenues for a business, and increased profitability. This therefore emphasises the importance of measuring customer satisfaction levels.

In relation to customer loyalty, the customer's perspective of whether they had received good service can often play a key role in determining whether they will continue to choose one company over another. Importantly, a company may **think** it is providing good-quality service, but if the customers disagree then they are less likely to remain loyal to it. This reiterates the importance of finding out what customers actually feel about the levels of service they have received; for example, by obtaining customer feedback.

Research conducted by the consultancy firm Bain & Company found that an increase of 5% in customer retention can increase profits by anywhere between 25% and 95%. The same study found that it costs between six and seven times more to gain a new customer than to keep an existing one.

Similarly, the International Customer Service Association reported that 68% of customers stop doing business with a company because of poor service. Yet 95% of dissatisfied customers would continue to do business with a company if their problem was solved quickly and satisfactorily.

2.3 Quality of service

Exam focus point

> In Chapter 4, we looked at the changing accounting needs of modern service-orientated businesses compared with traditional manufacturing businesses. Equally, however, a key aspect of performance in service businesses is the quality of service which they provide for their customers. Consequently, it is also important for such businesses to measure the quality of service which they are providing.

Service quality is measured principally by **qualitative measures**, although some quantitative measures are used by some businesses.

Service businesses, such as restaurants, hotels, airlines and software developers, need to research the **needs of their customers** to be able to measure how well they are performing.

These needs are likely to vary according to the nature of the business: for example, reliability is important in a bank; comfort is more likely to be important in a hotel.

The **SERVQUAL** methodology (developed by Zeithanl, Parasurman and Berry) covers five dimensions of service quality. Customer feedback is sought in relation to:

(a) **Tangibles**: For example, appearance of facilities; is equipment up to date; are staff well dressed?

(b) **Reliability**: For example, are bookings processed accurately; if services are promised by a certain time, are they delivered by that time?

(c) **Responsiveness**: Do staff react to queries quickly, and courteously?

(d) **Assurance**: Do staff inspire confidence; if customers have problems, are staff sympathetic and reassuring?

(e) **Empathy**: Are customers treated as individuals; do staff have the customers' best interests at heart?

The SERVQUAL methodology then allows businesses to improve their performance by gauging the gap between how well they think they are performing and customers' expectations of how well they should be performing. Staff and managers may believe they are delivering a good-quality service; however, customers may not agree.

The following table (based on Fitzgerald *et al*) identifies **factors** pertaining to service quality, the **measures** used to assess them, and the **means of obtaining the information** in the context of British Airports Authority (BAA), a mass transport service.

Service quality factors	Measures	Mechanisms
Access	Walking distances Ease of finding way around	Customer survey and internal operational data Customer survey
Aesthetics/appearance	Staff appearance Airport's appearance Quantity, quality, appearance of food	Customer survey Customer survey Management inspection
Availability	Equipment availability	Internal fault monitoring system and customer survey Customer survey and internal operational data

Service quality factors	Measures	Mechanisms
Cleanliness/tidiness	Cleanliness of environment and equipment	Customer survey and management inspection
Comfort	Crowdedness of airport	Customer survey and management inspection
Communication	Information clarity Clarity of labelling and pricing	Customer survey Management inspection
Competence	Competence of staff in performing duties and answering customer queries	Internal operational data Customer survey
Courtesy	Courtesy of staff in dealing with customers	Customer survey and management inspection
Friendliness	Staff attitude and helpfulness	Customer survey and management inspection
Reliability	Number of equipment faults	Internal fault monitoring systems
Responsiveness	Staff responsiveness	Customer survey
Security	Efficiency of security checks Number of urgent safety reports	Customer survey Internal operational data

Case Study — TNT

TNT is a leading global express distribution, logistics and international mail company which moves documents, consignments and business mail.

TNT's philosophy focuses on the customer and aims to be their business partner, devising solutions for all of their customers' distribution needs. TNT's mission is to exceed its customers' expectations in the transfer of their goods and documents around the world.

TNT is serious about providing distinctive levels of service quality and customer care to its customers, and works hard to derive improvements from problems and complaints. It uses a worldwide reporting system to identify all failures in detail, without exception. Then a weekly in-depth root-cause analysis is used to identify and solve problems.

By focusing on complaints data, TNT has been able to dramatically improve its performance, including a major improvement in the number of on-time deliveries, and a similarly dramatic reduction in missed pick-ups. This in turn resulted in fewer problems for staff, and led to a reduction in employee turnover and absenteeism.

3 Interpreting data about qualitative issues 12/14

FAST FORWARD

Whereas quantitative factors relate to quantities or amounts and so can be measured relatively easily, **qualitative factors** relate to quality and can often be more difficult to measure, and can be very difficult to express in monetary terms.

3.1 Qualitative information and difficulties in interpreting data

One of the major problems in interpreting qualitative data is that it is based on people's opinions and judgements, and therefore it is **subjective**.

For example, one person's assessment of the quality of service they have received could be different to another person's, despite the quality of service being provided remaining essentially the same.

Often the interpretation of qualitative issues is subject to **personal preference and taste**. For example, television talent shows (such as 'The X Factor') have a panel of judges who compare the quality of the performances they have seen and then provide feedback on them. However, the judges often differ as to which performances they thought were best, reflecting the subjective nature of comparing the quality of different performances.

There can also be problems in relation to how qualitative data is recorded and processed. One way to try to overcome the problems is by **converting qualitative data into quantitative data**. For example, continuing the idea of television talent shows, instead of just giving their comments on performances, the judges also give the different contestants a mark. Then the acts can be ranked according to the totals of the marks they have received.

Organisations can do something similar in order to measure performance in qualitative areas. For example, if they want to record customers' feedback about the quality of service they have received, they can ask the customers to complete a short survey on it.

Surveys often use scoring systems to capture data on service or staff attitudes. This can be aggregated for management to get a feel for, say, employee or customer satisfaction. For example, customer service surveys may ask customers to indicate how satisfied they are with the level of service they have received, on a scale of 1 to 5, with '1' representing 'Very satisfied' and '5' representing 'Not at all satisfied'. However, scoring systems are still subjective, and there is also a tendency to score towards the middle. In general, people tend to feel more comfortable selecting scores in the range 2 to 4, rather than using the extreme scores of 1 or 5.

3.2 Trends and time series

One way of reducing the impact of the subjectivity in qualitative non-financial data is to look at trends in performance rather than one-off metrics.

In this respect, the average scores from customer service surveys over a period of time can be recorded as a time series, and a trend line (a regression line) can be derived from them. This trend line will show whether performance is improving or getting worse over time.

However, as with any time series analysis, there are different **components of the time series** which it may be necessary to identify.

(a) An underlying **trend**

(b) **Seasonal variations** or fluctuations

(c) Cycles, or **cyclical variations**

(d) Non-recurring, **random variations** which may be caused by unforeseen circumstances, such as a technological change or a fire at a factory or warehouse

Exam focus point

Part of a question in the December 2014 exam asked candidates to discuss the difficulties of measuring qualitative factors of performance, and then to suggest ways these difficulties could be overcome.

4 Branding and brand awareness

FAST FORWARD

Brand strength can play an important part in generating customer loyalty and, as a result, repeat business.

4.1 Branding 12/12

Brand identity conveys a lot of information very quickly and concisely. This helps customers to identify the goods or services and thus helps to **create customer loyalty** to the brand. It is therefore a means of increasing or maintaining sales. (In some extreme cases, a strong brand could even act as a barrier to entry, preventing potential entrants from entering a market, if those potential entrants think customers will not be persuaded to move away from the brands they currently buy.)

Where a brand image promotes an idea of **quality**, a customer will be disappointed if their experience of a product or service fails to live up to expectations. Quality assurance and control is therefore of utmost importance. It is essentially a problem for **service industries**, such as hotels, airlines and retail stores, where there is **less possibility** than in the manufacturing sector of **detecting and rejecting the work of an operator before it reaches the customer**. Bad behaviour by an employee in a face to face encounter with a customer will **reflect on** the **entire company** and possibly deter the customer from using any of the company's services again.

According to the marketing guru Kotler, a brand is 'a name, term, sign, symbol or design or combination of them, intended to identify the goods or services of one seller or group of sellers and to differentiate them from those of competitors.'

Brands convey messages to customers, for example denoting quality or reliability, fashionability ('coolness') or tradition.

Branding messages are usually qualitative rather than focusing on price, and one of the perceived advantages of branding is that by creating an 'identity' for a product an organisation can reduce the importance of price differentials between their product and rival products. This may in turn allow them to charge a higher price for their product.

However, some brands will position themselves on the basis of value for money so branding does not necessarily mean charging premium prices. Moreover, certain consumers reject 'branded products' especially when considering **value for money**. This can be seen in supermarkets where shoppers choose generic (own label) products in preference to brand names, because the own label products are seen as being cheaper but having the same use.

In this respect, branding is perhaps most appropriate to organisations or products which are following a differentiation strategy. Branding is a form of **product differentiation** that can make it possible to charge premium prices for a product (or service) and therefore earn higher profits than if products had to be sold at a lower price. (Think, for example, of designer clothes labels. The kudos attached to the brand means that the clothes can be sold for significantly higher prices than non-branded equivalents.)

Luxury brands use quality and exclusiveness to appeal to consumers. Recent reinventions of 'tired' brands include Burberry where a new designer has extended the brand life by reinventing the house style and designing it into new products. Extending the brand life in this way means that the business can continue to benefit from the status of an existing brand. Burberry had a loyal customer base who bought the signature check products and these are still produced. It was also able to extend the brand life by attracting younger and high-spending customers who prefer modern interpretations but associated with established quality. This represents additional revenue.

4.1.1 Brand awareness and brand loyalty

When assessing the impact that a brand could have on business performance it is important to distinguish between brand awareness and brand loyalty.

Brand awareness indicates the likelihood that consumers will recognise a brand, or recognise the existence of a product or organisation in the market. **Recall tests** can be used to assess brand awareness – for example, showing consumers a brand logo and seeing if they know what brand the logo represents. Creating brand awareness is an important step in promoting a product or service, but simply making consumers aware of a product does not mean that they will buy it.

By contrast, **brand loyalty** means that consumers are committed to a brand and make repeated purchases of that brand over time. Brand loyalty (and the repeat business it generates) is very valuable to companies, so many will have marketing strategies to try to cultivate loyalty among their customers, thereby increasing **customer retention rates** and the level of repeat purchases.

An example of the way organisations try to increase brand loyalty is in the use of reward programmes by supermarkets (for example, Tesco's Clubcard or 'Nectar'), attracting customers by earning points each time they buy goods from that store or from a consortium of participating retailers.

However, as well as encouraging loyalty, these cards provide the retailer with valuable data about customer purchases and behaviours. The retailer can then use this data to create a profile of what kind of people its cardholders are; by using data mining techniques it can also identify patterns in their purchases. The resulting information can then be used by the retailer to target its marketing campaigns – for example, offering cardholders deals on the products which they are likely to buy, thereby increasing the likelihood they will continue to shop with that retailer, and continue to provide revenue for that retailer.

Case Study **Branding and perception**

The 2014 Interbrand Report of Top Global Brands identified Coca-Cola as the third most valuable global brand (behind Apple and Google) with a brand value of $81,563 million.

Coca-Cola itself has acknowledged that only a relatively small percentage of the company's value lies in its plant and machinery, because most of the value lies in its brands.

Strong brand names have positive effects on consumer perceptions and preferences.

Jobber, in *Principles and Practice of Marketing,* highlights a striking example of this.

Two matched samples of consumers were asked to taste Diet Coke and Diet Pepsi, and state a preference between the two drinks. The first group carried out a 'blind test' (that is, they tasted the drinks without being told which one was which). The second group carried out an 'open test' (that is, they knew which drink was which when tasting them).

The results of the tests were as follows.

	'Blind' tasting	'Open' tasting
Prefer Diet Coke	44%	65%
Prefer Diet Pepsi	51%	23%
No clear preference	5%	12%

The tests clearly show how a strong brand name influenced perceptions and preferences towards Diet Coke.

This kind of positive brand equity is likely to result in high customer loyalty and low price sensitivity, which in turn should enable market-leading brands to be able to sustain high profits.

4.2 Company profile

Company profile is **how an organisation is perceived by a range of stakeholders**. For example, stakeholders may have a negative attitude towards an organisation, perhaps as a result of an ethical issue or a crisis that has struck the organisation and the associated media comment.

Similarly, a company's profile could be affected by the **quality of its staff** (for example, how well they deal with customers or how promptly they respond to queries), and the **quality of its products**. This again highlights the importance of quality as a determinant of an organisation's performance – and we will look at quality in more detail in the next chapter of this Study Text.

Case Study **Toyota – product recalls**

Toyota has traditionally been admired for the quality of its manufacturing excellence. However, in recent years a number of product recalls have raised concerns that the quality level of Toyota's products has fallen in recent years.

In 2009 and early 2010 Toyota recalled approximately 12 million vehicles worldwide due to concerns about their accelerator pedals becoming 'stuck' (sometimes as a result of floor mats becoming stuck underneath them) and causing unintended acceleration.

Toyota's reputation and sales suffered badly in the aftermath of these recalls, largely because the problems had been linked to deadly accidents.

In October 2012 Toyota recalled more than 7 million vehicles worldwide in relation to faulty window switches. Four weeks later (November 2012), it recalled 2.7 million cars worldwide because of problems with the steering wheel and water pump system.

At the time of the recall in November 2012, a Toyota spokesperson said that no accidents had yet been reported due to this fault. Nonetheless, the total number of recalls in October and November 2012 was close to 10 million.

The recalls in 2012 were precautionary, but the scale of them still had the potential to cause significant damage to Toyota's brand and its reputation as a producer of high-quality cars.

However, some analysts felt that the impact of the 2012 recalls would be less damaging. Koichi Sugimoto, an auto analyst with BNP Paribas in Tokyo, said: 'Nobody is perfect. Vehicles nowadays are very complicated ... The company is taking appropriate measures to fix the problems, so I don't think this will cause significant damage to Toyota's reputation.'

Based on: Zuk, M. (2013), Yet another recall hits automotive giant's reputation. The New Economy. Online. Available from: http://www.theneweconomy.com/business/yet-another-toyota-recall-hits-automotive-giants-reputation

[Accessed 26 January 2016]

Market research can determine company profile and **marketing campaigns** can be used to improve a company's profile if necessary.

Exam focus point

A question in the December 2012 exam asked candidates to discuss the impact of brand loyalty and brand awareness on a company, from both a customer and an internal business process perspective. The question also asked candidates to evaluate suitable measures for brand loyalty and brand awareness.

In this respect, it was important to recognise that brand awareness plays an important role in attracting new customers, whereas the value of brand loyalty comes from the retention of existing customers. The performance measures suggested should have reflected this, although the examination team commented (in the post-exam report) that only a minority of candidates made this distinction.

Chapter Roundup

- If organisations concentrate solely on financial performance indicators, important goals and objectives may get overlooked. And, although financial indicators can be used to measure performance, they give little insight into the drivers which have caused an organisation to perform as it has.
- Non-financial performance indicators can usefully be applied to **employees**. This could be particularly important in service industries, where the staff providing a service, and the way that service is provided, can have a significant impact on a customer's impression of the service, and their satisfaction with it.
- Indicators such as **customer satisfaction scores** and **repeat business ratings** can act as useful surrogates for product/service quality. If customer satisfaction scores or customer retention levels are falling, this could be a warning that the underlying quality of an organisation's product/service is also deteriorating.
- Whereas quantitative factors relate to quantities or amounts and so can be measured relatively easily, **qualitative factors** relate to quality and can often be more difficult to measure, and can be very difficult to express in monetary terms.
- Brand strength can play an important part in generating customer loyalty and, as a result, repeat business.

Quick Quiz

1 Which of the following is/are true:

(i) Non-financial performance indicators are always qualitative.

(ii) Non-financial performance indicators are less open to manipulation than financial performance indicators.

A Neither of them
B (i) only
C (ii) only
D Both of them

2 What is the main difficulty in interpreting qualitative data?

3 Managers are increasingly using non-financial as well as financial performance indicators. List some reasons why you think this might be happening.

4 Why are non-financial performance indicators important in relation to employees?

5 Is the following statement true or false?

The main benefit of an increase in brand loyalty will be that it helps a company to increase its revenue through the acquisition of additional, new customers.

Answers to Quick Quiz

1 A

Although non-financial performance indicators focus on factors of a non-financial nature, they can still include both quantitative and qualitative measures. So (i) is not true.

Both financial and non-financial performance measures could be open to manipulation. However, if anything, the subjective nature of many non-financial measures makes them more open to manipulation than financial measures are. So (ii) is not true either.

2 The data is often based on a person's opinion or judgement and is therefore subjective, because opinions and judgements vary from person to person.

3 Three possible reasons are:

(a) Financial indicators concentrate on too few variables.
(b) Financial indicators give no information on quality.
(c) Financial indicators measure success but don't, in themselves, help businesses to be successful.

4 A number of the aspects of employees' performance (such as skill, morale and attitude) are qualitative and cannot be expressed in financial terms. However, these aspects of employee performance can have a significant impact on an organisation's performance. For example, poor morale and attitude may translate into poor customer service and, in turn, poor customer retention rates.

5 False

The main benefits of an increase in brand loyalty will be that it helps a company increase its retention rates or the level of repeat purchases among its existing customers; but brand loyalty in itself will not primarily help to attract new customers. An increase in brand awareness would be more likely to help attract new customers.

Now try the question below from the Practice Question Bank

Number	Level	Marks	Approximate time
Q12	Examination	20	40 mins

The role of quality in management information and performance measurement systems

13

Topic list	Syllabus reference
1 Quality overview	-
2 Modern Japanese business practices and techniques	D5(a)
3 Quality management and performance management	D5(b)
4 Quality in management information systems	D5(c)
5 The qualities of good information and good management information systems	D5(c)
6 Six Sigma and quality improvement	D5(d)

Introduction

The achievement of a consistent, desired level of quality is a vital feature of putting strategy into action.

In this chapter we will examine a range of approaches to quality management, derived from Japanese business practices.

However, as well as looking at the importance of quality in relation to an organisation's performance, we will look at the importance of having high - quality management information systems.

Study guide

		Intellectual level
D5	**The role of quality in management information and performance measurement systems**	
(a)	Discuss and evaluate the application of Japanese business practices and management accounting techniques, including: (i) Kaizen costing (ii) Target costing (iii) Just-in-time (iv) Total Quality Management	3
(b)	Assess the relationship of quality management to the performance management strategy of an organisation, including the costs of quality.	3
(c)	Justify the need for, and assess the characteristics of, quality in management information systems.	3
(d)	Discuss and apply Six Sigma as a quality improvement method using tools such as DMAIC for implementation.	2

Exam guide

Quality has been an important theme in management thinking for the last 50 years. Consideration of quality is a fundamental part of strategy, and the word 'quality' is often mentioned in organisations' mission statements. Equally, as we discussed in the previous chapter, product or service quality is likely to have a significant impact on customer satisfaction and customer retention. Questions on quality could either be standalone questions on quality issues and their impact on an organisation's performance, or they could be integrated with other topics, such as IT systems and the quality of management information available within an organisation.

Exam focus point

Part of one of the questions in the June 2013 exam asked candidates to assess how information about the various quality-related costs could be used, and improved, to assist cost reduction and quality management in an organisation.

The first section of the chapter provides some background context, explaining the history of quality management. This will help you see how modern approaches have developed. Some of the ideas here may be familiar, if only through phrases such as quality circles. However, you will not be expected to write on the history of quality management in your exam.

1 Quality overview

FAST FORWARD

Quality management has developed from an inspection-based process to a philosophy of business that emphasises customer satisfaction, the elimination of waste and the acceptance of responsibility for conformance with quality specifications at all stages of all business processes.

1.1 Traditional approaches to quality

There has been a rise in awareness of quality and the systems that support it, to the extent that it has become of **strategic significance**. Quality is now considered to be of fundamental importance to many organisations. Indeed, many firms pursue a **strategy of differentiation based on high quality**.

There was a time when quality was not measured as an output target, and when managers considered it something to be added onto a product rather than something that was integral to it. Quality control applied

largely to manufacturing and meant **inspection**, or identifying when defective items are being produced at an unacceptable level.

There are many problems with this approach.

(a) The inspection process itself **does not add value**: if it could be guaranteed that no defective items were produced, there would be no need for a separate inspection function.

(b) The **production of substandard products is a waste** of raw materials, machine time, human effort and overhead cost.

(c) The inspection department takes up possibly expensive **land and warehousing space**.

(d) The production of defects is **not compatible with newer production techniques** such as just-in-time: there is no time for inspection.

(e) **Working capital is tied up** in inventories that cannot be sold.

In other words, the inspection approach builds **waste** into the process, which is not acceptable: the resources it consumes can be put to better use.

1.2 The development of quality management

Quality management is not new. Below, we give a brief guide to some of the major ideas behind the development of quality management. An important theme running through this process is the gradual expansion of the quality idea from a **technique** forming part of the management of manufacturing output to its current status as a **philosophy of business** and vital component of strategy. Partly as a result of this development, the threshold level of quality capability has gradually risen, so that high quality standards are now taken for granted.

This last point is important. Threshold values of quality have increased in most organisations over the last few decades. Therefore, if an organisation wants to use 'high quality' as part of a differentiation strategy, then the levels of quality it must achieve must also increase, to maintain the differentiation from all the other organisations.

1.3 Deming

W Edwards Deming is one of the founding fathers of the quality movement. Deming's first job in this field was to use **statistical process control** to raise productivity in US factories during World War II. His ideas were adopted in Japan, once he was able to convince Japanese business leaders of their merits. Deming has asserted that over 90% of a company's problems can be corrected only by management, as management has the sole authority to change the system.

Deming's book *Out of the Crisis* listed 14 points for managers to adopt to improve quality and competitiveness. These are summarised as follows:

(a) Improving products and services must be a constant purpose of the organisation.

(b) Eliminate all waste. (This was especially important in Japan, which has few sources of raw materials.)

(c) Cease depending on mass inspection to achieve quality. This ties up resources and working capital in stocks.

(d) Price should not be the only consideration in choosing a supplier. Quality and reliability are also important.

(e) Improve the systems for production and service delivery. This reduces waste and enhances quality by ensuring the production system works optimally.

(f) Train people so they are better at working, and understand how to optimise production.

(g) Lead people.

(h) 'Drive out fear'.

(i) Break down barriers between staff areas.

(j) Get rid of slogans, exhortations, targets. These can be alienating.

(k) Get rid of numerical quotas. These encourage the wrong attitude to production.

(l) Enable people to take pride in work.

(m) Encourage 'education and self improvement for everyone'.

(n) Action should be taken to accomplish quality objectives.

The abandonment of mass inspection to assess quality implies that quality must be built in from the beginning, not added on at the end.

1.4 Crosby

Philip B Crosby is chiefly known for two concepts:

(a) **Zero defects**: There should never be any defects in a product. Some consider this to be an impossible ideal, and invoke the concept of diminishing returns. Alternatively, it can be seen as a slogan to employees.

(b) **Right first time**: This is another idea which holds that a product should not have to be corrected once it is built. It is thus a corollary of the zero defects concept.

Crosby proposes four standards that flesh out these concepts.

(a) Quality is **conformance to requirements**.
(b) The system for advancing quality is **prevention**, not appraisal.
(c) The **goal** should be zero defects.
(d) The importance of quality is measured by the cost of **not** having quality.

Crosby's ideas demonstrate a fundamental shift from a 'supervisory' culture of quality assurance to one where each individual takes full responsibility for his work: **quality is everyone's responsibility**.

1.5 Juran

Joseph Juran's book *Quality Control Handbook* was published in 1951. He also worked with Japanese industrialists in the years immediately after World War II and, with Deming, is credited with increasing Japan's industrial competitiveness.

While Deming's ideas are wide ranging and expand into considerations of leadership and management style, Juran was concerned with identifying **specific improvements for enhancing quality**. Juran's ideas are different in the following ways:

(a) The best approach to enhancing quality is to 'identify specific opportunities, evaluate their viability by using conventional methods such as return on investment, plan the selected project carefully, monitor their results'.

(b) Juran believes in the law of **diminishing returns**: there is an economic level of quality beyond which it is pointless to strive, because the costs outweigh the benefits.

(c) Juran believes that most quality problems derive from management systems and processes rather than poor workmanship.

Juran defines quality as 'fitness for use', which includes two elements:

(a) **Quality of design**, which can include the customer satisfactions built into the product
(b) **Quality of conformance**, in other words a lack of defects in the finished goods

1.6 Feigenbaum

Armand Feigenbaum appended the word 'total' to quality, thus emphasising the relevance of quality issues to **all areas of the operations of a business**. He is also noted for assessing the economic value of quality, as the value of many quality improvement measures is not exactly self-evident. In other words, he

stressed the importance of identifying the **costs** of quality, and the lack of quality, to prove that, in economic and accounting terms, 'prevention is better than cure'.

This involves changing the role of the quality control function (which inspected and rejected output) to one in which quality provided an effective system for quality maintenance.

(a) An **inspection role** is carried out after the event, after the wasteful and substandard production.

(b) A **planning role** would involve the design of systems and procedures to reduce the likelihood of sub-optimal production.

1.7 Ishikawa

The quality philosophy has been implemented most famously in Japan. According to some commentators, **design quality** rather than **conformance quality** has been responsible for much of the success of Japanese firms in some industries.

Ishikawa is noted for proposing **quality circles**, which are groups of selected workers delegated with the task of analysing the production process, and coming up with ideas to improve it. Success requires a commitment from the circle's membership, and a management willingness to take a back seat.

Quality circles are mainly management stimulated. Whatever the stated reasons are for instituting quality circles, the real reason for having quality circles is to motivate employees to improve quality.

2 Modern Japanese business practices and techniques

FAST FORWARD

Changes to the **competitive environment**, **product life cycles** and **customer requirements** have had a significant impact on the modern business environment.

2.1 Changing competitive environment

2.1.1 Management accounting and organisational culture

The relevance of organisational culture to management accounting can be explained in simple terms. The business of management accounting is to provide managers with information to help them run the business. **If the management accountant is not sensitive to the culture of their organisation they will not understand how it is run and will not know what sort of information to provide**. For example, a management accountant in a public sector organisation may need to focus on the effectiveness and efficiency of cost control, while a management accountant in a commercial entity may need to focus on how it is generating value for its shareholders.

Question **Management accounting and organisational culture**

Robert Waterman (co-author with Tom Peters of the classic text *In Search of Excellence*) published a book entitled *The Frontiers of Excellence* (1994), which argued that leading companies at the time, and those that had been successful over long periods, did not put the shareholders first. Instead, they concentrated on 'putting people first', the people in question being employees and customers.

How could a management accounting system foster such a culture, or undermine it?

Answer

A system to **foster** the 'people' culture would collect and analyse data about employee performance and customer reaction, provide the basis for rewards for what is good in these terms, and supply information that indicates to people how they could do better.

The culture would be **undermined** by a system that concentrates solely on reporting in figures and language aimed at the stock market.

Undoubtedly the most **profound influences** on Western corporate cultures since the 1990s have been ideas borrowed from **Japanese management**. 'Philosophies' such as just-in-time **(JIT)** and Total Quality Management (**TQM**) have a direct impact on business areas that have long been the preserve of accountants – purchasing and inventory control, quality costs, waste and scrap and so on.

Similarly, the Japanese **team working** approach is a radical change from the individualistic culture of the West, and this has further implications for performance measurement and reporting.

2.2 Total quality management (TQM)

One of the most significant developments in performance management has been the emphasis on quality. A key aspect of this has been a recognition of the **costs of quality**, which we will look at later in this chapter.

FAST FORWARD

In the context of **TQM**, quality means getting things right first time and improving continuously.

Key term

Total quality management (TQM) is the process of applying a zero defects philosophy to the management of all resources and relationships within an organisation as a means of developing and sustaining a culture of continuous improvement which focuses on meeting customers' expectations.

According to the Chartered Quality Institute, 'TQM is a way of thinking about goals, organisations, processes and people to ensure that the **right things are done right first time**.'

Importantly, the 'total' in TQM applies to the whole organisation, so it covers 'soft' issues (such as attitudes, cultures and behaviour) as well as operational systems and processes.

The following are key principles and characteristics of TQM programmes.

(a) **Customer focus**: Organisation-wide there must be acceptance that the only thing that matters is the customer. Organisations depend on their customers and so must strive to understand and meet customer needs and expectations.

(b) **Internal customers and internal suppliers**: All parts of the organisation are involved in quality issues, and need to work together. Every person and every activity in the organisation affects the work done by others. The work done by an internal supplier for an internal customer will eventually affect the quality of the product or service to the external customer.

(c) **Identify causes of defects**: Instead of relying on inspection to a predefined level of quality, the cause of the defect in the first place should be prevented.

(d) **Quality culture**: Every person within an organisation has an impact on quality, and it is the responsibility of all employees to get quality right. Each employee or group of employees must be **personally responsible** for defect-free production or service in their area of the organisation.

(e) **Zero defects**: There should be a move away from 'acceptable' quality levels. Any level of defects must be unacceptable.

(f) **Right first time**: All departments should try obsessively to get things right first time; this applies to misdirected phone calls and typing errors as much as to production.

(g) **Quality certification programmes** should be introduced.

(h) **Costs of poor quality**: The cost of poor quality should be emphasised; good quality generates savings (for example, through not having to rework items with defects, or through a reduction in the level of refunds or replacement products given to customers).

More generally, the following are also important principles of quality management:

Leadership. Management create an environment in which people become fully involved in achieving the organisation's objectives.

People. People are key assets across all levels of an organisation, so the organisation needs to ensure their talents and abilities are used to best effect for the organisation's benefit.

Process approach. Results can be achieved more efficiently when resources and activities are managed as a process.

Continuous improvement. An organisation should seek continuous improvement as one of its objectives.

Factual approach to decision making. Effective decisions are based on the logical analysis of data and information, rather than being based on intuition and guesswork.

2.3 Just-in-time (JIT) systems 12/11, 12/15

FAST FORWARD

JIT aims for zero inventory and perfect quality and operates by demand-pull. It consists of **JIT purchasing** and **JIT production** and results in lower investment requirements, space savings, greater customer satisfaction and increased flexibility.

Key terms

Just-in-time (JIT) is 'A system whose objective is to produce or to procure products or components as they are required by a customer or for use, rather than for inventory.

A JIT system is a "pull" system, which responds to demand, in contrast to a "push" system, in which inventories act as buffers between the different elements of the system, such as purchasing, production and sales.'

Just-in-time production is 'A production system which is driven by demand for finished products, whereby each component on a production line is produced only when needed for the next stage.'

Just-in-time purchasing is 'A purchasing system in which material purchases are contracted so that the receipt and usage of material, to the maximum extent possible, coincide.'

(Chartered Institute of Management Accountants (CIMA), *Official Terminology*)

Although often described as a technique, JIT is more of a **philosophy or approach to management** since it encompasses a **commitment to continuous improvement** and the **search for excellence** in the design and operation of the production management system.

In this respect, the aims of JIT are aligned with those of TQM, since both focus on eliminating waste and non value added activities, and on producing goods which have zero defects.

Exam focus point

Part of a question in the December 2011 exam asked candidates to evaluate the effect that moving to JIT purchasing and production systems has on a company, and what impact it would have on the performance measures the company uses.

Quality and reliability are key elements of a successful JIT system, so it will be important for a company which uses a JIT system to introduce measures to assess how well it is performing in these areas if it does not already do so.

2.3.1 Essential elements of JIT

The table below identifies the key elements of JIT systems.

Element	Detail
JIT purchasing	Parts and raw materials should be purchased as near as possible to the time they are needed, using small frequent deliveries against bulk contracts. Inventory levels are therefore minimised.
Close relationship with suppliers	In a JIT environment, the responsibility for the quality of goods lies with the supplier. A long-term commitment between supplier and customer should therefore be established. If an organisation has confidence that suppliers will deliver material of 100% quality, on time, so that there will be no rejects, returns and hence no consequent production delays, usage of materials can be matched with delivery of materials and inventories can be kept at near zero levels. However, flexibility and establishing good communication channels are also important aspects of the relationship with suppliers.
Uniform loading	All parts of the productive process should be operated at a speed which matches the rate at which the final product is demanded by the customer. Production runs will therefore be shorter and there will be smaller inventories of finished goods because output is being matched more closely to demand (and so storage costs will be reduced).
Set-up time reduction	No value is added during set-up times, so set-ups are non value added activities. Consequently, time spent setting up machinery should be minimised.
Simplification	There is a constant focus on the simplification of products and processes in order to maximise the utilisation of available resources.
Machine cells	Machines or workers should be grouped by product or component instead of by the type of work performed. Products can flow from machine to machine without having to wait for the next stage of processing or returning to stores. Lead times and work in progress are thus reduced.
Quality	Production management should seek to eliminate scrap and defective units during production, and to avoid the need for reworking of units since this stops the flow of production and leads to late deliveries to customers. Product quality and production quality are important 'drivers' in a JIT system. Also, note that the fundamental requirement in relation to quality is that the level of quality satisfies the customer.
Pull system ('kanban')	Products/components are only produced when needed by the next process. Nothing is produced in anticipation of need, to then remain in inventory, consuming resources.
Preventive maintenance	Production systems must be reliable and prompt, without unforeseen delays and breakdowns.
Employee involvement	Workers within each machine cell should be trained to operate each machine within that cell and to be able to perform routine preventive maintenance on the cell machines (ie to be multi-skilled and flexible). Employee involvement in JIT programmes is also important at a more general level. The successful operation of JIT requires workers to possess a flexibility of both attitude and aptitude.
Continuous improvement ('Kaizen')	The ideal target is to meet demand immediately with perfect quality and no waste. In practice, this ideal is never achieved. However, the JIT philosophy is that an organisation should work towards the ideal, and therefore continuous improvement is both possible and necessary.

JIT and service organisations

The JIT philosophy can be applied to service operations as well as to manufacturing operations. Whereas JIT in manufacturing seeks to eliminate inventories, JIT in service operations seeks to remove queues of customers.

Queues of customers are wasteful because:

- They waste customers' time
- Queues require space for customers to wait in, and this space is not adding value
- Queuing lowers the customer's perception of the quality of the service

The application of JIT to a service operation calls for the removal of task specialisation, so that the workforce can be used more flexibly and moved from one type of work to another, in response to demand and work flow requirements.

For example, postal delivery services often have specific postmen or postwomen allocated to their own routes. However, there may be scenarios where, say, Route A is overloaded while Route B has a very light load of post.

Rather than have letters for Route A piling up at the sorting office, when the person responsible for Route B has finished delivering earlier, this person might help out on Route A.

Teamwork and flexibility are difficult to introduce into an organisation because people might be more comfortable with clearly delineated boundaries in terms of their responsibilities. However, the customer is usually not interested in the company organisation structure because they are more interested in receiving a timely service.

In practice, service organisations are likely to use a buffer operation to minimise customer queuing times. For example, a hairdresser will get an assistant to give the client a shampoo to reduce the impact of waiting for the stylist. Restaurants may have an area where guests could have a drink if no vacant tables are available immediately; such a facility may even encourage guests to plan in a few drinks before dinner, thereby increasing the restaurant's revenues.

2.3.2 Problems associated with JIT 12/14

JIT should not be seen as a panacea for all the endemic problems associated with Western manufacturing. It might not even be appropriate in all circumstances.

(a) It is **not always easy to predict patterns of demand**.

(b) JIT makes the organisation **far more vulnerable to disruptions in the supply chain** (as the disruption to air freight in the aftermath of the volcanic eruption of Eyjafjallajokull in Iceland demonstrated – see the case study below).

(c) JIT, originated by Toyota, was designed at a time when all of Toyota's manufacturing was done within a 50 km radius of its headquarters. Wide geographical spread, however, makes this difficult.

Case Study — **JIT and supply chains**

Following the Eyjafjallajokull volcanic eruption in Iceland in April 2010, a number of flights across Europe were cancelled because airline companies were concerned about the potential impact of the volcanic ash on the engines of their planes.

This flight ban, in turn, threatened to force worldwide car production to grind to a halt, as manufacturers were unable to source key electronic components.

The flight disruption highlighted the car industry's dependence on complex, worldwide supply chains that need multiple modes of transport to deliver goods and components just in time, to where they are needed.

Although air freight accounts for a tiny amount of world trade by weight – about 0.5% for the UK – the disruption has highlighted how it plays a vital role in supplying key, high-value components to many manufacturers. In spite of its tiny volume, it accounts for 25% of UK trade by value.

Among the carmakers, BMW and Nissan said they planned to suspend some production because of disruption to supplies. Audi said it might have to cancel shifts because of missing parts.

Although all three mainly use suppliers based near their factories and use road and sea for most deliveries, they depend on air freight for a small number of high-value electronic components. Nissan UK, for example, said it might have to halt production of its Cube, Murano SUV and Rogue crossover models because it lacked supplies of a critical sensor made in Ireland.

Although some components could be transported by sea freight (instead of air freight) this is a much slower means of transport, and so would lead to a delay in the components becoming available.

Some commentators have questioned whether this disruption will make companies re-examine their arrangements for sourcing goods. Companies have become more vulnerable to disruption since moving to JIT production methods, where hardly any inventory of products is held.

On the other hand, it would make little sense to carry large quantities of excess inventory given the very slim chance of further severe disruption of this kind. Carrying excess inventory is a cost in itself.

However, there is an argument that companies should set up supply chains that reduce their reliance on a single mode of transport, and could be adapted to meet different circumstances. As Emma Scott from the Chartered Institute of Purchasing & Supply in the UK commented, 'It's a case of taking a sensible approach and having a flexible approach to your supply chain.'

Adapted from: Wright, R. & Reed, J. (2010) 'Pressure grows on supply chains,' *Financial Times*. Online. Available from: http://www.ft.com/cms/s/0/481eb8d6-4cdc-11df-9977-00144feab49a.html#axzz3yM5HBnov

[Accessed 26 January 2016]

Exam focus point

Part of a question in the December 2014 exam asked candidates to explain the problems a company would face in moving towards JIT manufacturing. The examining team noted that many candidates discussed how to implement JIT, or explained what the benefits of JIT might be, rather than focusing specifically on the problems the company would face when introducing JIT.

2.3.3 Modern versus traditional inventory control systems

There is no reason for the newer approaches to supersede the old entirely. A restaurant, for example, might find it preferable to use the traditional economic order quantity approach for staple non-perishable food inventories, but adopt JIT for perishable and 'exotic' items. In a hospital a stock-out could, quite literally, be fatal, and JIT would be quite unsuitable.

2.3.4 Costing implications of JIT

The implications of JIT for costing methods can be summarised as follows:

'Just-in-time manufacturing enables purchasing, production, and sales to occur in quick succession with inventory being maintained at minimum levels. The absence of inventory renders decisions regarding cost-flow assumptions (such as weighted average or first-in, first-out) or inventory costing methods (such as absorption or marginal costing) unimportant. This is because all of the manufacturing costs attributable to a period flow directly into cost of goods sold. Job costing is simplified by the rapid conversion of direct materials into finished goods that are then sold immediately.'

(Shane Johnson, 'Just-in-time operations', originally published in ACCA *Student Accountant*, 2004)

Shane Johnson's article also stresses that, while minimising costs will always remain an important consideration for businesses, the focus is no longer simply on minimising costs but also on **value appreciation**. This has important implications for performance measurement and performance management. Performance information can no longer simply look at costs, but financial and non-financial information will also be required looking at supplier performance, on-time deliveries, cycle times and the number of defective items manufactured.

This again highlights the importance of non-financial performance indicators and multi-dimensional performance measurement systems. In particular, the references to information about on-time deliveries, cycle times, waste and defective items highlight a link to the **performance pyramid**, because they are very similar to the types of measure recommended at the operational level in the pyramid.

(We will look at the performance pyramid in more detail in Chapter 15 of this Study Text.)

2.4 Life cycle costing and target costing

FAST FORWARD

Life cycle costing assists in the planning and control of a product's life cycle costs by monitoring spending – and commitments to spend – during a product's life cycle.

2.4.1 What are life cycle costs?

Life cycle costs are incurred for products and services **from their design stage through development to market launch, production and sales, and their eventual withdrawal from the market**.

Traditional management accounting systems in general only report costs at the physical production stage of the life cycle and do not accumulate costs over the entire life cycle. They **assess a product's or project's profitability on a periodic basis**. Life cycle costing, on the other hand, considers a product's/project's entire life.

Key term

Life cycle costing tracks and accumulates actual costs and revenues attributable to each product or project over the entire product/project life cycle.

The **total profitability** of any given product/project can therefore be determined.

Traditional management accounting systems usually total **all non-production costs** and record them as a **period expense**. **Using life cycle costing**, such costs are **traced to individual products over complete life cycles**.

(a) The total of these costs for each individual product can therefore be reported and compared with revenues generated in the future.

(b) The visibility of such costs is increased.

(c) **Individual product profitability can be more fully understood** by attributing **all** costs to products.

(d) As a consequence, **more accurate feedback information** is available on the organisation's success or failure in developing new products. In today's competitive environment, where the ability to produce new and updated versions of products is paramount to the survival of an organisation, this information is vital.

2.4.2 The importance of the early stages of the life cycle

It is reported that some organisations operating within an advanced manufacturing technology (**AMT**) **environment** find that approximately **80–90% of a product's life cycle cost is determined by decisions made early in the cycle** at the design stage. Life cycle costing is therefore particularly suited to such organisations and products, monitoring spending and commitments to spend during the early stages of a product's life cycle.

In order to compete effectively in today's competitive market, organisations need to **redesign continually their products** with the result that **product life cycles** have become much **shorter**. The **planning, design and development stages of a product's cycle** are therefore **critical to an organisation's cost management process**. Cost reduction at this stage of a product's life cycle, rather than during the production process, is one of the most important ways of reducing product cost.

Here are some **examples of costs that are determined at the design stage:**

(a) The number of different components
(b) Whether the components are standard or not
(c) The ease of changing over tools
(d) Type of packaging

Case Study **Car manufacturing**

The following case study illustrates the benefits of increasing the amount of standardisation in the car manufacturing process.

In August 2011, General Motors Co announced plans to become leaner in the future, cutting costs so it could make stronger profits.

GM said it plans to cut costs by halving the number of frames it bases its vehicles on around the globe. In 2010, GM had 30 frames, known in the industry as 'platforms'. By 2018 it plans to cut that number to 14. It will also sell more of the cars and trucks built on those platforms around the globe, saving on manufacturing, engineering and design costs. The company also planned to cut the number of engines it develops.

The Chairman and CEO noted, 'There's a lot of complexity. We need to simplify it. More of our components will be common, and more of our vehicles will be built on global architectures.'

At the time (2011) GM said just 6% of its cars and trucks were currently built off of global platforms. However, GM's intention was that this figure should rise to 90% by 2018.

Japanese companies developed **target costing** as a response to the problem of **controlling and reducing costs over the product life cycle.**

2.4.3 Target costing

FAST FORWARD

Target costing is a proactive cost control system. The target cost is calculated by deducting the target profit from a predetermined selling price, based on customers' views. Techniques such as value analysis are used to change production methods and/or reduce expected costs so that the target cost is met.

Key term

Target cost is an estimate of a product cost which is derived by subtracting a desired profit margin from a competitive market price.

One of the key drivers in target costing is that once a target cost has been established, costs – in the design and manufacture of the product – have to be reduced to provide a product that can be made for the desired (target) cost.

'Target cost management has been defined as a system that is effective in managing costs in new-product design and development stages. It has also been viewed as allowing the production cost of a proposed product to be identified so that when sold it generates the desired profit level. ... Target cost management has also been viewed as playing a useful role in enabling an enterprise to set and support the attainment of cost levels to effectively reflect its planned financial performance. ... What appears to be evident is that there are almost as **many conceptions of target costing** as there are companies deploying the approach and there are probably many **companies engaging in various aspects of target cost management without referring to the term.**

Target cost management has been posited to assist in the pursuit of product development time reduction, as well as the quality definition for a new product and cost containment generally. It has therefore been perceived as a managerial tool simultaneously to **address time, quality and cost issues.**'

Bhimani and Okano, 'Targeting excellence: target cost management at Toyota in the UK', *Management Accounting,* June 1995 (with BPP's emphasis)

Question

Target costing

Can you see any problems with adopting target costing as a tool in a not-for-profit organisation?

Answer

Target costing can lead to **increased pressure on the workforce**, as cost targets can be demanding and require a reduction in times taken to do jobs. This can be more difficult to achieve in the not–for-profit sector where employees can be the largest cost, and they are often the means of delivering the services. Over time savings become increasingly difficult to achieve.

Case Study

Breast cancer drugs

One of the functions of NICE (the National Institute for Health and Care Excellence) in the UK is assessing the most appropriate treatments for different diseases, based on the medical outcome and potential result for patients and the economic implications of the treatments.

NICE has been appraising 'Kadcyla' as a treatment option for people with breast cancer that has spread to other parts of the body, cannot be surgically removed and has stopped responding to initial treatment.

However, despite some evidence of Kadcyla's clinical efficacy, in August 2014, NICE issued a statement that it should not be recommended for routine use by the National Health Service (NHS).

A major factor was cost – because a course of treatment using Kadcyla could cost more than £90,000 per patient. As such, NICE assessed that Kadcyla was not sufficiently effective to justify the price the NHS was being asked to pay for the drug.

When making the announcement, NICE's Chief Executive said 'We had hoped that Roche (the manufacturers of Kadcyla) would have recognised the challenge the NHS faces in managing the adoption of expensive new treatments by reducing the cost of Kadcyla to the NHS.'

NICE had previously encouraged Roche to consider if there was anything it could do to reduce the price of the drug. However, Roche decided not to offer the treatment at a price which was sufficiently lower to enable Kadcyla to become available for routine use.

www.nice.org.uk

Target costing requires managers to change the way they think about the relationship between cost, price and profit.

(a) The **traditional approach** is to **develop a product, determine the expected standard production cost** of that product and **then set a selling price** (probably based on cost) with a resulting profit or loss. Costs are controlled through variance analysis at monthly intervals.

(b) The **target costing approach** is to develop a **product concept** and the primary specifications for performance and design and then to **determine the price customers would be willing to pay** for that concept. The **desired profit margin is deducted from the price leaving a figure that represents total cost**. This is the target cost and the product must be capable of being produced for this amount otherwise the product will not be manufactured. **During the product's life the target cost will constantly be reduced** so that the **price can fall**. **Continuous cost reduction techniques** must therefore be employed.

2.4.4 The target costing process

Step 1 **Analyse the external environment** to ascertain what customers require and what competitors are producing. Determine the **product concept**, the price customers will be willing to pay and thus the **target cost**.

Step 2 **Split the total target cost into broad cost categories**, such as development, marketing and manufacturing. **Then split up the manufacturing target cost per unit across the different functional areas of the product. Design the product so that each functional product area can be made within the target cost.** If a functional product area cannot be made within the target cost, so that a **cost gap** exists between the currently achievable cost and the target cost, the targets for the other areas must be reduced, or the product redesigned or scrapped. The product should be developed in an atmosphere of **continuous improvement** using **value engineering techniques** and **close collaboration with suppliers**, to enhance the product (in terms of service, quality, durability and so on) and reduce costs.

Key term

Value engineering aims to help design products which meet customer requirements at the lowest cost while assuring that the required standards of quality and reliability are maintained.

Step 3 Once it is decided that it is feasible to meet the total target cost, **detailed cost sheets** will be prepared and **processes formalised**.

The target costing process

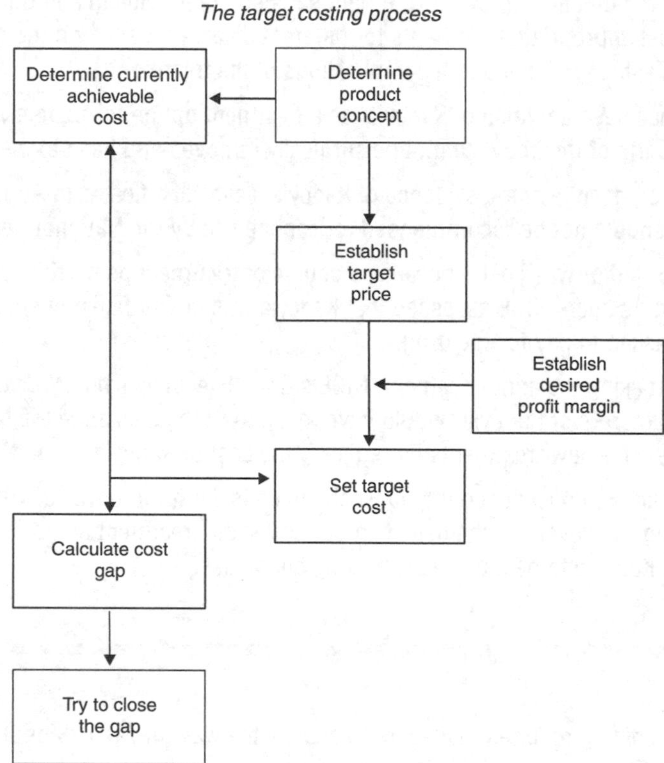

2.4.5 Attaining the target cost

It is possible that management may decide to go ahead and manufacture a product whose target cost is well below the currently attainable cost (so that there is a **cost gap**), the currently attainable cost being determined by current technology and processes. If this is the case management will **set benchmarks for improvement** towards the target costs, by specified dates.

Options available to reduce costs

(a) **Training** staff in more efficient techniques
(b) Using **cheaper staff**
(c) Acquiring new, more **efficient technology**
(d) Cutting out **non value added activities**

Even if the product can be produced within the target cost, the story does not end there. **Once the product goes into production target costs will gradually be reduced**. These reductions will be incorporated into the budgeting process. This means that cost savings must be actively sought and made continuously. Value analysis will be used to reduce costs if and when targets are missed.

Key term

Value analysis involves examining the factors which affect the cost of a product or service, so as to devise ways of achieving the intended purpose most economically at the required standards of quality and reliability.

Question

Standard costing vs target costing

Fill in the blank spaces ((a) to (d)) in the table below to show how standard costing and target costing differ.

Stage in product life cycle	Standard costing approach	Target costing approach
Product concept stage	No action	(a)
Design stage	(b)	Keep costs to a minimum
Production stage	Costs are controlled using variance analysis	(c)
Remainder of life	(d)	Target cost reduced, perhaps monthly

Answer

(a) Set the selling price and required profit and determine the resulting target cost
(b) Set standard cost and a resulting standard price
(c) Constant cost reduction
(d) Standards usually revised annually

2.5 Kaizen costing 12/11, 12/15

Key term

Kaizen costing focuses on obtaining small incremental cost reductions during the production stage of the product life cycle.

Kaizen costing has been used by some Japanese firms for over 20 years and is now widely used in the electronics and automobile industries, for example. 'Kaizen' translates as **continuous improvement**.

FAST FORWARD

The aim of **Kaizen costing** is to reduce current costs by using various tools such as value analysis and functional analysis.

2.5.1 The Kaizen costing process

Functional analysis is applied at the design stage of a new product, and a **target cost for each function** is set. The functional target costs are added together and the total becomes the **product target cost**. Once the product has been in production for a year, the **actual cost of the first year becomes the starting point for further cost reduction**. It is this **process of continuous improvement, encouraging constant reductions by tightening the 'standards'**, that is known as Kaizen costing.

The following Kaizen costing chart is based on one used at Daihatsu, the Japanese car manufacturer owned in part by Toyota, and reported in Monden and Lee's 'How a Japanese Auto Maker Reduces Costs' (*Management Accounting*, 2002).

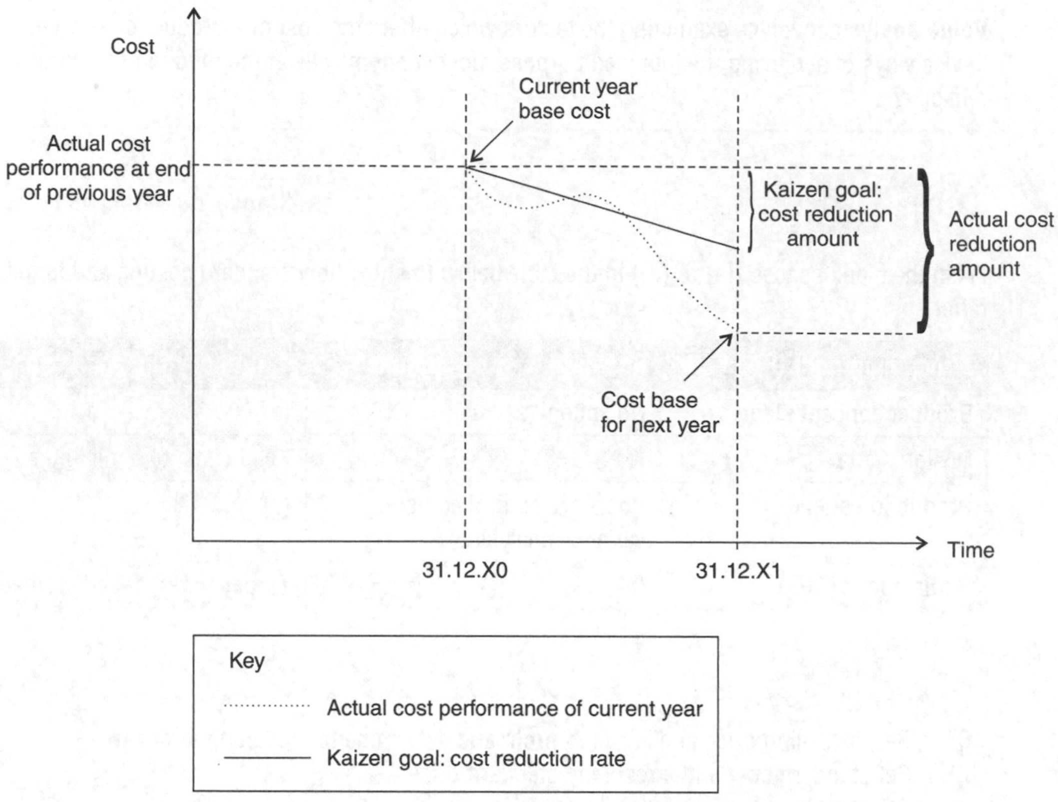

Kaizen costing and cost reduction

The previous year's actual production cost serves as the cost base for the current year's production cost. A reduction rate and reduction amount are set (**Kaizen cost goals**). **Actual performance** is **compared** to the **Kaizen goals** throughout the year and **variances are monitored**. At the end of the current year, the current actual cost becomes the cost base for the next year. New (lower) Kaizen goals are set and the whole process starts again.

2.5.2 Kaizen costing vs standard costing

Standard costing is used in conjunction with management by exception (management's attention is directed towards situations where actual results differ from expected results). The expected results are based on standards which have been derived from the capability of current organisational processes. **Standard costing** therefore **reflects current levels of performance** and **fails to provide any motivation to improve**.

The following table sets out the **principal differences between Kaizen costing and standard costing techniques**.

	Standard costing	Kaizen costing
Concepts	It is used for cost **control**. It is assumed that current manufacturing conditions remain unchanged. The cost focus is on standard costs based on static conditions. The aim is to meet cost performance standards.	It is used for cost **reduction**. It assumes **continuous improvement**. The cost focus is on actual costs assuming dynamic conditions. The aim is to achieve cost reduction targets.

	Standard costing	Kaizen costing
Techniques	Standards are set every 6 or 12 months. Costs are controlled using variance analysis based on standard and actual costs. Management should investigate and respond when standards are not met.	Cost reduction targets are set and applied monthly. Costs are reduced by implementing **continuous improvement** (Kaizen) to attain the target profit or to reduce the gap between target and estimated profit. Management should investigate and respond when target Kaizen amounts are not attained.
Employees	They are often viewed as the **cause of problems**.	They are viewed as the **source of**, and are empowered to find, the **solutions**.

(Adapted from Monden and Lee: 'Kaizen Costing: Its Function and Structure Compared to Standard Costing')

Exam focus point

One of the questions in the December 2011 exam picked up on the contrast between Kaizen costing and standard costing approaches. The question scenario highlighted that a company's existing performance reporting system used a standard costing approach, but that the management planned to improve financial performance through the use of Kaizen costing and JIT purchasing and production.

Candidates were then asked to discuss and evaluate the impact the Kaizen costing approach would have on the costing system and on employee management in the company.

In effect, the question was asking candidates to highlight the contrast between traditional costing systems which focus on cost control (against standard, fixed targets), and Kaizen costing systems which focus on cost reduction and performance improvement.

It is also important to note the impact that the change in systems has on employees and employee management.

A standard costing system doesn't provide any motivation to improve performance levels, but the whole focus of Kaizen costing is on performance improvement. And crucially, instead of being seen as the cause of problems, as they are in traditional systems, employees will be seen as the source of solutions under a Kaizen system, and they will be empowered to find, and then implement, those solutions. This, in turn, should help increase staff motivation.

2.5.3 How are Kaizen goals met?

(a) Reduction of non value added activities and costs
(b) Elimination of waste
(c) Improvements in production cycle time

2.6 Continuous improvement

FAST FORWARD

The essence of **continuous improvement** is the use of an organisation's human resources to produce a constant stream of improvements in all aspects of customer value, including quality, functional design, and timely delivery, while lowering cost at the same time.

In today's highly competitive environment, performance against static historical standards is no longer appropriate and successful organisations must be **open to change** if they are to **maintain their business advantage**. Being **forward looking** and **receptive to new ideas** are **essential elements of continuous improvement**. The concept was popularised in Japan, where it is known as Kaizen.

Key term

Continuous improvement is an 'ongoing process that involves a continuous search to reduce costs, eliminate waste, and improve the quality and performance of activities that increase customer value or satisfaction'. (Drury, *Management and Cost Accounting*)

The implementation of continuous improvement does not necessarily call for significant investment, but it does require a great deal of **commitment and continuous effort**.

Continuous improvement is often associated with **incremental changes** in the day to day process of work **suggested by employees** themselves. This is not to say that continuous improvement organisations do not engage in radical change. **Quantum leaps in performance** can occur when cumulative improvements synergise, the sum of a number of small improvements causing a profound net effect greater than the sum of all the small improvements.

However, because the improvements are continuous they are, by definition, **ongoing**. The process must never stop and sustained success is more likely in organisations which regularly review their business methods and processes in the drive for improvement.

Case Study **Oxford Instruments**

Oxford Instruments

Oxford Instruments is a leading provider of high technology tools and systems for industry and research.

The following extracts are taken from its preliminary results for the year to 31 March 2014:

'Across the world, people are focused on addressing the great challenges of the 21st century. Constant advances are needed to keep pace with our rapidly evolving world. With finite resources, we need to achieve more with fewer raw materials ... The continued expansion of our capabilities and expertise allows us to address customers' needs in a wide variety of markets ...'

'Improvement of our operational excellence forms a key part of our strategy. Following the successful introduction of continuous improvement and lean six sigma activities in selected ... businesses [within the Group], we have initiated a global Operational Excellence programme that develops and deploys best practice lean six sigma methodologies throughout the Group to ensure our processes are continually improved and deliver the benefits of economies of scale as the business grows.'

www.oxford-instruments.com

2.6.1 Essential factors for continuous improvement

(a) Total **commitment from senior management**

(b) The **opportunity for all employees to contribute** to the continuous improvement process. Tactical and operational level staff, rather than senior management, usually have the information required. The most successful continuous improvement programmes are the ones that have the highest staff involvement.

(c) Good, objective **information about the organisation's environment** so that its outcomes (what it does) and its processes (how it does it) can be evaluated

(d) **Employees' awareness of their role** in the achievement of the organisation's strategy

(e) **Management of the performance and contribution of employees**

(f) **Good communication** throughout the organisation

(g) Implementation of **recognised quality management systems and standards**

(h) **Measurement and evaluation of progress against key performance indicators and benchmarks.** Some organisations have found that simply displaying productivity and quality data every day or week raises production and quality because staff can tell when they are doing things right, and so find themselves in a personal continuous improvement cycle.

It is claimed that if these areas are regularly **reviewed**, change can be managed effectively and **continuous improvement becomes a natural part of the organisational processes.** It should create steady growth and development by keeping the organisation focused on its aims, priorities and performance.

Management accounting also supports continuous improvement by identifying ways to improve, and then reporting on the progress of the methods for improvement which have been implemented.

2.6.2 Quality circles

A quality circle consists of a **group of employees**, often from different areas of the organisation, who meet regularly to **discuss problems of quality and quality control** in their area of work, and perhaps to suggest **ways of improving quality**. It is also a way to **encourage innovation**. The aim of quality circles is to **improve employee development and morale** so as to create a **sense of ownership of the quality** of products and services.

Teamwork, in the form of quality circles and **group problem-solving activities**, is the cornerstone of continuous improvement.

2.6.3 Benefits of continuous improvement

(a) Better performance, which produces increased profits
(b) Improvements in customer satisfaction
(c) Increases in staff morale
(d) Improvement on a continual, step by step basis is more prudent than changing things all at once
(e) Better communication within the organisation
(f) Improvements in relations with suppliers
(g) Better use of resources
(h) More efficient planning

2.7 Quality systems documentation

TQM is a management philosophy. However, implementing TQM is not simply a matter of involving employees and encouraging a quality culture. There is also a need for systems and procedures for ensuring quality. Quality systems should be documented thoroughly.

(a) A company quality manual may summarise the quality management policy and system.

(b) A procedures manual sets out the functions, structures and responsibilities for quality in each department.

(c) Detailed work instructions and specifications for how work should be carried out show how to achieve the desired quality standards.

2.8 Adverse feedback on TQM

Although many organisations continue to implement TQM programmes, TQM is susceptible to various adverse perceptions.

(a) In practice, TQM initiatives are not introduced or implemented effectively, and the job is 'botched' by management.

(b) After obtaining short-term benefits from introducing TQM the benefits wear off over time, due to 'quality disillusionment'.

TQM programmes can also suffer from:

(a) A lack of top-management commitment

(b) A failure to understand the full range of quality issues and quality costs

(c) Vested interests and organisational politics

(d) The slow speed of introducing new initiatives in an organisation, especially a large bureaucratic organisation

(e) General cynicism about quality and fulfilling customer needs

3 Quality management and performance management

FAST FORWARD

'Quality' does not mean 'high quality'. Rather, 'quality' is the degree to which a set of inherent characteristics fulfils requirements.

The notion of 'quality' is used in several ways in everyday speech: it is used most precisely to mean simply the **nature** of a thing or to refer to one of its specific **characteristics**. However, 'quality' is also used, rather imprecisely, to indicate that a thing possesses a high degree of excellence or is of **good** quality, the word **good** being implied. Thus, if people speak of 'a quality product', we understand them to mean that the product is made to high standards and will give good service.

In the context of business and performance management we need to be careful to define what we mean by 'quality' more carefully. This is because – as the concepts of generic strategies and market segmentation remind us – in business there is often scope for a wide range of different products, each providing a **different combination of price and relative quality**. People flying first class expect a greater degree of comfort and service than is provided to passengers in business class, and rightly so: they have paid a much higher fare. But this does not mean that business class passengers are not equally entitled to the proper level of service that they, in turn, have paid for. **Quality** does not mean 'the best': it means what is right and proper under the circumstances.

This concept of quality is adopted in the International Organization for Standardisation (ISO) definition.

Key term

Quality is 'the degree to which a set of inherent characteristics fulfils requirements'. (ISO)

The ISO definition is a little open-ended, in that its full meaning depends on what the 'requirements' are, but we can deal with that.

(a) In a **retail context**, we might suggest that those requirements are the same thing as **reasonable customer expectations**, bearing in mind that these will inevitably reflect the price paid, to some extent at least.

(b) Within the organisation or within a value system or network, the concept of the **internal customer** is relevant, and we may say that proper requirements reflect **fitness for purpose**, which must, in turn, reflect the same reasonable expectations of the **strategic customer**. Here we might usefully introduce the concept of **design specification**, which should provide a clear specification of what is required.

(c) In a **not-for-profit** scenario, a similar concept applies, though we might speak of the reasonable expectations of the relevant **stakeholders**.

3.1 Managing quality

If an organisation is to consistently deliver products and services of the level of quality expected by its customers (or other key stakeholders), it must actively manage all the factors that have an impact on quality. In fact, there are very few aspects of any organisation that can be regarded as having no influence on quality, so an effective **quality management system** (QMS) is likely to have complex ramifications.

Key term

> A **quality management system** is the organisational structure of responsibilities, activities, resources and events that together provide procedures and methods of implementation to ensure the capability of an organisation to meet quality requirements. (Tricker and Sherring-Lucas)

This definition gives a good indication of what is involved in a QMS. Many of the components will be present in organisations that do not even claim to have a QMS as such. However, the organisations which consciously use a QMS manage these common elements in a way that contributes to quality management. For example, any manufacturing organisation, no matter how rudimentary, will perform the activity of **procurement**. Procurement as part of a QMS will, for example, take positive steps to ensure that purchased materials conform consistently to the appropriate quality standards; non-QMS procurement may or may not do the same, but even if it does, it is unlikely that the procedures concerned will be documented and applied consistently.

The QMS pervades the whole organisation since it is unlikely that there will be any of its aspects that do not have the potential to affect the quality of its outputs.

However, an effective QMS should be designed around the eight quality management principles given in ISO 9001:2005 (a series of standards used for the accreditation of organisations' QMS):

- Customer focus
- Leadership
- Involvement of people [(1)]
- Process approach [(2)]
- Systems approach to management [(3)]
- Continual improvement
- Factual approach to decision making
- Mutually beneficial supplier relationships

Notes

1 When we discuss job design in another chapter, you will see how the influence of Japanese management practice has led to the now commonly adopted principle that **quality is everybody's concern**. An important result of this approach is increased employee involvement in quality management through such mechanisms as **quality circles**.

2 This means managing related activities and resources as integrated processes.

3 This means managing groups of related processes as integrated systems.

The ISO standards also stress four other principles (which resonate with a number of the aspects of performance management we have been discussing in this Study Text so far):

(a) Quality management should be **customer-focused**.

(b) Quality performance should be **measured**. Measures should relate both to **processes** that create products or services, and to **customer satisfaction** with those products or services.

(c) Quality management should be **improvement-driven**. Improvement must be demonstrated in both process performance and customer satisfaction.

(d) **Senior management** must demonstrate their **commitment** to maintaining and continually improving management systems.

3.2 Costs of quality and cost of quality reports

FAST FORWARD

Costs of quality can be analysed into **prevention, appraisal, internal failure** and **external failure** costs and should be detailed in a **cost of quality report**.

The costs associated with quality management can be classified into four types:

(a) Prevention costs
(b) Appraisal costs
(c) Internal failure
(d) External failure

The skill of quality management lies in minimising these costs **in total**. For example, the more rigorous the QMS, the lower the eventual costs of failure are likely to be, but the higher the costs of prevention and appraisal. So the aim must be to achieve a sensible balance between the two categories.

Key term

The **cost of quality** is 'The difference between the actual cost of producing, selling and supporting products or services and the equivalent costs if there were no failures during production or usage'.

The cost of quality can be analysed into the following:

- **Prevention costs** – costs which are incurred to prevent the production of products that do not conform to specification being produced.
- **Appraisal costs** (or **cost of inspection)** – costs incurred in order to ensure that outputs produced meet required quality standards.
- **Cost of internal failure** – costs incurred as a result of outputs not meeting required quality standards, but where these deficiencies are identified before a product is transferred to the customer
- **Cost of external failure** – costs resulting from products or services failing to meet requirements or to satisfy customer needs, but where these deficiencies are only identified after the products or services have been delivered to the customer.

Note that the first three 'costs' (prevention; appraisal; internal failure) are all **internal** to an organisation: for example, the inspections and analysis take place within the organisation before a product leaves the factory.

However, the fourth cost (external failure) only occurs once a product leaves the factory, and the quality problems or issues are identified by the **customer**.

Quality-related cost	Example
Prevention costs	Quality engineering Design/development of quality control/inspection equipment Maintenance of quality control/inspection equipment Administration of quality control Training in quality control Extra costs of acquiring higher quality raw materials
Appraisal (or inspection) costs	Acceptance testing Inspection of goods inwards Inspection costs of in-house processing Performance testing
Costs of internal failure	Costs of scrap Costs of repair and re-inspection Downtime and work stoppages caused by defects Losses due to lower selling prices for sub-quality goods Costs of reviewing product specifications after failures

Quality-related cost	Example
Costs of external failure	Costs of handling customer complaints Warranty replacements Cost of repairing products returned from customers Cost of replacing items due to substandard products/marketing errors Damage to reputation and potential loss of future sales

3.3 Views on quality costs

3.3.1 View one – the traditional view

Key terms

Cost of conformance is the cost of ensuring that products conform to specification and achieve the required quality standards. (This can be seen as prevention costs and appraisal (or inspection) costs).

Cost of non-conformance is the cost which arises as a result of failing to deliver the required standard of quality. (This can be seen as internal and external failure costs).

The **cost of conformance** is a **discretionary** cost which is incurred with the intention of **eliminating the costs of internal and external failure**.

The **cost of non-conformance**, on the other hand, can **only be reduced by increasing the cost of conformance**.

The **optimal investment in conformance costs** is when **total costs of quality reach a minimum** (which may be below 100% quality conformance). This is illustrated in the following diagram.

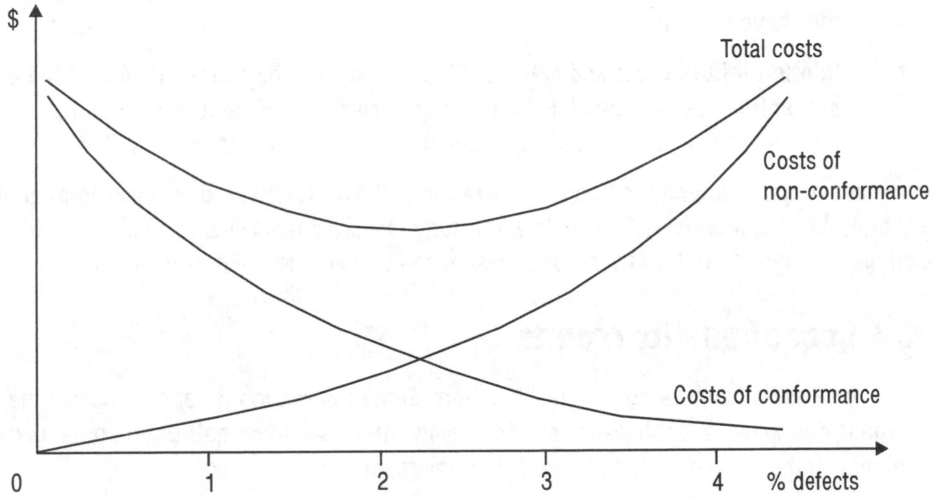

Costs of quality (Costs of conformance and costs of non-conformance)

To achieve **0% defects, costs of conformance must be high**. For example, if every single item that comes off a production line in a factory is subjected to a detailed quality check before it leaves the factory, this should lead to a very low level of defects, but it will mean the costs of conformance are high. As a greater proportion of defects are accepted, however, the costs of conformance can be reduced; for example, if only a sample of the items coming off the production line are checked, this will reduce the time (and cost) spent on checking.

At a level of **0% defects, costs of non-conformance** should be **nil** (because there are no defects to remedy) but the costs of non-conformance will increase as the accepted level of defects rises. There should therefore be an **acceptable level of defects** at which the **total costs of quality are at a minimum**.

3.3.2 View two – TQM philosophy

A 'traditional' approach to quality management (view one above) is that there is an **optimal level of quality effort, that minimises total quality costs**, and there is a point beyond which spending more on quality yields a benefit that is less than the additional cost incurred. Diminishing returns set in beyond the optimal quality level.

The **TQM philosophy** is different.

(a) Failure and poor quality are unacceptable. It is **inappropriate to think of an optimal level of quality** at which some failures will occur, and the **inevitability of errors is not something that an organisation should accept**. The target should be zero defects.

(b) Quality costs are difficult to measure, and failure costs in particular are often seriously underestimated. The **real costs of failure include** not just the cost of scrapped items and reworking faulty items, but also the **management time spent sorting out problems** and the **loss of confidence** between different parts of the organisation whenever faults occur.

(c) A TQM approach does not accept that the prevention costs of achieving zero defects becomes unacceptably high as the quality standard improves and goes above a certain level. In other words, **diminishing returns do not necessarily set in**. If everyone in the organisation is involved in improving quality, the cost of continuous improvement need not be high.

(d) If an organisation **accepts an optimal quality level** that it believes will minimise total quality costs, there will be **no further challenge** to management to improve quality further.

The **TQM quality cost model** is based on the view that:

(a) **Prevention costs and appraisal costs** are **subject to management influence** or control. It is **better to spend money on prevention**, before failures occur, than on inspection to detect failures after they have happened.

(b) **Internal failure costs and external failure costs** are the **consequences of the efforts spent on prevention and appraisal**. Extra effort on prevention will reduce internal failure costs and this in turn will have a knock-on effect, reducing external failure costs as well.

In other words, **higher spending on prevention will eventually lead to lower total quality costs**, because appraisal costs, internal failure costs and external failure costs will all be reduced. The emphasis should be on 'getting things right first time' and 'designing in quality' to the product or service.

3.4 Cost of quality reports

Shown below is a typical cost of quality report. **Some figures** in the report, such as the contribution forgone due to sales lost because of poor quality, may have to be **estimated**, but it is better to include an estimate rather than omit the category from the report.

The report has the following **uses**:

(a) By expressing each cost category as a percentage of sales revenue, **comparisons** can be made with previous periods, divisions within the group or other organisations, thereby highlighting problem areas. A comparison of the proportion of external failure costs to sales revenue with the figures for other organisations, for example, can provide some idea of the level of customer satisfaction.

(b) It can be used to make senior management aware of **how much is being spent** on quality-related costs.

(c) It can provide an indication of **how total quality costs could be reduced by a more sensible division of costs between the four categories**. For example, an increase in spending on prevention costs should reduce the costs of internal and external failure and hence reduce total spending.

COST OF QUALITY REPORT
YEAR ENDING 31 DECEMBER 20X0

	$'000	$'000	*Cost as % of annual revenue* ($10 million)
Prevention costs			
Design of quality control equipment	80		
Quality control training	80		
		160	1.6
Appraisal costs			
Inspection of goods inwards	90		
Inspection of WIP	100		
		190	1.9
Internal failure costs			
Scrap	150		
Rework	200		
		350	3.5
External failure costs			
Returns	500		
Contribution forgone on lost sales	400		
Handling customer complaints	100		
		1,000	10.0
		1,700	17.0

Although cost of quality reports provide a useful summary of the costs, effort and progress of quality, **non-financial quality measures** may be more appropriate for **lower levels of management**. Here are some examples of such measures:

(a) Number of customer complaints
(b) Number of warranty claims
(c) Number of defective units delivered to customers as a percentage of total units delivered

Question

Quality costs

LL designs and makes a single product, the X4, used in the telecommunications industry. The organisation has a goods received store which employs staff who carry out random checks to ensure materials are of the correct specification. In addition to the random checks, a standard allowance is made for failures due to faulty materials at the completion stage and the normal practice is to charge the cost of any remedial work required to the cost of production for the month. Once delivered to the customer, any faults discovered in the X4 during its warranty period become an expense of the customer support department.

At the end of each month, management reports are prepared for the board of directors. These identify the cost of running the stores and the number of issues, the cost of production and the number of units manufactured, and the cost of customer support.

Required

(a) Briefly discuss why the current accounting system fails to highlight the cost of quality.

(b) Identify four general categories (or classifications) of LL's activities where expenditure making up the explicit cost of quality will be found and provide an example of a cost found within each category.

(c) Give one example of a cost of quality not normally identified by the accounting system.

Answer

(a) **Failure of the current accounting system to highlight the cost of quality**

Traditionally, the costs of scrapped units, wasted materials and reworking have been **subsumed within the costs of production** by assigning the costs of an expected level of loss (a normal loss) to the costs of good production, while accounting for **other costs of poor quality** within **production or marketing overheads**. Such costs are therefore not only considered as **inevitable** but are not **highlighted** for management attention. Moreover, traditional accounting reports tend to **ignore the hidden but real costs of excessive inventory levels** (held to enable faulty material to be replaced without hindering production) and the facilities necessary for storing that **inventory**.

(b) **Explicit costs of quality**

There are four recognised categories of cost identifiable within an accounting system which make up the cost of quality:

(i) **Prevention costs** are the costs of any action taken to investigate, prevent or reduce the production of faulty output. Included within this category are the costs of training in quality control and the cost of the design/development and maintenance of quality control and inspection equipment.

(ii) **Appraisal costs** are the costs of assessing the actual quality achieved. Examples include the cost of the inspection of goods delivered and the cost of inspecting production during the manufacturing process.

(iii) **Internal failure costs** are the costs incurred by the organisation when production fails to meet the level of quality required. Such costs include losses due to lower selling prices for sub-quality goods, the costs of reviewing product specifications after failures and losses arising from the failure of purchased items.

(iv) **External failure costs** are the costs which arise outside the organisation (after the customer has received the product) due to failure to achieve the required level of quality. Included within this category are the costs of repairing products returned from customers, the cost of providing replacement items due to substandard products or marketing errors and the costs of a customer service department.

(c) **Quality costs not identified by the accounting system**

Quality costs which are not identified by the accounting system tend to be of two forms:

(i) Opportunity costs, such as the loss of future sales to a customer dissatisfied with faulty goods

(ii) Costs which tend to be subsumed within other account headings, such as those costs which result from the disruption caused by stock-outs due to faulty purchases

Exam focus point

While it is important to be aware of the different costs of quality, it is also important not to lose sight of the bigger picture and **why** 'quality' is important for an organisation. The following could all be important in this respect:

- 'Costs' of quality will affect the organisation's profitability.
- Quality (high quality) may be used as a differentiating factor by an organisation pursuing a differentiation strategy.
- The quality of the goods or services that customers receive is likely to affect customer satisfaction, and in turn customer retention and revenues.

- Ultimately, if the quality of an organisation's products or services regularly falls below the required standard, the organisation will not be able to survive, because customers will not want to buy products from it, or use its services.
- An organisation will not be able to meet its strategic objectives consistently if doesn't have any control over the quality of the products or services it offers.

3.5 The advantages of having a QMS

An effective QMS, as well as minimising quality-related costs, will have other important advantages:

(a) An improvement in the organisation's ability to deliver outputs of consistently satisfactory quality
(b) An improved level of staff commitment based on pride in work
(c) Improved customer relationships, with fewer complaints and increased turnover

3.6 Quality management and performance management

Earlier in the chapter we defined quality as: 'the degree to which a set of inherent characteristics fulfils requirements'. However, we could also add to that definition that quality also reflects the degree to which a product or service consistently **conforms to customers' expectations**.

Equally, as we have already suggested, 'quality' should be a key concern in all organisations. High-quality goods and services can give an organisation a competitive edge over its rivals. Good quality also reduces the costs of rework, waste, complaints, and returns an organisation incurs; and – perhaps most importantly – good quality generates satisfied customers.

In this respect, quality improvements can have a major effect on other aspects of an organisation's performance. For example, revenues can be increased by better sales and being able to charge higher prices (relative to poorer-quality products). At the same time, costs can be reduced through improved efficiencies and productivity.

However, adding a reference to meeting customer expectations into our definition of quality reinforces the importance of the customer in any discussion of quality. From the customer's perspective, quality problems arise when the customer's perception of a product or service fails to match their expectations of it. Therefore a key aspect of quality management is ensuring that products or services meet customers' expectations of them.

However, in order to do this, an organisation has to know:

(a) What the customers' expectations of its product or service are

(b) What the key processes and success factors are that will enable it to achieve customers' expectations

For example, let us consider some quality characteristics for an online grocery shopping service.

Quality characteristics	Examples
Product characteristics	Product range Product availability Shelf life/durability of products Products not damaged (Also, possibly more generally, the taste/flavour of the products)
Delivery service characteristics	Reliability of service (turns up when scheduled) Accuracy of delivery (what is delivered agrees to what was ordered) Products not damaged when delivered Attitude of delivery driver; and physical appearance (of driver and delivery vehicle) Coping with any errors (eg response if customer notices any differences between what was ordered and what is delivered)

Quality characteristics	Examples
Website characteristics	Ease of use Reliability of website (eg doesn't crash) Security of website

Importantly, however, once these quality characteristics have been identified, they also indicate the areas of the operation's performance which are **important to measure**, to ensure that quality levels are maintained against acceptable standards.

This is a point we will return to later in the chapter when we look at Six Sigma as a method of quality improvement. The first stage in implementing a Six Sigma programme is 'Defining customer requirements'.

More generally, this idea of identifying the aspects of performance which are important to measure also reminds us of our discussion of critical success factors in Chapter 2 of this Study Text. Critical success factors (CSFs) are those aspects of a product or service particularly valued by customers, and therefore the ones which a business must excel at to outperform its competitors. In turn, the business then needs to use its key performance indicators (KPIs) to measure how well it is performing against its CSFs.

4 Quality in management information systems

FAST FORWARD

Four aspects of quality are particularly important in software:

- Functionality
- Reliability
- Usability
- Build quality (flexibility, expandability, portability, ease of maintenance)

Low quality in IS development produces systems that are difficult to use, maintain and enhance.

Your syllabus requires you to have some knowledge of quality management in information systems (IS) development. The complexity and internal integration of many IS makes them particularly susceptible to undesirable effects caused by defects of design and coding in particular. If you have used a PC at all you are likely to have had experience of the frustration and delay caused by defects in even such well-established systems as Microsoft Windows.

4.1 Consequences of low quality in information systems (IS)

Poor design and coding produce IS that are difficult to use, maintain and enhance. This has undesirable consequences:

(a) **Excessive costs** are incurred in correcting defects and adding or improving features to make the systems usable.

(b) **User confidence** is undermined.

(c) **Business efficiency** is harmed, with harmful effects on customer satisfaction and therefore on profitability and even on the continuing existence of the organisation.

4.2 Features of good software

Four aspects of quality are particularly important in software:

(a) **Functionality** is the ability of the system to perform the tasks expected of it. It should do what the user wants it to do.

(b) **Reliability** means that the system keeps working and is not out of service frequently or for extended periods. Also, it does not produce unexpected or bizarre outputs.

(c) **Usability** means that the system is easy to use effectively.

(d) **Build quality** is evidenced by such features as ease of **maintenance**, **flexibility** in use, **expandability** and **portability** between platforms.

Failures of **functionality** and **reliability** give rise to the undesirable consequences already mentioned. Lack of **usability** will make operation of the system complex and costly in staff time; it will also require the provision of **extensive training** to users. Poor **build quality** will damage prospects for further overall system development in the future, as well as complicating maintenance and upgrades.

Software quality could be very important for managers if they are using the software to produce management information. If managers are unable to review reports which give them relevant, timely and accurate information about how their business is performing, this will make their job of managing performance much harder.

5 The qualities of good information and good management information systems

FAST FORWARD

As well as ensuring that it has good-quality information systems, an organisation needs to ensure that it produces good quality management information.

Just because an organisation has good-quality information systems does not guarantee that the reports or information those systems produce will be useful for management.

Earlier in this Study Text we have highlighted some of the characteristics that good management information should demonstrate: for example, it should be timely, accurate and relevant to its recipients.

'Good' management information is information that adds to management's understanding of performance or a particular issue, and can help them control the business.

The qualities of good information are outlined in the following table. You can use the mnemonic ACCURATE to help you remember the qualities of good information.

Quality	Example
Accurate	Figures should add up, the degree of rounding should be appropriate, there should be no typos, items should be allocated to the correct category, assumptions should be stated for uncertain information.
Complete	Information should include everything that it needs to include, for example external data if relevant, comparative information or qualitative information as well as quantitative. Sometimes managers or strategic planners will need to build on the available information to produce a forecast using assumptions or extrapolations.
Cost-beneficial	It should not cost more to obtain the information than the benefit derived from having it. Providers of information should be given efficient means of collecting and analysing it. Presentation should be such that users do not waste time working out what it means.
User-targeted	The needs of the user should be borne in mind, for instance senior managers need strategic summaries periodically, junior ones need detail.
Relevant	Information that is not needed for a decision should be omitted, no matter how 'interesting' it may be.
Authoritative	The source of the information should be a reliable one (not, for instance, 'Joe Bloggs Predictions Page' on the internet unless Joe Bloggs is known to be a reliable source for that type of information). However, subjective information (eg expert opinions) may be required in addition to objective facts.
Timely	The information should be available when it is needed. It should also cover relevant time periods, the future as well as the past.

Quality	Example
Easy to use	Information should be clearly presented, not excessively long, and sent using the right medium and communication channel (email, telephone, hard-copy report etc).

Exam focus point

In Chapter 8 we looked at the dangers of information overload, and when assessing the quality of information (eg relevance; ease of use) it could be useful to think whether there is a danger that too much information is being provided.

5.1 Improvements to information

However, as well as being able to identify the qualities of good information, you may also need to identify the problems that an organisation is having with the information it currently produces, and to suggest potential ways that information can be improved.

The table below contains some suggestions as to how poor information can be **improved**.

Feature	Examples of possible improvements
Accurate	Use computerised systems with automatic input checks rather than manual systems. Allow sufficient time for collation and analysis of data if pinpoint accuracy is crucial. Incorporate elements of probability within projections so that the required response to different future scenarios can be assessed.
Complete	Include past data as a reference point for future projections. Include any planned developments, such as new products. Information about future demand would be more useful than information about past demand. Include external data.
Cost-beneficial	Always bear in mind whether the benefit of having the information is greater than the cost of obtaining it.
User-targeted	Information should be summarised and presented together with relevant ratios or percentages. Consider use of graphics or dashboards for summarised data for senior management.
Relevant	The purpose of the report should be defined. It may be trying to fulfil too many purposes at once. Perhaps several shorter reports would be more effective. Information should include exception reporting, where only those items that are worthy of note – and the control actions taken by more junior managers to deal with them – are reported.
Authoritative	Use reliable sources and experienced personnel. If some figures are derived from other figures, the method of derivation should be explained.
Timely	Information collection and analysis by production managers needs to be speeded up considerably, probably by the introduction of better information systems (possibly even systems that can provide real-time information).

Feature	Examples of possible improvements
Easy to use	Graphical presentation, allowing trends to be quickly assimilated and relevant action decided on. Alternative methods of presentation should be considered, such as graphs or charts, to make it easier to review the information at a glance. Numerical information is sometimes best summarised in narrative form or vice versa. A 'house style' for reports should be devised and adhered to by all. This would cover such matters as number of decimal places to use, table headings and labels, paragraph numbering and so on.

6 Six Sigma and quality improvement 6/12, 12/15

FAST FORWARD

Six Sigma is a quality management system that grew out of statistical quality techniques. The overall aim is to ensure a very high and consistent standard of quality output. Six Sigma tends to take the form of specific improvement projects that follow a standard five phase pattern.

- **Define** requirements
- **Measure** performance
- **Analyse** the process
- **Improve** the process
- **Control** the new process

Six Sigma is a quality management methodology developed at Motorola in the late 1980s. Originally, it was a set of statistics-based techniques used by managers to assess manufacturing process performance. It has evolved into a widely applicable process improvement system with links to **process re-engineering**. Both Harmon and Pande and Holpp describe Six Sigma as the latest development in an evolutionary process that began with Scientific Management and continued through lean manufacturing and TQM.

There are three classifications of **process change work** which we will introduce here briefly.

(a) **Process improvement** is a tactical-level incremental technique that is appropriate for developing smaller, stable existing processes.

(b) **Process re-engineering** is used at the strategic level when major environmental threats or opportunities mandate fundamental rethinking of large-scale, core processes that are critical to the operation of the value chain.

(c) **Process redesign** is an intermediate scale of operation appropriate for middle-sized processes that require extensive improvement or change.

Pande and Holpp think that Six Sigma is applicable to all three approaches and declare that 'achieving the goal of Six Sigma requires more than small, incremental improvements; it requires breakthroughs in every area of an operation'. They emphasise Six Sigma's track record of producing major return on investment and its effects on management methods.

On the other hand, Harmon describes Six Sigma as typically employed in **process improvement projects**. He goes on to say that it is very good at 'describing how to think about measuring process and activity outcomes' and 'how to use statistical techniques to analyse the outcomes and decide on corrective action'.

Pande and Holpp identify six themes in Six Sigma:

- Genuine focus on the customer
- Data- and fact-driven management
- Processes as the key to success
- Proactive management
- Boundaryless collaboration
- Perfectionism combined with tolerance of failure

Exam focus point

The following section is useful background which explains the theory behind Six Sigma. You will not need to know this for the exam but it helps you understand how Six Sigma was developed.

You will not need to do any calculations in the question which test Six Sigma.

6.1 The Six Sigma concept

The essence of Six Sigma is to improve a process to the extent that there is only the tiniest probability that it will produce unsatisfactory outputs. Note that we speak of probability: there are no certainties in this sort of work and we need to look a little further at **probability** to understand what is going on.

6.1.1 The normal distribution

The kind of probability we are concerned with is based on variation of a characteristic within a population. The population might be, say, men in the UK and the characteristic might be, say, height. Equally well, the population might be all the widgets a factory produces in a year and the characteristic might be their weight in grams. The important point about these two characteristics is that they **vary** from individual to individual and their variation is **normally distributed**.

Normal distribution of a population variable implies that its magnitude tends to clump around the mean, but there are also likely to be individual cases that are quite a long way from the mean. If we draw a graph to show the **frequency** with which actual measurements occur in a normally distributed variable, it will be a **bell shaped curve**, such as the one below.

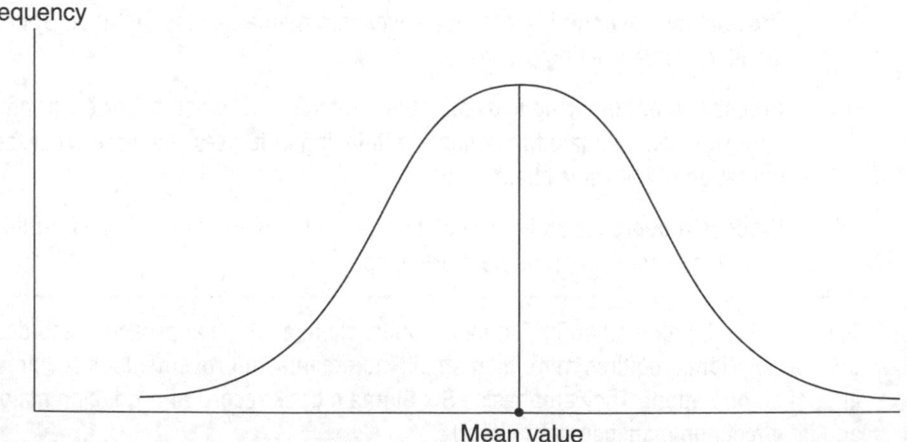

Normal distribution curve

A good way to visualise the way the normal distribution works is to imagine **looking down vertically on a football pitch** with a large number of people standing on it. We have measured all these people's height and worked out the mean.

We persuade all the people whose height is **equal to the mean** to line up one behind the other **along the halfway line**, starting from one of the touch lines; then the people who are one centimetre taller than the mean line up immediately to their right and those who are one centimetre shorter line up on their left, both starting from the same touch line. Then we repeat the process with those who are two centimetres taller and two centimetres shorter and so on, until everyone is in place.

If we then look down on the **shape of our crowd**, we will find that it is very close indeed to the curve shown above. We have drawn a graph using the touch line as the x axis and the centre line as the y axis. The people of mean height will be the most numerous and they will be at the centre of the curve. Taller and shorter people will be fewer in number and the greater the difference from the mean, the fewer people there will be. Eventually, as we move out towards the goal lines at either end, there might only be one or two people who are sufficiently tall or short to qualify.

It would probably take several thousand people to make this demonstration work. Even so, they would represent only a **sample** of the entire population of the country, so it is unlikely that we would encounter anyone who was outstandingly tall or short. But such people do exist and we cannot say for certain where the final limits of human height lie. The same is true of all normally distributed variables and so the tails of the normal curve never actually meet the x axis of our graph.

6.1.2 Standard deviation

However, we can say some other very precise things about our normally distributed variable. We can work out a measure of the variable called the **standard deviation**. How this is done need not concern us here, so long as we understand what it tells us. The standard deviation gives us an indication of the **dispersion** of the variable; that is to say, whether the curve is very tall and narrow, with most of the population values very close to the mean, or very low and flat, covering a wide range of measurements. The smaller the standard deviation, the taller and narrower the curve.

The standard deviation is interesting when we come to consider **probability**. The area under a part of the curve defined by a given number of standard deviations from the mean is easily obtained from mathematical tables. So, for example, if we take the part of the curve that lies within **two standard deviations** on either side of the mean, we find that approximately **95%** of the population will lie under it.

Going back to our height example, if the mean is 170 cm and the standard deviation is 10 cm, we can say that approximately 95% of people are between 150 cm and 190 cm tall. If we include everybody within **three standard deviations**, using the tables, we can say that over 99% of the population will be between 140 cm and 200 cm tall.

This is all very comforting and precise, but what does it have to do with **probability** which, you may recall, was why we started on the normal distribution in the first place?

6.1.3 Probability

To deal with probability, we have to turn the concept on its head. We started off by describing the normal curve in terms of a **very large number of people** and we have discussed how it defines one of their variable characteristics: height in our example. We now think about what it can tell us about a **single individual**. While it cannot tell us anything absolutely precisely, it can tell us something useful with a certain degree of probability.

If we know, for example, that a person is a member of the population whose height we measured earlier, we can say **with 95% probability** that their height must lie in the range 170 cm to 190 cm. That is, we know that 95% of the population lie within that range, so a randomly chosen individual must therefore have a **95% chance** of being in that section of the population and, equally, of lying in that height range. Another way of using the same facts would be to say that our randomly chosen person has **only a 5% chance of lying outside** that height range.

6.1.4 Probability and process quality

The probability aspect of the normal distribution becomes very important for **process quality** when we start to think about product characteristics. We said that the essence of Six Sigma is to improve a process to the extent that there is only the **tiniest probability** that it will produce **unsatisfactory outputs**. In other words, we want to **control** things like widget weight so that it has only a tiny percentage chance of lying outside the acceptable limits.

We have spoken of 95% and 99% probability, both of which are regarded as pretty close to certainty. However, for Six Sigma we want to do better. The area under the normal curve out to three standard deviations includes well over 99% of all individual occurrences. If we extended the curve out to six standard deviations, the occurrences that were not covered would be **very, very few** indeed. This is the principle of Six Sigma: reduce the probability of defects to the minute level defined by the area **more than six standard deviations from the mean**. (The Greek letter sigma in its lower case form (σ) is the usual mathematical symbol for standard deviation, hence Six Sigma.)

In fact, the distribution used in the statistical theory that underpins Six Sigma differs slightly from the normal curve because of a phenomenon called long run process drift. Using this approach, only **3.4 items in a million** will lie outside the limit of six standard deviations either side of the mean. The goal of Six Sigma, therefore, is to **reduce failures to a rate of less than 3.4 in a million**.

An important implication of this approach is that success is represented by a **band of quality** rather than a single specification. That band is defined as six standard deviations either side of the mean. Fairly obviously, if the measurements that correspond to those limits are close together, the standard deviation of the permitted measurements will be **very small** and the graph of the overall distribution will be very tall and thin.

6.1.5 Tolerances

It may be easiest to think about this in terms of a simple manufactured component, such as the piston in a single cylinder petrol engine. If the piston is too big, it will bind in the cylinder, or possibly not even fit into it at all. If it is too small, it will fail to capture the power generated from burning the fuel and it will also move in an irregular fashion and cause excessive wear in the cylinder.

However, this does not mean that all pistons must be absolutely identical to the limit of measurement. Between the unacceptable extremes outlined above, there will be **a range of dimensions that are acceptable**. This range will be very narrow indeed, but it will exist. In fact, the specification for the piston diameter will probably be given with a **tolerance** such as 'plus or minus four thousandths of an inch'.

Whatever the physical dimensions of the permitted tolerance, Six Sigma requires that they must equate to plus or minus six standard deviations from the mean of the entire output of pistons if the manufacturing process is to qualify as operating at the Six Sigma level of quality.

This principle can be extended to processes other than manufacturing so long as some form of quantitative measurement is possible.

6.2 Process improvement with Six Sigma

As indicated above, Harmon suggests that Six Sigma is best applied to the **incremental improvement of fairly narrowly defined processes and sub-processes**; it is not an appropriate approach to process re-engineering or radical redesign. However, it must always be clear how the target process relates to the wider functional and strategic background.

An important feature of the system is its emphasis on the importance of basing management on **well-substantiated data** rather than opinion and intuition.

Exam focus point

In Chapter 4 we looked at business process re-engineering (BPR), and noted it involves the fundamental rethinking and radical redesign of business processes to achieve dramatic performance improvements.

By contrast, Six Sigma process improvement is best applied to the **incremental** improvement of processes and is not appropriate for radical redesign.

Make sure you appreciate this distinction in the relative suitability of the two methodologies for different scenarios.

6.2.1 Organising Six Sigma

When an organisation decides to commit to Six Sigma, it will normally appoint an overall **implementation leader** and form a **steering committee** at a senior level to provide a vision for the process and to oversee it. One of the principal responsibilities of this committee will be to nominate process areas for improvement. Each area will constitute a separate project and will have its own Six Sigma **project team** and **sponsor** or **champion**. The sponsor will be a member of the steering committee or may be the

process sponsor. The project team will be made up of **staff experienced in the process** under review; for smaller-scale projects, they will be the staff actually operating the process.

Staff involved in the **leadership of projects** may possess varying grades of qualification in Six Sigma.

(a) **Master Black Belts** are in-house consultants in Six Sigma and spend all of their time on it. They are especially skilled in the statistical techniques involved and will contribute to several projects simultaneously.

(b) **Black Belts** also spend all of their time on Six Sigma and lead specific projects.

(c) **Green Belts** also lead projects. They are managers who retain other job responsibilities alongside Six Sigma.

A Six Sigma project is likely to entail a large amount of training, both for the various leader grades and for the process operating staff that make up the project teams. **Empowerment** is a feature of the system in that improvements are expected to flow from the bottom upwards. Team members are expected to commit to and take responsibility for the improvement work they are involved in.

Basic **project management techniques** are used in Six Sigma. Each improvement project will have a **charter** that defines its purpose, scope, assumptions and constraints in broad terms. This document will be subject to revision during the life of the project as its assumptions are challenged.

6.2.2 Six Sigma project phases

Six Sigma process improvement projects follow a **five phase** pattern known by the acronym DMAIC.

- **Define** customer requirements
- **Measure** existing performance
- **Analyse** the existing process
- **Improve** the process
- **Control** the new process

Exam focus point

A question in the June 2012 exam asked candidates to explain how Six Sigma could help improve the quality of performance in an organisation, and then to illustrate how the DMAIC method could be applied in that organisation in order to implement Six Sigma. Similarly, a question in the September/December 2015 exam asked how a Six Sigma project could be implemented using the DMAIC methodology.

Exam focus point

Notice that the 'D' in DMAIC relates to defining **customer** requirements, not defining the problem or issue. 'Customer' is actually the key word here. One of the key themes in Six Sigma is establishing a genuine focus on the customer, and what is important for the customer.

6.2.3 Define

The definition phase is a planning phase and includes project definition and the documentation of the existing process. Typically this will take one to two weeks, with the team meeting two or three times each week. A project charter may be provided by the project sponsor, but it may be necessary for the team to negotiate project scope and goals. The establishment of precise **customer requirements** from the process in question is an essential part of this phase. Kano divides customer requirements into three levels:

- **Basic** requirements are the minimum the customer will accept.
- **Satisfiers** improve the quality of the customer's experience.
- **Delighters** are totally unexpected by the customer.

Both external and internal customers may be vague in stating their requirements so careful research and logical definition are required.

A further important output from this phase is careful documentation of the process as it exists, probably using some form of **flow diagram**.

6.2.4 Measure

In the measure phase, statistical tools to assess current performance are selected using black belt expertise. Harmon, quoting Eckes, suggests three measurement principles:

- Only measure what the **customer** thinks is important.
- Do not measure things that the customer is satisfied with.
- Only measure things that **can be improved**.

There are three main areas for measurement:

- **Inputs** such as raw materials and product specifications
- **Process elements** such as cost, time, skills and training
- **Outputs and customer satisfaction**

Fairly clearly, outputs and customer satisfaction derive from and are determined by inputs and processes. According to Pande and Holpp, it is common to represent this relationship as an equation Y=f(X), where 'Y' represents outputs and 'X' represents inputs and processes. Y is then used in the jargon to mean goal or objective.

6.2.5 Analyse

Each element of the process may be assessed into one of three categories.

- **Value adding**
- **Necessary support** to value-adding activities
- **Non value adding**

Establishing the status of the various aspects of the process will require the use of a range of techniques including statistical analysis, and **fishbone analysis** (which you should be familiar with, from your P3 studies).

Analysis should produce a list of problem causes and potential areas for improvement.

6.2.6 Improve

It may be particularly appropriate to **revisit the project charter** at the beginning of this phase, so as to incorporate any implications of the information obtained.

Improving the process demands a degree of **creative thought**. This can, to some extent, be guided by the wider experience of the team and its expert consultants. The problems identified in the analysis phase will indicate fruitful areas for consideration.

It is common for the people closely involved with the operation of a process to develop ideas for its improvement almost as soon as the possibility is raised. There is often value in these ideas, not least because of the great intimacy their authors have with the details of the process and its organisational setting.

Nevertheless, it is important that all proposals for improvement are subjected to a **rational review** so that their implications may be considered in as much detail as possible. **Cost** and **resource** consequences are of particular importance.

Implementation of the agreed improvements will require careful planning, probably small-scale piloting and selling to stakeholders who were not involved in the project.

6.2.7 Control

Controlling processes is a **routine and continuing part of the management role**. When a process has been improved, it will probably be necessary to maintain some of the measurement processes used during the improvement effort in order to exercise control. However, the **cost of monitoring** must be considered, so it is likely that the extent of measurement will be minimised. Some processes can be monitored automatically, with control systems that generate exception reports automatically.

6.3 Example of DMAIC in context

We will now look at an example based on a restaurant ('The Foodhouse'), to illustrate how a Six Sigma project could be applied in practice.

The focus of The Foodhouse's project was on the customer satisfaction of customers who eat there. Their goal was ensuring customers are satisfied with the quality of their meal, and of the service they receive.

The project team identified a number of things about a dinner meal that **might** satisfy customers: quality of the food (taste, temperature); presentation of the food; variety of menu (number of items, daily specials); service (speed of food delivery, attention to customer's needs during the meal); ambience (room layout, cleanliness); and the price of the meal.

However, this list only showed the things that the project team thought might affect customer satisfaction. For their project to be effective, they had to determine the role that each of these possible requirements actually plays in customer satisfaction (that is, they had to **define** customer requirements).

They did this by asking all their customers to complete a short questionnaire survey after their meal.

The results of the survey showed that different types of customer have different requirements:

(a) For business customers, taste, temperature, speed of delivery and attentiveness during the meal were important factors.

(b) Elderly people indicated that taste, temperature and the availability of daily specials were most important to them.

(c) Customers with children indicate that taste, temperature and speed of delivery were most important to them.

The questionnaire responses gave the project team a clear idea of their customers' requirements.

They now had to identify **measures** to see how well they performed in satisfying these requirements.

One key measure The Foodhouse used to measure performance was the time it took for a customer to receive their meal (defined as the time between when the waiter took the order and when the meal is delivered to the table).

The total time is made up of the time it took the waiter to submit the order to the kitchen, the kitchen to cook the food and plate it up ready for service, and then for the waiter to deliver the meal.

The Foodhouse project team decided to split this process into two parts: the time it took waiters to place and deliver orders; and the time it took the kitchen to prepare and cook the food.

The team began to gather data on the time it took waiters to place and deliver orders, so that they could analyse it for trends as to what the most common causes of delay were when meals were delayed (the **analysis** phase).

The analysis indicated a number of things that took up a waiter's time and therefore interfered with the prompt placement of orders and delivery of food. These included: families with children wanting tables to be rearranged; multiple tables all requiring waiter service at the same time; and tables wanting to make frequent drink orders.

This highlighted to the project team that an important issue affecting the speed of service was the control and placement of families. The team decided that two groups of families with children should not be put in the same area if possible; or if there was no alternative to putting families together, the number of tables served by the waiter dealing with them should be reduced, and extra tables should be allocated to another waiter. (This is the **'improve'** stage.)

Overall, everyone was happy with the results obtained from the project. However, it was agreed that for one week every three months, follow-up customer feedback surveys would be distributed to all diners eating at the restaurant. The results from these surveys allow The Foodhouse's restaurant manager to monitor ongoing customer satisfaction (the **'control'** stage).

Exam focus point

Importance of measurement. An important theme in the P5 syllabus is the nature of measurement, and how it might be related to quality, efficiency and reward.

However, management theorists often acknowledge that 'what gets measured, gets done'. But this also raises the caution of whether the indicators which are actually being measured are the ones which **should** be being measured in order to control critical business processes, or to promote a desired outcome.

The question scenarios in your exam may include examples of the 'wrong' measures being applied, in which case you may need to suggest alternative measures which should be used instead.

6.4 Six Sigma and new processes

Although the 'DMAIC' methodology is the methodology most commonly associated with Six Sigma, this should be used for **improving existing processes** rather than designing and **implementing new processes** or activities which are free from defects.

If an organisation is looking to design and implement new processes or activities, then the methodology should be modified to 'DMADV'.

- **Define**. Define customer requirements, and the objective of the process or activity.
- **Measure**. Measure and identify product capabilities and process capabilities, and assess risks involved.
- **Analyse**. Analyse alternative ways of designing the process or activity and evaluate them to choose the best alternative.
- **Design**. Plan the design of the process or activity, optimise the design and then produce the design.
- **Verify**. Verify the actual process works as intended in the design, by carrying out trial runs. Then implement the process.

Chapter Roundup

- Quality management has developed from an inspection-based process to a philosophy of business that emphasises customer satisfaction, the elimination of waste and the acceptance of responsibility for conformance with quality specifications at all stages of all business processes.
- Changes to the **competitive environment**, **product life cycles** and **customer requirements** have had a significant impact on the modern business environment.
- In the context of **TQM**, quality means getting things right first time and improving continuously.
- **JIT** aims for zero inventory and perfect quality and operates by demand-pull. It consists of **JIT purchasing** and **JIT production** and results in lower investment requirements, space savings, greater customer satisfaction and increased flexibility.
- **Life cycle costing** assists in the planning and control of a product's life cycle costs by monitoring spending – and commitments to spend – during a product's life cycle.
- **Target costing** is a proactive cost control system. The target cost is calculated by deducting the target profit from a predetermined selling price, based on customers' views. Techniques such as value analysis are used to change production methods and/or reduce expected costs so that the target cost is met.
- The aim of **Kaizen costing** is to reduce current costs by using various tools such as value analysis and functional analysis.
- The essence of **continuous improvement** is the use of an organisation's human resources to produce a constant stream of improvements in all aspects of customer value, including quality, functional design and timely delivery, while lowering cost at the same time.
- 'Quality' does not mean 'high quality'. Rather, 'quality' is the degree to which a set of inherent characteristics fulfils requirements.
- **Costs of quality** can be analysed into **prevention**, **appraisal**, **internal failure** and **external failure** costs and should be detailed in a **cost of quality report**.
- Four aspects of quality are particularly important in software:
  - Functionality
  - Reliability
  - Usability
  - Build quality (flexibility, expandability, portability, ease of maintenance)
- Low quality in IS development produces systems that are difficult to use, maintain and enhance.
- As well as ensuring it has good-quality information systems, an organisation needs to ensure that it produces good-quality management information.
- Six Sigma is a quality management system that grew out of statistical quality techniques. The overall aim is to ensure a very high and consistent standard of quality output. Six Sigma tends to take the form of specific improvement projects that follow a standard five phase pattern.
  - **Define** requirements
  - **Measure** performance
  - **Analyse** the process
  - **Improve** the process
  - **Control** the new process

Quick Quiz

1 Why is standard costing not appropriate for budgeting in JIT production systems?

2 Which of the following statements about total quality management is/are true?

(i) Customer focus is vital for an organisation, because quality is measured in relation to meeting customers' needs and expectations.

(ii) An organisation's culture must demonstrate the importance of keeping defects to an acceptable level at all times.

A Neither of them
B (i) only
C (ii) only
D Both of them

3 Which of the following statements about Kaizen costing is/are true?

(i) Kaizen costing aims to reduce cost rather than just control it.
(ii) Employees are viewed as a source of solutions rather than as a cause of problems.

A Neither of them
B (i) only
C (ii) only
D Both of them

4 An organisation has recently noticed it has suffered an increase in the cost of scrapped parts and materials it is incurring, and it has seen a loss of production time as a result of coping with errors.

Which of the 'costs of quality' do these issues indicate the organisation needs to address?

A Prevention costs
B Appraisal costs
C Internal failure costs
D External failure costs

5 Which of the following is **not** one of the steps in the standard five phase pattern used in Six Sigma to improve existing processes?

A Analyse the process
B Measure performance
C Create a new process
D Define customer requirements

Answers to Quick Quiz

1 One of the key elements of JIT systems is continuous improvement. By definition, the idea of sticking to a standard cost is inconsistent with the concept of continuous improvement, and therefore would not be appropriate for a JIT environment.

2 B (i) only

TQM seeks to improve quality and performance to a level which meets or exceeds customer expectations. TQM recognises that organisations depend on their customers, and so must strive to meet customer needs. Therefore customer focus is vital for an organisation.

One of the core principles of TQM is that organisations should aim for zero defects. As such, any level of defects should be seen as unacceptable, so option (ii) is false.

3 D Both of them

Both of these are characteristics which distinguish Kaizen costing from standard costing. The aim of Kaizen costing is to reduce costs through continuous improvement (rather than looking to control costs against a standard base).

Similarly, Kaizen costing views employees as a source of solutions and empowers them to find those solutions (whereas standard costing often views employees as a cause of problems).

4 C Internal failure costs (costs associated with errors which are dealt with inside the operation) include: the costs of scrapped parts and materials, or reworked parts and materials, and the lost production time as a result of coping with errors.

5 C The 'C' in DMAIC stands for 'Control' the new process, not 'Create' the new process.

Now try the question below from the Practice Question Bank

Number	Level	Marks	Approximate time
Q13	Practice	20	40 mins

Performance measurement and strategic HRM issues

14

Topic list	Syllabus reference
1 Strategic human resource management	D6(b)
2 Performance management and appraisal	D6(b)
3 Reward management and reward schemes	D6(a)-D6(d)
4 Accountability	D7(a)
5 What gets measured, gets done	D7(b)
6 Management styles	D7(c)

Introduction

Human resource (HR) management plays a key role in enabling organisations to implement their strategies successfully – because strategy implementation requires the effective recruitment, training, organisation and retention of staff, coupled with effective leadership and performance measurement to ensure that employees' objectives and goals are aligned to those of their organisation.

In this chapter we will look first at the relationship between HR management and strategy implementation in general terms, before going on to look at the issues surrounding measuring and managing employees' performance in more detail. An important element of this is the impact that reward systems – and performance measurement systems more generally – can have on employees' behaviour.

We explore the behavioural aspects of performance measurement in more detail in the latter sections of the chapter.

Study guide

		Intellectual level
D6	**Performance measurement and strategic Human Resource Management issues**	
(a)	Advise on the relationship of HR management to performance measurement (performance rating) and suitable remuneration methods.	3
(b)	Advise on the link between achievement of the corporate strategy and the management of human resources (eg through the Building Block model).	2
(c)	Discuss and evaluate different methods of reward practices.	3
(d)	Assess the potential beneficial and adverse consequences of linking reward schemes to performance measurement, for example how it can affect the risk appetite of employees.	3
D7	**Other behavioural aspects of performance measurement**	
(a)	Discuss the accountability issues that might arise from performance measurement systems.	3
(b)	Assess the statement; 'What gets measured, gets done.'	3
(c)	Demonstrate how management style needs to be considered when designing an effective performance measurement system.	3

Exam guide

Although the overall focus of Section D of the syllabus is on strategic performance measurement, it is important to remember that an organisation's performance will be strongly influenced by the performance of the people working within it.

As such, human resource management (HRM) plays a key role in enabling an organisation to implement its strategy successfully – and Section D6 of the syllabus highlights these links between HRM and corporate strategy. A key element of this involves ensuring that the performance measurement systems used to assess employees, and the reward systems in place, motivate employees to help the organisation achieve its objectives.

Equally, in the context of an exam question, you need to be prepared to look critically at an organisation's remuneration and reward systems to assess whether they are helping the organisation to implement its corporate strategy successfully, or whether there are elements of them which could be improved. For example, Section D6 (c) identifies that candidates need to be able to 'evaluate' different methods of rewards practices – which means you may need to identify both the advantages and limitations of different methods being described in a case study scenario.

Element (d) of Performance objective 14 identifies that you should 'Use review and reward systems to monitor and assess performance.'

Reward systems are not only a key part of human resource management; they can also play a key role in helping an organisation to achieve its strategic objectives (by motivating employees). Equally, however, poorly designed reward systems could have a detrimental impact on an organisation's performance.

Issues to do with HRM more generally are also relevant to element (c) of Performance objective 5 – Leadership and management: 'Manage human ... resources within your control or allocated to your department to deliver your objectives to agreed deadlines, seeking opportunities to motivate or assist in the development of others.'

Overview of HRM

The diagram below, adapted from Fombrun, Tichy and Devanna's model of HRM, is a useful way of illustrating how HRM activities link together. Try to keep this diagram – and the linkages between the activities – in your mind as you read through this chapter, and if you have to answer a question about HRM in your exam.

Remember also HRM's role in business strategy overall. Bratton and Gold's definition of HRM is very useful here for highlighting its strategic importance.

> 'HRM is a strategic approach to managing employment relations, which emphasises that leveraging people's capabilities is critical to achieving sustainable competitive advantage, this being achieved through a distinctive set of integrated employment policies, programmes and practices.'

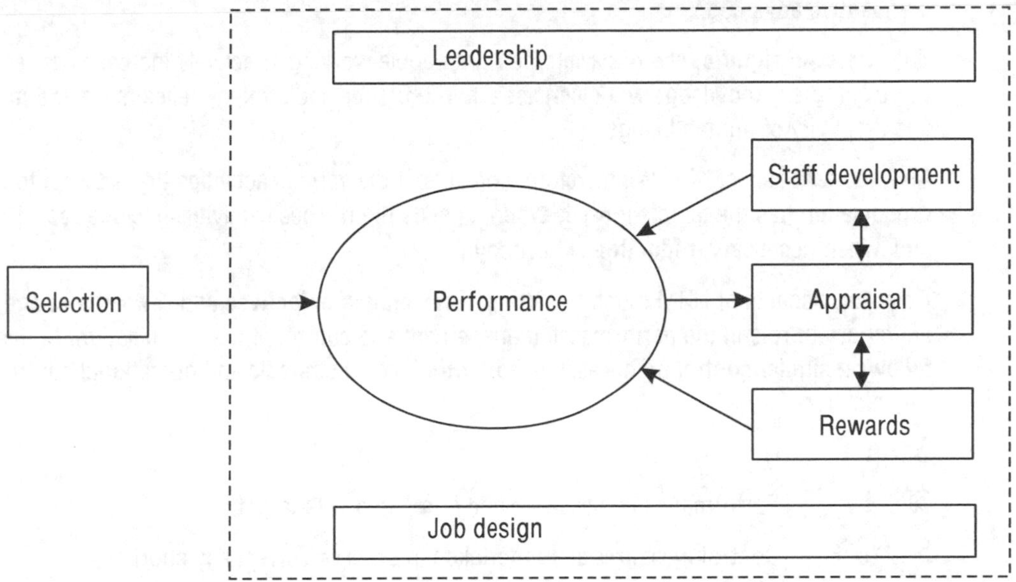

Strategic Human Resource Management (after Fornbrun, Tichy & Devanna)

Exam focus point

> The Technical Articles section of the resources available for Paper P5 on ACCA's website contains two articles about HRM and reward systems:
>
> - 'Human resource management and the appraisal system'
> - 'Reward schemes for employees and management'
>
> These articles supplement the material in this chapter, and you are strongly advised to read them as part of your preparation for your P5 exam.

Exam focus point

> One of the questions in the December 2012 exam described a company's remuneration policy, and the remuneration packages for different grades of staff within the company. Candidates were then asked to evaluate the remuneration policy and suggest changes where appropriate.

1 Strategic human resource management

FAST FORWARD

People are fundamental to any organisation, and therefore **human resource management** needs to be integrated with, and **aligned** to, an organisation's **corporate strategy**. An organisation also needs to ensure that its **employees are motivated** to help it achieve its corporate objectives.

1.1 People and strategic success

Bratton and Gold's definition of HRM (on the previous page) highlights that human knowledge and skills are a strategic resource for an organisation, and that they can play a vital role in achieving sustainable competitive advantage.

The **strategic significance** of having the right people working effectively increases as technology becomes more complex, knowledge work increases in importance and strategy relies more and more on the talents and creativity of human beings.

An important aspect of HRM, therefore, consists of the various activities that attempt to ensure that the organisation has the people it needs when it needs them. These activities include **recruitment**, **retention** and, when necessary, **reduction** of headcount.

However, aspects of HRM (such as setting **performance objectives** and **reward management**) also play an important role in the performance management and control of the organisation. In this respect, HRM follows a similar control model as is used for the overall strategic and operational control of an organisation.

Step 1 Goals are set.

Step 2 Performance is measured and compared with target.

Step 3 Control measures are undertaken in order to correct any shortfall.

Step 4 Goals are adjusted in the light of experience.

However, it is crucial to recognise that these goals link to both strategic and operational success. Effective performance management requires that the strategic objectives of the organisation are broken down into layers of more and more detailed sub-objectives, so that **individual performance** can be judged against personal goals that support and link directly back to corporate strategy.

In this respect, it is important to recognise the links between HRM and an organisation's objectives and critical success factors (CSFs). For example, if an organisation identifies excellent customer service as a CSF, then its recruitment process, training, appraisal and reward systems should all be geared towards promoting customer service skills in its staff.

More generally, the HRM process within an organisation also needs to support the organisation's corporate strategy by ensuring that the right number of employees are in place, with the necessary skills and knowledge, and whose behaviour and approach to their work is consistent with the organisation's culture.

1.2 People and operational success

Recruitment and selection

Operational success relies on the ability of people to do their jobs properly. This could be their ability to perform a range of activities, such as being able to operate machinery correctly, use computers, manage others and perform specific technical routines. In this respect, operational success requires the proper **recruitment** and **selection** of people with the right skills for the particular job, and the provision of further training as the requirements may dictate.

An organisation's staff are a very important resource, and they are likely to play a crucial role in an organisation achieving its strategic objectives. Therefore, it is vital that an organisation has the right number (**quantity**) and the right **quality** of staff to achieve its objectives.

In this respect, human resource planning is very important; not only in forecasting the numbers and levels of staff an organisation is likely to need, but also in deciding whether, for example, the staff should all work 'in house' or whether it might be more appropriate to outsource some functions, or to move to a more 'network' based organisation rather than using a more formally structured one.

In this way, recruitment and human resource planning play a vital role in ensuring that organisations have the necessary quantity and quality of staff to facilitate their success.

Objectives and performance targets

Staff should also have individual work **objectives** and **performance targets** (for example the number of sales calls made) and their performance against these objectives should be measured. These individual objectives and targets should be derived from department and organisation objectives. This should then mean that, in theory, if every individual achieves their objectives then their department will achieve its objectives and, if every department achieves its objectives, then the organisation as a whole will achieve its objectives.

Two factors that play an important role in determining whether employees achieve their objectives are **management** and **motivation**. We will look at a number of aspects of employee performance management later in this chapter, but in general terms we can highlight the link between performance and motivation by reference to the following equation (after Vroom).

Performance = Ability × Motivation

(where Motivation = Desire × Commitment)

In this equation, desire is seen as enthusiasm for a task, and commitment is about putting in effort. Therefore, as well as ensuring that employees have the necessary abilities to carry out their jobs, managers also need to make sure that their staff have the desire and commitment to do so efficiently and successfully.

Staff retention

Keeping staff motivated can also help an organisation retain staff more effectively, and in doing so can reduce the costs associated with **staff turnover**. These include: the time and costs spent in advertising for and recruiting new staff; time and money spent training new staff, and the 'learning curve' associated with new staff getting up to speed with their jobs; and the loss of organisational knowledge which occurs when individuals (particularly key employees) leave an organisation.

1.3 Rational planning and diagnostic planning

Early attempts to systematise staff planning in the 1960s and 1970s relied on a top-down, 'manpower planning' approach that fitted well with the then-popular rational planning approach to strategy. This attempted to forecast future requirements for all grades and types of staff, to analyse existing staff into the various categories required and to forecast the resulting surpluses or shortfalls. Recruitment, retention and reduction were then planned as required to meet the overall requirement. Extensive work was done on statistical tools and measures to support this method, leading to **PC-based personnel information systems** that could provide extensive detail on such matters as staff turnover, absenteeism and retention.

This approach suffered from the same disadvantages that we have seen in connection with the rational approach to strategy itself. In particular, it failed to pay sufficient attention to the **complexity of human behaviour**, emphasising systems rather than actually managing people in an effective way. As a result, a more **diagnostic** approach was developed. This attempts to look behind the raw data and to discern the factors that lead to variation in such matters as turnover, retention and absenteeism. As a result, 'planning becomes integrated into the whole process of management of the employment relationship ... Importantly, manpower planning has a part to play in bridging the gap between the needs of the organisation (as defined by senior management) and the needs of individual employees' (Gold).

1.4 Human resource planning

Both the rational and diagnostic approaches are used to support an existing strategy. The use of the term 'human resource planning' to replace 'manpower planning' reflects a move to a co-ordinated bundle of

HRM practices that make the links between strategy, structure and people more explicit. One important result of this change is an acknowledgement that HR practices based on high involvement, commitment and reward tend to be more effective than the alternative approach based on low pay, low job security and work intensification. However, basing HRM methods on the former approach requires that senior management accept that individual and collective knowledge and skill constitute an important element of strategic capability. Many organisations do not accept this and see their people mainly as a cost driver that must be controlled.

1.5 Psychological contracts

A **psychological contract** exists between individuals in an organisation and the organisation itself.

(a) The individual expects to derive certain benefits from membership of the organisation and is prepared to expend a certain amount of effort in return.

(b) The organisation expects the individual to fulfil certain requirements and is prepared to offer certain rewards in return.

Three types of psychological contract can be identified:

(a) **Coercive contract**. This is a contract in which the individual considers that they are being forced to contribute their efforts and energies involuntarily, and that the rewards they receive in return are inadequate compensation.

(b) **Calculative contract**. This is a contract, accepted **voluntarily** by the individual, in which they expect to do their job in exchange for a readily identifiable set of rewards. With such psychological contracts, motivation can only be increased if the rewards to the individual are improved. If the organisation attempts to demand greater efforts without increasing the rewards, the psychological contract will revert to a coercive one, and motivation may become negative.

(c) **Co-operative contract**. This is a contract in which the individual identifies themselves with the organisation and its goals, so that they actively seek to contribute further to the achievement of those goals. Motivation comes out of success at work, a sense of achievement, and self-fulfilment. The individual will probably want to share in the planning and control decisions which affect their work, and **co-operative contracts are therefore likely to occur where employees participate in decision making**.

Motivation happens when the psychological contract is viewed in the same way by the organisation and by the individual and when both parties are able to fulfil their side of the bargain: the individual agrees to work, or work well, in return for whatever rewards or satisfactions are understood as the terms of the 'contract'.

An important aspect of how employees perceive the equity of their relationship with their employers lies in the way they perceive their material rewards. Adams and Salomon suggest that this perception will always be coloured by comparisons with other people. There are many classes of person with whom comparison could be made, such as employees doing the same work, those doing different work and those working for other organisations. Comparisons will also be made between the employee's pay and the company's profits; between the employee's pay and their perception of their needs; and so on.

1.5.1 Impact of psychological contracts on recruitment and selection

The psychological contract comes into existence during the processes of recruitment and selection. The co-operative contract may be considered to be the most appropriate for highly skilled knowledge workers, such as professionally qualified accountants, but the calculative contract is probably at least as important. The potential for the calculative contract to degenerate into a coercive contract emphasises the importance of a clear understanding of the **mutual obligations** that exist within employment. This understanding should be based on equitable recruitment and selection procedures and developed within the employment relationship.

2 Performance management and appraisal 6/14

FAST FORWARD

Appraisal is a key part of performance management, forming a link between individual members of staff and an organisation's overall strategy.

However, within this overall setting, appraisal has two different purposes – **judgement** and **development** – and there is an inherent conflict between these two which has never been satisfactorily resolved.

2.1 Introduction

While the need for some kind of performance assessment is widely accepted, appraisal systems are frequently criticised as bureaucratic, ineffective and largely irrelevant to the work of the organisation. Partly as a response to this view, modern approaches attempt to enhance the relevance of appraisal by linking it to organisational strategy and objectives. This emphasises the use of appraisal as an **instrument of control over the workforce**.

The technical article 'Human resource management and the appraisal system' (available via ACCA's website) highlights:

> 'Appraisal is, therefore, seen as part of management control. By measuring the performance of employees against targets, management is seen to be proactively managing the performance of employees and therefore improving the performance of the organisation.'

2.1.1 The purpose of appraisal

Exam focus point

Part of a question in the June 2014 exam asked candidates to advise what the purpose of a staff appraisal scheme is and how the appraisal process could improve a company's performance. The question scenario referred specifically to the 'balance between control and staff development' in the appraisal process, which should have been a reminder that appraisals are both judgemental and developmental.

Appraisal is a process that provides an analysis of a person's overall capabilities and potential. An important part of the appraisal process is assessment – collecting and reviewing data on an individual's work.

The purpose of appraisal is usually seen as the **improvement of individual performance**, but it may also be regarded as having close links to a wide range of other HR issues, including discipline, career management, identifying training and development opportunities, motivation, communication, selection for promotion and determining rewards. It is also fundamental to the notion of **performance management**, which may be regarded as trying to direct and support individual employees to work as effectively and efficiently as possible so that the individual's goals are aligned with the organisation's goals and business strategy.

Within this wider view, regular appraisal interviews can be seen as serving two distinct purposes.

(a) **Judgement**: Judgemental appraisals are undertaken in order for decisions to be made about employees' pay, promotion and work responsibilities.

These decisions have to be made on the basis of judgements about the appraisee's behaviour, talent, industry and value to the organisation. Such judgements can be uncomfortable for both appraiser and appraisee and lead to hostility and aggression.

(b) **Development**: The focus of developmental appraisals is to assess employees' training and development needs.

Development appraisal can contribute to **performance improvement** by establishing individuals' development needs, progress and opportunities. This is the more supportive aspect of appraisal, but still requires the appraiser to make decisions about the appraisee.

'The tension between appraisal as a judgemental process and as a supportive development process has never been resolved and lies at the heart of most debates about the effectiveness of appraisal at work.' (Bratton and Gold)

Feedback on performance has been widely regarded as an important aspect of the participative style of management which, in turn, has been promoted as having potential to motivate higher performance. However, the link between feedback and motivation is not simple and an important aspect of the judgemental part of appraisal is its **potential to demotivate**.

The classic study which highlighted this was carried out by Meyer *et al* at the General Electric Company (GEC) in 1965. Bratton and Gold suggest that the findings from Meyer *et al*'s study are still relevant, and provide a summary of them.

(a) Criticism often has a negative effect on motivation and performance.

(b) Praise has little effect, one way or the other.

(c) Performance improves with specific goals.

(d) Participation by the employee in goal-setting helps to produce favourable results. (Don't forget the whole point of performance management is to improve performance!)

(e) Interviews designed primarily to improve performance should not at the same time weigh salary or promotion in the balance.

(f) Coaching by managers should be day to day rather than just once a year.

This last point could have useful implications for overcoming the problems faced in relation to many appraisals, where a formal appraisal process is carried out on an annual basis only. In addition to the formal appraisal process, however, it could be beneficial for managers to give employees informal feedback throughout the year. Employees are generally more likely to accept this feedback more readily, in which case constructive feedback given on an informal basis throughout the year is more likely to lead to improvements in employees' performance than formal feedback given in an end of year appraisal.

Opinions about performance

From their research in the 1980s into the effectiveness of self-appraisal as a means of evaluating performance, Campbell and Lee have pointed out another potential issue which can arise during the appraisal process: discrepancies between people's own opinions of their performance and the opinions held by their supervisors.

Campbell and Lee point out three ways in which these discrepancies may arise;

(a) **Information**. There may be disagreement over what work roles involve, standards of performance and methods to be used.

(b) **Cognition**. The complexity of behaviour and performance leads to different perceptions.

(c) **Affect**. The judgemental nature of appraisal is threatening to the appraisee and, possibly, to the appraiser.

Since Meyer *et al's* study there has been a long search to find a way of appraising employees which reduces the feeling that feedback is about criticism.

One approach to mitigating the undesirable effects of judgemental appraisal has been the use of **multi-source feedback**, including 360 degree appraisal, in order to provide a demonstrably more **objective** review. Such approaches have tended to be used principally for appraisal of managers. Multisource feedback can be seen as empowering for staff. It may also be seen as reinforcing for good management behaviour (since it shows managers how they are seen by others) and likely to improve the overall reliability of appraisal. However, research has shown that the effects can vary significantly.

2.1.2 Appraisal as control or development?

The last of Meyer *et al's* findings – 'coaching by managers should be day to day rather than just once a year' – also highlights the role of managers in the **development** of their staff on a continual basis.

However, any shift towards a more developmental view of appraisal sits uncomfortably with the traditional management objectives of having a means of measuring, monitoring and controlling performance.

As we have already noted, most appraisal schemes are still ultimately **performance control schemes**, assessing actual performance against predetermined targets.

This somewhat rigid approach, based on the drive for rationality and efficiency in organisations, highlights what Mintzberg has called '**machine bureaucracy**'. 'Getting organised', 'being rational' and 'achieving efficiency' are felt to be the best ways for an organisation to be structured.

This mechanistic view of organisations will, almost inevitably, mean that appraisal is seen as a control system, and will lead to employees feeling that they are being controlled by appraisal systems. However, this is unlikely to motivate employees or to generate trust, commitment and high productivity.

Employees' trust and commitment to an organisation will come about through management creating a culture that supports the long-term development of people. Assessment and appraisal could play a key part in this shift, but only if human resource managers can convince organisations that, while control remains important, development needs to play a much greater role in the appraisal process.

2.2 HRM and performance management

FAST FORWARD

Performance management attempts to integrate HRM processes with the strategic direction and control of the organisation by incorporating agreed goals and control measures. There are several approaches to performance rating.

- Inputs and personal qualities
- Results and outcomes
- Behaviour in performance

As we mentioned at the start of the chapter, performance management systems represent the rational, efficiency-driven aspect of HRM. They attempt to integrate HRM processes with the strategic direction and control of the organisation.

Step 1 Goals are set.

Step 2 Performance is measured and compared with target.

Step 3 Control measures are undertaken in order to correct any shortfall.

Step 4 Goals are adjusted in the light of experience.

You should be familiar with this kind of management control in business organisations, where the balanced scorecard, for example, is often used as the basis for such an approach. Ultimately, management control involves managers taking steps to ensure that employees do what is best for their organisation.

Performance management requires that the strategic objectives of the organisation are broken down into layers of more and more detailed sub-objectives, so that individual performance can be judged against personal goals that support and link directly back to corporate strategy. This kind of cascade of goals and objectives was discussed earlier in this Study Text.

The performance management system, though it emphasises the control aspects of appraisal, must also allow for the **development** aspect of appraisal, providing for coaching and training where needed.

2.3 Performance rating

Intimately linked with the definition of goals is the creation of suitable **performance indicators** against which to measure employees' performance.

Three different approaches can be used: measurement of inputs; measurement of results and outcomes; and behaviour in performance.

2.3.1 Inputs or personal qualities

Measurement of inputs focuses on the personality traits and competences of an individual to determine whether that person has the characteristics or competences required for a job. For example, attributes such as leadership, commitment, team working and loyalty are often viewed as desirable traits in this respect.

However, the nature of these traits means they cannot be measured quantitatively. Therefore, when managers attempt to assess performance on the basis of personal qualities, subjectively and bias (whether real or perceived) can undermine the reliability of the output.

Therefore many organisations now use psychometric tests designed by suitably qualified professionals, rather than relying on the judgements of their own managers.

2.3.2 Results and outcomes

Where the cybernetic model is implemented, objective assessment of performance against work targets can be a **reliable method of rating**. Targets are set for individuals – for example, the level of sales achieved by a salesperson – and then their performance will be judged against those targets. Have they reached their targets or not?

However, a fundamental problem with this approach is the importance of the way in which objectives are set. Ideally, they should be agreed at the outset, but this requires a degree of understanding of the complexity and difficulty of the work situation that neither party to the appraisal may possess.

Additionally, this approach does not take account of external factors which may have affected performance. For example, a general slowdown in the economy may affect a salesperson's ability to achieve sales targets in a way that may not have been anticipated when those targets were set.

These points highlight two key issues in relation to setting targets.

Achievable – any targets set should be realistic and achievable. If targets are perceived to be unrealistic, staff will not attempt to achieve them, and they are also likely to be demotivated as a result of the targets set.

Controllable – staff should not be judged on targets which are outside their control.

Exam focus point

The 'results and outcomes' approach can be used effectively in the context of both quality management and business process redesign, which we have considered earlier in this Study Text.

Note the importance of measurement here, and remember that 'measure' is one of the DMAIC project phases in Six Sigma.

However, the reference to 'measurement' should also be a reminder that 'what gets measured, gets done'. This could be particularly important when determining what aspects of their performance will be included in employees' appraisals. For example, if call centre staff are being measured purely on the volume of calls they handle (without any measure of customer satisfaction), this is likely to encourage them to conclude each call as quickly as possible, regardless of how well they have addressed a customer's query.

2.3.3 Behaviour in performance

In this approach, the focus is more on how staff carry out their roles, rather than simply looking at quantified measures of achievement. A 'behaviour in performance' approach is often particularly relevant to managerial and professional activities, such as communication, planning, leadership and problem solving, where qualitative data is as important as quantitative data in evaluating performance.

Behaviour-anchored rating scales (BARS) enable numerical scoring of performance of such activities. A numerical scale from, say, one to five is 'anchored' against descriptions of the kind of behaviour that would lead to a maximum or minimum score, and the appraiser then gives the score which they think is appropriate.

For example, at the end of an accountancy training course, students could be asked to grade their tutor according to such criteria as 'how clearly they explained topics' and 'how approachable they were' – where '5' is excellent and '1' is very poor.

Behavioural observation scales (BOS) identify specific actions, and staff are then judged accordingly to how frequently they perform those actions, relative to the frequency of opportunities they had to perform them.

For example, the actions might be 'providing constructive feedback', 'giving praise where due' or 'sharing best practice'. Scores are then recorded on a numerical scale, graded from 'never' at one extreme to 'always' at the other.

Problems of subjectivity

A major problem with measuring 'behavioural' performance is the subjectivity involved. For example, one student may feel that a tutor has explained a topic clearly, while another may not. In this respect, BOS are slightly less subjective than BARS, because BOS are based on the frequency with which behaviour is observed, rather than on an assessment of the quality of the behaviour itself.

2.4 Target selection

In relation to appraisals and performance rating, we have considered how performance management acts as a control system in measuring people's achievement against targets. However, in order for performance management to be beneficial, it is important to select the right measures or targets at the outset when setting performance goals.

We have noted the phrase 'What gets measured, gets done' several times already in this Study Text – in relation to corporate performance – but it is equally relevant here. If the 'wrong' performance measures or targets are set, this could lead to staff behaviour being different to that originally intended, and ultimately adversely affecting performance.

Case Study — **Banks' mis-selling scandals**

UK banks have been embroiled in a spate of mis-selling scandals in recent years: payment protection insurance (PPI), interest swaps and unnecessary insurance against credit card theft.

Part of the reason for the mis-selling is likely to be the fact that banks' bonus schemes were tied solely to short-term goals. Speaking at a conference in May 2014, Erik Charles, a pay scheme expert, said that it was 'not surprising ... that staff had mis-sold thousands of financial products to customers' because the incentive schemes that the banks had put in place encouraged this.

Mr Charles also argued that, in addition to encouraging mis-selling, bonuses with short-term goals that are paid quarterly or annually do little to improve a bank's long-term productivity or health.

An employee can book the revenue from a deal, meet their short-term goal, earn their bonus, and then leave the company. However, the bank might only realise later that the deal is riddled with problems that it has to deal with – and which could potentially also have significant financial implications for it.

In 2013, the *Financial Times* reported that the cost of the PPI scandal to UK banks (in terms of compensation claims) was already in excess of £15bn and still rising, while banks had set aside a £2bn compensation plan for mis-sold interest rate swaps, and £1.3bn for mis-sold credit card theft insurance.

Sources: Brinded, L. (2014) UK Financial Mis-selling Was Caused By Short Term Bank Bonus Goals, says Pay Scheme Expert, *International Business Times*, Online. Available from: http://www.ibtimes.co.uk/uk-financial-mis-selling-was-caused-by-short-term-bank-bonus-goals-says-pay-scheme-expert-1449201 [Accessed 26 January 2016]

Jenkins, P. (2013) Another mis-selling scandal rocks UK banks' reputation, *Financial Times*, 23 August.

The individual performance measures selected should be relevant to the overall objectives of the organisation. Individuals' objectives must reflect the overall strategic initiatives management are taking. For example, if management is focusing on quality, performance measures must reflect this by measuring employees on their contribution to achieving quality targets.

2.4.1 Targets and motivation

Some employees respond well to difficult targets and are motivated to attain them. Others may find the targets daunting and feel they are unachievable, and indeed there may be valid reasons why they believe this. For example, in an economic downturn, a number of businesses are reducing the amount they are spending on their IT budgets. Therefore, if a salesperson in an IT company was given a target of increasing sales 25% on the previous year, they would appear to be justified in thinking this target is unachievable.

Equally, care must be taken when using certain measures, for instance numbers of sales, as the basis for rewarding employees. As an example, here are some possible negative consequences of using sales numbers as a primary performance measure.

(a) The salesperson might offer potential customers large discounts in order to make the sale (but with the effect that the company makes a loss on the sale).

(b) The salesperson is concerned solely with the immediate sale, which may lead to poor after-sales service, low customer satisfaction levels and poor customer retention.

(c) The salesperson might use expensive promotions that actually generate less in sales value than they cost, but which allow the salesperson to register a number of sales.

(d) Once a salesperson has reached their target figure for a period they might look to defer future sales into the next period.

It may be better to use a balanced mix of targets – for example, setting customer care and customer profitability targets as well as the number of sales made.

It is also important to make sure that whatever goals are set are capable of being controlled by the individual, otherwise the individual is likely to become demotivated.

In addition, if processes are being redesigned, and job roles are changing, performance measures must be adapted to reflect the new jobs and responsibilities.

However, it is important that people are not given too many objectives and targets. There is a danger that people could become overwhelmed by the sheer number of goals they are expected to meet, but with the result that they do not know what their priorities are or what aspects of their work they should give most attention to.

Finally, it is useful to remember the acronym SMART when setting performance targets: are the targets specific, measurable, achievable, relevant and time-bounded?

3 Reward management and reward schemes 12/12

FAST FORWARD

Employment is an economic relationship: labour is exchanged for reward. **Extrinsic rewards** derive from job context and include pay and benefits. **Intrinsic rewards** derive from job content and satisfy higher-level needs. Reward systems interact with many other aspects of the organisation. Reward policy must recognise these interactions, the economic relationship and the psychological contract.

A reward system should also fulfil three key behavioural objectives: supporting the recruitment and retention of staff; motivating employees to high levels of performance; and promoting compliance with workplace rules and expectations.

3.1 Reward

Employment is fundamentally an economic relationship: the employee works as directed by the employer and, in exchange, the employer provides reward. The relationship inevitably generates a degree of tension between the parties, since it requires **co-operation** if it is to function, but it is also likely to give rise to **conflict** since the employee's reward equates exactly to a cost for the employer.

Key term

> A **reward system** encompasses 'all of the monetary, non-monetary and psychological payments that an organisation provides for its employees in exchange for the work they perform'. (Bratton)

The rewards provided for employees may be seen as **extrinsic** or **intrinsic**.

(a) **Extrinsic rewards** derive from the **job context**: such extrinsic rewards include pay and other material benefits as well as such matters as working conditions and management style.

(b) **Intrinsic rewards** derive from **job content** and satisfy higher-level needs, such as those for self-esteem and personal development.

The organisation's reward system is based on these two types of reward and also includes the policies and processes involved in providing them.

Reward systems are a fundamental aspect of HRM and of the way the organisation functions. An organisation's reward system interacts with many other systems, objectives and activities.

The following are all important characteristics of reward systems:

- They should support the overall strategy of the organisation.
- They should help to align the goals of individual employees with the goals of the organisation.
- They are a vital part of the psychological contract.
- They influence the success of recruitment and retention policies.
- They must conform with law.
- They consume resources and so must be affordable.
- They affect motivation and performance management within an organisation.
- They should help to align the risk preferences of managers and employees with those of the organisation – and its owners.
- They should be easy to administer efficiently and correctly.

The dual nature of reward mentioned earlier – a benefit for the employee, a cost for the employer – means that the parties in the relationship have divergent views of its purposes and extent. Employees see reward as fundamental to their standard of living: inflation, comparisons with others and rising expectations put upward pressure on their notion of what its proper level should be. Employers, on the other hand, seek both to control their employment costs and to use the reward system to influence such matters as productivity, recruitment, retention and change.

Case Study — Barclays

Barclays

Consider the following case, and whether you think the bonus payments are justified or not.

In 2013, despite a fall in annual pre-tax profits of 37% in Barclays' investment bank, and return on equity falling from 12.7% to 8.2%, bonuses increased by 13%. Barclays' investment bankers enjoyed bonuses of £1.6bn compared to £1.4bn in 2012. Total bonus pay across the Barclays group as a whole increased from £2.2bn in 2012 to £2.4bn in 2014.

Announcing these figures, Barclays' chief executive said: 'At Barclays, we believe in paying for performance and paying competitively.'

Barclays is trying to compete directly, on a worldwide basis, with JP Morgan and Goldman Sachs to hire and retain the investment bankers it values most highly. As Barclays' chief executive pointed out: 'We compete in global markets for talent. If we are to act in the best interests of our shareholders, we have to make sure we have the best people in our firm.'

Consequently, the chief executive insisted that the bonuses needed to be paid, because Barclays had no control over market-led pay. In other words, if Barclays pays less than rival banks, it will not be able to retain its staff.

As such, Barclays' chief executive argued that the increase in the incentive pool was required in order to build the business in the long-term interests of shareholders. This suggests that it is more important to retain talented employees to support the business's future growth than to tie annual rewards to annual performance.

But is this really how performance-related pay should work? Critics argued that, instead of rewarding past performance, Barclays' bonuses are more akin to a reward for performance that the bank hopes will occur in the future – provided that JP Morgan (and others) don't increase their bonuses even higher, and in the hope that trading bonds becomes interesting again.

Similarly, critics have argued that these bonuses are not consistent with the general principle that bonuses are meant to reflect financial performance – that is, bonus awards increase as [financial] performance increases, and go down if [financial] performance worsens.

Moreover, after the results were announced, Barclays faced a revolt among its institutional investors, and 34% of its shareholders voted against the remuneration report at the Group's annual meeting in June 2012.

In its 2012 annual report, Barclays had pledged to take 'a different approach to the balance between directors' and employees' remuneration, and returns for shareholders.'

However, the corporate governance director at the Institute of Directors was very critical of the impact of this new balance. In the light of the bank proposing to pay £2.4bn in bonuses compared with £860m in dividends to shareholders, he questioned who Barclays was being run for – its staff or its owners?

Based on: Pratley, N. (2014), 'Barclays' bonuses: back to the bad old days', *The Guardian*. Online. Available from: http://www.theguardian.com/business/nils-pratley-on-finance/2014/feb/11/barclays-bonuses-pay-for-performance [Accessed 26 January 2016]

Treanor, J. (2014), 'Barclays condemned over £2.4bn bonuses', *The Guardian*. Online. Available from: http://www.theguardian.com/business/2014/feb/11/barclays-hikes-bonuses-profits-slide [Accessed 26 January 2016]

3.2 A reward management model

The effective reward system should facilitate both the **organisation's strategic goals** and also the goals of **individual employees**.

Within this, an organisation has to make three basic decisions about monetary reward:

(a) How much to pay
(b) Whether monetary rewards should be paid on an individual, group or collective basis
(c) How much emphasis to place on monetary reward as part of the total employment relationship

However, there is no single reward system that fits all organisations.

Bratton proposes a model of reward management based on five elements:

(a) The **strategic perspective**
(b) Reward **objectives**
(c) Reward **options**
(d) Reward **techniques**
(e) Reward **competitiveness**

3.3 The strategic perspective

Knowledge brought forward from earlier studies

You will recall from your studies for Paper F1 that contingency theory as applied to management suggests that techniques used should be appropriate to the circumstances they are intended to deal with: there is unlikely to be a single best option that is appropriate to any context.

A **contingency approach to reward** accepts that the organisation's strategy is a fundamental influence on its reward system and that the reward system should support the chosen strategy.

Thus, for example, cost leadership and differentiation based on service will have very different implications for reward strategy (and, indeed, for other aspects of HRM). This is because each strategy needs a reward which is appropriate for it. The closer the alignment between the reward system and the strategic context, the more effective the organisation. The following example illustrates this.

3.3.1 Example of strategic perspective

Bratton and Gold in *Human Resource Management* provide an illustration of how two different businesses with different generic strategies have completely different reward systems.

The first business produces high-quality, custom-made machine tools for a high-tech industry. The production process is complex and workers are highly skilled, capable of performing various different jobs. The workers all work in self-managed teams.

In contrast to the industry norm, these skilled machine operators are not paid an hourly wage, but instead they receive a base salary which is increased as they learn new skills. The employees receive an excellent benefits package and profit-sharing bonuses. Not surprisingly, staff turnover is very low.

Labour costs at this company are above the industry average, but the company is successful nonetheless because its reward system is aligned to its strategy. It is following a differentiation strategy, and its reward system encourages commitment from its staff. The system also encourages higher productivity than its competitors, because of the increased functional flexibility which having multi-skilled staff offers. The incentive of their salary increasing as they learn new skills encourages the staff to become multi-skilled. In turn, having a multi-skilled workforce reduces machine downtime and scrap rates. Because the teams are self-managed, the company does not need to employ supervisors or quality inspectors (the teams self-regulate their own quality). Because staff turnover is low, recruitment and training costs are similarly low.

Therefore, although the company's labour costs are above the industry average, these additional costs deliver benefits elsewhere and support its differentiation strategy.

Against this, Bratton and Gold contrast a production process producing frozen food. The work is low-skilled and monotonous, and requires little employee commitment. The production line is automated and managers, not workers, control the speed of the line.

The workers are paid an hourly wage marginally above the minimum wage, and there are no additional payments or benefits. Not surprisingly, labour turnover is very high.

However, again this company is successful, because its reward system is aligned to its strategy. It is following a cost leadership strategy and so low-cost production is essential. The high labour turnover is not a problem because unskilled workers are easy to recruit, and training costs are low. Therefore, the company's policy of paying near-minimum wage only is appropriate to a strategy in which little commitment or loyalty is required from the employees.

Exam focus point

It is important that reward systems are aligned to an organisation's objectives and its critical success factors, as well as to the job in question. As the example from Bratton and Gold (above) illustrates, if the organisation has highly skilled employees who are crucial to its competitive success, then the reward system should be designed to try to retain such staff.

However, it is also important to recognise the impact that implementing a reward system can have on employees' day to day performance. Once again, the adage 'What gets measured, gets done' could be relevant here. In particular, if a reward system is based primarily around individual performance, then staff will focus on their own individual results and teamwork could suffer as a result.

In your exam, a case study scenario may describe a reward management system which is not appropriate for the context in which it is being used, and you may need to evaluate the system and the impact it could have on an organisation's performance.

Similarly, if an organisation is looking to redesign jobs as part of a change initiative (for example, to introduce new technologies), you may be asked to consider what impact this could have on the reward system.

3.4 Reward objectives

The reward system should pursue three behavioural objectives:

(a) It should support **recruitment and retention**.

(b) It should **motivate** employees to high levels of **performance**. This motivation may, in turn, develop into commitment and a sense of belonging, but these do not result directly from the reward system.

(c) It should promote **compliance** with workplace rules and expectations.

3.4.1 Recruitment and retention

The reward system should support **recruitment and retention**. Several influences are important here. Employees will certainly assess their pay and material benefits against what they believe to be the prevailing market rate. They will also take account of disadvantageous factors, such as unpleasant working conditions in their assessment of the degree of equity their reward achieves for them. Finally, they will be very sensitive to comparisons with the rewards achieved by other employees of the same organisation. Failure to provide a significant degree of satisfaction of these concerns will lead to enhanced recruitment costs.

3.4.2 Motivation

The reward system should **motivate employees** to high levels of performance.

Knowledge brought forward from earlier studies

You will recall from your studies for Paper F1 that motivation has been the subject of much research and many theories. It is a very complex topic and impossible to sum up in a few words. However, we can say with reasonable confidence that the relationship between reward and motivation is far from simple and that there is no more than a very limited degree of correlation between pay levels and work performance and motivation.

Also remember **Maslow's hierarchy of needs** and **Herzberg's 'Motivation-hygiene' theory**.

Maslow's hierarchy of needs suggests that monetary rewards are more likely to motivate low-paid staff (because the money they earn will enable them to meet their physiological and safety needs – for example, for food and housing). However, as employees become progressively better paid, money is less likely to be a motivating factor for them. Instead, a sense of respect and achievement ('esteem'), and a sense of fulfilment ('self-actualisation') are likely to be more important for such employees.

Similarly, although Herzberg's theory suggests that employees will be dissatisfied if they have a poor salary, monetary rewards alone do **not** generate satisfaction and motivation in the longer term. Instead, non-financial factors, such as a sense of achievement, recognition, increased responsibility and opportunities for advancement and growth, plus the nature of the work itself, are more likely to motivate employees.

Despite the apparently tenuous link between performance and level of pay, traditional pay systems have featured incentives intended to improve performance; there has also been a tendency for British and North American companies to adopt systems of individual performance-related pay intended to support overall organisational objectives rather than simply to incentivise individual productivity.

3.4.3 Compliance

The reward system should **promote compliance** with workplace rules and expectations. The psychological contract is complex and has many features, including material rewards. The incentives included in the reward system play an important role in **signalling to employees the behaviour that the organisation values**. It is also an important contributor to the way employees perceive the organisation and their relationship with it.

3.5 Reward options

Material reward may be divided into three categories.

(a) **Base pay** is a simply established reward for the time spent working.

(b) **Performance-related pay** is normally added to base pay and is intended to reward the performance of either the individual or of a team of employees.

(c) **Indirect pay** is made up of benefits such as health insurance and child care and is provided in addition to base pay or performance pay.

3.5.1 Base pay

Base pay is usually related to the value of the job, as established by a simple estimate, a scheme of **job evaluation** or reference to prevailing employment market conditions. A distinction may be made between hourly or weekly paid **wages** and monthly paid **salary**.

Base pay is easy to administer, although for many employees it is more likely to be a hygiene factor than a motivating factor (in Herzberg's terms).

Base pay can be supplemented by other types of remuneration – for example, overtime or performance-related pay.

3.5.2 Performance-related pay

In performance-related pay (PRP) schemes, remuneration is linked to an assessment of performance, usually measured against pre-agreed objectives. These schemes (which can also be known as 'merit pay') usually relate to output and quality of work, but may sometimes include an element of evaluation of behavioural characteristics.

Performance-related pay can either be based on an individual's performance against their own objectives (individual PRP) or it can be based on a team's performance against its objectives (group PRP).

Individual PRP schemes have the benefit of controllability, since each employee has control over their own rewards rather than being dependent on the effort (or lack of effort) of other members of their team. However, a danger of individual PRP schemes is that they may lead to a lack of teamwork as each member of the team seeks to maximise their own performance.

Conversely, while group PRP schemes should encourage teamwork, they have the potential disadvantage that members of a team who work less hard benefit from the efforts of those members of the team who work harder.

More generally, there is a danger that PRP schemes will lead employees to focus on those aspects of their performance which they know are being measured, to the detriment of other parts of their role. Once again this is the idea that 'What gets measured, gets done.'

Performance-related pay takes many forms. As well as merit pay, it can include commissions, piecework, and knowledge- or skill-related pay.

Commissions are often used as a form of remuneration for sales staff. These staff are likely to receive a relatively low basic salary, supplemented by a commission based on the level of sales they make.

One advantage of commission schemes is that they should help to motivate sales staff to achieve higher sales, thereby aligning the interests of individual staff members with those of the organisation.

Another advantage (for an organisation) is that they mean that a proportion of staff costs become variable costs; so if a salesperson only makes a relatively low level of sales, the amount the organisation pays them is also relatively low.

However, a potential disadvantage of commission schemes is that they may lead to dysfunctional behaviour. For example, they could adversely affect teamwork as each individual tries to maximise their own commission. They could also encourage sales staff to 'put the sales target above the customer', and pressurise a customer to buy something before they have time to think about the purchase, or possibly even if they don't really want to make the purchase. This is likely to be disadvantageous to a company in the long run, though, because a customer is unlikely to buy from them again, if they are unhappy with the way they have been treated.

Under a **piecework scheme**, an individual is paid a price for each unit of output, so the higher their output the more they receive. However, the inherent danger of such a scheme is that the payment is based on quantity, not quality, so some kind of quality control will also be necessary to ensure that an individual is not paid for substandard work.

Knowledge- or competence-related pay reflects a situation where an employee receives a pay increase, or a bonus, in return for increasing their competences or knowledge. Such a situation frequently occurs in the accountancy profession, where trainee accountants receive a higher salary once they have passed their exams.

Profit-related pay

Profit-related pay can also be seen as a type of group PRP scheme. In a profit-related pay scheme, part of an employee's remuneration is linked to the profitability of their organisation. So, for example, a profit target could be set at the beginning of each year; then, if the organisation's profit for the year exceeds that target figure, employees will become eligible for their bonuses.

The logic of profit-related pay schemes is that rewarding employees for the success of their organisations should help motivate them to increase their performance – in order to contribute to the success of the organisation overall. They may also encourage loyalty to an organisation, since in many cases employees lose their entitlement to a bonus when they leave the organisation.

However, a significant disadvantage of profit-related pay is that it could lead to a conflict between short-term and long-term performance, and hence between the directors or managers of a company and its shareholders.

If the managers of a company know that their bonuses depend on annual (short-term) profits, they may be motivated to take actions to boost the short-term profitability of the company. However, those actions may not generate value for the company in the longer term, and may end up damaging the longer-term profitability of the company. As such, the managers' actions will also be inconsistent with the primary objective of their companies – which is to maximise the wealth of their shareholders.

3.5.3 Target setting and performance-related pay

The logic of performance-related pay should be pretty clear: if an organisation can find a way of linking the personal objectives of its employees to its corporate objectives, then better goal congruence should result. If employees' performance is then linked to financial reward, for example in the form of bonuses, then there should be a mutual benefit for employees, employers and owners resulting from objectives being met.

However, a key factor in the success of PRP schemes will be the performance measures and targets actually set.

Fitzgerald and Moon (in their 'building block' model) suggest that effective targets (or performance standards) should have the following three characteristics:

(a) **Fairness** (equity) – When targets are being set across an organisation (for various managers and staff across a range of departments or functions) care needs to be taken to ensure that the targets set are equally challenging, rather than being easier for some managers/staff to achieve than others.

(b) **Ownership** – The targets should be accepted and agreed by the managers or staff they relate to. Where individuals participate in the setting of their targets they are more likely to accept them – and be motivated by them – rather than simply having the targets imposed on them.

(c) **Achievability** – The most effective targets are ones which are challenging yet achievable. If employees feel that a target is too difficult and is therefore unachievable, their inability (either real or perceived) to achieve the target is likely to demotivate them.

Exam focus point

We will look at Fitzgerald and Moon's building block model in more detail in Chapter 15, in our review of multi-dimensional performance models. The building blocks were designed as a framework for performance measurement specifically in service industries.

However, the characteristics of 'standards' and 'rewards' which Fitzgerald and Moon identified can usefully be considered in relation to reward systems as a whole.

The effectiveness of standards (or targets) is affected by the principles of fairness, ownership and achievability.

The effectiveness of reward schemes is affected by the principles of clarity, ability to motivate, and controllability.

The issue of clarity also links back to the ideas of 'SMART' and performance objectives being 'specific' and 'measurable' – if an employee's performance objectives are not clearly defined, how can the employee be assessed on whether they have achieved them or not?

A question in the June 2013 exam asked candidates to evaluate the standards and rewards which were being proposed for use in a performance reward system for hotel managers. The scenario specifically referred to Fitzgerald and Moon's model; so, in effect, the examination team was asking candidates to evaluate the reward scheme using the principles we have noted above: fairness, ownership, achievability, clarity, ability to motivate, and controllability.

3.5.4 Share options

One further type of reward option we should consider is share options (or employee share option plans (ESOP)). Note, however, that share options tend to be most appropriate for the directors and senior management of an organisation, because they are the people who have most influence over the organisation's share price. Share options give directors – and possibly other managers and staff – the right to purchase shares at a specified exercise price after a specified time period in the future.

The options will normally have an exercise price that is equal to, or slightly higher than, the market price on the date that the options are granted. The time period (vesting period) that must pass before the options can be exercised is generally a few years. If the director or employee leaves during that period the options will lapse.

In this respect, share options can be seen as a way of rewarding directors and employees for remaining with a company. In turn, this could mean that they are concerned with the longer-term success of the company, rather than simply focusing on short-term performance.

Share options will generally be exercisable on a specific date at the end of the vesting period. In the UK, the Corporate Governance Code states that shares granted, or other forms of remuneration, should not vest or be exercisable in less than three years. Directors should be encouraged to hold their shares for a further period after vesting or exercise. If directors or employees are granted a number of options in one package, these options should not all be able to be first exercised at the same date.

If the price of the shares rises so that it exceeds the exercise price by the time the options can be exercised, the directors will be able to purchase shares at lower than their market value, which is clearly advantageous for the directors exercising the options. Share options can therefore be used to **align management and shareholder interests**, because the directors have an interest in ensuring that the share price increases over time such that it is higher than the exercise price when the options come to be exercised. This is particularly relevant for options held for a long time when value is dependent on long-term performance.

However, the main danger with share options is that they could give directors an incentive to manipulate the share price if a large number of options are due to be exercised.

Alternatively, granting options could be used as a way of encouraging cautious (or risk averse) directors to take positive action to increase the value of the company.

Again, this could help align the interests of directors and shareholders, if the directors would not otherwise be prepared to accept the same risks which the shareholders would tolerate by themselves.

The upside risk of share options is unlimited – because there is no restriction on how much the share price can exceed the exercise price. However, there is no corresponding downside risk for the directors. If the share price is less than the exercise price, the intrinsic value of options will be zero and the options will lapse. In these circumstances it will make no difference how far the share price is below the exercise price.

If directors hold options, the value of their options will rise if a strategic investment succeeds and they will not suffer any loss on their options if the investment fails. Therefore, granting the options might encourage the directors to take actions they would not otherwise be prepared to take.

However, the absence of downside risk for the directors means that **share options still leave a mismatch** between the risks faced by the organisation (and its owners) and the risk borne by the directors who hold the options. The directors (option holders) benefit if share prices increase, but do not bear any losses if the share price falls. However, although an organisation's shareholders benefit if the share price rises, they **will** incur losses if the share price falls.

This could be a particular issue if the exercise price looks like it may not be met. Directors may be motivated to implement high-risk strategies in the hope that the strategies will increase the share price if they are successful. The directors can afford to do this, safe in the knowledge that they will not lose out if the share price falls any further below the exercise price. However, shareholders could suffer significant losses following a subsequent fall in the price of the shares which they already hold.

Another significant issue with share options as a reward scheme is that share prices may be determined by **external factors** and market movements as much as by the performance of the directors and senior management of a company. If share prices are rising across a stock market, a company's price may rise as a result of this general movement, rather than because of any strategies introduced by the directors. In this respect, share options do not reflect the principle of '**controllability**' which is one of the characteristics of an effective reward scheme.

In this respect, the use of an **indexed exercise price** might be more acceptable to the shareholders of a company. That is, the price at which the director can buy the shares will be equal to the market price of the shares when the options are granted, adjusted for the increase in the stock market index between the date the options were granted and the exercise date. This 'indexed' approach reflects the controllability principle better, because it means directors will not be rewarded for risks in the stock market in general.

As such, the indexed approach will also help to align the directors' interests with the shareholders' interests better, because shareholders will ultimately want the companies in which they hold shares to outperform the market as a whole.

Exam focus point

> Part of the question about remuneration policies in the December 2012 exam asked candidates to suggest appropriate improvements to a company's existing remuneration policy. The examination team commented that although the question was answered quite well overall many candidates seemed 'to be under the misapprehension that share schemes solve all remuneration policy issues'.
>
> It is important to realise that, while employee share schemes **can** improve the alignment of staff interests with those of shareholders, they do not necessarily address the short-sighted nature of many bonus schemes.

3.5.5 Risk, reward and performance

Although we have noted that share options could encourage cautious directors to be less cautious, it is equally important that reward systems do not encourage directors and managers to take excessive risks. One of the essential characteristics of reward systems is that they should align the risk preferences of managers and staff with those of the organisation and its owners. In this respect, reward systems should not encourage managers and staff to take too much risk, just as they should discourage them from being too risk averse.

Since the collapse of Northern Rock bank (in 2007), and throughout the ensuing financial crisis, there was a great deal of political and media interest in the issue of reward management. This focused on the role that reward structures were perceived to have played in encouraging excessive risk taking in the financial services sector and, in turn, what role this risk taking played in the problems which have affected the sector.

Additionally, there has been increasing concern about the extent to which the level of remuneration given to senior executives reflects (or does not reflect) the value their companies are generating for their shareholders.

In the UK, in a speech to the High Pay Commission and the Institute for Public Policy Research (January 2012) the Labour MP, Chuka Umunna, highlighted the extent to which the value of incentive packages for executives has risen disproportionately to improvements in company performance. In the first decade of the 21st century, FTSE 350 firms increased their pre-tax profits by 50% and their earnings per share by 73%, while year-end share prices fell by 5%. Over the same period, bonuses for executives in these companies rose by 187% and long-term incentive plans by 254%.

And, as Mr Umunna pointed out, in the worst cases 'you end up with perverse incentive structures which encourage the wrong kind of decision making, as the failures in many financial institutions in the wake of the 2008/9 financial crises so clearly illustrated.'

Another issue which is causing increasing anger and frustration among shareholders is the level of bonuses being awarded by companies that were rescued by taxpayer funds.

This is perhaps symptomatic of a potentially wider issue: the extent to which companies are perceived to be **rewarding failure**. The senior executives of failed companies often walk away with significant payouts, while large numbers of other managers and staff lose their jobs and their incomes.

Critics have argued that if companies are serious about improving performance, then they need to stop rewarding failure.

Case Study — **Tesco – payments to former directors**

Following payouts of more than £2 million to two former directors of Tesco in February 2015, City investors are looking at ways to reduce contractual payments to departing company bosses.

Philip Clarke and Laurie McIlwee, formerly chief executive and finance director of Tesco respectively, received the payments despite the £263m accounting scandal which was uncovered by Mr Clarke's successor in September 2014.

Tesco had previously sought to withhold the payments – £1.2m to Mr Clarke and £970,800 to Mr McIlwee – but in February 2015 it announced it would have to pay them, after being told it had no legal grounds to continue withholding them. Tesco said it was contractually obliged to make the payments to the former directors unless it could 'legally establish a case misconduct' against them.

Following Tesco's announcement, investors have argued it is time to review the length of directors' contracts. Old Mutual – a leading investment group – has called for directors' contracts to be 'substantially shorter' than the current norm of 12 months. The head of UK stewardship and governance at Old Mutual Global Investors said that 12-month contracts, and the requirement to give departing directors a year's pay, were 'an anachronism' in today's business environment.

Based on: Treanor, J. (2015) City bosses' 12-month contract rule should be reviewed, say investors, *The Guardian*, Online. Available from: http://www.theguardian.com/business/2015/feb/17/city-bosses-12-month-contract-rule-should-be-reviewed-say-investors [Accessed 26 January 2016]

3.5.6 Indirect pay

Indirect pay is often called 'employee benefits'.

Benefits can form a valuable component of the total reward package. They can be designed so as to resemble either base pay or, to some extent, performance pay. A benefit resembling base pay, for example, would be the use of a subsidised staff canteen, whereas the common practice of rewarding high-performing sales staff with holiday packages or superior cars looks more like performance pay. Again, though, the extent to which an organisation offers indirect pay should reflect whether this type of reward supports its strategy.

There is a trend towards a **cafeteria** approach to benefits. Employees select the benefits they require from a 'menu' – showing the cost to them of each benefit – up to the total value they are awarded. This means that employees' benefits are likely to match their needs and be more highly valued as a result.

Types of indirect pay include:

- Pension plans
- Private healthcare
- Private dental care
- Car allowance
- Discounted insurance
- Extra vacation days
- Child care
- Shopping/entertainment vouchers

Exam focus point

One of the questions in the December 2012 exam described the remuneration policy applied to different grades of staff in an organisation, and then asked candidates to evaluate the policy and suggest what changes were appropriate.

The majority of the staff grades were paid a basic salary plus some kind of bonus – but the evaluation involved looking at the basis on which the salaries and bonuses were determined.

3.6 Reward techniques

Two factors need to be taken into account when deciding how much employees should be paid.

(a) **Internal equity** – This means that when staff members compare their rewards and remuneration with other people within the organisation, they conclude that the overall remuneration system is fair. If internal equity is not achieved, employees will conclude that the psychological contract has been breached, and their behaviour is likely to be affected as a result. They may become less motivated, or less co-operative, or they may leave the organisation completely.

(b) **External competitiveness** – Unless the level of rewards an organisation offers is competitive compared with those offered by other organisations, it will be difficult for the organisation to recruit and retain staff – particularly skilled staff. Equally, however, it is important that an

organisation doesn't offer rewards which are too high because this will inflate its costs, and reduce profits accordingly. To this end, it will be important for an organisation to benchmark its reward schemes against those offered by competitors.

3.7 Internal equity

Three techniques contribute to the establishment of internal equity.

3.7.1 Job analysis

Job analysis is the 'systematic process of collecting and evaluating information about the tasks, responsibilities and the context of a specific job' (Bratton). The data collected during job analysis identifies the major tasks performed by the job-holder, the outcomes that are expected, and how the job links to other jobs in the organisation. This data is used to prepare job descriptions, job specifications and job performance standards. (Note that in practice the terms job description and job specification may be used loosely and a **job specification** is often referred to as a **person specification**.)

This information is useful in itself for a range of HRM purposes, including recruitment and training needs analysis, and it also forms the basis for **job evaluation**.

Note also that job analysis is an important aspect of quality and process redesign initiatives and is almost certainly required when e-business methods are adopted.

3.7.2 Job evaluation

Job evaluation is 'a systematic process designed to determine the relative worth of jobs within a single work organisation' (Bratton). The process depends on a series of subjective judgements and may be influenced by organisational politics and personal preconceptions. In particular, it can be difficult to separate the nature of the job from the qualities of the current incumbent.

Evaluation may be carried out in four ways.

(a) **Ranking** simply requires the arrangement of existing jobs into a hierarchy of relative value to the organisation.

(b) **Job-grading** starts with the definition of a suitable structure of grades in a hierarchy. Definitions are based on requirements for skill, knowledge and experience. Each job in the organisation is then allocated to an appropriate grade.

(c) **Factor comparison** requires the allocation of monetary value to the various factors making up the content of a suitable range of benchmark jobs. This method is complex and cumbersome.

(d) **Points rating** is similar to factor comparison, but uses points rather than monetary units to assess the elements of job content.

Whichever method is used, the end point of a job evaluation exercise is the production of a **hierarchy of jobs** in terms of their relative value to the organisation. The **pay structure** is then set by reference to this hierarchy of jobs.

3.7.3 Performance appraisal

Performance appraisal has already been discussed in detail.

3.8 Reward competitiveness

The level of rewards an organisation offers will inevitably be subject to factors external to the organisation.

(a) The **labour market** as it exists locally, nationally and perhaps globally, as relevant to the organisation's circumstances

(b) The pressure for **cost efficiency** in the relevant industry or sector

(c) **Legislation** such as the level of any applicable minimum wage

3.9 Setting reward levels in practice

Many companies use commercially available **survey data** to guide the overall level of the rewards they offer. This approach can be combined with the reward techniques outlined above.

An element of **flexibility** must be incorporated to reflect both the different levels of skill, knowledge and experience deployed by people doing the same work and their effectiveness in doing it.

Governments influence pay levels by means other than outright legislative prescription.

(a) They affect the demand for labour by being major employers in their own right.

(b) They can affect the supply of labour by, for example, setting down minimum age or qualification requirements for certain jobs.

(c) Their fiscal and monetary policies can lead them to exert downward pressure on public sector wage rates.

3.9.1 Problems with reward systems

Reward systems are subject to a range of pressures that influence their working and affect the psychological contract.

(a) Where **trade unions** are weak, as in the UK, employers have more freedom to introduce performance-related pay.

(b) **Economic conditions** may prevent employers from funding the rewards they might wish to provide in order to improve commitment. The result would be disappointment and dissatisfaction.

(c) Performance pay systems are prone to **subjective and inconsistent** judgement about merit; this will discredit them in the eyes of the employees.

3.10 Benefits and adverse consequences of linking reward schemes to performance measurement

3.10.1 Benefits for the organisation

It is clear how objectives set at higher levels are being translated into individual goals thereby linking strategy to outcomes for the individual. This is explained in Bratton's model where the strategic perspective explains that the reward system should support strategy, and the two should be closely aligned.

A reward scheme should also provide an incentive to achieve a good level of performance, and the existence of a reward scheme can help to both attract and retain employees who are making favourable contributions to the running of the organisation.

A reward scheme can also help emphasise the key performance indicators (KPIs) of the business, if these are incorporated into the performance measures which underpin the scheme. This will help reinforce to employees the key aspects of their performance which contribute most to the organisation's success.

3.10.2 Drawbacks for the organisation

However, the global financial crisis of 2007 to 2008 showed the dangers of linking reward schemes to performance measures if those **performance measures are poorly designed**. We highlighted this in the case study earlier in the chapter, suggesting that bank bonuses encouraged a focus on short-term decision making and risk taking.

A European Commission report into the financial crisis suggested that 'Excessive risk taking in the financial services industry ... has contributed to the failure of financial undertakings ... Whilst not the main cause of the financial crises that unfolded ... there is widespread consensus that inappropriate remuneration practices ... also induced excessive risk taking.'

In this case, there appears to be a direct link between the profit measures (short-term profitability) and the **risk appetite of employees**. Employees were prepared to take greater risks in the hope of making higher profits and therefore getting larger bonuses.

However, a second potential drawback for an organisation arises if it is unable to reward individuals for good performance (for instance, due to a shortage of funds) because then the link between reward and motivation may break down.

3.10.3 Benefits and drawbacks for the individual

If an individual's goals are linked to the objectives of the organisation, then it is clear to the individual how their performance is measured and why their goals are set as they are. However, on occasions there may be a problem in linking individual rewards directly to organisational outcomes, especially if the latter is uncertain.

Another drawback is that, in striving to meet targets, some individuals may become cautious and reluctant to take risks given that they have a stake in the outcome. Conversely, other individuals may choose riskier behaviour, especially if reward is linked to, say, revenue generation or levels of output.

3.10.4 Risk and reward

Overall, a reward system needs to achieve a balance between risk and reward.

Recruitment and retention: Rewards need to be structured in such a way that they attract and retain key talent. If an organisation's reward system is not deemed to be attractive, then there is a risk it will not be able to attract or retain the staff it needs to be successful.

Alignment with business strategy and culture: If reward strategy is not aligned to organisational goals then there is a risk the organisation will not achieve those goals. Equally, the reward system needs to encourage styles of behaviour that fit with the organisation's culture.

Reputation/brand: If the organisation's reward systems generate negative press coverage (as has been the case with some banks in the recent financial crisis) there is a risk that this will adversely affect the organisation's reputation or brand.

4 Accountability

FAST FORWARD

Hard accountability involves consideration of financial and quantitative information. **Soft accountability** considers the human input to the system and its role in shaping, evaluating and implementing goals.

4.1 Agency theory

Key term

Agency theory considers the relationship between a principal (such as the owners of a company, the shareholders) and an agent (such as an organisation's managers and employees).

The dilemma at the heart of the agency relationship is highlighted in the following extract.

> 'The problem is "how can the agent be motivated and monitored?". The motivation may be achieved by the payment of ... a reward. The monitoring may be through the submission of regular accounts ... (as a measure of performance). The key requirements are that:
>
> (a) The **agent** must have to **give an account of performance** to the principal; and
> (b) The **principal** must be able to **hold the agent to account**.'
>
> (George Brown, 'Accountability and performance measurement', originally published in ACCA *Student Newsletter,* August 1998)

In the corporate sector, the identification of agents (managers and employees) and principals (shareholders) is comparatively straightforward. In public sector and non profit seeking organisations there are likely to be multiple principals (such as the Government and students in the higher education sector), making identification more difficult.

The theory makes certain **assumptions about individuals as agents**, listed in Wilson and Chua, *Managerial Accounting: Method and Meaning*, as follows:

(a) They behave rationally in seeking to maximise their own utility.

(b) They seek financial and non-financial rewards.

(c) They tend to be risk averse and, hence, reluctant to innovate.

(d) Their individual interests will not always coincide with those of their principals.

(e) They prefer leisure to hard work.

(f) They have greater knowledge about their operating performance and actions than is available to their principals.

Key issues in agency theory are **attitudes to risk** and the **observability of effort**.

(a) Conventional management accounting assumes that principals protect agents from risk – it only makes managers responsible for things they can control. Agency theory suggests that if principals are risk averse then they should share the risk with agents and this can increase the utility of both parties. Making a large part of an executive's potential reward subject to some profit target is a simple example of such a contract.

(b) The principal may find it difficult to observe the agent's efforts. Alternatively the principal may not be able to evaluate the effort because they do not possess the information on which the decision to expend that much effort was based.

Accountability requires and assumes that the agent (manager or employee) is motivated and monitored to do what the principal wants them to do. The reward system has to incorporate the means of **monitoring** (performance measurement) and **motivating** the agent to do what is required of them. If the reward system aligns the agent's goals with those of the organisation (ie it promotes goal congruence) it should be successful in monitoring and motivating the agent to perform as desired. The problem is ensuring that the agent is motivated and monitored, or else they may not do what is required.

Another potential complication comes from identifying who the principal is.

In **commercial organisations**, this is relatively straightforward: the principals are the shareholders, and the agents are the management and staff of the organisation. However, in the **public sector and not-for-profit** organisations this relationship can be more complex because there are often multiple principals.

For example, in the public health sector (hospitals) principals may include the Government (as providers of funds) and patients (as recipients of healthcare). The agents are the hospital management, surgeons and staff. The achievement of accountability (holding the agent to account) is an important aspect of the relationship. However, this can be difficult if the principals have differing aims: for example, is the hospital primarily judged according to the quality of its medical treatment (patient as principal), or how well it stays within budget (government as principal)? Moreover, any such uncertainty can lead to uncertainty over the key performance measures for an organisation to focus on.

4.1.1 Pressure for short-term results

Another difficulty that managers (agents) can sometimes face is how to achieve a target level of result without increasing the level of risk they are prepared to take. This can particularly be the case if managers are under pressure to achieve short-term performance targets.

For example, if a manager is being assessed against an annual revenue target, and they know they will not achieve that target if they continue with their current (relatively low-risk) strategy, then the manager may consider alternative strategies (which may be higher risk, but have the potential for greater rewards) in order to try to achieve the revenue target.

4.2 Accounting and accountability

Accountancy via the use of **management control systems** (budgeting and standard costing) has a key role to play in the development of regimes of accountability. Such control systems provide two forms of accountability.

4.2.1 Hard accountability

This involves consideration of financial and quantitative information and covers three areas.

(a) **Counting** (that is, **converting activities and outcomes into numbers**), such as the number and type of warranty claims.

(b) **Ensuring that the numbers are accounted for** (in other words, **reporting on activities and outcomes** and providing a discussion of **how and why they have occurred**). For example, an organisation could report that 'we achieved 20% new customers through promising a just-in-time (JIT) delivery of orders (**how**) and 80% of complaints related to an inability to meet the JIT timetable because of internal failure of the 'pull-through' system due to lack of a synchronised manufacturing system (**why**)'.

(c) **Being held accountable for** accounting and also for the events and circumstances leading to the records, such as being held responsible for failing to meet unrealistic production schedules, and for failing to take action, such as implementing overtime working to try to meet the schedules.

4.2.2 Soft accountability

This involves consideration of the human input to the system and its role in shaping, evaluating and implementing goals. **Self accountability** achieved by employees, for example, will be affected by financial and non-financial rewards offered, training and development programmes and the way in which employees are grouped in order to achieve specific business outcomes (such as multi-disciplinary project teams and quality circles).

4.2.3 Implementing accountability

George Brown suggests that **accountability requires** the implementation of the following **steps**:

(a) 'Choose and make public a range of accepted performance measures;
(b) Ensure that the benefits of the performance measures have been identified;
(c) Identify and understand possible problems in the use of performance measures;
(d) Consider ways in which to counter perceived problems in the use of performance measures.'

4.3 Accountability and control

In Section 4.2 above we introduced the idea that management control systems have an important role to play in developing accountability, and we will now look at this idea of accountability and control further.

There are three broad categories of control mechanism which companies can use to cope with the problem of organisational control:

- Behavioural (or action) control
- Personnel and cultural control
- Results (or output) control

4.3.1 Behavioural control

The aim of behavioural (or action) controls is to ensure that only those behaviours and actions which are desirable occur, and those which are undesirable do not occur.

For example, in a highly automated and repetitive process (such as a production line), the supervisor watches over the production line staff to ensure they carry out their tasks as they are meant to – knowing that if they do, this should guarantee the quality of the end product.

Action accountability involves defining actions and behaviours that are acceptable or unacceptable, observing the actions and behaviours of employees and then rewarding those which are acceptable and preventing or punishing those which are unacceptable.

In this way, action accountability sets limits on employee behaviour. For example, setting budgets for different categories of expenditure makes the budget holder accountable if they exceed the budget limit, such that they have to explain or justify their actions. In this way, budgets, acting as an action control, should help to prevent excess expenditure which is not in the best interests of the organisation.

4.3.2 Personnel control

The aim of personnel controls is to help employees do a good job, by ensuring they have the capabilities and the resources needed to do that job.

In this respect, we can highlight three major methods of implementing personnel controls:

- **Recruitment and selection** (finding the right people to do a specified job)
- **Training and job design** (where job design includes making sure that jobs are not too complex, onerous or badly designed so that employees do not know what is expected of them)
- **Providing the necessary resources** for people to do their jobs

Cultural controls represent a set of values or social norms that are shared by members of an organisation and influence their actions. These could include codes of conduct, or group-based reward schemes. Part of the logic behind group-based reward schemes (such as profit sharing schemes) is that they encourage employees to work together to enhance the collective achievements of the group.

More generally, one of the aims of personnel or cultural controls could also be to ensure that staff believe in the objectives that an organisation is trying to achieve so that they are motivated to work towards those objectives and accordingly do not require detailed supervision and monitoring.

4.3.3 Results control

The focus of results control is on collecting and reporting information about the outcomes of work effort.

Drury identifies four stages of results control:

(a) Establishing results measures (performance measures) that maximise desirable behaviour or minimise undesirable behaviour

(b) Establishing performance targets for those measures

(c) Measuring performance

(d) Providing rewards or punishment based on performance

The key value of results controls for organisations is that they identify deviations from desired performance measures (eg variances to budget) and then allow corrective actions to be taken to try to improve performance. (In this respect, results controls resemble feedback controls which we looked at in Chapters 1 and 7 earlier in this Study Text.)

However, results measures work most effectively where the individuals whose behaviours are being controlled are able to control and influence the results. If uncontrollable factors cannot be separated from controllable factors, then results control measures are unlikely to provide useful information for evaluating the actions taken by individuals.

Moreover, if the outcomes of desirable behaviours are offset by the impact of uncontrollable factors, then results measures will lose any motivational impact and create the impression that they are unfair.

For example, a sales manager's target may be to increase annual sales by a given percentage, continuing the pattern of growth experienced in previous years. However, if during the course of the current year a new rival company joins the market, and overall economic growth slows down significantly, the sales manager is unlikely to achieve their performance target. However, this failure to achieve the target does not necessarily reflect any undesirable behaviour on the part of the sales manager, or any decline in their own performance. Rather, it is likely to be due to the new, uncontrollable factors that have emerged.

Exam focus point

> We looked at the idea of controllability in Chapters 3 and 7 earlier in this Study Text, and we highlighted the key principle that managers should only be responsible for those aspects of performance they can control.
>
> It is important to remember that principle when designing reward systems.
>
> One of the case study scenario questions in the December 2011 exam highlighted a situation in which managers were unhappy with their remuneration. One of the main reasons for this was that their bonuses were dependent on achieving performance targets (performing above budget) but they had no control over a number of the factors which affected whether or not their shops reached their budget targets.
>
> Part of the question requirement asked students to suggest suitable improvements to the company's reward system for the shop managers. One such improvement was the need to focus on controllable aspects of performance.
>
> Another point to consider in relation to controllability is whether it might be more appropriate to use relative targets as a means of assessing performance, rather than absolute targets.
>
> So, for example, rather than setting a sales manager an absolute target (ie sales of $x million for the year), it would be better for the target to be set in relation to market share (%).
>
> This immediately improves the controllability of the measure. Whereas a sales manager cannot control the overall increase or decrease in the total market size, they can control the level of sales they achieve relative to other players in the market.

4.4 Selecting appropriate control mechanisms

In his journal article 'A Conceptual Framework for the Design of Organizational Control Mechanisms', William Ouchi identifies that an important element underlying the majority of formal management controls is the assumption that it is feasible to measure, with reasonable precision, the performance which is required from employees.

The ability to measure the outputs or behaviours which are relevant to the desired performance is crucial to the 'results and outcomes' or the 'behaviour in performance' approaches to performance rating which we discussed earlier in this chapter.

Ouchi also highlights the importance of having a control system which is appropriate for the organisation or the task at hand. In this respect, Ouchi suggests that the type of control which is most appropriate in any situation is likely to depend on two key variables:

(a) The **ability to measure output**
(b) The **knowledge of the transformation process** required to produce that output

The matrix figure below shows the types of control system which Ouchi suggests are most appropriate for different processes or functions in an organisation.

		Knowledge of the transformation process	
		Perfect	*Imperfect*
Ability to measure output	*High*	Behavioural or output controls	Output control
	Low	Behavioural control	Personnel control

Factors determining the measurement of behaviour and output

(Based on a figure in Ouchi, 'A Conceptual Framework for the Design of Organizational Control Mechanisms')

Knowledge of the transformation process will be high for routine or standardised processes which have been carried out many times before (such as a routine manufacturing process). Given that it is also easy to measure the output from the process (the number and quality of units produced), behavioural control or output control would both be appropriate for employees carrying out this kind of routine, standardised task (represented by the top left quadrant of the matrix).

By contrast, consider a control system for a 'buyer' for a high-end fashion store. It is not possible to create a set of rules for the buyers to follow which could assure success, so managers are unlikely to be able to assess the behaviour of a successful 'buyer'. However, managers can measure the sales volume and profit margins which are achieved on the buyer's product lines, suggesting that an output control mechanism is more appropriate here (top right quadrant in the matrix).

One problem with Ouchi's matrix in this respect, however, is that it does not look at any **external factors**. While the 'buyer' may have selected good products, the fashion store may have struggled to make sales for other reasons – for example, a rival store opening close by. This again raises the issue of **controllability**, and whether it is fair to appraise employees on aspects of performance they cannot control.

While in the case of the manufacturing process or fashion buyer it is relatively easy to measure output, in other cases it may be much harder to measure output. For example, when scientists are engaged in research work it may take many years to identify whether their research has been successful or not. Equally, where people are working as a team, any 'output' more accurately reflects the collective effort of the team rather than individuals within the team – particularly if some individuals put in more than others.

If, as may be the case with the research laboratory, it is not possible to rationally evaluate the outputs of its work, nor the behaviour of staff due to the variety and uniqueness of their work, there may be few controls available to the organisation apart from ensuring it recruits the best scientists available so that it can be assured of having an able and committed set of people working for it (bottom right quadrant in the matrix).

5 What gets measured, gets done

FAST FORWARD

The notion that '**What gets measured, gets done**' suggests that people will make a greater effort to perform well in aspects of their roles which they know are being measured, compared to those which are not.

The quotation 'What gets measured, gets done' is often raised in relation to performance measurement, and highlights the fact that people will typically be motivated to put more effort into performing well in areas of performance which they know are being measured, compared to those which are not.

For example, if one of an employee's **objectives** focuses on providing high quality of customer service, the logic is that the employee will focus on the quality of customer service they are providing in order to help them achieve their objective. Conversely, their attitude to other aspects of their roles (which are not covered by their objectives) could be that those aspects are less important – because they are not part of the employee's objectives, and therefore the employee will not be assessed as to how well they perform them.

In this respect, the quotation also highlights one of the potential problems with performance measurement – **tunnel vision** (ie staff focus on one particular aspect of performance at the expense of others, knowing that they are being assessed on that particular area).

Exam focus point

We noted a similar idea in Chapter 11 in relation to public sector league tables. If organisations know that some aspects of performance have a greater weighting than others in the calculation of the league table, then they are likely to concentrate their efforts in performing well in the areas with the higher weighting – potentially at the expense of the areas which are given less weighting in the tables.

Although tunnel vision could be a problem for organisations, the notion that 'What gets measured, gets done' could also have more positive implications. In particular, in the context of CSFs and objectives, if an organisation correctly identifies its CSFs and then establishes organisational and individual objectives which are aligned to them, the existence of those objectives should encourage people to try to perform well in those key areas.

More generally, the idea of giving people targets and goals could, in itself, help to motivate them to improve their performance. Again, the idea of '**achievability**' (in Fitzgerald and Moon's building block model) is relevant here. If people are set targets which are challenging yet achievable this should be an effective way of motivating them to improve their performance – and thereby to achieve the target.

Nonetheless, it is debatable whether measuring something will actually ensure that it is achieved. For example, one of a company's objectives could be to increase revenue by 5% over a year; and related to this, the company could measure revenue as one of its KPIs. However, although the focus on revenue growth could encourage marketing initiatives and other initiatives to increase sales, there is no guarantee that they will lead to increased revenue. Similarly, linking back to the example of school league tables which we discussed in Chapter 11, critics have questioned to what extent (if any) the existence of league tables actually improves the quality of teaching in schools – which is arguably the most important aspect of performance in a school.

Some commentators suggest that the adage 'What gets measured, gets done' is adapted a derivation of the similar phrase 'If you can measure it, you can manage it.'

The reference to measurement and management is perhaps more useful than looking at something 'getting done' in terms of the results achieved. If managers can't gather any information about certain processes or activities (ie the processes can't be measured) this will make it much more difficult for the managers to assess how well those processes are operating, or to identify any actions which might be required to improve performance. By contrast, if performance is being measured, then managers should have the information they need to make sure that the processes are operating at the desired level.

Nonetheless, whichever way the quotation is presented – 'What gets measured, gets done' or 'If you can measure it, you can manage it' – it is important to remember the potential dangers of **information overload** (as we discussed in Chapter 8). If managers are presented with performance information about too many different aspects of performance, the key messages may get lost amidst the volume of information. As such, what has been measured may well not get done, because managers will not have sufficient time to analyse the information they have been given in order to identify the most important issues.

Exam focus point

The benefits of performance measures and the potential problems of performance measurement are discussed in one of the Technical Articles for P5 on ACCA's website – 'The Pyramids and Pitfalls of Performance Measurement'. Section 5.2 of this chapter (about the potential problems of performance measurement) is based on that article, but you are advised to read the article in full as part of your preparation for your P5 exam.

5.1 Benefits of performance measures

Berry, Broadbent and Otley suggest the benefits of using performance measures are as follows:

(a) Clarify the objectives of the organisation
(b) Develop agreed measures of activity
(c) Greater understanding of processes
(d) Facilitate comparison of performance in different organisations
(e) Facilitate the setting of targets for the organisation and its managers
(f) Promote accountability of the organisation to its stakeholders

5.2 Problems of using performance measures

However, Berry, Broadbent and Otley also suggest that there can be a number of possible problems accompanying the use of performance measures.

(a) **Tunnel vision** (undue focus on the aspects of performance being measured to the detriment of other aspects of performance). For example, if a performance measure for an accountancy firm is the staff utilisation ratio in terms of chargeable hours as a proportion of total hours, this may lead to an insufficient amount of time being spent on staff development or training.

(b) **Sub-optimisation** (focus on some objectives so that others – which could bring greater success – are not achieved). For example, if an audit partner focuses too much on winning new clients, this may lead to inadequate time being given to managing relationships with existing clients and supervising the work being done on the audits of those clients.

(c) **Myopia** (focusing on short-term success or goals at the expense of longer-term objectives and long-term success). For example, the audit firm might be focused on maximising client revenues rather than investing in the technology to provide automated audit software which will generate efficiency savings in the future.

(d) **Measure fixation** (a focus on measures and behaviour in order to achieve specific performance indicators which may not be effective; in effect, focusing more on the measures themselves, rather than underlying goals and objectives). For example, if the audit firm knows that the cost of the audit is being measured, this could mean it focuses on reducing the costs of its audits. However, this may lead it to use staff who are too junior for the complexity of the work involved at particular clients. This may also lead to client dissatisfaction (and loss of clients) or extra costs when a more senior member of staff has to re-do work which is unsatisfactory or incomplete.

(e) **Misrepresentation** ('creative' reporting or deliberate manipulation of data to make a result appear better than it actually is). For example, the audit firm may produce a report saying that 90% of its clients have expressed complete satisfaction with the service they have received. But if the firm only sent its client satisfaction survey to a carefully selected number of clients, rather than all its clients, the satisfaction score is misleading.

(f) **Misinterpretation** (misunderstanding the performance data; for example, due to a failure to recognise the complexity of the environment in which an organisation operates and therefore the influences on performance). Within the accountancy firm, one partner might be focused on winning new business from large, national clients, another might be focused on winning new business from small, local clients, while a third might be focused on selling additional services to existing clients. In this scenario, the motives of the different partners create a complex environment in which the objectives of the firm's key players may conflict. If the firm wins lots of business from large, national clients, how will this affect its capacity to take on extra business from small, local clients?

(g) **Gaming** (deliberate distortion of performance to secure some strategic advantage). This might include deliberate underperformance in the current period to avoid higher targets being set in future periods. For example, assume an audit manager spots an opportunity to sell some additional services to a client, but knows the audit firm is already on target to exceed budgeted profit for the current period. The manager may suggest that the consultancy work begins in the next period, with the hope that the additional services help create a favourable performance to budget in that period as well.

(h) **Ossification** (an overly rigid system, or an unwillingness to change the performance measure scheme once it has been set up). For example, the questions in the audit firm's questionnaire may be poorly designed and don't give clients the opportunity to comment on some aspects of the firm's offering. However, because the firm gets good responses from the questionnaire in its current form, it may be unwilling to change the questionnaire.

Exam focus point

> The scenario in one of the questions in the December 2013 exam referred specifically to the problems of myopia, gaming and ossification, and candidates were then asked to assess whether those problems applied to the company being described in the scenario. Candidates were then asked to suggest appropriate performance management solutions to the three problems.

5.2.1 Tunnel vision and performance targets

As we mentioned earlier in Section 5, Berry, Broadbent and Otley's concept of tunnel vision reiterates the point that 'What gets measured, gets done'.

If particular performance targets or objectives have been set, employees will know that their performance will be appraised against those targets. Therefore employees will concentrate on the areas in which their performance is being measured in preference to other possible aspects of their role. This could have negative side effects, though.

For example, in recent years in the UK, there have been concerns that passengers have had to wait too long to pass through passport control at airports. If performance targets were set in relation to passenger waiting times (or the length of the queues) staff might respond by trying to speed up the passenger checks they carry out. However, this could lead to a reduction in the quality or thoroughness of the checks being carried out, which in turn could lead to an increased risk of failing to detect passengers who are trying to pass through passport control without valid documentation.

The following two short examples also illustrate the potential negative side effects of setting inappropriate targets.

The manager of a fast food restaurant was striving to achieve a bonus which was dependent on minimising the amount of chicken pieces and burgers which were wasted. The manager earned the bonus, but did so by instructing staff to wait until the chicken pieces or burgers were ordered before cooking them. However, the long waiting times which resulted led to a huge loss of customers in the following weeks.

Sales staff at a company met their sales targets by offering discounts and extending payment terms. In some cases, they even made credit sales to customers they felt might never pay. As a result, the sales staff achieved their targets at the expense of the company's profitability. However, the sales staff were not concerned by profits, because they were motivated by a bonus scheme which was based solely on the level of sales they achieved.

Case Study **Reward systems and IT transformation**

The following scenario, adapted from the business technology website ZDNet, looks at some examples of failings in reward systems in relation to IT projects.

An organisation had a plan for an enterprise-wide service-orientated approach which was well thought through and should have worked well. But when the project was implemented it turned out to be a failure. One of the reasons for the failure was the way in which IT professionals and managers were rewarded, highlighting the importance of rewarding the right behaviour in any IT-driven transformational project.

The article highlights four common misconceptions in reward systems.

- **Rewarding programmers for lines of code produced, or based on program complexity**. This type of reward system will encourage programmers to develop more complex or difficult programs without considering what the organisation needs. It may not need – or want – complex or difficult programs.
- **Rewarding developers based on long hours worked**. There is a danger with this kind of measure that **quantity** gets rewarded rather than **quality**. A programmer may end up working very long days simply because they did a poor job of estimation and planning upfront, or the long hours could be an indication that there is a lot of code rewriting going on, to correct mistakes which the programmer had made initially.

- **Rewards based on salary surveys**. Basing IT salaries on industry averages means that some of the competitor companies in the market are paying more (although some are also paying less). However, if you simply pay an average rate as soon as the economy becomes more buoyant, and demand for workers heats up, programmers will defect and move to higher-paying rival companies.
- **Rewarding people based on the number of problem statements they close**. A problem statement is a description of the issues which need to be solved by the problem-solving team. The difficulty with this as a basis of reward is that some people will solve multiple problems within one problem statement, while others will open and solve as many problem statements as they can to inflate the number of problems solved.

Source: McKendrick, J. (2010) *Why reward systems fail to deliver IT transformation*, ZDnet. Online. Available from: http://www.zdnet.com/article/why-reward-systems-fail-to-deliver-it-transformation/#!

[Accessed 26 January 2016]

More generally, the problems of performance measurement highlighted by Berry, Broadbent and Otley also highlight the issue of **congruence between the goals of individuals and the goals of the organisation**.

Individual goals may be financially or non-financially orientated and relate to remuneration, promotion prospects, job security, job satisfaction and self-esteem. Each **individual** may face a **conflict** between taking action to ensure organisational goals and action to ensure personal goals.

Exam focus point

Although we have looked at the problems of performance measurement here in the context of the way they could adversely affect the behaviour of individuals within an organisation, they could equally be used as a summary of the potential dangers of performance measurement in organisations as a whole.

For example, if an organisation concentrates on measuring the aspects of performance which are easily measurable, rather than those which support its achievement of its critical success factors, this could be an illustration of sub-optimisation.

Also, if environmental factors change, but an organisation does not change its performance measures or targets to reflect the changed environment, the organisation's performance measures can quickly become ossified. The danger here could be that the organisation thinks it is performing well (because it is achieving its performance targets) but those targets may no longer be relevant (for example, due to new technologies which have enabled competitors to improve their performance to a higher level).

5.2.2 Ways in which the problems may be reduced

(a) **Involvement of staff** at all levels in the development and implementation of the scheme should help to reduce gaming and tunnel vision.

(b) A **flexible use** of performance measures should help to reduce measure fixation and misrepresentation.

(c) Keeping the performance measurement system under **constant review** should help to overcome the problems of ossification and gaming.

(d) Give careful consideration to the **dimensions of performance**. Quantifying all objectives should help to overcome sub-optimisation, while a focus on measuring customer satisfaction should reduce tunnel vision and sub-optimisation.

(e) Consideration should be given to the **audit of the system**. Expert interpretation of the performance measurement scheme should help to provide an idea of the incidence of the problems, while a careful audit of the data used should help to reduce the incidence and impact of measure fixation, misinterpretation and gaming.

(f) **Recognition of the key feature** necessary in any scheme (a long-term view/perspective among staff, a sensible number of measures, benchmarks which are independent of past activity) should help to overcome the range of problems listed above.

6 Management styles

FAST FORWARD

Hopwood identified three distinct management styles: **budget-constrained style; profit-conscious style;** and **non-accounting style**. It is important that the management style employed is appropriate to an organisation's context.

6.1 Hopwood's management styles

Style	Hopwood says ...
Budget-constrained style	'The manager's performance is primarily evaluated upon the basis of his ability to continually **meet the budget** on a **short-term basis** ... stressed at the expense of other valued and important criteria and the manager will receive unfavourable feedback from his superior if, for instance, his actual costs exceed the budgeted costs, regardless of other considerations.'
Profit-conscious style	'The manager's performance is evaluated on the basis of his ability to **increase the general effectiveness** of his unit's operations in relation to the **long-term purposes** of the organisation.' If the manager can prove their actions will benefit the company in the future, they will be rewarded rather than punished (even if the actions have a short-term cost).
Non-accounting style	'The budgetary information plays a **relatively unimportant** part in the superior's evaluation of the manager's performance.' Other non-financial factors are deemed more important when appraising the manager's performance.

With the **profit-conscious** style of evaluation, budget reports are not dealt with in the rigid sense of analysing the size and direction of variances: the information in budget reports is supplemented with **information from other sources** and **interpreted in a wider sense**.

Short-term vs long-term performance

On a number of occasions in this Study Text we have highlighted the contrast between focusing on short-term performance targets or longer-term objectives. The distinction between 'budget-constrained style' and 'profit-conscious style' is another illustration of this contrast.

In an organisation which has a **budget-constrained management** style, the focus will be on **short-term financial performance**, and managers will be assessed on their ability to achieve budgets and other short-term targets.

The main focus of performance measures under a budget-constrained style is on **cost control**. However, again this might hinder future performance in the longer term. For example, if a firm reduces marketing expenditure there is a danger that its future revenue growth or market share may be reduced as a result.

By contrast, an organisation which has a **profit-conscious style** focuses more on **long-term performance**, and increasing an organisation's ability to achieve its longer-term objectives (eg growth).

Moreover, the main focus of performance measures under a profit-conscious style is **profitability** rather than cost control.

However, there is a possible danger that short-term performance could suffer if an organisation focuses too much on the long term rather at the expense of any more short-term measures.

Hopwood's summary of the effects of the three styles of evaluation

	Style of evaluation		
Effects	**Budget-constrained**	**Profit-conscious**	**Non-accounting**
Involvement with costs	HIGH	HIGH	LOW
Job-related tension	HIGH	MEDIUM	MEDIUM
Manipulation of accounting reports	EXTENSIVE	LITTLE	LITTLE
Relations with the supervisor	POOR	GOOD	GOOD
Relations with colleague	POOR	GOOD	GOOD

The **profit-conscious style appears to be optimum** in terms of the variable examined but Hopwood pointed out this may **differ between organisations** and **between activities in the same organisation**.

Otley carried out a separate study and found **no significant difference** in job-related tension and so on, whichever managerial style was adopted. However, Otley's study considered managers who were comparatively independent, had a high degree of control over cash and resources and operated in a more predictable environment than the managers studied by Hopwood.

6.2 The importance of context

Otley's research indicates that the **context** in which budgetary control is used is as **important** as the style in which it is used. For example, some managers (like those studied by Hopwood) are highly interdependent and face a good deal of uncertainty, so that good performance depends on others' co-operation and favourable external circumstances. Such situations do not match well with the budget-constrained style.

A **budget-constrained** style can be appropriate in a business with cash flow problems where management are focusing on keeping costs reined in. So, for example, making unplanned expenditure to get a machine repaired quickly so that an important order could be completed and shipped to a customer would be criticised because it led to the repair budget being exceeded. Not surprisingly, this approach leads to very **poor manager/subordinate relationships** and also encourages the manipulation and misreporting of information.

This style might be used in a **mature business**, where there is limited scope for growth so **cost control** becomes increasingly important to maximising profit. A business in decline may possibly also use this style. (We consider business failure in a later chapter.)

A **profit-conscious** style may suit a business which has devolved operations and managers assume a high level of discretion. Short-term profit remains important but it is balanced against **longer-term performance** objectives. In the previous example, the employee who arranged for the machine to be repaired would be more likely to be praised for this because it enabled the organisation to meet customer requirements, thereby increasing the likelihood of generating further business from them in the future.

This style is likely to be used by businesses which are in the **growth phase** of their life cycle.

A **non-accounting** style may suit managers with operational priorities rather than a cost or profit focus, because it prioritises non-financial performance measures above financial ones.

For example, the quality control department for an airline company has to ensure that its planes are safe to fly before they take to the air. If an inspection requires that a plane needs some repair work before it can take off safely, that repair work has to be done, because the consequences of not doing it could be disastrous.

Equally, this style may be appropriate in some medical research and development teams. The teams' performance could be evaluated on the basis of the quality of the research they carry out and the number of potentially valuable new discoveries they make rather than the amount of profit made by the department.

A non-accounting style could also be appropriate for public sector organisations where financial parameters are less important than non-financial ones.

However, if an organisation focuses too much on non-financial performance at the expense of financial performance (as would be the case in a non-accounting style) there is a danger that financial performance will suffer as a result.

6.3 Management culture and generic strategy

In Section 3.2 of this chapter we identified the importance of ensuring that an organisation's reward system is aligned to its chosen strategy.

However, more generally, it is also important that an organisation's overall culture is aligned to its strategy. In essence, organisations that are pursuing cost leadership strategies would be expected to have elements of Financial Control Cultures, while organisations that are pursuing differentiation strategies would be expected to be more aligned to Excellence/Service Cultures.

Exam focus point

There is a technical article on ACCA's website – 'Accounting and organisational cultures' – which explores these ideas in more detail. The text here only provides a brief summary of some of the key points from the article, but you are advised to read the full article as part of your preparation for your exam.

The full article also notes that the Financial Control Culture and Excellence/Service Culture represent the two ends of a continuum; and in practice there are many interim positions between these two extremes.

Financial Control Culture

The Financial Control Culture is based on the belief that an organisation's success depends on it achieving efficiency through being well managed and having good management information systems which support cost planning and control systems.

The managerial structure in this kind of culture is hierarchical, and top-down, and can be characterised as having a 'command and control' philosophy. Management's fundamental objective for departments in the organisation is for them to achieve the annual budget targets which have been set for them.

The emphasis on financial performance also places the short-run interests of shareholders as the primary goal of the business. Performance measures will focus on maximising the efficiency of fixed assets, with reference to profitability measures, such as return on capital employed.

Excellence/Service Culture

By contrast, the Excellence/Service Culture is based on the belief that success depends on delivering high levels of customer satisfaction. To this end, customer needs are clearly understood and the organisation continually aims to improve value for customers, and develop relationships with them.

The management structure is much looser in an Excellence/Service Culture compared with a Financial Control Culture. Management's emphasis is on creating autonomous, customer-orientated teams, which are accountable for customer profitability – the key measure of performance. Authority and decision making are delegated to operational managers who are closer to customers than head office staff would be.

In contrast to Financial Control Culture, which focuses on achieving short-term financial targets, in an Excellence/Service Culture intangible assets, knowledge systems and brands are all seen as being crucial to long-term success. Moreover, performance is evaluated and rewarded by comparing teams against benchmarks, peers and previous years – rather than against a budget target set at the start of the year.

The overall orientation of performance management is on 'managing the business' rather than 'managing the numbers'. Although financial performance measures are still important, they are not the dominant measure of success. Instead they are integrated into wider performance measurement frameworks, such as the balanced scorecard.

Chapter Roundup

- People are fundamental to any organisation, and therefore **human resource management** needs to be integrated with, and **aligned** to, an organisation's **corporate strategy**. An organisation also needs to ensure that its **employees are motivated** to help it achieve its corporate objectives.
- Appraisal is a key part of performance management, forming a link between individual members of staff and an organisation's overall strategy.
- However, within this overall setting, appraisal has two different purposes – **judgement** and **development** – and there is an inherent conflict between these two which has never been satisfactorily resolved.
- Performance management attempts to integrate HRM processes with the strategic direction and control of the organisation by incorporating agreed goals and control measures. There are several approaches to performance rating.
  - Inputs and personal qualities
  - Results and outcomes
  - Behaviour in performance
- Employment is an economic relationship: labour is exchanged for reward. **Extrinsic rewards** derive from job context and include pay and benefits. **Intrinsic rewards** derive from job content and satisfy higher-level needs. Reward systems interact with many other aspects of the organisation. Reward policy must recognise these interactions, the economic relationship and the psychological contract.
- A reward system should also fulfil three key behavioural objectives: supporting the recruitment and retention of staff; motivating employees to high levels of performance; and promoting compliance with workplace rules and expectations.
- **Hard accountability** involves consideration of financial and quantitative information. **Soft accountability** considers the human input to the system and its role in shaping, evaluating and implementing goals.
- The notion that '**What gets measured, gets done**' suggests that people will make a greater effort to perform well in aspects of their roles which they know are being measured, compared to those which are not.
- Hopwood identified three distinct management styles: **budget-constrained style; profit-conscious style;** and **non-accounting style**. It is important that the management style employed is appropriate to an organisation's context.

Quick Quiz

1. What are the two main purposes of appraisal?
2. What are the five elements of Bratton's model of reward management?
3. At the end of a training course, students were asked to grade their tutor's performance (on a scale of 1 to 5) against a number of criteria, such as how clearly they explained topics.

   What type of scale is being used to assess the tutor's performance?

   A Behaviour-anchored rating scale
   B Behavioural observation scale
4. One potential disadvantage of the fact that 'What gets measured, gets done' is that organisations could suffer from tunnel vision.

   Which of the following best describes tunnel vision?

   A A focus on short-term objectives at the expense of longer-term objectives

   B Undue focus on the aspects of performance being measured to the detriment of other aspects of performance

   C A reluctance to change the measures in a performance measure system once it has been set up

   D Failure to recognise the complexity of the environment in which an organisation operates
5. Relationships between managers and staff at AQ Co have become increasingly strained recently, with staff being concerned at the number of cutbacks that are being made. They feel that the managers need to look at longer-term objectives rather than focusing solely on short-term cost targets, which they seem to be doing at the moment.

   Which of Hopwood's management styles best describes the style being used at AQ Co?

   A Budget-constrained style
   B Profit-conscious style
   C Non-accounting style
   D Judgemental style

Answers to Quick Quiz

1 Judgement; and development

Remember, the tension between judgement (control) and development is at the heart of most debates about the effectiveness of appraisal at work.

2 Strategic perspective, reward objectives, reward options, reward techniques and reward competitiveness. Remember, strategic perspective is very important because a reward system must be properly aligned to the job and the organisation's overall strategy.

3 A Behaviour-anchored rating scale

Behaviour-anchored rating scales enable numerical scoring of performance.
Behavioural observation scales are used to judge how frequently somebody performs a desired activity (eg never; rarely; sometimes; always).

4 B Undue focus on the aspects of performance being measured to the detriment of other aspects of performance

The other options describe myopia (Option A), ossification (C) and misinterpretation (D),

5 A Budget-constrained style

The focus on short-term results and cost cutting is characteristic of a budget-constrained style.
A budget-constrained style also tends to lead to poor relationships between managers and subordinates.

Now try the question below from the Practice Question Bank

Number	Level	Marks	Approximate time
Q14	Examination	25	50 mins

PART E

Performance evaluation and corporate failure

Alternative views of performance measurement and management

Topic list	Syllabus reference
1 The balanced scorecard	E1(a)
2 The performance pyramid	E1(b)
3 Building blocks (Fitzgerald and Moon)	E1(c)
4 Activity-based management	E1(d)
5 Value-based management (VBM)	E1(e)

Introduction

One of the key themes in this Study Text has been that it is no longer sufficient for organisations to look at performance measurement solely in terms of financial results. Instead, they also need to look at the performance of the activities and operations that ultimately generate those financial results.

In this chapter, we look at a range of models and approaches which can be used to measure performance. Importantly though, these approaches look at 'performance' not only from a financial perspective but also from a non-financial one.

You should already be aware of the balanced scorecard, the building block model, and activity-based management from your previous studies (since they are covered in Paper F5). However, we will recap them here, as well as looking at two models which may be new to you – the performance pyramid, and value-based management.

For each model, we will first explain it and then evaluate its usefulness in measuring performance.

Study guide

		Intellectual level
E1	**Alternative views of performance measurement and management**	
(a)	Apply and evaluate the 'balanced scorecard' approach as a way in which to improve the range and linkage between performance measures.	3
(b)	Apply and evaluate the 'performance pyramid' as a way in which to link strategy, operations and performance.	3
(c)	Apply and evaluate the work of Fitzgerald and Moon that considers performance measurement in business services using building blocks for dimensions, standards and rewards.	3
(d)	Discuss and evaluate the application of activity-based management.	3
(e)	Evaluate and apply the value-based management approaches to performance management.	3

Exam guide

One of the overall syllabus aims for P5 is that candidates should be able '**to advise ... on strategic business performance evaluation...**'. So you must think about how you could use the models here in a report to advise management on how well an organisation is performing.

You must also think about the action words used in the Study Guide, so you may need to **'apply and evaluate'** different models or frameworks in your exam answer. For example, a question scenario may describe the current performance measurement system and then you may be asked how that would change if the organisation introduced one of the models or frameworks listed in the Study Guide. What impact will introducing the model have? How could the organisation introduce it? What benefits could the organisation gain from introducing it?

However, as the Study Guide requires you to be able to '**evaluate**' the different models, you need to be able to analyse the potential limitations of using each model in any given circumstance, as well as the potential benefits from doing so.

Exam focus point

The **balanced scorecard** and Fitzgerald and Moon's **building blocks** model both featured in the June 2011 exam. The question on the balanced scorecard required candidates to evaluate the measures proposed for use in the scorecard, and to describe how the scorecard could affect a company's strategic approach, rather than simply describing the scorecard itself. Similarly, the question about the building block model required candidates to apply their knowledge to a specific case study scenario, to advise how introducing the model could allow an organisation to improve its performance management.

The balanced scorecard featured again in the June 2013 exam, when candidates were asked to evaluate an outline balanced scorecard which a company had developed, and then to suggest possible improvements to it. The question then asked candidates to describe the difficulties the company could face in implementing and using the scorecard.

One of the questions in the December 2011 exam asked candidates how the **performance pyramid** could be used to help evaluate the current performance management system in an organisation (whose key performance indicators (KPIs) are currently only financial). The question then asked candidates to explain how the pyramid could be used to help the organisation develop a coherent set of performance measures.

The performance pyramid was examined again in the December 2013 exam, where candidates were asked to use the pyramid to evaluate the performance measurement system being used by an organisation.

Activity-based management (ABM) featured in the June 2013 exam, when candidates were asked whether introducing an activity-based costing system would enable it to control costs more effectively than its existing – very simple – method of cost allocation.

Value-based management (VBM) featured in the June 2014 exam, where candidates were asker explain how VBM could be implemented in an organisation, and to evaluate its potential impact organisation.

Exam focus point

Given the frequency with which the models in this chapter have been examined in recent sittings, make sure you look out for any articles about them in the Technical Articles section of ACCA's website.

There is an article about 'Activity-based Management' which, amongst other things, looks at some of the issues raised in the June 2013 exam question. We will discuss activity-based management later in this chapter, but you are also advised to read the article about it in full.

Two of the elements you need to fulfil Performance objective 14 are:

- Analysing and providing appropriate information to measure performance (PO 14 (b))
- Advising on appropriate ways to maintain and improve performance (PO 14 (e))

One of the key features of the models we discuss in this chapter is that they address non-financial aspects of performance as well as financial ones. This could be an issue to consider in relation to the performance measurement systems in your own organisations. For example, do they have a suitable balance between the financial and the non-financial? Might it be beneficial to monitor different aspects of performance which are not currently being measured?

1 The balanced scorecard 6/11, 6/13, 12/15

FAST FORWARD

The **balanced scorecard** approach to performance measurement focuses on four different perspectives – financial, customer, internal business process, and innovation and learning. By including a combination of non-financial indicators as well as financial ones, the scorecard highlights the fact that these non-financial areas play a key role in shaping an organisation's financial performance.

In Chapter 12 we noted that it is important for organisations to look at measures of **non-financial performance** (non-financial performance indicators) as well as looking at measures of **financial performance**.

There, we highlighted the contrast between leading and lagging indicators, and that distinction is made again here in the context of the multi-dimensional performance models we are discussing in this chapter. The non-financial factors which are monitored in models such as the balanced scorecard help to shape performance, whereas the financial indicators only measure it.

Equally, however, although financial measurements do not capture all the strategic realities of the business, it is still important that they are not overlooked. A failure to attend to the 'numbers' can rapidly lead to a failure of the business. This therefore reiterates the importance for organisations to use multi-dimensional performance measurement systems which look at both financial and non-financial aspects of performance. The balanced scorecard is one such model.

Knowledge brought forward from earlier studies

The **balanced scorecard** approach emphasises the need to provide management with a set of information that covers all relevant areas of performance in an objective and unbiased fashion. The information provided may be both financial and non-financial and cover such areas as **profitability**, **customer satisfaction**, **internal efficiency** and **innovation**.

The balanced scorecard focuses on **four different perspectives**, as follows.

Perspective	Question	Explanation
Financial	How does our performance look to our shareholders? How do we create value for our shareholders?	Covers traditional measures such as growth, profitability and shareholder value but set through talking to the shareholder or shareholders direct
Customer	How do our customers see us? What do existing and new customers value from us?	Gives rise to targets that matter to customers: cost, quality, delivery, inspection, handling and so on
Internal business	What process must we excel at to achieve our financial and customer objectives?	Aims to improve internal processes and decision making
Innovation and learning	Can we continue to improve and create future value?	Considers the business's capacity to maintain its competitive position through the acquisition of new skills and the development of new products

By asking these questions, the organisation can establish its **major goals for each of the four perspectives**, and can then set performance measures and performance targets, based on these major goals, in relation to each of the perspectives.

The scorecard is **'balanced'**, as managers are required to think in terms of **all four** perspectives, to prevent improvements being made in one area at the expense of another.

An example of how a balanced scorecard might appear is offered below.

Balanced Scorecard

Financial Perspective

GOALS	MEASURES
Survive	Cash flow
Succeed	Monthly sales growth and operating income by division
Prosper	Increase market share and ROI

Customer Perspective

GOALS	MEASURES
New products	Percentage of sales from new products
Responsive supply	On-time delivery (defined by customer)
Preferred supplier	Share of key accounts' purchases Ranking by key accounts
Customer partnership	Number of cooperative engineering efforts

Internal Business Perspective

GOALS	MEASURES
Technology capability	Manufacturing configuration vs competition
Manufacturing excellence	Cycle time Unit cost Yield
Design productivity	Silicon efficiency Engineering efficiency
New product introduction	Actual introduction schedule vs plan

Innovation and Learning Perspective

GOALS	MEASURES
Technology leadership	Time to develop next generation of products
Manufacturing learning	Process time to maturity
Product focus	Percentage of products that equal 80% sales
Time to market	New product introduction vs competition

Philips Electronics

Philips Electronics

(Based on a case study in Johnson, Scholes and Whittington, *Exploring Corporate Strategy*)

Philips Electronics uses the balanced scorecard to manage its diverse product lines and divisions around the world.

The company has identified four critical success factors (CSFs) for the organisation as a whole:

- Competence (knowledge, technology, leadership and teamwork)
- Processes (drivers for performance)
- Customers (value propositions)
- Financial performance (value, growth and productivity)

Philips applies these four scorecard criteria at four levels: overall strategy review, operations review, business unit level, and for individual employees.

In each case, criteria from one level are cascaded down to more detailed criteria at the level below, such that employees can understand how their day to day activities ultimately link back to overall corporate goals.

At the business unit level, for example, the management team determine the local CSFs and then agree indicators for each. Targets are then set for each indicator.

Examples of the indicators at the business unit level include:

Financial perspective	**Customer perspective**
Economic profit Income from operations Working capital Operational cash flow Inventory turns	Rank in customer surveys Market share Repeat order rate Level of complaints Brand index
Processes (internal business perspective)	**Competence (innovation and learning perspective)**
Percentage reduction in process cycle time Number of engineering changes Capacity utilisation Order response time Process capability	Leadership competence Percentage of patent-protected turnover Training days per employee Quality improvement team participation

1.1 Advantages of the balanced scorecard

Important features of this approach are as follows:

(a) It looks at both **internal and external** matters concerning the organisation.

(b) It is related to the key elements of a company's **strategy**, and in this respect links **to long-term objectives** as well as **short-term ones**.

(c) **Financial and non-financial** measures are linked together.

By encouraging managers to consider a mixture of internal and external matters, long-term and short-term objectives, and financial as well as non-financial measures, the scorecard helps them obtain a **balanced view** about an organisation's performance.

Kaplan and Norton (who developed the balanced scorecard) have found that organisations are using it to:

- Identify and align strategic initiatives
- Link budgets with strategy

- Align the organisation (structure and processes) with strategy
- Conduct periodic strategic performance reviews with the aim of learning more about, and improving, strategy

This is consistent with Kaplan and Norton's original intention of how the scorecard should be used. They saw the scorecard as a means **of translating mission and strategy into objectives**, and measures into four different perspectives. They also say it is a means of communicating mission and strategy and using the measures to inform employees about the key drivers of success.

However, interestingly Kaplan and Norton intended the scorecard to be a **communication** and **information** system, **not a control system**.

1.2 Problems with using the balanced scorecard

As with all techniques, problems can arise when the balanced scorecard is applied.

Problem	Explanation
Conflicting measures	Some measures in the scorecard may naturally conflict (for example, a business process measure might be to speed up processing times, but cost control measures in financial perspectives may prevent the introduction of the new equipment needed to do this). It is often difficult to determine the balance between measures which will achieve the best results, but an organisation should always seek **goal congruence** between the different measures in its scorecard.
Selecting measures	Not only do appropriate measures have to be devised, but the number of measures used must be agreed. Care must be taken that the impact of the results is not lost in a sea of information. The innovation and learning perspective is, perhaps, the most difficult to measure directly, since much development of human capital will not feed directly into such crude measures as rate of new product launches or even training hours undertaken. It will, rather, improve economy and effectiveness and support the achievement of customer perspective measures. When selecting measures it is important to measure those which actually add value to an organisation, not just those that are easy to measure.
Expertise	Measurement is only useful if it initiates appropriate action. Non-financial managers may have difficulty with the usual profit measures. With more measures to consider, this problem will be compounded. Measures need to be developed by someone who understands the business processes concerned.
Interpretation	Even a financially trained manager may have difficulty in putting the figures into an overall perspective.
Management commitment	The scorecard can only be effective if senior managers commit to it. If they revert to focusing solely on the financial measures they are used to, then the value of introducing additional measures will be reduced. In this context, do not overlook the **cost** of the scorecard. There will be costs involved in measuring the performance of additional processes.

It may also be worth considering the following issues in relation to using the balanced scorecard:

(a) It doesn't provide a single aggregate summary performance measure; for example, part of the popularity of return on investment (ROI) or return on capital employed (ROCE) comes from the fact that they provide a convenient summary of how well a business is performing.

(b) In comparison to measures like economic value added (EVA), there is no direct link between the scorecard and **shareholder value**.

(c) **There are practical issues with implementation**: introducing the scorecard may require a shift in corporate culture, for example in understanding an organisation as a set of processes rather as departments. Therefore, there may be practical difficulties in introducing the scorecard into an organisation.

Equally, implementing the scorecard will require an organisation to move away from looking solely at short-term financial measures, and focus on longer-term strategic measures instead.

The scorecard should be used **flexibly**. Although there are four given perspectives, these may need to be adapted to fit the particular characteristics of a business. However, the process of deciding **what to measure** forces a business to clarify its strategy. For example, a manufacturing company may find that 50–60% of costs are represented by bought-in components, so measurements relating to suppliers could usefully be added to the scorecard. These could include payment terms, lead times, or quality considerations.

1.3 Linkages

If an organisation fails to look at all measures in their **scorecard as a whole**, this might lead to **disappointing results**. For example, increasing productivity means that fewer employees are needed for a given level of output. Excess capacity can be created by quality improvements. However, these improvements have to be exploited (eg by increasing sales). The **financial element** of the balanced scorecard 'reminds executives that improved quality, response time, productivity or new products benefit the company only when they are translated into improved financial results', or if they enable the firm to obtain a sustainable competitive advantage.

1.4 Strategy maps

As an extension to the balanced scorecard, Kaplan and Norton also developed the idea of strategy maps, which could be used to help implement the scorecard more successfully.

Strategy maps identify six stages:

(1) Identify **objectives**. Identify the key objectives of the organisation.

(2) **Value creation**. In the light of the key objectives identified, determine the main ways the organisation creates value.

(3) **Financial perspective**. Identify financial strategies to support the overall objective and strategy.

(4) **Customer perspective**. Clarify customer-orientated strategies to support the overall strategy.

(5) **Internal processes**. Identify how internal processes support the strategy and help to create value.

(6) **Innovation and learning**. Identify the skills and competencies needed to support the overall strategy and achieve the objectives.

The sequence of these stages also suggests there is a **hierarchy among the different perspectives**. The financial perspective is the highest level perspective, and the measures and goals from the other perspectives should help an organisation achieve its financial goals.

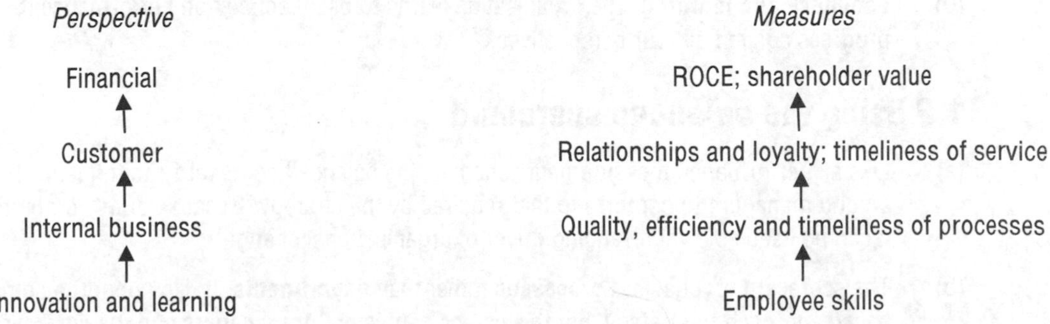

In this way, the strategy map highlights how the four perspectives of the scorecard help create value, with the overall aim of helping an organisation achieve its objectives. It can also help staff appreciate the way that different elements of performance management are linked to an organisation's overall strategy.

However, it is also important to recognise that the balanced scorecard only measures performance. **It does not indicate that the strategy an organisation is employing is the right one.** As Kaplan and Norton highlighted from the outset:

'A failure to convert improved operational performance... into improved financial performance should send executives back to their drawing boards to rethink the company's strategy or its implementation plans.'

(Kaplan, R. & Norton, D., (1992), The Balanced Scorecard: measures that drive performance, *Harvard Business Review*)

1.4.1 Practical steps in developing a scorecard

As with any other projects or changes, if an organisation is going to implement a scorecard successfully, it will need to think carefully about the steps involved in developing a scorecard.

Identify key outcomes – Identify the key outcomes critical to the success of the organisation (this is similar to identifying the organisation's CSFs).

Key processes – Identify the processes that lead to those outcomes.

KPIs – Develop key performance indicators for those processes.

Data capture – Develop systems for capturing the data necessary to measure those key performance indicators.

Reporting – Develop a mechanism for communicating or reporting the indicators to staff (for example, through charts or graphs or on a dashboard).

Performance improvement – Develop improvement programmes to ensure that performance improves as necessary.

1.5 Implementing the balanced scorecard

The introduction and practical use of the balanced scorecard is likely to be subject to all the problems associated with balancing long-term strategic progress against the management of short-term tactical imperatives. Kaplan and Norton recognise this and recommend an iterative, four-stage approach to the practical problems involved.

(a) **Translating the vision**: The organisation's mission must be expressed in a way that has to have clear operational meaning for each employee.

(b) **Communicating and linking**: The next stage is to link the vision or mission to departmental and individual objectives, including those that transcend traditional short-term financial goals.

(c) **Business planning**: The scorecard is used to prioritise objectives and allocate resources in order to make the best progress towards strategic goals.

(d) **Feedback and learning**: The organisation learns to use feedback on performance to promote progress against all four perspectives.

1.6 Using the balanced scorecard

(a) Like all performance measurement schemes, the balanced scorecard can influence behaviour among managers to conform to that required by the strategy. Because of its comprehensive nature, it can be used as a wide-ranging driver of organisational change.

(b) The scorecard emphasises **processes** rather than **departments**. It can support a competence-based approach to strategy, but this can be confusing for managers and may make it difficult to gain their support. (Moreover, although the scorecard looks at processes, it focuses mainly on an

organisation's own process, rather than comparing performance with other organisations, for example through benchmarking.)

(c) Deciding just what to measure can be especially difficult, particularly as the scorecard **vertical vector** lays emphasis on customer reaction. This is not to discount the importance of meeting customer expectations, purely to emphasise the difficulty of establishing what they are.

1.6.1 A word of warning

Kaplan and Norton never intended the balanced scorecard to replace all other performance measurement systems a business may use. They acknowledge that financial measures and financial results remain important, but suggest that businesses can use the scorecard to help deliver strategic goals.

Kaplan and Norton have also acknowledged that the scorecard needs to recognise the linkages between **strategic**, **tactical** (management) and **operational levels** in organisations. In this context, they recognise that indicators measured in the scorecard often focus on the strategic level, rather than looking at the practical, day to day operational levels. Operational managers need far more detail about performance than is given in the scorecard.

Increasingly, organisations are looking to be able to identify the linkages between these levels, and to be able to drill down and identify the sources and root causes behind the underperformance at a strategic level.

Exam focus point

Part of the compulsory question in the June 2013 exam asked candidates to evaluate a draft balanced scorecard at an organisation, and suggest suitable improvements to it, before describing the difficulties which the organisation could face in implementing and using the scorecard.

One of the issues which the examination team hoped candidates would consider (when suggesting improvements) was how well the performance metrics included in the scorecard linked to the organisation's mission. This idea of linkages is very important in the balanced scorecard. However, the post-exam report suggested that candidates did not successfully identify the link between the scorecard metrics and the organisation's mission. The examination team suggested that candidates would have scored more marks if they had considered how the metrics being used in the scorecard would help the organisation achieve its mission.

The examination team also commented that answers to the question about implementing and using the scorecard were surprisingly poor. It is vital that you appreciate the advantages and disadvantages of using the balanced scorecard, and the likely difficulties an organisation could face when introducing (or using) one.

2 The performance pyramid 12/11, 12/13

FAST FORWARD

The **performance pyramid** highlights the linkages between an organisation's corporate vision and its day to day operations. The different levels in the pyramid all need to support each other in order for an organisation to successfully achieve its corporate vision.

Key term

The **performance pyramid** derives from the idea that an organisation operates at different levels, each of which has different concerns which should nevertheless support each other in achieving business objectives. The pyramid therefore links the overall strategic view of management with day to day operations.

The performance pyramid (developed by Lynch and Cross) stems from an acknowledgement that traditional performance measures which focused on financial indicators, such as profitability, cash flow and return on capital employed, did not address the driving forces that guide an organisation's ability to achieve its strategic objectives.

Instead of focusing purely on financial objectives, the pyramid focuses on a range of **objectives** for both **external effectiveness** (related to customer satisfaction) and **internal efficiency** (related to flexibility and productivity), which Lynch and Cross propose are the driving forces on which company objectives are based. The status of these driving forces can then be monitored and measured by the indicators at the lower levels in the pyramid – measures of quality, delivery, cycle time and waste.

However, a crucial point behind the presentation of the model as a pyramid is that, although the organisation operates at different levels, each of which has a different focus, it is vital that each different level supports each other. In this way, the pyramid explicitly makes the link between **corporate level strategy** and the **day to day operations** of an organisation. (We have looked at this idea of a performance hierarchy on several occasions already in this Study Text, and the performance pyramid provides a framework for an organisation to incorporate this hierarchy into its performance measurement system.)

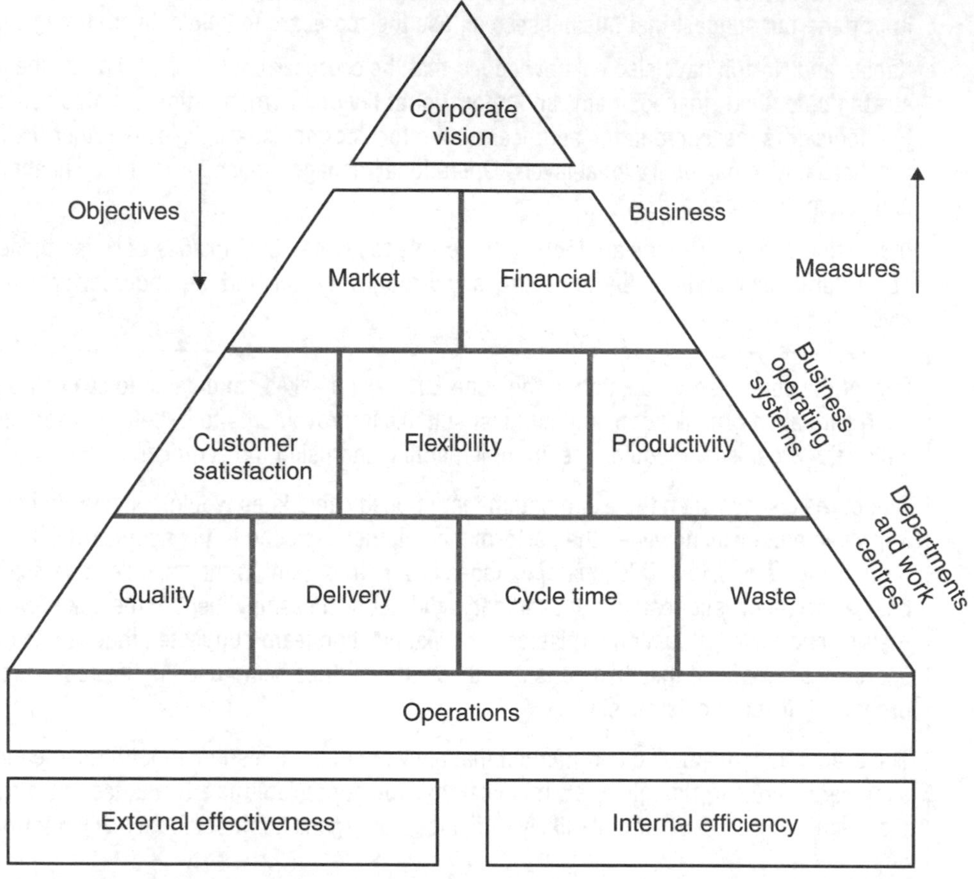

Performance Pyramid (Source*:* ACCA, December 2011 P5 exam: Solutions)

Note. When looking at any appraisal of costs it is crucial to understand the **processes driving** the costs, rather than simply looking at the costs as figures in the management accounts.

(a) At **corporate level**, the vision is developed and financial and market objectives are set in accordance with the **vision**.

(b) At **strategic business unit** level, strategies are developed to achieve these financial and market objectives.

  (i) **Customer satisfaction** is defined as meeting customer expectations.
  (ii) **Flexibility** indicates responsiveness of the business operating system as a whole.
  (iii) **Productivity** refers to the management of resources, such as labour and time.

(c) These in turn are supported by more specific **operational** criteria.

  (i) **Quality** of the product or service, consistency of product and fit for the purpose
  (ii) **Delivery** of the product or service (the method of distribution, its speed and ease of management)
  (iii) **Process time** (or cycle time) of all processes from cash collection to order processing to recruitment
  (iv) **Waste**, meaning the elimination of all non-value-added activities

The pyramid highlights the **links** running between the **vision for the company** and **functional objectives**. For example, a reduction in process time should lead to increased productivity and hence improved financial performance. The links within the pyramid help to ensure not only **goal congruence** but also a **consistency of performance** across all business areas, and a balanced approach.

2.1 Strengths and weaknesses of the performance pyramid

The performance pyramid clearly links the performance measures at the different hierarchical levels of the organisation, and encourages operational performance measures to be linked to strategic goals. Individual departments need to be aware of the extent to which they are contributing to strategic aims, and their performance measures should link operational goals to strategic goals. This in itself is a strength, but perhaps the key strength of the model is the fact that it links this **hierarchical view** of performance measurement with an appreciation of **business processes** and the need to focus all business activities on the **requirements of the customer**. (In this respect, the model contains echoes of Porter's value chain which highlights the importance of business processes creating **value** for the customer.)

The model also makes clear the measures that are of interest to **external** parties (such as customer satisfaction, quality and delivery) and those that the business focuses on **internally** (such as productivity, cycle time and waste).

However, the model does not suggest how key performance indicators may be identified.

Moreover, as with the balanced scorecard, critics have pointed to problems with applying the performance pyramid.

(a) Applying it may significantly increase the **cost** of organisational control.

(b) An organisation should measure the factors which are **most important to achieving its objectives**, rather than simply the ones which are **easy to measure**. However, the factors which are crucial to success may be difficult or expensive to measure.

(c) **Management effort**, which could otherwise be devoted to running the business, could be used in devising performance measures and responding to reports.

(d) Measures may **conflict** (for example could there be a trade-off between quality and cost?). Any such conflict could demotivate managers who feel they are caught in a 'no win' situation.

(e) Staff turnover may increase if staff feel they are being checked up on all the time or have to spend lots of time inputting data.

Exam focus point

Performance pyramids are discussed further in the article 'The Pyramids and Pitfalls of Performance Measurement' which is available in the P5 Technical Articles section of ACCA's website. You are strongly advised to read the article if you have not already done so.

Exam focus point

A question in the December 2013 exam asked candidates to use the performance pyramid to evaluate the performance measurement system currently being used in an organisation. In other words, did the measures in the current system link to the main aim of the business, and support its achievement, in the way that the pyramid suggests measures should?

3 Building blocks (Fitzgerald and Moon) 6/11

FAST FORWARD

Fitzgerald and Moon's **building blocks** for **dimensions, standards** and **rewards** attempt to overcome the problems associated with performance measurement of **service businesses**. The 'dimensions' building block is split into **results** and the **determinants** which affect those results (quality of service, flexibility, resource utilisation and innovation).

Exam focus point

The building block model was tested in a Section B question in the June 2011 exam. The first part of the question (for 4 marks) was purely a test of knowledge in which candidates were asked to briefly describe the model. However, the majority of the question (the remaining 16 marks) required candidates to apply the model to a case study scenario, in order to evaluate the current performance management system in an organisation and then suggest how the building block model could help to improve that system.

Question — Services vs manufacturing

In Chapter 4 we looked at five major characteristics of services that distinguish services from manufacturing. Can you relate them to the provision of a haircut?

Answer

(a) **Intangibility**. A haircut is intangible in itself, and the performance of the service comprises many other intangible factors, like the music in the salon and the personality of the hairdresser.

(b) **Simultaneity/inseparability**. The production and consumption of a haircut are simultaneous, and so cannot be inspected for quality in advance, nor returned if it is not what was required.

(c) **Perishability**. Haircuts are perishable, so they cannot be stored. You cannot buy them in bulk, and the hairdresser cannot do them in advance and keep them in inventory in case of heavy demand.

(d) **Heterogeneity/variability**. A haircut is heterogeneous and so the exact service received will vary each time: not only will Justin and Nigel cut hair differently, but Justin will not consistently deliver the same standard of haircut.

(e) **No transfer of ownership**. A haircut does not become the property of the customer.

Question — Characteristics of services

Consider how the factors intangibility, simultaneity, perishability, no transfer of ownership and heterogeneity apply to the various services that you use: public transport, your bank account, meals in restaurants, the postal service, your annual holiday and so on.

Knowledge brought forward from earlier studies

Performance measurement in service businesses has sometimes been perceived as difficult because of the five factors listed above, but the modern view is that if something is difficult to measure this is often because it has not been clearly enough defined. Fitzgerald and Moon identify **building blocks** for **dimensions, standards** and **rewards** which can be used as the elements in effective performance measurement systems for **service businesses**.

Dimensions are the areas of performance which yield the specific performance metrics for a company. The dimensions are split into **results** (competitive performance and financial performance) and the **determinants** which affect those results (quality of service, flexibility, resource utilisation and innovation).

Results

(a) **Competitive performance** focuses on such factors as sales growth and market share.
(b) **Financial performance** concentrates on profitability, capital structure and so on.

Determinants

(c) **Quality of service** looks at matters like reliability, courtesy and competence.

(d) **Flexibility** is an apt heading for assessing the organisation's ability to deliver at the right speed, to respond to precise customer specifications, and to cope with fluctuations in demand.

(e) **Resource utilisation**, not surprisingly, considers how efficiently resources are being utilised. This can be problematic because of the complexity of the inputs to a service and the outputs from it and because some of the inputs are supplied by the customer (they bring their own hair, for example). Many measures are possible, however, for example 'number of customers per hairdresser'. Performance measures can be devised easily if it is known what activities are involved in the service.

(f) **Innovation** is assessed in terms of both the innovation process and the success of individual innovations.

Focusing on the examination and improvement of the determinants should lead to improvement in the results.

There is no need to elaborate on **competitive performance**, **financial performance** and **quality of service** issues, all of which have been covered already. The other three dimensions deserve more attention.

Flexibility

Flexibility has three aspects.

Speed of delivery

Punctuality is vital in some service industries like passenger transport: indeed, punctuality is currently one of the most widely publicised performance measures in the UK, because organisations like railway companies are making a point of it. **Measures** include waiting time in queues, as well as late trains. In other types of service it may be more a question of **timeliness.** Does the auditor turn up to do the annual audit during the appointed week? Is the audit done within the time anticipated by the partner or does it drag on for weeks? These aspects are all easily measurable in terms of **'days late'**. Depending on the circumstances, 'days late' may also reflect on inability to cope with fluctuations in demand.

Response to customer specifications

The ability of a service organisation to respond to **customers' specifications** is one of the criteria by which Fitzgerald *et al* distinguish between the three different types of service. Clearly a professional service such as legal advice and assistance must be tailored exactly to the customer's needs. Performance is partly a matter of customer perception and so **customer attitude surveys** may be appropriate. However, it is also a matter of the diversity of skills possessed by the service organisation and so it can be measured in terms of the **mix of staff skills** and the amount of time spent on **training**. In **mass service** business customisation is not possible by the very nature of the service.

Coping with demand

This is clearly measurable in quantitative terms in a mass service like a railway company which can ascertain the extent of **overcrowding**. It can also be very closely monitored in service shops: customer **queuing** time can be measured in banks and retailers, for example. Professional services can measure levels of **overtime** worked: excessive amounts indicate that the current demand is too great for the organisation to cope with in the long term without obtaining extra human resources.

Resource utilisation measures

Resource utilisation is usually measured in terms of **productivity**. The ease with which this may be measured varies according to the service being delivered.

The main resource of a firm of accountants, for example, is the **time** of various grades of staff. The main output of an accountancy firm is **chargeable hours**.

In a restaurant it is not nearly so straightforward. Inputs are highly **diverse**: the ingredients for the meal, the chef's time and expertise, the surroundings and the customers' own likes and dislikes. A **customer**

attitude survey might show whether or not a customer enjoyed the food, but it could not ascribe the enjoyment or lack of it to the quality of the ingredients, say, rather than the skill of the chef.

Innovation

In a modern environment in which product quality, product differentiation and continuous improvement are the order of the day, a company that can find innovative ways of satisfying customers' needs has an important **competitive advantage**.

Fitzgerald *et al* suggest that **individual innovations** should be measured in terms of whether they bring about **improvements in the other five 'dimensions'**.

The innovating **process** can be measured in terms of how much it **costs** to develop a new service, how **effective** the organisation is at generating new processes (how innovative the organisation is), and how **quickly** the organisation can develop new services. This might translate into looking at measures relating to:

(a) The amount of R&D spending, and whether (and how quickly) these costs are recovered from new service sales

(b) The proportion of new services to total services provided

(c) The time between identifying the need for a new service and making it available

Standards

Standards are the measures chosen for each of the dimensions being measured. In order to be effective, employees must view standards as **fair** and **achievable**, and must take **ownership** of them.

(a) To ensure that employees take **ownership** of standards, they need to **participate** in the budget and standard-setting processes. They are then more likely to **accept** the standards and feel more **motivated**, as they perceive the standards to be achievable, and **morale** is improved. The disadvantage to participation is that it offers the opportunity for the introduction of **budgetary slack**.

(b) **Achievability** – Standards need to be set **high enough** to ensure that there is some **sense of achievement** in attaining them, but **not so high** that there is a **demotivating** effect because they are unachievable. It is management's task to find a **balance** between what the organisation perceives as achievable and what employees perceive as achievable.

(c) **Fairness** – It is vital that equity is seen to occur when applying standards for performance measurement purposes. The performance of different business units should not be measured against the same standards if some units have an inherent advantage unconnected with their own efforts. For example, divisions operating in different countries should not be assessed against the same standards.

Rewards

Rewards are the motivators which encourage employees to work towards the standards set.

Three issues need to be considered if the performance measurement system is to operate successfully: **clarity**, **motivation** and **controllability**.

(a) The organisation's objectives need to be **clearly understood** by those whose performance is being appraised; that is, they need to know what goals they are working towards.

(b) Individuals should be **motivated** to work in pursuit of the organisation's strategic objectives. Goal clarity and participation have been shown to contribute to higher levels of motivation to achieve targets, providing managers accept those targets. Bonuses can be used to motivate.

(c) Managers should have a certain level of **controllability** for their areas of responsibility. For example, they should not be held responsible for costs over which they have no control.

Exam focus point

Note the overlap between 'Standards' and 'Rewards' and the issues we discussed in Chapter 14 in relation to reward and remuneration schemes. The characteristics of effective 'Standards' and 'Rewards' identified here would provide a useful framework for evaluating a performance-related pay scheme, for example.

Now try the question below using your knowledge of the model.

Question

Competitiveness and resource utilisation

A service business has collected some figures relating to its year just ended.

		Budget	*Actual*
Customer enquiries:	New customers	6,000	9,000
	Existing customers	4,000	3,000
Business won:	New customers	2,000	4,000
	Existing customers	1,500	1,500
Types of services performed:	Service A	875	780
	Service B	1,575	1,850
	Service C	1,050	2,870
Employees:	Service A	5	4
	Service B	10	10
	Service C	5	8

Required

Calculate figures that illustrate competitiveness and resource utilisation.

Answer

Competitiveness can only be measured from these figures by looking at how successful the organisation is at converting enquiries into firm orders.

Percentage of enquiries converted into firm orders

	Budget	*Actual*
New customers (W1)	33%	44%
Existing customers (W1)	37.5%	50%

Resource utilisation can be measured by looking at average services performed per employee.

	Budget	*Actual*	*Rise*
Service A (W2)	175	195	+11.4%
Service B (W2)	157.5	185	+17.5%
Service C (W2)	210	358.75	+70.8%

Workings

1 For example 2,000/6,000 = 33%

2 For example 875/5 = 175

What comments would you make about these results? How well is the business doing?

3.1 Points to consider

There is some debate as to **how far the links between the financial results and the determinants** of those results **can be precisely identified**. Better quality will please customers, but there is a problem of **short-term versus long-term** benefits. Quality costs money now, while the benefits may take a long time to come through.

There is also the question of **how much quality** is enough: endless improvements that cost a lot of money, but are not necessarily sought by the customers (who may indeed be unwilling to pay for them) will harm long-term profitability.

Exam focus point

In the exam, you may be required to suggest appropriate performance measures for different areas of an organisation's business. Remember to make sure the measures you suggest are relevant to, and suitable for, the organisation in question. For example, there is little point in suggesting measures such as waiting times in queues to assess the quality of the service provided by an educational establishment.

Question

Performance indicators

Suggest two separate performance indicators that could be used to assess each of the following areas of a fast food chain's operations.

(a) Food preparation department
(b) Marketing department

Answer

Here are some suggestions.

(a) Material usage per product
Wastage levels
Incidences of food poisoning

(b) Market share
Sales revenue per employee
Growth in sales revenue

3.2 Strengths and weaknesses of the building blocks model

The model is clear when it explains how to encourage employee participation in setting budgets and standards and links these to the reward system. It also sets a range of financial and non-financial 'dimensions' similar to the balanced scorecard but specifically tailored to service activities. For instance, quality of service is a measure included under dimensions.

However, it can be difficult to see how the building blocks relate to strategic objectives. Although employees are encouraged to take part in budget setting, how the overall objectives of the organisation relate to budgets is not clear.

Finally, remember the model is designed for service businesses so it is difficult to apply elsewhere.

4 Activity-based management 12/10, 6/13

FAST FORWARD

Activity-based management (ABM) includes performing activities more efficiently, eliminating the need to perform certain activities that do not add value for customers, improving the design of products and developing better relationships with customers and suppliers. The goal of ABM is to enable customer needs to be satisfied while making fewer demands on organisational resources.

Exam focus point

Note the potential links between activity-based management and Porter's value chain which we looked at in Chapter 4 earlier in this Study Text.

Activity-based management encourages managers to view businesses as a set of linked activities which add value for a customer. This then encourages managers to eliminate unnecessary activities (and thereby reduce costs) and improve the performance of value-adding activities and processes.

The idea of process improvement also links back to the ideas of continuous improvement and Six Sigma which we discussed in Chapter 13 and possibly, if more radical improvements are required, to business process re-engineering (which we discussed in Chapter 4).

Exam focus point

A question scenario in the June 2013 exam described a company which currently uses a very simple system of cost allocation, but which is planning to introduce activity-based costing (ABC). Candidates were then asked to evaluate the impact of using ABC.

One of the issues which the evaluation raises is whether the difference in the cost allocations under ABC are sufficiently different than those under the current system to justify the additional time and effort involved in implementing an ABC system.

This could be an important consideration for companies in real life too. Will the benefits from introducing ABC justify the costs of doing so?

The article in the P5 Technical Articles section of ACCA's website called 'Activity-based Management' looks at the way ABC information can be used in ABM, and also includes an illustrative example based on the exam question from June 2013. You are strongly advised to read this article as part of your preparation for your P5 exam.

4.1 Definitions of activity-based management

Activity-based costing (ABC) was originally introduced as a method of working out the cost of producing a product. However, organisations can now also use ABC information to help manage costs, and to focus on those activities which add value.

In essence, the emphasis has switched away from using activity-based approaches for product costing to using it to **improve cost management**. The terms activity-based management (ABM) and activity-based cost management (ABCM) are used to describe the cost management applications of ABC. In effect, ABM is ABC in action.

There are a great many different definitions of ABM.

Here is Drury's definition (from *Management and Cost Accounting*), with BPP's emphasis.

> 'ABM views the business as a set of linked activities that ultimately add value to the customer. It focuses on managing the business on the basis of the activities that make up the organisation. ABM is based on the premise that activities consume costs. Therefore **by managing activities costs will be managed in the long term**. The **goal of ABM is to enable customer needs to be satisfied while making fewer demands on organisation resources**. The measurement of activities is a key role of the management accounting function. In particular, activity cost information is useful for prioritising those activities that need to be studied closely so that they can be eliminated or improved.
>
> In recent years ABM information has been used for a variety of business applications. They include cost reduction, activity-based budgeting, performance measurement, benchmarking and business process re-engineering.'

Horngren, Foster and Datar in *Cost Accounting: A Managerial Emphasis* 'define it broadly to include pricing and product-mix decisions, cost reduction and process improvement decisions, and product design decisions'.

In *Managerial Accounting*, Raiborn, Barfield and Kinney include **activity analysis**, **cost driver analysis**, **continuous improvement**, **operational control and performance evaluation** as the concepts covered by ABM. 'These concepts help companies to produce more efficiently, determine costs more accurately, and control and evaluate performance more effectively.'

Clark and Baxter (*Management Accounting,* June 1992) provide a description, which appears to include every management accounting buzzword.

> 'The aim of activity-based management (ABM) is to provide management with a method of introducing and managing process and organisational change.'

It focuses on activities within a process, decision making and planning relative to those activities and the need for continuous improvement of all organisational activity. Management and staff must determine which activities are critical to success and decide how these are to be clearly defined across all functions.

Everyone must co-operate in defining:

(a) Cost pools
(b) Cost drivers
(c) Key performance indicators

They must be trained and empowered to act; all must be fairly treated and success recognised.

Clearly, ABM and employee empowerment take a critical step forward beyond ABC by recognising the contribution that people make as the key resource in any organisation's success.

(a) It nurtures good communication and teamwork.
(b) It develops quality decision making.
(c) It leads to quality control and continuous improvement.

Some accountants do not appear to understand that ABM provides an essential link to total quality management (TQM) and its concepts of 'continuous improvement'.

ABM helps to deliver:

(a) Improved quality
(b) Increased customer satisfaction
(c) Lower costs
(d) Increased profitability

'It provides accountants and other technical managers with a meaningful path into the business management team.'

Perhaps the clearest and most concise definition of ABM, however, is offered by Kaplan *et al* in *Management Accounting.*

Key term

Activity-based management (ABM) is '... the management processes that use the information provided by an activity-based cost analysis to improve organisational profitability. Activity-based management (ABM) includes performing activities more efficiently, eliminating the need to perform certain activities that do not add value for customers, improving the design of products, and developing better relationships with customers and suppliers. The goal of ABM is to enable customer needs to be satisfied while making fewer demands on organisational resources.'

In the following paragraphs we examine some of the aspects of ABM mentioned in the definitions above.

4.2 Cost reduction and process improvement

Traditional cost analysis analyses costs by types of expense for each responsibility centre. ABM, on the other hand, analyses costs on the basis of cross-departmental activities and therefore provides management information on why costs are incurred and on the output of the activity in terms of cost drivers. **By controlling or reducing the incidence of the cost driver, the associated cost can be controlled or reduced.**

This is fundamental to ABM. At its heart is the recognition that the activities people undertake (to produce products or deliver services) consume resources, so controlling these activities allows managers to control costs at their source.

The difference between traditional cost analysis and activity-based analysis is illustrated in the example below of the activity of processing customer orders.

Traditional analysis

	$
Salaries	5,700
Stationery	350
Travel	1,290
Telephone	980
Equipment depreciation	680
	9,000

ABC analysis

	$
Preparation of quotations	4,200
Receipt of customer orders	900
Assessment of customer creditworthiness	1,100
Expedition of orders	1,300
Resolution of customer problems	1,500
	9,000

Suppose that the analysis above showed that it cost $250 to process a customer's order. This would indicate to sales staff that it may not be worthwhile chasing orders with a low sales value. By eliminating lots of small orders and focusing on those with a larger value, demand for the activities associated with customer order processing should fall, with spending decreasing as a consequence.

4.2.1 Problems associated with cost reduction and ABM

(a) The extent to which activity-based approaches can be applied is very dependent on an organisation's ability to identify its main activities and their associated cost drivers.

(b) If a system of 'conventional' responsibility centres has been carefully designed, this may already be a reflection of the key organisational activities. For example, a despatch department might be a cost centre, but despatch might also be a key activity.

(c) In some circumstances, the 'pooling' of activity-based costs and the identification of a single cost driver for every cost pool may even hamper effective control if the cost driver is not completely applicable to every cost within that cost pool. For example, suppose that the cost of materials handling was allocated to a cost pool for which the cost driver was the number of production runs. Logically, to control the cost of materials handling the number of production runs should be controlled. If the cost is actually driven by the weight of materials being handled, however, it can only be controlled if efforts are made to use lighter materials where possible.

4.3 Activity analysis

The activity-based analysis above provides information not available from a traditional cost analysis. Why was $1,500 spent on resolving customer orders, for example? An **activity analysis** usually **surprises managers** who had not realised the amount being spent on certain activities. This leads to **questions** about the **necessity for particular activities** and, if an activity is required, whether it can be carried out more effectively and efficiently.

Such questions can be answered by classifying activities as value added or non value added (or as core/primary, support or diversionary/discretionary).

4.3.1 Value-added and non value added activities

Key term

> An activity may increase the worth of a product or service to the customer; in this case the customer is willing to pay for that activity and it is considered **value-added**. Some activities, though, simply increase the time spent on a product or service but do not increase its worth to the customer; these activities are **non value added**. (Rayborn, Barfield and Kinney, *Managerial Accounting*)

As an example, getting luggage on the proper flight is a value-added activity for airlines; dealing with the complaints from customers whose luggage gets lost is not.

The time spent on non value added activities creates additional costs that are unnecessary. If such activities were eliminated, costs would decrease without affecting the market value or quality of the product or service.

The processing **time** of an organisation is made up of four types.

(a) **Production** or **performance time** is the actual time that it takes to perform the functions necessary to manufacture the product or perform the service.

(b) Performing quality control results in **inspection time**.

(c) Moving products or components from one place to another is **transfer time**.

(d) Storage time and time spent waiting at the production operation for processing is **idle time**.

Production time is value added. The other three are not. The time from receipt of an order to completion of a product or performance of a service equals production time plus non value added time.

Just-in-time (JIT) would of course eliminate a significant proportion of the idle time occurring from storage and wait processes but it is important to realise that **very few organisations can completely eliminate all quality control functions and all transfer time**. If managers understand the non value added nature of these functions, however, they should be able to **minimise** such activities as much as possible.

Sometimes non value added activities arise because of inadequacies in existing processes and so they cannot be eliminated unless these inadequacies are addressed.

(a) The National Health Service (NHS) is a classic example of this. Some heart patients on the NHS wait up to four months for critical heart surgery. During this time they are likely to be severely ill on a number of occasions and have to be taken to hospital where they spend the day receiving treatment that will temporarily relieve the problem. This non value added activity is totally unnecessary and is dependent on an inadequate process: that of providing operations when required.

(b) Customer complaints services can be viewed in the same way: eliminate the source of complaints and the need for the department greatly reduces.

(c) Setting up machinery for a new production run is a non value added cost. If the number of components per product can be reduced, the number of different components made will reduce and therefore set-up time will also reduce.

Normally one of the **costliest** things an organisation can do is to **invest in equipment and people to make non value added activities more efficient**. The objective is to eliminate them altogether or subject them to a major overhaul, not make them more efficient. For example, if a supplier of raw materials makes a commitment to supply high-quality materials, inspection is no longer required, and buying testing equipment and hiring more staff to inspect incoming raw material would waste time and money.

However, there are occasions when non value added activities are essential to remain in business. For instance, pharmaceutical companies need to meet Food and Drug Agency regulation on quality assurance which add nothing to the product or process.

4.3.2 Core/primary, support and diversionary/discretionary activities

This is an alternative classification of activities.

Key terms

A **core activity** or **primary activity** is one that adds value to a product, for example cutting and drilling materials and assembling them.

A **secondary activity** is one that supports a core activity, but does not add value in itself. For example, setting up a machine so that it drills holes of a certain size is a secondary activity.

Diversionary activities or **discretionary activities** do not add value and are symptoms of failure within an organisation. For instance, repairing faulty production work is such an activity because the production should not have been faulty in the first place.

The aim of ABM is to try to eliminate as far as possible the diversionary activities but, as with non value added activities, experience has shown that it is usually impossible to eliminate them all, although the time and cost associated with them can be greatly reduced.

4.4 Design decisions

In many organisations today, roughly 80% of a product's costs are committed at the product design stage, well before production begins. By **providing product designers with cost driver information** they can be encouraged to **design low-cost products that still meet customer requirements**.

The identification of appropriate cost drivers and tracing costs to products on the basis of these cost drivers has the potential to **influence behaviour to support the cost management strategies of the organisation**.

For example, suppose product costs depend on the number and type of components. A product that is designed so that it uses fewer components will be cheaper to produce. A product using standard components will also be cheaper to produce. Management can influence the action of designers through overhead absorption rates if overheads are related to products on the basis of the number of component parts they contain. Hitachi's refrigeration plant uses this method to influence the behaviour of their product designers and ultimately the cost of manufacture.

4.5 Cost driver analysis

To reflect today's more complex business environment, recognition must be given to the fact that costs are created and incurred because their cost drivers occur at different levels. Cost driver analysis investigates, quantifies and explains the relationships between cost drivers and their related costs.

Classification level	Cause of cost	Types of cost	Necessity of cost
Unit level costs	Production/acquisition of a single unit of product or delivery of single unit of service	Direct materials Direct labour	Once for each unit produced
Batch level costs	A group of things being made, handled or processed	Purchase orders Set-ups Inspection	Once for each batch produced
Product/process level costs	Development, production or acquisition of different items	Equipment maintenance Product development	Supports a product type or a process
Organisational/facility costs		Building depreciation Organisational advertising	Supports the overall production or service process

(Cost driver analysis - Adapted from Raiborn *et al*)

Traditionally it has been assumed that if costs did not vary with changes in production at the unit level, they were fixed rather than variable. The analysis above shows this assumption to be false, and that costs vary for reasons other than production volume. To determine an accurate estimate of product or service cost, **costs should be accumulated at each successively higher level of costs**.

Unit level costs are allocated over number of units produced, batch level costs over the number of units in the batch and product level costs over the number of units produced by the product line. These costs are all related to units of product (merely at different levels) and so can be gathered together at the product level to match with revenue. Organisational level costs are not product related, however, and so should simply be deducted from net revenue.

Such an approach gives a far greater insight into product profitability.

4.6 Using ABC in service and retail organisations

ABC was first introduced in manufacturing organisations, and for a long time it was only considered to be relevant to manufacturing.

However, to varying degrees, all organisations have processes and activities in place which allow them to provide the products or services required by their customers or users. ABC can therefore be used equally well in other types of organisation, including service companies, public sector organisations and not-for-profit organisations.

For example, when the management of the US Post Office introduced ABC they analysed the activities associated with cash processing as follows.

Activities	Examples	Possible cost driver
Unit level	Accept cash	Number of transactions
	Processing of cash by bank	Number of transactions
Batch level	'Close out' and supervisor review of clerk	Number of 'close outs'
	Deposits	Number of deposits
	Review and transfer of funds	Number of accounts
Product level	Maintenance charges for bank accounts	Number of accounts
	Reconciling bank accounts	Number of accounts

Retail organisations are considered in more detail in the context of direct product profitability later in this Study Text, but they too **can use ABC**.

Question — ABC and retail organisations

Complete the following table to show activities and drivers that might be used in a retail organisation.

Activities	Possible cost driver

Answer

Activities	Possible cost driver
Procure goods	Number of orders
Receive goods	Number of orders or pallets
Store goods	Volume of goods
Pick goods	Number of packs
Handle returnables/recyclables	Volume of goods

4.7 Continuous improvement

Continuous improvement **recognises the concept of eliminating non value added activities** to reduce lead time, make products or perform services with zero defects, reduce product costs on an ongoing basis and simplify products and processes. It focuses on including employees in the process, as they are often the best source of ideas.

4.8 Operational control

'**To control costs, managers must understand where costs are being incurred and for what purpose**. Some of this understanding will come from differentiating between value-added and non value added activities. Some will come from the better information generated by more appropriate tracing of overhead costs to products and services. Some will come from viewing fixed costs as long-term variable overheads and recognising that certain activities will cause those costs to change. Understanding costs allows managers to visualise what needs to be done to control those costs, to implement cost reduction activities, and to plan resource utilisation.

... By better understanding the underlying cost of making a product or performing a service, managers obtain **new insight into product or service profitability**. Such insight could **result in management decisions** about expanding or contracting product variety, raising or reducing prices, and entering or leaving a market. For example, managers may decide to raise selling prices or discontinue production of low-volume speciality output, since that output consumes more resources than does high-volume output. Managers may decide to discontinue manufacturing products that require complex operations. Or, managers may reap the benefits from low-volume or complex production through implementing high-technology processes.'

(Raiborn *et al*, with BPP's emphasis)

Innes and Mitchell (*Activity Based Costing)* report that in some organisations:

'ABCM has also been used in **make-or-buy decisions** and has led to the sub-contracting of certain activities. In another engineering company the ABCM information on purchasing **concentrated** managers' **attention** on problems such as **late deliveries, short deliveries and poor-quality raw materials**. This information enabled this engineering company to identify 20 problem suppliers and take the necessary corrective action, which varied from changing suppliers to working with others to overcome the existing problems.'

4.9 Performance evaluation

ABM encourages and rewards employees for developing new skills, accepting greater responsibilities, and making suggestions for improvements in plant layout, product design and staff utilisation. Each of these improvements reduces non value added time and cost. In addition, by focusing on activities and costs, ABM is better able to provide more appropriate measures of performance than are found in more traditional systems.

To monitor the effectiveness and efficiency of activities, performance measures relating to volume, time, quality and costs are needed.

(a) Activity **volume** measures provide an indication of the throughput and capacity utilisation of activities. For example, reporting the number of times an activity such as setting-up is undertaken focuses attention on the need to investigate ways of reducing the volume of the activity and hence future costs.

(b) To increase customer satisfaction, organisations must provide a speedy response to customer requests and reduce the time taken to develop and bring a new product to the market. Organisations must therefore focus on the **time** taken to complete an activity or sequence of activities. This time can be reduced by eliminating (as far as is possible) the time spent on non value added activities.

(c) A focus on value chain analysis is a means of enhancing customer satisfaction. The value chain is the linked set of activities from basic raw material acquisition all the way through to the end-use product or service delivered to the customer. By viewing each of the activities in the value chain as a supplier-customer relationship, the opinions of the customers can be used to provide useful feedback on the **quality** of the service provided by the supplying activity. For example, the quality of the service provided by the processing of purchase orders activity can be evaluated by users of the activity in terms of the speed of processing orders and the quality of the service provided by the supplier chosen by the purchasing activity. Such qualitative evaluations can be supported by quantitative measures, such as percentage of deliveries that are late.

(d) **Cost** driver rates (such as cost per set-up) can be communicated in a format that is easily understood by all staff and can be used to motivate managers to reduce the cost of performing activities (given that cost driver rate × activity level = cost of activity). Their use as a measure of performance can induce dysfunctional behaviour, however. By splitting production runs and therefore having more set-ups, the cost per set-up can be reduced. Workload will be increased, however, and so in the long run costs could increase.

4.10 Strengths and weaknesses of ABM

ABM focuses on managing the activities in the organisation that ultimately bring **value to the customer**. In this respect, ABM can focus management attention on key value-added activities, to help an organisation maintain or increase its competitive advantage. ABM also highlights the need for businesses to be focused on quality and continuous improvement.

To the extent that ABM highlights the importance of analysing the way activities add value for the customer, it has a degree of overlap with some of the other models we have looked at in this chapter (for example, the balanced scorecard and the performance pyramid, which also highlight the importance of creating value for the customer).

More specifically, ABM could be useful to organisations in helping to:

(a) Design products and services that meet or exceed customers' expectations and can be produced and delivered at a profit

(b) Identify where improvements (either continuous, or one-off transformations) are required in quality, efficiency and speed

(c) Negotiate with customers about prices, product features, quality, delivery and service

However, ABM should not be seen as a panacea.

(a) **ABM will not, by itself, reduce costs**. It can help organisations understand their costs better in order to know what activities they have to address to reduce costs. However, the necessary actions still have to be taken to improve or redesign these activities in order to reduce the costs.

(b) Also, the **amount of work** required to set up the ABC system and in data collection must be considered, to assess whether the cost of setting up the system outweighs the benefits of having it.

(c) **Organisational and behavioural consequences**. Selected activity cost pools may not correspond to the formal structure of cost responsibilities within the organisation (the purchasing activity may spread across purchasing, production, stores, administrative and finance departments) and so determining 'ownership' of the activity and its costs may be problematic. We have already mentioned the behavioural impact of some performance measures.

Moreover, it is important not to forget the point (which is a weakness of ABC in general) that it can sometimes be difficult to find out what costs apply to a particular activity. Some areas of activity overlap and may be difficult to separate.

Exam focus point

An exam question on activity-based management could be written, or require calculations, or be a mixture of both.

Exam questions may also test your knowledge of ABC (which is assumed knowledge brought forward from F5).

The December 2010 exam required candidates to evaluate an absorption costing system compared with an ABC system, and then comment on any action that management should take in relation to product pricing. This question combined calculations and a written report, because candidates had to perform an ABC calculation on the figures given in the scenario, and then use their findings from the calculation to identify what action management should take.

5 Value-based management (VBM) 6/14

FAST FORWARD

Value-based management (VBM) aligns an organisation's overall aspirations, analytical techniques, and management processes with the **key drivers of value**. So, VBM takes the idea of creating value through return on future cash flow and embeds this in the organisational culture in its strategy, as well as making this a performance measure to be used throughout the organisation.

The explanation of value-based management in this section is based on the article 'What is Value-Based Management?' published in *The McKinsey Quarterly*, 1994; Volume 3. In turn, that article was adapted from a book, *Valuation: Measuring and Managing the Value of Companies,* by Tom Copeland, Tim Koller and Jack Murrin.

(Note that return on invested capital (ROIC) is equivalent to ROCE in the UK.)

5.1 What is value-based management?

Value-based management (VBM) starts with the philosophy that the **value of a company** is measured by **its discounted future cash flows**. Value is created only when companies invest capital at returns that exceed the cost of that capital.

VBM **extends this philosophy** by focusing on how companies use the idea of value creation to make both major strategic and everyday operating decisions. So VBM is an approach to management that **aligns the strategic**, **operational** and **management processes** to focus management decision making on the activities that **create value for the shareholder**.

5.2 Principles

VBM focuses on better decision making at all levels in an organisation. Hierarchical command and control structures cannot work well, especially in large multi-divisional organisations. Managers need to use **value-based performance measures** for making better decisions. This means that they must manage the statement of financial position (balance sheet) as well as the income statement, and maintain a balance between long- and short-term perspectives. This approach to performance measurement is known as the **value mindset**.

5.2.1 The value mindset

VBM requires companies to move on from only using traditional financial performance measures, such as earnings or earnings growth, as these do not focus enough on value creation. Companies should also set **goals** in terms of **discounted cash flow value**, the most direct measure of value creation. These targets can then be cascaded down the organisation as shorter-term, more objective financial performance targets.

However, non-financial goals such as customer satisfaction, product innovation and employee satisfaction are also important, as these inspire and guide the entire organisation.

The most prosperous companies are usually the ones that combine their financial and non-financial goals to have a balanced approach to performance review and measurement.

Key term

A **value mindset** means that senior managers are fully aware that their ultimate financial objective is maximising value. They have clear rules for deciding when other objectives (such as employment or environmental goals) outweigh this objective; and they have a solid analytical understanding of which performance variables drive the value of the company.

Planning, target setting, performance measurement and incentive systems need to be linked to value creation at the different levels of the organisation. Management processes and systems encourage managers and employees to behave in a way that maximises the value of the organisation.

(a) **For the head of a business unit**, the objective may be stated as value creation measured in financial terms.

(b) **A functional manager's goals** could be expressed in terms of customer service.

(c) A **manufacturing manager** might focus on operational measures such as cost per unit, cycle time and defect rate.

The focus of VBM should be on the **why** and **how** of **changing the organisation's corporate culture**. A value-based manager balances an awareness of organisational behaviour with using valuation as a performance metric and decision-making tool.

Case Study — **VBM in practice**

'When VBM is working well, an organisation's management processes provide decision makers at all levels with the right information and incentives to make value-creating decisions.

Take the **manager of a business unit**. VBM would provide them with the information to quantify and compare the value of alternative strategies and the incentive to choose the value-maximising strategy. Such an incentive is created by specific financial targets set by senior management, by evaluation and compensation systems that reinforce value creation, and – most importantly – by the strategy review process between manager and superiors. In addition, the manager's own evaluation would be based on long- and short-term targets that measure progress towards the overall value creation objective.

Line managers and supervisors can have targets and performance measures that are tailored to their particular circumstances but driven by the overall strategy.

A **production manager** might work to targets for cost per unit, quality, and turnaround time. At the top of the organisation, on the other hand, VBM informs the board of directors and corporate centre about the value of their strategies and helps them to evaluate mergers, acquisitions, and divestitures. Value-based management can best be understood as a marriage between a value creation mindset and the management processes and systems that are necessary to translate that mindset into action. Taken alone, either element is insufficient. Taken together, they can have a huge and sustained impact.'

(From: Koller, T., *What is value-based management?*)

5.2.2 Value drivers

VBM requires that management understand the performance variables that create the value of the business that are the key **value drivers**. Management cannot act directly on value, but can respond to things it **can** influence, such as customer satisfaction, cost and capital expenditure.

Key term

A **value driver** is any variable that affects the value of the company.

Value drivers need to be ranked in terms of their **impact on value** and **responsibility assigned** to individuals who can help the organisation meet its targets.

Value drivers must be matched to the appropriate level of management so that they are consistent with the decision variables that are directly under the control of line management.

Value drivers are useful at three levels in the organisation:

(a) **Generic**, where operating margins and invested capital are combined to compute ROIC

(b) **Business unit**, where variables such as customer mix are particularly relevant

(c) **Grass roots**, where value drivers are precisely defined and tied to specific decisions that front-line managers have under their control

So value drivers are usually cascaded in 'trees' down the organisation so that each layer of management has clear targets relevant to areas under their control.

These 'trees' are then usually linked into ROIC trees, which are in turn linked into multi-period cash flows and valuation of the business unit.

It can be difficult to **identify key value drivers** because it requires an organisation to think about its processes in a different way and existing reporting systems are often not equipped to supply the necessary information. Mechanical approaches based on available information and purely financial measures rarely succeed. What is needed instead is a creative process involving much trial and error. Nor can value drivers be considered in isolation from each other. The article suggests that a good way of relating a range of value drivers is to use **scenario analysis**. It is a way of assessing the impact of different sets of mutually consistent assumptions on the value of a company or its business units.

5.2.3 Management processes

VBM also requires that managers must establish **processes** that ensure all line managers **adopt value-based thinking** as an improved way of making decisions. VBM must eventually involve every decision maker in the company.

The article notes that there are **four essential management processes** that collectively govern the adoption of VBM. These four processes are linked across the company at the **corporate, business-unit and functional levels**. The four processes which run in order are expressed below as steps.

Step 1 A company or business unit **develops a strategy** to maximise value.

Step 2 This strategy translates into short- and long-term **performance targets** defined in terms of the key value drivers.

Step 3 **Action plans and budgets** are drawn up to define the steps that will be taken over the next year or so to achieve these targets.

Step 4 Finally **performance measurement and incentive systems** are set up to monitor performance against targets and to encourage employees to meet their goals.

(a) **Strategy development**

Corporate level. Under VBM, senior management devises a corporate strategy that explicitly maximises the overall value of the company, including buying and selling business units as appropriate. This should be built on a thorough understanding of business-unit strategies.

Business-unit level. Alternative strategies should be weighed up and the one with the highest value chosen. The chosen strategy should spell out how the business unit will achieve a competitive advantage that will permit it to create value. The VBM elements of the strategy then apply. They include:

(i) **Assessing the results of the valuation** and the key assumptions driving the value of the strategy.

(ii) Assessing the value of the alternative strategies that were discarded, along with the reasons for rejecting them.

(iii) **Looking at resource requirements**. Business-unit managers need to focus on the statement of financial position (balance sheet) and also consider human resource requirements.

(iv) **Summarising the strategic plan projections**, by focusing on the key value drivers. These should be supplemented by an analysis of the ROIC over time and relative to competitors.

(v) **Analysing alternative scenarios** to assess the effect of competitive threats or opportunities.

(b) **Target setting**

The next step after strategies for maximising value are agreed is to translate these into specific targets. In applying VBM to target setting, several general principles are helpful.

(i) **Base targets on key value drivers**. This should cover both financial and non-financial targets. The latter serve to prevent manipulation of short-term financial targets.

(ii) **Tailor the targets to the different levels within an organisation**. So that senior business-unit managers should have targets for overall financial performance and unit-wide non-financial objectives. Functional managers need functional targets, such as cost per unit and quality.

(iii) **Link short-term targets to long-term ones**. The article gives the example of setting linked performance targets for ten years, three years, and one year. The ten-year targets express a company's aspirations; the three-year targets define how much progress it has to make within that time in order to meet its ten-year aspirations; and the one-year target is a working budget for managers.

The article notes that 'Ideally, targets should be expressed in terms of value, but since value is always based on long-term future cash flows and depends on an assessment of the future, short-term targets need a more immediate measure derived from actual performance over a single year.

Economic profit is a short-term financial performance measure that is tightly linked to value creation. It is defined as: Economic profit = Invested capital × (Return on invested capital – Weighted average cost of capital)

Economic profit measures the gap between what a company earns during a period and the minimum it must earn to satisfy its investors. Maximising economic profit over time will also maximize company value.'

Exam focus point

Value-based management and economic value added (EVA)

Although value-based management is a much broader concept than EVA (which is ultimately only a way of **measuring** financial performance), the notion of economic profit in EVA can still be useful to a value-driven firm.

As we saw in our discussion of EVA in Chapter 9, economic profit (unlike accounting profit) makes an allowance for **value-building expenditure**. Economic profit also recognises that wealth is only created when a company covers all of its operating costs and the cost of capital (including both debt and equity).

As such, if managers evaluate potential investments on the basis of their ability to increase an organisation's EVA in the future, this should also help to ensure that they seek out and implement value-creating investments.

(c) **Action plans and budgets**

Then, management must translate strategy into the specific steps an organisation will take to achieve its targets, particularly in the short term through action plans. The plans must identify the actions that the organisation will take so that it can pursue its goals in a methodical manner.

(d) **Performance measurement**

Finally performance measurement and incentive systems will track progress in achieving targets and motivate managers and other employees to achieve them. VBM may force a company to modify its traditional approach to these systems by linking performance measures to long-term value creation and strategy. In particular, it shifts performance measurement from being **accounting driven** to being **management driven**. Key principles include:

(i) **Tailor performance measurement to the business unit**. Each business unit should have its own performance measures which it can influence.

(ii) **Link performance measurement to a unit's short- and long-term targets**. Performance measurement systems are often based almost exclusively on accounting results. By contrast, VBM systems focus on the creation of shareholder wealth.

(iii) **Combine financial and operating performance in the measurement**. Financial performance is often reported separately from operating performance, whereas an integrated report would better serve managers' needs.

(iv) **Identify performance measures that serve as early warning indicators**. Early warning indicators might be simple non-financial indicators, such as market share and sales trends. Once performance measurements are an established part of corporate culture and managers are familiar with them, it is time to revise the compensation system.

In addition to these key principles, the following aspects are relevant to performance measurement (and management) under a VBM system:

(i) **Management remuneration** – Rewards should be linked to the key value drivers, and how well these targets are achieved.

(ii) **Internal communication** – The background to the programme, and how VBM will benefit the business, need to be explained to staff.

(iii) **External communication** – Management decisions, and how they are designed to achieve value, must be communicated to the market. The market's reaction to these decisions will help determine movements in the organisation's share price (and hence the value of the company).

5.3 Evaluation of VBM

Identifies value not profit

VBM highlights that management decisions designed to lead to higher profits do not necessarily **create value for shareholders**. Often, management are under pressure to meet short-term profit targets, and they are prepared to sacrifice long-term value in order to achieve these short-term targets. For example, management might avoid initiating a project with a positive net present value if that project leads to their organisation falling short of expected profit targets in the current period.

Profit-based performance measures may therefore obscure the true state of a business. By contrast, VBM seeks to ensure that analytical techniques and management processes are all aligned to help an organisation **maximise its value**. VBM does this by focusing management decision making on the key drivers of value, and making management more accountable for growing an organisation's intrinsic value.

(Note, the focus on shareholder value and future cash flows suggests that the VBM would be very unlikely to be used in not-for-profit organisations where value creation is not measured by future cash flow.)

Forward looking

Therefore, whereas profit-based performance measures look at what has happened in the past, VBM seeks to maximise **returns on new investments**. What matters to the shareholders of a company is that they earn an acceptable return on their capital. They are interested in not only how a company has performed in the past but also how it is likely to perform in the future.

Need for good information

Although it is easy to identify the logic that companies ought to be managed for shareholder value, it is much harder to specify how this can be achieved. For example, a strategy to increase market share may not actually increase shareholder value.

Good-quality information is essential in a VBM system, so that management can identify where value is being created – or destroyed – in a business. For example, continuing the previous example, there is no value in increasing market share in a market if that market is not profitable. (Consequently, if an organisation currently has poor management information systems it is unlikely to be able to implement a VBM system effectively. One particular problem could be **identifying value drivers**, as an organisation's reporting systems may not be set up to be able to identify these.)

An organisation will need to identify its value drivers, and then put strategies in place for each of them. When identifying its value drivers, an organisation may also find that its organisational structure needs reorganising, to ensure that it is aligned with the processes which create value. (However, note that any such reorganisation could be expensive and time consuming to implement in the short term.)

Need to redefine performance metrics

VBM will lead to a change in the performance metrics used in a company. Instead of focusing solely on historical returns, companies also need to look at more forward-looking contributions to value: for example, growth and sustainability. The performance measures used in VBM are often non-financial.

Aligning agents and principles

In many companies today, the intellectual capital provided by employees plays a key role in generating value. VBM attempts to align the interests of the employees who generate value and the shareholders they create value for.

If it didn't do this, VBM could drive a wedge between those who deliver economic performance (employees) and those who harvest its benefits (shareholders). In practice, the solution to this problem is to introduce remuneration structures which include some form of share-based payments.

Cultural change

However, successfully implementing VBM may also involve cultural change in an organisation. The employees in the organisation will need to commit to creating shareholder value. Value is created throughout the company, not just by senior management, so all the employees need to appreciate how their roles add value.

Nonetheless, visible leadership and strong commitment from senior management will be essential for a shift to VBM to be successful.

However, as with any change programme, implementing VBM could be expensive and potentially disruptive, particularly if extensive restructuring is required.

Case Study **Problems with VBM**

The following extract from the article 'What is Value-Based Management' published in *The McKinsey Quarterly* (1994; Vol. 3) highlights that VBM is not without some problems, however.

'A few years ago, the chief planning officer of a large company gave us a preview of a presentation intended for his chief financial officer and board of directors. For about two hours we listened to details of how each business unit had been valued, complete with cash flow forecasts, cost of capital, separate capital structures, and the assumptions underlying the calculations of continuing value.

When the time came for us to comment, we had to give the team A+ for their valuation skills. Their methodology was impeccable. But they deserved an F for management content. None of the company's significant strategic or operating issues were on the table. The team had not even talked to any of the operating managers at the group or business-unit level. Scarcely relevant to the real decision makers, their presentation was a staff-captured exercise that would have no real impact on how the company was run. Instead of value-based management, this company simply had value veneering.'

Exam focus point

One of the question scenarios in the June 2014 exam highlighted that an organisation's shareholders had expressed concern that it lacked focus, and they had suggested the introduction of VBM using EVA as the measure of value.

The question requirement asked candidates to explain how VBM could be implemented and to evaluate its potential impact on the organisation. The post-exam report suggested that the majority of candidates appeared to have little knowledge of what VBM was, and many appeared to confuse VBM with ABM, despite its being presented alongside EVA in both the scenario and the requirements.

Chapter Roundup

- The **balanced scorecard** approach to performance measurement focuses on four different perspectives – financial, customer, internal business process, and innovation and learning. By including a combination of non-financial indicators as well as financial ones, the scorecard highlights the fact that these non-financial areas play a key role in shaping an organisation's financial performance.
- The **performance pyramid** highlights the linkages between an organisation's corporate vision and its day to day operations. The different levels in the pyramid all need to support each other in order for an organisation to successfully achieve its corporate vision.
- Fitzgerald and Moon's **building blocks** for **dimensions, standards** and **rewards** attempt to overcome the problems associated with performance measurement of **service businesses**. The 'dimensions' building block is split into **results** and the **determinants** which affect those results (quality of service, flexibility, resource utilisation and innovation).
- **Activity-based management** (**ABM**) includes performing activities more efficiently, eliminating the need to perform certain activities that do not add value for customers, improving the design of products and developing better relationships with customers and suppliers. The goal of ABM is to enable customer needs to be satisfied while making fewer demands on organisational resources.
- Value-based management (VBM) aligns an organisation's overall aspirations, analytical techniques, and management processes with the **key drivers of value**. So, VBM takes the idea of creating value through return on future cash flow and embeds this in the organisational culture in its strategy, as well as making this a performance measure to be used throughout the organisation.

Quick Quiz

1 Which of the following are the four perspectives of the balanced scorecard?

A Innovation and learning, customer, financial, competitive
B Financial, quality, innovation, internal
C Financial, customer, internal business, innovation and learning
D Customer, quality, competitive, flexibility

2 Label the performance pyramid below.

3 Which of the following statements about performance measurement frameworks (such as the balanced scorecard and the performance pyramid) are true?

(i) Performance measures should be linked to corporate strategy.

(ii) Performance measures should only focus on non-financial performance.

(iii) Performance measures should include important but difficult to measure factors and not just easily measurable ones.

A (i) and (ii)
B (i) and (iii)
C (ii) and (iii)
D All of them

4 Fitzgerald and Moon's standards for performance measurement systems are ownership, achievability and controllability. True or false?

5 Complete the table below for the four levels of classification of cost driver under an ABC/ABM analysis of costs.

Classification level	Cause of cost	Types of cost	Necessity of cost

Answers to Quick Quiz

1 C The four perspectives of the balanced scorecard are: Financial, customer, internal business, and innovation and learning.

2

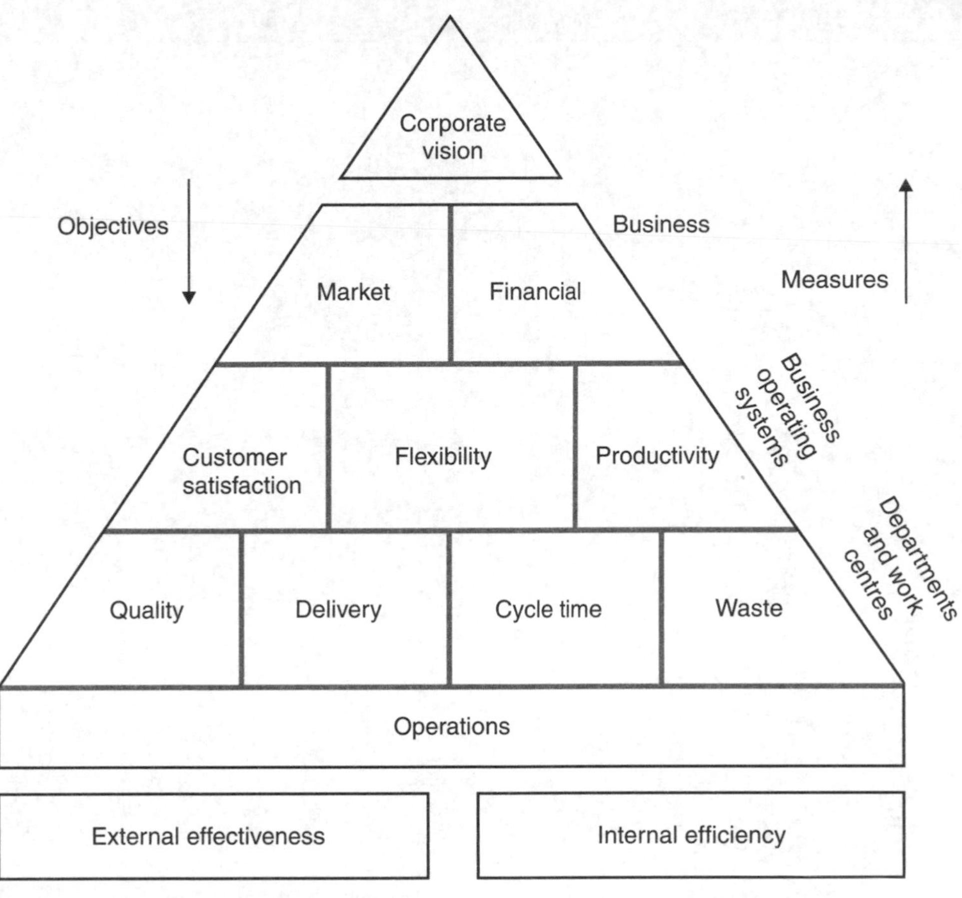

3 B

Option (ii) is incorrect. Performance measures should include non-financial **and** financial measures.

4 False. They are ownership, achievability and equity.

5

Classification level	Cause of cost	Types of cost	Necessity of cost
Unit level costs	Production/acquisition of a single unit of product or delivery of single unit of service	Direct materials Direct labour	Once for each unit produced
Batch level costs	A group of things being made, handled or processed	Purchase orders Set-ups Inspection	Once for each batch produced
Product/process level costs	Development, production or acquisition of different items	Equipment maintenance Product development	Supports a product type or a process
Organisational/ facility costs		Building depreciation Organisational advertising	Supports the overall production or service process

Now try the questions below from the Practice Question Bank

Number	Level	Marks	Approximate time
Q15	Examination	25	50 mins
Q16	Examination	50	100 mins

16

Strategic performance issues in complex business structures

Topic list	Syllabus reference
1 Performance measurement in complex business structures	E2(a)
2 Impact of different business models on performance management	E2(b)

Introduction

A recurring theme throughout this Study Text has been the importance of selecting performance measures (both financial and non-financial) which are suitable for an organisation and the context in which it is operating.

In this chapter, we are going to consider the particular issues which relate to measuring and controlling performance in complex business structures (such as strategic alliances, **joint ventures** and **network organisations**).

Study guide

		Intellectual level
E2	**Strategic performance issues in complex business structures**	
(a)	Discuss the problems encountered in planning, controlling and measuring performance levels, eg productivity, profitability, quality and service levels, in complex business structures.	3
(b)	Discuss the impact on performance management of the use of business models involving strategic alliances, joint ventures and complex supply chain structures.	3

Exam guide

In Chapter 1 we identified that performance management is a way of trying to direct and support the performance of employees and departments within an organisation so that they work as efficiently and effectively as possible, and so that their individual goals are aligned with the organisation's overall goals and business strategy. However, one of the key issues which can arise in relation to complex business structures (such as joint ventures) is deciding what the organisation's goals and objectives are. The decision-making process can be particularly difficult if the strategic partners involved have different approaches – for example, if one partner in a joint venture wants to pursue high-risk, high-return approach to growth, but the other would prefer a more cautious approach.

Similarly, if different facets of performance are important to the venture partners in a joint venture, this could make it difficult to decide what the performance metrics for the venture should be.

Exam focus point

The potential difficulties in managing performance in a joint venture where the venture partners had differing goals were examined in a question in the June 2014 exam.

Complex business structures can also present difficulties in relation to controlling the performance of individuals or organisations within the value system. One of the points often raised as a disadvantage of outsourcing is that it is harder to control the performance of a third-party (outsourced) service provider, than it is to control an in-house division or department.

Once again, though, it is important to note the difference in approach between Paper P5 and Paper P3 in this respect. In Paper P3 you might be expected to advise whether an organisation should outsource a function or retain it in-house. By contrast, in Paper P5, the focus will be more on how an organisation can measure the level of service it is receiving from an outsourced partner.

1 Performance measurement in complex business structures

FAST FORWARD

The complex nature of business structures, such as joint ventures, strategic alliances, multinational companies and network organisations, can lead to problems in measuring and controlling performance; for example in relation to productivity, quality and service levels.

Exam focus point

You may recall that in Chapter 4 we looked at the information requirements for different business structures (functional, division, network) and how information needs vary according to the type of structure an organisation adopts.

As we look now at the performance measurement problems which might arise in complex business structures, remember that an organisation's ability to measure and control performance effectively might be adversely affected by the availability of suitable management information, and the quality of that information.

Complex business structures include joint ventures, strategic alliances, multinational companies, virtual organisations and divisionalised structures.

The nature of the structures may lead to problems in planning, controlling and measuring performance. In this respect, a number of different aspects of performance may be important: **productivity, profitability, quality**, and **service levels**.

Traditional performance indicators and performance management activities focus on optimising the **internal workings** of a business, to maximise the value it generates for its shareholders.

However, in many organisations it is no longer sufficient for performance measurement to focus solely on internal activities. In complex business structures a wider range of stakeholders and activities (both internal and external) contribute to an organisation's performance.

When a business operates through a network of interrelated organisations, the performance of all these different organisations should be measured, not simply the performance of the business's own internal operations.

For example, most Nike shoes never see the inside of a Nike facility because they are manufactured by outsourced suppliers. The flow of information between Nike and the suppliers is critical – from Nike, to identify the design and quantity of shoes; and from the suppliers to identify the progress of the orders. However, the productivity of the suppliers and the quality of the shoes they produce are still important aspects of performance that Nike needs to manage. For example, if there is a problem with the quality of the shoes, it is the Nike brand which will suffer with the customers.

Consequently, performance management has to be applied between organisations and among parts of the same organisation. Companies need to monitor success within the context of their performance network. Moreover, performance measurement now also needs to focus on building **trust and relationships** between partner organisations, instead of just controlling internal value-adding activities.

1.1 Joint ventures 6/14

Part of the problem of measuring performance in joint ventures is establishing what the goals of the joint venture are. The different joint venture partners may have different **goals**, depending on their past experience, knowledge of local markets, or their understanding of product/process technology issues.

Performance measures are likely to include a variety of **financial indicators**, such as profitability, growth and cost positions. However, difficulties may arise in establishing accountability for different elements of performance.

One of the most common problems in joint ventures as a whole is that of ensuring smooth **co-ordination and control** among the venture partners. Problems arise when there is no clear pattern for decision making, or a lack of overall leadership. For example, if one partner wants to focus on **short-term performance** and another is more interested in the **longer-term prospects** of the venture, it will not be clear what the key performance metrics for the venture will be. **Quality** may also be an issue if the venture partners have different ideas about the level of quality which is acceptable.

In addition, the respective **cultures** of the venture partners could have an important impact on the success of the ventures. If there is a mismatch between the cultures of the partners, this could reduce the chances of the joint venture being successful.

Another potential issue in joint ventures is that, as well as sharing resources (such as capital, staff and facilities), organisations share **information** and **intellectual property**. However, it is likely to be more difficult to measure the contribution of these intangible elements to the performance of a venture than it is to measure more tangible aspects, such as the productivity of different processes.

Moreover, the venture partners may be reluctant to share too much information about their own businesses with their partners. In this respect, developing the strength of the relationship between the venture partners and the **trust** between them could be very important for the success of a joint venture, and is therefore just as much a part of performance management as is controlling the efficiency of any production processes within the venture.

Exam focus point

> One of the scenarios in the June 2014 exam featured a joint venture in which one of the joint venture partners was owned by venture capitalists and managed by an ambitious and dynamic group of managers, while the other venture partner was a family-owned company operating in a mature market, but whose survival has been threatened by cash flow difficulties.
>
> Part of the question asked candidates to discuss the problems encountered in managing performance in a joint venture such as this (where the venture partners clearly had different goals and objectives for the venture, as well as different attitudes to risk).

1.2 Strategic alliances

The organisations in the alliance remain independent organisations. Therefore they will retain their own internal procedures and behaviours, and there is little scope for the alliance to enforce and analyse common performance measures.

Equally, the individual alliance partners will retain their own individual business practices, cultures and management objectives. If the cultures and objectives vary between alliance partners this could lead to differences in the focus of their performance measurement and control. It may even lead to conflicts between the alliance partners.

Moreover, because the alliance partners are separate individual entities they could all have different management information styles and produce different management information. Therefore it may be difficult to compare and collate information.

Communication and collaboration. The 'loose' nature of the alliance structure means that success will be achieved through communication and collaboration rather than through a formal set of goals and objectives which can be cascaded throughout a single organisation. The efficient sharing of information in a performance network will enable stakeholders to identify bottlenecks in a production process or opportunities to improve process efficiency.

Reciprocity. The key distinction between joint ventures and strategic alliances and conventional hierarchical organisations is the way a number of stakeholder organisations (venture partners or alliance partners) contribute to the alliance's success. However, this could also raise sensitive issues for performance measurement.

In a conventional hierarchical organisation, performance measurement focuses on the organisation's own performance. However, within a JV or alliance, partner organisations will each be interested in the returns the venture is generating relative to the amounts they are investing in it. In this respect, it may be difficult to assess how much one partner is contributing relative to another. Equally, if one partner feels that another partner's performance (for example, poor-quality output) is damaging the overall performance of the venture this will create tensions, because ultimately the performance of the venture affects the bottom line of both partners.

1.3 Multinational companies

While the issues facing joint ventures and alliances come from bringing together different companies, the issues facing multinational companies arise from operating in different locations.

Managers in multinational companies need to establish systems of measurement and accountability which enable them to create and maintain a common organisational 'language', embedded in a corporate culture, which in turn enables them to co-ordinate the diverse elements of the company, operating in different countries.

Multinational companies have to deal with local currencies and tax systems before reporting a single set of consolidated results. However, trying to compare the performance of divisions or subsidiaries operating in different countries can be very challenging.

The relative **profitability of different divisions** may depend on local factors outside the control of division management; for example, government policy (eg tax rates) or economic circumstances (eg recession vs economic growth; levels of domestic competition) may vary from country to country. More generally, different **social** or **cultural factors** could affect performance in different countries. However, these differences make it harder for the corporate centre to compare the performance of different divisions in a multinational.

Comparing divisions or subsidiaries operating in different countries raises a number of performance measurement issues.

(a) **Realistic standards**. It may be difficult to establish realistic standards for each different country. Performance standards should take account of local conditions, considering local opportunities as well as any restrictions on the activities of an operating unit in a particular country. For example, if one subsidiary is operating in a rapidly growing economy, but another is operating in a country suffering from recession, is it realistic to expect both to grow at a similar rate?

(b) **Controllable cash flows**. Care must be taken to determine which cash flows are controllable and to separate these from those outside the control of local management. In particular, the distortions caused by local taxation laws should be eliminated.

(c) **Currency conversion**. Considerable friction and difficulty in measuring performance can be caused by the use of inappropriate currency conversion rates.

As a more general point, multinational companies could also be faced with issues around how they reconcile long-term strategic goals with short-term operational targets. For example, if a company has a strategic goal to expand in a certain region, how is this translated into targets for the local operations? And how will these targets affect the behaviour of the local managers in the foreign subsidiaries?

Performance information

Multinational organisations also have to consider the procedures they use to obtain performance information from the subsidiaries.

(a) **Reports**

 (i) Need to be **standardised** to allow comparative analysis between subsidiaries

 (ii) Should use an agreed **common language** and **currency**

 (iii) **Frequency**, as necessary to allow proper management

 (iv) Must be designed to ensure they include all the **information needs of the corporate centre** (head office)

(b) **Meetings**
Meetings between head office executives and subsidiary management allow for more intensive information exchange and monitoring, and minimise misunderstandings. They do, however, take up time and resources (eg travel costs for managers from foreign subsidiaries) and are generally not as regular as reports.

(c) **Information technology**
The transmission speed of email and internet communications makes close monitoring of marketing and financial performance much easier. Videoconference meetings allow both cost and time savings to be made, provided both the head office and the relevant subsidiaries have the necessary technology in place to enable videoconferencing to take place.

1.4 Virtual organisations 6/12

Exam focus point

One of the question scenarios in the June 2012 exam describes a company which describes itself as a 'virtual company' because it has outsourced many of its business processes to strategic partners.

Candidates were then asked to assess the difficulties of measuring and managing performance in complex business structures, which in this case related to home-working employees and strategic outsourcing partners.

The exact definition of virtual organisations (and network organisations) may vary, but crucial features include **geographical dispersion** and the centrality of **information technology** to the production process. Many definitions also agree that a virtual organisation only has a temporary character. Other characteristics are a **flexible structure** and a **collaborative culture**.

IT systems will be crucial to measuring performance: for example, the core organisation may create a knowledge database capturing the performance of its partners.

Productivity. Measuring productivity could be a problem because it relies on the performance of remote workers as well as those who are 'on site'. The problems in measuring, controlling and planning performance relate to capturing data from dispersed sources and controlling and monitoring the performance of remote workers. Key performance questions and issues will be: are the network partners fulfilling the tasks given to them? Are the network partners meeting the standards and goals assigned to them? What is the contribution of different partners? How are the partners collaborating with the central organisation?

A key element of performance indicators in a network relationship is that they need to reflect the results of **service delivery** by the network partners. Are they delivering the agreed quantity and quality of goods and services on time? However, in order to measure whether the partners are meeting such requirements, the requirements first have to be established.

This highlights the importance of establishing **service level agreements** between the core organisation and their network partners. Once a service level agreement is in place, then both partners have a structure against which to measure their performance in the relationship, and to assess whether a satisfactory level of service is being provided.

1.5 Remote working

Some of the issues which may be faced in virtual organisations may also be faced in relation to managing remote workers (or home workers).

On the one hand, a situation in which employees are working without a manager monitoring what they are doing involves a high degree of trust – because the manager has little way of knowing what the employees are doing.

However, perhaps more importantly, managers will need to provide their employees with clear goals and expectations for their work.

In order to manage remote employees, managers will have to adopt a '**management by objectives**' approach, as opposed to managing by observation. This will involve setting goals and action plans, and then evaluating employees' performance based on the outputs or results they achieve.

Or, to use Ouchi's terminology in relation to control mechanisms – which we discussed in Chapter 14 – employees' performance will have to be rated in terms of **results and outcomes**, because managers will not be able to monitor **behaviour in performance**.

1.6 Divisionalised structures

We looked at performance measurement issues in divisionalised structures in Chapter 10.

2 Impact of different business models on performance management

FAST FORWARD

A **supply chain** is the network of suppliers, manufacturers and distributors that is involved in the process of moving goods for a customer order from the raw materials stage through the production and distribution stages to the customer. Every organisation operates somewhere within a supply chain.

A **commonly held view** by management is that **to improve profitability** it is necessary to **get the lowest prices from suppliers** and to **obtain the best prices from the customers** next in line down the supply chain.

Supply chain management looks at the supply chain as a whole, and starts with the view that all organisations in the supply chain collaborate to produce something of value for the end customer.

Supply chain managers need to consider **production, supply, inventory, location, transportation and information**.

Strategic alliances are formed by two or more businesses when they wish to share their resources and activities to pursue a particular strategy. They decide to do this rather than set up a new company or buy access to resources and competences.

Joint ventures are a common form of strategic alliance where the partners remain independent setting up a collaborative venture usually for a longer term than a consortium. This arrangement is popular in countries such as China, where Western companies would provide technical expertise and finance and a Chinese company would offer a workforce and entry into the local market.

A supply chain is a network of facilities and distribution options that performs the functions of procurement of materials, transformation of these materials into intermediate and finished products and the distribution of these finished products to customers.

(Ganeshan and Harrison, *Supply Chain Management*)

Within a supply chain, many processes might take place between the origination of raw materials to the eventual delivery of the finished product or service to the end customer. For each organisation inside a supply chain, some of the processes are carried out by the organisation itself, and others are carried out by suppliers or by other organisations further down the supply chain.

Case Study

Supply chain

A company manufacturing motor vehicles might have a plant where the vehicles are assembled and finished. It might manufacture some parts itself and produce the car body work, but most sub-assemblies and the tyres will be purchased from outside suppliers. The suppliers of sub-assemblies might make some components themselves, but will also purchase many of their components from other suppliers. The manufacturer, suppliers and sub-suppliers might all purchase raw materials, such as steel, from other suppliers. The manufacturer will also purchase capital equipment from equipment suppliers, who are another part of the supply chain. The finished cars will not be sold directly to the end customer, but to distributors, and the distributors will sell to the end customer.

How performance management is affected by these business models

Where a business is sharing information and resources with another business there is always a concern over **the confidentiality and security of the information passed between them**. The businesses also need to **agree how profits and losses will be apportioned**. Legal contracts should make clear what each business is due under a joint venture agreement.

Joint ventures and performance management

The impact on performance management of a **joint venture** structure includes:

(a) **Sharing costs**. As the capital outlay is shared, joint ventures are especially attractive to smaller or risk-averse firms, or where very expensive new technologies are being researched and developed (such as in the civil aerospace or petrochemical industries).

(b) **Cutting risk**. A joint venture can reduce the risk of government intervention if a local firm is involved. However, in practice joint venture (JV) partners do not always deliver the level of performance which had been expected.

(c) Participating enterprises benefit from all sources of profit.

(d) Close control over marketing and other operations.

(e) Overseas JVs provide local knowledge, quickly.

(f) **Synergies**. One firm's production expertise can be supplemented by the other's marketing and distribution facility. However, it is also important to understand the partner's needs and expectations before entering into a JV. The JV is likely to work most effectively when the needs of the JV partners are aligned.

Case Study **Telstra – Telkom Indonesia joint venture**

In August 2014, the Australian telecommunications and information services company Telstra finalised a JV agreement with Telkom Indonesia (the largest telecommunications and network services provider in Indonesia) to provide Network Application and Services (NAS) support to Indonesian businesses, multinationals and Australian companies operating in Indonesia.

NAS support provides businesses with managed network and cloud-based communications services, and the JV will be able to offer an integrated end to end service which is unique in the Indonesian market. NAS will be bundled with Telkom's connectivity and sold through Telkom Indonesia and Telstra's enterprise sales team.

From Telstra's perspective, the JV accelerates Telstra's growth in the rapidly growing Indonesian market (South-East Asia's largest economy) and across the South-East Asian region more generally.

Announcing the venture, a Telstra executive said, 'We are looking forward to partnering with Telkom Indonesia, a well-respected market leader, which has a large enterprise and government customer base and the broadest reach of domestic connectivity in Indonesia. Indonesia is a fast-growing NAS market and we believe the best way to make inroads is by partnering a well-recognised and respected local player.'

He continued by saying that the JV is also aligned to Telstra's strategy of supporting its business customers around the world. The venture forms part of Telstra's expansion plans for Asia, and Telstra is 'looking forward to giving our [business] customers local support, allowing them to focus on their business rather than managing information technology and telecommunication as a business cost.'

Telkom highlighted that the deal will enable it to bring proven NAS solutions to Indonesia to assist businesses to be more productive and competitive. Telkom's CEO also stated 'We believe the JV ... will grow significantly not only because of the partnership with Telstra, but also considering Telkom's capabilities in network and data centre, as well as [its] strong position in the enterprise market segment which is the target market of NAS.'

An important feature of JVs (particularly international JVs) is that they are often formed between firms with **different organisational and cultural characteristics**. This can lead to problems in managing the venture. In particular, conflicts can arise as a result of differences between the partners, such as incompatible management styles and approaches, and cultures.

The differences between venture partners may even extend to them having different goals when they enter the JV. If the partners have incongruent goals this is likely to lead to reduced performance by the venture.

The concept of **business relatedness** is also important in managing the performance of a JV. If the business activities of the parent and the JVs are similar, then the JV could lead to increased economies of scale and scope, by increasing learning opportunities and reducing production cost.

However, if a JV is unrelated to a firm's existing operations the partners will have to keep close control over the JV to make sure that it develops in the desired direction. Performance management (and planning) is likely to be critical to the success of the JV in such a situation.

Strategic alliances and performance management

Strategic alliances share resources. They will need to share information in order to measure outcomes that are measuring and controlling performance. They may have concerns over sharing data; whether IT systems are compatible and who is accountable for what outcomes also needs to be made clear.

Supply chains and performance management

Supply chains are regulated in one of two ways. If there is a **given amount of profit** in a particular market for a finished product, this profit will be **shared out between all the organisations involved in the supply chain**. In this sense, suppliers and their customers **compete** with each other for **a bigger share of the available profit**. This 'traditional' **adversarial arms' length** attitude is evident in negotiations between an organisation and its suppliers, and efforts by the organisation to get the best terms possible and the lowest prices in their purchasing negotiations.

This view of the supply chain is **challenged by** the concept of **supply chain management**. This looks at the supply chain as a whole, and starts with the view that all organisations in the supply chain collaborate to produce something of value for the end customer.

This has two advantages.

(a) By **adding value** within the supply chain, **customer satisfaction** will be **improved** and **customers** will **pay more** for what they buy.

(b) **Organisations can also benefit collectively by reducing waste and inefficiency**. A lot of **wasteful activity** (activity that does not add any value to the final product) **occurs at the interface between organisations within the supply chain**. For example, a supplier might spend money on checking outwards supplies for quality, and the same goods will be checked by the organisation buying them when they are delivered. Inspection costs could be reduced by closer collaboration between the organisations, both to improve quality and to reduce inspection activities.

By looking at the supply chain as a collaborative effort, managers can look for ways of enhancing the profitability of the supply chain as a whole, so that everyone, including the end customer, benefits.

2.1 Developing relationships

However, developing strong relationships is not an easy task. The arms' length supplier-purchaser relationship has been based on both sides winning as much short-term gain as possible, and so sharing sensitive information and developing long-term ties is often difficult.

There are a number of practices which can be used to foster improved relationships with key suppliers.

(a) **Power balancing**. This occurs if the proportion of a supplier's total output that is sold to a customer roughly equals the proportion of total purchases acquired by the customer from that supplier. Maintaining relative dependence between suppliers and buyers increases the likelihood that both parties will have a vested interest in the success of the other.

(b) **Co-dependency.** When a supplier commits substantial specialised resources to meeting the demands of a purchaser and the purchaser chooses to single-source from that supplier, both parties have a vested interest in the success of the purchaser.

(c) **Target costing.** Suppliers can be rewarded when targets are reached.

(d) **Personal ties.** The establishment of teams of employees from both supplier and purchaser helps foster good working relationships and develop trust.

Key terms

Supply chain management (or **pipeline management** or **value stream management**) views all the buyers and sellers in this chain as part of a continuum, and the aim should be to look at the supply chain as a whole and seek to optimise the functioning of the entire chain. In other words, a company should look beyond its immediate suppliers and its immediate customers to add value, for example by improving efficiency and eliminating waste.

2.1.1 Adding value

The overall supply chain can be thought of as a **sequence of operations, each of which should add value**. An activity has value if it gives the customer something that the customer considers worth having (ie values), but an activity only adds value if the amount of value added exceeds the cost of creating it. Value is therefore added by making something worth more (in terms of the price the customer will pay, or the quality the customer perceives) or by reducing the cost of the operation (without sacrificing quality).

2.2 Elements of supply chain management

To apply the concept of supply chain management fully, there has to be **close collaboration** between organisations within the supply chain. A company must be able to work constructively with its suppliers. At the same time, it should continually **look for ways of improving the supply chain structure**, and this could involve switching to **different suppliers**, or selling **output through new channels**. The internet has opened up new possibilities for identifying new suppliers worldwide and for **selling direct to customers** instead of through distributors.

There is no single model for the ideal supply chain, and supply chain management can involve:

(a) Decisions about improving collaboration with suppliers by sharing information and through the joint development of new products

(b) Switching to new suppliers by purchasing online

(c) Outsourcing some activities that were previously performed in-house

2.3 Issues facing supply chain managers

2.3.1 Production

The customer often wants suppliers to respond to their particular requirements, and to customise orders to their specific needs. A supply chain that can **respond quickly to individual customer requirements** is known as an **'agile' supply chain**.

Issues for management include deciding **what** products or components to make, and **where** to make them. Should the production of components, sub-assemblies or even the final product be done in-house or by external suppliers?

Management **focus** is on **capacity**, **quality** and **order volume**. Production has to be scheduled so as to provide a sufficient workload for the production resources, and to achieve workload balance (so as to avoid both production bottlenecks and underutilisation of resources). Quality control is an issue, because producing poor-quality output has implications for both cost and customer dissatisfaction.

The **challenge** is to **meet customer orders immediately**, **without** having to invest heavily in **inventories** of finished goods, which are wasteful and expensive.

2.3.2 Supply

Most manufacturing companies cannot make everything themselves and still keep the quality of their output high. Decisions have to be made about how much should be purchased from 'outside'. Some companies have chosen to **close in-house production facilities** and **switch to external suppliers**, so that they can **concentrate on their 'core competences' where they add most value**.

In choosing external suppliers, management need to consider the capabilities of the supplier, and the extent to which close collaboration will be necessary. (Collaboration is much more important for key supplies, and much less important for low-cost general supplies that can be purchased from numerous sources.) **Distinctive competences** of the supplier and the organisation should be **similar**. An organisation selling 'cheap and cheerful' goods will want suppliers who are able to supply 'cheap and cheerful' subcomponents. The management focus should be on the **speed, quality and flexibility of supply**, as well as on cost.

2.3.3 Inventory

If a firm holds large amounts of inventory, it should be able to meet many customer orders immediately out of inventory and should not suffer hold-ups due to inventory shortages. Holding inventory is expensive, however, and there is no certainty that finished goods inventories will ever find a customer, unless they have been made to satisfy specific customer orders. **Ideally, inventory levels should be**

minimised, but without damaging the ability of the firm to meet customer orders quickly or holding up work flow due to a stock-out of key supplies.

In managing inventory levels, organisations need to know, with as much certainty as possible, the **lead time** for delivery of supplies and for the production of goods. Unknown lead times increase the chance of too little or too much inventory, both of which are costly for organisations.

2.3.4 Location

Decisions need to be made about where to locate production facilities and warehousing facilities. Cost and tax issues might result in production facilities being constructed in **emerging market economies**.

2.3.5 Transportation

Logistics management is another aspect of supply chain management. Supplies need to be delivered to a firm's premises and finished goods delivered to customers **efficiently, reliably** and at a **low cost**.

2.3.6 Information

Information resources throughout the supply chain need to be **linked together**, for speed of information exchange and to reduce wasteful paperwork. Some firms link their computer networks, or share information over the internet.

2.3.7 Overall management

Managing the supply chain therefore calls for an **understanding of** and **knowledge about**:

(a) **Customer demand patterns** (eg seasonal variations in demand)
(b) **Service level requirements** (speed of delivery expectations, quality expectations, and so on)
(c) **Distance considerations** (location and logistics)
(d) **Cost**

2.3.8 Responsiveness vs efficiency in supply chains

In addition, the characteristics of a supply chain which are most important will depend on an organisation's overall supply chain strategy.

In this respect, organisations have to evaluate the trade-off between responsiveness and efficiency: meeting customer orders quickly, but without investing heavily in inventories of finished goods (which tie up working capital).

The following table summarises the differences between responsive and efficient supply chains.

	Responsive supply chains	Efficient supply chains
Primary goal	Respond quickly to changes in demand	Supply demand at the lowest cost
Product design strategy	Create modularity, so that product differentiation comes as late in the product process as possible	Maximise performance at a minimum product cost
Pricing strategy	Higher margins because price is not a prime consideration for customers	Lower margins, because price is a key driver for customers
Manufacturing strategy	Maintain capacity flexibility to buffer against uncertainty in demand and/or supply	Lower costs through high utilisation
Inventory strategy	Maintain buffer inventory to deal with uncertainty in demand and/or supply	Minimise inventory to lower cost

	Responsive supply chains	Efficient supply chains
Lead-time strategy	Reduce aggressively, even if the costs of doing so are significant	Reduce where possible, but not at the expense of increasing costs
Supplier strategy	Select suppliers based on speed, flexibility, reliability and quality	Select suppliers based on cost and quality

(Table adapted from Chopra, S. and Meindl, P. *Supply Chain Management*)

Although we have presented the contrasts between responsiveness and efficiency in a supply chain, in reality entities will try to structure their supply chain in a way that maximises responsiveness **and** efficiency. However, it is also very important that organisations choose supply chain strategies in which the **balance between responsiveness and efficiency fits with their overall competitive strategy**. For example, a retailer whose strategy is based on a low-cost model for a wide variety of mass-consumption goods is likely to emphasise the elements of efficiency in their supply chain.

2.4 Using information and technology

A firm can **share** its **information** about expected customer demand and orders in the pipeline, so that the **suppliers can get themselves ready** for orders that might come to them from the firm. 'Modern' supply chain management uses the internet to share information as soon as it is available. A firm might have an integrated **enterprise resource planning (ERP)** system sitting on a website or on a server running on the internet. The ERP runs the supply chain database, holding information about a wide range of items, such as customer orders, inventory levels and pricing structures.

The use of Electronic Data Interchange, internet technology and software applications means that **suppliers know what a customer needs before the customer asks**. A supplier that 'knows' what their customers want does not have to guess or wait until the customer places an order. It will be able to **better plan its own delivery systems**. Technology has made the concept of the **'seamless' supply chain** a reality. The development of creative links with suppliers and customers provides organisations with the chance of **competitive advantage over competitors unwilling or unable to invest the time and resources in improving their supply chains.**

A critical issue for successful supply chain management is the **speed** with which activities can be carried out and customer demands met. If a firm, helped by its suppliers and sub-suppliers in the chain, can **respond quickly and flexibly** to customer requirements, the benefits will come from **lower inventories, lower operating costs, better product availability and greater customer satisfaction**.

Case Study — Zara

As a chain of fashion stores, Zara operates in an industry in which customer demand is rapidly changing and fickle. However, Zara has been able to grow successfully by employing a strategy that combines affordable prices with being highly responsive to changing trends.

Across the apparel industry as a whole, 'design-to-sales' cycle times have traditionally averaged more than six months. However, Zara has achieved cycle times of four to six weeks. This speed allows Zara to introduce new designs every week and to change 75% of its merchandise display every three to four weeks. As a result, the clothes on display in Zara's shops match customer preferences much more closely than the clothes in competitors' shops do. Consequently, Zara sells most of its products at full price, rather than having to apply markdowns to clear old stock.

Zara manufactures its clothes using a combination of flexible and quick suppliers in Europe and low-cost suppliers in Asia. This model contrasts with the majority of clothing manufacturers which have moved most of their manufacturing to Asia. About 40% of the manufacturing capacity is owned by Zara's parent company (Inditex), with the remainder outsourced.

Products with highly uncertain demand Zara sources from its European suppliers, whereas those with more predictable demand are sourced from Asian suppliers.

More than 40% of Zara's purchases of finished goods, and most of its in-house production, occur after a sales season starts. This compares with less than 20% production after the start of a sales season for a typical clothes retailer. This responsiveness, and the postponement of decisions until after seasonal trends are known, allows Zara to reduce inventories and to reduce the risk of error in forecasting demand.

In addition, Zara has invested heavily in information technology to ensure that the latest sales data are available to drive replenishment and production decisions.

2.5 Collaboration with customers

One of the key features of supply chain management is that it involves a closer relationship between producers and customers. And it is important to acknowledge the extent to which the role of the customer has changed in recent years.

Traditional business models – for example, in Porter's value chain – show businesses creating value **for** the customer, yet the customer is external to the value creation process.

However, increasingly, customers are now becoming integrated with an organisation's process. We can see this at an operational level through examples such as internet banking, or online check-in for air travel. In such a model, business becomes a process of continuous interaction and collaboration between an organisation and its customers. Customers can also monitor aspects of operational performance, for example, by tracking the status of orders made from online businesses (such as Amazon).

However, customers also now have an increasing involvement in the design of products – for example, new car orders allow customers to choose different options for their car, such as the colour of the roof and body, and the type of wheels.

A key feature in all of these collaborative relationships is information. Communication and collaboration with customers help provide businesses with information, and in turn information becomes an asset for businesses, just as capital or materials are assets.

2.5.1 Joint development projects

In the previous section, we have highlighted the scope for collaboration between businesses and their customers. However, the examples we looked at focused on collaboration between businesses and individual customers. But collaboration could equally well take place between two businesses.

In markets where competition between suppliers is becoming increasingly intense, rather than approaching customers with a standardised, generic product (or service) firms could instead offer to collaborate directly with the customer to create new products (or services) that are specifically suited to that customer's requirements and their sales and marketing objectives.

If the customer organisation is interested in the offer, then both firms could work together in a project that involves both parties contributing ideas, feedback, and technical and financial resources.

Working with customers on joint development projects could be advantageous for the following reasons:

(a) If the customer is willing to contribute towards the cost of developing new products or technologies, this will help the manufacturer maintain its research and development competences but at a **lower cost** than if the manufacturer had to fund its research and development budget itself.

(b) **Customer insight**. The manufacturer will gain an insight into how the customer operates; in particular, how the customer views its relationships with suppliers, and with its own customers. As well as providing information about the specific relationships in question, such an insight could help the manufacturer understand more about the overall business environment in which it is operating.

(c) If the customer has invested time and other resources in developing a product, the customer will have a **vested interest** in making the finished product commercially successful, which should hopefully translate into a sustained revenue stream for the manufacturer.

Nonetheless, there are also potential risks and disadvantages to such a relationship between manufacturers and customers.

(a) **Exploitation of technology and core competences**. The manufacturer needs to safeguard its core technology and ensure that a customer doesn't simply want to exploit whatever technical know-how is available from the manufacturer and then let the relationship lapse. Intellectual property rights which will be used in, or created by, the joint development project should also be identified in advance, and clear rules should be established about who owns any such intellectual property and how it can be used in future.

(b) Conversely, the manufacturer needs to be confident that the **standard of its functional resources** (eg its equipment and processes) is high enough to withstand the scrutiny that may come from working closely with a customer, and giving the customer access to its operational activities. If the customer discovers any major weaknesses in the manufacturers' processes during the project, this may not only cause it to abandon the project, but also, more importantly, may lead the customer to remove the manufacturer from its list of preferred suppliers for other items as well.

(c) The manufacturer needs to ensure the customer can fulfil whatever commitments it makes to the project. For example, if the customer doesn't deliver the promised funding or personnel, then this will place an unexpected burden on the manufacturer.

Chapter Roundup

- The complex nature of business structures, such as joint ventures, strategic alliances, multinational companies and network organisations, can lead to problems in measuring and controlling performance; for example in relation to productivity, quality and service levels.
- A **supply chain** is the network of suppliers, manufacturers and distributors that is involved in the process of moving goods for a customer order from the raw materials stage through the production and distribution stages to the customer. Every organisation operates somewhere within a supply chain.
- A **commonly held view** by management is that **to improve profitability** it is necessary to **get the lowest prices from suppliers** and to **obtain the best prices from the customers** next in line down the supply chain.
- **Supply chain management** looks at the supply chain as a whole, and starts with the view that all organisations in the supply chain collaborate to produce something of value for the end customer.
- Supply chain managers need to consider **production, supply, inventory, location, transportation and information**.

Quick Quiz

1 A potential difficulty when managing the performance of a joint venture is the need for the joint venture partners to agree the performance measurement metrics to be used.

Identify **two** factors which could be a source of disagreement between the venture partners when trying to set performance measures for a joint venture.

2 An organisation is experiencing problems in measuring and managing performance, due to differences in the national economic circumstances in which its various divisions are operating, as well as currency differences between the divisions. Which of the following is the organisation most likely to be?

A Virtual organisation
B Joint venture
C Multinational organisation
D Strategic alliance

3 Why is a 'management by objectives' approach necessary when managing remote employees?

4 Is the following statement true or false?

A service level agreement should include an explanation of the service the supplier has agreed to provide to a company, and details of any information the company has agreed to provide to the supplier.

5 Which of the following are characteristics of responsive supply chains as opposed to efficient supply chains?

(i) Goods are supplied in order to meet demand at the lowest cost.
(ii) Buffer inventory is maintained in order to deal with uncertainty in demand.
(iii) Suppliers are selected on the basis of cost and quality.

A (ii) only
B (i) and (ii)
C (i) and (iii)
D (ii) and (iii)

Answers to Quick Quiz

1 Two possible sources of disagreement are:

- Differences in the venture partners' goals and objectives for the venture
- Differences in the venture partners' attitude to risk

(The potential issues involved in managing joint ventures are discussed in Section 1.1 of the chapter.)

2 C The profitability of different divisions in a multinational may depend on local factors, such as tax rates and economic circumstances (eg recession vs economic growth), which the corporate centre cannot control. Currency conversion rates also create problems for measuring performance in multinational organisations.

3 Because remote employees do not work at the same location as their manager, they cannot be managed 'by observation'. Instead, a manager can only judge an employee's performance according to the outputs, or results, the employee achieves in relation to their goals and objectives.

4 True

The purpose of a service level agreement is to enable **both parties** (the company and the supplier) to have a structure against which to measure their performance in the relationship, and to assess whether a satisfactory level of performance is being achieved. In this respect, it is important to know what the company agrees to provide to the supplier, as well as knowing what the supplier agrees to provide to the company.

5 A (ii) only

Responsive supply chains maintain buffer inventory to deal with uncertainty in demand and/or supply, whereas efficient supply chains look to minimise inventory in order to lower costs.

The primary goal of efficient supply chains is to meet demand at the lowest cost, but responsive supply chains seek to respond quickly to changes in demand.

Suppliers in responsive supply chains are selected on the basis of speed, flexibility, reliability and quality. Selecting suppliers on the basis of cost and quality characterises efficient supply chains, not responsive ones.

Now try the question below from the Practice Question Bank

Number	Level	Marks	Approximate time
Q17	Examination	25	50 mins

Predicting and preventing corporate failure

17

Topic list	Syllabus reference
1 Organisational survival and life cycle issues	E3(a)
2 Predicting business failure	E3(b)
3 Evaluating corporate failure prediction models	E3(c)
4 Performance improvement strategies and corporate failure	E3(d)
5 Implementing performance improvement strategies	E3(e)

Introduction

In general terms, the focus of this Study Text so far has been on how organisations can measure and manage their performance in order to help them achieve their corporate goals.

However, not all businesses achieve their goals successfully, and it is important that managers can identify situations where there is a risk of corporate failure so that they can take action to try to prevent that failure from happening.

One reason for failure is that a product (or industry) is reaching the end of its life cycle. As such, companies need to consider their products' positions in their life cycles, and try to achieve a balanced portfolio. We begin the chapter by looking at **life cycle issues**.

Then we move on to discuss the performance measures which could be used to **assess whether a business is underperforming**.

The fourth section of the chapter looks at **performance improvement strategies** that can be used to try to prevent corporate failure.

In the final section we look at how performance management systems may need to be amended to support the changes and initiatives which are required to improve an organisation's performance.

Study guide

		Intellectual level
E3	**Predicting and preventing corporate failure**	
(a)	Discuss how long-term survival necessitates consideration of life cycle issues.	3
(b)	Assess the potential likelihood of corporate failure, utilising quantitative and qualitative performance measures and models (such as Z-scores and Argenti).	3
(c)	Assess and critique quantitative and qualitative corporate failure prediction models.	3
(d)	Identify and discuss performance improvement strategies that may be adopted in order to prevent corporate failure.	3
(e)	Identify and discuss operational changes to performance management systems required to implement the performance improvement strategies.	3

Exam guide

The material in this chapter could easily be examined, either in its own right or as part of a longer scenario in one of the compulsory Section A questions.

You should be prepared to show a variety of skills in answering exam questions linked to topics covered in this chapter.

First, you should be able to discuss the models themselves, including their strengths and weaknesses.

Second, you should be able to discuss these strengths and weaknesses in the specific context of a scenario given in the question.

Third, you need to be able to apply the models, to assess the likelihood of corporate failure in a particular scenario.

Finally, you need to identify and discuss appropriate performance improvement strategies to combat corporate failure for the scenario organisation.

Exam focus point

There is an article in the P5 Technical Articles section on ACCA's website entitled 'Business Failure'. This article covers the main models in this chapter and gives other useful background information in corporate failure, so you should read it as part of your preparation for the exam.

A question in the December 2010 exam asked candidates to discuss the strengths and weaknesses of quantitative and qualitative models for predicting corporate failure, and it then went on to ask candidates to identify the problems evident in an organisation's structure and performance, and to explain why these are relevant to possible failure.

Part of a question in the December 2012 exam asked candidates to explain a qualitative model for predicting corporate failure (such as Argenti's model) and then to comment on an organisation's position using that model.

A question in the December 2014 exam asked candidates to evaluate the results of a Z-score calculation, and also to assess the appropriateness of the model for the organisation in the scenario. The question then also asked candidates to examine the impact that life cycle issues have on the Z-score and the probability of failure.

1 Organisational survival and life cycle issues

The dynamism and complexity of the contemporary business environment, coupled with high levels of technological innovation and increasingly sophisticated customer demands, are combining to shorten the life cycles of many products. Organisations can often no longer rely on a sustained period of high demand for their products, and so, to compete effectively, they need to continually improve or redesign their products, or develop new products.

Case Study **Apple**

Apple

In its Annual Report, the consumer electronics and software giant Apple identified the risk factors which could affect its business. One of the factors identified in the 2014 Report was that the markets for the company's products and services are highly competitive and are subject to rapid technological change:

> 'The Company's products and services compete in highly competitive global markets characterized by aggressive price cutting and resulting downward pressure on gross margins, frequent introduction of new products, short product life cycles, evolving industry standards, continual improvement in product price/performance characteristics, rapid adoption of technological and product advancements by competitors, and price sensitivity on the part of consumers.
>
> 'The Company's ability to compete successfully depends heavily on its ability to ensure a continuing and timely introduction of innovative new products and technologies to the marketplace ... As a result, the Company must make significant investments in R&D. The Company currently holds a significant number of patents and copyrights and has registered and/or has applied to register numerous patents, trademarks and service marks. In contrast, many of the Company's competitors seek to compete primarily through aggressive pricing and very low cost structures, and emulating the Company's products and infringing on its intellectual property. If the Company is unable to continue to develop and sell innovative new products with attractive margins or if competitors infringe on the Company's intellectual property, the Company's ability to maintain a competitive advantage could be adversely affected.'

The 2014 Annual Report showed that the company's R&D expenditure for the fiscal year 2014 was $6.0 billion; up from $4.5 billion in 2013. However, the Report noted that Apple expects to continue making further investments in R&D in the future to remain competitive.

Net sales rose 7% during 2014 compared to 2013, due in part to the successful launch of iPhone 6 and 6 Plus, and strong demand for MacBook Air and MacBook Pro which were updated in 2014 with faster processors and offered at lower prices.

During the first quarter of 2014, the company introduced iPad Air – its fifth generation iPad, with Retina display (for improved viewing quality).

In October 2014, the company launched Apple Pay in the US (enabling shoppers to make payments using some of the latest Apple products, such as the iPhone 6), and also previewed Apple Watch, its first new product category for five years.

However, although Apple has continued to generate impressive profits, some analysts are concerned that the company's performance is too heavily dependent on the iPhone.

www.apple.com

Exam focus point

In Chapter 1, we looked at the BCG matrix as a model for analysing an organisation's product portfolio. The vertical axis of the matrix is market growth; and the matrix highlights that a balanced portfolio should include some products in the market which are growing quickly as well as some in those which are more stable.

This idea links with the points we will be discussing here in relation to life cycles. Products which are in the earlier stages of their life cycle typically offer greater scope for growth than those which are more mature.

This also has important implications for the selection of performance measures. Business units or products which are in the mature or decline stages of their life cycles cannot expect to use revenue growth as a basis for increasing profits; instead they should look at increasing efficiency and reducing costs; therefore measures which focus on cost control are likely to be very important for them.

By contrast, business units or products which are in the earlier stages of their life cycles should be focusing more on growth, in which case additional expenditure may sometimes be needed in order to generate future revenues (for example, through marketing and promotions).

FAST FORWARD

The **product life cycle** describes the financial and marketing life of a product from introduction, through growth to maturity and decline. The life cycle can be determined by technology or customer demand. The strategies which are appropriate for a product will vary throughout its life cycle.

1.1 Stages of the life cycle

The **product life cycle model** suggests that a **product** goes through **stages** – launch (introduction), growth, maturity and decline – each of which has **different financial and operating characteristics**.

Key term

The **product life cycle** is the period which begins with the initial product specification, and ends with the withdrawal from the market of both the product and its support. It is characterised by defined stages including introduction, growth, maturity, and decline.

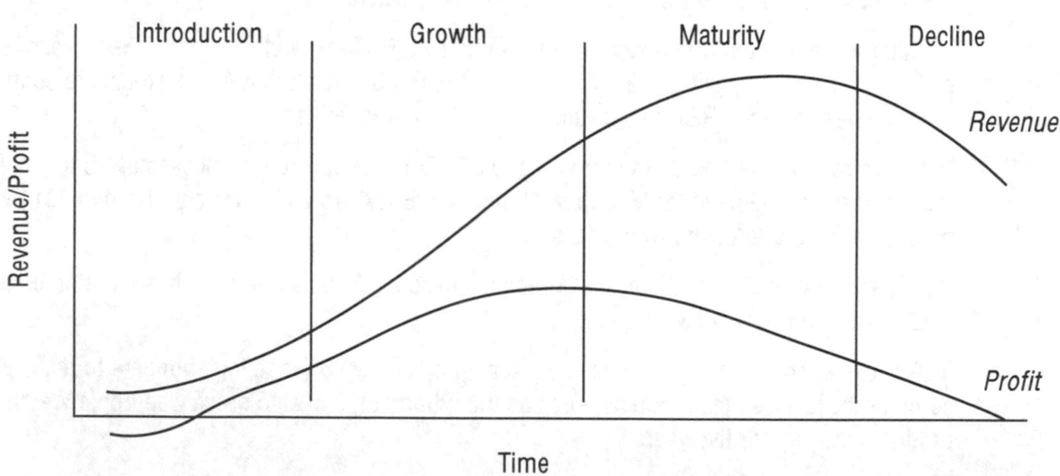

Product life cycle

1.1.1 Introduction

(a) A new product takes time to be accepted by would-be purchasers. There is a slow growth in sales. Unit costs are high due to low output and costly promotions. High marketing costs are required in order to get the product recognised by customers.

(b) The product for the time being is a loss-maker, and has negative cash flows.

(c) The product is high risk because it is new and has not yet been accepted by the market.

(d) The product has few, if any, competitors (because they are not willing to take similar risks).

Pricing strategy will be influenced by price elasticity of demand. If demand is likely to be inelastic, **price skimming** is appropriate. If demand is expected to be elastic and/or gaining market share is an important objective, **penetration pricing** is likely to be appropriate.

1.1.2 Growth

(a) If the new product gains market acceptance, sales will eventually rise more sharply and the product will start to make profits.

(b) Capital investments are needed to fulfil levels of demand, meaning cash flows remain lower than profit. However, cash flows increase as sales increase and the market becomes profitable.

(c) Competitors are attracted with similar products, but as sales and production rise, unit costs fall (eg due to economies of scale).

(d) Sales for the market as a whole increase.

(e) Need to add additional features to differentiate from competitors as buyers become more sophisticated. Product complexity is likely to rise. Alternatively, firms may choose to lower prices and compete on price grounds.

expenditure is required to differentiate the firm's product from competitors'
et segments may be developed.

in the market slows down significantly. Purchases are now based on repeat or
ıases, rather than new customers.

npetition, because in order to increase sales a firm needs to capture market share
;.

the longest period of a successful product's life as customers buy to replace
ts when they reach the end of their useful lives.

even most, products on the market will be at the mature stage of their life cycle.

good, and levels of investment are low, meaning cash flow is also positive.

s more sensitive. Prices are likely to start to decline, as firms compete with one
to increase their share of a fixed-size market.

(g) Equally, companies need defensive strategies to protect their current position from competitors.

(h) Firms try to capitalise on existing brand name by launching spin-off products under the same name. By now, buyers are sophisticated and fully understand the product.

(i) Environmental analysis is important. Companies need to detect or anticipate changes in the market so that they can be ready to undertake modifications in product-market strategies to lengthen the life cycle.

(j) The number of firms in industry reduces again, due to consolidation in the industry in an attempt to restore profitability.

1.1.4 Decline

Eventually, products are superseded by **technically superior substitutes**. Sales begin to decline and there is overcapacity of production in the industry. Prices are lowered in order to try to attract business. Severe competition occurs, **profits fall** and some **producers leave the market**. The remaining producers try to prolong the product life by modifying it and searching for new (niche) market segments. Investment is kept to a minimum. Although some producers are reluctant to leave the market if they haven't found alternative industries to move into, many inevitably do because of falling profits.

1.2 Control measures

FAST FORWARD

Assuming the life cycle pattern applies, then in order to survive and prosper firms need new products to take the place of declining ones. Different **control measures** are appropriate at different stages of the life cycle.

It is possible to summarise the different information and financial control needs of different stages of the product life cycle.

	Introduction	Growth	Maturity	Decline
Financial characteristics	- High business risk - Negative net cash flow - DCF evaluation for overall investment	- High business risk - Neutral net cash flow	- Medium business risk - Positive cash flow	- Low risk - Neutral/positive cash flow
Critical success factors	Innovative product	- Market share growth - Sustaining competitive advantage - Products can be mass produced	- Efficiency in operations (to keep overheads low) - Customer retention	- Low overheads - Brand loyalty - Timely exit
Information needs	Market research into demand	- Market growth/ share - Competitors' marketing strategies	- Comparative competitor costs - Limiting factors	- Rate of decline - Best time to leave - Reliable sale values of assets
Financial and other controls	- Strategic 'milestones' - Physical evaluation - Mainly non-financial measures owing to volatility (eg rate of take up by consumers)	- DCF - Market share - Marketing objectives	- ROI - Profit margin - Maintaining market share	Free cash flow (for investment elsewhere)

1.3 The life cycle and long-term survival

The **returns** expected from a product are likely to depend on where that product is in its life cycle.

Performance measure	Stage in the life cycle			
	Introduction	Growth	Maturity	Decline
Cash	Net user	Net user	Generator	Generator
Return on capital	Not important	Not important	Important	Important
Growth	Vital	Vital	Grow with new uses	Negative growth
Profit	Not expected	Important	Important	Very important

Ideally, firms should therefore have a **number of products at different stages** in the life cycle.

(a) New products at the introduction and growth stages which, when mature, will generate cash.

(b) Mature products, which generate cash for new investment. Mature products generate most of the profits and cash.

(c) Products in decline to be harvested.

A product portfolio should also contain products with life cycles of different lengths.

1.3.1 Product life cycle and the BCG matrix

The **Boston Consulting Group (BCG) matrix** (which we discussed in Chapter 1) is also closely linked to the idea of the product life cycle, and highlights the importance of businesses having a balance of products (or strategic business units) at different stages in their life cycles.

In effect, we could suggest that the products in the BCG matrix align to the stages of the product life cycle as follows:

- Introduction – Question mark
- Growth – Star
- Maturity – Cash cow
- Decline – Dog

The BCG matrix highlights that, in order to ensure long-term success, a business needs to combine high-growth products which need cash inputs (stars; question marks) and low-growth products which generate cash (cash cows).

The best way to achieve a stable revenue in the long term is by having **cash cows** in a portfolio (products which command a large market share in mature markets). However, as the BCG matrix indicates, to maintain the presence of cash cows in its portfolio over the long term, a business also needs to have 'star' products in its current portfolio. In time, the current 'stars' will become 'cash cows' and will then be able to replace the current cash cows when they decline and become 'dogs'.

Managers should look at three criteria when reviewing product or business unit portfolios:

(1) The **balance of the portfolio** in relation to the organisation's markets and overall strategy

(2) The **attractiveness of the individual portfolio**; that is, strengths and profitability in the individual market(s)

(3) **The fit within the organisation**; that is, synergy

A product's **life cycle** can be '**extended**' by the use of **technology**. Demand for recorded music has been met by vinyl, CD, DVD and internet downloads via MP3, different technological solutions to the same customer need.

Interestingly, though, although technology can be used to extend an individual product's life cycle, overall the pace of technological developments in recent years has led to a shortening of product life cycles. In turn, the short product life cycles associated with fast-moving technology becomes both a problem and an opportunity for manufacturers. The 'problem' for manufacturers is that the rapid rate of changes translates into a critical need to stay at the leading edge of technology and to stay ahead of their competitors. If they fail to do so, their products will quickly become obsolete, and they will lose market share. By contrast, the 'opportunity' is that if a manufacturer can develop a new technology in advance of their competitors this might enable them to increase market share.

Exam focus point

You could be given information in a case study scenario about a range of products and then asked to use life cycle analysis to assess how a company can manage its performance. To do this you would need to assess where the products are in their life cycles, and therefore what strategies would be appropriate for managing them.

2 Predicting business failure

FAST FORWARD

Corporate decline arises from the decline in the industry and from poor management. It is still possible to make money in declining industries, just as it is possible to **'turn round'** declining companies. However, it is crucial to identify the **symptoms** and **causes** of corporate decline in order for them to be addressed.

It is easy to rattle off a list of successful companies, and to ascribe to them a whole variety of factors which have fuelled their success. It is less easy, however, to assess precisely those factors which cause industries and companies to fail. Decline has two aspects:

(a) What should a company do to be successful in a **declining industry**, if it cannot realistically withdraw (for example, if there are significant barriers to exit)?

(b) How do **corporations 'go bad'** and what can be done to turn them round?

Case Study **Comet**

Comet

One of the more high-profile retail failures in the UK in recent years was that of Comet (which went into administration in 2012).

The company's profit figures since 2007 give an indication of its decline. In 2007, profit before tax was £56m. This fell to £25m in 2008, and in subsequent years it posted losses of £8m, £3m and then £39m in 2011.

The Chief Executive of rival retailer, Dixons, was very clear about the reasons for Comet's demise, though.

- While Dixons reacted very aggressively to 'the existential shift' in the retail industry, he said, Comet did not pursue that journey.
- In addition, he believes that the sale of Comet by Kesa Electrical to private investment firm OpCapita earlier in 2012 was 'structurally unsound'. OpCapita 'didn't have enough oomph behind it. There was not enough capital, will, desire or push', he said.

The rise in online retailers has clearly had a major impact on the retail industry. However, other commentators have argued that simply blaming the online retailers for Comet's failure does not capture the full picture.

An alternative – or at least additional – explanation is that Comet set its customer service standards far too low, and customers have simply voted with their feet. In a competitive marketplace, a company cannot deliver poor customer service and then expect a customer to return or to recommend them. In this respect, Comet's poor customer service and insistent selling of extended and expensive after-sales warranties, coupled with a deficient delivery service, can all be seen as major contributors to its downfall.

An article about Comet by John Roberts in the *Huffington Post* highlights that customer service needs to be integral to any business, whether purchasing in person, online or through mobile devices. Roberts argues that customers 'should be able to use their computer, telephone or tablet to find out everything they need to know in order to make an informed purchasing choice. They should be able to order any time before 10pm, seven days a week, and have their product delivered the next day, at a time that suits them, not the company. And they should expect the company to keep them up to date on the day of the delivery regarding the time it will arrive.'

Good customer service needs to be integral to any business, whether it is a traditional bricks and mortar firm, or an online retailer.

Roberts, J. (2012) Comet has failed because it did not put the customer first, *Huffington Post.* Online. Available from: http://www.huffingtonpost.co.uk/john-roberts/comet-demise-online-retailers-are-not-to-blame_b_2091626.html [Accessed 26 January 2016]

Ruddick, G. (2012) Comet failed after 'structurally unsound' OpCapita deal, Dixons boss says, *The Telegraph*, Online. Available from: http://www.telegraph.co.uk/finance/newsbysector/retailandconsumer/9712417/Comet-failed-after-structurally-unsound-OpCapita-deal-Dixons-boss-says.html [Accessed 26 January 2016]

2.1 Declining industries

Determining the causes of decline will help companies assess future demand and the profitability of serving a diminishing market. One approach might be to look at a company in the context of its corporate life cycle, and the industry life cycle more generally. However, not all companies follow the conventional life cycle pattern, since companies can be revitalised or transformed at any time.

So, instead of simply looking at decline in terms of the life cycle overall, it will be useful to look for more specific reasons. The reasons for declining demand might include:

- Technological advances leading to the growth of substitute products, often of lower cost and higher quality
- Rising costs of inputs of complementary products
- Regulatory changes or changes in legislation
- Shrinking customer groups (caused, for example, by demographic changes)
- Changes in lifestyle, buyers' needs, tastes or trends
- Customers are in financial difficulty (for example, due to economic hardship in a recession)

In her article 'Strategies for Declining Industries', Kathryn Harrigan (a student of Michael Porter) suggested that there are two types of industrial decline.

(a) **Product revitalisation** occurs when the decline is temporary (eg owing to a recession in consumer demand).

(b) **Endgame** occurs when a firm (and the industry) is confronted with substantially lower demand for its products.

2.1.1 Strategies for declining industries

(a) In **endgame** conditions, firms which had not competed with each other were drawn into **price wars**. This kneejerk response should encourage managers to consider their competitive behaviour before the endgame.

(b) The **characteristics of declining industries differ** (eg some have high exit barriers, some are concentrated, others are fragmented), so **different strategies** are appropriate.

(c) The **expectations** of competitors about future demand, and the expectations of their customers about future supplies, can have a powerful **influence** on the nature of the **competitive environment**.

(d) Forecasting techniques can help firms identify the **type** of competitor that will leave the industry and the types most likely to remain.

(e) If the industry is falling to a **substitute product**, then firms should innovate to capture the new technology.

(f) If products become commodity-like (ie differentiation is not all that significant) then **all but the lowest cost competitor will lose market share**. In these conditions a cost leadership strategy is appropriate. On the other hand, it might be a good idea to **differentiate** a product, if this is feasible, to build the security of a niche.

(g) Unless a company has the lowest costs, a strong distribution system relative to competitors, or a loyal niche of customers, it might be **worth selling the business to a competitor** who can make better use of it.

(h) Finally, a firm which is part of a **conglomerate** might be retained because of strategic relationships with other areas of the conglomerate.

2.2 Declining companies

As well as identifying the types of decline, managers need to be aware of the indicators which could indicate that a company is in decline. Based on an analysis of UK companies during the severe recession of the early 1980s, Stuart Slatter identified ten **symptoms of corporate decline**:

(a) Decrease in the company's profitability
(b) Decreasing sales volume (ie sales revenue adjusted for inflation)
(c) An increase in gearing (debt as a proportion of equity)
(d) A decrease in liquidity, as measured by accounting ratios
(e) Restrictions on the dividend policy
(f) Financial engineering (eg changes in accounting policies and periods)
(g) 'Top management fear'
(h) Frequent changes in senior executives
(i) Falling market share
(j) Evidence of a lack of planning

These are all observable externally. Internally, however, there may be a **severe crisis**, whose severity for the long term depends on the **behaviour of managers**. Slatter identifies **four stages in the crisis**.

(a) **Blinded stage** or **crisis denial**. Managers are complacent, ignore warning signs or do not appreciate their significance. This may result from poor control systems and poor environmental monitoring. Managers might rest on their laurels. They might be **blinded** to the situation. Prompt action would reverse the trend.

(b) **Inaction** or **hidden crisis**. When the signs of crisis appear, managers explain them away, or say that there is nothing they can do. The problem is that if they admit something **is** wrong they will be blamed. If a radical change is required, it might adversely affect their position. This second stage sadly means **inaction**. Again corrective action, more severe, might reverse the trend.

(c) **Faulty action** or **disintegration**. Managers decide that things are amiss and act to do something about them – too little, usually. Moreover, management becomes more autocratic, reducing alternative sources of information. This faulty action might not be enough.

(d) **Crisis** and **collapse** (or **dissolution**). Slatter says that, in the end, action is impossible. An expectation of failure increases, the most able managers leave, and there are power struggles for the remaining spoils. Eventually, the receiver is called in.

A more recent survey by Marius Pretorius (2008) also reviewed the evidence on business failure, and classified the **causes of business failure** into four main categories. These are similar to Slatter's symptoms.

Human causes
These causes include leadership and management failures. They broadly fall into self-deception, a rigid organisation culture and a tendency to conform and compromise. The symptoms of human causes may be seen in low morale and loss of leadership credibility. Competent staff leave while the remaining staff start scapegoating or blaming others for failure.

Internal and external causes
Firms often fail due to internal causes rather than external ones. **Internal factors** (like human causes) can include human resources issues, such as a lack of appropriate management action and discipline, but internal factors may also include high operating expenses, a lack of cash control, a lack of capital, a lack of knowledge about the company's product or service, and an inappropriate marketing strategy. **External factors** exist in the firm's operating environment and include recession and fiscal policy.

Structural causes
These causes include a lack of long-term planning, a lack of innovation, and simply the stage of the life cycle the business is at.

However, rather than simply thinking that it is older businesses that decline, Pretorius highlights that younger firms are more likely to suffer from resource and capability deficiencies than older firms, leading to the 'liability of newness' – for example, where a firm has yet to establish credibility or legitimacy with suppliers, clients, customers and other organisations in the industry. In this respect, the failure of older firms is more likely to be a function of internal market forces, while the failure of younger firms may well be a function of internal structural causes.

Financial causes
Pretorius suggests weak cash flow is not a cause of failure but suggests it arises from business-related causes. Working capital may suffer if customers fail to pay on time or inventories lie unsold.

Case Study

Phones 4u

The British mobile phone retailer, Phones 4u, went into administration in September 2014, leading to the closure of more than 550 stores and more than 2,500 staff being made redundant. Another 2,000 employees transferred to Vodafone, EE and Dixons Carphone after those three businesses took over 358 Phones 4u stores and concessions.

The collapse of a large independent mobile phone retailer, like Phones 4u, came as something of a shock because the mobile phone market seemed to be a good market to be in. The company had generated revenues of £1 billion in 2013.

The immediate cause of the company's collapse was the decision by Britain's largest mobile phone operator, EE, not to renew a contract to sell its products in Phones 4u stores. This followed a similar decision by Vodafone earlier the same month (September 2014), and previous decisions by two other operators, O2 and Three, not to sell their products in the company's stores.

As Phones 4u's Chief Executive noted, 'If the mobile network operators decline to supply us, we do not have a business.' The entrepreneur who founded Phones 4u (in 1987) blamed Vodafone and EE for the company's demise, saying the operators 'assassinated' the retailer by withdrawing their business from it. He suggested their motive for doing this was to knock a competitor out of the market (because the phone operators also had stores selling mobile phone contracts for their own networks).

However, Vodafone and EE both denied any wrongdoing, and blamed the owners of Phones 4u for weakening the company financially, so that it did not have capacity to be flexible when negotiating new contracts with the operators. (The company's owners – the private equity firm, BC Partners – had taken a special dividend of £223 million out of it in 2013, thereby increasing the level of debt in a company which already had a very heavy burden of debt.)

More generally, commentators noted that Phones 4u had failed to adapt to a changing market, in which the mobile phone operators had been building up their own retail networks so that they could deal directly with consumers rather than using intermediaries, like Phones 4u. Selling through their own outlets enables the operators to capture more of the margin on their own products.

Based on: *The Economist,* (2014), Death of a salesman – The collapse of Phones 4u. Online. Available from: http://www.economist.com/news/britain/21618864-row-over-another-high-street-casualty-time-mobile-phone-business-death
[Accessed 26 January 2016]

2.2.1 Feedback failure

The acquisition of feedback information is the final stage of the rational decision-making model (which you should be familiar with from your studies at Paper P3). In other words, the final stage of the decision process – once a strategy has been implemented – is the monitoring of whether the intended results from the strategy have been achieved.

Some organisations and individuals persist in activities which are undoubtedly failing. In other words, they **escalate their commitment to a decision.**

Why might managers escalate their commitment to a bad decision?

(a) **Managers block out negative information, when they themselves are responsible**. In other words, they refuse to believe the decision was wrong but claim instead, for example, that it was badly implemented, and that an injection of money will put things right. In part this is a **cultural problem**, if it means that past ways of working no longer apply.

(b) **Managers or decision makers do not wish to suffer the humiliation of a climb down**, as it might have a wider effect on their reputation. If compromise is seen as a weakness, moral, political or intellectual, then a manager is unlikely to be prepared to risk the poor 'publicity'. In companies whose corporate cultures do not tolerate failure, it might be better for the manager to soldier on in the hope that the situation will sort itself out; but when this involves committing more and more resources, such nervous wishful thinking can prove very expensive.

(c) **Consistency is valued**. Studies of leadership situations indicate that subordinates prefer managers whose leadership style is consistent. Failing to be consistent smacks of weakness or opportunism, even though such a course may be rational. Consistency in a person is valued, as it allows people to predict their behaviour.

(d) **Mistakes are viewed as failures to be punished rather than opportunities for organisational and/or personal learning**. Innovation inevitably involves experimentation: experiments often fail. A company that is not innovative is unlikely to tolerate failure.

(e) **The outcome of the project is uncertain**. It is easy to criticise with hindsight, and the bad decision may have been the best one taken with the information available at the time.

(f) **A failure to understand the principles of relevant costs for decision making**. As management accountants, you should already know that sunk costs are excluded from decision making. Not everybody finds this point easy to grasp. People will spend more, to turn a project round.

2.3 Strategic failure

FAST FORWARD

The **Icarus paradox** arises when a successful model becomes over-rigid, hampering innovation and reducing flexibility.

Failure of strategic management is likely to lead to rapid corporate decline. A common route to failure is **strategic drift**. Ironically, this often derives from success. Unfortunately, success can have the effect of making the organisation overconfident such that, in effect, an organisation's own success brings about its downfall. The organisation continues to revolve around what has worked in the past, hampering innovation and reducing flexibility. Danny Miller calls this the **Icarus paradox**. The organisation develops its strategy in accordance with its unchanged assumptions and gradually drifts away from environmental fit. It is very difficult to detect the difference between the deployment of core competences to achieve competitive advantage and the constraining effect of an obsolete model.

2.3.1 The Icarus paradox

Miller suggests that when companies succeed, their success can lead to a kind of dislocated feedback of the qualities that made them succeed; this distortion then leads to failure.

Miller diagnoses four important aspects of this distortion.

(a) **Leadership failures** occur when success reinforces top management's preconceptions, makes them overconfident, less concerned for the customer's views, conceited and obstinate.

(b) **Cultural domination** by star departments and their ideologies leads to intolerance of other ideas and reduces the capacity for innovative and flexible response.

(c) **Power games and politics** are used by dominant managers and departments to resist change and amplify current strategic thinking.

(d) **Corporate memory**, consisting of processes, habits and reflexes, is substituted for careful thought about new problems.

The interplay of these factors leads to decline, usually along one of four **trajectories**.

(a) **Craftsmen become tinkerers**. Quality-driven engineering farms become obsessed with irrelevant technical detail.

(b) **Builders become imperialists**. Acquisitive, growth-driven companies over-expand into areas they cannot manage properly.

(c) **Pioneers become escapists**. Companies whose core competence is technically superb innovation and state of the art products lose focus and waste their resources on grandiose and impractical projects.

(d) **Salespeople become drifters**. Marketing-orientated companies with portfolios of valuable brands become bureaucratic pursuers of sales figures whose market offerings become stale and uninspired.

2.4 Quantitative models for predicting business failure 12/14

Quantitative models

Quantitative models for predicting business failure look at financial ratios that differ when a company is failing from when it is healthy. These ratios are based largely on published financial data so comparisons can be easily and validly made.

Commonly accepted **financial indicators of impending failure** include:

- Low profitability compared to assets and commitments
- Low equity returns (both dividend and capital)
- Poor liquidity
- High gearing (though this varies from country to country depending on the local characteristics of debt and equity funding)
- Highly variable income

Models of quantitative scoring emerged in the 1960s with Beaver's model predicting failure based on cash flow to total debt. Later models became more sophisticated looking at a combination of ratios, or range of variables. This is described as 'multiple discriminant analysis' (MDA). In the MDA model, the ratios are combined into a single discriminant score – termed a **Z-score**. We look at the Z-score model later in this section.

The Z-score technique was later adapted to develop the **Performance Analysis Score** (PAS) which forms a ranking of Z-scores, measuring relative performance on a scale of 0 to 100. Monitoring the PAS score over time shows the relative performance trend of a company, highlighting any downward trends which should be investigated.

A final quantitative model is the **'H-score'** devised by Company Watch (www.companywatch.net). The H-score is a measure of financial health, compiled from looking at a company's published financial results. As with the Z-score, the H-score model is based on discriminant analysis, looking at the characteristics of companies which subsequently failed compared with those which survived. The discriminating factors look at profit management, asset management and funding management.

Then, similar to the PAS method, the scores are ranked, and the H-score indicates a company's position in the ranking. So, for example, a score of 15 indicates that only 15% of companies have characteristics which are more indicative of failed companies than the company under review. The lower the H-score, the weaker the company's financial health can be judged to be.

Overall, these quantitative techniques have proved 'generally impressive' in predicting failure, but that they must be tailored to the sample under consideration.

Exam focus point

The text in this section is summarised from the P5 Technical Article we mentioned at the start of the chapter: 'Business Failure'.

The full text of the article is available on ACCA's website, and you are strongly advised to read it.

2.5 Financial stability

The analysis of financial ratios is largely concerned with the efficiency and effectiveness of the use of resources by a company's management, and also with the financial stability of the company. Investors will wish to know:

(a) Whether additional funds could be lent to the company with reasonable safety
(b) Whether the company would fail without additional funds

2.6 Liquidity ratios

One method of predicting business failure is the use of **liquidity ratios** (the current ratio and the quick ratio). A company with a current ratio well below 2:1 or a quick ratio well below 1:1 might be considered illiquid and in danger of failure. Research seems to indicate, however, that the current ratio and the quick ratio and trends in the variations of these ratios for a company are poor indicators of eventual business failure.

2.7 Z-scores 12/14

FAST FORWARD

The likelihood of business failure can be assessed using quantitative or qualitative prediction models. **Z-scores** is a **quantitative** model based around a number of **financial indicators. Argenti's A-score** model is a **qualitative** model which assesses **defects, mistakes and symptoms** of decline within an organisation.

In the late 1960s, Edward Altman researched the extent to which analysis of different financial ratios could be used to **predict business failure** and **bankruptcy**.

Altman analysed 22 accounting and non-accounting variables in relation to a selection of failed and non-failed firms in the US. From this analysis, he identified five key indicators of the likely failure or non-failure of businesses:

(a) Liquidity
(b) Profitability
(c) Activity/efficiency
(d) Leverage
(e) Solvency

These five indicators were then used to derive a **Z-score**. The Z-score represents a combination of different ratios, weighted by coefficients (derived from Altman's analysis of firms which had declared bankruptcy compared with firms in similar industries and of similar size which had survived).

The Z-score is calculated as follows:

$$Z = 1.2X_1 + 1.4X_2 + 3.3X_3 + 0.6X_4 + 1.0X_5$$

where

X_1 = working capital/total assets (to measure liquidity)

X_2 = retained earnings/total assets (to measure cumulative profitability)

X_3 = earnings before interest and tax/total assets (to measure activity/efficiency, by looking at the productivity of assets)

X_4 = market value of equity/book value of total debt (a form of gearing ratio, to measure leverage)

X_5 = sales/total assets (to measure solvency, by looking at revenue-generating capacity)

The Z-score model suggests that firms with a Z-score of **3.0 or more** are likely to be **financially sound** and **relatively safe**, so they should be expected to survive, based on the financial data.

(However, there is still a danger that mismanagement, fraud, a major economic downturn, or other unexpected factors could cause an organisation's performance to decline, and could lead to it failing.)

At the other end of the scale, the Z-score model suggests that firms with a Z-score **of 1.8 or less are likely to fail** and are headed for bankruptcy. It is very rare for a firm with financial conditions generating a score below 1.8 to recover. The lower a firm's score, the greater likelihood there is of it going bankrupt.

Obviously, however, these scoring predictions leave a 'grey area' between 1.8 and 3.0 where the eventual failure or non-failure of an organisation could not be predicted with certainty. Further investigation is likely to be required to assess whether the firm is financially sound or in danger of failing.

For firms whose Z-scores are between 2.7 and 3.0 it is probably safe to predict survival, even though they are in the grey area and so fall below the threshold of relative safety (ie 3.0).

However, firms whose Z-scores fall within the range 1.8–2.7 are at risk of going bankrupt unless dramatic action is taken to ensure their survival. But, even if the necessary action **is** taken, there is a chance that these firms will not survive.

2.8 Argenti's A-score **12/12**

From historical data on a wide range of actual cases, Argenti developed a model that is intended to predict the likelihood of company failure.

Argenti believed that business failure followed a predictable system.

Defects ⟶ **Mistakes** ⟶ **Symptoms** ⟶ **Failure**

As such, Argenti argued that symptoms of failure only become apparent in the later stages of failure, so failure could better be predicted – and then, possibly, prevented – by looking at the root causes of failure ('defects' and 'mistakes'). In this respect, he believed that the main cause of business failure lay in management's ability to lead a business.

FACTORS IN ARGENTI'S MODEL	
Defects	Autocratic Chief Executive Passive board Lack of budgetary control
Mistakes	Over-trading (expanding faster than cash funding) Gearing – high bank overdrafts/loans Failure of large project jeopardises the company
Symptoms	Deteriorating ratios Creative accounting – signs of window-dressing Declining morale and declining quality

The model uses a management-scoring approach that explicitly seeks to rate the risks of poor management causing corporate failure. The model takes the qualitative problems associated with management and assigns a score for each problem area. These scores are judgemental, but aim to provide a means of comparing the situation with the possible worst-case scenario.

Source of problem	*Observed variable*	*Score*
Group A	**Management defects**	
	• Chief Executive is an autocrat	8
	• Chief Executive also holds position of Chairman	4
	• Passive board of directors	2
	• Unbalanced board of directors, not representing all business functions, or dominated by directors whose background is in the same business function	2
	• Weak Finance Director	2
	• Lack of 'management in depth'	1
	• Poor response to change: old-fashioned product or service, obsolete production facilities, out of date marketing methods; old directors	15
	Accounting defects	
	• No budgets or budgetary controls	3
	• No cash flow forecasts, or not up to date	3
	• No costing system: costs and contribution of each product or service are not known	3
	Σ	**= 43**
Group B	**Management mistakes**	
	• High gearing; inability to service debt	15
	• Overtrading: company expanding faster than funding; capital base too small for level of activity, or capital base unbalanced for type and nature of the business	15
	• Big project that has gone wrong; any obligation that the company will be unable to meet if something goes wrong	15
	Σ	**= 45**
Group C	**Symptoms of trouble**	
	• Financial analysis appears to indicate failure or difficulties (eg poor Z-score)	4
	• Creative accounting (eg gaming; misrepresentation)	4
	• Any non-financial signs of problems: uncleaned and untidy offices and factory, high staff turnover, low morale, rumours and so on	4
	Σ	**= 12**

Argenti's A score factors

The maximum score allotted is 100 (being 43 from Group A, 45 from Group B and 12 from Group C).

The criteria require that, for a firm to be cleared as healthy, it meets certain standards.

Category of score	*Maximum permitted*
Group A	10
Group B	15
Group C	0
Total score	25

The system sets a **maximum acceptable score of 25** overall, with 10 and 15 being the maximum acceptable scores in Group A (defects) and B (mistakes) respectively. If a firm scores anything in Group C this is immediately seen as an indicator that the firm is at risk.

A firm that scores more than 25 overall, even if it scores below the individual thresholds in either of Group A (10) or Group B (15), would still be considered at risk.

However, as with the Z-score, there is a degree to which 'A scores' are graded rather than it being suggested that firms simply 'pass' or 'fail'.

Usually companies which are not at risk of failure have fairly low scores, with a range of 0–18 being common for such firms.

Conversely, firms which are at risk usually score well above 25, and are often in the range 35–70.

However, there is still potentially a 'grey area' around 18–25, where firms can often show some warning signs of decline, even though they remain within the maximum permitted levels overall.

Exam focus point

Note that with Argenti's A-score model, the **higher** a firm's score the greater the likelihood of it failing and going bankrupt.

However, with the Z-score model, the risk of a firm going bankrupt increases the **lower** a firm's score is.

Exam focus point

The exam question linked to Argenti's model (December 2012) did not require candidates to give scores, but rather to explain the model and then use it to comment on an organisation's position and weaknesses more generally.

However, the examination team noted that few candidates could **explain** what defects, mistakes and symptoms of failure were – although they could list what the headings were. There is an important distinction here: at P5 level, you won't simply be expected to list the headings in a model; you will also be expected to use the model as a framework for understanding or analysing the information provided in a case study scenario.

2.9 Other indicators of financial difficulties

You should not think that **ratio analysis of published accounts** and **Z-score analysis** are the only ways of spotting that a company might be running into financial difficulties. There are other possible indicators too.

2.9.1 Other information in the published accounts

Some information in the published accounts might not lend itself readily to ratio analysis, but still be an indicator of financial difficulties, for example:

(a) Very **large increases in intangible non-current assets**
(b) A **worsening net liquid funds** position, as shown by the funds flow statement
(c) Very large **potential or contingent liabilities**
(d) Important **post statement of financial position (balance sheet) events**
(e) **Excess** of **current liabilities** over **current assets**
(f) Imminent **debt repayment** and **limited cash resources**

2.9.2 Information in the chairman's report, the directors' report and the audit report

The **report of the chairman** or chief executive that accompanies the published accounts might be very revealing. Although this report is not audited, and will no doubt try to paint a rosy picture of the company's affairs, any difficulties the company has had and not yet overcome will probably be discussed in it. There might also be warnings of problems to come in the future. The **audit report** itself may indicate difficulties.

2.9.3 Information in the press

Newspapers and financial journals are a source of information about companies, and the difficulties or successes they are having and the **markets** in which they operate. There may be reports of strikes, redundancies and closures.

2.9.4 Credit ratings

Ratings from specialist agencies or banks may be useful.

2.9.5 Published information about environmental or external matters

There will also be published information about matters that will have a direct influence on a company's future, although the connection may not be obvious. Examples of external matters that may affect a company adversely are:

(a) **New legislation**, for example on product safety standards or pollution controls, which affect a company's main products

(b) **International events**, for example political disagreements with a foreign country, leading to a restriction on trade between the countries

(c) **New and better products** being launched onto the market by a competitor

(d) A big **rise in interest rates**, which might affect a highly geared company seriously

(e) A big **change in foreign exchange rates**, which might affect a major importer or exporter seriously

3 Evaluating corporate failure prediction models

FAST FORWARD

The accuracy of corporate failure models (like any other model) can only be as good as the **quality of information** they use. It is likely that there will be **limitations to the data** collected. There will also be **limitations on the application of the model** and care needs to be taken when adopting a 'one size fits all' approach.

3.1 Weaknesses of using financial information to predict failure

There are the following problems in using available **financial information** to predict failure:

(a) **Significant events** can take place between the end of the financial year and the publication of the accounts. An extreme example of this would be the collapse of the Barings merchant bank. A further feature of the Barings case that is worthy of comment is the fact that the factors that led up to the collapse were essentially internal to the business and would never have become apparent in the published accounts.

(b) The information is essentially **backward looking** and takes no account of current and future situations. An extreme example would be the Central American banana producers. There would be nothing in their published accounts to predict the effect on their businesses of Hurricane Mitch.

(c) The **underlying financial information** may not be reliable.

The use of **creative, or even fraudulent, accounting** can be significant in situations of corporate failure. Similarly, the **pressure to deliver earnings growth** (and therefore short-term results) may result in companies making poor decisions that eventually lead to their downfall.

3.2 The value of Z-scores

A current view of the link between financial ratios and business failure would appear to be as follows:

(a) The financial ratios of firms which fail can be seen in retrospect to have **deteriorated significantly** prior to failure, and to be worse than the ratios of non-failed firms. In retrospect, financial ratios can be used to suggest why a firm has failed.

However, an individual Z-score is only valid for a single point in time. A single Z-score does not indicate whether a firm's financial condition is improving or deteriorating (but such information would be useful to know).

(b) No fully accepted **model for predicting** future business failures has yet been established, although some form of Z-score analysis would appear to be the most promising avenue for progress. In the UK, several Z-score type failure prediction models exist.

(c) It can be difficult to draw conclusions about the future of companies whose score falls within the '**grey area**' (1.8–3.0) because the model does not provide a prediction for them.

(d) Equally it may not be appropriate to apply Z-scores uniformly to all companies across different industries. Firms in different industries face different problems and issues, and also financial ratios may vary in different industries (for example, depending on the levels of working capital which are required).

(e) Because of the use of X_4 ('Market value of equity/book value of debt'), Z-score models cannot be used for unquoted companies which lack a market value of equity.

(f) Some Z-score models have been developed specifically for **individual industries** or **sizes of organisation**.

(g) The Z-score model was originally designed for use in **manufacturing companies**. Therefore it may not be appropriate to use the model on non-manufacturing companies without some modification. In particular, the Z-score model is not recommended for use with financial service companies.

Nonetheless, Z-score models are used widely by banks and financial institutions for assessing the credit risk of companies which are seeking funding. The models are also used by accountancy firms, management consultants, and companies wanting to acquire other companies. (The companies looking to make the acquisition use the models to assess the financial health of their target companies.)

Importantly, though, while a Z-score can indicate the likelihood of financial distress, and possible corporate failure, it does not provide any suggestions or solutions as to how a firm could try to overcome its financial distress.

Moreover, Altman found that while the Z-score model proved an accurate forecaster of failure up to two years prior to distress, its accuracy diminished substantially as the lead time increased beyond that. Therefore, in 1977 Altman and two colleagues (Haldeman and Narayanan) developed the Z-score model further into **the ZETA score model**, which demonstrated higher accuracy over a longer period of time (up to five years prior to distress).

The ZETA score model included the five original variables of the Z-score model, but also added 'stability of earnings' and 'size' (measured by a firm's total assets) to them.

3.2.1 Other quantitative models

While Altman's Z-score model (and the later ZETA score model) are important quantitative models to help predict business failure, they are by no means the only such models which have been developed. In fact, there have been a large number of quantitative models developed.

We have noted a few of these in Section 2 earlier, but an additional type of model to be aware of is that which looks specifically at the **probability** of a company failing. These models again look at different performance indicators, but then instead of producing a 'score' they calculate a probability of failure.

3.3 Argenti's A-score

Argenti's model uses **judgement** to assign scores to each problem area so therefore the scores chosen are subjective. This makes it clear that the model should only be used as a guideline when attempting to predict the likelihood of company failure.

3.4 Other corporate models

Beaver conducted a study which found the following:

(a) The **worst predictor** of failure is the current ratio (current assets/current liabilities).

(b) The **best predictor** of failure (sometimes called Beaver's ratio) is the ratio of cash flow from operations to total debt (**operating cash flow / total debt**), where total debt includes both long-term and short-term debt.

This ratio indicates the length of time it will take an organisation to repay its debt, assuming all the cash flow from operations is devoted to repaying the debt. The lower the ratio, the less ability an organisation has to service the principal (debt) and the related interest payments. Consequently, the lower the ratio, the more likely it is that problems will arise for the organisation in the future. All the organisations in Beaver's study with a ratio below 0.2 subsequently failed within five years, while all the organisations he studied which had a ratio above 0.4 did not fail in the next five years.

3.5 Advantages and disadvantages of qualitative models

Qualitative models (such as Argenti's A-score) may **augment quantitative models** giving a further range of factors to consider when assessing failure.

They typically include behaviours that have been observed in failing companies, for instance an autocratic chairman or poor budgetary control, and can be readily observed inside organisations before the organisation reaches a terminal state.

However, qualitative measures need to be used carefully, as **one or two measures on their own do not constitute terminal decline**. For example, an autocratic chairman does not necessarily signal the company is going to decline, but it could raise the possibility of this if it is combined with other qualitative and quantitative measures which could indicate failure.

A further complication of using qualitative measures is that they can be **subjective**, **are not easily comparable**, and can be based on **impressions**, as in our example, of what an autocratic chairman is.

Finally, we should note that models such as 'A-score' focus mainly on internal factors and indicators of performance. They do not incorporate **environmental analysis** (PESTEL) or considerations about the performance of an **industry as a whole**. However, these could also have an impact on the likelihood of corporate failure.

Western companies in China

eBay

In 2004, the online auctioning giant eBay decided to enter the Chinese market. It bought a local company, switched it to the eBay platform, and expected to expand its presence in China in quick time. eBay's logic was that it had dominated the online auction markets in other countries, so why wouldn't it be able to do the same in China?

Two years later, in 2006, eBay shut down its portal and abandoned the Chinese auction market. By contrast, the local competitor Taobao Marketplace (operated by the Alibaba group) was able to become the undisputed market leader. By 2010, Taobao served more than 80% of China's e-commerce market, with 170 million registered users and revenues of more than 20 billion renminbi from online advertising and fee-paying services such as shop design and sales training.

One of the main differences between eBay and Taobao is that, while Taobao developed an instant messaging facility – Aliwangwang – to enable potential buyers and sellers to chat, and for buyers to get to know sellers, eBay didn't offer any similar facility.

eBay had failed to appreciate the power of 'guanxi' (social connections) in China. And the fact that eBay's platform had no mechanism for promoting social connections between buyers and sellers was a crucial error which led to its failure in China.

Importantly also, Taobao noted that eBay in China was charging users to list products and services, but it allowed users to list for free in order to develop a large cohort of buyers and sellers. It recognised that critical mass would be crucial for attracting revenue-generating activities, such as online advertisements.

In addition, Taobao presented itself as very much a Chinese enterprise.

Based on: Greeven, M., Yang, S., Yue, T., van Hech, E. and Krug B., (2012), How Taobao bested Ebay in China, *Financial Times*, 12 March.

Home Depot

Home Depot is a US home improvement (DIY) retailer which operates large out of town stores selling home improvement and construction products. The growth of the middle class and millions of new homeowners in China attracted Home Depot to enter the Chinese market in 2006, and it opened 12 stores in the country.

However, by September 2012, the company had closed all of its stores in China. Commentators have noted there were several reasons for the failure.

First was the timing: Home Depot came late to China, after its competitors already had a foothold. By the time it arrived China's growth was slowing down.

Second was the nature of China's housing market. Many people buy homes for investment and speculation, not to improve.

Third was the store format. As other US retailers have also found, Chinese consumers don't like 'big-box' warehouses in suburban areas far away from a city centre. This was a particular issue for Home Depot because women in China make the final decision in buying home décor products, and the 'warehouse' concept store was less attractive to female shoppers than urban boutique shops.

Finally, and most fatally, Home Depot tried to bring US notions of DIY to a market where labour was so cheap that most people simply hired a handyman' (Carlson, 2013). As a Home Depot spokesperson noted, China was, in essence, a 'do it for me' market, rather than a 'do it yourself' market.

Based on:

Carlson, B., (2013), 'Why big American businesses fail in China' *CNBC*, Online. Available from: http://www.cnbc.com/2013/09/26/why-big-american-businesses-fail-in-china.html

[Accessed 26 January 2016]

4 Performance improvement strategies and corporate failure

FAST FORWARD

Leadership can be very important in allowing an organisation to avoid failure, but leaders need to be aware of the causes of decline which might lead to corporate failure.

4.1 Possible causes of decline and strategies to deal with them

Causes of decline and the **strategies** to deal with them:

(a) **Poor management**. This should be dealt with by the introduction of new management and perhaps organisational restructuring (this should only be embarked on once the new executive knows how the firm **really** works, including its informal organisation). More generally, management weaknesses can also be addressed through improvements to an organisation's corporate governance structure.

(b) **Poor financial controls**. This can be dealt with by new management, financial control systems which are tighter and more relevant and, perhaps, decentralisation and delegation of responsibility to first-line management of all aspects except finance.

(c) **High cost structure**. Cost reduction is important in improving margins in the long term. New product-market strategies are adopted for the short term (to boost profitability and cash flow). Growth-orientated strategies (eg product or market development, as in Ansoff's matrix) are only suitable once survival is assured. A focus strategy (whether cost-focus or differentiation-focus) is perhaps the most appropriate; focusing on a profitable niche in the market.

(d) **Poor marketing**. The marketing mix can be redeployed. Slatter believes that the sales force of a crisis-ridden firm is likely to be particularly demotivated.

(e) **Competitive weakness**. This is countered by cost reduction, improved marketing, asset reduction (eg disposing of subsidiaries, closure of poorly performing divisions, selling redundant non-current assets), even acquisition, and, of course, a suitable product-market strategy.

An assessment of an organisation's product portfolio (BCG matrix) could also be useful for helping areas of competitive weakness which need to be addressed through potential acquisitions or disposals.

Equally, a consideration of product life cycles could be useful; for example, for identifying the need to develop 'new' products if the majority of an organisation's existing products are reaching the latter stages of their life cycles.

(f) **Big projects/acquisitions**. Mergers and acquisitions can go bad (as was famously the case with AOL-Time Warner's disastrous merger in 2000), or there can be a failure of a major project. Too often, CEOs succumb to an undisciplined lust for growth, accumulating assets for the sake of accumulating assets. To guard against this, any potential acquisitions need to be evaluated critically; for example, to assess what synergies or other benefits they will generate and to assess the risk involved (for example, how compatible are the organisations involved and their respective cultures).

(g) **Financial policy**. Firms might suffer because of high gearing. Arguably many of the firms subject to management buyouts financed by interest-bearing loans are acutely vulnerable. Converting debt to equity and selling assets are ways of dealing with this.

Case Study — Nokia

At the beginning of 2011, Nokia was the world's leading smartphone vendor by sales volume.

However, its market share had fallen by 10% during 2010, as the company struggled to provide devices which could match the high-end smartphones offered by Apple, Samsung and HTB, or else to compete with cheaper manufacturers such as ZTE and Huawei.

In February 2011, chief executive Stephen Elop described Nokia as 'a company in crisis' because Nokia's Symbian operating system was unable to compete with Google's Android system.

By 2013, Nokia had fallen to tenth place in the ranks of smartphone sales.

How did Nokia respond?

- In April 2014, it sold 'substantially all' of its Devices and Services business to Microsoft, to enable Nokia to concentrate on building three strong businesses in networks, locations and technologies. (**Competitive weakness – Sale of poorly performing business**)
- It introduced a new governance structure and appointed a new leadership team from 1 May 2014. (**Addressing management weakness**)
- It announced plans for a €5 billion plan to optimise its capital structure, through distributing excess capital to shareholders and reducing interest-bearing debt. (**Financial policy – Addressing financial weakness**)

4.2 Strategic drift and strategies to deal with it

FAST FORWARD

Strategic drift occurs when strategies develop **incrementally** but fail to keep up with the changing environment of the organisation.

Companies that recovered did so largely because of the way in which the recovery strategy was implemented.

(a) **Contraction** in order to cut the cost base while maintaining revenue
(b) **Reinvestment** in organisational capability and efficiency
(c) **Rebuilding** with a concentration on innovation

Turning a company around requires an able top management, with the right mix of skills and experience, to stand outside of the culture of the organisation. Substantial changes at the top may be needed, and one of the most important **symbols of a new order is the change of personnel**. The development of an effective top management team depends on three things:

(a) What resources does the team have to work with, in the **context** of the industry and of the firm?

(b) What is **the ideal management** team given the nature of the crises facing the organisation? For example, a firm with poor financial controls may require a team with a financial or systems bias, whereas a firm whose problem was lacklustre products may need a team with a marketing bias.

(c) Against this **ideal team**, how does the **current team** shape up? New expertise may need to be imported, or a plan may be needed to enhance the capability of the existing team.

4.2.1 Leadership roles

(a) **Charismatic leaders** lead by force of personality, which will only be exercised in difficult situations.

(b) **Transformational leaders** not only have charisma, but also use it to some purpose:

  (i) To create a new vision for the organisation
  (ii) To gain acceptance of the new vision
  (iii) To force through and 'refreeze' the change

There are, of course, **corporate governance** issues involved. An overly powerful leader can be a danger to the good governance of the firm. This is why the Cadbury Committee recommended that the **roles of Chairman and Chief Executive should be split**.

(a) The **Chairman** should have no day to day operating responsibilities but should represent the interests of shareholders, deal with the audit committee and so forth.

(b) The Chief Executive Officer has direct responsibility for the operations of the company.

Such an arrangement has four useful features.

(a) It avoids **overconcentration** of power.
(b) Two senior members offer **different perspectives** on the businesses.
(c) The Chairman represents the **shareholders**.
(d) The Chairman deals with **key external stakeholders**.

4.2.2 Importance of leadership

Regardless of whether the detailed characteristics of business failure are analysed using quantitative or qualitative measures, it has often been suggested that the **ultimate reason for business failure is poor leadership**. The business guru Brian Tracy has suggested that 'Leadership is the most important single factor in determining business success or failure in our competitive, turbulent, fast-moving economy'.

Similarly, a study by a US bank has suggested that the main reasons why businesses fail are:

(a) **Poor business planning** – failing to develop a properly thought-out business plan

(b) **Poor financial planning** – starting out with too little capital or money, failing to control cash flow effectively, failing to balance liquidity and profitability, and failing to take financial responsibility

(c) **Poor marketing** – failing to understand (and meet) customer needs, failing to promote the business effectively and/or create demand for products and services, and failing to take account of (and respond to) competitors' activities

(d) **Poor management** – leaders not recognising their own failings and not seeking any help or advice (or ignoring help and advice they are given); having insufficient relevant business experience, delegating poorly, and hiring the wrong people

(Note the link here back to Argenti's A-score model, which highlighted 'Management defects' as one of its three key headings.)

4.3 Avoiding failure

There have been many books and articles which have focused on identifying the reasons for failure, and then sought to provide remedies for these reasons. We have already looked at a number of possible reasons for business failure, so we are not going to review any of these books in detail.

However, one relatively early work whose ideas are worth noting is that by Ross and Kami, who identified 'Ten Commandments' which could lead to business failure if they are not kept. These 'Ten Commandments' were:

(a) You must have a strategy.
(b) You must have controls.
(c) The board must participate.
(d) You must avoid one-man rule (for example, having an autocratic CEO).
(e) There must be management in depth.
(f) You must ensure you are informed of, and react to, change.
(g) The customer is king.
(h) Do not misuse computers.
(i) Do not manipulate your accounts.
(j) Organise to meet employees' needs.

Exam focus point

Some of the 'Ten Commandments' may seem obvious and even simplistic, but they could still provide a useful framework for assessing the features of a company which is failing. In such a situation, it could be useful to ask yourself how many of the 'Commandments' the company has failed to keep, and then equally what could be done to help ensure it does keep them.

5 Implementing performance improvement strategies

In the previous section, we identified some of the possible ways in which organisations could look to improve their performance and avoid corporate failure.

However, one specific way in which an organisation could respond to the threat of failure or closure is through a turnaround strategy.

5.1 Turnaround

When a business is in terminal decline and faces closure or takeover, there is a need for rapid and extensive change in order to achieve cost reduction and revenue generation. This change could be achieved through a **turnaround strategy**. We can identify **seven elements of such a strategy**.

5.1.1 Crisis stabilisation

The emphasis is on reducing costs and increasing revenues. An emphasis on reducing direct costs and improving productivity is more likely to be effective than efforts to reduce overheads.

(a) **Measures to increase revenue**

- Tailor marketing mix to key market segments
- Review pricing policies to maximise revenue
- Focus activities on target market segments
- Exploit revenue opportunities if related to target segments
- Invest in growth areas

(b) **Measures to reduce costs**

- Cut costs of labour and senior management
- Improve productivity
- Ensure clear marketing focus on target market segments
- Financial controls
- Strict cash management controls
- Reduce inventory
- Cut unprofitable products and services

Severe cost cutting is a common response to crisis but it is unlikely to be enough by itself. The **wider causes of decline** must be addressed.

5.1.2 Management changes

It is likely that new managers will be required, especially at the strategic apex. Important reasons for this include:

(a) The old management allowed the situation to deteriorate and **may be held responsible by key stakeholders.**

(b) **Experience of turnaround management** may be required.

(c) Managers brought in from outside will not be **prisoners of the old culture and ways of working** within the organisation (which had led to the turnaround situation), so they will be able to identify fresh approaches and strategies.

5.1.3 Communication with stakeholders

The support of key stakeholder groups – groups with both a high level of power and a high degree of interest in an organisation such as the workforce and providers of finance – is likely to be very important in a turnaround. It is likely that stakeholders did not receive full information during the period of deterioration. A **stakeholder analysis** (for example, using Mendelow's matrix, as in Chapter 5 earlier in this Study Text) should be carried out so that the various stakeholder groups can be informed and managed appropriately.

5.1.4 Attention to target markets

A **clear focus on appropriate target market segments** is essential; indeed a lack of such focus is a common cause of decline. The organisation must become customer orientated and ensure that it has good flows of marketing information.

5.1.5 Concentration of effort

Resources should be concentrated on the best opportunities to create value. It will almost certainly be appropriate to **review products and the market segments** currently served and eliminate any distractions and poor performers. A similar review of internal activities would also be likely to show up several candidates for **outsourcing**.

5.1.6 Financial restructuring

Some form of **financial restructuring** is likely to be required. In the worst case, this may involve trading out of insolvency. Even where the business is more or less solvent, capital restructuring may be required, both to provide cash for investment and to reduce cash outflows in the shorter term.

5.1.7 Prioritisation

The eventual success of a turnaround strategy depends in part on management's ability to **prioritise necessary activities**, such as those noted above.

5.2 Performance management systems

The first two stages of the turnaround process clearly identify the need to increase revenues and reduce costs. However, by doing so, they also suggest the need for suitable performance measures and a suitable performance management system to be in place to assess how well these goals are being achieved.

One of the causes behind an organisation's decline prior to the turnaround could have been management's lack of focus on performance management. In which case, a key part of the turnaround will also be introducing a performance management system which identifies the key performance drivers (for example, production output, sales, quality) required to improve the organisation's performance.

For example, the need to reduce costs suggests the organisation may need to reduce its workforce and increase the efficiency of the remaining staff. However, to do this, the organisation will need to analyse its existing activities and processes to work out where staff savings can be made in a way which minimises any negative impact on the value it provides for its customers.

Equally, the need to improve efficiency may, in the longer term, encourage the organisation to look at such techniques as target costing, business process re-engineering, or total quality management.

5.2.1 Linking strategies and targets

Importantly, once an organisation has identified a strategy and objectives for improving its performance, it also needs to ensure that it sets **operational targets** which are **directly linked to its strategic objectives**. This should increase the chance of business operations – and specifically employees – delivering the performance improvements which are required.

Equally importantly, however, the organisation needs to **monitor performance** against those targets.

5.2.2 Accountability

Establishing a culture of accountability could also be an important part of a performance improvement strategy; encouraging everyone in an organisation to take ownership of results.

However, this does not mean that employees should be held accountable for results they cannot influence. For example, expecting a mechanic in a factory to influence 'profit' is a meaningless target. Instead, individual staff should set specific objectives and targets for their functional areas (for example, for the mechanic, these might relate to productivity, wastage and quality).

In addition, employees could be empowered to take action to influence the targets they have set. This combination of target setting and empowerment should encourage employees to be more accountable for results.

5.2.3 Employee rewards

We looked at some of the issues surrounding performance management and employee reward systems in Chapter 14. One of the key messages from that is of the need to integrate human resource management processes (recruitment, retention or reduction of staff) with the strategic direction and control of an organisation.

These issues are particularly important in the context of performance improvement strategies. Management should consider what **goals are chosen for employees** and how performance is measured and rewarded in a performance management system. The goals must align with the overall objectives of the organisation as it seeks to improve its performance.

Clearly an organisation in crisis working hard to survive will have some demanding goals and targets to attain. These may well be set for a short period of time with the recognition that once the business recovers, new goals will be drawn up. Rewards could be deferred until the business had recovered to provide incentives to perform even where the immediate reward is not available.

As an example of organisational restructuring, during the 2007–2010 global financial crisis, some businesses asked workers to opt for shorter working weeks in the short term to help the business cash flow and ensure people were not idle when there was a downturn in activity. This amendment to working conditions would be reflected in the performance management of these employees.

Chapter Roundup

- The **product life cycle** describes the financial and marketing life of a product from introduction, through growth to maturity and decline. The life cycle can be determined by technology or customer demand. The strategies which are appropriate for a product will vary throughout its life cycle.
- Assuming the life cycle pattern applies, then in order to survive and prosper firms need new products to take the place of declining ones. Different **control measures** are appropriate at different stages of the life cycle.
- **Corporate decline** arises from the decline in the industry and from poor management. It is still possible to make money in declining industries, just as it is possible to **'turn round'** declining companies. However, it is crucial to identify the **symptoms** and **causes** of corporate decline in order for them to be addressed.
- The **Icarus paradox** arises when a successful model becomes over-rigid, hampering innovation and reducing flexibility.
- The likelihood of business failure can be assessed using quantitative or qualitative prediction models. **Z-scores** is a **quantitative** model based around a number of **financial indicators**. **Argenti's A-score** model is a **qualitative** model which assesses **defects, mistakes and symptoms** of decline within an organisation.
- The accuracy of corporate failure models (like any other model) can only be as good as the **quality of information** they use. It is likely that there will be **limitations to the data** collected. There will also be **limitations on the application of the model** and care needs to be taken when adopting a 'one size fits all' approach.
- Leadership can be very important in allowing an organisation to avoid failure, but leaders need to be aware of the causes of decline which might lead to corporate failure.
- **Strategic drift** occurs when strategies develop **incrementally** but fail to keep up with the changing environment of the organisation.

Quick Quiz

1. 'Product X commands 50% in a market that is no longer growing. We are able to earn $Y per unit of scale resource, owing to economies of scale, and are pleased that our customer retention rate is increasing, reducing 'churn' costs.'

   What stage of the product life cycle is described above?

   A Introduction
   B Growth
   C Maturity
   D Decline

2. Identify four typical causes of corporate decline.

3. Argenti devised a scoring system to predict company failure based on three factors. List these factors and give an example of each.

4. Three years ago, a company's Z-score was calculated as 3.3, but it has now been recalculated as 2.9 based on the company's latest financial results.

   According to the Z-score model, which of the following best describes the company?

   A The company's financial performance is deteriorating, and it seems likely to be heading for bankruptcy and corporate failure.
   B The company's financial performance is deteriorating, but whether it is going to fail or survive cannot be predicted with any certainty.
   C The company's financial performance is improving, but whether it is going to fail or survive cannot be predicted with any certainty.
   D The company's financial performance is improving, and it is now relatively safe from the risk of corporate failure.

5. Why can Altman's Z-score not be used by unquoted companies to predict business failure?

Answers to Quick Quiz

1 C Maturity

The fact that the market is no longer growing means the product has to be in either the mature or decline phases of its life cycle. The focus on retention rates indicates the importance of capturing (and retaining) market share from competitors, which is an important feature of mature markets.

2 Poor financial controls; high cost structure; failure of a major project; high gearing

3 We have given more than one example of each but you are only asked for one.

FACTORS IN ARGENTI'S MODEL	
Defects	Autocratic Chief Executive Passive board Lack of budgetary control
Mistakes	Over-trading (expanding faster than cash funding) Gearing – high bank overdrafts/loans Failure of large project jeopardises the company
Symptoms	Deteriorating ratios Creative accounting – signs of window-dressing Declining morale and declining quality

4 B The company's financial performance is deteriorating, but whether it is going to fail or survive cannot be predicted with any certainty.

A Z-score of 3.0 or higher suggests that a company is likely to be financially sound and relatively safe from corporate failure.

Three years ago, the company was in this position (with a score of 3.3) but its score has deteriorated to below 3.0.

The Z-score model predicts that companies with a score below 1.8 are heading for bankruptcy and corporate failure.

However, companies with a Z-score between 1.8 and 3.0 are in the 'grey area' where their eventual failure or survival cannot be predicted with any certainty. The company's score of 2.9 means it is currently in this 'grey area'.

5 Because of the use of **X_4: market value of equity/book value of debt**, Z-score models cannot be used for unquoted companies which lack a market value of equity.

Now try the question below from the Practice Question Bank

Number	Level	Marks	Approximate time
Q18	Examination	15	30 mins

Mathematical tables

Present Value Table

Present value of 1 ie $(1 + r)^{-n}$

Where r = discount rate
n = number of periods until payment

Discount rate (r)

Periods (n)	1%	2%	3%	4%	5%	6%	7%	8%	9%	10%	
1	0·990	0·980	0·971	0·962	0·952	0·943	0·935	0·926	0·917	0·909	1
2	0·980	0·961	0·943	0·925	0·907	0·890	0·873	0·857	0·842	0·826	2
3	0·971	0·942	0·915	0·889	0·864	0·840	0·816	0·794	0·772	0·751	3
4	0·961	0·924	0·888	0·855	0·823	0·792	0·763	0·735	0·708	0·683	4
5	0·951	0·906	0·863	0·822	0·784	0·747	0·713	0·681	0·650	0·621	5
6	0·942	0·888	0·837	0·790	0·746	0·705	0·666	0·630	0·596	0·564	6
7	0·933	0·871	0·813	0·760	0·711	0·665	0·623	0·583	0·547	0·513	7
8	0·923	0·853	0·789	0·731	0·677	0·627	0·582	0·540	0·502	0·467	8
9	0·914	0·837	0·766	0·703	0·645	0·592	0·544	0·500	0·460	0·424	9
10	0·905	0·820	0·744	0·676	0·614	0·558	0·508	0·463	0·422	0·386	10
11	0·896	0·804	0·722	0·650	0·585	0·527	0·475	0·429	0·388	0·350	11
12	0·887	0·788	0·701	0·625	0·557	0·497	0·444	0·397	0·356	0·319	12
13	0·879	0·773	0·681	0·601	0·530	0·469	0·415	0·368	0·326	0·290	13
14	0·870	0·758	0·661	0·577	0·505	0·442	0·388	0·340	0·299	0·263	14
15	0·861	0·743	0·642	0·555	0·481	0·417	0·362	0·315	0·275	0·239	15

(n)	11%	12%	13%	14%	15%	16%	17%	18%	19%	20%	
1	0·901	0·893	0·885	0·877	0·870	0·862	0·855	0·847	0·840	0·833	1
2	0·812	0·797	0·783	0·769	0·756	0·743	0·731	0·718	0·706	0·694	2
3	0·731	0·712	0·693	0·675	0·658	0·641	0·624	0·609	0·593	0·579	3
4	0·659	0·636	0·613	0·592	0·572	0·552	0·534	0·516	0·499	0·482	4
5	0·593	0·567	0·543	0·519	0·497	0·476	0·456	0·437	0·419	0·402	5
6	0·535	0·507	0·480	0·456	0·432	0·410	0·390	0·370	0·352	0·335	6
7	0·482	0·452	0·425	0·400	0·376	0·354	0·333	0·314	0·296	0·279	7
8	0·434	0·404	0·376	0·351	0·327	0·305	0·285	0·266	0·249	0·233	8
9	0·391	0·361	0·333	0·308	0·284	0·263	0·243	0·225	0·209	0·194	9
10	0·352	0·322	0·295	0·270	0·247	0·227	0·208	0·191	0·176	0·162	10
11	0·317	0·287	0·261	0·237	0·215	0·195	0·178	0·162	0·148	0·135	11
12	0·286	0·257	0·231	0·208	0·187	0·168	0·152	0·137	0·124	0·112	12
13	0·258	0·229	0·204	0·182	0·163	0·145	0·130	0·116	0·104	0·093	13
14	0·232	0·205	0·181	0·160	0·141	0·125	0·111	0·099	0·088	0·078	14
15	0·209	0·183	0·160	0·140	0·123	0·108	0·095	0·084	0·074	0·065	15

Annuity Table

Present value of an annuity of 1 ie $\frac{1-(1+r)^{-n}}{r}$

Where r = discount rate
n = number of periods

Discount rate (r)

Periods (n)	1%	2%	3%	4%	5%	6%	7%	8%	9%	10%	
1	0·990	0·980	0·971	0·962	0·952	0·943	0·935	0·926	0·917	0·909	1
2	1·970	1·942	1·913	1·886	1·859	1·833	1·808	1·783	1·759	1·736	2
3	2·941	2·884	2·829	2·775	2·723	2·673	2·624	2·577	2·531	2·487	3
4	3·902	3·808	3·717	3·630	3·546	3·465	3·387	3·312	3·240	3·170	4
5	4·853	4·713	4·580	4·452	4·329	4·212	4·100	3·993	3·890	3·791	5
6	5·795	5·601	5·417	5·242	5·076	4·917	4·767	4·623	4·486	4·355	6
7	6·728	6·472	6·230	6·002	5·786	5·582	5·389	5·206	5·033	4·868	7
8	7·652	7·325	7·020	6·733	6·463	6·210	5·971	5·747	5·535	5·335	8
9	8·566	8·162	7·786	7·435	7·108	6·802	6·515	6·247	5·995	5·759	9
10	9·471	8·983	8·530	8·111	7·722	7·360	7·024	6·710	6·418	6·145	10
11	10·37	9·787	9·253	8·760	8·306	7·887	7·499	7·139	6·805	6·495	11
12	11·26	10·58	9·954	9·385	8·863	8·384	7·943	7·536	7·161	6·814	12
13	12·13	11·35	10·63	9·986	9·394	8·853	8·358	7·904	7·487	7·103	13
14	13·00	12·11	11·30	10·56	9·899	9·295	8·745	8·244	7·786	7·367	14
15	13·87	12·85	11·94	11·12	10·38	9·712	9·108	8·559	8·061	7·606	15

(n)	11%	12%	13%	14%	15%	16%	17%	18%	19%	20%	
1	0·901	0·893	0·885	0·877	0·870	0·862	0·855	0·847	0·840	0·833	1
2	1·713	1·690	1·668	1·647	1·626	1·605	1·585	1·566	1·547	1·528	2
3	2·444	2·402	2·361	2·322	2·283	2·246	2·210	2·174	2·140	2·106	3
4	3·102	3·037	2·974	2·914	2·855	2·798	2·743	2·690	2·639	2·589	4
5	3·696	3·605	3·517	3·433	3·352	3·274	3·199	3·127	3·058	2·991	5
6	4·231	4·111	3·998	3·889	3·784	3·685	3·589	3·498	3·410	3·326	6
7	4·712	4·564	4·423	4·288	4·160	4·039	3·922	3·812	3·706	3·605	7
8	5·146	4·968	4·799	4·639	4·487	4·344	4·207	4·078	3·954	3·837	8
9	5·537	5·328	5·132	4·946	4·772	4·607	4·451	4·303	4·163	4·031	9
10	5·889	5·650	5·426	5·216	5·019	4·833	4·659	4·494	4·339	4·192	10
11	6·207	5·938	5·687	5·453	5·234	5·029	4·836	4·656	4·486	4·327	11
12	6·492	6·194	5·918	5·660	5·421	5·197	4·988	4·793	4·611	4·439	12
13	6·750	6·424	6·122	5·842	5·583	5·342	5·118	4·910	4·715	4·533	13
14	6·982	6·628	6·302	6·002	5·724	5·468	5·229	5·008	4·802	4·611	14
15	7·191	6·811	6·462	6·142	5·847	5·575	5·324	5·092	4·876	4·675	15

Practice question and answer bank

1 SCC **Approx. 40 mins**

The Specialist Clothing Company (SCC) is a manufacturer of a wide range of clothing. Its operations are organised into five divisions which are as follows.

(i) Fashion
(ii) Industrial
(iii) Leisure
(iv) Children
(v) Footwear

The Fashion division manufactures a narrow range of high-quality clothing which is sold to a leading retail store which has branches in every major city in its country of operation. The products have very short life cycles.

The Industrial division manufactures a wide range of clothing which has been designed for use in industrial environments. In an attempt to increase sales volumes, SCC introduced an online ordering facility for these products (through its website) with effect from 1 June 20X5.

The Leisure division manufactures a narrow range of clothing designed for outdoor pursuits, such as mountaineering and skydiving, which it markets under its own, well-established 'Elite' brand label.

The Children's division manufactures a range of school and casual wear which is sold to leading retail stores.

The Footwear division manufactures a narrow range of footwear.

The management accountant of SCC has gathered the following actual and forecast information relating to the five divisions.

Year ending 31 May	*20X4 Actual*	*20X5 Actual*	*20X6 Actual*	*20X7 Forecast*	*20X8 Forecast*
Fashion					
Market size ($m)	200.00	240.00	280.00	305.00	350.00
Revenue ($m)	10.00	14.40	22.40	30.50	35.00
Industrial					
Market size ($m)	150.00	158.00	166.00	174.00	182.00
Revenue ($m)	5.00	5.10	5.20	5.30	5.40
Leisure					
Market size ($m)	20.0	20.50	21.00	21.50	21.80
Revenue ($m)	13.60	14.20	14.70	15.00	15.20
Children					
Market size ($m)	60.00	70.00	80.00	90.00	100.00
Revenue ($m)	2.00	2.10	2.20	2.30	2.40
Footwear					
Market size ($m)	20.00	20.20	20.40	20.60	21.00
Revenue ($m)	0.50	0.52	0.54	0.52	0.50

The management accountant has also collated the following information relating to the market share held at 31 May 20X6 by the market leader or nearest competitor in the markets in which each division operates.

Division	*Market share (%) held by market leader/nearest competitor*
Fashion	8
Industrial	15
Leisure	70
Children	28
Footwear	33

Required

(a) Use the Boston Consulting Group matrix to analyse SCC's business and its performance. **(10 marks)**

(b) Explain the implications of the BCG analysis for the choice of performance measures used at SCC. **(6 marks)**

(c) Discuss **two** limitations of the Boston Consulting Group matrix as a performance management system. **(4 marks)**

(Total = 20 marks)

2 Southside College — Approx. 40 mins

Southside College (SC) offers a wide range of courses aimed at vocational and professional qualifications. It has been operating for over 30 years now, and is well established. It has been accredited as an approved training provider by a number of the qualification-awarding bodies.

Although it competes with not-for-profit universities and colleges in some of its markets, SC is a limited company. Throughout its history, SC has always traded profitably.

In recent years, there have been a number of new entrants into the professional qualifications market. However, to date, SC has managed to retain the largest market share. SC's students consistently achieve higher pass rates than the national averages for the qualifications they are sitting.

SC has always concentrated on the quality of the teaching on its courses and the accompanying study materials. In recent years, however, a number of SC's competitors have begun to offer their students online tutorials to supplement their taught courses and these have proved very popular. SC's customer services team is receiving an increasing number of enquiries from prospective students about whether SC offers similar online tutorials. SC is developing its own online tutorials, but the development process is taking longer than had been hoped.

SC's management team has never been convinced of the need for market research or customer research, arguing that the company has always achieved its sales targets and has always been profitable. Similarly, they point out that SC has established a good reputation and a position as a market leader, despite investing relatively little in marketing activities.

Historically, SC has had a very low rate of employee turnover, but in recent years this has begun to increase as some of SC's tutors have left to join the new entrants in the market. This increase in employee turnover has concerned SC's management team.

Accordingly, SC's management team are keen to identify the critical success factors which will enable SC to maintain its performance levels in the future.

Required

(a) Identify four critical success factors which it would be appropriate to use at SC. **(4 marks)**

(b) For each critical success factor you have identified, recommend, with reasons, two key performance indicators which could be used to support that critical success factor. **(16 marks)**

(Total = 20 marks)

3 Kitch Co — Approx. 50 mins

Kitch Co manufactures and markets a range of small electronic kitchen appliances, including coffee makers and toasters. The company currently earns revenues of $55 million per annum, and has a functional organisational structure.

Kitch prepares annual budgets, and it currently operates an incremental budgeted system. The budgets are set by the budget committee which is comprised of six members of the senior management team: the Chief Executive, the Finance Director, the Marketing Director, the IT Director, the HR Director and the Operations Director.

No other members of staff apart from these six senior managers are involved in the budget setting process.

In recent years, all the members of Kitch's senior management team have received annual bonuses of between 10% and 25% of their annual salary. The amount of bonus each manager receives is based on a comparison of the actual costs for their functional area compared with the budgeted costs for that function. All the managers in the company are eligible for these bonuses, not just the senior management team.

Kitch has just appointed a new finance director, who previously held a senior management position within a large retail organisation. The new finance director was shocked when they heard about the way Kitch sets its budgets, and said they felt this should be changed as a matter of urgency.

The new finance director is keen that Kitch should introduce a zero-based budgeted system instead of its current incremental system, and they believe it is vital that the budget holders for all the cost centres are involved in the budgeting process.

Required

(a) Discuss the problems with Kitch's current system of budgeting and the factors Kitch should consider before implementing a system of zero-based budgeting. **(15 marks)**

(b) Analyse the behavioural problems that Kitch might encounter when implementing a system of zero-based budgeting, and recommend how these problems may be addressed. **(10 marks)**

(Total = 25 marks)

4 SPS sports shop **Approx. 50 mins**

SPS is a medium-sized retailer of sports equipment and leisure clothing. SPS was established in the early 1990s, and currently operates from three retail shops in town centre locations.

The management team at SPS is very careful about how it recruits staff. In addition to the specific skills required to do the job, any applicant must have a 'passion' for sport. This has resulted in SPS gaining a reputation for excellent customer service and enthusiastic staff.

A large proportion of staff time is also devoted to training, both on the product range and on customer service techniques. According to a recent survey conducted by the store managers, the customers believe that SPS employees are 'helpful and knowledgeable'. The customers also praised the SPS shops for being 'well designed' and said that it was 'very easy' to find what they were looking for.

Another feature of SPS that is appreciated by the customers is the range of goods stocked. By developing close relationships with the major manufacturers of sports goods and clothing, SPS is able to stock a far wider range of items than its rivals. Control of this stock (inventory) was made easier, last year, by the development of a sophisticated computerised inventory control system. Using the system, any member of staff can locate any item of inventory in any of the shops or the warehouse. If the required item is not 'in stock' at SPS, it is also possible to automatically check the availability of inventory with the manufacturer.

At a recent management meeting, one of the store managers suggested that SPS consider developing its very basic website into one capable of e-retailing. At present, the website only gives the location of stores and some very basic details of the range of stock carried. Although the development of the website would be expensive, the managers have decided to give the suggestion serious consideration.

Required

(a) Using the value chain model, analyse the activities that add value in the SPS organisation, **before** the e-retail investment. **(10 marks)**

(b) Identify those activities in the value chain of SPS that may be affected by the e-retail investment, explaining whether the value added by each of them may increase or decrease as a result of the e-retail investment. **(15 marks)**

(Total = 25 marks)

5 Nadir Products **Approx. 40 mins**

John Staples is the Finance Director of Nadir Products, a UK-based company which manufactures and sells bathroom products – baths, sinks and toilets – to the UK market. These products are sold through a selection of specialist shops and through larger 'do it yourself' stores. Customers include professional plumbers and also ordinary householders who are renovating their houses themselves. The company operates at the lower end of the market and does not have a strong reputation for service. Sales have been slowly declining whereas those of competitors have been improving. In order to encourage increased sales the board of directors has decided to pay senior staff a bonus if certain targets are achieved. The two main targets are based on profit levels and annual sales. Two months before the end of the financial year the Finance Director asks one of their staff to check through the orders and accounts to assess the current situation. They are informed that without a sudden improvement in sales before the year end the important sales targets will not be met and so bonuses will be adversely affected.

The Finance Director has proposed to other senior staff that this shortfall in sales can be corrected by taking one of the following decisions.

(1) A significant discount can be offered to any retail outlet which takes delivery of additional products prior to the end of the financial year.

(2) Scheduled orders due to be delivered at the beginning of the next financial year can be brought forward and billed before the end of this year.

(3) Distributors can be told that there is a risk of price increases in the future and that it will be advisable to order early so as to circumvent this possibility.

The board is not sure of the implications associated with such decisions.

Required

(a) As a consultant, prepare a report for the board of Nadir Products examining the commercial and ethical implications associated with each of the proposed options mentioned above. **(8 marks)**

(b) Assess the significance of the corporate social responsibility model for Nadir Products. **(12 marks)**

(Total = 20 marks)

6 Lithio Car **Approx. 40 mins**

The Lithio Car company was formed six years ago to commercially exploit the pioneering work of two professors at Beeland University. Over a number of years, the professors had developed and then patented processes which allowed them to use Lithium-ion batteries to power an electric car, which could travel up to 180 kilometres before it needed recharging.

Together with two other colleagues from the university, the professors founded Lithio Car to put the car into commercial production.

At the same time, the area around Beeland was suffering from major industrial decline, and the former factory of Royston Cars had recently been shut down by its parent company, after over 50 years of continuous vehicle manufacturing on that site. Many skilled production workers were made redundant as a result, in an area which was already suffering from high unemployment.

However, Lithio Car was able to benefit from grants from the regional council and interest-free loans from the Government to purchase and refurbish part of the Royston Cars factory, and employ 50 of the skilled workers that had been made redundant by Royston Cars. A number of the other workers, who had worked at the Royston factory for a long time, chose to retire when the factory closed.

As a result, although unemployment remains high in the area, Lithio Car has found it difficult to recruit skilled labour, and this shortage has been reflected in increased wages and staff costs in its factory.

Table 1 compares the Lithio Car with a similar petrol-fuelled car (the Gassio) and a hybrid car (Hybrid1) where the petrol engine is supplemented by power from an electric motor.

Model	Lithio Car	Gassio	Hybrid1
Power source	Lithium-ion batteries; electric motor	Petrol	Petrol with assistance from an electric motor
Price	$9,999	$7,999	$9,500
CO_2 emissions	Zero	180 grams / kilometre	95 grams / kilometre
Economy	Approximately $5 per 100 kilometres (electricity charge)	Approximately $40 per 100 kilometres	Approximately $25 per 100 kilometres
Performance	0–100 kph: 18 seconds Max speed: 120 kph	0–100 kph: 10 seconds Max speed: 180 kph	1–100 kph: 12 seconds Max speed: 170 kph
Range	160 kilometres until battery needs recharging	550 kilometres on a full tank of petrol	1,200 kilometres on a tank full of petrol

Table 1: Comparison of the Lithio car with petrol and hybrid cars

Hybrid cars are a popular way of reducing emissions and fuel consumption. There are also experimental cars not yet in production, which are fuelled by other low-emission alternatives to petrol, such as hydrogen.

The Lithio Car can be recharged from a domestic electricity supply. However, to supplement this, the Government has recently funded the development of 130 charging stations for electric cars spread throughout the country. The Government of Exland (in which Beeland is situated) has also given businesses tax incentives to switch to electric cars and is heavily taxing cars with high CO_2 emissions because of the detrimental effect of excess CO_2 on the environment.

Despite the industrial decline around Beeland, Exland remains a prosperous, developed country with a well-educated population. The Lithio Car is largely bought by 'green' consumers in Exland, who are prepared to pay a price premium for such a car. However, some consumers are also attracted to the Lithio car by the high price of petrol, which currently costs about $5 per litre in Exland. Only 5% of Lithio Car's production is currently exported.

Last year, Mega Motors, the second largest car manufacturer in the world, made an offer to buy Lithio Car, which the professors rejected. Although car production at Lithio Car is currently still very low, Mega Motors believes that demand for electric cars will be very significant in the future, and buying Lithio Car would be a way of entering this market. Mega Motors believes that the Lithium-ion batteries (which power the Lithio Car) will eventually become lighter, cheaper and give better performance and range.

Required

Using Porter's five forces model, assess the impact that the external business environment could have on Lithio Car's performance and the implications this has for performance management at Lithio Car.

(Total = 20 marks)

7 KLL **Approx. 40 mins**

KLL is a large health and fitness complex located in a capital city. Started seven years ago, the business has been profitable. The introduction of a much wider range of activities over the past few years has led to increased complexity of administration and difficulty in interpreting the rapidly growing basic data generated daily. This data remains largely unstructured and this in turn leads to uncertainty in decision making.

The present management information system (MIS) is able to produce monthly reports on the performance overall but can only break down the key indicators of revenue and gross profit into six broad categories: water sports, sports hall activities, fitness training, beauty treatments, squash courts and outdoor sports. Thus there is no detail on specific activities, such as table tennis, sauna room, badminton or soccer. The managing director and the board cannot distinguish the profitable activities from the unprofitable ones. The managing director tells the board 'we must have a management information system that can cope with our complex business; there are so many variables it is becoming impossible to make decisions with confidence. Sometimes we have detail we cannot interpret and sometimes we simply do not have enough good information'. The finance director points out that 'the staff are doing their best but they have limited technical knowledge and the software support company is often slow to help'.

Recognising that it is important to build an MIS to serve the company well into the future, the board decides to ask you to submit a proposal to them for a new system.

Required

Prepare a memorandum to the board explaining the main purposes of a new MIS and the benefits the company could expect such a system to bring.

(Total = 20 marks)

8 Cobra Golf Club — Approx. 40 mins

The Cobra Golf Club is one of the largest and most successful members' golf clubs in its country. It is administered by a general manager, who is supported by an accountant. Monthly performance reports are prepared for the board of directors, which consists of the general manager and non-executive directors who are elected from the club membership.

The board of directors has recently been accused by the membership of failing to control the club's finances, and there is strong opposition to rumoured plans for a large increase in annual subscriptions next year.

At a recent board meeting, the directors agreed that financial control could be improved, but argued that it was very difficult to monitor the club's income and expenses because the monthly management accounts were not as helpful as they could be.

The monthly management accounts consist of a nine-page report. An example of the first page of a report is as follows:

	Current month		*Year to date (YTD)*		*Budget*			*% increase on YTD*
	This year	*Last year*	*This year*	*Last year*	*Current month*	*Year to date*	*Annual*	
Income								
Subscriptions	127,800	129,200	383,400	387,600	129,200	383,400	1,550,400	(1.1)
Entrance fees	9,000	3,000	15,000	12,000	7,500	22,500	90,000	25.0
Green fees	16,800	12,100	45,900	44,300	14,000	42,000	48,000	2.5
Hire of rooms	2,000	4,400	5,600	7,200	3,000	9,000	36,000	(22.3)
	155,600	148,700	449,900	451,100	153,700	456,900	1,724,400	(0.3)
Bar and catering								
Total sales	52,800	50,700	142,300	140,200	50,000	150,000	720,000	1.5
Cost of sales	27,100	26,800	74,000	74,500	25,000	75,000	360,000	(0.1)
Gross profit	25,700	23,900	68,300	65,700	25,000	75,000	360,000	4.0
Wages	23,900	23,200	70,200	68,900	24,000	72,000	300,000	1.9
Net contribution	1,800	700	(1,900)	(3,200)	1,000	3,000	60,000	(59.3)

Expenditure								
Course expenditure (see page 3)	73,200	64,700	132,100	127,400	50,000	150,000	600,000	3.7
Club house expenditure (see page 4)	52,200	53,600	116,000	116,300	45,000	145,000	540,000	(0.3)
Administration								
Staff costs	18,500	18,200	55,500	54,600	18,000	54,000	216,000	1.6
Golf professional	8,000	7,600	24,000	23,000	7,800	23,400	93,600	2.7
Insurance	1,800	1,600	5,400	4,800	1,750	5,250	21,000	12.5
Stationery, postage	700	2,100	1,800	2,600	800	2,400	9,600	(30.8)
Telephone	3,800	3,400	10,500	9,100	3,300	9,900	39,600	15.4
Prizes and competitions	500	700	2,100	2,000	700	2,100	8,400	5.0
Marketing	100	900	3,500	3,900	1,000	3,000	12,000	(10.3)
Training	1,200	0	1,200	1,000	700	2,100	8,400	20.0
IT costs	1,500	1,400	4,200	4,000	1,200	3,600	14,400	5.0
Miscellaneous	9,400	7,300	31,800	25,000	8,000	24,000	96,000	27.2
	45,500	43,200	140,000	130,000	43,250	129,750	519,000	7.7
Depreciation								
Course improvements	4,000	3,900	12,000	11,700	4,000	12,000	48,000	
Course machinery	8,200	8,000	24,600	24,000	8,000	24,000	96,000	
Clubhouse building	3,100	2,900	9,000	8,700	3,000	9,000	36,000	
Fittings and furniture	800	700	2,300	2,100	700	2,100	8,400	
	16,100	15,500	47,900	46,500	15,700	47,100	188,400	
Net income	(29,600)	(27,600)	12,000	27,700	750	(11,950)	(63,000)	(56.7)

Page 2 of the report provides a more detailed analysis of bar and catering services. Page 3 and page 4 provide a detailed analysis of expenditure of the golf course and the club house, analysed in the same columns as page 1.

Page 5 provides a statement of financial position (balance sheet) as at the end of the month, and page 6 provides a review of capital expenditure (budget and actual for the year to date). Page 7 provides a cash flow analysis, month by month. Page 8 provides a rolling forecast of results for the year, which is prepared by adding actual results for the year to date to the budget for the rest of the year. Finally page 9 provides a list of aged receivables (debtors), which are mainly companies that have hired the course for corporate golf days.

Required

(a) Explain the nature of information overload in management reporting. **(5 marks)**

(b) Analyse the weaknesses in the reporting system used by the Cobra Golf Club and recommend changes that might be made. **(15 marks)**

(Total = 20 marks)

9 Aqua Holdings

Approx. 80 mins

Water Supply Services (WSS) and Enterprise Activities (EA) are two wholly owned subsidiaries of Aqua Holdings. You have recently qualified as an accountant and have joined the finance team of Aqua Holdings at headquarters. Your finance director is not satisfied with the performance of these two subsidiaries and has asked you to prepare a report covering the following issues.

(a) The profitability of the two subsidiaries
(b) The competence of the Enterprise Activity manager to make financial decisions
(c) The consequences of having a common management information system serving both companies

The finance director has also provided you with the following background information on the two companies.

Water Supply Services

The company holds a licence issued by the Government to be the sole supplier of drinking water to a large town. The business necessitates a considerable investment in infrastructure assets and is therefore highly capital intensive. To comply with the licence the company has to demonstrate that it is maintaining guaranteed service standards to its customers. WSS is extensively regulated, requiring very detailed annual returns concerning costs, prices, profits and service delivery standards. The Government enforces a price-capping regime and therefore the company has limited freedom in tariff determination – the Government will normally only sanction a price increase following a demonstrable rise in costs.

Enterprise Activities

In contrast to Water Supply Services, Enterprise Activities operates in a very competitive market offering a plumbing service to domestic properties. The business has the following characteristics.

(a) Rapidly changing market conditions
(b) A high rate of new entrants and business failures
(c) Occasional shortages of skilled plumbers
(d) Fluctuating profits

In addition to this background information you also have the following.

(a) Summarised income statements and statements of financial position (balance sheets) for the last two years for both companies

(b) Service contract costing information from Enterprise Activities

(c) Notes from a meeting that you have had with the manager responsible for the profitability of the three service contracts offered by Enterprise Activities

Water Supply Services
Summary statement of profit or loss

		20X0		*20W9*
		$m		$m
Revenue		31		30
Less: staff costs	3		2	
general expenses	2		2	
depreciation	12		9	
interest	5		5	
		(22)		(18)
		9		12

Summary statement of financial position (balance sheet)

	20X0	20W9
Assets	$m	$m
Non-current asset	165	134
Current assets	5	6
Total assets	170	140
Equity and liabilities		
Equity	120	87
Non-current liabilities	47	47
Current liabilities	3	6
	170	140

Enterprise Activities
Summary statement of profit or loss

		20X0		20W9
		$m		$m
Revenue		20		35
Less: staff costs	5		6	
general expenses	10		10	
materials	3		6	
depreciation	1		1	
		(19)		(23)
Profit		1		12

Summary statement of financial position (balance sheet)

	20X0	20W9
Assets	$m	$m
Non-current asset	23	22
Current assets	12	12
	35	34
Equity and liabilities		
Equity	31	30
Current liabilities	4	4
	35	34

Enterprise Activities
Service contract costing data

The company offers three service contracts: standard, super and economy.
You have been provided with the following information.

	Standard	*Super*	*Economy*
Budgeted demand for contracts	1,000	800	2,000
Raw material cost per contract	$100	$150	$80
Direct labour hours per contract ($10 per hour)	5	8	2

Fixed overheads are allocated to the contracts at 150% of total direct costs.
The selling price is arrived at by adding 50% to the total costs.

Notes of meeting

(a) The manager states that his prime objective 'is to maximise the total profit that the three service contracts earn'.

(b) You discover that there is currently an unavoidable shortage of labour that has resulted in the available hours being limited to 80% of those originally planned in the budget.

(c) The manager responds to the shortfall in labour hours by 'concentrating sales on our most profitable service contracts, surely this is the obvious thing to do'.

(d) The manager is provided with the fixed overhead figure (150% of direct costs) from the finance department and assumes that it remains 'fixed' irrespective of the contract volume and contract mix. This overhead arises only as a consequence of operating the service contract business.

(e) The manager would never knowingly 'supply a service contract that did not cover the total cost, otherwise the company's profits would decline'.

(f) The manager estimates the volume of contracts for budgetary purposes and provides these figures to the finance team. You have compared their past estimates with the actual sales and conclude that they are very accurate with the sales forecast – you can assume that the actual number of contracts sold for any of the three contract types will not be exceeded.

Required

(a) Prepare a report on the comparative financial performance of Water Supply Services and Enterprise Activities from the above financial statements. Your report should incorporate an assessment of the potential limitations of undertaking such a comparison. **(16 marks)**

(b) Your finance director has asked you to provide a consultancy service to the newly appointed profit centre manager responsible for the service contract business.

Describe the advice you would give them to assist the achievement of their financial target. **(10 marks)**

(c) Calculate the maximum profit that the service contract business could earn if only 80% of the budgeted labour hours were available. **(10 marks)**

(d) Identify the likely differences in the two companies' management information needs. **(4 marks)**

(Total = 40 marks)

Approaching the answer

Look for key words and ask questions of the information given to you. This is illustrated here.

Water Supply Services (WSS) and Enterprise Activities (EA) are two wholly owned subsidiaries of Aqua Holdings. You have recently qualified as an accountant and have joined the finance team of Aqua Holdings at headquarters. Your finance director is not satisfied with the performance of these two subsidiaries and has asked you to prepare a report covering the following issues.

(a) The profitability of the two subsidiaries
(b) The competence of the Enterprise Activity manager to make financial decisions
(c) The consequences of having a common management information system serving both companies

The finance director has also provided you with the following background information on the two companies.

Not non profit making

WSS's market – monopoly

Important

Water Supply Services

How is this financed?

Government sets service levels

The company holds a licence issued by the Government to be the sole supplier of drinking water to a large town. The business necessitates a considerable investment in infrastructure assets and is therefore highly capital intensive. To comply with the licence the company has to demonstrate that it is maintaining guaranteed service standards to its customers. WSS is extensively regulated, requiring very detailed annual returns concerning costs, prices, profits and service delivery standards. The Government enforces a price-capping regime and therefore the company has limited freedom in tariff determination – the Government will normally only sanction a price increase following a demonstrable rise in costs.

Areas of regulation

Implication of regulation

Enterprise Activities

In contrast to Water Supply Services, Enterprise Activities operates in a very competitive market offering a plumbing service to domestic properties. The business has the following characteristics.

- Rapidly changing market conditions
- A high rate of new entrants and business failures
- Occasional shortages of skilled plumbers
- Fluctuating profits

EA's market

Risky!

Information for two years

In addition to this background information you also have the following.

(a) Summarised profit and loss accounts and balance sheets for the last two years for both companies

(b) Service contract costing information from Enterprise Activities

(c) Notes from a meeting that you have had with the manager responsible for the profitability of the three service contracts offered by Enterprise Activities

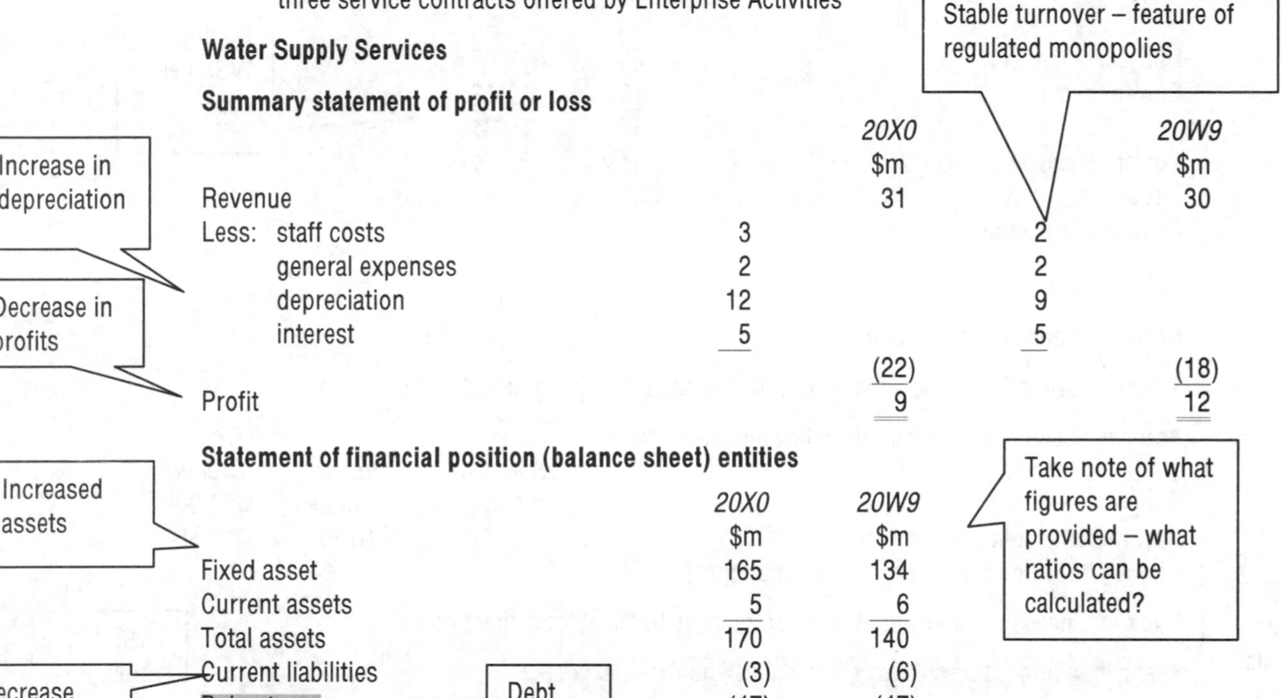

Water Supply Services

Summary statement of profit or loss

			20X0		20W9
			$m		$m
Revenue			31		30
Less:	staff costs	3		2	
	general expenses	2		2	
	depreciation	12		9	
	interest	5		5	
			(22)		(18)
Profit			9		12

Statement of financial position (balance sheet) entities

	20X0	20W9
	$m	$m
Fixed asset	165	134
Current assets	5	6
Total assets	170	140
Current liabilities	(3)	(6)
Debentures	(47)	(47)
Net assets	120	87
Shareholders' equity	120	87

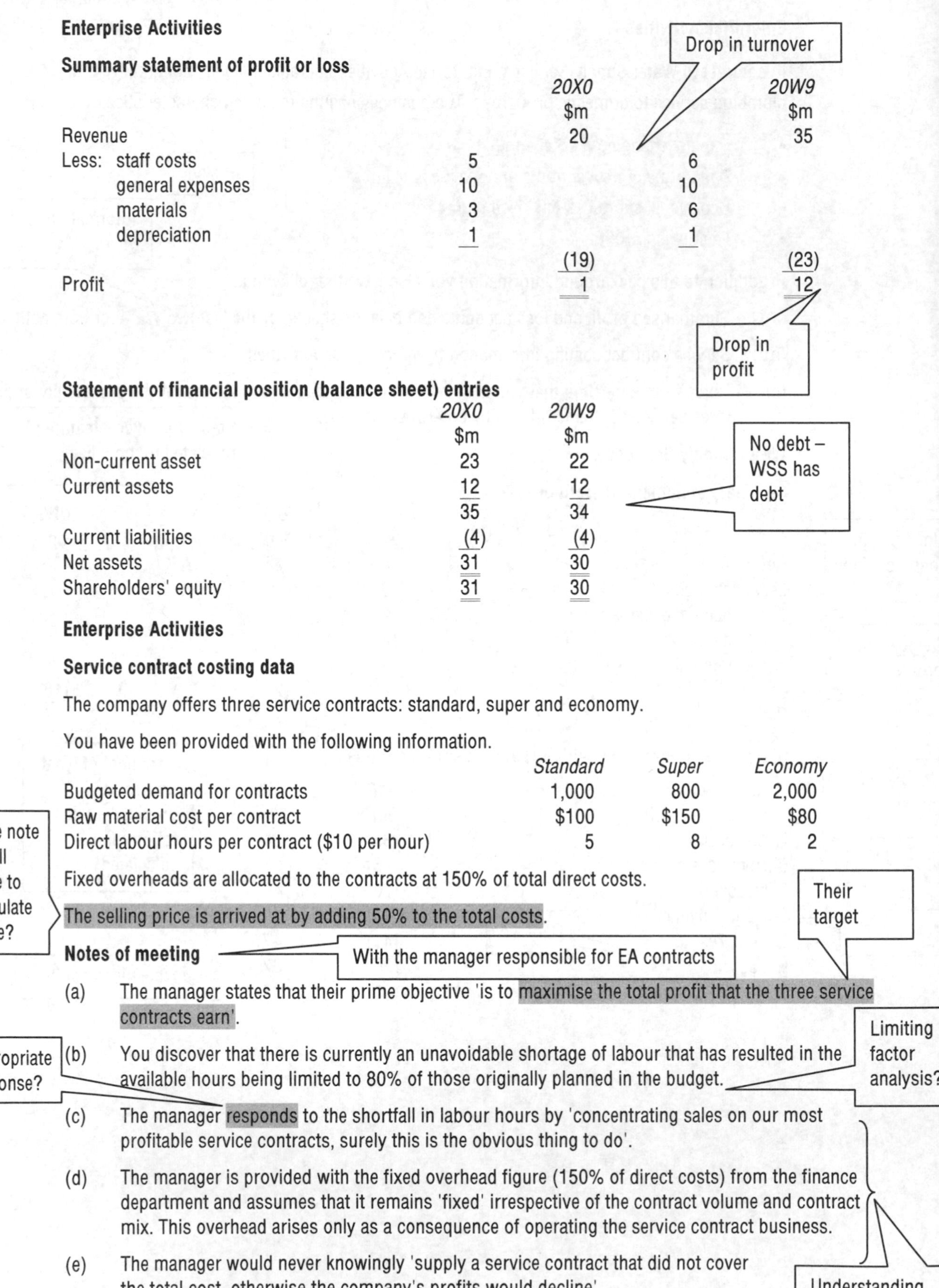

Enterprise Activities

Summary statement of profit or loss

		20X0		20W9
		$m		$m
Revenue		20		35
Less: staff costs	5		6	
general expenses	10		10	
materials	3		6	
depreciation	1		1	
		(19)		(23)
Profit		1		12

Statement of financial position (balance sheet) entries

	20X0	20W9
	$m	$m
Non-current asset	23	22
Current assets	12	12
	35	34
Current liabilities	(4)	(4)
Net assets	31	30
Shareholders' equity	31	30

Enterprise Activities

Service contract costing data

The company offers three service contracts: standard, super and economy.

You have been provided with the following information.

	Standard	Super	Economy
Budgeted demand for contracts	1,000	800	2,000
Raw material cost per contract	$100	$150	$80
Direct labour hours per contract ($10 per hour)	5	8	2

Fixed overheads are allocated to the contracts at 150% of total direct costs.

The selling price is arrived at by adding 50% to the total costs.

Notes of meeting

(a) The manager states that their prime objective 'is to maximise the total profit that the three service contracts earn'.

(b) You discover that there is currently an unavoidable shortage of labour that has resulted in the available hours being limited to 80% of those originally planned in the budget.

(c) The manager responds to the shortfall in labour hours by 'concentrating sales on our most profitable service contracts, surely this is the obvious thing to do'.

(d) The manager is provided with the fixed overhead figure (150% of direct costs) from the finance department and assumes that it remains 'fixed' irrespective of the contract volume and contract mix. This overhead arises only as a consequence of operating the service contract business.

(e) The manager would never knowingly 'supply a service contract that did not cover the total cost, otherwise the company's profits would decline'.

(f) The manager estimates the volume of contracts for budgetary purposes and provides these figures to the finance team. You have compared their past estimates with the actual sales and conclude that they are very accurate with the sales forecast – you can assume that the actual number of contracts sold for any of the three contract types will not be exceeded.

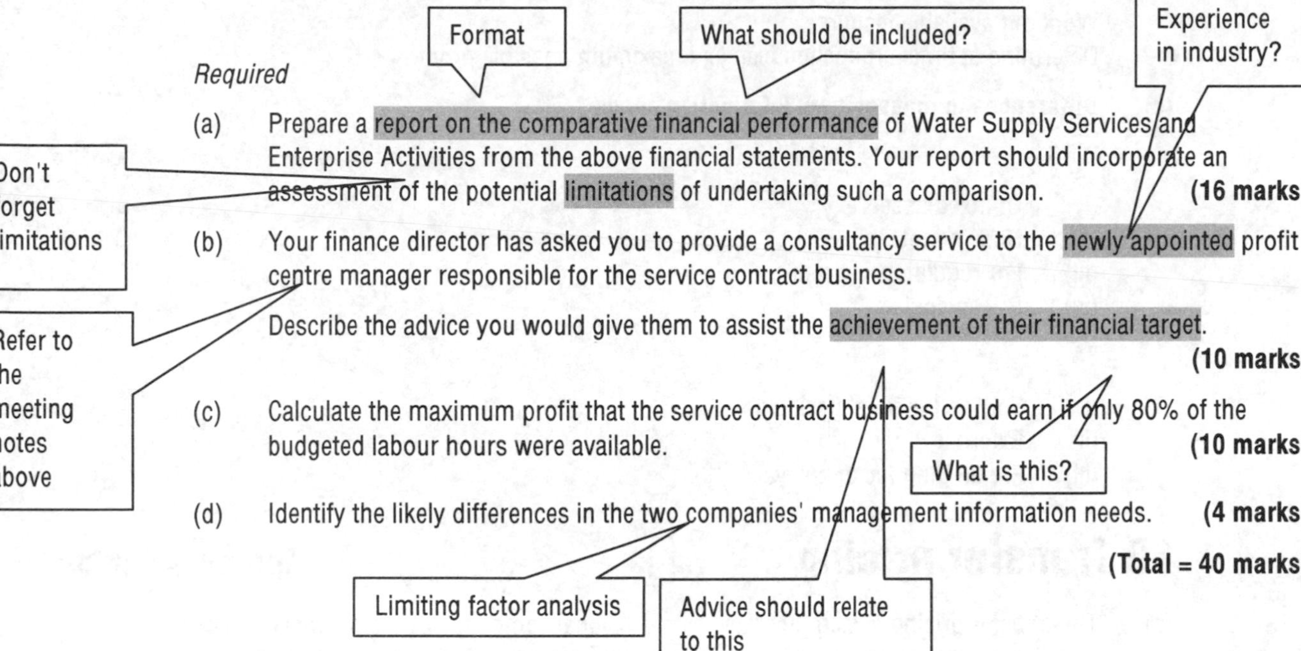

Required

(a) Prepare a report on the comparative financial performance of Water Supply Services and Enterprise Activities from the above financial statements. Your report should incorporate an assessment of the potential limitations of undertaking such a comparison. **(16 marks)**

(b) Your finance director has asked you to provide a consultancy service to the newly appointed profit centre manager responsible for the service contract business.

Describe the advice you would give them to assist the achievement of their financial target. **(10 marks)**

(c) Calculate the maximum profit that the service contract business could earn if only 80% of the budgeted labour hours were available. **(10 marks)**

(d) Identify the likely differences in the two companies' management information needs. **(4 marks)**

(Total = 40 marks)

Answer plan

Not all the points you notice will necessarily be relevant and you may also find that you do not have time to mention all the points in your answer. Now you should prioritise your points in a more formal answer plan and then write your answer.

(a) **Calculation of ratios for each subsidiary for each of the two years**

- (i) Profit margin
- (ii) ROCE
- (iii) Asset turnover
- (iv) Current ratio
- (v) Gearing ratio – not for EA

Analysis of each subsidiary's ratios

Limitations of comparison

- (i) Different markets ⇒ different levels of financial and business risk
  different levels of regulation
  different ways of setting quality standards
- (ii) Focuses on the short term

(b) **What is their target?**

What do they need to understand?

- (i) Relationship between costs/profit/activity level
- (ii) Environment

What advice do they need?

- (i) Pricing policy
- (ii) Budget preparation
- (iii) Limiting factor analysis
- (iv) General business/management eg TQM

(c) **Limiting factor analysis**

Calculate total cost and hence selling price
Calculate contribution per unit of limiting factor
Rank
Work out available resource
Determine optimal production plan and maximum possible profit

(d) **Differences in management information needs**

WSS

(i) On fixed assets
(ii) Non-monetary
(iii) For regulatory reporting
(iv) Prices/costs

EA

(i) For 'on the spot' decisions
(ii) External
(iii) For limiting factor analysis

10 Transfer pricing

Approx. 40 mins

(a) The transfer pricing system operated by a divisional company has the potential to make a significant contribution towards the achievement of corporate financial objectives.

Required

Explain the potential benefits of operating a transfer pricing system within a divisionalised company. **(6 marks)**

(b) A company operates two divisions, Able and Baker. Able manufactures two products, X and Y. Product X is sold to external customers for $42 per unit. The only outlet for product Y is Baker.

Baker supplies an external market and can obtain its semi-finished supplies (product Y) from either Able or an external source. Baker currently has the opportunity to purchase product Y from an external supplier for $38 per unit. The capacity of division Able is measured in units of output, irrespective of whether product X, Y or a combination of both are being manufactured. The associated product costs are as follows.

	X	*Y*
Variable costs per unit	32	35
Fixed overheads per unit	5	5
Total unit costs	37	40

Required

Using the above information, provide advice on the determination of an appropriate transfer price for the sale of product Y from division Able to division Baker under the following conditions.

(i) When division Able has spare capacity and limited external demand for product X **(3 marks)**

(ii) When division Able is operating at full capacity with unsatisfied external demand for product X **(4 marks)**

(c) The design of an information system to support transfer pricing decision making necessitates the inclusion of specific data.

Identify the data that needs to be collected and how you would expect it to be used. **(7 marks)**

(Total = 20 marks)

11 Not-for-profit organisations **Approx. 40 mins**

(a) The absence of the profit measure in non profit seeking organisations causes problems for the measurement of their efficiency and effectiveness.

Required

(i) Explain why the absence of the profit measure should be a cause of the problems referred to. **(7 marks)**

(ii) Explain how these problems extend to activities within business entities which have a profit motive. Support your answer with examples. **(3 marks)**

(b) A public health clinic is the subject of a scheme to measure its efficiency and effectiveness. Among a number of factors, the 'quality of care provided' has been included as an aspect of the clinic's service to be measured. Three features of 'quality of care provided' have been listed.

(i) Clinic's adherence to appointment times
(ii) Patients' ability to contact the clinic and make appointments without difficulty
(iii) The provision of a comprehensive patient health monitoring programme

Required

(i) Suggest a set of quantitative measures which can be used to identify the effective level of achievement of each of the features listed. **(8 marks)**

(ii) Indicate how these measures could be combined into a single 'quality of care' measure. **(2 marks)**

(Total = 20 marks)

12 Abbott and Bartram **Approx. 40 mins**

A company sells a large number of products that are accessories for a certain class of machine. In the UK it has nine salespeople, each of whom is responsible for sales in a separate territory.

Estimates of total market potential are $6.0 million and $7.1 million for 20X1 and 20X2 respectively.

Data for two individual salespeople and for the company as a whole is shown in the box below.

Required

(a) For the average of all nine salespeople and for each of salespeople Abbott and Bartram for 20X2 do the following.

(i) Calculate the following.

(1) Sales potential
(2) Sales penetration percentages
(3) Sales potential per account

(ii) Calculate **eight** relevant measures that would help assess the performance of each salesperson. These measures should be developed from the data given under the following five headings.

(1) Customers
(2) Gross margin
(3) Calls made
(4) Remuneration
(5) Expenses

At least one measure should be calculated for each heading. **(12 marks)**

(b) Assess the performance of Bartram for 20X2 based on a combination of the data in (a) above plus any other data that you consider relevant. **(8 marks)**

	Territory 1	Territory 2	Total UK (including territories 1 and 2)
Territory area ('000 sq km)	7.30	15.40	230.90
Number of machines in territory (millions)	1.65	0.83	12.80
Potential number of accounts	699	423	5,965
Salespeople	Abbott	Bartram	
20X1			
Sales ($'000)	97	101	1,211
Customers (number of accounts)	412	323	3,318
Gross margin ($'000)	34	39	426
Calls made	1,410	1,163	10,901
20X2			
Sales ($'000)	112	123	1,460
Customers (number of accounts)	398	364	3,271
Gross margin	39	47	498
Calls made	1,450	1,220	11,030
Salary ($)	7,100	6,000	60,800
Commission ($)	1,680	1,845	21,585
Total remuneration ($)	8,780	7,845	82,385
Expenses ($)	1,940	3,200	28,060

(Total = 20 marks)

13 JIT systems **Approx. 40 mins**

(a) SW is a member of the SWAL Group of companies. SW manufactures cleaning liquid using chemicals that it buys from a number of suppliers. In the past SW has used a periodic review inventory control system with maximum and reorder levels to control the purchase of the chemicals and the economic order quantity model to minimise its costs.

The Managing Director of SW is considering a change by introducing a just-in-time (JIT) system and has asked you to provide him with some more information about this.

Required

Explain how a JIT system differs from the system presently being used at SW, and the extent to which its introduction would require a review of SW's quality control procedures. **(10 marks)**

(b) The X Group is a well-established manufacturing group that operates a number of companies using similar production and inventory holding policies. All of the companies are in the same country though there are considerable distances between them.

The group has traditionally operated a constant production system whereby the same volume of output is produced each week, even though the demand for the group's products is subject to seasonal fluctuations. As a result there is always finished goods inventory in the group's warehouses waiting for customer orders. This inventory will include a safety inventory equal to two weeks' production.

Raw material inventories are ordered from suppliers using the Economic Order Quantity (EOQ) model in conjunction with a computerised inventory control system which identifies the need to place an order when the reorder level is reached. The purchasing department is centralised for the group. On receiving a notification from the computerised inventory control system that an order is to be placed, a series of quotation enquiries are issued to prospective suppliers so that the best price and delivery terms are obtained for each order. This practice has resulted in there being a large number of suppliers to the X Group. Each supplier delivers directly to the company that requires the material.

The managing director of the X Group has recently returned from a conference on World Class Manufacturing and was particularly interested in the possible use of just-in-time (JIT) within the X Group.

Required

Explain how the adoption of JIT might affect profitability within the X Group. **(10 marks)**

(Total = 20 marks)

14 Connie Head **Approx. 50 mins**

Connie Head was the recently appointed HR manager in a medium-sized accounting firm. Her appointment was a belated recognition by the senior partners of the firm that their ambitious corporate growth goals were linked to the performance of the individual business units and the accountants working in those units. Connie was convinced that performance management and an appraisal system were integral elements in helping the firm achieve its strategic objectives. This reflected her experience of introducing an appraisal system into the corporate finance unit for which she was responsible. The unit had consistently outperformed its growth targets and individual members of the unit were well motivated and appreciative of the appraisal process.

However, the senior partner of the firm remained unconvinced about the benefits of appraisal systems. He argued that accountants, through their training, were self-motivated and should have the maximum freedom to carry out their work. His experience of appraisal systems to date had shown them to lack clarity of purpose, be extremely time consuming, involve masses of bureaucratic form filling and create little benefit for the supervisors or their subordinates. Certainly, he was resistant to having his own performance reviewed through an appraisal system. Connie, however, was convinced that a firm-wide appraisal system would be of major benefit in helping the achievement of growth goals.

Required

(a) Evaluate the extent to which an effective appraisal system could help the accounting firm achieve its goals. **(15 marks)**

(b) Using models where appropriate, assess the contribution, if any, of performance management to the strategic management process. **(10 marks)**

(Total = 25 marks)

15 Eatwell Restaurant

Approx. 50 mins

The owners of The Eatwell Restaurant have diversified business interests and operate in a wide range of commercial areas. Since buying the restaurant in 20X0 they have carefully recorded the data below.

	20X1	*20X2*	*20X3*	*20X4*
Total meals served	3,750	5,100	6,200	6,700
Regular customers attending weekly	5	11	15	26
Number of items on offer per day	4	4	7	9
Reported cases of food poisoning	4	5	7	7
Special theme evenings introduced	0	3	9	13
Annual operating hours with no customers	380	307	187	126
Proposals submitted to cater for special events	10	17	29	38
Contracts won to cater for special events	2	5	15	25
Complimentary letters from satisfied customers	0	4	3	6
Average number of customers at peak times	18	23	37	39
Average service delay at peak times (mins)	32	47	15	35
Maximum seating capacity	25	25	40	40
Weekly opening hours	36	36	40	36
Written complaints received	8	12	14	14
Idle time	570	540	465	187
New meals introduced during the year	16	8	27	11
Financial data				
	$	$	$	$
Average customer spend on wine	3	4	4	7
Total revenue	83,000	124,500	137,000	185,000
Revenue from special events	2,000	13,000	25,000	55,000
Profit	11,600	21,400	43,700	57,200
Value of food wasted in preparation	1,700	1,900	3,600	1,450
Total revenue of all restaurants in locality	895,000	1,234,000	980,000	1,056,000

Required

(a) Assess the overall performance of the business and submit your comments to the owners. They wish to compare the performance of the restaurant with their other business interests and require your comments to be grouped into the key areas of performance such as those described by Fitzgerald and Moon. **(14 marks)**

(b) Identify any additional information that you would consider of assistance in assessing the performance of The Eatwell Restaurant in comparison with another restaurant. Give reasons for your selection and explain how they would relate to the key performance area categories used in (a). **(6 marks)**

(c) Briefly discuss the factors which determine the effectiveness of performance standards used in service organisations. **(5 marks)**

(Total = 25 marks)

16 Glasburgh Trust **Approx. 100 mins**

The Royal Laurel Hospital (RLH) and The King Hardy Hospital (KHH) are government-funded institutions which are managed by the Glasburgh Trust. The following information is available for the year ended 31 May 20X9.

	RLH Actual	*RLH Budget*	*KHH Actual*
Total inpatients	37,000	36,500	40,000
Number of inpatients waiting >5 weeks for admission	3,330	365	320
Number of inpatients waiting >11 weeks for admission	740	0	0
Total outpatients	44,000	43,800	44,000
Number of outpatients waiting >5 weeks for treatment	4,400	2,190	352
Number of outpatients waiting >11 weeks for treatment	1,320	438	220
Number of outpatients waiting >13 weeks for treatment	220	0	0
Achievement (%) of target maximum waiting time of 2 weeks for admission to Rapid Access Chest Pains Clinic	70	98	100
Number of emergency admissions	300	400	300
Number of 12 hour 'trolley' waits for emergency admissions	4	0	0
Achievement (%) of target of 4 hours or less time spent in Accident and Emergency ward	96	98	100
Number of complaints received	1,620	803	420
Number of complaints responded to within 25 days	1,539	803	416
Number of deaths (all inpatients)	600	730	800
Infection control – number of instances of infections reported	2	6	0
Number of drug administration errors	80	100	20
Number of staff shortages	80	60	20
Staff productivity measure (number of patient days per staff member)	8.4	7.4	9.2
Number of times of Government or agency staff usage	80	60	20
Bed occupancy (number of inpatient bed days)	138,750	146,000	134,320
Theatre utilisation (%)	?	?	?
% of inpatients requiring a single operation	80%	80%	80%
Number of operations performed	29,008	?	31,840
Revenue from clinical and non-clinical activities ($m)	54.2	55.2	60.2
Medical staff costs ($m)	22.3	22.2	19.6
Other staff costs ($m)	5.5	5.5	4.0
Income and expenditure surplus margin	(1.0)	0.0	4.0
Number of days cash in hand	31	30	35

Additional information:

(1) Both hospitals were in operation for 365 days during the year.

(2) Each hospital has 42 wards, each of which accommodates 10 beds.

(3) RLH budgeted that each inpatient would require a stay of four days and nights in hospital.

(4) Each hospital has ten operating theatres in each of which an average of nine operations per day were undertaken.

(5) No outpatient required an operation during the year.

(6) The management of the trust uses a 'balanced scorecard' approach in order to assess the performance of each hospital. Their balanced scorecard has four dimensions which are as follows:

(i) Access to services
(ii) Clinical
(iii) Efficiency
(iv) Financial management

In recent years, there has been growing pressure to reduce the financial resources allocated to government-funded organisations across the country in which Glasburgh is located. Increasingly, these organisations are being required to provide an effective service while making more efficient use of scarce resources. Comparative performance indicators are being applied by the providers of resources to organisations which operate within the same sector, such as healthcare provision. These performance indicators provide statistics on expenditure and service delivery and frequently attempt to portray levels of efficiency by producing league tables which rank the organisations being compared.

Required

(a) Discuss the limitations of assessing performance by using comparative data drawn from organisations operating in the same government-funded service sector. **(10 marks)**

Prepare a report to the management of the Glasburgh Trust which:

(b) Critically assesses, on the basis of the above information, the performance of both hospitals for the year ended 31 May 20X9. You should use the four dimensions to perform your assessment as per note (6) above. **(20 marks)**

(c) Evaluates the balanced scorecard used by the Glasburgh Trust and provides recommendations which would improve its usefulness as a performance measurement tool. **(11 marks)**

Professional marks will be awarded for the appropriateness of the format and presentation of the report and the quality of its content. **(4 marks)**

Performance reports, containing detailed performance information similar to that at the beginning of this question, are provided for the hospital Trustees' management meetings which take place every three months.

One of the Trustees has commented that he feels the reports are too detailed, and he finds it difficult to identify the key performance issues which need to be managed. He has asked the management accountant to consider whether any improvements could be made to the content or presentation of the report.

(d) Recommend, with reasons, three improvements which could be made to the content and/or presentation of the current quarterly management report. **(5 marks)**

(Total = 50 marks)

17 CHN Retail chain **Approx. 50 mins**

CHN is a major retail chain based in a European country. The company's competitive strategy is based around emphasising the quality of its products and its customer service, even if this means its products are sometimes more expensive than those sold by other supermarkets.

CHN has recently introduced a vendor managed inventory (VMI) relationship with 15 of its main suppliers. Under the VMI relationship, CHN's suppliers replenish products automatically without CHN raising purchase orders for them. The suppliers have access to CHN's sales quantities and inventory data (via an Electronic Data Interchange (EDI)) and use this to work out when replenishment is needed.

The data available via the EDI is updated on a real-time basis, by the sales data recorded on the electronic point of sale (EPoS) systems in all of CHN's stores. The suppliers also have access to CHN's sales forecasts to allow them to adjust replenishment quantities according to demand predictions.

When the VMI system was introduced, CHN's Operations Director argued that it should allow CHN to reduce inventory levels yet still improve availability, because the suppliers can plan their production and deliveries more efficiently than us in order to supply products as they are needed. The Operations Director pointed out that suppliers typically only deal with a relatively small number of stock lines, whereas CHN's buying department deals with thousands of product lines overall.

At the time the Marketing Director remained critical of the system. He said it would only work if CHN's suppliers are agile and adaptable. He said he felt it was a risk shifting responsibility for the quantity and timing of product deliveries to the suppliers, particularly in the absence of any service level agreements with the suppliers. In addition, he added, 'Only about half of our main suppliers actually deliver what we want, every week. Others continually fail.'

However, initial performance reports suggest that CHN's VMI system is working well, and the company is now looking to add additional suppliers into the relationship. The procurement manager is currently evaluating two existing suppliers who supply similar goods, but he only wants to add one of them onto the list of preferred suppliers under the VMI relationship.

He has rated them on a number of characteristics (below) on a scale from 1 to 10, where 1 is 'very poor', and 10 is 'excellent'.

	Supplier BY	*Supplier KA*
Cost performance	10	8
Quality record	8	9
Reliability (orders fulfilled correctly)	9	10
Dependability of supply (on time deliveries)	7	9
Volume flexibility	8	9
Range of products provided	9	8
Scope to develop new products	7	10
Ease of doing business with	8	8

Required

(a) Evaluate the extent to which the VMI system adds value for CHN's customers. **(6 marks)**

(b) Assess the importance of CHN establishing service level agreements with the suppliers using the VMI system, and identify **two** measures of supplier performance which CHN should include in a service level agreement. **(8 marks)**

(c) Recommend, with reasons, which of the two suppliers CHN should select as its preferred supplier. **(6 marks)**

(d) Briefly discuss the impact which CHN's competitive strategy will have on the performance information which the directors should monitor. **(5 marks)**

(Total = 25 marks)

18 NewsPrint Co

Approx. 30 mins

NewsPrint Co (NPC) is a long-established publisher of local and national newspapers in a European country. In recent years, NPC, like the other major newspaper publishers in its country, has started providing online versions of its newspapers. These are free to view, but they generate advertising revenue from the banner adverts in them.

However, tough economic conditions in NPC's country have led to a decline in advertising revenues since 20X7.

An extract of some key figures from NPC's financial statements is given below.

	20X4 ($m)	*20X9* ($m)
Revenue	382	345
Operating profit	86	72
Net cash flow from operations	46	45
Total debt	175	195

At present, four major publishers have an aggregate market share of 90% of the newspaper market in NPC's country. The current market leader has a 27% market share. The market shares of the other three major publishers, including NPC, are equal in size. All the publishers offer a similar range of newspapers, including both broadsheet newspapers and tabloids, and daily and weekly papers.

The latest market research figures show that the newspaper market for printed newspapers in NPC's country grew 1% in the last year. Despite this finding, some of NPC's directors feel that the newspaper market is declining because fewer people can make time to read printed publications. They are concerned that people are increasingly more likely to watch a television news channel than read a newspaper.

Five years ago, NPC was the market leader with a market share of 29%. However, NPC was slower to develop online versions of its newspapers than its competitors. The main reason for this is that the Chief Executive felt strongly that people would prefer to read printed copies of a paper, and so they resisted the move to develop online versions, despite the remainder of the directors being keen to do so. The reluctance to develop online versions has had an adverse impact on printed sales, rather than protecting them.

However, NPC has now introduced new IT systems across the business, which have enabled it to re-engineer how it publishes content across the printed and online versions of the newspapers. As a result, the business expects to be able to achieve efficiencies and cost savings without any detriment to quality. The new IT systems cost $30m, and NPC took out additional loan financing in 20X8 to pay for them.

However, a number of shareholders have expressed concern that NPC's loss of market share might lead to the end of the company as an organisation, and they have called on the directors to address this issue as a matter of urgency.

Required

Identify and evaluate the problems or indicators which could identify that NPC might fail as a corporate entity.

(Total = 15 marks)

1 SCC

Top tips. The requirement in **part (a)** to **'use'** the BCG matrix to analyse SCC's performance is important because it highlights your primary focus should be on SCC, not on describing the matrix in general terms.

In other words, you need to use the data provided in the scenario to analyse market growth rates and SCC's relative market share for each of the divisions, and then consider what impact this will have on their performance.

Part (b) provides a good example of the difference in the way models are examined in Paper P5 compared to Paper P3. Whereas in P3 the focus is on an organisation's **strategy** (for example, whether to acquire new business units or to divest existing ones), in P5 the focus is on how **performance** is managed and measured.

The key issue in part (b) is to recognise that the performance measures which would be appropriate for one division (eg in a fast-growing market) may not be appropriate for one in a mature or declining market.

Whereas the focus in part (a) is on SCC's performance, the focus in **part (c)** is on the BCG matrix itself. This highlights another important aspect of the P5 syllabus – the need to be able to assess the advantages or disadvantages of different models which could be used in performance management.

Here, you need to focus specifically on the limitations of the BCG matrix, but note you can discuss them in general terms – there is no requirement to link your answer specifically back to SCC.

(a) The BCG matrix can be used to classify business units in relation to the growth rates of the markets they operate in, and their relative market share.

The four categories of classification are:

Stars, which are in a high growth market, with a high relative market share

Cash cows, which are in a low growth market, but with a high relative market share

Question marks, which exist in a high growth market but have a low relative market share

Dogs, which are in markets with low growth, and have a low relative market share

Division	*Five-year market growth*	*Market share – own at 31 May 20X6*	*Relative market share at 31 May 20X6 (*)*
	%	%	
Fashion	75	8.0	8.0 / 8 = 1
Industrial	21	3.1	3.1 / 15 = 0.21
Leisure	9	70.0	70.0 / 70 = 1
Children	67	2.8	2.8 / 28 = 0.1
Footwear	5	2.6	2.6 / 33 = 0.08

* Relative market share is the division's market share divided by the market share of the market leader (as given in the question).

Analysis of SCC's business and performance

Star

Fashion is operating in a market with high growth and it appears to be the market leader (or at least the joint market leader). As such it is a star according to the BCG matrix. By 20X8 it is predicted to have 10% of the market, so it is increasing its market share in a growing market.

However, the short life cycles of individual products means that the division's ability to achieve the growth it wants is likely to depend on its ability to continue to produce popular designs and products – which appeal to the retail store's customers – and which maintain the quality standards expected of them.

Question marks

Industrial is operating in a market with a reasonably high level of growth (21% over five years), but it only has a relatively low market share. Therefore it should be classified as a question mark.

Although it has only been a year since the online ordering facility was introduced, it appears to have little impact on revenues so far. In addition, the Industrial division's overall market share in 20X8 (3.0%) is forecast to be marginally lower than in 20X6 (3.1%), which might suggest that the e-commerce facility has not been very successful.

The **Children's clothing** division also has a low relative market share, but it is operating in a market with very high growth. Currently the market leader controls over one-quarter of the market (28%), and SCC appears to be struggling to break into the market. Its market share is expected to fall from 3.3% in 20X4 to 2.4% in 20X8, despite it selling to the leading retail stores. It seems likely that the division will need additional investment – for example, in marketing and promotions – to help it increase its market share.

Cash cow

Leisure. The leisure division earns 70% of the sales in its market, therefore it is a clear market leader (high relative market share). However, the market itself is only growing slowly, meaning that the division should be classified as a cash cow.

The Leisure division's ability to generate cash to support the growth of other divisions (particularly the Fashion division) is likely to be crucial for the group's continuing success.

Dog

The **Footwear** division has a very low relative market share, and it is operating in a market with low growth, meaning that it should be classified as a dog. The fact that SCC only manufactures a narrow range of footwear limits its opportunities for growth, and the division's revenue as well as its market share is forecast to decline over the next two years.

Overall portfolio

SCC should review its overall product portfolio in the light of this analysis. Within its five divisions, it currently has one dog and two question marks. These will require management's attention to decide about their future. SCC will need to consider whether it can convert the question marks into stars, and what strategies will be required to help them increase their market share. Similarly, management will need to consider whether there is anything which can be done to improve the performance of the footwear divisions, or whether it should be disposed of, or closed.

The leisure division (as a cash cow) is likely to be the key source of funds to invest elsewhere in the group, but it may not produce sufficient cash to sustain the growth of the fashion division (star) as well as the industrial and children's clothing divisions (question marks).

(b) **Context** – The differences in the opportunities for growth between the divisions suggest that it would also be appropriate to focus on different strategies across the divisions. Some of SCC's divisions should be focusing on growth strategies, while others should be focusing on controlling costs.

Performance measures – By recognising these differences in context, managers can then also tailor the performance measures used in each division to their particular circumstances.

The financial performance measures for the high growth divisions (in particular, Fashion, but also Children's clothing) should be based on profit or return on investment. By contrast, the financial performance measures for the low growth divisions (in particular Leisure) should focus on maintaining margins and cash control.

As the amount of net cash generated by the Leisure division is likely to be crucial for supporting growth in the other divisions, this could be a specific measure applied to the Leisure division.

Market share – The BCG analysis also highlights the importance of market share as a performance measure in its own right – particularly in relation to stars or question marks which are pursuing a '**build**' strategy. If SCC is investing in divisions in order to promote their growth, it will be important to monitor whether this investment is paying off (and whether the divisions are growing).

The fast-moving nature of the Fashion division's market means that market share is likely to be a particularly important indicator for it. If the new product ranges are not successful, this is likely to be reflected in a fall in the division's market share.

Market share will also be an important metric for the Leisure division, where SCC should adopt a '**hold**' strategy. Since there is relatively little growth in the market as a whole, SCC will only be able to maintain its revenues if it also maintains its market share. In turn, this also highlights other aspects of performance such as brand reputation and brand loyalty, or customer retention which are likely to be important in the Leisure division.

(c) **Limitations of the model as a performance management tool**

Note. Only two were required, but for tutorial purposes we have included a range of limitations you could have included here.

Problems of definition – Although the BCG matrix can be useful in providing a context for performance management, its usefulness is limited by its simplicity. For example, a business unit is only considered to have a high relative market share if it is greater than 1. By definition, however, this means that only the market leader can have a high market share, and therefore there can only be one star or one cash cow in each market sector.

Choice of axis – The axes themselves are also too simplistic. A high market share is assumed to indicate competitive strength, but this is not necessarily true. A strong brand may yield competitive strength despite a relatively low market share.

Equally, the matrix uses market share to estimate costs associated with given products or business units. The implication here is that there is a link between higher market share and lower costs (for example, due to economies of scale). However, this is not necessarily always the case.

Assumptions behind axes – Similarly, high market growth is deemed to indicate an attractive industry. However, **fast-growing industries are likely to require significant investment**, so they may not be attractive to a firm with limited capital available. Conversely, markets which are declining or not growing significantly can still provide profit potential for firms, particularly if there are high barriers to entry into the markets. However, if a firm focuses its attention on high growth markets this may lead to the profit potential of declining markets being ignored.

Focus on cash resources – The BCG matrix appears to assume that cash is the critical resource for organisations (meaning that 'cash cows' are needed to generate cash to fund the growth of question marks or stars). However, cash is not the only resource organisations need to grow successfully. Question marks and stars are also very demanding on the innovative capacity of managers, designers, engineers etc to underpin growth.

Overlooks possible synergies and relationships between business units – Another issue which arises from the simplicity of the model is that it treats business units in isolation, and in doing so can overlook possible synergies between them. For example, adults who buy SCC's Fashion range may also look to buy clothes from its Children's ranges for their children.

Assumptions about behaviour – The model makes assumptions about behaviour that do not fit every business case. Organisations may choose to stay in certain markets and sectors to avoid risk or to benefit from the interrelationship between businesses.

Defining the market – Although in the scenario, the markets SCC operates in appear to be clearly defined, that is not always the case. Even in this scenario, we could suggest that instead of operating in a range of different 'sub-markets' SCC operates in one large market for 'clothing'.

2 Southside College

Top tips. Part (a) requires you to 'identify' four relevant CSFs. The verb requirement is important here, as is the mark allocation. There are only four marks available for part (a). So you should not have spent time discussing, explaining or justifying the CSFs you choose. You just need to identify them and then move on. The opportunity for explaining and justifying comes in (b).

Nonetheless, make sure you identified CSFs rather than KPIs in part (a).

Similarly, in **part (b)** did you identify KPIs rather than CSFs? KPIs need to be measures of performance, not activities or processes. The key point of a KPI is that it has a measurable aim.

To score well in part (b) it was also important that you gave clear reasons why each of the KPIs you chose were relevant and appropriate to each CSF identified. This is reflected in the relative mark allocations for the two parts of this question: 16 for part (b), compared to 4 for part (a).

The solution below is only a suggestion, and you may well have identified other KPIs to the ones we have in our suggested solution. Provided the KPIs you selected are relevant and appropriate, you would have scored marks for them.

(a) Four critical success factors which would be appropriate to use at SC are:

(i) **Students' satisfaction** with courses and learning materials
(ii) **Staff satisfaction**
(iii) **Quality** of teaching and materials
(iv) **Reputation** and brand image

(b) KPIs for each of the CSFs could be:

Student satisfaction

Student satisfaction rating – At the end of a course, or at the end of a module within a course, students could be asked to complete a questionnaire rating their satisfaction with various aspects of the course (for example, the knowledge levels of the staff, the quality of the supporting materials, and the approachability/availability of staff to ask them questions).

If students are happy with the level of tuition they receive, they are more likely to book on subsequent courses with SC than if they are dissatisfied with the courses or the materials. Similarly, they may share their experiences with their peers, in turn influencing their decision about where to book courses. Consequently, SC needs to ensure that student satisfaction levels are maintained as high as possible, particularly with the increasing number of competitors in entering the professional qualifications market. In this respect, it is important that TDM knows how its students (its customers) feel about the services it offers so that it can improve any areas where it is not performing well.

Percentage of modules with online tutorials available – The online tutorials being offered by SC's competitors appear to be very popular, and may lead students who would otherwise have studied with SC to choose one of its competitors instead. If SC cannot offer the online tutorials it may lead students to think that the level of tuition and service they will receive from SC may be inferior to that offered by the competitors, even though this may not actually be the case.

Staff satisfaction

Staff turnover – The quality of SC's teaching staff is vital in maintaining customer satisfaction, so it is important for SC to retain its best staff. SC has been experiencing an increasing rate of employee turnover, and this could be indicative of dissatisfaction among the staff. The management at SC should be keen to prevent this upward trend in staff turnover from increasing, particularly if SC's best staff are leaving to join competitor organisations. The increase in staff turnover is a problem in itself, but even more so if staff are joining direct competitors – making this a crucial measure to look at.

Staff absenteeism – High levels of absence are likely to also indicate dissatisfaction among the staff. If absenteeism is rising in conjunction with employee turnover, then there is a danger that the quality of service provided to students will suffer. For example, if an experienced lecturer phones in 'sick' at short notice their classes may have to be taken by an inexperienced lecturer who is not such an expert in a subject, meaning the students could receive lower-quality tuition.

Quality of teaching and materials

Market share – SC currently has the largest market share in its sector, despite carrying out relatively little marketing activity, and despite the number of new entrants joining the professional qualifications market in recent years. It will be important for SC to monitor its market share, because the share of the market it can capture will have a direct impact on its revenues and consequently on the wealth of its shareholders.

Customers will only continue to use SC if they feel it is providing courses and materials which are high quality, and also which offer value for money. If its market share starts to fall, it may be an indication that the students feel SC's competitors are offering courses which are better value for money.

Accreditations – SC's courses are accredited by a number of qualification-awarding bodies. SC has always concentrated on the quality of its courses and the accompanying study materials, so external accreditations will provide an independent corroboration of this quality. The quality of course tuition and study materials, in turn, is likely to feed back into the level of customer satisfaction with SC's courses, and the pass rates.

The scenario does not indicate what the accrediting bodies think about the use of online tutorials. However, it is possible that, in time, providing some kind of online tutorial support may become one of the conditions for accreditation.

Reputation and brand image

Brand reputation – SC's management team has never seen the need for market and customer research, given that SC has managed to establish a good reputation and a market-leading position without doing so. However, given the entrance of new competitors into the market, SC will need to ensure that its brand reputation is maintained. This will be very important if SC is to ensure that potential customers will choose to come on its courses rather than going to one of its competitors. Equally, SC will need to ensure that the lack of online tutorials does not damage its reputation; for example, if students think that SC is out of touch with current practices and the new developments in the industry.

Pass rates – SC's students consistently achieve pass rates that are higher than the national average for the qualifications they are sitting. The level of pass rates achieved could be a key factor in students deciding where to study (or for employers deciding where to send their employees to study). If students, or their employers, think that selecting one college in preference to another can affect their chances of passing their exam, they are likely to select the college with the highest pass rate.

Equally, if some of SC's rivals regularly achieve pass rates that are even further above the national average than SC's, the competitors could use this as a marketing message to try to gain market share from SC. Conversely, if SC continues to deliver higher pass rates than its competitors (despite not offering tutorials) this could be an equally powerful marketing message in SC's favour.

3 Kitch Co

Top tips. Make sure you read the requirements carefully before answering this question. Both parts of the requirement have two parts to them, so you must ensure you address all of them.

You should have identified that Kitch Co's current system of budgeting is an incremental. In effect, therefore, **part (a)** requires you to discuss the problems of incremental budgeting, and then consider whether moving to a system of zero-based budgeting would be an appropriate way of solving them. However, your answer should not have been a theoretical discussion of the relative advantages and disadvantages of the different systems of budgeting; instead, it should have been linked directly to the context of the scenario.

Similarly, your answer to **part (b)** also needs to be linked to the scenario. If Kitch does move to a system of zero-based budgeting, this will mean the budgeting process is very different to how it is now. How will the staff react to this change? And how can any resistance to the change be overcome?

(a) **Current system of budgeting**

Lack of staff involvement – The current budgeting system means that Kitch's budgets are set solely by the six directors. However, it appears that the staff who are directly involved in producing and selling Kitch's appliances are not involved in the budget planning process, despite them potentially being more aware of things that could happen to affect costs in the forthcoming year than the directors.

Equally, none of the operational budget holders are involved in the planning system, but instead the budget seems to be imposed on them and they are then expected to achieve it. However, this is **less likely to motivate the staff** to want to achieve the budget than if they had been involved in the budget-setting process, particularly if they feel that some of the budget figures are no longer realistic.

It is possible that, in some cases, staff do not even know what their budget figures are. The scenario does not indicate how the budgets are communicated to the staff, or how widely they are communicated.

Incremental adjustments – The current system means that incremental adjustments are added to the current year's results to allow for known changes. However, unless Kitch's current operations and processes are as efficient and effective as they can be, simply adding incremental adjustments to the current year's figures will **perpetuate any existing inefficiencies**. Equally this approach doesn't give Kitch any incentives to look for ways of **improving performance**.

Encourages slack – The incremental adjustments provided can only take account of known changes but the managers will also be aware that they cannot predict all the possible changes in the next year compared with the current year. Consequently, they may be tempted to **build some slack into the budget**, particularly as their bonuses depend on actual costs being less than budget. The fact that the six managers have earned bonuses in recent years suggests that actual costs have been less than budget, but this may be due to the amount of slack in the budget, rather than efficient cost control. However, in this respect, if a budget contains too much slack then its **value as a control mechanism** is reduced.

Zero based budgeting (ZBB)

Challenges existing cost patterns – In contrast to an incremental approach, a ZBB approach would require individual budget holders to **begin preparing each budget afresh** each year, rather than using the previous year as a base. In addition, managers are required to consider **alternative ways of achieving their objectives**, which may lead to resources being used more efficiently and effectively.

Factors to consider about implementing ZBB at Kitch

The role of budget holders – Currently operational budget holders are not involved in the planning and budgeting process, but they will be integral to the new process. However, their involvement should result in improved forecasts since they have a more detailed knowledge of their areas of the business than the directors.

However, the ZBB planning process is much more **time consuming** than Kitch's current process, which makes it a more costly process in terms of staff time. Moreover, because Kitch has not employed this approach before, the **staff may need training** before it can be introduced.

Cultural issues – If Kitch decides to move to a ZBB approach, there may also need to be a degree of cultural shift involved. Under Kitch's current approach, the budgeting process remains the sole responsibility of the six members of the senior management team, and the budget is then passed down to the rest of the company, in a **top-down approach.**

However, ZBB requires a more **participative approach**, in which operational managers are directly involved in planning and budgeting, which may feel somewhat alien to the senior management team given the current top-down approach. On the other hand, though, if the operational managers are involved in preparing their own budgets, they are likely to accept **more ownership** of the budgets and have a **greater commitment** to ensuring that the budgets are achieved.

More challenging targets – The Finance Director's enthusiasm to move to a ZBB system suggests they believe it will lead to greater efficiency within Kitch Co. Consequently, the budgets under the new system may be more challenging than under the existing system. However, it is important that the managers appreciate that the driver behind the changes is the desire to increase efficiency, rather than to reduce the amount of bonuses payable. This point needs to be communicated clearly (see part (b)), otherwise the managers will resist the new approach.

Impact on Kitch's costs – One of the benefits of adopting a ZBB approach is that it should lead to Kitch's processes becoming more efficient and effective, and therefore costs being reduced. However, there will inevitably be costs associated with introducing ZBB – for example, the additional time taken to prepare the budgets, and the cost of any training. Therefore, before implementing ZBB, Kitch will need to assess whether the potential operational benefits of ZBB (through cost reduction) outweigh the costs of introducing it (through staff and management time spent on budget preparation).

The allocation of resources – One of the biggest differences between the ZBB approach and the existing incremental approach at Kitch is that departments will no longer be entitled to resources simply because they had similar resources the previous year. Under the new approach, each process or cost will have to be justified before it will be included in the next year's budget. However, in order to make these resource allocation decisions, Kitch will need to **establish clear criteria** against which to rank potentially conflicting requests for resources. It is possible that, even with clear criteria, the allocation of resources will require **subjective value judgements**, but this will become inevitable if clear criteria are not established.

Quality and availability of data – Another feature of introducing ZBB will be that it requires Kitch to **analyse its cost behaviour patterns much more closely** than it currently does. As we mentioned in the previous point, every cost has to be justified in order to be included in the next year's budget.

However, in order to do this, Kitch's management information systems need to be able to **produce information in sufficient detail** so that expenditure can be accurately allocated to different functions, or attributed to different processes and products. If Kitch's current information systems are not capable of providing the level of cost information required, then it will be very difficult for Kitch to implement a ZBB system effectively.

(b) **Impact of existing culture** – As we noted in part (a), the ZBB approach will require managers to get involved in their own budgets. However, a legacy of Kitch Co's current approach may be that the managers still try to build in **budgetary slack** in order to try to generate more easily achievable targets, and consequently get as much bonus as they can.

Explanations required – However, this potential problem should be addressed by the nature of the ZBB process itself. The requirement that all costs or processes be justified (for example in terms of the revenues they will generate) should help identify any slack which managers are trying to build into their budgets (for example, where a cost line is disproportionately high in relation to related revenues).

Fear of blame culture – The managers may also be concerned that if they have prepared the detailed budgets themselves, they will then be blamed if the forecast results are not achieved.

However, it is important that this type of blame culture does not develop. The logic of changing the budget model is not to apportion blame, but to involve the people who best understand the costs and processes in each area of the business in setting the budgets for their area of the business.

Importance of communication – In this respect, communication will be very important. It is vital that the FD communicates the message that the change in budget approach is driven by the desire to make Kitch more successful and more competitive, not to make life more difficult for the managers, or to blame them if budget targets are not achieved. By contrast, Kitch should highlight to the managers that the changes give them a greater opportunity to use their knowledge of the business to set the budget targets. If the managers feel they are **more involved in the business decision making**, in the longer term this could actually help increase their motivation.

Resistance to changes in the system – A number of the managers may be sceptical about the motives behind the introduction of a ZBB system. They are likely to be aware that the change in approach could **affect their bonuses**, and may therefore view the change in approach as an attempt to reduce their bonuses.

Importance of communication – Again, **effective communication** will be vital for overcoming this problem. The FD should give the managers a full explanation of the ZBB process, and its potential advantages – both to Kitch as a whole (through increased efficiency or effectiveness) and to the individual managers, by having more realistic budgets. Also, it is very important that the managers still have the opportunity to earn bonuses under the new approach, even if the mechanism for earning them is different.

Changes to bonus scheme – In order to maintain staff morale, the bonus scheme should not be changed without **first consulting the managers and budget holders**. However, the changes to the bonus scheme need not necessarily be seen as a bad thing. At the moment, it appears that bonuses depend on a single measure of performance compared to budget. However, with the more detailed analysis of costs and processes which will be necessary to support the ZBB approach, it should be possible to establish much clearer links between performance outcomes and bonuses received. In this respect, there may even be opportunities for managers to earn increased bonuses if performance exceeds expectations in key performance areas.

The additional workload – The time-consuming nature of the ZBB process is likely to represent a **significant increase in individual managers' workloads**. Managers are likely to resent this, particularly if they have to fit the additional workload around their existing duties.

Phased reviews – One option Kitch Co should consider here is the possibility of staggering the full ZBB budgets over a number of years. A number of functions could be selected to prepare a full ZBB budget each year so that, for example, each function only has to carry out a full ZBB analysis once every three years. In the intervening years, the functions budget could still be prepared on an incremental basis.

4 SPS sports shop

Top tips. The scenario should provide you with plenty of examples of the way that SPS adds value. The trick is to analyse these examples in terms of the value chain model. However, the value chain is actually most applicable to manufacturing businesses so it can be more difficult to apply it to a service business such as a retailer.

In addition, SPS's value activities could be classified in more than one way, 'according to interpretation' so there isn't a single 'right' answer to this question. Although you must avoid obvious errors, such as calling an HRM activity a logistics one, if you can establish a link of some kind between an activity and an aspect of the value chain, you can base your analysis on it, even if another interpretation is possible (eg the allocation of recruitment both to HRM or to procurement (because it is procuring labour to work in the shop).

In effect, **part (a)** of this question required you to look at SPS's current value chain, while part (b) requires you to think about how it may change in the future. So, for **part (b)** you needed to identify, from the activities discussed in part (a), those which may be affected by the e-retail investment. Then you need to 'explain' the effects of the e-retail investment in terms of whether the value added would increase or decrease.

It is obvious that any e-commerce operation dealing with physical goods needs an appropriate system to deliver the items ordered online. This is known as fulfilment, and would be analysed in value chain terms as outbound logistics, an activity that does not currently appear to exist in SPS as described in the narrative.

(a) **Value chain activities**

Value chain activities, using Porter's model, can be depicted as follows:

(i) **Firm infrastructure**

The location, design and layout of SPS's shops enhance customer convenience and satisfaction and are therefore important sources of value. Firm infrastructure, as described by Porter, includes such continuing administrative activities as planning and accounting, while buildings and furnishings are assets rather than activities. However, the decision-making processes that resulted in the current benefit derived by SPS from its fixed assets certainly qualify as important value activities.

(ii) **Human resource management**

SPS's staff are enthusiastic and knowledgeable; they are helpful and provide excellent customer service. As is heavily emphasised by the extended marketing mix, the degree of success achieved by a service business such as SPS is heavily dependent on the people it employs. SPS has both recruited and trained its employees with great care and the company's shops are now staffed by people who make a major contribution to the value it creates through the way that they do their work.

(iii) **Procurement**

SPS's range of goods in stock is far wider than those of its competitors, which provides its customers with a greater degree of choice and an improved likelihood that they will be able to purchase items suited to their needs and wants. These factors are likely to have a positive effect on both footfall (the rate at which potential customers visit the premises) and on actual sales. SPS is in this position as a result of developing close relationships with major manufacturers, which is an important procurement activity. The potential downside to this is that SPS's inventory holding costs are likely to be higher than those of its rivals.

(iv) **Technology development and inbound logistics**

The company has developed a sophisticated inventory control system that can be used to locate any desired item that is in stock in SPS's shops or warehouse; it can also be used to check the availability of stock with the manufacturer. This system is likely to provide significant enhancement to customer satisfaction and thus to sales. The potential downside to this advantage is the cost of developing the system.

(v) **Marketing**

The managers of SPS's shops have recently carried out a customer survey. This is an important aspect of customer communications and a proper customer focus: it is important to know what customers think of the company's market offering.

(b) (i) **Firm infrastructure**

The location, design and layout of SPS's shops will remain an important source of value, although this may be reduced as physical stores give way to 'virtual' online displays and sales. In essence, SPS would move from having a purely physical infrastructure to having a mixed physical and online infrastructure. Sales revenue through the stores will decrease as some existing customers choose to shop online, but the associated costs of operating the stores will substantially remain. However, it is likely that SPS's overall turnover will increase as a result of starting its online store. Although there will be some cannibalisation of the existing shop sales, it should expect the online store to also generate some new, incremental business. The e-retail avenue may increase the added value of point of sale infrastructure, by enhancing the perceived offering to customers (in terms of convenience, empowerment and potentially an entertaining online experience), generating additional sales revenue at lower administrative cost.

(ii) **Human resource management**

Given that customers continuing to use the retail stores will be doing so primarily because of the human service element, the capacity of SPS's staff to add value within the offline retail segment should be increased. This will, however, be diluted in overall terms by the shift in sales to e-retail, where customer value is not significantly added by human intervention. The focus of HR added value may shift to skills in the design and implementation of the e-retail system: the ability of IT staff to deliver a quality service at lower administrative/maintenance cost to the firm.

(iii) **Procurement**

The e-retail system should increase the added value of SPS's supply strategies and inventory control systems. It will enable the full range of goods stocked to be visible to all customers, regardless of location, maximising the value of an attribute highly valued by customers.

The e-retail system should also support better-quality information sharing with suppliers, enabling better demand forecasting and delivery performance throughout the supply chain. This may enable SPS to add further value through just-in-time supply strategies, thereby reducing the amount of working capital tied up in inventories.

Meanwhile, procurement has potential to add new value through the procurement of IT infrastructure, equipment and services – perhaps through managing an outsourced IT support. There may be a further role in managing outsourced fulfilment activities: many e-retail organisations outsource their warehousing and distribution systems to specialists who can cope with the greater volume of small transactions.

(iv) **Technology development and inbound logistics**

Integration of the e-retail system with the existing inventory control system should increase its potential to add value. It will empower customers to access stock availability information, generate orders and track orders at lower cost than via sales staff intervention. The system should also allow real-time updating of inventory figures – and triggering of stock replenishment – in response to online purchases: this increases the potential for reduced costs through fully automated and integrated e-procurement.

(v) **Marketing**

The addition of an e-retailing capacity has the potential to add considerable value to the firm's marketing activities. It presents highly flexible, controllable and cost-efficient opportunities for information, advertising, purchase incentives (eg online loyalty schemes and sales promotions), public relations (eg posted media releases), relationship marketing (eg gathering customer data, encouraging registration, site personalisation, email permission marketing) and so on. It particularly enhances market/customer research, by replacing customer survey data with data about actual customer browsing and purchase patterns and preferences.

(vi) **Additional value-adding activities**

It should also be noted that e-retail will create potential for new value-adding activity in the area of outbound logistics, which currently operates within the internal supply chain only (warehouse to outlets) and represents cost without generating revenue. This is a 'waste' activity, which can be reduced by supplying direct from the warehouse to the customer. Prompt, reliable and trackable delivery is a major contributor to customer satisfaction, so outbound logistics has the potential to create significant value – although the greater frequency and smaller value of deliveries will also create new costs.

In value chain terms, service means after-sales service. This is likely to be minimal at the moment and consists largely of dealing with returned faulty goods. With e-retailing, it will be necessary to offer a more comprehensive reverse-logistics service – which again both adds value and incurs cost.

5 Nadir Products

Part (a)

Top tips. While this question clearly has an important ethical slant, it is important to deal with the commercial impact of the proposed courses of action. If you feel your experience has not prepared you to do this, think in terms of stakeholder theory and ask yourself what connected stakeholder groups (such as an organisation's customers) are reasonably entitled to expect and how **you** would react to these ploys.

Do not spend more than a minute on dealing with the report form requirement: a suitable heading and, perhaps, numbered paragraphs are all that is required. A short introductory paragraph giving the reason for the report is a good way to get started.

REPORT

To: Board Members, Nadir Products
From: A Consultant
Date: December 20X6
Subject: Proposed adjustments to revenue reporting

You asked me to comment on the commercial and ethical implications of suggestions that had been made about the value of this year's revenue. There was concern that a current decline in sales will adversely affect the level of bonuses paid to senior staff.

My first comment is that the **assumption behind the suggestions appears wrong**. The aim of the bonus scheme was surely to provide an incentive for senior staff to take appropriate action to improve performance. If performance has not improved, it would be perverse to adjust the numbers so that they receive the bonuses anyway. There is an element of **moral hazard** here: if the bonuses are in effect guaranteed and not dependent on improved performance, the incentive effect disappears and the scheme might as well be abandoned.

I understand that there is concern that staff will be adversely affected by the downturn in sales value. However, I must point out the **questionable nature of the suggestions** from an ethical point of view. It is likely that the detailed proposals will create a **conflict of interest** since each has the potential to disadvantage shareholders. It would be ethically inappropriate to pursue any course of action that reduced shareholder value in order to enrich senior staff.

I will now examine the individual proposals.

Discount for additional sales. A discount is an unexceptional sales promotional device that may be used, for instance, to increase or defend market share or to shift excess inventory. It has a cost, in the form of reduced margin, and it is a matter of commercial judgement to decide whether the benefit is greater than the cost. It may also have the effect of merely bringing sales forward in time, so that later trading periods suffer.

Of the three suggestions, this is the most defensible. However, it is quite **indefensible** if it is undertaken solely in order to boost bonuses, because of the conflict of interest discussed above.

Bringing forward scheduled orders is a form of window dressing. Your auditors will deploy checks on such activities as a matter of course, and may succeed in detecting this. The accounts would then have to be adjusted, since there is no commercial justification for the practice. It can be seen as detrimental to shareholders since the reported profit would be overstated and, while this may have a positive effect on share value in the short term, were it ever discovered, it would bring into question the company's **corporate governance**. Such a scheme is also likely to irritate customers who may respond by delaying payment and even seeking a new supplier. This would clearly disadvantage the company.

This suggestion is **unacceptable** on both ethical and practical grounds.

Warning of possible price rises. I take it as read that there are no actual plans to raise prices? If this is the case, to say that such plans exist is **untruthful** and therefore inappropriate for a company that wishes to maintain high ethical standards. Further, to hide behind a form of words such as 'there **may** be price rises' would be equally dishonest, since the intention would be to create a specific, incorrect impression in customers' minds. When the warning is eventually shown to be spurious, customers' estimation of the company will fall, with an eventual knock-on effect on revenue.

This ploy is comparable to the previous one in its potential effect on shareholders and customers but is even more unethical.

Conclusion. None of the suggestions is acceptable ethically or commercially as a solution to the senior staff bonus problem.

Part (b)

Top tips. You will have realised that there is very little in the scenario that is directly related to the issue of corporate social responsibility.

One of our aims in preparing the suggested solution below was to demonstrate how it is possible to relate an answer to such a question. You will notice that we have used a little deduction and suggestion to achieve this effect. By using this technique you can include some (relevant) points which are not directly referred to in the scenario.

However, you must use such an approach with caution! You must stick to the point and not wander off into regions you like the look of but which have no connection to the question as set.

The **stakeholder view** is that many groups have a stake in what the organisation does. This is particularly important in the business context, where shareholders own the business but employees, customers and government also have particularly strong claims to having their interests considered. It is suggested that modern corporations are so powerful, socially, economically and politically, that unrestrained use of their power will inevitably **damage other people's rights**. Under this approach, the exercise of corporate social responsibility constrains the corporation to act at all times as a **good citizen**. Particular emphasis is laid on the preservation of employment and protection of the environment.

We are not told the extent of Nadir Products' operations. If, as seems likely, they are largely confined to the UK, or at least to the EU, the company's activities will be subject to fairly demanding **legal requirements** concerning such basic aspects of good corporate citizenship. They must conform or court legal sanctions.

Another argument points out that corporations exist within society and are dependent on it for the **resources** they use. Some of these resources are obtained by direct contracts with suppliers but others are not, being provided by **government expenditure**. Examples are such things as transport infrastructure, technical research and education for the workforce. Clearly, Nadir Products contributes to the taxes that pay for these things, but the relationship is rather tenuous and the tax burden can be minimised by careful management. The company can do as much or as little as it cares to in this connection.

Mintzberg suggests that simply viewing organisations as **vehicles for shareholder investment** is inadequate, since in practice, he says, organisations are rarely controlled effectively by shareholders. Most shareholders are passive investors. We do not know whether or not this is the case with Nadir Products.

Many organisations regard the exercise of corporate social responsibility as valuable in promoting a **positive corporate image**. The management of Nadir Products therefore may feel that it is appropriate to take an **instrumental approach** to such matters as sponsorship and charitable giving. Charitable donations and artistic sponsorship are useful media of public relations and can reflect well on the business. They can be regarded as another form of promotion which, like advertising, serves to enhance consumer awareness of the business. It would be necessary for the company to ensure that the recipients of its generosity were appropriate to its operations at the bottom end of the market: grand opera would probably be inappropriate.

The arguments for and against social responsibility are complex ones. However, ultimately they can be traced to different assumptions about society and the relationships between the individuals and organisations within it. It is unlikely to be something that needs to occupy a great deal of the time of Nadir Products' directors.

6 Lithio Car

Top tips. Although this question clearly requires you to identify the strength of the competitive forces (as described in the scenario), it is important that you think specifically about the impact these could have on Lithio Car's performance, rather than, for example, how they could be used to assess the attractiveness of the industry as a whole.

Similarly, where the competitive forces are strong, this could indicate areas where it is particularly important for Lithio to measure its performance – to see how it is coping with the threat of those forces. Remember, the question requirement asks about the implications that the business environment could have on performance management at Lithio Car, not just on the company's performance.

Importantly, although the requirement mentioned Porter's five forces model by name, you needed to use the model as a framework for answering the question, and so you should not have spent time discussing each of the forces in general terms. Instead, a useful way of approaching this question would have been to use each of the forces as a heading for your answer, and then to look in turn at the potential impact each force could have on Lithio Car's performance.

One final point to note: Porter's five forces model is traditionally used to assess the state of competition in an industry, and therefore the level of profitability which can be sustained in that industry. But what industry does Lithio Car actually compete in? The new car industry as a whole? Or does it have a narrower focus (ie environmentally friendly cars)?

Scope of industry – Before looking at the detail of each of the five forces, it is important to identify the potential differences in the scope of the industry which Lithio Car is competing in, because these differences in scope will affect the extent of the competition in the 'industry'. The 'industry' could be seen as the car industry as a whole, or just that sector of the car industry which makes vehicles with reduced emissions (such as the hybrid car); it could possibly even be extended to mean the 'transport' industry as a whole, thereby including public transport or (motor)cycles. When analysing the five forces in relation to Lithio Car, it is therefore important to recognise the different levels at which the competitive forces could be acting.

Substitute products

Existence of substitutes – The threat of substitute products is linked, in part, to developments in technology. For the car industry as a whole, there is currently no clear successor to conventional petrol and diesel fuelled cars, although a number of alternatives (such as the Lithio Car and hybrid cars) are available, or under development (such as the hydrogen car). However, the production of these new alternatives remains very low, so the threat to the profitability of the industry remains relatively low.

Low emission cars – Nonetheless, if we define petrol cars and reduced emission cars as being different industries, then petrol cars are substitutes for low emission cars. In this respect, Lithio Car's performance will depend on how attractive its cars are compared with traditional petrol cars. The figures in Table 1 indicate that the Lithio Car is more expensive, is slower, and has a lower range. By contrast, the Lithio Car is much cheaper to run and is more environmentally friendly.

Consequently, it depends on which aspects of performance customers value more as to whether they will view the Lithio Car as an attractive substitute to a petrol car. In turn, the nature of customer preference in this respect will also affect Lithio Car's performance: if demand for low emission cars in general increases, then Lithio Car should likewise see its volume of sales and its revenues increasing.

Public transport and cycling – Furthermore, there may be a popular movement to 'do without cars' completely. If there is a cheap, reliable and frequent public transport system available, people could choose to use this in preference to cars, which would lead to lower demand for private cars overall. Such an option may be attractive to 'green' consumers, who might otherwise look to buy a Lithio Car in preference to a traditional car. Cycling could also pose a threat to cars, combining a non-polluting alternative with exercise and addressing problems of obesity and associated health issues.

Bargaining power of consumers

Switching costs – If we take the car industry as a whole, then the switching costs for a consumer are relatively low: the consumer simply sells their existing car and purchases a different one.

However, by targeting a specific niche in the market, Lithio Car may be reducing the bargaining power of consumers in this respect. The Lithio Car appeals to a segment of buyers who are prepared to pay a **premium price for the more environmentally friendly product**. Therefore, although the cost of the product is relatively higher than traditional cars, consumers do not actively seek out cheaper alternatives. The consumers know these alternatives exist, but they choose not to purchase them because of their 'green' ideals.

This has important **performance management implications** for Lithio Car. First, it suggests that Lithio Car's critical success factors need to focus on producing the most environmentally friendly car, rather than the cheapest or fastest. Second, it also suggests that the scope for increasing market share of the total car market over time is likely to depend on the number of consumers who value having an environmentally friendly car.

Threat of new entrants

Scope for new entrants – In the same way that Lithio Car was a new entrant to the market following the development of its patented process, so technological developments mean there will always be a threat of new entrants into this market. And the uncertainty about what type of car will prove the long-term successor to petrol cars may increase this threat.

Barriers to entry – However, establishing a car manufacturing factory will require considerable capital investments, and this is likely to deter some potential entrants. Lithio Car was able to overcome these barriers to entry with the help of grants and interest-free loans. These incentives are unlikely to be available in all countries, or even in all regions of Exland, given that the grants Lithio Car attracted are likely to be linked to the high unemployment and industrial decline in its region.

Threat of acquisitions – However, Mega Motors' offer to buy Lithio Car is interesting here, because it highlights the threat of existing 'traditional' car manufacturers entering the market for low emission cars. In such a case, the capital requirements are not likely to be a barrier to entry.

The possible entry of larger manufacturers into what is currently a niche market could have very important implications for Lithio Car. The presence of larger manufacturers is likely to lead to an increase in the production of low emission cars, but more importantly it could also lead to the price of the cars being lowered as the large manufacturers take advantage of their existing economies of scale in car production more generally.

Assuming that Lithio Car remains an independent company, then two aspects of performance management could become crucial here. On the one hand, Lithio Car could look at whether it could improve the efficiency (and therefore lower the cost) of any aspects of its production, such that it could lower its prices if necessary.

On the other hand, Lithio Car may look at whether it could develop and patent any additional processes which would further differentiate it from any potential new entrants. In this respect, monitoring the number of patents Lithio Car holds could be an important performance metric.

Bargaining power of suppliers

The scenario does not indicate the strength of the bargaining power of suppliers in the industry. In general terms, supply chains in the car industry are often tightly linked which makes it harder to switch suppliers. Therefore, although it may not be a problem for large car manufacturers to switch suppliers, since they are much larger than their supplier companies, it could be a problem for a small manufacturer like Lithio Car.

Labour supply – The availability of skilled labour appears to be a problem for Lithio Car. Labour can also be seen as a supply, and the shortage of skilled labour is leading to an increase in the bargaining power of skilled workers. This has been reflected in the increased wages and staff costs at the factory.

In this respect, monitoring staff costs as a proportion of total costs will be important for Lithio Car, because the increasing staff costs are likely to put pressure on the company's profit margins. If staff costs continue to increase, Lithio may have to investigate whether any of its production processes can be automated (if they are not already), or whether any of them can be outsourced to reduce the company's demand for in-house labour.

Competitive rivalry

Industry structure – In the car industry as a whole there are many competing firms, and buyers can switch easily from one make of car to another. The industry has high fixed costs and the cost of leaving the industry is high. Thus competitive rivalry in the car industry is high.

Scope of industry – Again, however, the question of scope is important here. In the environmentally friendly sector, there are not as many competing firms, and they tend to be fairly well differentiated (as, for example, between the Hybrid1 and the Lithio Car). Therefore, the competitive rivalry would appear to be lower in the environmentally friendly sector than in the car marketplace as a whole.

In this respect, as with substitutes, the prevailing notion of 'the industry' may play an important part in shaping Lithio Car's performance. If the consumers view low emission cars as a separate market, then Lithio Car is likely to be able to sustain higher profits than if consumers treat low emission cars as direct competitors for traditional cars.

Competitor analysis – Nonetheless, competitive rivalry within Lithio Car's niche of the market will increase if competitors start producing similar cars. Therefore, it will be important for Lithio Car to monitor its competitors' activities, to gauge whether any of them are planning to launch rival products.

7 KLL

Top tips. You have probably been told this many times already since you started your ACCA studies, but always make sure you provide an answer in the **format requested**. Here you are asked to provide a memo, which is normally used for fairly informal situations. However, note the recipients: board members will expect a certain level of **formality** in terms of both language and structure.

You may find that your answer did not cover all the points mentioned in ours and that you needed to rely to a large extent on knowledge picked up in other papers. Don't worry at all if this is the case. By the time you have worked through Part C of this Study Text you should feel far more confident about discussing information systems in terms of the requirements of **this** paper.

The **qualities of good information** could have been used as a framework for an answer plan. By comparing the type of information provided by the existing MIS to the information actually required by employees and management in terms of the qualities, you could have covered the second part of the requirement in particular (ie the benefits the MIS could bring).

Importantly, though, note that the requirement asks you to explain two different things in your memorandum: (i) the purposes of a new MIS; and (ii) the benefits that it could be expected to bring. Make sure you address both of these different elements in your answer.

MEMORANDUM

To: All board members
From: Your name
Subject: Purposes and benefits of a Management Information System
Date: December 20X1

KLL requires a new management information system to provide more detailed information on the various activities of the company. The existing MIS is limited in the information that it can provide, and the directors have identified additional information that would help them control and develop the business. This memo summarises the purposes and benefits that can be obtained from a modern management information system.

Purposes of a management information system

A MIS is a system to convert data from internal and external sources into information and to communicate that information, in an appropriate form, to managers at all levels in all functions to enable them to make timely and effective decisions for planning, directing and controlling the activities for which they are responsible. The MIS is therefore established in a company to satisfy the information needs of management.

Within KLL, the directors will already be aware of this objective of a MIS because the company already has a MIS. The limitations of that MIS are now apparent, however, because activities cannot be split between those that are profit making and those that are loss making.

Benefits of a MIS

The benefits of a MIS are summarised below, focusing particularly on the requirements of KLL.

(a) **Provision of financial information**

The existing MIS can provide some financial information, although the limitations of this information have been recognised by the directors. This limitation may well be a function of an older MIS being designed to produce specific reports rather than holding the data in some form of database and then different reports being generated from that data as required.

A new MIS should store data in a less rigorous format, enabling different reports to be produced as required. Details of profit- and loss-making sports can therefore be obtained.

(b) **Provision of more timely information**

The current MIS produces reports on a monthly basis. It is not clear whether this is a system limitation or whether reports have not been requested on a more frequent basis. However, monitoring the profitability of individual sports activities may benefit from more frequent provision of information. For example, if a competitor starts pricing activities below the price charged by KLL, then an immediate response will be required, rather than waiting up to a month to amend prices.

A modern MIS should be able to provide information on a daily, if not real-time, basis to enable the directors to make quicker and more effective decisions.

(c) **Provision of summary information**

The managing director is concerned about the inappropriate level of detail being provided by the MIS. If the detail cannot be interpreted (per the question) then it is likely that the MIS is producing information at an operational level, rather than a strategic or tactical level. The detail is available, but this has not been summarised appropriately. It is possible, for example, that income from individual games of squash can be seen, but not the total income for each court or for the sport squash itself for each week or month.

The new MIS will provide a summary of income initially, with the ability to provide more operational information as necessary using the 'drill down' ability of many information systems. Focusing the information at the strategic level first, rather than the operational, should provide the managing director with the appropriate level of detail.

(d) **'Better' information**

The managing director is also concerned about the lack of 'good' information. This appears to be linked to the comment concerning the limited technical knowledge of staff and poor support from the software company. It is therefore possible that staff either have a lack of training in the use of the MIS or they are producing bespoke reports, and are not receiving the support from the supplier to help them do this. The board is not receiving good information because reports are not sufficiently focused on the activities of KLL.

Whether the situation actually needs a new MIS to resolve it remains unclear. It is possible that appropriate training or support would enable staff to provide the appropriate reports for the board. Alternatively, more recent MIS programmes normally provide an easy to use report generator so staff should find it easier to produce the necessary reports.

Alternatively, data can be exported into a spreadsheet package for additional analysis and production of visual aids, such as charts and graphs, as necessary.

(e) **Staff morale**

Providing a new MIS will have other benefits for the company, such as increased staff morale and a better working environment. Staff are likely to be more motivated because the company is providing the software that is needed to carry out their job.

8 Cobra Golf Club

Top tips. The key to this answer is given in **part (a)** of the question – information overload. The extract from the golf club accounts is an example of reporting that provides too much detail and too little information. This is all you need to extract from the figures; do not waste any time trying to analyse the numbers in the extract from the accounts. Remember, this question is about the performance report itself, not about the golf club's performance.

Notice that part (a) does not require any application to the scenario: it is simply asking you to explain what information overload is.

However, you do then need to apply your knowledge to **part (b)**. Clearly one of the weaknesses of Cobra's reporting system is that of information overload, but it is not the only one. Note also that once you have identified the weaknesses, you then need to recommend changes that could be made – to help address the weaknesses.

(a) **Information overload**, as the term suggests, refers to the provision of excess amounts of information. In management reporting information overload occurs when management are given excessive amounts of detail in their reports.

Problems of excess information – Excessive information can significantly reduce the value of the information actually provided. This is because a manager receiving the reports may not identify significant items of data that are 'hidden' by large quantities of unimportant data. Unless key items of information are identified, they will not be acted upon, and the value of the information will be lost.

Impact on management time – Information overload can also waste management time, by requiring managers to try to absorb all the information in a report. Greater quantities of information take longer to read and understand. For this reason, managers may restrict reading reports to looking at one or two figures that they consider to be important.

Although supporting information may be provided in extensive detail, an important principle of management reporting is to draw management attention to the critical aspects of performance. This may be done through **exception reporting** or the use of **key performance indicators**.

(b) The main weakness of the reporting system at Cobra is information overload. The club has a problem with insufficient income or excessive expenditure, but it is not clear from the report where the problem exists.

There are several ways in which the information overload may be reduced.

(i) Some of the columns of information on page 1 (and so possibly on pages 2, 3 and 4 as well) may be superfluous and add little, if anything, of value. The annual budget figures service no purpose, because there is nothing to compare them with and for most items the annual budget is the monthly budget for the item multiplied by 12. It is not clear why figures for both the budget and last year are required. One or the other should be sufficient for control reporting; therefore the columns for the current month and the year to date should probably be removed for 'last year', leaving just the budget figures for comparison in the report.

(ii) Some of the line items seem quite small in value. It may be appropriate to combine these into a 'miscellaneous' items line, provided that variances between actual and budget are not. (In this report, however, there is quite a large line item for miscellaneous administrative expenditure and the variance for the month and year to date is fairly large. This is consequently an item where more management information rather than less might be appropriate.)

(iii) It is not clear why an end of month balance sheet (statement of financial position) should be required.

(iv) Similarly, the value of a comparison between budgeted and actual capital expenditure for the year to date does not provide anything of obvious practical value.

(v) Finally, on the subject of information overload, it is not clear that the board should be concerned with a detailed list of aged debtors. Collecting money from customers (either corporate or individual) should be a responsibility for the accountant, not the board, and the board should only be informed if a serious problem arises with collections or bad debts.

Feedforward control – It would seem to be useful to provide feedforward control information, comparing the budgeted results for the year with a current forecast. Unfortunately, the current forecast appears to be constructed using weak assumptions – adding actual results for the year to date to the budget for the remainder of the year. If the budget figures are known to be 'wrong' and unachievable, using budgeted figures to produce a revised forecast will simply produce an unreliable current forecast. This could provide very misleading control information.

Exception reporting – A monthly reporting system should make use of exception reporting. Exceptional differences between budget and actual figures, or between budget and current revised forecast, can be highlighted, for example in a different colour. In addition, a covering report from the general manager should refer to the exceptional items and their apparent causes. Exception reporting will enable management to focus on what appears to be significant in the monthly results.

9 Aqua Holdings

(a) **WSS**

	20X0	*20W9*
ROCE = $\left(\frac{\text{profit before interest}}{\text{capital employed}} \times 100\%\right)$	$\frac{14}{167} \times 100\% = 8.4\%$	$\frac{17}{134} \times 100\% = 12.7\%$
Sales margin = $\left(\frac{\text{profit before interest}}{\text{sales}} \times 100\%\right)$	$\frac{14}{31} \times 100\% = 45\%$	$\frac{17}{30} \times 100\% = 57\%$
Asset turnover = $\frac{\text{sales}}{\text{capital employed}}$	$\frac{31}{167} = 0.19$	$\frac{30}{134} = 0.22$

	20X0	20W9
Gearing ratio = $\frac{\text{long-term debt}}{\text{long-term debt + equity}}$	$\frac{47}{120 + 47} = 0.28$	$\frac{47}{87 + 47} = 0.35$
Current ratio = $\frac{\text{current assets}}{\text{current liabilities}}$	$\frac{5}{3} = 1.7$	$\frac{6}{6} = 1.0$
EA		
ROCE	$\frac{1}{31} \times 100\% = 3.2\%$	$\frac{12}{30} \times 100\% = 40.0\%$
Sales margin	$\frac{1}{20} \times 100\% = 5.0\%$	$\frac{12}{35} \times 100\% = 34.3\%$
Asset turnover	$\frac{20}{31} = 0.65$	$\frac{35}{30} = 1.17$
Gearing ratio	0	0
Current ratio	$\frac{12}{4} = 3$	$\frac{12}{4} = 3$

Water Supply Services

WSS's profits have fallen both in absolute terms (due to the $3 million increase in depreciation) and in relative terms. The organisation's rate of asset turnover has also fallen, although this is to be expected, as it often takes time for new assets to generate sales.

A fall in the level of the organisation's current liabilities has led to a marked increase in the current ratio and so the organisation's liquidity gives no immediate cause for concern.

The increase in shareholders' equity has lowered the gearing ratio but a significant proportion of the organisation's assets are funded by debt.

Shareholders may not have been too impressed by the fall in profits given the increase in their holdings.

Enterprise Activities

In contrast with the relative stability of WSS's revenue (an established feature of a regulated monopoly), EA's sales revenue has dropped dramatically, with a consequent substantial decline in profit in relative and absolute terms.

Unlike WSS, EA has no long-term debt. This may be because EA management felt that fixed interest payments would be impossible, given the rapidly changing market and the volatility of profits.

Like WSS, EA appears to be able to meet its future commitments to pay off its current liabilities (as indicated by the current ratio).

Limitations of undertaking comparisons of financial performance

(i) The markets in which the two organisations operate are completely different.

(1) **The markets are subject to different levels of financial and business risk**. This will have a significant impact on the expectations of shareholders and their required level of organisational performance and return.

(2) **The highly regulated nature of WSS's operating environment** means that high profits resulting from effective management might lead to the imposition of price cuts if profits are subject to regulation and are deemed excessive. On the other hand, inefficiency and high levels of costs might be hidden if price increases are allowed and hence fairly constant levels of profit are reported. **EA's financial performance** is **not subject to control in this way**.

(3) **A regulatory framework monitors service standards offered by WSS** and requires it to maintain these at a certain level at prices which are to a large degree determined by government. **The level of service provided to customers by EA and the price** at **which it is provided are set by the market**.

These differences make comparisons between the two organisations fraught with difficulties.

(ii) Given that the above analysis concentrates on relatively short-term performance, it is not a particularly appropriate means of assessing long-term organisational success.

(1) The asset acquisitions of WSS should produce future profits.

(2) We have no indication of whether the widely fluctuating profit levels of EA are part of a long-term trend or a one-off 'blip' in performance.

Such analysis does not therefore provide the full picture of how the organisations have performed.

(b) The manager's financial **target** is to maximise the total profit that the three service contracts earn.

Most importantly, to assist them in achieving this aim, the manager needs to have a **deeper understanding of the basic relationships between costs, profits and levels of activity**, especially in respect of the following:

(i) The overall cost structure of the organisation

(ii) The nature of fixed and variable costs

(iii) The difference between general fixed overheads and directly attributable fixed overheads

(iv) The concept of contribution

(v) The way in which optimal resource allocation decisions should be made when there is a limiting factor

(vi) Appropriate methods of allocating overheads

This understanding will improve the manager's decision-making skills.

The manager should also attempt to gain a **greater understanding of the environment** in which Enterprise Activities operates. Knowledge of the current business environment, a review of possible future operating scenarios and assimilation of detail on competitors will assist the manager in making appropriate decisions in a rapidly changing competitive environment.

The manager could also benefit from information and advice about a number of **management accounting methods**, such as pricing policy and budget preparation.

Advice on the following **general business/management areas** would also be of use:

(i) TQM programmes and the associated costs and benefits
(ii) Methods of overcoming labour shortages
(iii) Diversification of services offered (to reduce profit volatility)

(c) We begin by calculating total cost in order to work out selling price.

	Standard	*Super*	*Economy*
	$	$	$
Raw material	100.00	150.00	80.00
Direct labour	50.00	80.00	20.00
Variable cost	150.00	230.00	100.00
Fixed overheads	225.00	345.00	150.00
Total cost	375.00	575.00	250.00
Profit (50% of total cost)	187.50	287.50	125.00
Selling price	562.50	862.50	375.00

Step 1 **Calculate contribution per unit of limiting factor and rank products in order of production**

	Standard	*Super*	*Economy*
Contribution per unit	$412.50	$632.50	$275.00
Labour hours per unit	5	8	2
Contribution per unit of limiting factor	$82.50	$79.06	$137.50
Priority for production	Second	Third	First

Step 2 **Work out available resource**

Budgeted hours = (1,000 × 5) + (800 × 8) + (2,000 × 2) = 15,400

Available hours = 15,400 × 80% = 12,320

Step 3 **Work out optimal production plan and maximum possible profit**

	Units	*Hours used*	*Hours remaining*	*Contribution* $
Economy	2,000	4,000	8,320	550,000.00
Standard	1,000	5,000	3,320	412,500.00
Super	415*	3,320		262,487.50
Total contribution				1,224,987.50
Fixed overheads**				801,000.00
Maximum profit				423,987.50

*3,320 / 8

**$((225 × 1,000) + (345 × 800) + (150 × 2,000))

(d) **Differences in the two organisations' information needs**

The differences in the business environments of the two organisations will have a significant impact on the information needs of the two organisations.

Water Supply Services

(i) The information system will need to provide extensive detail on non-current assets.

(ii) Non-monetary information is needed to show that guaranteed service standards for customers have been maintained.

(iii) Information for regulatory reporting requirements must be readily available.

(iv) Detailed price and cost information is required to demonstrate equity of prices adopted and/or to justify price increases.

Enterprise Activities

(i) Information to make 'on the spot' decisions in response to rapidly changing market conditions must be available.

(ii) Externally sourced information about competitors, their prices and activities will allow the organisation to compete effectively.

(iii) Information is needed to allow profit-optimising allocations of scarce resources (skilled plumbers) to be made.

10 Transfer pricing

Top tips.

Part (a) is a test of knowledge, rather than application, so provided you understand the rationale behind transfer pricing you should have been able to score at least four of the six marks available.

If you can answer **part (b)** successfully then there is every chance that you really understand transfer pricing. The reasoning required is not at all difficult but goes to the very **heart of the topic**. If you couldn't answer part (b) yourself, work through our answer really carefully until you understand what's going on.

Part (c) picks up on a point which occurs quite frequently in P5 questions: in order for management to make decisions or monitor performance, they need relevant information so an organisation's information systems need to be able to provide them with that information. In this case, the question is what data managers will need to determine transfer prices. This might seem a difficult requirement at first, but if you think about the different ways transfer prices can be calculated this should give you some ideas about the sorts of data required.

(a) **Potential benefits of operating a transfer pricing system within a divisionalised company**

(i) It can lead to **goal congruence** by motivating divisional managers to make decisions, which improve divisional profit and improve profit of the organisation as a whole.

(ii) It can prevent **dysfunctional decision making** so that decisions taken by a divisional manager are in the best interests of their own part of the business, other divisions and the organisation as a whole.

(iii) Transfer prices can be set at a level that enables divisional performance to be measured 'commercially'. A transfer pricing system should therefore report a level of divisional profit that is a **reasonable measure of the managerial performance** of the division.

(iv) It should ensure that **divisional autonomy** is not undermined. A well-run transfer pricing system helps to ensure that a balance is kept between divisional autonomy to provide incentives and motivation, and centralised authority to ensure that the divisions are all working towards the same target, the benefit of the organisation as a whole.

(b) (i) **Division Able has spare capacity and limited external demand for product X**

In this situation, the incremental cost to the company of producing product Y is $35. It costs division Baker $38 to buy product Y from the external market and so it is cheaper by $3 per unit to buy from division Able.

The transfer price needs to be fixed at a price above $35 both to provide some incentive to division Able to supply division Baker and to provide some contribution towards fixed overheads. The transfer price must be below $38 per unit, however, to encourage division Baker to buy from division Able rather than from the external supplier.

The transfer price should therefore be set in the range above $35 and below $38 and at a level so that both divisions, acting independently and in their own interests, would choose to buy from and sell to each other.

(ii) **Division Able is operating at full capacity with unsatisfied external demand for product X**

If division Able chooses to supply division Baker rather than the external market, the **opportunity cost** of such a decision must be incorporated into the transfer price.

For every unit of product Y produced and sold to division Baker, division Able will lose $10 ($(42–32)) in contribution due to not supplying the external market with product X. The relevant cost of supplying product Y in these circumstances is therefore $45 ($(35 + 10)). It is therefore in the interests of the company as a whole if division Baker sources product Y externally at the cheaper price of $38 per unit. Division Able can therefore continue to supply external demand at $42 per unit.

The company can ensure this happens if the transfer price of product Y is set above $38, thereby encouraging division Baker to buy externally rather than from division Able.

(c) **Data to be collected for an information system to support transfer pricing decision making**

Type of data	How it would be used
Unit variable costs	To show the incremental cost of making various products/providing various services
External selling prices	To provide guidance as to market value transfer prices To indicate contribution that could be earned if products were sold externally rather than transferred internally
Capacity levels	To give guidance as to whether opportunity costs of lost sales need to be incorporated in transfer prices
Limiting factors	To highlight how capacity can be expanded

Type of data	How it would be used
Shadow prices	To determine whether or not additional resources should be obtained
Availability/prices of external prices	To make or buy decisions

11 Not–for-profit organisations

Top tips. The wording of the requirement for **part (a)** should help provide you with a logical and structured framework for your answer. You can address **efficiency** and **effectiveness** in turn (this solution opts to deal with effectiveness first) and explain why, for each of them, the absence of a profit measure causes problems. This then also suggests that you need to explain why the **presence of a profit measure** helps with the assessment of efficiency and effectiveness.

Take note of the **examples about objectives** we have provided in **part (a)(i)**. Questions looking at the implications of the lack of a profit measure in not-for-profit organisations have featured in P5 exams before and being able to relate a case study scenario to a real-life context could help you identify the issues to discuss in your answer.

Note the need to provide **examples** in **part (a)(ii)** – you should try to identify at least one example for each problem. As well as the given similarity between profit-seeking and not-for-profit organisations, don't forget that the **distinctions between the two types of organisation are becoming blurred.**

For **part (b)**, remember that indicators need to be **compared against a target or benchmark** to be useful for performance measurement purposes. The fact that 8% of appointments were cancelled has, by itself, relatively little use in terms of evaluating performance. When considered in conjunction with a target of 5%, it becomes much more useful!

(a) (i) **Effectiveness** refers to the use of resources so as to achieve desired ends or objectives or outputs.

In a profit-making organisation, objectives can be expressed financially in terms of a target profit or return. The organisation, or profit centres within the organisation, can be judged to have operated effectively if they have achieved a target profit within a given period.

In non profit seeking organisations, effectiveness cannot be measured in this way. The organisation's objectives cannot be expressed in financial terms at all, and non-financial objectives need to be established. The effectiveness of performance could be measured in terms of whether targeted non-financial objectives have been achieved, but there are several **problems** involved in trying to do this.

(1) The organisation might have several **different objectives** which are difficult to reconcile with each other. Achieving one objective might only be possible at the expense of failing to achieve another. For example, schools have the objective of providing education. They teach a certain curriculum but, by opting to educate students in some subjects, there is no time available to provide education in other subjects.

(2) A non profit seeking organisation will invariably be **restricted in what it can achieve by the availability of funds**. The health service, for example, has the objective of providing healthcare, but since funds are restricted there is a limit to the amount of care that can be provided, and there will be competition for funds between different parts of the service.

(3) The objectives of non profit seeking organisations are also difficult to establish because the **quality** of the service provided will be a significant feature of their service. For example, a local authority has, among its various different objectives, the objective of providing a rubbish collection service. The effectiveness of this

service can only be judged by establishing what standard or quality of service is required.

(4) With differing objectives, none of them directly comparable, and none that can be expressed in profit terms, **human judgement** is likely to be involved in deciding whether an organisation has been effective or not. This is most clearly seen in government organisations where political views cloud opinion about the Government's performance.

Efficiency refers to the rate at which resources are consumed to achieve desired ends. Efficiency measurements compare the output produced by the organisation with the resources employed or used up to achieve the output. They are used to control the consumption of resources, so that the maximum output is achieved by a given amount of input resources, or a certain volume of output is produced within the minimum resources being used up.

In profit-making organisations, the efficiency of the organisation as a whole can be measured in terms of return on capital employed. Individual profit centres or operating units within the organisation can also have efficiency measured by relating the quantity of output produced, which has a **market value** and therefore a quantifiable financial value, to the resources (and their costs) required to make the output.

In non profit seeking organisations, output does not usually have a market value, and it is therefore more difficult to measure efficiency. This difficulty is compounded by the fact that since these organisations often have **several different objectives**, it is difficult to compare the efficiency of one operation with the efficiency of another. For example, with the police force, it might be difficult to compare the efficiency of a serious crimes squad with the efficiency of the traffic police, because each has its own 'outputs' that are not easily comparable in terms of 'value achieved'.

In spite of the difficulties of measuring effectiveness and efficiency, control over the performance of non profit seeking organisations can only be satisfactorily achieved by assessments of **'value for money'** (economy, efficiency and effectiveness).

(ii) The **same problems extend** to **support activities** within profit-motivated organisations, **where these activities are not directly involved in the creation of output and sales**. Examples include research and development, the personnel function and the accountancy function.

(1) Some of the outputs of these functions **cannot be measured in market values**.
(2) The **objectives** of the functions are **not easily expressed** in quantifiable terms.

Examples

(1) Within the personnel department, outputs from activities such as training and some aspects of recruitment can be given market price values by estimating what the same services would cost if provided by an external organisation. Other activities, however, do not have any such market valuation. Welfare is an example. Its objective is to provide support for employees in their personal affairs, but since this objective cannot easily be expressed as quantifiable targets, and does not have a market price valuation, the effectiveness and efficiency of work done by welfare staff cannot be measured easily.

(2) Within the accountancy department, outputs from management accountants are management information. This does not have an easily measured market value, and information's value depends more on quality than quantity. The contribution of management accounting to profitability is difficult to judge, and so the efficiency and effectiveness of the function are difficult to measure.

(b) (i) To measure effectiveness, we need to establish objectives or targets for performance. Since these cannot be expressed financially, **non-financial targets** must be used. The effective level of achievement could be measured by comparing actual performance against target.

Adherence to appointment times

(1) Percentage of appointments kept on time
(2) Percentage of appointments no more than 10 minutes late
(3) Percentage of appointments kept within 30 minutes of schedule
(4) Percentage of cancelled appointments
(5) Average delay in appointments

A **problem** with these measures is that there is an implied assumption that all patients will be at the clinic by their appointed time. In practice, this will not always be the case.

Patients' ability to contact the clinic and make appointments

(1) Percentage of patients who can make an appointment at their first preferred time, or at the first date offered to them

(2) Average time from making an appointment to the appointment date

(3) Number of complaints about failure to contact the clinic, as a percentage of total patients seen

(4) If the telephone answering system provides for queuing of calls, the average waiting for answer times for callers and the percentage of abandoned calls

Comprehensive monitoring programme

Measures might be based on the definition of each element or step within a monitoring programme for a patient. It would then be possible to measure the following:

(1) Percentage of patients receiving every stage of the programme (and percentage receiving every stage but one, every stage but two, and so on)

(2) If each stage has a scheduled date for completion, the average delay for patients in the completion of each stage

(ii) A **single quality of care** measure would call for subjective judgements about the following:

(1) The key **objective**/objectives for each of the three features of service
(2) The relative **weighting** that should be given to each

The objectives would have to be measured on comparable terms and, since money values are inappropriate, an index based on percentage or a points-scoring system of measurement might be used. A target index or points score for achievement could then be set, and actual results compared against the target.

12 Abbott and Bartram

Top tips. Even if you do not get a question in the exam which concentrates to such an extent on the calculation of non-financial performance indicators (NFPIs), this question provides you with lots of practice in thinking up relevant NFPIs.

It was important to note that **each of the company's territories was the responsibility of one salesperson**, with Abbott being the salesperson for territory 1 and Bartram being the salesperson for territory 2. Once you had this clear in your mind it should have made **part (a)(i)** more straightforward.

- **Total sales potential** is **allocated** to individual salespeople on **the basis of the proportion of the total number of machines requiring the accessories in each territory**. So, for example, Abbott should be able to achieve 1.65/12.8 of total sales potential.
- **Sales penetration** is the **proportion of potential sales achieved**.

We have suggested 11 indices in **part (a)(ii)**, although only 8 were required for your answer. Don't worry if you didn't get the same as us; others might have been equally acceptable. **Gross margin** ((a)(ii)(2)) **as a percentage of sales** would **not be a suitable measure to evaluate the performance of salespeople**. Rather, it would be a measure of the profitability of the products sold and the performance of production (production costs).

We have assessed the performance of Bartram in terms of the five headings in (a)(ii). It was not necessary to do this but it does ensure that you cover a wide range of performance.

(a) (i) Sales potential in total is $7.1 million for 20X2.

		Average of all nine salespeople	*Abbott*	*Bartram*
(1)	**Sales potential**	$\frac{\$7.1\text{m}}{9}$	$\frac{1.65}{12.80}\times\$7.1\text{m}$	$\frac{0.83}{12.80}\times\$7.1\text{m}$
		= $788,889	= $915,234	= $460,391
(2)	**Sales penetration**	$\frac{\$1,460,000}{9\times£788,889}$	$\frac{\$112,000}{\$915,234}$	$\frac{\$123,000}{\$460,391}$
		= 20.6%	= 12.2%	= 26.7%
(3)	**Sales potential per account**	$\frac{\$788,889\times 9}{5,965}$	$\frac{\$915,234}{699}$	$\frac{\$460,391}{423}$
		= $1,190	= $1,309	= $1,088

(ii)

		Average of all nine salespeople	*Abbott*	*Bartram*
Customers				
(1)	Number of accounts per salesperson as a percentage of potential accounts	$\frac{3,271}{5,965}$	$\frac{398}{699}$	$\frac{364}{423}$
		54.8%	56.9%	86.1%
(2)	Average sales per customer account	$\frac{\$1,460,000}{3,271}$	$\frac{\$112,000}{398}$	$\frac{\$123,000}{364}$
		= $446	= $281	= $338
(3)	Average sales per customer as a percentage of average sales potential per account	$\frac{\$446}{\$1,190}$	$\frac{\$281}{\$1,309}$	$\frac{\$338}{\$1,088}$
		= 37.5%	= 21.5%	= 31.1%
Gross margin				
(1)	Gross margin per customer	$\frac{\$498,000}{3,271}$	$\frac{\$39,000}{398}$	$\frac{\$47,000}{364}$
		= $152	= $98	= $129
(2)	Gross margin per call	$\frac{\$498,000}{11,030}$	$\frac{\$39,000}{1450}$	$\frac{\$47,000}{1220}$
		= $45	$27	$39
Calls made				
(1)	Calls per customer	$\frac{11,030}{3,271}$	$\frac{1,450}{398}$	$\frac{1,220}{364}$
		= 3.4	= 3.6	= 3.4
(2)	Sales per call	$\frac{\$1,460,000}{11,030}$	$\frac{\$112,000}{1,450}$	$\frac{\$123,000}{1,220}$
		= $132	= $77	= $101

Remuneration

(1)	Remuneration as a % of sales	$\frac{\$82,385}{\$1,460,000}$ = 5.6%	$\frac{\$8,780}{\$112,000}$ = 7.8%	$\frac{\$7,845}{\$123,000}$ = 6.4%
(2)	Commission % (workings not shown)	1.5%	1.5%	1.5%

Expenses

(1)	Expenses as a % of sales	1.9%	1.7%	2.6%
(2)	Expenses per call	$2.54	$1.34	$2.62

(b) **Assessment of performance of Bartram for 20X2**

(i) **General**

Despite gaining 41 customers in the year, and increasing calls made by 5% and gross margin by $195 per customer, their results are below average, with net margin 18% below the average of the other salespeople.

However, the market potential of their area is relatively low.

(ii) **Customers**

Despite the low market potential they increased the number of their customers by 13% despite an overall fall in the UK of 1%. However, they are selling to 85% of potential by 20X2, which compares favourably with the 20X2 UK average of 55% and their own 20X1 figure of 75%. Consequently, their sales penetration of 27% is well above the UK average of 21%.

(iii) **Gross margin**

These were below the UK averages of $152 per customer, and $45 per call.

(iv) **Calls made**

Sales per call were below the UK average although calls as a percentage of customers was around the average.

(v) **Remuneration and expenses**

Both salary and total remuneration were below the UK average as were their remuneration per call. Expenses per call were average.

13 JIT systems

Part (a)

Top tips. The principal areas you would need to cover to score well would be:

(a) Explanation of present system of inventory control
(b) Explanation of JIT system
(c) Explanation of need for quality supplies of material
(d) Explanation of need for quality during processing

Objectives of JIT

The objective of a JIT system is to produce products or components as they are needed by the customer or by the production process, rather than for inventory.

A JIT production system therefore only produces a component when needed in the next stage of production.

In a JIT purchasing system, purchases of raw materials are contracted so that, as far as possible, the receipt and usage of material coincides.

Comparison of current inventory control system to a JIT system

A JIT **inventory** control system for the purchase of chemicals would be fundamentally different to the one currently being used.

Raw materials would not be ordered when a reorder level is reached but when they were actually needed in production.

Inventory levels would therefore be reduced to near zero levels; there would be no maximum and minimum levels.

Supplies would be delivered on a long-term contract basis as soon as they were needed, but in small quantities. This would obviously increase ordering costs.

However, the costs of space for holding inventories of chemicals, and costs such as damage or deterioration in stores, stores administration and security, would be dramatically reduced. In particular the interest cost and opportunity cost of tying up working capital in large inventories would be avoided.

The economic order quantity model would therefore not be relevant, not only because the exact quantity needed would be delivered, but also because holding costs would be kept to a minimum while no direct effort would be made to minimise ordering costs.

JIT and the implications for quality control procedures

JIT purchasing

If raw material inventories were to be kept at near-zero levels, the company would need to have confidence that suppliers would deliver on time and that they would deliver chemicals of 100% quality. There could be no rejects or returns; if there were, production would be delayed because no inventories are held.

The reliability of the organisation's suppliers would therefore be of the utmost importance and hence we would have to build up close relationships with them. This could be achieved by doing more business with fewer suppliers and placing long-term orders so that the supplier would be assured of sales and could produce to meet the required demand.

A supplier quality assurance programme (such as ISO 9001) should be introduced. The quality of the chemicals delivered would be guaranteed by suppliers and the onus would be on the supplier to carry out the necessary quality checks, or face cancellation of the contract.

JIT production

Since inventories of components would not be held, production management within a JIT environment would seek both to eliminate scrap and defective chemicals during production and avoid the need for reworking. Defects would stop the production line, thus creating rework and possibly resulting in a failure to meet delivery dates.

Quality control procedures would therefore have to be in place to ensure that the correct cleaning liquid was made to the appropriate level of quality on the first pass through production.

- Products would need to be designed with quality in mind.
- Controls would have to be put in place within processes to prevent the manufacture of defective output.
- Quality awareness programmes would need to be established.
- Statistical checks on output quality both during production and for finished goods would be required.
- Continual worker training would be necessary.

Part (b)

Top tips. It could be useful to start by defining what JIT is before going on to apply your knowledge to the scenario, by stating how JIT would affect profitability in X Group.

It is important that you focus specifically on the requirement set – how JIT might affect profitability in the Group – rather than discussing the potential advantages or disadvantages of adopting JIT in more general terms.

JIT definition

JIT is a customer-led production system, also known as a 'pull' system. The objective is to produce products as they are required by the customer rather than build up inventory to cater for demand.

Just-in-time production

A JIT production system is driven by demand for finished products whereby each component in a process is only made when needed for the next stage.

Just-in-time purchasing

A JIT purchasing system requires material to be purchased so that as far as possible it can be used straightaway.

The effect on X Group's profitability

The introduction of a JIT production and purchasing system could have the following impacts:

(i) **Increased efficiency** – One of the key principles in JIT production is the elimination of waste (for example through the elimination of defects, and the reduction of idle time). Reducing waste – and, correspondingly, increasing the efficiency of its production processes – should help X to increase its profitability.

Similarly, if throughput time is reduced, and X can satisfy customer demand more quickly, this could help it to increase revenue – particularly during periods of high demand.

(ii) **Customer satisfaction** – Reducing the level of defects should also help to increase customer satisfaction levels. If X is able to increase its levels of customer retention (as a result of these increased satisfaction levels) this should also boost revenue and profitability.

(iii) **Supplier relationships** – X Group currently uses a large number of suppliers. However, the increased importance of on-time deliveries and supplier reliability required to implement JIT successfully means it is likely that X will need to reduce the number of suppliers it works with, and develop stronger relationships with the ones it retains. On the one hand, this could increase the bargaining power of the suppliers, and if they increase their prices accordingly this could reduce X's profitability. On the other hand, dealing with a smaller number of suppliers could enable X to benefit from greater economies of scale in purchasing which could help it to increase its profitability.

(iv) **Quality control costs** – Particularly in the short term, as it adjusts to the new system, X may need to incur additional quality control costs to monitor the quality of materials received from suppliers and the finished goods it produces for customers. However, in the longer term, these costs should be outweighed by the benefits X experiences by continuously improving quality and reducing the level of defects.

(v) **Potential impact of disruption** – The absence of any inventories means that X could become vulnerable to any disruptions in its supply chain. For example, if one of its suppliers fails to deliver component parts when they are due, this could force production to stop at very short notice, and is also likely to mean that X is unable to fulfil customer orders. In turn, this could lead to a fall in revenues and profits.

(vi) **Inventory holdings costs** – Introducing JIT should mean that X enjoys a significant reduction in its inventory holding costs, because it will no longer be holding two weeks' safety inventory. However, while a reduction in inventory levels will help X's working capital management, this will not, in itself, have any impact on profitability (unless X currently has to write off substantial amounts of slow-moving or obsolete inventory).

14 Connie Head

Top tips. This is quite a difficult question, which requires consideration of both performance management and the process of appraisal, together with its potential to assist with strategic management. Effectively, you need to consider the ways reward and development are combined through an appraisal system. Note also in **part (a)** you are asked to 'evaluate the extent ...' so you should include any limitations as well as the benefits of the appraisal system in helping the firm achieve its goals.

The only easy marks were available in part (a), for discussing the uses to which appraisal is put: that is to say, basically, assessment of performance, potential and training needs. To score well, you would also need to discuss how effective implementation of an appraisal scheme can be achieved.

Technical article. As we have already mentioned in the chapter, there is an article in the P5 Technical Articles section on ACCA's website about reward schemes and their effect on an organisation's performance and employees' behaviour – 'Reward Schemes for Employees and Management'. You are strongly advised to read this article as part of your preparation for your exam if you have not already done so.

(a) The Senior Partner and Connie emphasise the aspects of appraisal schemes that **support their own favoured policies**. Such schemes should support the organisation's overall objectives without incurring excessive administrative and management costs.

In an organisation such as an accounting practice, the professional staff should indeed be highly **self-motivated**, able to judge the effectiveness of their own performance, and bring to their work a commitment to high professional standards. On the other hand, it is inevitable that their **talents and performance will vary** and they will need **guidance and help with their future development**. Dealing with these issues would be the role of an appraisal scheme.

The overall aim of such a scheme would be to **support progress towards the achievement of corporate objectives** and it would do this in three ways: performance review, potential review and training needs review.

Performance review. Performance review should provide employees with an **impartial and authoritative assessment of the quality and effect of their work**. Individuals should have personal objectives that support corporate goals via intermediate objectives relevant to the roles of their work groups. A reasoned assessment of performance can have a **positive motivating effect**, simply as a kind of positive, reinforcing feedback. It can also provide an opportunity for analysing and addressing the **reasons for sub-optimal performance**.

Potential review. Any organisation needs to make the best use it can of its people. An accountancy practice is typical of many modern organisations in that its people are its greatest asset and its future success depends on managing them in a way that makes the best use of their skills and aptitudes. An important aspect of this is **assessing potential for promotion and moves into other positions of greater challenge and responsibility.**

Training needs review. A further aspect of the desirable practice of enabling staff to achieve their potential is the provision of training and development activities. The appraisal system is one means by which **training needs can be assessed** and training provision initiated.

In this context, the reviews within the appraisal system would seem to be a supportive developmental process.

However, there is a tension at the heart of an appraisal system between appraisal as a **judgement process** and a **developmental process**. Whereas development will help motivate, the judgemental aspect of appraisal may **demotivate**, and this will hinder the firm in trying to achieve its goals.

The appraisal system

An appraisal system must be properly administered and operated if it is to make a proper contribution to the organisation's progress.

The appraisal cycle. Formal appraisal, with interviews and written assessments, is typically undertaken on an **annual cycle**. This interval is commonly regarded as too long to be effective because of the speed with which individual roles can evolve and their holders can develop, so the annual appraisal is often supplemented with a less detailed review after six months. Sometimes the procedure is sufficiently simplified that the whole thing can be done at six monthly intervals. Much modern thinking on this topic is now suggesting that any frequency of periodic appraisal is unsatisfactory and that it should be replaced by a **continuous process of coaching and assessment**.

This aspect of 'continuous improvement' will be more likely to help the firm achieve its goals.

Objectivity and reliability. Appraisal involves an element of direct personal criticism that can be stressful for all parties involved. If the system is to be credible its outputs must be seen to be objective and reliable. These outputs should be used to motivate individuals to achieve their goals.

Setting targets. Past performance should be reviewed against **objective standards** and the performance against these targets should form the basis of the employee's reward.

If the appraisal system acts to motivate the staff by rewarding them for achieving their **individual goals**, and these individual goals are properly **aligned to the firm's goals**, then the appraisal can be effective in helping the firm achieve its goals.

However, the goals in themselves must be **realistic and achievable**. If they are not, then staff will become demotivated and the appraisals will be counter-productive.

However, overall an effective appraisal system can help manage the workforce in a rational way, thereby helping the firm achieve its goals, via the feedback loop illustrated below.

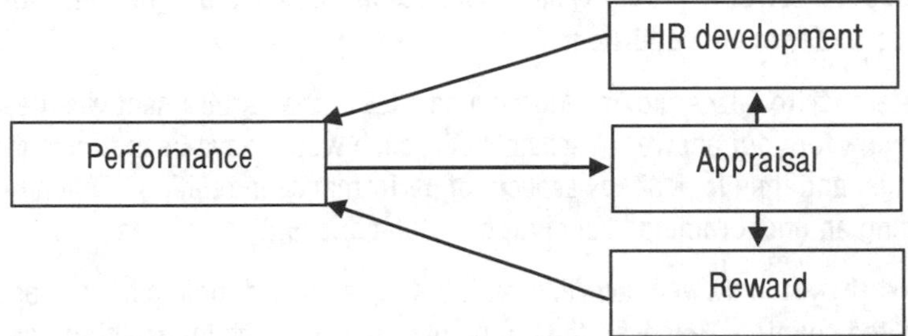

(b) **Performance management** involves the establishment of clear, agreed individual **goals and performance standards**; continuous leadership action to both **motivate and appraise subordinates**; and a **periodic review** of performance at which the goals and performance standards for the next cycle are set.

Performance management is an application of the **rational model** of strategic management, in that individual goals are intended to form the lowest echelon of a **hierarchy of objectives** that builds up to support the **overall mission** of the organisation. It is an essential aspect of the system that individual goals should be **agreed and internalised** so that true **goal congruence** is achieved.

This overall approach was first described by Peter Drucker, and is seen most clearly in the system of **management by objectives** (MbO). MbO as a management system has fallen somewhat from favour with the rise of quality management methods that emphasise processual and procedural conformance rather than the attainment of overall performance goals. Nevertheless, it has much to offer.

MbO and strategic analysis

Under a formal MbO system, the process of setting goals is part of the **implementation phase** of strategic management and follows consideration of resources, overall objectives and SWOT analysis. In this way, MbO resembles the strategic analysis stage of the rational planning model.

Strategic choice

Top level subordinate goals are agreed for heads of departments, divisions or functions: these goals should be specific, measurable, attainable, relevant and time-bounded (SMART). It is particularly important that the achievement of a goal can be established by objective **measurement**. There may be different timescales for different objectives, with short-term goals supporting longer-term ones. Again there is a parallel here to the notions of suitability, acceptability, and feasibility of the rational planning model.

Strategic implementation

Departmental heads then agree SMART goals for their subordinates in discussion with them, that support their own personal goals, and so on down the hierarchy to the level of the individual employee. All members of the organisation thus know what they are expected to achieve and how it fits into the wider fabric of the organisation's mission.

Periodic **performance review** is based on the objective appraisal of success against agreed goals, the agreement of goals for the next period and an assessment of the resources, including training, that the reviewee may require to reach those goals. The MbO system thus closes the **feedback loop** in the corporate control system.

15 Eatwell Restaurant

Top tips. To score well in **part (a)** of this question you need to cover a good number of the key areas of performance in the 25 or so minutes available. It would have been very easy to go into too much depth on one or two areas – as you were provided with a wealth of data.

Although you need to make use of the data given in the scenario, don't worry if you did not use all of it. As you will see in our answer we made no reference to the value of food wasted in preparation, for example, and yet **our answer is probably still more comprehensive and longer than one you could aim to produce under exam conditions**.

The reference to Fitzgerald and Moon in part (a) of the requirement was designed to provide you with a framework for your answer. A sensible approach would have been to use the results and determinants as headings, and then look at key aspects of performance in relation to each of them – rather than simply providing an uncoordinated list of ratio calculations and comments.

For **part (b)** you may well have different, but equally valid, points in your answer than we have in the suggested solution. However, the key point here is that the information/data you suggest is new, and not simply a duplication of what was given in the question.

Part (c) – The building block model specifically identifies that, in order for standards to be effective, employees must view the standards as fair and achievable, and must take ownership of them. These three qualities (fairness, achievability and ownership) are the three factors you should have discussed here. You are not required to apply your answer to the scenario. This part of the question is purely a test of knowledge.

(a) **Competitive performance**

Over the last four years, **market share** (the business's share of the revenue of all restaurants in the locality) has **increased** year on year from 9% in 20X1 to 18% in 20X4.

	20X1	*20X2*	*20X3*	*20X4*
Market share	(83/895) 9%	(124.5/1,234) 10%	(137/980) 14%	(185/1,056) 18%

The restaurant is therefore taking an increasing proportion of the area's restaurant business, doubling its market share over the four-year period.

The number of proposals submitted to cater for special events has increased dramatically, from 10 proposals submitted in 20X1 to 38 submitted in 20X4, whilst the **percentage of contracts won as a percentage of proposals submitted** has shown remarkable **growth**.

	20X1	*20X2*	*20X3*	*20X4*
Contracts won as % of proposals submitted	20%	29%	52%	66%

The restaurant appears to be **increasingly effective in winning business** in this developing area.

Financial performance

	20X1	*20X2*	*20X3*	*20X4*	*20X1–20X4*
Change in revenue		+50%	+10%	+35%	+123%
Change in profit		+84%	+104%	+31%	+393%
Profit margin	14%	17%	32%	31%	

The analysis above shows **continuous growth in revenue** and an even **stronger growth in profitability**. The **increase in profit margins** may be a result of **improved resource utilisation**, with fixed costs as a percentage of revenue falling.

It is clear that **20X2** was a **successful** year compared with 20X1, and that **20X3** results were **even better**. While there was a significant increase in revenue in **20X4**, the increase in profitability was less than in previous years and the **profit margin fell** (admittedly only by 1%). This could indicate the need for **tighter cost control**.

Quality of service

Just under 7% ((5 × 52)/3,750) of meals served in 20X1 were to regular customers compared with over 20% ((26 × 52)/6,700) in 20X4. The business therefore has a **growing number of regular customers** who can be assumed to be happy with the price, level of service, quality of food or, indeed, the total package offered by the restaurant.

The data about **complimentary letters, written complaints** and **cases of food poisoning** does **not paint a clear picture** about quality of service as no definitively clear trends are evident, even when the number of meals served is taken into account.

	20X1	*20X2*	*20X3*	*20X4*
Meals served per complimentary letter	3,750	1,275	2,067	1,117
Meals served per written complaint	469	425	443	479
Meals served per reported case of food poisoning	938	1,020	886	957

Without a yardstick such as rates achieved by competitors it is therefore **difficult to draw firm conclusions** on the quality of service provided by the restaurant, especially as the number of customers almost doubled over the period. More accurate information could possibly be gathered from a large-scale customer satisfaction survey.

Flexibility

One measure of a business's flexibility is **how well it copes with varying levels of demand**. The restaurant's average service delay at peak times shows no clear trend but has fluctuated widely from 47 minutes in 20X2 to less than one-third of that in 20X3. When these figures are analysed in conjunction with the average number of customers at peak times, however, it is clear that performance was particularly poor in 20X2 (with a low level of customers but the longest delay), while performance in 20X3 was better. Overall, however, it is clear that there are **problems in flexing resources to meet demand at peak times**.

The number of **items on offer each day**, the **new meals introduced** during the year, the **special theme evenings introduced** and the **weekly opening hours** also indicate improving levels of flexibility, reflecting the **increasing choice available to customers.** The number of items on offer has more than doubled over the 4-year period, from 4 to 9, the number of new meals introduced has varied between 8 and 27, the number of special theme evenings has increased from 0 to 13, and opening hours increased in 20X3.

Resource utilisation

This is usually measured in terms of **productivity** (output relative to some form of input). Given the information available and assuming the restaurant is open 52 weeks a year, one measure of productivity is **total meals served/opening hours.** This ratio has steadily increased from 2 in 20X1 to 3.6 in 20X4.

And **levels of non-productive time** (measured by idle time rates and proportion of operating hours with no customers) **declined.**

	20X1	*20X2*	*20X3*	*20X4*
Idle hours	570	540	465	187
Opening hours (weekly × 52)	1,872	1,872	2,080	1,872
Idle time %	30%	29%	22%	10%
Operating hours with no customers as % of opening hours	20%	16%	9%	7%

In conjunction with the increase in the number of meals served (the year on year increases being 36%, 22%, and 8%), these measures would tend to indicate overall improvements in resource utilisation.

The **increase in capacity** by 60% in 20X3 allowed more customers to be seated during peak times (although we do not know if this was due to increasing floor space or to seating more customers in the same space), but it was **not matched by similar increases in overall activity level**, and did in fact correspond with a **drop number of meals served per seat**.

	20X1	*20X2*	*20X3*	*20X4*
Meals served per seat	150	204	155	168

Weekly **opening hours** were **increased** in 20X3 but, as the figures above demonstrate, there was **no corresponding increase in meals served per seat**.

Innovation

The business appears to have been **particularly successful in this area**, attempts at innovative ways of satisfying customer needs including the introduction of **special theme evenings**, **increased items on offer** and the successful development of **catering for special events**.

A number of **new meals** have also been **introduced**, although the degree of experimentation has varied considerably from year to year.

(b) **Additional information for assessing performance**

Competitiveness

(i) Any similar data from one or more restaurants in the locality would enable the business to determine how well it was performing in relation to competitors.

(ii) It would also be useful to have data about total meals served in all restaurants in the same price band in the locality in order to assess market share in terms of volume.

Additional answers

(iii) More general information about national trends in eating out and restaurant prices, and market research (particularly customer surveys) on similar restaurants would provide a broader context to the performance assessment.

(iv) Details of the cost of catering for special events would allow the profitability (or otherwise) of this area of business to be determined.

Financial performance

(i) Cost data on labour, food and overheads, which is missing at the moment, would enable a more in-depth profitability analysis.

(ii) Details of assets would enable the calculation of ROCE.

Quality of service

(i) Especially useful would be any customer feedback received by or systematically collected by the restaurant (in addition to the complaints and compliments already detailed).

(ii) Any reviews of the restaurant that might have appeared in guides, newspapers and so on would provide an expert's analysis of the service provided.

Additional answer

(iii) Data on intangible factors such as courtesy of staff, ambience of the restaurant and so on would enable a fuller assessment of the quality of service.

Flexibility

(i) Details of the ease with which the restaurant deals with requests for non-menu items (such as those connected with special dietary needs) would give additional information with which to assess this area.

(ii) It would be useful to know whether any staff training to promote multi-skilling (which should improve the business's ability to cope with fluctuations in demand) has ever, or could, take place.

Resource utilisation

(i) A number of useful measures could be calculated if information about staffing levels was provided (eg meals served per hour per member of the waiting staff or revenue per member of staff).

(ii) If information about floor area was also provided, measures such as revenue per square metre could be calculated.

Additional answer

(iii) It would be useful to know how seat numbers were increased (additional space or more seats in the same space).

Innovation

(i) An analysis of the popularity of new meals introduced would provide an assessment of the menu planner's ability to tap into customer preferences.

(ii) The popularity of the theme evenings could be established with details of the numbers of meals served during them. There is little point running a theme evening if the number of customers is less than on a non-theme evening.

However, focusing on special events could be the reason for the **lack of innovation** in the restaurant. Following 27 new meals in 20X3, only 11 were introduced in 20X4. This cutback could also be due to the lack of success here. In 20X3, $3,600 of food was wasted. This was reduced to $1,450 in 20X4.

(c) **Performance measurement** in service businesses has sometimes been perceived as difficult, but the modern view is that if something is difficult to measure this is because it has not been clearly enough defined. Fitzgerald and Moon provide the elements of performance standards in service businesses. These are **ownership**, **achievability** and **equity**.

(i) **Ownership**. One of the most important factors in setting up a system of performance measurement is that those who are being measured must feel that they 'own' the standards that have been established. People who participate are more likely to feel comfortable with, and committed to, the targets that they have. This will make working relationships much more effective. It will be hard for people to be motivated to achieve targets set by someone else.

(ii) **Achievability**. Performance measures need to be realistic, and balance the need to perform to the best standards against the need to make sure that employees are not discouraged by impossible targets. Employees must accept their targets and consider them to be attainable.

(iii) **Equity**. Measurement must be fair ('equitable') across all business units. Two business units operating in very different regulatory environments, for example, could not be fairly compared if one unit had far higher compliance-related costs than another.

16 Glasburgh Trust

Top tips. Part (a). Although the question requirement doesn't specifically mention 'league tables', the requirement is effectively asking you to discuss the potential problems with public sector league tables, and the reference to 'comparative performance indicators' should have helped to identify this.

However, although you could use examples relating to a hospital (as we have done in our solution), there isn't any specific requirement to link your answer to this part of the question to Glasburgh, so you could have drawn on examples from other public services (schools; police forces etc) if you preferred.

In **part (b)** read the requirements carefully. You are asked to **assess** the performance of each hospital, but the additional requirement to do it critically means you have to comment on your calculations and what they mean. This means you mustn't simply copy data from the question scenario without then commenting on what it illustrates about the hospitals' performance. So, for instance, if you mention medical staff costs in both hospitals, try to draw some useful comparisons between them – don't simply say that RLH's actual costs were $22.3m and KHH's were $19.6m. That is not an assessment of performance, because you have not given any insight into what the figures tell us about how well the hospitals are performing.

A useful approach could be to draw up a table with the four dimensions and three columns for actual and budget. Make this your appendix to the report to keep your calculations and initial thoughts separate. Calculate measures for each dimension, making any notes that occur to you, as this is a critical assessment. These can be very simple observations, such as one hospital has far better performance on waiting times, but then you need to ask why this might be so. Might better performance on, say, financial management be at the expense of clinical standards?

Never take things at face value: use your experience and skills as an accountant to analyse the data. Remember, the balanced scorecard is meant to consider an all-round view so some of the categories may conflict eg a better financial measure may be at the expense of a service measure because cost cutting has reduced a service but improved the budget. You may consider a measure to be inappropriate or more information may be required before it can be used, so state this in your answer and say why.

The key to a good answer is:

- Classifying performance under the correct dimension: eg in-patient admissions under access to services
- Including relevant information on each performance measure from the table in the question or calculated
- Making comparisons in your report
- Critically assessing the performance based on your comparisons: are they relevant or useful? Is there anything else the management needs to know?

In **part (c)** you are asked to **evaluate** the balanced scorecard used by the Trust. Does it provide the information the Trust needs to assess performance or is it flawed? What other performance measures would you use? Don't launch into a review of the balanced scorecard using the perspectives in the Study Text. Use the scenario's categories for assessing performance, which are broadly similar to the scorecard's perspectives, and cover financial and non-financial performance measures.

Finally, remember to write this as a **report.** There are up to four marks available for format, presentation and quality.

We have placed extra comments in additional answer boxes where we see these as useful in rounding out your discussion but more than you would realistically be able to produce in the hour you have to do this question.

Part (d). The question requirement is relatively open-ended here. You could either recommend improvements to the content of the report, or to the presentation of the report, or a mixture of both. Either way, make sure you recommend three improvements in total and, crucially, explain what the benefit of the recommended improvement will be.

It is more than likely that you have recommended different improvements to the ones we have suggested in our solution. However, provided they are relevant to the scenario, and you have explained what their benefit will be, you can score the marks available.

(a) **Limitations of comparative performance data in the public sector**

As part of the trend towards greater **openness** and **accountability** in government, many public sector organisations are required to publish **performance indicators** to assess how well they are doing in comparison with others in the same sector.

For example, hospitals are assessed on the number of people on their waiting lists, or the length of time patients have to wait for operations. In other sectors, schools, for example, can be assessed in **league tables** based on exam results (eg the percentage of pupils achieving certain grades in their exams).

The **purpose** of these indicators is to give information allowing **choice to members of the public** and thus **encourage underperformers** to improve their performance.

Problems with performance indicators, especially if applied in a simplistic way, are these.

(i) **Context**. League tables compare organisations on a like for like basis. However, it may not always be appropriate to treat organisations as being alike. For example, small hospitals often achieve higher ratings for patient care than larger hospitals because it is easier for doctors and nurses to know their patients.

Equally, for example, schools have different catchment areas, and so a school itself may not be solely responsible for educational performance. Schools in areas with profound social problems are likely to score worse in league tables than schools in more affluent areas, despite the quality of teaching pupils in the respective schools are given.

(ii) **Mix of indicators**. One of the main problems in producing league tables is the choice of indicators which are used for measuring performance. As is suggested by the number of performance indicators which Glasburgh uses, no single indicator is likely to be sufficient to judge performance; so public sector bodies need to be judged on a mix of indicators. For example, typical hospital performance indicators include waiting times, as well as care and treatment. Hospitals can reduce waiting lists by rushing operations and sending people home sooner. However, this is likely to reduce the quality of treatment patients receive, and could also subsequently lead to a rise in emergency readmissions, so it will be counter-productive.

(iii) **Tunnel vision**. The adage that 'what gets measured, gets done' is also relevant here. If an organisation knows that performance league tables are based on only certain aspects of performance, it could focus on performance in these areas, to the detriment of performance in other areas. For example, if a hospital is judged on the cleanliness of its wards, rather than on the quality of meals it provides for its patients, it is likely to focus more on the quality of its cleaning than on its meals.

(iv) **Information collection**

(1) The validity of any league tables depends on the **quality of information** collected at operational level, and the integrity of the data and the people who deal with it.

Statistical information is prone to **manipulation**, and those who are judged on its performance may have an incentive to misclassify data. For example, if hospitals don't add people onto their waiting lists until the month they are due to have an operation, this would reduce the waiting time. Alternatively, hospitals can offer patients appointments at times they cannot make (for example, because they are away on holiday). However, because the patient has been offered – and declined – an appointment, this adjusts the length of time the patient is recorded as waiting for an appointment.

(2) Even ignoring the possibility of interference, the data collection systems need to capture the **right data for accurate indicators** to be prepared.

(b) **To:** Management of Glasburgh Trust

From: Management Accountant

Date: 5 June 20X9

Subject: Performance of the Royal Laurel Hospital (RLH) and King Hardy Hospital (KHH) using a balanced scorecard approach for the year ended 31 May 20X9

This report will summarise the performance of the two hospitals using a balanced scorecard approach.

The four dimensions used in the assessment of performance of the two hospitals are:

- Access to services (measured by waiting time before treatment)
- Clinical (measured by medical measures such as drug errors and infection control)
- Efficiency assessed by output for any given input
- Financial management

RLH will be compared to KHH for actual performance and budgeted performance.

It may be unclear what the measures relate to. Access to services is measured by the waiting time taken before treatment. Clinical is measured by 'medical' measures such as drug errors and infection control. Efficiency is assessed by the outputs for any given input.

Access to services

The **total inpatients** at each hospital in the year to 31 May 20X9 were 37,000 at RLH and 40,000 at KHH. KHH has lower waiting times for inpatients than RLH at 0.8% for five weeks or more so 99.2% of inpatients are admitted within five weeks and all inpatients by 11 weeks. By comparison, 9% of patients for RLH have at least a five-week wait, which is significantly poorer than the 1% budgeted. By week 11, the number of patients still waiting has gone down to 2%.

Both hospitals had the same number of outpatients, at 44,000 in the year. **Outpatient waits** show a similar pattern where, at 5 weeks, RHH has 10% of patients still waiting compared with 0.8% for KHH and at 11 weeks the figures are 3% and 0.5% respectively.

KHH performs better despite having 3,000 more inpatients and the same number of outpatients as RLH.

Additional answer

Lower waiting times may mask a sacrifice in standards as more patients are 'processed' through the system or a focus on service at any cost. A decline in standards in KHH is not borne out by the clinical measures on infection or by complaints received, though there is a slightly higher incidence of deaths at 200 more than RLH. Of course KHH attended to 3,000 more patients in the year and the two hospitals have similar percentage mortality rates (1.6% for RLH and 2% at KHH).

On other measures of access to services, RLH admitted 70% of patients within two weeks to the **chest pain clinic** which was 28% below target whilst KHH admitted all of its patients within two weeks. This could have serious consequences as chest pains may be life threatening.

Figures for emergency services show KHH performed better than RLH again. Both hospitals had the same number of emergency admissions but RLH was unable to find beds for 4 patients by 12 hours whereas KHH admitted all emergency patients in that time. The quality of care in RLH was compromised by having to leave patients on trolleys. KHH managed to move all of its emergency admissions out of emergency and onto wards within four hours but RLH undershot its target of

98% by 2%. It is not known how complex the emergency admissions were across the two hospitals. However, on raw data KHH has performed far better.

Turning to operations, 80% of inpatients required a single operation in each hospital. This means 29,600 patients in RLH and 32,000 in KHH were scheduled to have an operation. Actual operations performed were less than this in both hospitals. In RLH 592 patients were not operated on despite being scheduled and in KHH there were 160 patients who didn't receive an operation. In percentage terms these are 2% and 0.5% respectively.

Clinical

KHH **responds quicker to complaints** than RLH as 99% of complaints received being responded to within 25 days compared to 95% for RLH (5% below target). At 1,620 complaints, the number received by RLH is twice that budgeted and nearly four times that of KHH. This is despite KHH having 3,000 more patients than RLH.

Additional answer

Nonetheless, what 'responds to complaints' means is not defined and whether the two hospitals measure this the same way.

Inpatient deaths (%) may be low for both hospitals at 1.6% for RLH and 2% for KHH but in absolute terms is 600 deaths in RLH compared to 800 in KHH. What is not known is whether this is better than the norm for all hospitals and how the two hospitals compare on the sickness of the patients they admit.

Problems arising in clinical care include 2 **infections reported** at RLH which is an improvement on the target of 6. There were no infections reported in KHH which is clearly superior and may suggest a focus or priority in this area. Both hospitals reported **errors in administering drugs** with RLH having 80 errors (20% better than target) and KHH 20 errors. These are small figures but serious in their consequences and suggest a review of how drugs are prescribed is needed.

Efficiency

RLH had actual **bed occupancy** of 91% compared to 95% as target. KHH had an actual bed occupancy rate of 88%. This is lower than RLH but we do not know how it compares with target. This measures 'throughput' of patients so higher occupancy implies more patients are being treated. It doesn't in itself reveal how long individual patients have stayed and if some are taking up beds for longer than expected. However, taking this with the numbers of days stayed (below) reveals patients are staying a shorter time than expected (on average) so the lower occupancy for RLH than target means fewer are being treated.

Inpatients stayed on average less than the 4-day target in both hospitals. Thus patients stayed for an average of 3.75 bed days in RLH and 3.36 bed days in KHH. These measures need to be combined with clinical measures to assess the actual quality of the care received.

KHH staff are dealing with more patients each (9.2 patient days) compared with 8.4 actual and 7.4 target for RLH which may suggest they are more efficient but does not reveal the quality of care given to each patient. Clinical data can give some idea.

Finally, looking at the **utilisation of the operating theatres**, both hospitals had 80% of inpatients needing a single operation (target and actual). In reality, 88% of this total were operated on at RLH and 97% at KHH. Again KHH performs better than RLH.

Financial management

KHH earns more revenue from its activities than RLH at $60.2m compared with $54.2m and has a surplus of $4m compared to a deficit of $1m. As trust hospitals it may be assumed that they don't have to make a profit but this does show a better control of costs. From a financial viewpoint, KHH spent less than RLH in the year overall at $23.6m on staff when RLH spent $27.8m. More information on the types of staff would be useful. KHH has a higher cash buffer than RLH at 35 days compared with 31 days.

(c) **Evaluation of the balanced scorecard used by the Trust and recommendations to improve its usefulness**

Evaluation

The balanced scorecard measures performance across four dimensions, one of which is purely financial. The balanced scorecard must use dimensions that are important to the particular organisation. Thus clinical performance is vital in a hospital but far less so (in fact irrelevant) in a fast food chain. Hospitals must measure targets that reveal quality of the service they provide and also those favoured by the Government such as waiting lists and mortality rates.

What is essential is that the scorecard captures data in a variety of areas and not just financial data. The data in different areas may reveal a conflict between, say, keeping costs down and maintaining a good level of clinical service. A pure financial focus would not highlight the need to balance different considerations when making decisions.

The **access to services** dimension captures the ability of patients to access services. This is a key measure given patients are the main reason for the existence of the hospitals. They are the 'client'. **Clinical measures** are those reflecting the operational ability of the hospitals. The hospitals perform operations and the measures here capture the extent to which patients get infections or are prescribed the wrong drugs or the wrong dosage of drugs.

Efficiency measures measure the use of resources or outputs for given inputs. Public bodies are accountable to the Government and taxpayers for their funding rather than competing in the open market. As funding comes through grants then efficiency is important as the use of the grant monies is scrutinised for value for money. The hospitals need to look at how well resources are managed. For instance, staff manage the 'throughput' of patients in both hospitals so why are there differences between the two hospitals in the number of patient days per member of staff?

The hospitals also need to show they can manage their funding in a way that gives the most value for money. **Financial measures** reveal how the hospitals manage their costs and ask questions on how well funds are managed. Trusts must also balance their books and so financial measures are useful and may reveal where more funding is needed or where a hospital is especially good at keeping within budget.

Recommendations to improve usefulness

The Trust could consider looking at strategic forward-looking measures, as the scorecard only measures operational and historical data.

From the analysis in the first part of the report, certain measures need more refinement, for instance the relative sickness of patients admitted to each hospital or the degree of seriousness of infections reported. Financial data would benefit from more detail on the types of staff employed, a breakdown of the operational costs and the classes of income received.

Staff are key in the hospitals and a staff dimension could capture staff turnover, absenteeism and sickness for example. This may reveal the extent of staff motivation, or lack of it, and increase stress if staff are overworked or not trained properly for their jobs.

Service quality is another dimension which looks deeper into non-financial performance measures. Measures such as number of complaints could be linked to the number of patients cared for to get a measure of the percentage of complaints received.

Please contact me if you want any more information or clarification of the contents of this report.

Appendix

Performance measure	RLH (A)	RLH (B)	KHH (A)	Comments
Access to services Waiting time % – inpatients				KHH had 3,000 more inpatients and significantly lower % waiting times than RLH actual but similar to RLH budget. Per note 3 RLH budgets for 4 days and nights per inpatient. In fact both hospitals have a faster turnover of patients at 3.75 days and 3.36 days for RLH and KHH. (See below)
5 weeks or more	9	1	0.8	
11 weeks or more	2	0	0	
Waiting time % – outpatients				Both hospitals had the same number of actual outpatients but KHH had far lower waiting times.
5 weeks or more	10	5	0.9	
11 weeks or more	3	1	0.5	
13 weeks or more	0.5	0	0	
				Overall: KHH performs better than RLH on actual and RLH actual is worse than budget. Is KHH using more staff? There were 80 staff shortages in RLH compared to KHH's 20 in the year.
Inpatient stays (days)	138,750/ 37,000	146,000/ 36,500	134,320/ 40,000	Note 3 states this should be 4 days and nights. This is also a measure of efficiency which shows that both hospitals are passing patients through quicker than anticipated. The speed of throughput may clash with clinical care, however, so measures including deaths and errors must be looked at too.
Operations scheduled/actually performed	(80% × 37,000) –29,008 = 592 or 98%	0	(80% × 40,000) –31,840 = 160 or 99.5 %	Total inpatients × 80% compared with actual operations done
Other waiting time measures	70%	98%	100%	RLH had 70% of admissions to the chest pains clinic within 2 weeks compared with 100% for KHH.

Performance measure	RLH (A)	RLH (B)	KHH (A)	Comments
Number of emergency admissions	300	400	300	Both hospitals had the same number of emergency admissions but RLH had 4 trolley waits and 96% achievement of a 4-hour target turnaround in A&E compared to nil and 100%. It appears KHH is more efficient. However, without knowing the types of injuries or whether the hospitals have different admissions policies, KHH may admit these patients to other wards to ensure they meet the target or have more resources in A&E.
Clinical Complaints responded to within 25 days %	(1,539/1,620) = 95	(803/803) = 100	(416/420) = 99	KHH clearly responds quicker to complaints. What is more worrying is that the number of complaints received by RLH is twice that budgeted and nearly 4 times that of KHH at 1,620. Remember KHH has slightly more patients at around 84,000 compared to 81,000.
Inpatient deaths as % of inpatients	1.6	2	2	RLH performs better here than KHH but only slightly. The absolute difference is 200 deaths. Does KHH admit patients who are more critically ill, or merely more patients so deaths are more likely to occur? KHH performed 2,832 more operations than RLH in the year and had 3,000 more inpatients. The % includes waiting list patients so it seems longer waiting lists don't affect mortality though it would be expected that patients will deteriorate waiting for treatment.
Drug errors	80	100	20	RLH had better performance than budget but worse than KHH.

Performance measure	RLH (A)	RLH (B)	KHH (A)	Comments
Infections reported	2	6	0	These are tiny figures but don't inform how serious the infections were – did they lead to death or contagion? Did they take place at the end of the year and may numbers become higher at the start of the following year?
Efficiency				
Number of operations as % of total poss.	(29,008/ 32850) = 88	–	(31,840/ 32,850) = 97	Note 4 gives 90 ops per day × 365 days = 32,850 maximum. KHH has higher throughput, though of course there may be a trade-off in quality with 200 more deaths in inpatients.
Staff productivity number of patient days per member of staff	8.4	7.4	9.2	This means KHH staff are dealing with more patients each.
Bed occupancy (inpatient bed days)	138,750	146,000	134,320	Total possible bed occupancy is 42 wards × 10 beds × 365 days = 153,300. So as a percentage of total occupancy, RLH (A), RLH (B) and KHH (A): 91%, 95% and 88%.
Financial management				
Staff costs $m	27.8	27.7	23.6	Raw data suggest KHH staff are paid less so need to know numbers and mix of staff.
Revenue $m	54.2	55.2	60.2	Is KHH attracting more grant funding or does it have other sources of income? Could RLH learn from this?

(d) **Potential improvements to the report**

Comparative figures – The report currently focuses on actual performance against a target or budget. However, this does not give any indication of how the hospital's performance has changed over time, and therefore whether it is improving or getting worse. Therefore, the report should also include figures for the prior years to compare against.

Graphical information – The Trustee's comment highlights that, although the report is intended as a summary report, it contains a lot of numerical information. One way of highlighting key issues or trends in performance might be to use graphs or charts, rather than simply presenting a list of figures. For example, the percentage figure for the number of patients who have to wait two weeks or less for admission to the Rapid Access Chest Pains Clinic could be plotted as a graph over time (for example, on a monthly or quarterly basis). This could then highlight whether Glasburgh's performance is improving over time, and whether there are any trends (eg seasonality) in the figures.

Functional areas – The layout of the report – as a continuous series of data – does not provide any insight into how different functional areas or processes within the hospital are working. One way in which this could be improved is by grouping measures of performance together according to the different perspectives of the balanced scorecard. Alternatively, measures could be grouped according to the performance areas which they relate to; for example: admissions and access to services; quality of care and treatment; communication with patients; wards and facilities; and financial aspects.

17 CHN Retail chain

Top tips. Part (a). Make sure you read the requirement very carefully here. You need to evaluate the extent to which the VMI system adds value for CHN's **customers**, not for CHN itself. Therefore, the fact that it will mean CHN is holding lower inventory is not relevant here. The focus needs to be on the customer.

Part (b). There are two different parts to this requirement: (i) why is it important for CHN to establish service level agreement with its suppliers; (ii) identify **two** measures which should be included in such an agreement.

The key point here is that if CHN hasn't established what its requirements are, then it cannot assess whether its suppliers are meeting them or not. A service level agreement will allow CHN and the suppliers to formalise what each expects of the other and what they will undertake to supply.

Part (c). The key here is establishing how CHN's competitive strategy will affect what characteristics it is looking for in a supplier. CHN competes on the basis of quality rather than cost leadership. Therefore issues of quality, reliability and dependability are very important in choosing a supplier, not simply choosing the supplier who promises the lowest price.

Part (d). We have already identified that CHN is pursuing a differentiation strategy, based on quality. Therefore it will be important for the directors to have performance information relating to quality. However, it will also be important for the directors to know how CHN is performing financially, so don't overlook this. In addition, if CHN is going to gain competitive advantage from the quality of its products and services, they need to be superior to its competitors. So, for example, could it try to benchmark its performance against theirs?

(a) **Supply Chain Management** – CHN is looking to use the VMI system as a way of improving the way it meets its customers' needs. In this way, it is an example of supply chain management and the way in which technology can be used to enable the exchange of information and goods across organisational boundaries (between CHN and its suppliers).

Closer relationships – The VMI system is designed to improve the links in CHN's value chain and the relationships between CHN and its suppliers, so that the right products can be delivered to the right places at the right times. Having the correct item in stock when the end customer needs it benefits all parties involved (the customer, CHN and the supplier).

The Marketing Director's comment that 'only about half of our main suppliers actually deliver what we want, every week' identifies the scope for the VMI system to improve the efficiency of CHN's current value system.

Customer satisfaction – If the value chain process operates effectively in this respect, this should help CHN increase its customer satisfaction levels – for example, by reducing the risk of a product they want being out of stock at any time.

However, it could be argued that it is CHN's supply chain in general, rather than the VMI system specifically, which adds the majority of the value for CHN's customers.

In addition, it could be argued that the VMI has a number of **benefits for CHN**: a decrease in stock-outs, a decrease in inventory levels, and a reduction in planning and ordering costs due to responsibility for them being shifted to the supplier.

(b) **Performance measurement** – The VMI system means that CHN will be relying on its key suppliers to forecast the quantity and timing of deliveries required accurately. However, it will also require them to make the deliveries as required, because if they don't this could leave CHN with a shortage of products to sell.

A key element of performance indicators in the relationship between CHN and its suppliers is that they need to reflect the results of the suppliers' deliveries. Are the suppliers delivering the quantity and quality of goods that CHN needs, on time, in order to meet customer requirements?

However, in order to measure whether the suppliers are meeting CHN's requirements, these requirements first have to be established. A service level agreement will allow CHN and the suppliers to formalise these requirements.

Once the agreement is in place, then both CHN and its suppliers have a structure in place against which to measure the supplier's performance and to assess whether a satisfactory level of service is being provided.

However, it is important that the service levels agreed strike a suitable balance between 'carrot and stick' measures in order to encourage supplier performance. If the levels are too onerous, the supplier may feel they are not achievable, which will be demotivating.

The service levels chosen should be within the supplier's influence and should be important measures of the success of the VMI system. Two such measures could be:

Quantity – To ensure that the number of times each month a product line is out of stock remains below an agreed figure.

Responsiveness – To ensure that if a product line does become out of stock then inventories are replenished within an agreed amount of time.

(c) **Cost performance** – CHN's competitive strategy is based around the high quality of its products rather than selling them at a lower price than its competitors. Therefore, cost performance is potentially less important than a number of the other areas being measured.

Quality, reliability and dependability – By contrast, quality, reliability and dependability are very important, because they link directly to key areas of CHN's performance. One of the main benefits of the VMI system should be that it enables CHN to have the right products in stock as customers need them. Reliability and dependability of supply will be very important to achieving this.

In all three of the areas of quality, reliability and dependability KA is deemed to perform better than BY.

Flexibility – Flexibility gives an indication of the supplier's ability to respond to unexpected variations in demand. This is important in helping to avoid a stock-out, and again KA performs better than BY.

Short-term vs long-term indicators – The VMI system should allow CHN and its preferred suppliers to develop long-term relationships in which they work closely together. In this respect, the vendor selection process needs to look at longer-term indicators as well as short-term ones. The 'Scope to develop new products' and 'Ease of doing business with' are long-term indicators, while all the other indicators can be seen as short-term ones.

So, although BY currently appears to supply a wider range of products than KA does, KA has significantly greater scope to supply new products.

Recommendation – KA seems to meet CHN's key vendor selection criteria better than BY, so therefore KA should be selected as the preferred supplier.

(d) **Differentiation** – CHN seems to be pursuing a differentiation strategy, based around the quality of its products and its customer service. Therefore, it will be very important for the directors to monitor customer satisfaction in relation to product quality and customer service. In this respect, it is also likely to be important to monitor the level of customer complaints and product returns.

It would be useful for the directors to identify the critical success factors which will help CHN pursue its strategy successfully, because once the CSFs have been identified the directors can identify the key performance indicators to measure and, in turn, these will dictate the performance information which needs to be monitored.

Reliability – Also, as we mentioned in part (c), reliability will also be important, to ensure that customers can buy the goods they want to, when they want to, rather than any goods being out of stock. If customers cannot buy the products they want, this will reduce their satisfaction with CHN's service. Therefore, it will be important for CHN's performance information to monitor products which are out of stock, in terms of both the number of products which are out of stock and how long they remain out of stock for. If there are products which are regularly out of stock, CHN may need to identify whether it can find an alternative supplier for those products that is more reliable.

Financial performance – CHN is not competing as a cost leader, and therefore it will not place as much emphasis on obtaining products as cheaply as possible as a cost leader would. Nonetheless, it will still be important for the directors to monitor financial information, such as gross margin, to ensure that its costs are kept under control. Although CHN competes on the basis of quality rather than price, it is still important for it to operate as cost effectively as possible so that it can generate as high a margin as possible.

Competitor performance – As well as looking at its own performance, the directors should assess how well CHN is performing relative to its competitors. In particular, for CHN's strategy to be successful, it needs to obtain higher customer satisfaction scores in relation to quality and service than its competitors. In this respect, the directors should try to compare CHN's performance against competitors' performance, or industry surveys. Therefore the directors should look at external information as well as internal performance information.

18 NewsPrint Co

Top tips. You should have been able to identify a number of characteristics in the scenario which could be indicators of corporate failure. For example, falling profitability and sales volume could be **symptoms** of corporate decline, while an autocratic Chief Executive is a **defect**.

Importantly, you should address both financial and non-financial issues, but you also need to consider external factors as well as internal ones. For example, where is the industry in its life cycle?

Note, however, that many of the indicators in the scenario do not necessarily mean that the company will fail, and you should acknowledge this in your evaluation.

Declining market share: Five years ago, NPC was the market leader, holding 29% of the newspaper market in its country. However, its market share has fallen to 21%, and it is no longer the market leader. NPC has seen a decline in its share of the market of 8% in five years, which should be a cause for concern. However, by itself this does not indicate that the NPC is in danger of corporate failure.

Late entry into online market: NPC's late entry into the online (digital) newspaper market seems to have had a significant impact on NPC's revenues and market share. However, it is not clear whether NPC will be able to regain this market share now that it has developed digital versions of its papers, or whether the loss of market share is permanent. If the loss of market share proves to be temporary, then it is not an indicator that NPC is in danger of corporate failure.

There are several other performance indicators (both financial and non-financial) which NPC could analyse to assess the risk of corporate failure.

Financial indicators

Declining revenues: NPC has suffered a $37m (10%) fall in revenues in the five years from 20X4 to 20X9. As with the loss of market share, this downward trend will become a major cause for concern if it continues. However, part of the decline may be attributable to a downturn in advertising revenues in the recession which is currently affecting NPC's country. The scenario does not indicate how much of NPC's revenues come from advertising and therefore how much of the fall in revenue can be attributed to the downturn in advertising revenues. However, this downturn will hopefully only be temporary and so should not, by itself, be treated as an indicator of corporate failure.

Profit margin: Given the fall in revenue, and the loss of market share in a slow-growing market, we would expect NPC's operating profit to have fallen over the period 20X4–20X9. However, operating profits have fallen by 16%, which is greater than the fall in revenues, and consequently the profit margin has fallen from 22.5% to 20.8%. This fall in profit margin is a serious concern for NPC. However, if the new IT systems deliver the **efficiencies and cost savings** which are expected, then this should help improve the profit margin. If they do not, though, and margins continue to fall, this could ultimately lead to NPC becoming loss making.

Cash flows and net debt: The ratio of cash flow to net debt has been suggested as a useful indicator of the likelihood of corporate failure. NPC's ratio has fallen from 0.26 (46/175) to 0.23 (45/195) over the period, so this could be a cause for concern.

However, although NPC's total debt has increased by $20m over the period, we know it borrowed an additional $30m to pay for the new IT systems in 20X8. Without this additional loan, NPC's total debt would have actually fallen $10m over the period, in which case the ratio in 20X9 would have increased slightly to 0.27 (45/165).

Moreover, NPC appears to be managing its cash flows quite successfully. Despite the fall in revenue and operating profits, net cash flow from operations has remained largely the same between 20X4 and 20X9. **Tight management of working capital and cash flows** should be seen as indicators that the company is being well run, which may in turn lower the risk of corporate failure.

Non-financial indicators

Stage in life cycle – The market for printed newspapers in NPC's country appears to be, at least, in the mature phase of its life cycle, with the likelihood that it is about to enter the decline phase if it has not already done so. The low growth rates in the market suggest it will be hard for NPC to increase revenues significantly within this market.

However, the market research figures only relate to the printed newspapers. It is likely that the market for **digital media (eg iPads, tablets) will be growing** and so NPC may be able to achieve more significant growth in this area of its business. In this respect, rather than looking at the business as a whole it may be more useful to separate it into two business units. Printed papers have been a **cash cow**, but have now become dogs, while digital media are more likely to be **question marks**. If NPC can successfully grow its digital media operations and the associated advertising (and possibly subscription) revenues, this will reduce the risk of corporate failure.

Lack of innovation – In this respect, NPC's late entry into the digital market should be a cause for concern. Although it appears to be primarily a result of the Chief Executive's reluctance to enter the market, it may also be an indicator that NPC is less innovative than some of its rivals. As the newspaper market becomes increasingly digitalised, innovation and change are likely to become increasingly important. If NPC is consistently left behind by its rivals then this could increase the risk of its failing.

Autocratic Chief Executive – The presence of an Autocratic Chief Executive in a company is often seen as a major corporate **defect** which can lead to corporate failure. In this case, NPC's failure to develop online newspapers at the same time as its competitors appears to be the result of an Autocratic Chief Executive ignoring the views of the other directors. The Chief Executive seems to have resisted the move in line with their personal views, despite the rest of the directors all being keen that NPC should develop online versions of its newspapers. If the Chief Executive's approach to this issue is characteristic of the way they run the company, this is perhaps the strongest of all the indicators in the scenario as to why NPC may fail as a corporate entity.

Index

Note. Key Terms and their page references are given in **bold**.

BPP
LEARNING MEDIA

Review Form – Paper P5 Advanced Performance Management (02/16)

Please help us to ensure that the ACCA learning materials we produce remain as accurate and user-friendly as possible. We cannot promise to answer every submission we receive, but we do promise that it will be read and taken into account when we update this Study Text.

Name: ______________________ **Address:** ______________________

____

____

How have you used this Study Text?
(Tick one box only)

☐ On its own (book only)
☐ On a BPP in-centre course ______________
☐ On a BPP online course
☐ On a course with another college
☐ Other ______________

Why did you decide to purchase this Study Text? *(Tick one box only)*

☐ Have used BPP Study Texts in the past
☐ Recommendation by friend/colleague
☐ Recommendation by a lecturer at college
☐ Saw information on BPP website
☐ Saw advertising
☐ Other ______________

During the past six months do you recall seeing/receiving any of the following?
(Tick as many boxes as are relevant)

☐ Our advertisement in *ACCA Student Accountant*
☐ Our advertisement in *Pass*
☐ Our advertisement in *PQ*
☐ Our brochure with a letter through the post
☐ Our website www.bpp.com

Which (if any) aspects of our advertising do you find useful?
(Tick as many boxes as are relevant)

☐ Prices and publication dates of new editions
☐ Information on Study Text content
☐ Facility to order books off-the-page
☐ None of the above

Which BPP products have you used?

Study Text ☑ *Passcards* ☐ *Kit* ☐
Other ☐

Your ratings, comments and suggestions would be appreciated on the following areas.

	Very useful	*Useful*	*Not useful*
Introductory section	☐	☐	☐
Chapter introductions	☐	☐	☐
Key terms	☐	☐	☐
Quality of explanations	☐	☐	☐
Case studies and other examples	☐	☐	☐
Exam focus points	☐	☐	☐
Questions and answers in each chapter	☐	☐	☐
Fast forwards and chapter roundups	☐	☐	☐
Quick quizzes	☐	☐	☐
Question Bank	☐	☐	☐
Answer Bank	☐	☐	☐
Index	☐	☐	☐

Overall opinion of this Study Text *Excellent* ☐ *Good* ☐ *Adequate* ☐ *Poor* ☐

Do you intend to continue using BPP products? *Yes* ☐ *No* ☐

On the reverse of this page is space for you to write your comments about our Study Text. We welcome your feedback.

The author of this edition can be emailed at: accaqueries@bpp.com

Please return this form to: Head of ACCA & FIA Programmes, BPP Learning Media Ltd, FREEPOST, London, W12 8AA

TELL US WHAT YOU THINK

Please note any further comments and suggestions/errors below. For example, was the text accurate, readable, concise, user-friendly and comprehensive?